A HISTORY OF UNITARIANISM

LONDON : GEOFFREY CUMBERLEGE
OXFORD UNIVERSITY PRESS

A History of Unitarianism

Socinianism and its Antecedents

BY

EARL MORSE WILBUR, D.D.

CAMBRIDGE, MASSACHUSETTS

HARVARD UNIVERSITY PRESS

1946

Second Printing

PRINTED AT THE HARVARD UNIVERSITY PRINTING OFFICE

CAMBRIDGE, MASSACHUSETTS, U.S.A.

In Memory of
A dearly beloved Son

THOMAS LAMB ELIOT WILBUR
1912–1932

in whose life, too soon cut short
were finely exemplified the principles of
Freedom in thought
Reason in conduct and
Tolerance in judgment
crowned by uprightness of character

PREFACE

THIS HISTORY is the fruit of attention that I have given the subject more and more intensively during forty years. The first incentive to it was received when, to fill a gap in a student's required schedule, I offered an elementary one-hour course, the study for which at once discovered a lamentable want of works dealing with the subject save in the most superficial way. The only work in English attempting to cover the entire field (J. H. Allen, *Historical Sketch of the Unitarian Movement*, 1894) was in fact only a 'sketch,' hastily done and with little use of primary sources. For the Continental section only two works were at all satisfactory, and they were dated far back in the previous century (F. Trechsel, *Die protestantischen Antitrinitarier*, 1839–'44; and Otto Fock, *Der Socinianismus*, 1847). For England there was nothing at all, and for America only one work (G. W. Cooke, *American Unitarianism*, 1902) besides a series of popular lectures by different persons, wholly done at second hand (*Unitarianism: Its Origin and History*, 1895).

The reasons for this surprising neglect were two: first, the failure clearly to recognize that here were not four separate though similar movements, arising in Poland, Transylvania, England, and America, but rather four connected phases of one single movement nearly as old as Protestantism, whose significance can not be clearly grasped until they are considered together; and secondly, the widely scattered location of the primary authorities and the forbidding barriers of the languages in which many of them are written. For, in addition to extensive sources in Latin and in the more familiar languages of western Europe, a rich store of quite indispensable material is buried in Polish and Hungarian, two difficult languages practically unknown to English-speaking scholars; and these works, moreover, are for the most part to be found only in remote libraries which have seldom been explored by western scholars. The whole subject, in fact, can not be adequately investigated without a working knowledge of some thirteen different languages (witness the footnotes). Nor, strangely enough, had any library in either Europe or America ever attempted to collect more than a casual fraction of the works necessary for a proper study of the subject.

With a distant goal thus glimpsed I long ago began compiling a comprehensive bibliography of the subject and, on the basis of this bibliography, collecting as opportunity offered all obtainable items bearing on any phase of it, including photostats of a considerable number of the rarest and most important items. The result, now in the library of the Starr King School for the Ministry at Berkeley, may confidently be regarded as by far the most comprehensive collection of Unitariana in the world, comprising practically all works on the subject now obtainable in any language.

As my studies progressed year by year, I sharpened the language tools required in them, while sabbatical leaves enabled me to explore half a hundred libraries in Europe and America in order to discover where to find important authorities, widely scattered and in many cases exceedingly rare, and incidentally also to gain a vivid sense of the background of the history by visiting in person nearly every spot having any intimate connection with it. Finally, generous grants from the Guggenheim Foundation and the Hibbert Trust made it possible for me to spend three years in working over this material in the quiet interval between the World Wars, with full access to libraries which have since been either destroyed or hopelessly scattered. The copious notes thus taken (together with the bibliography) are now deposited in the library of the Starr King School for the Ministry, where they constitute what may perhaps be the only surviving remnant of many works now irrevocably lost to scholarship.

Since the beginning of the present century many researches in various details of this subject have been made, especially by Polish scholars, which are practically unknown to the English-speaking world. Of these I have taken full advantage. To the present work my *Our Unitarian Heritage* (1925) was in a sense a preliminary study, though designed for young people and greatly restricted in scope. Any discrepancies from it discovered here should of course be taken as corrections called for by more recent studies. The composition of this history from such a mass of materials has proved unexpectedly difficult and time-consuming, and has more than once been interrupted by illness; but I have steadfastly refused to be hurried into doing slipshod work.

The gathering of materials for such a book as this makes one indebted to countless persons who have shown him courtesy, done him kindness, or given him active help. To most of these I can make only this general acknowledgment; but I would especially mention my debt to Professor

George R. Noyes of the University of California, who in teaching me Polish gave me the key to rich sources on Socinianism hitherto unexplored and has for a generation been unfailingly helpful; to Professors Wacław Sobieski (now deceased), Stanisław Kot, and Roman Dyboski of the University at Kraków for their unstinted helpfulness and their valued friendship; to Dr. W. H. Drummond of Oxford, Dr. Henry Wilder Foote of Cambridge, Massachusetts, and Professor Roland H. Bainton of Yale University for repeated acts of kindness; to the administration of the Jagellonian and Czartoryski libraries at Kraków, the Unitarian College at Kolozsvár, the Preussische Staatsbibliothek in Berlin, the University libraries at Leiden and Jena, the British Museum and the Dr. Williams's Library in London; to the Principals of Manchester College, Oxford, and the Unitarian College at Manchester, and the librarians of Harvard University and the University of California, all of whom have been unfailingly helpful. The Trustees of the Guggenheim Foundation, New York, and of the Hibbert Trust, London, by their opportune grant of fellowships enabled me to complete my researches at a time when the whole work must otherwise have fallen to the ground, and have left me forever grateful to them. The Trustees of the Starr King School for the Ministry (succeeding the institution in whose service most of this work was done) have made this history to a special degree their own by a most generous subvention toward the expense of publication, in which numerous others have also assisted. But besides and above all others my wife deserves acknowledgment for the unwavering and solicitous interest and the constant encouragement and helpfulness with which she has through long years followed every phase and step of my work, though it has, alas, robbed us both of many hours of happy companionship.

Particular pains have been taken with the bibliographical references, which have been designed not only to cite authorities used but also to indicate literature in which the subject can be pursued in further detail. An index to the full titles of works cited in abbreviated form, and a table giving the pronunciation of names likely to be otherwise troublesome, may be found at the end of the text.

E. M. W.

BERKELEY, CALIFORNIA
    APRIL, 1945

CONTENTS

A HISTORY OF UNITARIANISM
SOCINIANISM AND ITS ANTECEDENTS

CHAPTER I

INTRODUCTION

IT IS THE PURPOSE of this work to set forth a comprehensive and well documented account, from its earliest origins through the first quarter of the twentieth century, of that free and progressive movement in Christian history since the Reformation which, though it has at different times and in different lands borne a variety of names, has on the Continent of Europe (save in Transylvania) been most widely known as Socinianism, and in Transylvania, England and America as Unitarianism.[1] This movement is most often conceived by the world at large, and frequently even by its own adherents, as one confined to England and America, and limited to the past century and a half, definitely dating in England from the opening of Lindsey's Unitarian chapel in London in 1774, and in America from Channing's sermon at Baltimore in 1819. In reality, however, its beginnings were only a few years later than those of Protestantism itself; and it had on the Continent an organized existence of more than two centuries before it took form in England — a history of great dramatic interest, and of significant influence upon the thought and life of the whole period. For while the Protestant Reformation began in 1517 when Luther posted his theses at Wittenberg, it was only fourteen years later that Servetus in 1531, by publishing his first book in criticism of the doctrine of the Trinity, ini-

[1] Its names, when taken from heresies with which its opponents sought to identify it, have been Ebionism, Sabellianism, Samosatenianism, Arianism, Photinianism. Its adherents, named from their leaders, have been called Servetians, Budnaeans, Farnovians, Socinians, Bidellians; from the chief seats of their activity, Pinczovians or Racovians; if from their distinctive doctrines, Monarchians, Antitrinitarians, Tritheists, Bideites, Trinitarians! Unitarians. They themselves have preferred to be called simply Christians, Polish Brethren, Rational Christians, Catholic Christians, Liberal Christians, and Unitarians. Of these names, Arians is the one that was (and still is) most widely current in Poland; Unitarians, throughout in Transylvania; Socinians, in western Europe and for some time in England; while controversialists in Germany freely employed the term Photinians. The name Unitarian, as will be seen, has had different connotations at different times; but though by many not too willingly borne, as giving undue emphasis to a single doctrine, it has now by the usage of more than a century in England and America become well established.

tiated the movement here treated. The springs of this movement in Italy, Switzerland and Germany ran together in that decade and those next following, into a stream that was to some extent to wash the shores of almost every country of western Europe; though its main current was to flow from Poland and Transylvania through Germany and Holland to England and America, in a continuity which, though it has not often been clearly recognized, is yet indisputable.

I have spoken of this as of a single movement in religious history. For although its developments in the countries with which it has been chiefly associated — Poland, Transylvania, England, America — have been so loosely connected or so little dependent upon one another that they might indeed easily be treated as distinct movements, yet they are in fact all joined together by very clear, even if sometimes slender, threads of historical sequence; and it will be shown that throughout their course they exhibit in common certain distinctive marks and principles which fundamentally characterize the movement as a whole.

It may be well at the outset to state the conception of this movement which will underlie the treatment of it here attempted. Whatever names it has borne, it has usually been regarded, alike by its adherents and its opponents, from the standpoint of doctrinal theology, as a movement or a sect characterized primarily by certain beliefs about the being of God and the person of Christ. It is true that it has from the beginning generally had such doctrinal associations. It has from first to last been anti-trinitarian, or at least un-trinitarian, if the Nicene and Athanasian doctrine of the Trinity be taken as the standard. But beyond this it would not be easy to name another doctrine on which those adhering to this movement have not at one time or another held the widest differences of opinion. It has been thus with the doctrines relating to Christ, the Holy Spirit, revelation, man, sin, the atonement, salvation, and the future life. Indeed, its consistent adherence to the unipersonality of God and the subordinate rank of Christ, may almost be said to be incidental to the movement rather than essential to it. Had the chief doctrinal controversies in the early Church happened to be waged over the doctrine of man rather than the doctrines of God and Christ, the separation from the main stream of Christian tradition might have come about on quite other grounds; and this indeed came near happening in the Pelagian controversy of the fifth century. In the few and brief periods when this movement has been suffered to exist free from persecution or from the necessity of defending itself against attack, doctrine has almost invariably retired into the background, and the emphasis has by preference been laid on conduct and character. Its primary psychological character is thus best described in terms not of the intellect or of the emotions, but of the will.

It is intended here, therefore, to present not so much the history of a particular sect or form of Christian *doctrine*, as to consider broadly the development of a movement fundamentally characterized instead by its steadfast and increasing devotion to these three leading *principles*: first, complete mental freedom in religion rather than bondage to creeds or confessions; second, the unrestricted use of reason in religion, rather than reliance upon external authority or past tradition; third, generous tolerance of differing religious views and usages rather than insistence upon uniformity in doctrine, worship or polity. Freedom, reason and tolerance: it is these conditions above all others that this movement has from the beginning increasingly sought to promote; while if emphasis upon certain doctrinal elements has often or for long periods seemed to characterize it or even to dictate its name, it has been largely because insistence upon contrary doctrines seemed to conflict with the enjoyment of the conditions above named.[2] For the movement has throughout its whole course strenuously resisted any attempt at dogmatic fixity, has made reason its ultimate court of appeal, and has normally been hospitable to changes and restatements in its forms of thought; being at all times far more concerned with the underlying spirit of Christianity in its application to the situations of practical life than with intellectual formulations of Christian thought.

Yet though not intending to treat of this movement in any narrow or sectarian spirit, I do not undertake here to present a history of liberal Christian tendencies in general, tracing their manifestation in the various confessions or denominations, Protestant or Catholic. That would be a task quite too broad and ill-defined. I must content myself with the more modest attempt to follow them in the narrower stream, flowing in a channel largely separate from the others, in which the distinctive characteristics of which I have just spoken have therefore been more fully and clearly developed.

[2] For a fuller development of this view, see the author's article, 'The Meaning and Lesson of Unitarian History,' in the *Proceedings of the Unitarian Historical Society* (London, 1926), iii. 350.

This movement may be said to have some peculiar claims upon our interest. It has been carried on by bold and adventurous spirits that have habitually insisted upon being free and independent. Setting small store by traditions of past ages or the codified opinions of past generations, they have in the field of religion tended to seek out new truth or new interpretations of old truths. The interest that their story invites may be compared with that with which we follow those explorers of a New World who, dauntless and unafraid, left all familiar headlands behind them and made for the open sea and the ever-receding horizon. In such a quest for new worlds, even in the sphere of thought, there is bound to be much of dramatic interest. This history, in so far as it deals with leading personalities, will have to do with some of the bravest, boldest and most heroic pioneers of religious thought. Perhaps no other extant movement in the Christian Church has had a larger proportion of martyrs and confessors. Until near the beginning of the eighteenth century men suffered imprisonment or death for this faith, and civil disabilities attended it until almost the middle of the nineteenth; while such names as Servetus, Socinus, Dávid, Biddle, Emlyn, Lindsey, Priestley, Martineau, Channing, Emerson and Parker may well be ranked with almost any others that Christian history can show, for the compelling interest of their lives, and their faithfulness to convictions of truth and duty. With a great price purchased they this freedom.

The movement whose history we are to explore was in its full development a fusion or amalgamation of various factors or elements which, arising from widely diverse sources, eventually combined in various proportions in a single stream that superficially often bore certain doctrinal marks, but was fundamentally characterized by the three broad principles spoken of above. It may therefore be well to speak in advance of the elements out of which the whole movement was gradually composed. Earliest in point of time was the element of deep personal devotion in many choice spirits of the mediaeval Church, which had comparatively little interest in speculative doctrines or doctrinal systems, and is preserved for us in such devotional classics as the *Imitation of Christ* and the *Theologia Germanica*. This element strongly influenced our movement by way of the Anabaptist tradition. There is also, some think, a strain from late scholastic philosophy, inducing a sceptical attitude toward the dogmas of the church. Servetus betrays some acquaintance with thinkers of this school, though it may be doubted whether this stream of thought penetrated deeply into Socinianism. But overshadowing all other elements that helped to shape Socinianism was the tendency to look directly to the word of Scripture itself as the sole pure source of religious truth, and to ignore as unimportant whatever could not be traced to this source. These various elements were emphasized in varying degree by the various leaders of the movement, each of whom made his contribution to it, until at length, when the competent leader appeared at the opportune time, all the streams became mingled in one, and what had been an irregular succession of individual influences became consolidated into a coherent movement.

The proper history of the Socinian-Unitarian movement begins, as has been said above, very early in the period of the Protestant Reformation. While it is true that in the thousand years preceding the Reformation we find occasional outbreaks of heretical opinion as to the received doctrine of God and of Christ, which seem in a way to anticipate this movement, yet they do not form part of any historically continuous development of thought. They must rather be regarded merely as sporadic instances, often widely separated in time and space, of independent and inquisitive minds applying themselves to difficult topics of theology. It was not until the Renaissance brought emancipation of the minds of men from the long slavery of the Middle Ages, and the invention of printing made the ideas of thinkers the common property of all that could read, that the way was opened for a new school of thought to become rapidly and widely diffused.

Nor can it be successfully maintained that this movement is simply a return to an earlier form of Christianity as it was in the fourth century. This interpretation of it has, it is true, often been made both by the adherents of this movement and by its opponents. On the one hand, the earlier Socinians and Unitarians contended that their faith was simply a revival of that of primitive Christianity, a return to the original pure teaching of Jesus and his Apostles, and of the Ante-Nicene Fathers, which had for twelve centuries been obscured and corrupted by admixture with pagan doctrines of Greek philosophy.[3] It was thought demonstrable that Peter and Paul were in fact first-century Unitarians, whose true successors had now at length recovered 'the faith once delivered to the saints.' On the other hand, their opponents contended that the new

[3] For the classic statement of this view, see Joseph Priestley, *History of the Corruptions of Christianity* (London, 1782).

interpretations of Christianity were only a modern revival of ancient heresies long since condemned and discarded: these modern Socinians or Unitarians were only the ancient Ebionites, Samosatenians, Sabellians, Arians or Photinians under a new name, old foes with a new face. In both these contentions there was a certain measure of truth. It was easy enough for Socinians to demonstrate that nothing like the Athanasian or even the Nicene doctrine was to be found in the New Testament, and that these were elaborated in the fourth century or later when adjustment was sought between Christian faith and Greek philosophy; and that the primitive faith was expressed rather in the Apostles' Creed and its successors. But this did not establish an identity between New Testament Christianity and Socinianism. It was easy on the other hand for orthodox theologians to find points of similarity between Socinian and Unitarian doctrines and the ancient heresies; and there was of course a tactical advantage in calling attention to the likeness. But there were also cardinal points of difference, and the so-called 'Arians' in Poland or in England indignantly and rightly insisted that they did not accept the doctrinal system of Arius. The key to a just understanding of the prolonged controversies that were to ensue can therefore be best gained through a brief résumé of the development of Christian doctrine, from the beginning of Christianity down to the period of the Renaissance when the pioneers of our movement, in their effort for greater freedom and a fuller use of reason in religion, began to make their protest against a religion of blind obedience to authority and a servile following of tradition.

There is an immense gap between the religion of the Sermon on the Mount and the parables of Jesus as reported to us in the first three Gospels, on the one hand, and the orthodox Christianity of the fourth and fifth centuries as stated in the Nicene and Athanasian Creeds, on the other. In the former, while belief in God and recognition of man's duty to obey him are everywhere taken for granted, the essence of religion is summed up in love to God and one's neighbor; and the whole emphasis is laid upon a life of reverent trust in God and brotherly relations with men. In the latter, while piety and virtue may doubtless be presupposed in a Christian, yet they are hardly once mentioned, still less are they insisted on as of vital importance; while the entire emphasis is laid upon profession of belief in abstruse speculative dogmas which were finally arrived at only after generations of hair-splitting controversy. The difference is that between a religion of the heart and life, and one of the head. Nevertheless in the literature and history of early Christianity we may trace every step of the process by which the one was transformed into the other. This transformation was the outcome of a long-continued effort to express the philosophy of a religion of Jewish origin in terms satisfactory to those whose habits of thinking had been cast in the mold of Greek philosophy.[4]

The primitive Christian religion of the first century was that of a Jewish sect. Its distinctive mark was the belief that Jesus was the promised Messiah. His credentials were the mighty works that he did and the prophecies that were fulfilled in him; and these were confirmed by his resurrection from the dead. Belief in God was in a divine being of the simplest unity: no other would have found a moment's acceptance with any Palestinian Jew of the first century, nor would the belief that the Messiah shared the attributes of divinity. He was a man, chosen indeed for an exceptional office, endowed with exceptional powers, but yet limited in knowledge, authority, power and even goodness. Evidences of this primitive belief are numerous in the Gospels, and it survived for more than four centuries in the Jewish Christian sect known as Ebionites. But long before the end of the first century, as Christians became increasingly alienated from Judaism, and were now seeking converts in the gentile world, this earliest Christian belief began to be transformed. For Christianity encountered in the world of Greek thought the conception of a personified *Logos* or Word, a kind of world-soul intermediate between infinite and holy deity and finite and sinful man; and the critical step was taken when the Jewish Messiah or Christ came gradually to be identified with this Greek Logos. Thus a Christianity of Jewish origin was fitted into the frame of Greek philosophy, and the wide spread of the religion into the Greco-Roman world was assured.[5]

The problem facing the Christian Apologists of the second century as they tried to organize their religious beliefs into a tenable system was as to just how this Logos was related to Jesus of Nazareth on the one

[4] For the full development of this thought, see Edwin Hatch, *The Influence of Greek Ideas and Usages upon the Christian Church* (Hibbert Lectures), London, 1890.

[5] For a lucid account of the following development of Christian thought, see Albert Réville, *History of the Dogma of the Deity of Jesus Christ* (London, 1905), chaps. iii–iv.

hand and the eternal God on the other. Various solutions were tentatively put forth by Justin Martyr, Irenaeus, Clement of Alexandria, Tertullian and others, none of them finally satisfactory, yet all agreeing that the Logos or Son of God was inferior to the Father, though all tending to regard him as in some sense divine. To guard, however, against Christianity's relapsing into a religion with more than one divinity, two further views were presented in the third century. Paul of Samosata suggested that though Jesus was originally a man, he gradually became divine until at length he was completely one with God; while Sabellius sought to preserve the unity of God by the view that Father, Son and Holy Spirit were simply three modes in which the one God manifested himself. Both these views long showed great vitality, but they were at length rejected by the Church as unsatisfactory, and were condemned as heretical.

The next and yet more important step was taken in the Arian controversy of the fourth century. The Bishop of Alexandria thought to simplify the problem by saying that the Son of God was possessed of *eternal* divinity, having *always* been of the same 'substance,' or essential nature, with God; whereas Arius, one of his priests, considering this as merely Sabellianism in another form, proposed the view that Christ, though a created being less than God, had yet existed before the world and ranked far above man, and that his nature was something between divine and human. Controversy between these two views became so heated in Alexandria, and grew so violent throughout the Empire, that it threatened to undermine the very throne. As a measure of political safety, therefore, and in order to bring the controversy to permanent settlement, the Emperor Constantine felt forced to convene at Nicaea in 325 a general council of all the churches in the Roman Empire. The council lasted six weeks, and was marked by great bitterness and even violence. Three parties were involved: followers of Arius, holding that in his essential nature Christ was *different* from God; followers of Athanasius, holding that he was *the same* as God; and an intermediate party, in the great majority, holding that he was *similar* to God. The Arians, being a small minority, were soon outvoted; but the Athanasians, though also a minority, proved so unwilling to make the least concession, that at length the Emperor threw his weight into the balance, and insisted on the adoption of their statement of doctrine, which nearly all now signed. This was the Nicene Creed, affirming the eternal deity of Christ. Those opposing it were declared to be enemies of Christianity.

Nevertheless Arianism did not at once become extinct. In a few years it became even dominant, for forty years it was in the saddle in the East, and it was for a time the official religion of the whole Empire. The Emperor Theodosius, however, was of the opposite view, and in 380, in order once and for all to put an end to doctrinal controversies, he decreed that all nations in the Empire should adhere to the orthodox belief in the Trinity, and that all that would not do so should be branded as heretics and be punished as should seem best.[6] Thus Arianism, though it still survived among the barbarian nations of invaders for two centuries more, was finally outlawed in the Roman Empire.

From this account thus briefly given, it will be seen how it was that the primary emphasis of the Christian religion came to be laid upon an intellectual belief about a speculative question as to which Christians had been widely divided and had long wavered. If it is remembered, however, that this question distracted the whole Roman Empire more or less violently for two centuries, it will be the more readily understood why the question of belief came to be regarded as one of primary importance, taking precedence over all others. Henceforth for centuries the question of crucial importance was to be not, How does one act, what is his character? but, How does he believe, what is his creed?

In the fifth century the Emperor Justinian incorporated the doctrine of the accepted creed into the Roman law,[7] and the door was closed to freedom of belief or teaching on these subjects. The appeal might no longer be to reason, but only to tradition. Tolerance was a sin, toleration was treason, heresy was a crime to be punished at the stake; and to propagate heretical views was deemed as much worse than murder as the eternal life of a human soul is of greater importance than the temporal life of a human body. Such was the background of religion in Europe early in the sixteenth century, when the spirit of the Renaissance roused men's minds to fresh inquiry in every field of thought, and the Reformation was re-opening many questions in religion long since regarded as closed.

[6] We, the three Emperors, will that all our subjects . . . believe the one divinity of the Father, Son and Holy Spirit, of majesty co-equal, in the Holy Trinity. We will that those that embrace this creed be called Catholic Christians. We brand all the senseless followers of other religions by the infamous name of heretics, and forbid their conventicles to assume the name of churches, etc. *Codex Theodosianus*, xvi, 1, 2.   [7] *Codex Justinianeus*, I, i, 5.

CHAPTER II

LATENT ANTITRINITARIANISM AMONG THE EARLY REFORMERS

THE EFFORT to confine theological thinking within the limits set by creeds and conciliar decrees was not entirely successful. If heretics were so outspoken as to their speculations that they attracted attention and threatened to become a popular danger, they could indeed be suppressed, but behind closed doors speculation and questioning still went on. The decidedly skeptical tendency of the Scotist philosophy tended to undermine the arguments by which the great mysteries of the Christian faith were commonly supported, even though, relying on the higher authority of the Church, men still professed to accept the traditional dogmas nevertheless. The dogma of the Trinity was the subject of much debate in the Middle Ages among Catholic theologians, including even Popes themselves.[1] The scholastics trifled with it and admitted its difficulties, but held that though it was beyond all reason it must be accepted on blind faith in the Church's authority.[2] In the twelfth century Peter Lombard in his *Sentences* raised questions as to the Trinity which could not be answered. Abélard was decidedly unsound on this article. Jerome of Prague in his university days publicly set forth with great boldness theses in which he rejected this doctrine. Pico della Mirandola late in the fifteenth century held it as a fundamental point that God is an absolute unity, in which one can not speak of number, since that is appropriate only to multiplicity. The unknown author of the *Theologia Germanica* at about the same time, and Reuchlin in 1494, taught the absolute unity of God.[3] It is therefore no wonder that shortly after the beginning of the Reformation similar views should have found even freer expression in Protestant circles. Nevertheless at the beginning of the sixteenth century in the Church at large Christian

---

[1] cf. Friedrich Thudichum, *Die deutsche Reformation* (Leipzig, 1909), ii, 151; *id.*, *Papsttum und Reformation* (Leipzig, 1903), p. 333.

[2] cf. Robert Holkot, *Super quatuor libros Sententiarum*, I, quaest. 5.

[3] cf. Thudichum, *Papsttum*, pp. 101, 371.

thought had been for more than a thousand years practically stagnant at the point to which the creeds and councils of the fourth and fifth centuries had brought it. The doctrines of Christianity appealed to the sole authority of tradition. One was not supposed to examine them in the light of reason, or even of Scripture, but humbly to accept them on faith as divine mysteries. Intolerance of divergent opinions in religion was deemed a Christian duty, and persecution of heretics a cardinal civic virtue.

This condition of stagnation was now to be disturbed by new forces too widespread to be longer resisted. Many such forces were asserting themselves at the end of the Middle Ages, and they culminated in the period of the Renaissance, when the revival of the ancient learning and the spirit of intellectual Humanism conspired to encourage men to independent thinking and acting in every department of life. New forms of literature arose, new traditions in art were established, new tendencies in government appeared, and new methods were used and new paths followed in science. In no field was the new spirit more marked than in that of religion; and now that the invention of printing had made the Bible accessible to all that wished to read it, educated men were no longer content to leave it as the monopoly of the clergy, but were exploring it with the same enthusiasm with which they devoted themselves to the rediscovered ancient classics; and even common folk were laying its teachings to heart as never before.

This general breaking-up of a condition long-standing in the religious world was greatly accentuated by the Protestant Reformation, which went much further than was at first meant or wished. It was by no means intended as a revolution or a revolt from the Church, but only as a reform of certain flagrant abuses and corrupt practices, in order that the Church might better meet the religious needs of the people at large. The dogmas of the Church were not in question, nor was there as yet any disposition to revise them. This point was especially insisted upon at the outset of the Reformation. After the reformers had presented their statements for imperial approval at the Diet of Augsburg, Melanchthon took particular pains to say in behalf of his fellow reformers that they did not differ from the Roman Church on any point of doctrine.[4]

[4] Dogma nullum habemus diversum ab ecclesia Romana. Letter of July 6, 1530, to Cardinal Campeggio. Melanchthon, *Opera*, ed. Bretschneider (Braunschweig, 1834–1860),

Nevertheless, when Protestantism presently found itself in the enjoyment of a separate, independent existence, no longer acknowledging the authority of the Roman Church, the whole field of doctrine was bound to lie open for review. The Roman Catholics had indeed regarded Holy Scripture as supreme authority; but in any question as to how Scripture was to be interpreted, they fell back upon the authoritative traditions and declarations of the Church, very much as members of a civil State may regard the Constitution as final authority, yet in any case of doubt will look to the Supreme Court for interpretations of its meaning. When Protestants, however, no longer accepted Catholic traditions as binding, and substituted the principle of private judgment, under the guidance of the Holy Spirit, the way was open to a wide variety of opinion. Diversity of view soon showed itself even among the sober and enlightened leaders of the Reformation, and before long it was seen also among the unlettered and undisciplined, where it often went to scandalous lengths. Hence Protestantism was driven in self-defence to set up its own standards of teaching, and then to adopt a form of organization by which it might secure a good measure of adherence to them.

Modification of the dogmas that had been accepted in the Roman Church was thus bound to come as soon as Protestants began seriously to inquire how far those were supported by the Scriptures which they had adopted as their standard of faith and practice; and the dogmas concerning the Trinity and the person of Christ, which had been agreed upon only after such prolonged controversies in the early Christian centuries, were naturally among the first to attract attention. Even before the outbreak of the Reformation under Luther, the foundation for inquiry into these dogmas had been laid by Erasmus. For in the edition of the Greek New Testament which he published in 1516 he had omitted as an interpolation the strongest proof-text for the doctrine of the Trinity;[5] and in his Annotations on the New Testament he also helped to undermine belief in scriptural support for this doctrine.[6]

---

ii, 170. On the genuineness of this passage, cf. Benrath in *Jahrbücher für protestantische Theologie*, viii (1882), 179 f.

[5] I. John v. 7. Compare the Revised English Version with the Authorized Version, noting the omission.

[6] For many citations of his antitrinitarian tendencies, cf. Henri Tollin, 'Der Verfasser De Trinitatis Erroribus und die zeitgenossischen Katholiken,' *Jahrbücher für protestantische Theologie*, xvii (1891), 389–412; Étienne Chastel, *Histoire du Christianisme*

This fresh inquiry into the scriptural foundation of the traditional doctrines was pursued even by the more conservative leaders of the Reformation. Thus Luther disliked the term *homoousios* as being a human invention, not found in Scripture, and he preferred to say 'oneness.' Trinity, he said, has a cold sound, and it would be far better to say God than Trinity.[7] He therefore omitted these terms from his Catechism, and the invocation of the Trinity from his Litany. Hence Catholic writers did not hesitate to call him an Arian.[8]

The tendency of the first reformers was rather to pass over the doctrine as unscriptural and therefore unessential, than to deny it as unreasonable or untrue. Thus Melanchthon, in his first attempt to give the teaching of Protestantism a systematic statement in his *Loci Communes*, 1521, said, 'Surely there is no reason why we should spend such pains on these sublime matters, God, unity, trinity, the mystery of creation, or the mode of incarnation. Why, what have the scholastic theologians gained in all these centuries by their handling of such themes? . . . How many of them indeed, seem to tend to heresy rather than to the Catholic doctrine. . . . Paul did not philosophize . . . on the mystery of the Trinity, or the mode of incarnation, or active or passive creation, did he?'[9] He too had to meet the charge of Arianism. Viret, minister at Lausanne, in 1534 presented a confession accepted as perfectly orthodox, without using the dogmatic expressions Trinity, substance, person, etc.[10]

Calvin himself in his Commentaries on the Gospels frankly recog-

---

(Paris, 1881–'83), iv, 380, and all along here, iv, 379–385; G. Bonet-Maury, *Sources of English Unitarian Christianity* (London, 1884), pp. 41–44; Charles Beard, *Reformation of the Sixteenth Century* (Hibbert Lectures), London, 1883; pp. 149–152. See Erasmus's annotations on John i, 1; Rom. ix, 5; I. John v. 7; cf. his *Opera* (Leiden edition), ix, 1040B, 1050D.

[7] Vocula haec Trinitas nusquam in divinis scriptoribus reperitur, caeterum humanitus tantummodo inventa. Unde omnino etiam frigide sonat; ac multo praestabilius foret, si Deus potiusquam Trinitas dicatur. *Postilla major super Dominicam Trinitatis.* cf. Bonet-Maury, *op. cit.*, pp. 12–14, 221; T. M. Lindsay, *History of the Reformation* (New York, 1910), i, 471 f; Maurice Schwalb, *Luther, ses opinions religieuses* (Strasbourg, 1866), p. 72.

[8] cf. Christopher Sandius, *Nucleus Historiae Ecclesiasticae* (ed. 2, Coloniae, 1676), p. 423.

[9] *Loci theologici*, 1521, ed. Plitt (Erlangen, 1864), p. 103 ff. Text and translation also in Bonet-Maury, *op. cit.*, p. 10 ff; Chastel, *op. cit.*, iv, 380.

[10] cf. Friedrich Trechsel, *Die Protestantischen Antitrinitarier vor Faustus Socin* (Heidelberg, 1839), i, 160; Abraham Ruchat, *Histoire de la Réformation de la Suisse* (Nyon, 1836), V, 27 ff.

nized human limitations in Jesus;[11] and in his earlier career he declared that the Nicene Creed was better fitted to be sung as a song than to be recited as a confession of belief.[12] He disapproved of the Athanasian Creed, disliked the usual prayer to the Holy Trinity, and in his Catechism touched but lightly on the doctrine.[13] He taught that the Holy Spirit is not so much a person in the proper sense of the term as a power of God active in the world and in man.[14] At Lausanne in 1537, therefore, both he and the other Geneva pastors were charged by Pierre Caroli with Arianism and Sabellianism.[15] Farel, Calvin's predecessor at Geneva, made about 1525 the earliest statement in French of the chief points of Christian doctrine, which had great popularity. In this he made not the slightest reference to the Trinity or the dual nature of Christ.[16] Finally, Zwingli at Zürich held that Christ was not a proper object of worship, and this view influenced the practice of the Reformed Church. Oecolampadius at Basel was also under suspicion.[17]

These instances of wavering orthodoxy among the most influential leaders of thought in the early Reformation do not indeed prove that they were all but ready to take the next step and deny outright the doctrines that they had inherited, and whose terms or expressions they thus

---

[11] cf. on Matt. xxvii. 34; Luke ii. 40; John x. 30, 36; xvii. 21. Aegidius Hunnius, *Calvinus judaizans*, etc. (Witebergae, 1595), examines and cites many passages in Calvin's commentaries in which he rejects the orthodox interpretation in favor of the doctrine of the Trinity, and approves one more acceptable to Antitrinitarianism, and thus lays a foundation for Arianism.

[12] Vides ergo carmen esse, magis cantillando aptum quam formulam confessionis. "Adversus Caroli calumnias," in Calvin, *Opera*, ed. Baum, Cunitz et Reuss (Brunsvigae, 1863–1900), vii, 316.

[13] Precatio vulgo trita: Sancta Trinitas unus Deus miserere nostri, mihi non placet, ac omnino barbariem sapit; "Epistola ad Polonos," April 30, 1563, Calvin, ix, 647. cf. Bonet-Maury, *op. cit.*, pp. 15–17; Chastel, *op. cit.*, iv, 381. The Geneva Confession of 1536 in art. ii. expresses belief in "ung seul Dieu," but gives no intimation of a Trinity; cf. Calvin, ix, 693.

[14] Ubique diffusus omnia sustinet, vegitat et vivificat, in coelo et terra. "Institutio" (1559), I. xiii. 14; ii, 202. cf. *La Rochelle Confession*, art. vi, "Le Saint-Esprit, sa vertu, puissance, et efficace."

[15] cf. Chastel, *op. cit.*, iv, 381; Philip Schaff, *History of the Christian Church* (New York, 1885–1907), vii, 351, 632; Ruchat, *op. cit.*, v, 16–24.

[16] Guillaume Farel, *Sommaire et briève déclaration d'aucuns lieux fort nécessaires a ung chacun Chrétien* (reprint of the ed. of 1534, Genève, 1867). cf. chap. i., "De Dieu"; ii., "De Jésus Christ."

[17] cf. Réville, *Deity*, p. 204 f. At Marburg Luther charged both Zwingli and Oecolampadius with encouraging denial of the Trinity. cf. Bonet-Maury, *op. cit.*, pp. 15, 55 n. For yet other examples, cf. Trechsel, *op. cit.*, i, 156–164.

criticised; for not only did they from the beginning give at least a nominal adherence to the Nicene and Athanasian Creeds, but after a few
years, for reasons that will be shown later, when faced by hostile criticism, they took especial pains to make their position on this point unmistakably orthodox. But they do show a disposition to question the
form in which these doctrines had been stated, and to regard them as
not essential to salvation because not clearly supported by Scripture authority; and the next step logically would have been to treat them as
optional, and let them be ignored or even denied by those that found
them superfluous or objectionable.

This next step, however, was not taken, for doctrinal controversy and
doctrinal history took such a turn that when the several Protestant confessions within a generation adopted their official standards of faith, they
with one consent reaffirmed their acceptance of the traditional views.
Freedom of inquiry on these lines was not to be longer possible, the appeal to reason or even to Scripture was to have no standing in opposition
to authoritative tradition, and tolerance of dissenting views was to be
frowned upon as opening the way to heresy, and to the ruin of immortal
souls. That the reconstruction of the doctrinal system of the Catholic
Church did not proceed further than it did is perhaps due most of all
to the fact that those that were most ready and eager to carry the reform
further proceeded too fast and went too far, in view of all the condition-
ing circumstances. It is the familiar phenomenon of a movement or reform being retarded, injured and all but ruined by the impatience, im-
prudence and recklessness of those that are most desirous of promoting
it. For the Protestant cause still had a precarious footing during the first
generation of the Reformation. Depending as it had to do upon the
sympathy and support of the German Protestant Princes as against the
Catholic Emperor, it could not afford to do anything to alienate the
former, nor to furnish the latter with gratuitous grounds of attack. But
unfortunately the earliest and most conspicuous leaders of the movement whose history we are tracing did both the one and the other, and
thus greatly compromised their cause. The more radical reformers in
Germany and the Low Countries were leaders in the sect of the Anabaptists, and were thus associated with fanatical radical tendencies in
that sect which threatened the overthrow of all social and religious order.
The Protestant movement could not afford to give them countenance
at the cost of losing the support of the Princes on which their success

obviously depended. On the other hand, Servetus, the first writer boldly to attack the traditional doctrine of the Trinity, ignored the fact that he was dealing with what had for a thousand years and more been deemed the central and most sacred dogma of the Christian religion, and made his attack so violent, and in a manner so ruthless, that even the reformers that more or less agreed with him shrank back from him and were forced to disown him, lest all Christendom rise in protest against such a reform. Hence for a generation doctrinal reform in this direction went into an eclipse, not to take a fresh start until saner thinkers and more sober leaders should arise to give it direction. Before proceeding, however, to trace the further development, it will be necessary to survey the more or less abortive attempts to which reference has just been made, since they were nevertheless like scattered springs which, lost in the ground for a time, were at length to contribute to a single permanent stream.

CHAPTER III

ANTITRINITARIAN TENDENCIES AMONG THE EARLY ANABAPTISTS IN GERMANY AND SWITZERLAND

IT HAS BEEN NOTED in the previous chapter that though the leading thinkers of the Protestant Reformation at the outset showed a clear tendency to waver about including in their doctrinal system the dogmas with which we are here most concerned, yet they were before long led by force of circumstances to affirm them with the utmost positiveness. Orthodox Protestant theology did indeed divest itself of the current scholastic terminology, but it retained without wavering the Nicene and Athanasian form of doctrine. After the leading reformers had abandoned any plan for a thorough and consistent reform of the Christian doctrines, and had become absorbed in other aspects of Protestantism, there remained, however, an unorganized but by no means uninfluential minority of those that continued to follow that quest. These were forerunners of the movement whose history we are here tracing, though it was not until a generation later that it assumed a coherent, organized form. These forerunners were found in two separate camps, quite different in composition and character, and widely separated in space, though in the ultimate development they were destined to unite and bear fruit as the one fertilized the other.

The one group was found among those known as Anabaptists. Although among their leaders there were a few able scholars, their following as a rule was among the humbler classes both intellectually and socially. Originating in Switzerland, they spread northward into Germany and Holland, and eastward into Moravia and Poland, and to a small degree into northern Italy. They had an enormous number of adherents. In temperament they were mystics, fervent in piety, and for the most part they had little interest in doctrinal theology. Their primary concern in religion was practical, and their aim was to live Christian lives, and form a Christian community which should strictly conform to the commands of Jesus and the practice of the primitive Church.

The other group was found among the Humanists south of the Alps. They were cultivated intellectuals of high social position and superior education. At first they were still in nominal communion with the Roman Church; and it was not until the Inquisition began to put them in peril that they fled from Italy and sought refuge in Switzerland, Moravia or Poland. They were relatively as few in number as they were important in influence. In temperament they were rationalists, and their primary interest in religion was intellectual. The Christian religion was to them a system of philosophy, and the Church a school of definite and reasonable opinions.

It will at once be imagined that if these two groups could in the course of time and by natural processes be somehow fused, a very interesting religious movement might result, and one stronger than either of its component parts. Such a fusion was in fact destined to take place in Poland, where, as we shall see, these two strains eventually coalesced, Anabaptist elements furnishing the most of the material, and Italian liberals providing the stimulus and leadership, for a nascent Socinianism. Before we arrive at that point, however, it is necessary to give a little further consideration to these two contrasted lines of development, and to the ground of their conflict with the conservative majority.

The Protestant Reformation early began in another respect to develop in two radically different directions. On the one hand were the more conservative spirits, who wished to form out of those that had left the Roman communion a new Church, in which of course the abuses of the old one should be corrected, but with the general form, purpose and spirit very much the same as of old. It was to be systematically organized, its worship was to be sacramental, its faith was to be strictly defined, and membership in it was to be conditioned on conformity to an orthodox standard of belief, and to accepted usages. On the other hand were those that wished a spiritual fellowship of free spirits, with little formal organization, with no prescribed form of worship, with no inflexible standard of belief, but with primary emphasis upon personal religious experience in a direct communion of the soul with God. Out of the former tendency came the Lutheran and Reformed Churches; out of the latter, the Anabaptist movement.

It lay in the nature of things that in the former case individual freedom would be considerably restricted by the spirit of the organization, that tradition would weigh more heavily than reason, and that there would be little tolerance of those that did not conform to the accepted standards; and that if spiritual freedom were to be found and reason and tolerance to be widely exercised, it would be rather in the other camp. Moreover, it might naturally be expected that in case of conflict between the two contrasted systems, the churches of organization and discipline would prevail over a movement that preferred freedom of the individual soul to a régime of discipline and restraint. It would have been well for the history of Christianity in Europe had both types of religion been able, or been permitted, to exist normally side by side, each making its contribution to the total of Europe's spiritual life. The persecution and repression of the Anabaptist movement, therefore, though no doubt in the circumstances unavoidable, is one of the most regrettable phases of the history of the modern Church.

The very widespread but ill-defined body that came to be known as Anabaptists were called by this name because what seemed to the common mind most conspicuously to distinguish them from other Christians was the fact that they rejected infant baptism, and insisted that the rite should be administered only to adults upon confession of personal faith in Christ. This involved that any that had been baptized in infancy must upon reaching maturity be *re*-baptized: hence the name *Ana*-baptists, which they themselves never accepted, since they did not admit that baptism of infants was real baptism at all. The spiritual roots of this very important movement lay far back of Protestantism, in circles of devout mystics and humble believers in the bosom of the Catholic Church, such as had in the Middle Ages given the world devotional classics like the *Imitation of Christ* and *Theologia Germanica*. Never regarded with too much favor in ecclesiastical circles, they were stimulated by the Reformation into fresh vitality and activity. After a few years this movement, which was essentially one devoted to the cultivation of personal religious experience and the development of Christian character, became in certain quarters more or less infiltrated and blended with a strain of a quite different origin and character: a movement of the poor and oppressed classes, whose primary interest in religion seemed to be social and political, and whose aim was, along with the Reformation to bring about a radical reconstruction of the social order.

This phase of the Anabaptist movement soon attracted to it a large and unruly following; and as they had no leader strong enough and wise enough to guide them or to hold them in restraint, they presently got out of hand, and in the belief that the millennium was soon to come they ran into the wildest excesses of superstition, fanaticism and immorality. The Peasants' War and the social chaos at Münster followed, and had to be mercilessly checked by the sword in 1535. The result upon the whole movement was that Anabaptism, which at the outset had great merits and no little promise, became deeply discredited, and was all but utterly wrecked by the impatience and excesses of its radical elements; so that Anabaptists were more bitterly hated and more harshly persecuted than the adherents of any other religious movement in the sixteenth century. The scattered remnants that survived persecution were at length gathered into an organized body under the sober leadership of Menno Simons in Holland, from whose followers have descended the Mennonites or Doopsgezinden in Holland, and the Baptists of England and America, who still continue many of the best traditions of the earlier Anabaptism.

Our concern here is with Anabaptism as a purely religious movement. It may fairly be said to have begun its separate existence as an outgrowth of the Reformation at Zürich, in 1525, when Zwingli's church there decided to enforce the practice of infant baptism, and banished the leaders of the party that opposed it. These therefore withdrew and organized a separate church of their own. The matter of baptism, however, was only an incidental and superficial symptom of more fundamental differences. Zwingli wanted to form a strong Protestant State Church; the Anabaptists demanded a church absolutely independent of the State. He wished to reform the old; they, to build something entirely new. He tolerated all that had been members of the old Church; they wanted a church of believers only.[1] They were diligent in their study of the Bible, were severely strict in their lives and in their church discipline, and tried in everything to conform to the precepts and practice of the New Testament as they understood it. Their views of a reformed Christianity corresponded to a desire very widely felt, and their movement spread with great rapidity. Holding strictly to the teaching of Scripture, they interpreted it according to what they deemed an inner light, upheld freedom of conscience, opposed religious persecution, cared little for speculative doctrines or outward ceremonies, and nothing for creeds or councils except as those agreed with Scripture. As they held aloof

---

[1] cf. H. E. Dosker, *The Dutch Anabaptists* (Philadelphia, 1921), p. 33.

from the existing Lutheran or Reformed Churches, which were trying
to unite the forces of Protestantism against Catholic opposition, and
were often sharply critical of them, they incurred their bitter hatred, and
were widely persecuted, even unto death, as turbulents dangerous to
the very existence of Protestantism. In their relations to civil society
their views varied according to locality and to the leaders they followed;
but they were in general non-resistants, opposed military service, oaths,
courts, capital punishment and usury, and often advocated community
of goods. Such views brought many of them into collision with the
State, and relentless persecution followed. At the Diet of Speyer in 1529
death was decreed against all Anabaptists, and during half a century
large numbers of them were put to death with all imaginable cruelty
in all the countries of Europe.

Inasmuch as the Anabaptists rejected all external authority in religion save Scripture, which each explained according to his own inner
conviction, the way was open for wide differences of opinion as to matters of belief; and these depended upon whether they tended to fall in
with current modes of thought, or to think independently of inherited
tradition and prevailing usage. Hence it is not surprising that we find
a tendency stronger among them than elsewhere to call received dogmas
in question, and to favor other views as more agreeable to Scripture,
more in accordance with reason, and more helpful to piety. Such independent thinkers would naturally be in the minority, and the free spirit
of the movement, with its inclination to emphasize the conduct of life
far more than details of belief, would discourage organized effort to
enforce this doctrine or that. In tracing the progress of thought we shall
therefore have to do not with the whole body of Anabaptists, but with
individual members of it. These individuals, however, may stand as
signs of a widespread ferment of thought which, when conditions become favorable, will cohere into the movement with whose history we
are here concerned, and of which they were the earliest pioneers.

Antitrinitarian views early made their appearance in Protestant circles. At Nürnberg in the autumn of 1524 and the following January
several (presumably Anabaptists) were arrested for teaching that there
is only one God, and that Jesus Christ is not God. The Council sought
counsel of Luther as to their punishment. He ascribed their doctrines
to the influence of the radical Anabaptists, Münzer and Karlstadt, and
replied that he regarded them not as blasphemers but as Turks and

apostates.[2] A little latter the Humanist Andreas Althamer complains in a little book,[3] 'And now comes Satan with a new rabble who say that Christ was only a prophet and a mere man and not very God, who also deny the whole New Testament; and some of these I have myself heard, and more or less known.' It is not certain whom he had in mind.

The first known Protestant, however, to express such views in print was Martin Cellarius.[4] He was born at Stuttgart in 1499, became an accomplished Hebraist at Tübingen under Reuchlin, studied philosophy at Heidelberg, and then proceeded to Wittenberg where he enjoyed the friendship of Melanchthon. Here, however, he embraced Anabaptist views, had a heated quarrel with Luther, and leaving in 1525 went to East Prussia, where he defended Anabaptism in print, and was for a time held in prison for his radical views. When released the following year he went to Strassburg, was befriended by Capito, leader of the Reformation there,[5] grew more conservative, and in 1527 published there a little book, *De operibus Dei*. In this he remarks, though only in passing, that Jesus is God because he shared fully in the deity which dwelt in him bodily, and in the Holy Spirit which he had without measure; but he adds that we too are all Gods and sons of the Most High, by our sharing in the same deity and Spirit.[6] This book was so highly esteemed by those that a generation later were just launching a Unitarian movement in Transylvania, that they republished a part of it there together with the commendatory preface by Capito.[7] Cellarius continued his studies at Strassburg, and won such a reputation that in 1536 he was made professor at the University of Basel, where he successively

---

[2] Thudichum, *Reformation*, ii, 151 f.

[3] *Das unser Christus Jesus warer Gott sey, zeugnüss der heyligen geschrifft, wider die newen Juden und Arrianer, unter Christlichem namen, welche die Gottheyt Christi verleugnen.* (Nürnberg, 1527), p. aa ii.

[4] See *Athenae Rauricae* (Basileae, 1778), p. 24 f; Camill Gerbert, *Geschichte der Strassburger Sektenbewegung* (Strassburg, 1889), pp. 64–70; Bernhard Riggenbach, article in *Basler Jahrbuch* (Basel, 1900), pp. 47–84; Stanislaus von Dunin Borkowski, 'Quellenstudien zur Vorgeschichte der Unitarier des 16. Jahrhunderts' (in *75 Jahre Stella Matutina, Festschrift*, Feldkirch, 1931), i, 121–125.

[5] cf. Zwingli, *Sämtliche Werke*, hrsg. Egli u. Finsler (Leipzig, 1905–), ix, 191 f; Ludwig Keller, *Ein Apostel der Wiedertäuffer* (Leipzig, 1882), p. 153.

[6] Sit ille Deus plene per plenam participationem Deitatis quae in eo habitat corporaliter, et per plenam participationem Spiritus Sancti quem ad mensuram non habet. At et nos Dei et filii excelsi omnes sumus, participatione Deitatis et Spiritus ejusdem. *op. cit.*, p. 28a.

[7] Under the title, *De restauratione ecclesiae*, as a part of Blandrata's *De Mediatore* (Albae Juliae, 1568.)

taught Rhetoric, Oratory, and the Old Testament, and was twice Rector.[8] Though discreet in expressing his views, he used in his Commentary on Isaiah (Basel, 1561) numerous expressions as to God and Christ which the early Unitarians adopted bodily, claiming him for one of their own.[9] He died of the plague at Basel in 1564.

A far more significant influence was that of Johann (or Hans) Denck,[10] the most important of the South-German Anabaptists. Outcast and persecuted in his own time, he has more recently come to be appreciated as one of the most gifted and noblest characters, and one of the profoundest religious thinkers, of the sixteenth century. Impressive and handsome in appearance and dignified in bearing, he made a favorable impression on all that heard him; and both his followers and his opponents bore testimony to his talents, spotless character and influence. His teachings were widely accepted in the Rhine cities, Franconia, Bavaria, Switzerland and Moravia; and leading conservative reformers styled him the Abbot or Pope of the Anabaptists.[11]

He was born probably in Bavaria about 1495, studied at Ingolstadt, and while earning his living as corrector for the press won a higher degree at Basel in the time of Erasmus's residence there, and established a reputation for his mastery of Latin, Greek and Hebrew. On the recommendation of his friend Oecolampadius, leader of the Reformation at Basel, he was appointed Rector of St. Sebald's School at Nürnberg, a position of much importance. He was at the time nominally a Lutheran, but he had already been much impressed by such mystical writings as *Theologia Germanica*, the sermons of Johann Tauler, and the *Imitation of Christ*. As his thought ripened he found himself growing out of sympathy with some of Luther's central doctrines, and into sympathy with some of the views of Anabaptist leaders.

---

[8] In entering upon his new career he gave up the name Cellarius which he had previously adopted, and resumed his original name of Borrhäus.

[9] For the proof, with citation of passages, cf. Dunin Borkowski, *op. cit.*, p. 121 ff.

[10] cf. Wilhelm Heberle, 'Johann Denk und sein Büchlein vom Gesetz,' *Theologische Studien und Kritiken*, xxiv (1851), 121–194, 412 f; do., 'Johann Denk und die Ausbreitung seiner Lehre,' *id. op.*, xxviii (1855), 817–890; Ludwig Keller, *op. cit.*; *Realencyklopädie von protestantischer Theologie und Kirche*, 3. Aufl., iv, 576; *Mennonitisches Lexikon* (Frankfurt a/M., 1913–), i, 401–414; Rufus M. Jones, *Spiritual Reformers in the 16th and 17th centuries* (New York, 1914), chap. ii., "Hans Denck and the Inward Word"; Frederick L. Weis, *Life, Teachings and Works of Johannes Denck* (Strasbourg, 1924).

[11] cf. Heberle, in *Studien und Kritiken*, xxviii, 847 ff.

When Osiander, the leader of the Lutheran church at Nürnberg, learned of this, he had Denck called to account before the city Council. Denck discussed his views before them with ability, but was required to submit a written confession of his beliefs. The outcome was that toward the end of January, 1525, he was suddenly ordered to leave the city before nightfall and never to come near it again. He obeyed the order, and during the remaining three years of his life was hounded from place to place as a homeless wanderer.

The rumor at once spread that he had been banished as a dangerous man, who held revolutionary ideas, disbelieved the Scriptures, and denied cardinal doctrines of Christianity. After a few months he appeared at St. Gallen in Switzerland, where he lived in the Anabaptist circle, maturing and discussing his views of religion. When trouble arose here, he removed to Augsburg, where the Anabaptists were very numerous. Here he was baptized into their communion and presently became a leader of great influence among them. The leaders of the Lutheran church felt their work much imperiled by the competition of another movement, for Denck was privately making many converts. They challenged him to a public debate, forbade his preaching at private meetings, and made bitter attacks upon him. Their power was too great for him to withstand successfully, and after a little more than a year he took the course of safety and left Augsburg for Strassburg, which was at the time the most hospitable place for free thought in religion. Here also the Anabaptists were numerous, and Capito, one of the leaders of the Protestant forces, which were still wavering between Luther and Zwingli, was well-disposed toward them. He had already given Cellarius a kind reception, and at first he showed himself friendly to Denck, whose irreproachable life and earnest moral teachings won him great respect. But Butzer, the other leader of the Protestants, feared that the whole Protestant cause there would be imperiled by further growth of Anabaptism. He therefore challenged Denck to a public debate, and then procured his banishment from the city after but two months' residence.

Leaving Strassburg the day before Christmas, 1527, Denck made his way down the Rhine valley, stopping for brief missionary efforts at two towns on the way, until he came to Worms. The Anabaptists here were engaged in a struggle with the Lutherans, and had already converted Jakob Kautz and another of their ministers. Denck quietly threw his strength into the struggle, but used his pen with good effect. He here found Ludwig Haetzer, an Anabaptist friend of earlier days. Both of them accomplished scholars, they brought to completion a translation of the Old Testament Prophets which had been begun at Strassburg.[12] This work was one of fine scholarship, and was made more or less the basis of the translation by the Swiss theologians in 1529, and of that by Luther three years later. It was so highly esteemed that within four years seventeen different editions of it appeared.[13] Though at Worms Denck had not come out in public, Kautz, fervent in his new faith, challenged the city preachers to a debate. The usual trouble followed. The Elector Ludwig intervened, the leaders of the movement had to leave the city, and within a short time several hundred of their followers were put to death in the Palatinate.[14]

Denck left Worms in July, and by midsummer was again at Augsburg, presiding over a gathering of Anabaptist leaders, and trying to organize the movement and to check the extreme tendencies toward which it was rapidly drifting. In this effort he apparently became discouraged, for at the end of September he addressed a pathetic appeal to his old friend Oecolampadius at Basel, begging that he might be suffered to stay there in quiet, undisturbing and undisturbed. His appeal was granted, and he now enjoyed a few weeks free from fear of persecution, during which he had many earnest conversations with Oecolampadius. But the plague was abroad, it seized upon a body worn by hardships and anxieties, and he died before the end of the year, hardly thirty-two years old.

During the three years of his public activity Denck published five little tracts, widely circulated in their time, though now extremely rare.[15] It is chiefly from these that we may learn his views. His view of religious truth was mystical: that God reveals it to us through an Inner Word, which Scripture may confirm but did not originate. Hence religious

---

[12] *Alle Propheten nach Hebräischer sprach verteutscht von Ludwig Hetzer und Hans Dengk* (Wormbs, 1527).

[13] cf. Frederick L. Weis, *Life, Teachings and Works of Ludwig Hetzer* (Lancaster, 1930), p. 141.

[14] cf. Keller, *Apostel*, p. 210.

[15] *Wer die warhait warlich lieb hat* (1525); *Was geredt sey, das die Schrifft sagt* (1526); *Ordnung Gottes, und der Creaturen werck* (1526); *Vom Gesatz Gottes* (1526); *Von der waren Lieb* (1527). Denck's tracts were reprinted in one volume at Amsterdam, 1680, under the title, *Geistliches Blumengärtlein.*

experience is a continuous revelation of God, and even Scripture can not be rightly understood save when illuminated by this inner authority. He thus gave a radically new interpretation of religion, setting up inner experience as superior to external authority or tradition. As against Luther, he defended freedom of the will, and held the Church to be not an external organization of all that hold the accepted doctrine, but a spiritual fellowship of all in whom the Spirit of God dwells. He also taught the ultimate salvation of all men.[16] In various other respects he set forth views that were little heeded by the dominant churches of his time, but have been more and more adopted since. Had he lived long enough to develop his thinking into a consistent system, and to spread it without being hindered by persecution, the Apostolic Brethren, as these moderate Anabaptists liked to call themselves, might have contributed to the Protestant movement of the sixteenth century a third form, along with the Lutheran and the Reformed Church, which would have had a wide and profound effect of the most wholesome sort upon the religious and moral life of Europe. Such freedom did at length come, to a restricted degree, to Menno Simons and his followers in Holland; but it was then too late for the Church of the Inner Experience to make the wide appeal that it had once bid fair to make, and the moral and spiritual life of Europe has therefore remained forever the poorer.

It was charged in his own time, and has been said repeatedly since, that Denck was an Antitrinitarian; but this can not be stated without reservation. In the confession that he presented at Nürnberg, and in a similar document drawn up just before his death for Oecolampadius, and published by the latter under the misleading title of *Widerruf* (Recantation), his views as to God and Christ are not included, though as his dissent from the prevailing views had been most marked on other topics of belief, it is perhaps of no particular significance that he did not touch upon the former. In the tenth chapter of his *Ordnung Gottes*, speaking of the Trinity, Unity, and Unity in Trinity of God, he says indeed that omnipotence, goodness and righteousness are the one and only Trinity of God;[17] but this must probably be taken rather as a symbolical expression than as a definite doctrinal statement. On the other hand, Capito wrote to Zwingli that Denck was banished from

---

[16] cf. Heberle, in *Studien und Kritiken*, xxviii (1855), 828–831.

[17] Allmacht, Güte und Gerechtigkeit, das ist die Dreifaltigkeit, einigkeit und einige Dreiheit Gottes.

Nürnberg for his doctrine about the Trinity;[18] Butzer wrote to him that Denck held that Christ is only an example for our imitation;[19] and Urbanus Rhegius, with whom he held a public disputation at Augsburg in 1526, bore similar testimony.[20] These charges can not be substantiated from any of his extant writings; but unless it is presumed that they are wanton fabrications of theological opponents, it may be believed that they are based upon what he had said in private conversation or public discussion. Such an inference is encouraged by his significant silence in his public writings as to doctrines which, if believed at all, should hold too important a place for them to be quite ignored; and further by the fact that he was on terms of intimacy with Haetzer and Kautz, whose rejection of these doctrines was well known. The fact that they lack quite satisfactory scriptural support would, to one holding his view of Scripture, be sufficient reason for leaving them out of account. It is therefore probably not unfair to consider Denck as having been (even if not in a positive and aggressive way) one of the pioneers of our movement.

In Denck's contemporary and fellow-worker Ludwig Haetzer (Hetzer) we find a man of more outspoken views, though of less stable character and of more tragic history.[21] He was born about 1500 at Bischofszell in Switzerland, not far from Constanz, and even before the Reformation was probably brought up as a Waldensian, and hence predisposed to join the Anabaptist movement when that arose. He perhaps studied at the German University of Freiburg, and knew his Hebrew uncommonly well. He began his public career as preacher at the charming village of Wädenschwyl on the Lake of Zürich. Zwingli at Zürich was beginning his efforts for the reform of the Church, and Haetzer took an active part with him; but he became dissatisfied that the reform was not pushed faster and further, and his sympathies were with the radical reformers who were soon to be exiled or put to death. He soon left Zürich for Augsburg, where he found influential friends. Before long he was again at Zürich actively siding with the Anabaptist radicals;

---

[18] Norimbergae ludimagister apud Theobaldi templum negavit spiritum sanctum et filium esse aequalem Patri, qui ob id pulsus et ejectus est. Capito to Zwingli, Feb. 6, 1525, Zwingli, *Werke*, viii, 302.

[19] Bucer to Zwingli, Aug. 13, 1527, Zwingli, *Werke*, ix, 185.

[20] Keller, *Apostel* p. 245.

[21] cf. Theodor Keim, 'Ludwig Hetzer', *Jahrbücher für deutsche Theologie*, i (1856), 215–288; *Realencyk.*, vii, 325; Weis, *Hetzer*.

and when they were driven out early in 1525 he returned to Augsburg where he found a party of radical Anabaptists now in full swing, and passionately espoused their cause. It was the tumultuous year of the Peasants' War, with which he sympathized, though he took no part in it. The Anabaptist cause grew amazingly, and was dreaded as dangerous. The religious authorities challenged him to a public disputation, at that time the usual means for settling doctrinal controversies. He failed to appear, and was therefore banished as a turbulent and dangerous man, but he left as a result of his mission the most numerous congregation of Anabaptists in all Germany.

Banished from both Zürich and Augsburg, Haetzer now turned to Basel, where he sought the friendship of Oecolampadius, and was taken into his house, where he lived for the best part of a year, broken by three visits to Zürich in the hope of a reconciliation with Zwingli. For a time he appeared to be wavering in his Anabaptism, but at length his mind was cleared, and he threw himself into the movement heart and soul. Late in the summer of 1526 he left Basel for Strassburg, where he found shelter in the home of Capito. He already had a reputation for eloquence and for fine scholarship, and did not here openly associate with the Anabaptists. Instead, he labored on a translation of the prophecy of Isaiah, in which he was assisted by Denck after the arrival of the latter in the autumn; and this work grew under their hands until it embraced all the Hebrew Prophets, as related above. Meantime the Anabaptist movement at Strassburg was assuming such proportions that the leaders of the city churches were alarmed. If Protestantism were to succeed in the face of the powerful Catholic opposition, it must have support from the civil government; but if Anabaptism grew much stronger this could not be hoped for. Prompt measures had to be taken. The usual course was followed. A public discussion was arranged, and on the basis of this Denck, as leader of the movement, was banished as we have already seen, and the Anabaptists were later put under the ban.[22] It was now time to take sides. Capito, who had hitherto sympathized with the Anabaptists enough to make him non-committal, now ranged himself along with Butzer against them; while Haetzer, who had hitherto remained inactive, took the part of Denck and soon followed him to Worms. What took place there during the next six months has already been told in connection with Denck. When the Protestants of the city had been

---

[22] For the decree of the Council in the case, cf. Weis, *Hetzer*, p. 135 f.

all but won over to Anabaptist views, the Elector intervened, the movement was crushed, and its leaders had to flee for their lives. The two went up the Rhine, quietly doing missionary preaching on the way, visited Nürnberg,[23] were present at the gathering of Anabaptist leaders of which mention has been made, and then separated, Denck going to Basel where he was soon to die.

Haetzer after a year's wanderings, and having again to flee from Augsburg, returned to his old haunts in Switzerland, and finally in the summer of 1528 came to Constanz. The little group of Anabaptists here had been severely persecuted, but he sought their company. After a few weeks he was arrested, not however as an Anabaptist, but unfortunately charged with flagrant and repeated breaches of the moral code. Legend greatly exaggerated his offences, but it probably must be admitted that his was one of those ill-assorted natures in which religious exaltation sometimes co-exists with weakness in face of temptation. The evidence against him was convincing, and he was condemned to death by beheading, and was executed February 4, 1529. His behavior in the last hours of his life was such as to win the sympathy and admiration of all that observed it, and even to persuade some then and since that he could not have been guilty as charged.[24]

Being by nature less reserved and moderate than Denck, Haetzer expressed his views more distinctly. Doubtless under Denck's influence, he denied the vicarious atonement, and rejected the doctrine of eternal punishment.[25] In a fragment of a hymn or poem of his entitled *Reime unter dem Kreuzgang Christi* which has been preserved to us, is a most explicit denial of the doctrine of the Trinity:[26]

[23] cf. J. H. Ottius, *Annales Anabaptistici* (Basileae, 1672), anno 1528, p. 46.

[24] cf. Thomas Blaurer, *Wie L. Hetzer zu Costenz mit dem Schwertgericht uss diesm zyt abscheyden ist* (Constanz, 1529); Sebastian Franck, *Chronica* (Strassburg, 1531), p. 415b; J. J. Hottinger, *Helvetische Kirchen-Geschichten* (Zürich, 1698–1729), iii, 498 f; J. Breitinger, 'Anekdota quaedam de Ludovico Haetzer' *Museum Helveticum* (Zürich, 1751), vi, 100–121; Tieleman J. van Braght, *Martyrology of the Churches of Christ commonly called Baptists*, etc. (London, 1850), i, 97–100 (Hanserd Knollys Society Publications, vol. vi).

[25] cf. Capito to Zwingli, July 7, 1527, Zwingli, *Werke*, ix, 167 f; quoted in Weis, *Hetzer*, p. 239.

[26] Preserved in Franck, *Chronica, loc. cit.*; reproduced also by Breitinger, *op. cit.*, p. 117; F. S. Bock, *Historia Antitrinitariorum* (Regiomonti et Lipsiae, 1776), ii, 235; Joseph Beck, *Geschichtsbücher der Wiedertäuffer in Oesterreich-Ungarn* (Fontes Rerum Austriacarum, ii. Abteilung, Bd. 43, Wien, 1883), p. 34; Weis, *Hetzer*, p. 214 f.

> Ich bin allein der einig Gott,
> Der on gehilff alle ding beschaffen hat.
> Fragstu wievil meiner sey?
> Ich bins allein, meinr seind nit drey.
> Sag auch darbey on allen won
> Da ich glat nit weiss von keinr person,
> Bin auch weder dis noch das:
> Wem ichs nit sag, der weisst nit was.

Haetzer is also said to have been the first to attack the doctrine of the deity of Christ, in a book which Zwingli suppressed,[27] and in which, according to Franck, he held that Christ was not equal to God, nor of one essence with the Father. This book remained in manuscript until Haetzer's death, after which at his request it was destroyed by Ambrosius Blaurer in 1532.[28]

The effect of views like these of Denck and Haetzer is seen in the publication at Nikolsburg in Moravia in 1527 of the so-called Nikolsburg Theses which were there proposed for discussion. The authorship of them was ascribed to Balthasar Hubmaier (Hübmeier, Hubmör), who belonged to the same circle as Denck and Haetzer. They proposed, *inter alia*, that Christ was born in sin; Mary was not mother of God but only mother of Christ; Christ was not God, but only a prophet to whom the word of God was committed; Christ did not make satisfaction for all the sins of the world.[29] Such views were calculated seriously to prejudice the Protestant cause in the eyes of the Christian world at large, and positive steps were taken to disown them. At once in 1530, therefore, the Augsburg Confession takes the first opportunity to say in the name of the reforming party (Article I., *De Deo*), ". . . Damnant et Samosatenos, veteres et neotericos, qui, cum tantum unam personam esse contendant, de Verbo et de Spiritu Sancto astute et impie rhetoricantur, quod non sint personae distinctae, sed quod Verbum significat verbum vocale, et Spiritus motum in rebus creatum." [30]

---

[27] cf. Ottius, *op. cit.*, *anno* 1529, sec. 4: Deitatem Christi ex illo hominum genere primus impugnavit libro scripto, quem suppressit Zwinglius.

[28] cf. Keim, *Hetzer*, p. 284.

[29] Printed in Johannes Heumann, *Documenta literaria* (Leipzig, 1758), p. 65; J. E. Gayler, *Historische Denkwürdigkeiten von Reutlingen* (Reutlingen, 1840), p. 317; Heberle in *Studien und Kritiken*, xxviii (1855), 854; Weis, *Hetzer*, p. 218.

[30] The reference has often been supposed to be to Servetus, or even to the Socinians. The dates make this impossible. Servetus did not publish until 1531, and the Socinians not until a generation later. The liberal Anabaptists must have been in mind. cf. Henricus

At Worms we found associated with Denck and Haetzer one of the city pastors, Jakob Kautz, a gifted and extraordinarily eloquent young preacher from Bockenheim.[31] He was a restless, fiery spirit, inclined to be radical, and had already two years before received as his guest the radical Anabaptist Melchior Hofmann, and been influenced by him. He and his colleague Hilarius had withdrawn from the Lutheran Church a few days before Denck and Haetzer arrived. They stayed at his house, and the three worked together in translating the Prophets and in making converts to their cause. Emboldened by success, Kautz early in June posted theses [32] on the cathedral door, challenging the Lutherans to a debate. Besides the characteristic Anabaptist positions, he proposed to defend the eternal salvation of all men, and declared that Christ's death made satisfaction for our sins only by showing us how to walk in the way of life. Whoever believes otherwise about him makes him an idol. The Lutherans presented opposing theses, and they and the Catholics banded together to oppose the Anabaptism which threatened to sweep the city. The Elector supported them with his power, the leaders of the movement fled for their lives, many of their followers were put to death, Anabaptism in Worms was crushed, and for a time all Protestantism as well. Kautz betook himself to Augsburg, where he again met Denck and Haetzer, and thence went to Rothenburg an der Tauber and perhaps to Moravia.

Meantime report of the doings at Worms had reached Strassburg and aroused no little concern among the reformers there. At the beginning of July therefore they issued a "Faithful Warning of the Preachers" (presumably written by Butzer) against the theses lately put forth by Kautz, and the serious errors of Denck and other Anabaptists.[33] The warning did not suffice as yet to stem the rising tide. Toward the end

---

ab Allwoerden, *Historia Michaelis Serveti* (Helmstadii, 1728), pp. 26–29; J. G. Walch, *Dissertatio de Samosatenianis neotericis quorum mentio fit in Confessione Augustana* (Jenae, 1730), pp. 14–25.

[31] cf. Heberle in *Studien und Kritiken*, xxviii (1855), 838–847; Weis, *Hetzer*, pp. 146–151.

[32] cf. Zwingli, *Opera*, ed. Schuler et Schulthess (Zürich, 1829–'42), viii. 77, n. 1; Heberle in article above cited, pp. 840–842; Thudichum, *Reformation*, ii, 162; Weis, *Hetzer*, p. 149 f.

[33] *Getrewe Warnung der Prediger des Evangelii zu Strassburg über die Artikel so Jacob Kautz, Prediger zu Worms, kürtzlich hat lassen aussgehn, die Frucht der Schrift und Gottes Worts, den Kinder Tauff und erlösung unsers Herrn Jesu Christi sampt anderm, darin sich Hans Dencken und anderer widertäuffer schwere yrthumb erregen betreffend* (Strassburg, 1527).

of the following year Kautz and a companion preacher came to Strassburg, as still the most tolerant of the Rhine cities,[34] and the most promising for spreading their views. They preached on the streets, and
raised such a disturbance that they were soon lodged in jail. They
asked for a public debate with the preachers, in which to defend their
views, but in the circumstances this was not deemed expedient. A written discussion was had, but to no purpose, and they were both required
to leave the city.[35] Again in 1532 Kautz sought permission to return to
Strassburg, promising to keep the peace; but the Magistrate was suspicious of him, and the preachers doubted his being able to keep his
promise.[36] He did not return.

Not long after the events above related of Anabaptist leaders in southern Germany and along the middle Rhine, a leader arose among the
Lutherans in northern Germany and along the lower Rhine who attracted considerable attention and exerted influence for well-nigh a century. This was Johannes Campanus.[37] He was born about 1500 at
Naeseyck in what is now the northeastern corner of Belgium, and was
educated at Düsseldorf and Cologne, where he had a reputation for
scholarship and high character, though for favoring Luther's ideas of
reform he was finally dismissed from the University. He may well have
got his start in heresy from radical Anabaptists who were at this time
active in the Netherlands;[38] but if so he kept his own counsel, and until
1530 was apparently a sincere and ardent Lutheran. In 1528 he went
to Wittenberg where he studied for nearly two years, esteemed for his
gifts and earnestness; but he disagreed with Luther about the Eucharist,
and sought an opportunity to lay before the conference at Marburg in
1529 a view that he felt sure would reconcile Luther and Zwingli and
prevent a division of the Protestant movement. He was not admitted,

[34] cf. Keim, *Hetzer*, i, 276; F. W. E. Roth, *Buchdruckereien zu Worms* (Worms, 1892),
p. 4.

[35] cf. T. W. Röhrich, *Geschichte der Reformation im Elsass* (Strassburg, 1830–32), i,
341; *id.*, 'Zur Geschichte der strassburgischen Wiedertäuffer', *Zeitschrift für die historische
Theologie*, xxx (1860), 43–48.

[36] cf. Röhrich, *Reformation*, ii, 76; *id.*, *Wiedertäuffer*, pp. 60–64.

[37] cf. J. G. Schelhorn, 'De Joanne Campano Anti-trinitario dissertatio' (*Amoenitates
Literariae*, Frankfurt, 1725–'31), xi, 1–92; Trechsel, *Antitrinitarier*, i, 26–34; Karl Rembert, *Wiedertäufer im Herzogtum Jülich* (Berlin, 1899), 161–302; *Mennonit. Lex.*, i,
317–324.

[38] cf. W. D. Tenzel, *Historischer Bericht . . der Reformation Lutheri*, ed. Cyprian
(Leipzig, 1717), p. 98. Campanus attacked the doctrine of the Trinity in Holland as early
as 1524; cf. Rembert, *op. cit.*, p. 164.

and soon left Wittenberg and went to the home of Georg Witzel, preacher at Niemeck, and engaged in study of the Fathers. Here he was ere long charged with unsoundness as to the Trinity. He himself made a hasty escape, and suspicion was transferred to Witzel who, though in fact innocent of the charge, was imprisoned, and so unfairly treated that he presently returned to the Catholic Church and became a determined foe of Luther's movement.

Campanus had meanwhile embraced Anabaptist and antinomian as well as antitrinitarian views. The Elector therefore caused his arrest, and for a time held him in confinement.[39] This treatment did not alter his opinions, and in 1530, when the Elector was preparing to go to the Diet of Augsburg to lay the reformers' views before the Emperor, Campanus ventured to present to him a written statement of his doctrines, which he desired to have publicly debated. His request was not granted, though the Elector was impressed, and took the statement with him to Augsburg. It denied, among other things, the deity of Christ and of the Holy Spirit, and the doctrine of original sin, and Melanchthon thought it a wicked lot of doctrines.[40] Melanchthon would have had him arrested, but the Elector refused. He for his part felt that Luther's reformation went only half way, while the Lutherans on the other hand henceforth regarded him as a fanatical blasphemer. Melanchthon wrote to the court at Cleve a letter of earnest warning against Campanus, and an edict was consequently issued against him as an Anabaptist; though so many of the nobles in his vicinity favored Anabaptist views that his agitation of them was long tolerated, and his fame spread so far that Sebastian Franck in 1531 sent him from Strassburg a long letter expressing sympathetic appreciation of his efforts.[41]

Other avenues of approach to the Lutheran world being now closed to him, Campanus took up his pen and wrote a book entitled, *Against the whole world since the Apostles*.[42] Though this circulated rather widely in manuscript, it is not known to have been printed; but it was presently followed in print by an abridged version in German.[43] The

---

[39] cf. Melanchthon, *Opera*, ii, 13.

[40] Attulit magnum acervum impiorum dogmatum . . disputat Christum non esse Deum, Spiritum Sanctum non esse Deum, peccatum originale nomen inane esse. cf. Melanchthon to Myconius, March 27, 1530, *Opera*, ii, 33.

[41] cf. Rembert, *op. cit.*, pp. 217–226.

[42] *Contra totum post Apostolos mundum*.

[43] *Göttlicher und heiliger Schrifft, vor vilen jaren verdunckelt, und durch unheylsame*

little book covers Campanus's whole system of theology, discussing the various points in the light of Scripture, and is distinctly anti-Lutheran. Luther thought the work not worth paying any attention to, and advised that the writer be not complimented with an answer; but Melanchthon was more agitated by it, and expressed the opinion that the author deserved to be hanged, and he so wrote to the Duke of Jülich.[44] Campanus's view of the Trinity is but a small part of the whole system of doctrine by which he proposed to restore the purity of Apostolic Christianity, though it is the most original part, and the one with which he sets out. The case of Adam and Eve, who though two persons were declared to be one flesh, is taken as a symbol of the Divine Being, in which there are two persons but only one God. One of these bears, the other is born. The Son is not eternal like the Father, but was born from the essence of the Father before all worlds; but he was not eternally begotten, and is subordinate to the Father. Scripture knows of no third person; and the Holy Spirit is the common being of Father and Son, the nature and power of God which inspires in us true faith and holy life.

Campanus continued for some twenty years to spread his notion of a reformed Christianity along the lower Rhine. Melanchthon kept watching him and writing the authorities letters against him; but his unbounded contempt for the Lutheran system won him favor and indulgence among a population largely Catholic. He gradually became more fanatical, and when at length he encouraged the peasants to quit work and live at ease in view of the approaching end of the world, he was arrested and imprisoned in the ducal castle at Angermund, about 1553.[45] Here he was kept in easy confinement for some twenty years until his death or release, after which he disappears from history.

It was noted above that when he was at the height of his activity in

---

leer und Leren (ausz Gottes zulassung) verfinstert, Restitution und besserung (1532). cf. Rembert, op. cit., pp. 238-264.

[44] Luther in his Table-talk said of him, Diesen verfluchten Unflat und Buben sol man nur verachten und sobald nicht wider ihn schreiben; denn da man wider ihn schreibe, so würde er desto kühner stolzer und mutiger . . . Da sprach M. Philip: Mein Bedencken were, dass man ihn an den liechten Galgen hienge, und solchs hette er seinem Herrn geschrieben. cf. Schelhorn, Campanus, p. 11. In his Table-talk for 1532 Luther also spoke of 'ein grewlich böss Buch wider die heilige Dreieinigkeit im Druck ausgegangen.' This has generally been supposed to refer to Servetus's book of 1531 on the Errors of the Trinity; but the reference fits Campanus equally well. (id., p. 56). cf. Melanchthon, Opera, ii, 29, 513.

[45] cf. Rembert, op. cit., p. 276, n.

behalf of a purer reformed religion Campanus received a sympathetic letter of encouragement from Sebastian Franck of Strassburg. Franck is one of the most engaging figures of his time, at once a mystic and a humanist, a keen observer and broad-minded judge of men and movements, an unsatisfied critic of all the reforming movements of his age, but addicted to none of them, though most sympathetic toward the Anabaptists. His soul was like a star that dwelt apart.[46] He was born in 1499 at Donauwörth in Bavaria, educated at Ingolstadt and Heidelberg, was for a short time a priest, then for a year or two was Lutheran preacher near Nürnberg, and for the rest of his life devoted himself to literary pursuits, writing numerous books on history or religion, and generally making them the medium for his own religious views. His books were among the most widely read in the Reformation age. At Nürnberg he was much influenced by the Anabaptists, and though he never joined their brotherhood he was inclined to them most of all the sects. Coming to Strassburg in 1529 he published his *Chronica*,[47] which had extraordinary popularity, and was often reprinted. It had escaped the vigilance of the censor, but its strong sympathy with heretics, its extracts from their writings, its espousal of the cause of the Anabaptists and its advocacy of unrestricted freedom of speech and of tolerance for them, gave so much offence that he was imprisoned, then sent away in perpetual banishment, and sale of the book was forbidden. The next eight years he lived as a wanderer, banished from place to place, unsuccessfully trying to make his living as a soap-maker, and devoting his spare time to his books. He came to rest at last at Basel as a printer, and died there in 1542 or 1543. In his beliefs he was a pronounced liberal, as appears most distinctly in his letter to Campanus. In this he speaks of Servetus, who had just published his book *On the Errors of*

---

[46] cf. H. W. Erbkam, *Geschichte der protestantischen Sekten im Zeitalter der Reformation* (Hamburg, 1848), pp. 286–357; C. A. Hase, *Sebastian Franck von Wörd der Schwarmgeist* (Leipzig, 1869); H. Ziegler, 'Kurze Darstellung Franck's theologischen Standpunkts,' *Zeitschrift für wissenschaftliche Theologie*, xii (1869), 383–421; J. F. Smith, 'Sebastian Franck, Heretic, Mystic and Reformer of the Reformation,' *Theological Review*, xi (1874), 158–179; Alfred Hegler, *Geist und Schrift bei Sebastian Franck* (Freiburg i/B, 1892); Edwin Tausch, *Sebastian Franck von Donauwörth und seine Lehrer*, (Berlin, 1893); Jones, *Reformers*, chap. iv., "Sebastian Franck: an Apostle of Inward Religion"; *Allgemeine Deutsche Biographie*, viii, 214; *Realencyk.*, vi, 142; *Mennonit. Lex.*, i, 668–674.

[47] *Chronica, Zeytbuch und Geschijchtbibel von anbegyn biss inn diss gegenwertig MDXXXI Yar* (Strassburg, 1531).

the Trinity, and was at Strassburg at this very time. Franck will certainly have known him personally, and he expresses approval of Servetus's doctrine of the Trinity.[48] He held that for pious Christians the Apostles' Creed and the Ten Commandments are enough.

In his letter to Campanus, Franck speaks in warm terms of commendation of Johannes Bünderlin,[49] a moderate, spiritually-minded Anabaptist. Very little is known of his life. He was from Linz in upper Austria, educated at the University of Vienna, and a good scholar. At first a Lutheran preacher, he became associated with the Anabaptists at their Augsburg conference in 1526, probably under the influence of Denck, though he later separated from them. We come across traces of his activity as an Apostle of the Anabaptists at Strassburg (where he was twice imprisoned) and Constanz, in Prussia and Moravia; but we lose track of him after 1533, when it is thought that he may have been put to death as a heretic. He published four little books, of which one was on the incarnation. He was in general agreement with Denck and Entfelder (see below), though it is hard to say decisively whether he was an Antitrinitarian. In his exposition of the doctrine of God he does not indeed deny the Trinity, but it seems significant that he wholly ignores it and avoids using the terms connected with it.

Of Bünderlin's contemporary and friend, Christian Entfelder,[50] even less is known. He was a disciple of Denck, was an Anabaptist preacher in Moravia, was with Bünderlin at Strassburg, and after separating from the Anabaptists was of some influence at the ducal court at Königsberg. Of his three published writings, one deals with the doctrine of the Trinity.[51] Dunin Borkowski calls this the first attempt to dissolve the dogma of the Trinity into a purely philosophical speculation. Entfelder is not such an Antitrinitarian as Campanus and Haetzer, for he tries to retain

---

[48] Strassburg, Feb. 4, 1531 . . . Der Spanier Servetus stellt in seinem Büchlein allein eine Person Gottes auf; Gott den Vater nämlich nennt er einen selbständigen Geist; keiner von beiden ist dagegen eine Person. Die Römische Kirche lehrt, dass da 3 Personen in einem Wesen sind. Ich halte lieber mit dem Spanier. Rembert, *Wiedertäuffer*, p. 225.

[49] cf. Alexander Nicoladoni, *Johannes Bünderlin von Linz und die oberösterreichischen Täufergemeinden in den Jahren 1525–1531* (Berlin, 1893); Jones, *Reformers*, chap. iii., "Two prophets of the Inward Word: Bünderlin and Entfelder"; Dunin Borkowski, *Quellenstudien*, pp. 110–112; *Mennonit. Lex.*, i, 298–300.

[50] cf. Georg Veesenmeyer, in *Neues theologisches Journal*, iv (1800), 309–334; Jones, *ut supra*; Dunin Borkowski, *op. cit.*, pp. 106–110; *Mennonit. Lex.*, i, 594 f.

[51] *Von Gottes unnd Christi Jesu unnseres Herren erkändtnuss*, etc., c. 1530. Bock, *Antitrinitar.*, ii, 240, erroneously attributes to a work of Denck a teaching clearly quoted from this book.

the doctrine in an intelligible form. He regards God as a three-fold power: first, as the power underlying all things — his Essence, the Father; second, as the power manifested in creation — his Activity, the Word or Son; third, as the divine spirit of love immanent in all creation — the Holy Spirit. It is an ingenious speculation, but a travesty of the historical doctrine of the Trinity.

Pilgram Marbeck also, a Tyrolean who was one of the active leaders of the Anabaptists at Strassburg in 1531, and after a discussion with Butzer suffered the usual fate of being banished from the city,[52] while he tries to retain at least a shadow of the doctrine by employing the traditional terms, uses the words in another sense than the current one, though he calls no attention to the fact.

Another Anabaptist is of a type so extreme that he deserves only passing mention, though like the rest he illustrates the doctrinal ferment of the time. One Conradin Bassen[53] of Heilbronn was arrested at Basel in 1530 for preaching that Christ was not our Savior, and was not God and man, nor born of a virgin; and also for not believing in prayer or the New Testament or a future life. As he would not recant, he was condemned to be beheaded, his head was impaled, and the rest of his body burned.

---

[52] cf. Röhrich, *Reformation*, ii, 72 ff; Dunin Borkowski, 'Untersuchungen zum Schrifttum der Unitarier vor Faustus Socini,' *75 Jahre Stella Matutina. Festschrift* (Feldkirch, 1931), ii, 110–112.

[53] Incorrectly, Conrad in Gassen. cf. Christian Wurstisen, *Baszler Chronik*, ed. 3 (Basel, 1883), p. 411; *Basler Chroniken* (Leipzig, 1872–1902), vi, 130, 201; Peter Ochs, *Geschichte der Stadt und Landschaft Basel* (Berlin, 1786), vi, 28.

CHAPTER IV

ANTITRINITARIAN ANABAPTISTS IN HOLLAND

A T THE TIME when the Anabaptist cause in southern Germany, Switzerland and along the Rhine was being steadily crushed under relentless persecution, it spread into a fresh field in Holland, where the Lutheran Reformation had failed to take vigorous root. Its leader here was Melchior Hofmann,[1] who has been called the father of the Dutch Anabaptists. He was born at Hall in Swabia in 1498, was a furrier by trade, and self-taught. He accepted the Reformation and became an earnest student of the Bible. He was a follower of Luther, to whom he went at Wittenberg, and by whom he was chosen to go to promote the Reformation at Dorpat in Russia, and as preacher to King Frederick of Denmark at Kiel. Later breaking with Luther on account of the Sacrament he was driven away by the Lutherans, and at length made his way to Strassburg, where he found himself at home in the company of the Anabaptists, and was baptized into their brotherhood in 1529. He soon became one of their leaders, and took their teaching to the North. He traveled widely in Germany and Holland, where he had wide influence and made great numbers of converts, who came to be known from him as Melchiorites. He was a lay-preacher *par excellence*; but he became increasingly obsessed with the conviction that the world was very soon to come to an end, and that he was the Elijah appointed to herald the impending doom. Amid the distressing social conditions then existing in Europe, this doctrine ran like wild-fire among the humbler classes, and helped to precipitate the terrible catastrophe at Münster in 1535. After four years of missionary preaching he returned to Strassburg in 1533, where he was soon arrested as an Anabaptist, tried and imprisoned for life. He died, after ten years' imprisonment, about

[1] cf. B. N. Krohn, *Melchior Hofmann und die Secte der Hofmannianer* (Leipzig, 1758); Hermann Krohn, *Essai sur la vie et les écrits de M. Hofmann* (Strasbourg, 1852); W. I. Leendertz, *Melchior Hofmann* (Haarlem, 1883); F. O. zur Linden, *Melchior Hofmann, ein Prophet der Wiedertäufer* (Haarlem, 1885); *Realencyk.*, viii, 222; *Allg. D. Biog.*, xii, 636 f. Three of his works in *Bibliotheca Reformatoria Neerlandica* ('s Gravenhage, 1909), v, 125–314.

1543. As to his beliefs, the judges at his trial found that he denied both the divinity and the humanity of Christ, for he held a peculiar view of the incarnation. He held that Christ had only one nature, and at his trial he said that prayer should be offered only to the Father, and not separately to the Son and the Holy Spirit.[2]

There was no part of Europe in which the Anabaptist movement became so widespread, or was so terribly persecuted, or has had so deep and permanent an influence, as in what was then northwestern Germany, in a territory of which a large part is now included in Holland. After the bloody collapse of the fanatical wing of their movement at Münster in 1535, persecution of the Anabaptists was so fierce that no fewer than 30,000 of them had by 1546 been put to death in Holland and Friesland.[3] Those that still survived in these parts, chastened and sobered, were gathered together into an organized body by Menno Simons and Dirk Philips, and came to be known first as Mennonites, and later as Doopsgezinden or Baptists. It is in the early history of this body that we find Adam Pastor,[4] the most brilliant man and scholar among the Dutch Anabaptists of his time, one of the two chief leaders of their movement, liberal, fearless, devout, the first real Unitarian in Europe, anticipating by twenty years the most advanced positions of the Unitarians in Poland and Transylvania.

Pastor was born at Dorpen in Westphalia about 1510, and originally bore the name of Roelof (Rudolf) Martens, which he probably changed when he left the Catholic priesthood and adopted his new faith. He was unusually well educated, and in 1543 became an elder, or missionary preacher, in Menno's brotherhood, where he was very active in opposing the wild and fanatical teachings of Hendrik Nicklaes and David Joris which were then infecting the movement. But in a discussion at Emden in 1547 he differed from Menno on the incarnation, and a little later in the same year in another disputation at Goch he expressed such open antitrinitarian views that with Menno's approval Philips deposed him

---

[2] cf. Röhrich, *Wiedertäuffer*, p. 65.

[3] cf. William Bradford, *Correspondence of the Emperor Charles V* (London, 1850), p. 471; H. T. Buckle, *History of Civilization* (London, 1873), i, 189.

[4] cf. *Bibliotheca Reformatoria Neerlandica*, v, 315–581, reprinting Pastor's *Underscheid*, and *Disputation*, with introductions. cf. A. H. Newman, 'Adam Pastor, Antitrinitarian Antipaedobaptist,' *Papers of the American Society of Church History* (second series, New York, 1917), v, 73–99; Dunin Borkowski, *Untersuchungen*, pp. 106–109; *id.*, 'Die Gruppierung der Antitrinitarier des 16. Jahrhunderts,' *Scholastik* (Bonn, 1932), vii, 487–493.

from his ministry and excommunicated him from the brotherhood. He sought reconciliation in vain, and never ceased to feel injured at the treatment he had received, which Menno himself lived to regret. An influential minority of the congregations took his side, and he became leader of the liberal Anabaptists, and was long active in the Duchy of Cleve, where he made many converts. He died at Emden (or perhaps at Münster) about 1552.[5]

Adam Pastor was little but a name until early in the twentieth century, when the only extant copy of his sole surviving work (published probably in 1552) was unearthed and republished with a valuable introduction.[6] It is from this that we get authentic knowledge of his teachings. While he may have been influenced by his contemporary Campanus who wrought in the same territory, his system of thought is essentially original, derived from his independent study of texts of Scripture, of which he had an extensive knowledge. His significance in this history lies in the fact that he represented and defended the Unitarian tendency of Anabaptism in northwestern Germany at a time when all the other leaders of the movement there had in general readopted the orthodox view. Passing by the whole traditional doctrine of the Trinity and avoiding its terms, he defends the simple unity of God, and the distinction of Christ from him. Trinitarianism is tritheistic. Christ is Son of God, miraculously born, and possesses all power; but he is later in time than the Father, and subordinate to him in power. The divinity of Christ is the Father's wisdom, word, will, power, and working in him. To regard him as co-eternal and co-equal with God and to worship him as such is to be guilty of idolatry. The Holy Spirit is not a separate or personal being, but only a breathing of God, inspiring in us everything good. It is possible that Budny, Dávid and others in Poland and Transylvania twenty years later, who held similar views, derived them from Pastor. At all events, the later Socinians claimed that he was the first to teach their doctrines in the Low Countries, and he certainly prepared the way for Socinianism there, especially among the Mennonites.

The persons thus far spoken of were on the whole representatives of

---

[5] cf. Bonet-Maury, *Sources*, p. 48.

[6] *Underscheid tusschen rechte leer unde valsche leer*, with an appendix, *Disputation van der Godtheit des Vader, Sone, unde Hilligen Geist*, both in the *Bibliotheca Reformatoria Neerlandica* above cited.

the more sober and conservative element in the Anabaptist movement. It remains now to speak finally of two others who, while holding similar doctrines of God and Christ, were in nature and temperament radically different from them, embodying the fanaticism and the loose social views that brought Anabaptism into such ill repute. The first of these was David Joris (or Georg).[7] His career is one of the most extraordinary, and his character one of the most puzzling, in modern Christian history. Between the accounts given by his opponents and by his apologists there is the widest discrepancy; and in his own conduct and character there seem to have been, either simultaneously or in succession, the most glaring contradictions. If we may trust the record, he combined in one person the characters of a sincere and earnest Christian and a calculating impostor, a profound mystic and a wicked blasphemer, a devout pietist and a rank antinomian, a self-denying ascetic and a self-indulgent sensualist, an intrepid hero and a visionary fanatic, a prudent man of the world and a mad millenarian.

He was born about 1501 probably in Flanders, perhaps at Bruges, though his early life was spent at Delft. His father seems to have been now a merchant at Delft, now a traveling showman. The son had a delicate, sensitive temperament and a keen intelligence, but he had not much better than an elementary education, and was always rather inclined to despise learning in favor of inward revelations of truth. For a trade he learned glass-painting, in which he became expert. At the age of twenty-two he first read the German Bible and passionately embraced the Reformation; but his zeal against the Roman Church carried him too far. He was arrested and publicly flogged, had his tongue pierced with an awl as a punishment for alleged blasphemy, and in 1528

---

[7] Joris is an obsolete Dutch form of Georg. His father was Joris de Koman; the son's name Joris is thus a patronymic. Of the voluminous literature, cf. (Johannes Acronius), *Davidis Georgii Holandi haeresiarchae vita et doctrina* (Basileae, 1559); Nicolaus Blesdijk, *Historia vitae, doctrinae, ac rerum gestarum Davidis Georgii haeresiarchae* (Daventriae, 1642); Friedrich Jessen, *Auffgedeckte Larve Davidis Georgii* (Kiel, 1670); Gottfried Arnold, *Unpartheyische Kirchen- und Ketzer Historie* (Franckfurt, 1729), ii, 750–778; IV, 534–737 (apologetic); A. M. Cramer 'Levensbeschrijving van David Joris,' *Nederlandsch Archiev voor kerkelijke Geschiedenis*, v, 1–145; vi, 289–368 (1845, 1846); Friedrich Nippold, 'David Joris van Delft, sein Leben, seine Lehre und seine Secte,' *Zeitschrift für die historische Theologie*, xxxiii, 3–166; xxxiv, 483–673; xxxviii, 475–591 (1863, 1864, 1868); Antonius van der Linde, *David Joris, Bibliografie* ('s Gravenhage, 1867); Paul Burckhardt, 'David Joris,' *Basler Biographien* (Basel, 1900), i, 91–157; Roland H. Bainton, *David Joris* (Leipzig, 1937).

was banished from Delft. During the wandering, hunted life that he now led for several years he saw much of the Anabaptists, who were just then arising in Holland as a result of Hofmann's mission; and though their disorderly doings at first repelled him, their behavior under persecution and in the face of martyrdom impressed him so much that he at length joined their sect in 1534 and was ordained to their ministry. Returning to Delft as preacher, he worked in greatest secrecy and made many converts.

After the Anabaptist débacle at Münster in 1535 the movement seemed in imminent danger of falling to pieces, so that a convention of the leaders of all parties was held at Bocholt in 1536. Joris took a prominent part in it, trying to moderate the extremists and to bring the separate divisions together; but though he won much reputation he failed in his effort and was finally repudiated by them all. The excitement of these strenuous years now began to tell upon his nature. Cut off from communion with the rest of the Anabaptists,[8] and living an extremely ascetic life, he began to see visions and to report them to his followers, and was soon surrounded by a sect of his own. They came to be known as Jorists, many of them too began to see visions, and all had a fanatical belief in their leader. Edicts were issued against them, persecutions increased, several score were put to death at Delft and the Hague, and among them Joris saw his own mother beheaded, while a price was set upon his head. He was constant in comforting his people in their sufferings, though to escape discovery he had often to change the style of his dress, appearing in turn as nobleman, peasant, merchant or priest, and with such success that it was believed that he had the power to render himself invisible. As his sense of his mission increased he came gradually to believe that he had been divinely appointed to herald the coming of the kingdom of God upon earth. His followers greatly increased in number, and looking upon him as a new embodiment of Christ they sold their property and brought the money to him. He expected to set up his kingdom after fifty years. Hunted in Holland, he sought to make converts in Strassburg, but in vain. As persecutions multiplied he appealed to various rulers for toleration, but they did not recognize his claims. He had an earnest discussion with Menno Simons, who would none of him. To give his notions wider currency he pub-

---

[8] He had been excommunicated by the Hofmannites at Strassburg and by the Mennonites in Friesland for his antitrinitarian opinions. cf. Bonet-Maury, *Sources*, p. 47.

lished the *Wonderbook*, his chief work,[9] a confused jumble of enthusiastic fancies and mystical interpretations of Scripture. He carried on a mission in East Friesland, and made approaches to John à Lasco, who was organizing the Reformation there; but persecutions made it impossible for him to stay. He wrote to Luther, only to be rebuffed. Nowhere could he make headway; and as it was unsafe for him to stay longer in Holland, and as he was everywhere baffled in efforts to spread his religion, he resolved upon a totally different course.

Counseling his followers to avoid further persecution by concealing their beliefs, he avoided it for himself by removing to another land and changing the form of his name, and then proceeded to wait patiently for the coming of the kingdom in which he had now come fervently to believe. In the spring of 1544 he left Holland and appeared at Basel as Johannes von Bruck (or Brügge), ostensibly a gentleman of high birth and great wealth, exiled from his own land for his religious faith. His stately person, lordly bearing and rich possessions commended him to the Council as a highly desirable citizen, and they granted him citizenship without hesitation or investigation. With the wealth he brought with him, constantly increased by rich gifts that his followers despite his protests kept sending him from Holland, he purchased a stately town house and several suburban estates,[10] lived in handsome style, was generous to the poor, regularly attended public worship, and was held by all in the highest esteem. Behind the scenes, with his family and the numerous followers in his train, who were solemnly pledged not to betray their secret, he was reverenced as a holy prophet; while he kept in communication with his sect in the Low Countries through incessant correspondence, and instructed and encouraged them by a succession of tracts which ran into the hundreds. Thus for twelve years until 1556 when he died, three days after his wife, and was buried with honor in St. Leonhard's church where he had used to worship.

Two years later dissension broke out among his followers, and a servant betrayed the secret. Basel was scandalized. The family were arrested, the house was searched, and large quantities of writings were found and examined. The family and other followers at first denied,

---

[9] *'t Wonderboeck, waerin dat van der Wereld aen ver sloten gheoperbaert is.* 1542 and later.

[10] The Spiesshof in town, and the Schloss zum Holée in the suburb of Binningen, are still extant. A fine portrait of Joris hangs in the public art museum near the Minster.

then evaded, and finally confessed all. The writings were laid before the university faculties of theology and law for an opinion and for in-structions how to proceed. They were judged to be full of dreadful heresies. Under the imperial law a heretic might still be tried and sen-tenced within five years after his death, and of such a procedure there were numerous instances. A public trial of David Joris was therefore held, and he was found guilty. Sentence was given that his body should be disinterred and burned together with his writings and por-trait, as he himself would have been if still living. The sentence was solemnly carried out, and his ashes were thrown into the Rhine. Joris now became more famous than ever, while the Catholics made merry with a mocking rhyme which ran: 'Basel verbrennt die toten Ketzer, und die Lebenden nit.' Joris's family and servants were required not long afterwards to appear in the Minster and publicly to renounce their errors and ask forgiveness, after which they were reconciled to the church. Some of his followers continued to reside at Basel, but the most of them removed to East Friesland. The Jorists long survived in the Netherlands, and continued to make converts and to reprint the works of their prophet; and they had followers also in France, Sweden and Holstein until nearly the middle of the eighteenth century, when the last remnants of their sect vanish from the scene.

Dramatic as is the story of Joris's life, our main concern here is with the teaching that he spread so widely.[11] He held that God is a simple and indivisible being. Of the Trinity he speaks very confusedly, but the sum of it is that in the Divine Being there is no distinction of persons except the embodiment of three periods of history in three historical persons, Moses, John the Baptist, and himself. In the strictest sense only the Father is God, and the word person should not be applied to him at all. He was well called the arch-heretic of the Anabaptists.

The last of the Anabaptists to be mentioned is Hendrik Nicklaes (Henry Nicholas).[12] Of his youth little is known, save that he was born about 1502 at Münster and in early manhood became a Lutheran. He was a merchant, but deeply interested in the Reformation, and was re-peatedly arrested on suspicion of heresy. In 1540 he began to get what

---

[11] cf. Dunin Borkowski, *Gruppierung*, p. 483 f; Nippold, *Joris*, xxxviii, 540.

[12] cf. Friedrich Nippold, 'Heinrich Nicklaes und das Haus der Liebe,' *Zeitschrift für die historische Theologie*, xxxiii (1862), 323–402, 473–563; Rufus M. Jones, *Studies in Mystical Religion* (New York, 1909), pp. 428–448.

he regarded as divine revelations, and removed from Amsterdam to
Emden in East Friesland, where he spent twenty years in preaching,
writing and publishing his many works. He taught a mystical system,
in which visions played an important part; and in trying to give Christianity a social application he held that all true Christians should be
united in one 'Family of Love.' His doctrines seem to have been mainly
derived from Joris, who was a kindred spirit, and they easily ran into
fanaticism on the one hand and loose morals on the other. The sect
that gathered about him came to be known as Familists; and he won
perhaps more converts in England, where he spent some time, than on
the Continent. While he often spoke of the Trinity, he used his words
in a sense quite different from the usual one, and he thus transformed
most of the other church dogmas. His teaching easily led to Antitrinitarianism. He died about 1580.

The persons whose history and teaching have here been passed in review represent widely different phases of that broad and vague movement known as Anabaptism, and include the most of the leaders of its
thought during the first eventful generation of its history. But however
widely they differ from one another in certain respects of temper or
teaching, they agree substantially in this: that they all departed more
or less widely from the historical doctrines of the Trinity and the deity
of Christ; some of them still keeping the old terms but using them in
a new and unauthorized sense, some virtually ignoring these doctrines
or passing them by without emphasis as of no vital importance, some
rejecting or denying them outright as unscriptural, unreasonable or misleading.

There is no sufficient warrant, however, for considering them doctri-
nally as pioneers of the general movement with which we are concerned
in this work, in the sense that the movement which eventually arose
was the direct outcome of their teaching. The contrary is the case. Not
one of these pioneer thinkers, so far as we can see, had confessed disciples among those that organized the first Socinian or Unitarian
churches, or appreciably stimulated their origin or influenced their development. Their significance in this history is rather this: that they
bear witness that in a large and influential, though oppressed and persecuted, minority of the Protestant world in its first generation, there
were great numbers on whom the doctrines named had lost their hold,

who had escaped from the rigorous bondage of traditional dogmas into the freedom of a religion of the spirit which laid its emphasis not upon theological beliefs but upon personal religious experience and practical Christian life, and which while not as yet emphasizing the value of reason in religion, did emphasize as fundamental the importance of tolerance.

In this respect these liberal Anabaptists took a long step toward realization of the principles which we said at the outset are to be regarded as the distinctive marks of the movement with which we are here concerned. In the countries where the Protestant Reformation first took root, bitter and persistent persecution by the civil power prevented Anabaptism from developing normally. But we shall presently see that when it was allowed to exist under conditions of even moderate toleration, it furnished fertile soil in which that further development might take place whose history is to be our theme. In the meantime, however, we must turn to a different quarter and trace another phase of pioneering, in which the characteristic contribution to our movement is to come from the intellectual side, and to place a permanent stamp upon it.

CHAPTER V

THE EARLY LIFE OF SERVETUS, 1511–1532

IN THE DEVELOPMENT of religious thought among the dissenting elements of the Protestant movement, that we have thus far traced, no positive results have been discovered. There has been indeed a widespread assertion and exercise of freedom from the Christian traditions and forms of thought hitherto dominant; there has been an even more significant demand for tolerance of thought and practice; but the main emphasis has been the practical one as realized in personal experience and character and in the institutions of society. There have also been individual leaders of great power and wide influence, and independent thinkers of originality, deep insight, and no little merit, who have thrown out pregnant truths and significant hints; but none of them attempted a systematic formulation of the Christian faith from a new point of view, or sought to carry out the full implications of a faith appealing to a new seat of authority. The relentless persecution of the Anabaptists would have made any such attempt untimely and barren.

Yet the daring thinkers with whom we have been concerned had most of them hardly been silenced by death or imprisonment, before there arose from an entirely different quarter a solitary figure who, though quite unconnected with them, was destined to go on beyond the point where they had been forced to stop, and who, having ignored the authority of the ancient creeds and the forms of mediaeval theology, was to work out, however crudely, a new system of belief based strictly on Scripture alone; and who, although he was to leave hardly a single disciple of his peculiar form of doctrine, was yet to leave an enduring impress upon the course of free Christian thought. This man was Michael Servetus,[1] whose dramatic life, tragic death, and cardinal relation to the

---

[1] The common Latin form of the name. The correct Spanish form is Miguel Serveto *alias* Reves; but this is in several respects so unusual a name that it was long and persistently conjectured that some other form must be the correct one: that the real name must have been Servede; that the *alias* must be a Latin equivalent for the Spanish *y*, and Reves therefore the mother's family name; that Reves was an anagram (ignoring the t) for Serve; while the forms de Reves, Renes, Rennes, and Revers also occur. The question

whole movement here considered entitle him to more than the ordinary measure of our attention. In the judgment of a biographer of Calvin not likely to be partial to him, Servetus 'was in intellectual endowments undoubtedly the peer of the greatest men of his century, Calvin included.'² As to his significance in the history of religious thought, Trechsel, a competent judge, states that 'Servetus personified the antitrinitarian spirit, and worked it out into a comprehensive system, giving it its first speculative and systematic form. Previous Antitrinitarians had either been merely negative, or their teaching had gone off on a tangent, and had left only sketches and hints, and were less concerned with dogma than with practical ends.'³ The German scientist Karl Vogt pronounced him 'the greatest savant of his century'; the French theologian Tollin called him one of the greatest mystics of all time; the Spanish littérateur Menéndez y Pelayo said, 'Of all Spanish heretics none surpasses Servetus in boldness and originality of ideas, in the order and consistency of his system, in logical vigor, and in the extreme character of his errors.'⁴ He made a conspicuous mark for himself not only in the history of Christian theology, but also in biblical criticism, in the

was at last settled by the discovery of seventeen documents in the archives of Santa Maria de Sigena, and attested 1511–'38 by his father, whose name is in each case given as above. Apparently the elder Serveto added *alias* Reves to his name when he became proprietor of the casa de Reves at Sigena. cf. Mariano de Pano, 'La Familia de Miguel Servet,' *Revista de Aragón*, ii (April, May, 1901), 119 ff., 151 ff.

Despite the great mass of Servetus literature, there is still far from being any satisfactory life. The chief sources are in his own works; in Calvin's *Opera* (*Corpus Reformatorum*), vol. viii, containing the records of the Geneva trial and much supplementary contemporary material; and in l'Abbé Antoine Gachet d'Artigny's *Nouveaux Mémoires d'histoire, de critique et de littérature*, vol. ii (Paris, 1749), giving records of the Vienne trial. Of subsequent works the most valuable are J. L. von Mosheim, *Anderweitiger Versuch einer . . . Geschichte . . . Michaels Serveto* (Helmstedt, 1748); supplemented by his *Neue Nachrichten von . . . Michael Serveto* (*ibid.*, 1750); Robert Willis, *Servetus and Calvin* (London, 1877); A. van der Linde, *Michael Servet, een brandoffer der gereformeerde Inquisitie* (Groningen, 1891); Sigismundo Pey-Ordeix, *Miguel Servet*, etc. (Madrid, 1911); José Goyanes, *Miguel Serveto, Teólogo, Geógrafo, y Médico*, etc. (Madrid, 1933). Also some seventy titles of works and periodical articles (1874–'94) by Henri Tollin, upon whom all later writers have largely based their writing. Though often suggestive, his statements and judgments, however positively given, deserve to be taken only with great critical caution. For a useful introduction to the literature, cf. Roland H. Bainton, 'The present state of Servetus Studies,' *Journal of Modern History*, iv (1932), 72–92.

² cf. E. Stähelin, *Johannes Calvin* (Elberfeld, 1863), i, 428.

³ cf. Trechsel, *Antitrinitarier*, i, 61.

⁴ Marcelino Menéndez y Pelayo, *Historia de los Heterodoxos Españoles* (Madrid, 1880), ii, 249.

history of medicine and anatomy, and in comparative geography, and his thought ranged over yet other wide and varied fields.

Comparatively little is known of Servetus's life before he entered the field of religious controversy at the age of twenty,[5] and from that little it is not always easy to discover the truth; for it is nearly all contained in his testimony given at trials at Vienne and Geneva where his life was at stake, and he had the strongest motive for concealing or misstating facts that might prejudice his case. He was perhaps born at the little town of Tudela in southern Navarre, but if so his father soon afterwards removed to Villanueva de Sigena,[6] whence the son later chose the disguising name of Michel de Villeneuve, or its Latin equivalent. As Spain has well-nigh three hundred places named Vilanova, Vilanoba, Villanueva, Vilanueba, Villanuova, etc.,[7] it was long uncertain from which of them Servetus came; but the place is now known to have been correctly described in his testimony at Geneva as Villanueva in the diocese of Lerida (though in the province of Huesca), a little village on the Alcanadre about sixty miles northeast of Saragossa. The ancestral home, the casa de Reves, is still standing, the most pretentious house in the village; and over the side-altar to Santa Lucia in the parish church of San Salvador hard by is a retablo believed to have been erected by the mother and brother of Servetus, and to bear their portraits.[8]

The date of Servetus's birth is also uncertain, but it was probably

[5] cf. Henri Tollin, 'Servet's Kindheit und Jugend' *Zeitschrift für die historische Theologie*, xiv (1875), 545–616.

[6] At Vienne he testified that he was a native of Tudela in Navarre, and also at his trial in Paris he said he was Navarrese (cf. Tollin, 'Kindheit'; *id*. 'Zur Servet-kritik,' *Zeitschrift für wissenschaftliche Theologie*, xxi (1878), 450; but at Geneva he said he was a native of Villanueva in Aragón. Reasons may easily be found for either answer. Opinion generally favors Tudela, but from early infancy his home was certainly at Villanueva. No parish records are extant for either place.

[7] cf. van der Linde, *Servet*, p. 235.

[8] cf. Dr. B. R. Barrios, 'Quelques notes sur Michel Servet', *Chronique Médical*, xii (Paris, Aug. 15, 1905), 556. Doubt is entertained whether any certainly authentic portrait of Servetus himself is extant. Allwoerden published as frontispiece to his work an engraving carefully made from a very old painting possessed by the Kirchenrat and Domprediger Peter Adoph Boysen of Halberstadt, whose provenance could be traced back to the famous Socinian scholar Johannes Crellius, who died eighty years after Socinus. Its further origin was unknown; but it was always regarded as authentic, and it was conjectured that it might have been made during Servetus's final imprisonment. Into whose hands it passed after Boysen's death is also unknown. cf. Allwoerden, *Servetus*, p. 147 ff; Mosheim, *Versuch*, p. 24 ff. The earliest printed portrait is the one engraved by Christoffel van Sichem (Amsterdam, 1607) and often reproduced. It is evidently derived from the same source. cf. J. P. Magnin, *Calvin et Servet* (Wiesbaden, 1886), p. 32.

1511.[9] His father was Antonio Serveto *alias* Reves,[10] who from 1511 until 1538 held the important office of Notary at Sigena, and was raised to the nobility in 1529. His mother was Catalina Conesa, and he had at least one brother, Juan, who entered the priesthood and became rector of Poliñino. The family Serveto was well known in Aragón, and numbered persons of distinction in state and church, among them Andrés Serveto of Aniñon, Professor of Law at Bologna and later Senator in Aragón, and Marco Antonio Serveto de Reves (a later style of the name), Canon of Saragossa and Abbot of Montearagón.[11]

When he published his first book at the age of twenty, Servetus had, besides his native Spanish, a ready writing and speaking knowledge of Latin, and knew Greek and Hebrew well enough to discuss intelligently the meaning of the Bible in its original tongues. He also had a considerable acquaintance with the Fathers of the Church and with scholastic philosophy. Where he acquired this knowledge is not definitely known, but as he was not physically strong he may have been originally intended for a religious life. If so, he would in all probability have been brought up in some cloister school,[12] or possibly (as has been suggested, though without the least proof) may have attended the University of Saragossa. It was early declared,[13] and often repeated, that he went to Africa to learn Arabic among the Moors; but for this there is no more evidence than the fact that in his first book he several times refers to the teachings of the Koran.

At the age of fifteen or sixteen, however, Servetus was sent by his father across the Pyrenees to Toulouse to study law, and he remained there two or three years.[14] The school of law at the University of

9 cf. van der Linde, *Servet*, p. 4 f. Servetus states his age only approximately, and the various data given are conflicting. From his testimony at Vienne the date would seem to be 1511; at Geneva, 1509, the same as Calvin's. There is no ground for making the day September 29 (as given on the Geneva monument) except the gratuitous assumption that he was named Michael from having been born on St. Michael's day.

10 Gordon's statement (*Encyclopaedia Britannica*, *s. v.* Servetus) that the father was Hernando Villanueva of San Gil rested upon a letter in the Record Office discovered in 1890, and was later acknowledged to be incorrect.

11 cf. de Pano, *Familia*.

12 Gordon very plausibly guesses the College of Huesca, cf. his *The Personality of Michael Servetus* (Manchester, 1910), p. 8.

13 As by W. Lindanus, *Tabulae grassantium haereseon* (Paris, 1562), cited by Socinus, *Opera*, ii, 535; cf. Allwoerden, *Servetus*, pp. 17–21; Mosheim, *Versuch*, pp. 8–11; Bock, *Antitrinitar.*, ii, 324–326.

14 cf. Calvin, viii. 767; Tollin, 'Michael Servet's Toulouser Leben,' *Zeitschrift für*

Toulouse was at this time the most celebrated in all Europe, while the theological atmosphere was of the narrowest type, and heresy was suppressed with ruthless cruelty. In such an environment Servetus began for the first time in his life secretly to read the Bible with some fellow-students;[15] and it is possible that here he first learned Greek and Hebrew in order the better to understand it. His enthusiasm over it as a book of vital religious experience knew scarcely any bounds, and is reflected in his first book published some three years later. Such religious teaching as he had hitherto received had been of the most abstract, speculative sort. Its central doctrine, and the one most strenuously insisted upon in the schools, conceived of God as a being existing in three distinct hypostases in one substance, and Christ was conceived of as one of these hypostases having had existence from all eternity. There was in such a doctrine more than enough to puzzle and confuse one's head, but nothing to warm his heart or inspire his life. In his newly discovered Bible, however, Servetus found something to which his whole religious nature responded, yet 'not one word about the Trinity, nor about its Persons, nor about an Essence, nor about a unity of the Substance, nor about one Nature of the several beings.' [16] It was because they were unwilling to profess this doctrine that in the generation just preceding 800,000 Jews had been banished from Spain, and many thousands of Moors had recently been burned at the stake in Andalusia.[17] Now, in contrast to all this, Servetus was relieved and inspired to find in the New Testament as the centre of Christian faith a historical being, the man Jesus of Nazareth. His religious problem was solved, and the wonderful Bible seemed to him no less than a book come down from heaven, in which he found all philosophy and all wisdom.[18] From this point on the vocation of Servetus was determined. He was destined to become not a jurist, nor yet a priest, but a religious reformer, who was to make known to the world his great discovery, supplement Luther's reform of abuses in the Church by simplifying its teachings and restoring the purity of its doctrines which the perverse subtlety of the Scholastics had rendered so confusing and sterile, and was thus, as he hoped,

---

wissenschaftliche Theologie, xx (1877), 342–386; *id.*, 'Toulouser Studentenleben im Anfang des 16. Jahrhunderts,' *Historisches Taschenbuch*, xliv (1874), 77–98.
[15] cf. Calvin, *loc. cit.* Reading of the Bible was forbidden at Toulouse.
[16] cf. Servetus, *De Trinitatis erroribus*, pp. 32a, 35b.
[17] cf. E. Rosseuw St. Hilaire, *Histoire d'Espagne* (Paris, 1837–'39), vi, 33 f.
[18] cf. *De Trin.*, pp. 107b, 78b, 79a.

to open the way to a general conversion of Mohammedans and Jews to Christianity.

At about the time when he went to Toulouse,[19] Servetus had entered the service of Juan de Quintana, a broad-minded, scholarly and eloquent Franciscan monk who was court preacher to the Emperor, and as such had distinguished himself at Worms during the Diet in 1521.[20] Servetus's service was that of a famulus, a sort of student-secretary, such as monks often employed. If student in some Franciscan cloister school, he may there have attracted the notice of Quintana by his talents and his excellent handwriting. His studies at Toulouse, however, were brought to an end early in 1529 when he was taken with his master into the suite of the Emperor who was about to go to Italy to receive from Pope Clement VII. coronation as Holy Roman Emperor.[21] He thus left his native land and never saw it again. This journey was of critical importance in shaping the rapidly developing religious thought of Servetus, for during the nearly six months that he was at Bologna,[22] he was able to get at close range many views of the conduct and character of the highest dignitaries in the Church.

Charles had already received the silver crown as Emperor of Germany at Aix-la-Chapelle ten years before, and now at Bologna he received the iron crown as King of Lombardy, and two days later, on Febuary 24, the Pope placed on his head the golden crown as Roman Emperor. The whole drama was preceded, accompanied and followed by a magnificence, a splendor, a luxury, an extravagance unprecedented in the history of Italy, and perhaps of the whole modern world.[23] Princes, nobles,

[19] This follows from Servetus's testimony at Vienne. cf. d'Artigny, *Mémoires*, ii, 102.

[20] Quintana was made confessor at Bologna in the spring of 1530, succeeding the bigoted Dominican, Garcia de Loyasa. Desiring if possible to conciliate the reforming party at the coming Diet at Augsburg, Charles wished as his spiritual adviser a more tolerant man than Loyasa, who was for taking the severest measures, and was therefore now transferred to Rome as Charles's representative at the Papal court. He was later recalled to service, and finally became Inquisitor-General of Spain. Quintana, after serving over two years as Confessor, returned to cloistered life in Spain as Prior of Montearagón and member of the Cortes, and died at Segovia in 1534. cf. Tollin, 'Die Beichtväter Kaiser Karls V.' *Magazin für die Literatur des Auslandes*, xliii (April 4– May 2, 1874), 201 ff.   [21] cf. d'Artigny, *Mémoires*, ii, 102.

[22] From Oct. 5 to March 22, 1530. cf. Vandesse's 'Itinerary of Charles V.,' in William Bradford, *Correspondence of Charles V.* (London, 1850).

[23] cf. contemporary accounts in Henricus Cornelius Agrippa, 'De duplici coronatione Caroli V. Caesaris apud Bononia historiola' in *Schardius Redivivus* (Giessae, 1674), ii, 266–275; and in Franck, *Chronica*, pp. ccxxvi a — ccxxviii a; Tollin, 'Eine italienische Kaiserreise,' *Historisches Taschenbuch*, xlvii (1877), 51–103.

legates from all the nations of Europe, cardinals, bishops were present in great numbers. This on the front stage for outward display. On the other hand, behind the scenes, where Servetus's office required him to be, and where his unsophisticated mind might have expected to find sincerest piety and spotless sanctity of life, he saw among ecclesiastical politicians and the highest dignitaries of the Church unmistakable evidences of worldliness, selfish ambition, cunning intrigue, cynical skepticism, and shameless immorality that made him sick at heart. Thoroughly disillusioned, he came to regard the official religion of the Church as hollow mockery, and to see in the Pope the Antichrist foretold in the New Testament. At the same time he saw the Pope treated with what seemed to him little less than idolatry. The Emperor knelt and kissed his feet, princes harnessed themselves to his chariot, the crowds in the streets knelt as he passed, or pressed to touch the hem of his garment as though even that could sanctify them. More than twenty years later as he recalled all this he boiled with mingled disgust and indignation in his last book:

He dares not touch his feet to the earth, lest his holiness be defiled. He has himself borne upon the shoulders of men, and adored as a God upon earth. Since the foundation of the world no one has ever dared try anything more wicked. With these very eyes we saw him carried with pomp on the necks of princes, making threatening crosses with his hand, and adored in the open squares by the whole people on bended knee; to such a degree that those that were able to kiss his feet or his shoes deemed themselves happy beyond others, said that they had got the greatest indulgences, and that for this the punishments of hell had been remitted for many years. O beast of beasts most wicked, harlot most shameless.[24]

All this, following so soon after his quickening experience of the simplicity and purity of native Christianity as discovered in the Bible, and in such shocking contrast with it, must inevitably have deepened whatever conviction he already had as to the need of a reformed Christianity, and have impressed upon him a determination to do whatever he could to promote it. If the chance of doing this through the dominant organization of the Church now seemed hopeless, there might be an opportunity of accomplishing something through those north of the Alps who were aiming at reformation. He may therefore well have looked forward with eager anticipation to the possibility of coming into touch with

[24] Servetus, *Christianismi Restitutio*, p. 462. The allusion evidently is not, as Mosheim conjectured (*Versuch*, p. 55), to an experience in Rome, but to the coronation at Bologna.

them at the approaching Diet at Augsburg, where their cause was to be laid before the Emperor.

Charles was at Augsburg from the middle of June until late in November; and if Servetus was there in his suite, as is entirely probable, though direct evidence on the point is wanting,[25] he is almost certain to have seen and heard Melanchthon, Butzer and Capito, leaders of the reforming party.[26] It is evident that in their quarter he saw much more hope for the reform he had in mind than in the old Church, for at this time he removed from a Catholic environment to a Protestant one. Just when his service with Quintana came to an end is not known, nor whether his leaving of it was voluntary, for definite data for his life at this period are wholly lacking; though his apparent implication at Vienne that it was occasioned by his master's death is misleading.[27] At all events, in October or earlier we find him at Basel in close personal intercourse with Oecolampadius, leader of the Reformation there.[28] His effort is now to be devoted to an attempt to get the leaders of the still plastic Protestant movement to see that the future of reformed Christian-

---

[25] cf. Tollin, *Michael Servet und Martin Butzer* (Berlin, 1880), p. 74 f.; *id.* 'Servet auf dem Reichstag zu Augsburg,' *Evangelisch-Reformirte Kirchenzeitung,* xxvi (1876), 155 ff., who builds too much on an indefinite reference of Spalatin.

[26] cf. Tollin, 'Der Reichstag von Augsburg,' *Historisches Taschenbuch,* i (1880), 61–108.

[27] If correctly reported, he did not literally say this, but: "dit qu'il demeura environ un an audit Allemagne, & depuis la mort dudit Quintaine demeura tout seul sans Maistre." *v.* d'Artigny, *Mémoires,* ii, 102. Quintana did not die until 1534.

[28] Tollin, whose imagination is ever fertile in making plausible conjectures where positive evidence is lacking, builds upon a single passage of uncertain meaning in a letter from Servetus to Oecolampadius — "aliter enim propriis auribus a te declarari audivi & aliter a Doctore Paulo & aliter a Luthero, & aliter a Melanchthone"; *v.* J. G. Fueslin, *Epistolae ab Ecclesiae Helveticae Reformatoribus* (Tiguri, 1742), p. 78; also in Mosheim, *Versuch,* p. 393 — the thesis that Servetus accompanied Butzer on a very hurried visit to Luther at Coburg, and even fixes the date as Sept. 19 and 20, 1530. He also makes him Butzer's amanuensis for a short time between his leaving Augsburg and his appearance at Basel. Though the thesis is cleverly argued, it can not be called more than pure conjecture. cf. Tollin, *Dr. M. Luther und Dr. M. Servet* (Berlin, 1875); *id., Servet und Butzer.* For trenchant criticism, see reviews by Kawerau, 'Luther und seine Beziehungen zu Servet,' *Studien und Kritiken,* li (1878), 479–498; and Knaake, *id. op.,* liv (1881), 317–350; also van der Linde, *Servet,* p. 240 ff. Marheinecke's statement (*Christliche Symbolik,* 1848) that Luther once took Servetus in as a fugitive is a mistake due to taking *servatus* for *Servetus* in a letter of Luther to Johann Brismann. cf. Tollin, 'Luther und Marheinecke,' *Zeitschrift für wissenschaftliche Theologie,* xxiii. (1880), 464–471. Luther mentions Servetus only twice by name and thrice by allusion (letter to the preachers of Erfurt, July 1, 1532; letter to Caspar Gürtel, Jan. 1539; and *Tischreden,* i. 297, 303; iv. 679, ed. Förstemann und Bindseil).

ity, and its acceptance in quarters that hitherto have remained impervious to Christianity at all, in large measure depends upon its being purified of the accretions of the centuries, relieved of the perverse subtleties of the scholastic theologians, and restored to the simplicities of its primitive state, especially as regards the doctrines about God and the nature of Christ, which have furnished the greatest difficulties to Christian faith.

At Basel Servetus sought repeated interviews with Oecolampadius. It must be remembered that he was as yet but a youth of nineteen, while Oecolampadius was forty-eight, professor at the University, and head of the city clergy, with a large part of the weight of the cause of the Reformation at Basel resting on his shoulders. But Servetus was precocious and eager, and obsessed with a certain sense of a divine calling in what he had undertaken. He was therefore less interested in learning from Oecolampadius than in instructing him as to the central dogmas of the Christian faith. The reformer at first received him kindly and, recognizing his talents, listened to him patiently; but when Servetus showed himself unteachable, and used language about Christ which seemed to him blasphemous, he lost patience. Servetus continued to crowd himself upon Oecolampadius's attention, only to be repulsed; whereupon he wrote complaining that he had been rudely and harshly treated, and wrote out for the reformer a confession of faith to reassure him. At first sight this seemed to be orthodox enough, but when Oecolampadius carefully scrutinized it he saw that it was calculated to deceive the unwary, for it gave no recognition to the three persons in the Godhead nor to the eternal divinity of Christ. He replied in a letter answering Servetus's complaints, refuting his arguments, criticizing his confession, and practically putting an end to any further discussion.[29] Servetus seems in his disappointment to have repeated his complaints to Butzer, with whom he was now evidently acquainted, and Butzer apparently interceded for Servetus. Oecolampadius replied, justifying his action on doctrinal grounds.[30]

---

[29] v. Oecolampadius's letter to Servetus (undated, but evidently of October, 1530), from which Servetus's letter to him, not extant, can be more or less reconstructed. cf. Oecolampadius & Zwingli, *Epistolae* (Basileae, 1536) (= *Epistolae doctorum virorum*, etc., *ibid.*, 1548); also in Calvin, viii, 857–862; Allwoerden, *Servetus*, pp. 12–17; Mosheim, *Versuch*, pp. 389–392.

[30] 'Jam dogmata nova nulli praescribo; facilis tamen sum ad recipienda ea, quae fidei non contradicunt; officiique nostri censeo eis, quae sanae doctrinae repugnant, contradicere.

Late in the same autumn a conference of leading reformers was held to discuss ways and means for spreading and defending their cause in the face of serious Catholic opposition. Zwingli, Bullinger, Oecolampadius, Butzer and Capito were present. Oecolampadius there reported the trouble he was having with Servetus and his Arian views, which he feared might infect others. Zwingli was much concerned, for he saw here a danger that their whole cause might be undone, and he urged that all pains be taken to convert or silence Servetus, and that his blasphemies be smothered.[31] They were however soon to be broadcast in another way. Servetus, it seems, had by now put his doctrinal views into writing, and he tried to secure attention for them in another quarter of highest influence. Erasmus had already become well known in Spain for his interest in the reform of the Church, and at just this period he was living at Basel. The fact that he was one of the most famous men in the world of his time, and now in his sixtieth year, did not prevent the youth Servetus from attempting to make a convert of him; but Erasmus would not listen.[32]

Thus rebuffed again, Servetus now determined upon a new line of procedure, by putting his views into print so that whether the reformers would heed them or no, the Christian world at large might read them and be convinced. The first step was to find a publisher. Since the book might be suspect, this was not quite easy. But there was at Basel a publisher and bookseller named Conrad Rous who also had shops at Strassburg and Paris.[33] Doubtless unwilling to run the risk of publishing the book himself, he arranged with Servetus for its printing abroad by the well-known printer Johann Setzer (Johannes Secerius) at Hagenau in

---

Quare audirem eum, qui negat filium coaetaneum vel consubstantialem Patri, nosque interim ut blasphemos reiicientem?' Oecolampadius & Zwingli, *Epistolae* (Basileae, 1592), p. 865 f. The letter is dated Oct. 25, 1530. cf. Mosheim, *Nachrichten*, p. 16 f.

31 (H. Bullinger), *Ministrorum Tigurinae Ecclesiae . . . Apologia* (Tiguri, 1575), pp. c3a–c4a. Quoted in Allwoerden, *Servetus*, p. 10 f; Mosheim, *Versuch*, p. 17; and in Latin translation in Calvin, viii, 744, n. 1.

32 Girolamo Aleandro (Aleander), papal representative with Charles V., speaking of Servetus's book on the Trinity, in a letter written from Ratisbon Apr. 17, 1532, says: 'Erasmo scrisse altre volte in una epistola, che questo Spagnolo ando per communicarli quest' opera, ma che non gli volle prestar orechie.' cf. Hugo Laemmer, *Monumenta Vaticana* (Friburgi, 1861), p. 109.

33 cf. Calvin, viii, 767. The name is variously given as Rous, Roux, Russ, Rouss, Rousch, Resch, Reich, and Rösch; and Trechsel even says he was called König (*Antitrinitarier*, i, 304). cf. E. Doumergue, *Jean Calvin* (Neuilly, 1926), vi, 200.

Alsace,[34] some fifteen miles north of Strassburg. Setzer had a high reputation for his work, and a wide patronage among scholars. Having once studied at Wittenberg, he was also an intense Lutheran, and had printed works of Luther and Melanchthon.[35] As Luther had fallen out with the theologians of the cities of the upper Rhine, who had sided with Zwingli in the controversy over the Lord's Supper, Setzer chuckled over the printing of a book from their quarter which would displease them, and confirm Luther's intimation at Marburg that they were unsound in the faith.[36]

Having now no hope of being able to accomplish anything by staying longer at Basel, Servetus in 1531 removed to Strassburg, where he might both be near the printer and thus easily see his book through the press, and also attempt if possible to succeed with the Strassburg reformers where he had failed with Oecolampadius. Servetus may well have hoped to find sympathy there. Strassburg was the most liberal of all the German cities, and had for some time been regarded as a paradise for freethinkers, if not even for heretics. We have already seen Cellarius, Denck, Haetzer, Kautz, Franck, Bünderlin, Entfelder, Marbeck, Hofmann and Joris gravitating thither when driven from other cities;[37] and whether Servetus knew it or not, the two leaders of the Reformation there had a reputation for liberalism which bordered on heresy.[38] Martin Butzer (Bucer), though by a dozen years the younger of the two, was the more influential. He was minister of a congregation of radical tendencies, and as Professor of New Testament Greek was founder of the University. He was a disciple of Erasmus, and disposed to wide toleration. Wolfgang Fabricius Capito as minister of another congregation was his colleague in the work of reform, and of even broader spirit, insomuch that his liberalism gave Butzer some concern.[39] Already in 1527 both had been accused to Luther of being unsound on the

34 Calvin, *ibid.*

35 cf. K. Stieff, 'Johannes Setzer.' *Centralblatt für Bibliothekswesen*, ix, 297–317, (Leipzig, 1892); also his article in *Allg. D. Biog.*, xxxiv, 49 f.

36 'Secerius gloriatus est, vel hoc nomine eximium librum quia nobis concionatoribus displiciturus sit; quasi scilicet Luthero probetur, qui Marpurgi obiiciebat de nobis tale quid sparsum esse.' cf. Oecolampadius & Zwingli, *Epistolae* (1536), p. 187; also Oecolampadius to Butzer, July 18, 1531, Calvin, viii, 866.

37 cf. chapters iii, iv, *supra.*

38 cf. Tollin, 'Strassburger kirchliche Zustände zu Anfang der reformationszeit', *Magazin für die Literatur des Auslandes*, xliv (1875), 333–336.

39 Butzer to Ambrose Blaurer, Dec. 29, 1531; Calvin, viii, 779, n. 2.

Trinity; and similar charges made at Marburg had aroused much feeling against them; while at the Marburg colloquy of 1529 Luther had bitterly charged Butzer with being unorthodox as to the Trinity and the deity of Christ.[40] Servetus had come to Strassburg to confer with Butzer and Capito about Scripture,[41] and he seems already to have known Butzer by correspondence if not in person. Despite the recent warnings from Oecolampadius and Zwingli, he was kindly received by the open-minded reformers, more than twice his age. Capito appeared at first to agree with him,[42] and Butzer, even after he had become his earnest opponent, addressed him in terms of affection.[43] But in the end he evidently made no better progress in discussion here than at Basel; so without attempting conference with any one else,[44] or taking his new friends into confidence as to what he was about to do,[45] he proceeded to his printer at Hagenau.

The book was published early in 1531,[46] and was entitled *De Trinitatis Erroribus, libri septem.*[47] The printer was too prudent to publish his name or the place of publication. Servetus, however, seems to have seen no reason why he should not propose a restatement of the doctrine of the Trinity with as much freedom as the reformers had used with regard to other time-honored doctrines. He therefore boldly, perhaps proudly,

---

[40] cf. Röhrich, *Reformation*, i, 346, citing Hedio's *Itinerarium*; and 456, quoting Gerbel's letter to Luther (1527): "Jam enim alas sumsere isti (Sacramentarii) et in secretissima Trinitatis archana penetrarunt: nescio quid de Personis excogitaturi, turbaturi sapientia sua miseram et novarum rerum cupidam plebem." Also in Trechsel, *Antitrinitarier*, i, 25, n. 2.

[41] cf. Calvin, viii, 767.

[42] *ibid.*, p. 768.

[43] "*Michael dilecte.*" Butzer to Servetus, July 8; Calvin, viii, 869; also in Röhrich, *Reformation*, ii, 272 f. cf. Gerbert, *Sectenbewegung*, pp. 114–132.

[44] cf. Calvin, viii, 768, 770.

[45] "Decuerat me ante editionem libri consulere," Butzer to Servetus, Calvin, viii, 868. "Nobis insciis liber alibi excusus," Oecolampadius to Butzer, Aug. 5, 1531; *ibid.*, p. 867 f.

[46] Sebastian Franck refers to it in his letter of Feb. 4, 1531 to Campanus, above cited, p. 38. Query, whether this date is not too early by several months.

[47] A counterfeit edition, often mistaken for the original, though easily distinguished from it, was issued about 1721 at Regensburg. For the origin of it, cf. J. H. Seelen, *Selecta Literaria* (Lübeck, 1726), pp. 52–54. A Dutch translation by Reinier Telle, *Van den Dolinghen in de Drievvldigheyd*, appeared in 1620, the printer of which is said to have been put to death (cf. Paul Henry, *Life of Calvin*, London, 1849, i, 38 n.). cf. Mosheim, *Versuch*, pp. 310–315, who also mentions an unpublished French translation. English translation, with introduction, life, bibliography and notes, by E. M. Wilbur, (Cambridge, 1932.) The original is extremely rare, and in 1935 was priced (together with the *Dialogues*) at 1200 francs.

placed his name on the title-page — *per Michaelem Serveto, alias Reves ab Aragonia Hispanum*. It was a little book of 238 small pages, neatly printed, but written in none too perfect Latin.[48] It was soon offered for sale at Strassburg, and later at Basel, Frankfurt, Bern and elsewhere;[49] but before going on to speak of the way in which it was received and the effect that it produced, it will be well to give some account of the contents of the book itself.

The work comprises seven books; but the gist of it is contained in the first book, which the remaining books for the most part merely supplement or amplify. Servetus's impulse toward writing this work dates back to his discovery of the Bible at Toulouse and his finding in it a view of the Christian faith very different from that which he had hitherto known. Christianity as he had been taught it was an abstruse system of doctrines, stated in the technical language of scholasticism, and centering about the Trinity as the doctrine of first importance, and the one most strenuously to be insisted upon. If we attempt to state this doctrine as simply as possible, it runs about as follows: the Divine Being is one in his substance or essence, but exists in three distinct hypostases or persons, known as the Father, the Word or Son, and the Holy Spirit, who are in all respects equal, and each of them God, and all of them eternally divine; yet there are not three Gods but one. The Word or Son had a divine existence from all eternity, but had two natures, a divine and a human, each of which, by a mysterious *communicatio idiomatum*, or mutual sharing of properties, possessed all the properties of the other.

Servetus had found this religiously a sterile doctrine. It confused his head, and failed to warm his heart or inspire his will. It not only was to Jews and Mohammedans an insuperable obstacle to accepting the Christian religion at all; but the average Christian, having no real comprehension of it, blindly accepted it as a holy mystery, which one must indeed profess, but was not expected to understand, or permitted to inquire into. Moreover, the professional theologians, the scholastics, at worst trifled with it and jested about it, and at best used it as a medium for hair-splitting distinctions and dialectical sleight-of-hand, as they set up theses and antitheses as to how the three could be one or

---

[48] cf. van der Linde, *Servet*, p. 237.

[49] Oecolampadius to Butzer, July 18, 1831, Calvin, viii, 866, 769; Oecolampadius to Zwingli, July 20, 1531, Zwingli, *Opera*, viii, 625.

the one three. Scholastic theologians of unquestioned orthodoxy, like Robert Holkot of England, John Major of Paris and others, not to mention also Pierre d'Ailly and Duns Scotus, frankly admitted that in this doctrine we really have three Gods, and might easily have had more, though adding that nevertheless it must be received on faith as an inscrutable mystery. As a matter of fact, whatever vitality or religious value this doctrine might once have had, it had at the beginning of the sixteenth century pretty much evaporated. Servetus saw this full well, and saw that in insisting on this scholastic doctrine as the central truth of Christianity, the Church was causing its members to miss Christianity's very heart as revealed by the New Testament in the person of Jesus.

Servetus did not mean in this book to deny the doctrine of the Trinity, for he believed in it to the very end. His intention was rather to point out the glaring errors in the *form* that perverse scholastics had given it, and instead to set forth the true form of the doctrine as taught in the New Testament. In place of a doctrine whose very terms — Trinity, hypostasis, person, substance, essence — were not taken from the Bible but invented by philosophers, and whose Christ was little more than a philosophical abstraction, he wished to get men to put their faith in a living God, in a divine Christ who had been a historical reality, and in a Holy Spirit forever working in the hearts of men. His method in doing this was at every step to place his feet solidly on clear teachings of Scripture, appealing also for confirmation to the authority of the Fathers of the Church who wrote before primitive Christianity had become corrupted by philosophy. He was a biblical literalist, amazingly familiar with the whole Bible, quotations from which are found on practically every page, and are applied in his arguments with great skill.

It would be neither interesting nor profitable to give in detail Servetus's criticism of the doctrine of the Trinity as it was held and taught in his time, nor to set forth at length what he deemed its true scriptural form. A brief statement of it in its essential features will be sufficient. Instead of approaching the doctrine from the standpoint of an abstract philosophical concept, as was usually done, Servetus begins with the concrete historical person of Jesus. He was first of all a human being. Beyond this, he was the Son of God, because supernaturally begotten. Furthermore, he was also God, sharing the fulness of deity, though without human imperfections; yet he was God in a different sense of the word from that applied to the Father. The Holy Spirit is not a third Divine Being (for this would land us in tritheism), nor indeed a distinct being at all, but an activity or power of God working within men. There is a certain harmony of power, though not a unity of nature, between Father, Son and Holy Spirit, and in this sense the three may be said to be one; but to invent the unscriptural terms of Trinity, persons, essence, substance and hypostases is only to introduce confusion. If one must use such terms, the simplest statement is that God's divinity is shown in each of three 'dispositions,' or characters, as Father, Son and Holy Spirit, and this is the true Trinity. The essence of Christian faith is that we should believe that Jesus is the Christ, the Son of God. This ensures our salvation, and makes us sons of God; whereas the Lutherans, with a different conception of faith, do not understand what justification really is. Servetus supports all positions taken by ample citations from scripture authority, and takes frequent flings at the traditional view, which he treats with repeated expressions of contempt, and with strong and offensive epithets against those that hold the traditional belief. The style is direct and personal, as though an argument were being aimed at an opponent.

Thus Servetus precipitated into the arena of public discussion a doctrine which had until now remained untouched. The Strassburg reformers had passively taken it over from Catholic Christianity without change; but, conscious that it had no clear support in Scripture, they had purposely avoided any discussion of it or emphasis upon it, lest to the controversies which they already had with Lutherans on the one hand and Catholics on the other, a worse one should be added, which by seeming to question the fundamental doctrine of Christian theology should prejudice their cause in all quarters.[50] And now came a book that was destined to drag this avoided doctrine into the very foreground.

If Servetus had hoped through his book to make his doctrines acceptable to the reformers, and through them to win favorable attention from the Protestant world at large, he was soon disillusioned. At Strassburg, where it was openly sold in the market-place, it was warmly received not by the adherents of the reformed churches, but by those

---

[50] In his apology for the Confessio Tetrapolitana written at just this time (summer, 1531), Butzer, while accepting the doctrine of the Trinity, took pains to avoid saying anything of it that might occasion controversy; and Ambrose Blaurer praised his prudence in this. cf. Butzer to Blaurer, Dec. 19, 1531; Blaurer to Butzer, Jan. 5 and 24, 1532; Röhrich, *Reformation*, ii, 83; Gerbert, *Sektenbewegung*, p. 116.

opposed to them and by them, namely the Anabaptist and other radical elements.[51] Capito reported this to Oecolampadius, who at once wrote Butzer deploring the probable effect upon the feeble churches in France and elsewhere, which might thus be alienated from the Reformation, and upon many of unstable mind whom the book might easily lead astray. He begged him to read the book and write him his opinion of it, and thought it would be well to nip the matter in the bud.[52] At the same time he also wrote Zwingli a letter expressing his feelings in no measured terms.[53]

Meantime Servetus had written Butzer, asking his support for the views expressed in the book. Butzer answered with considerable reserve, saying that in that case he should have been consulted before the book was published, as there were sundry things in it that he did not approve, which he would be glad to discuss with him when he had time. Servetus need look for no harm from him, but if he wished to stay at Strassburg he was advised to keep out of sight, for if the magistrate learned of his being there he would not allow it.[54] Servetus seems soon after this to have returned to Basel, and the discussion of which Butzer wrote did not take place, though he later wrote Servetus in a more cordial tone, taking up several points of difference.[55]

Sale of the book was soon forbidden at Strassburg,[56] and Butzer in a public lecture ere long confuted *pestilentissimum illum De Trinitate librum*;[57] but the poison of it had so affected some that while lecturing

---

[51] Oecolampadius to Butzer, July 18, 1531, Calvin, viii, 866. cf. also Oecolampadius & Zwingli, *Epistolae* (1536), p. 187.

[52] *ibid.*

[53] 'Circumfertur libellus Michaelis Serveti de Trinitatis erroribus terque quaterque blasphemus et impius, juxta meam quidem, h. e. ecclesiasticam, sententiam, tametsi ab Argentoratensibus quibusdam laudetur. Fortassis et isthuc pervenit. Quod si eo cares, fac ut sciam, et curabo communicari.' July 20, 1531. cf. Zwingli, *Opera*, viii, 625.

[54] Butzer to Servetus, summer of 1531, Calvin, viii, 868. Röhrich, *Reformation*, ii, 272.

[55] Butzer to Servetus, July 8, 1531, Calvin, viii, 869.

[56] For the censors' adverse report, cf. *Zeitschrift für die historische Theologie*, xxx (1860), 52.

[57] Oecolampadius felt too busy with his commentary on Job to prepare a confutation, much as he was inclined to do so, and urged Butzer to undertake it (cf. Calvin, viii, 866 f). Butzer's confutation was not published, but circulated in Ms among the reformers in the Oberland. Tollin found good reasons for believing it to be extant in a Ms bound in with a copy of *De Trinitatis erroribus* (No. D² 2437) in the Bibliothèque Nationale in Paris. cf. Tollin, 'Butzers Confutatio der Libri VII. de trinitatis erroribus', *Theologische Studien und Kritiken*, xlviii (1875), 711–736.

he was publicly contradicted by one of his neighboring colleagues in the clergy, Wolfgang Schultheiss, pastor at Schiltigheim;[58] and he suspected that Caspar Schwenckfeld might also be wavering, so that the latter felt called on to justify himself at the end of his book *Vom Ursprung des Fleisches Christi*.[59] The reaction of Capito himself was so equivocal as to cause Butzer uneasiness.[60]

Butzer was now beset from all quarters for his opinion and guidance. Wolfgang Musculus, preacher at Augsburg, wrote suggesting that he take Servetus in hand and find out his inmost thoughts.[61] Berthold Haller wrote from Bern a letter of anxious inquiry as to how things were going at Strassburg.[62] Ambrosius Blaurer wrote from Esslingen urging him by all means to bring Capito back to the right way, and strongly besought and adjured him to write him his judgment.[63] Simon Grynaeus, who had succeeded Oecolampadius at Basel, wrote wishing immediately to know what Butzer thought of the book: he himself had not read it, though he thought Servetus must be insane.[64] A little later, having read a page or two, but being unable to make anything of it, he wrote yet more urgently; and six months later yet Christopher Hoss, preacher at Speyer, wrote for information about Servetus, who had won ardent disciples in the Palatinate.[65] As soon as he could do so, Butzer answered these inquiries, and sent inquirers copies of his confutation, quieting their misgivings, dispelling their doubts, and ensuring their opposition to the new teaching. Butzer himself became so wrought up over the matter that he declared from the pulpit that Servetus deserved to be drawn and quartered.[66]

[58] Butzer to A. Blaurer, Dec. 29, 1531, Calvin, viii, 779, n. 2. cf. Tollin, *Servet und Butzer*, p. 207.

[59] Schwenckfeld admitted having had many conversations with Servetus, and having found something good in his books, though he thought him sorely astray as to the chief articles of the Christian faith, and judged his book on the Trinity to be *bös und verdamblich*. cf. Karl Ecke, *Schwenckfeld, Luther, und der Gedanke einer apostolischen Reformation* (Berlin, 1911), p. 210, n.

[60] cf. Butzer's letter to Blaurer cited above.

[61] Oct. 3, 1531; cited by Gerbert, *Sektenbewegung*, p. 120.

[62] Oct. 4, 1531, *ibid.*

[63] A. Blaurer to Butzer, Dec. 28, 1531, Calvin, viii, 870. cf. Gerbert, *op. cit.*, p. 119.

[64] Grynaeus to Butzer, Dec. 30, 1531, Calvin, viii, 779, n., 871 f. Oecolampadius had died Nov. 22.

[65] 'Plurimi apud nos sunt qui eundem Hispanum commendant, ad sidera tollunt, ut qui in materia Trinitatis ipsum scopum et veritatem attigerit et scripserit.' July 5, 1532. cf. Röhrich, *Reformation*, ii, 81 f; Gerbert, *op. cit.*, p. 120 f.

[66] This on the authority of Calvin, who many years afterwards (Sept. 9, 1553) wrote

At Basel also the sale of Servetus's book was soon prohibited by the Council, though not at the instigation of the clergy; but Oecolampadius was asked his opinion of it.[67] After reading it through carefully he reported that the work was carelessly done and had many minor faults, which were however of little consequence in comparison with his denial of the eternal deity of Christ, the personality of the Holy Spirit, and the accepted doctrine of the Trinity, though he had mingled some useful things with his errors.[68]

At Bern, so Oecolampadius reported,[69] some of the brethren that had seen the book were greatly displeased with it, and wished Butzer to write to Luther that the book had been published abroad without their knowledge. It was sheer impudence for Servetus to charge the Lutherans with knowing nothing about justification by faith.[70] Unless he was to be authoritatively answered, the churches would get a very bad name with the Emperor.

Thus the general impression which Servetus had made upon all the leading reformers of the upper Rhine and Switzerland was strongly adverse. There were distinct reasons for this. He had brought out into the open, where they were now practically forced to declare themselves upon it, a doctrine which the reformers, it is true, nominally believed and had tacitly accepted, but as to whose foundations they had many misgivings, and which they had therefore by common consent passed over with a bare mention; and he had attacked it in terms so rude and bald that his attacks must now be met with either implied approval or strong condemnation. In the second place, his reference to the favorite doctrine of Luther, that of justification by faith, though brief, had been so offensive as to raise great fear lest the serious breach between Lutherans and Zwinglians over the doctrine of the Lord's

---

to Simon Sulzer, chief minister at Basel: "Servetus . . . is est de quo fidelis Christi minister et sanctae memoriae D. Bucerus, quum alioqui mansueto esset ingenio, pro suggestu pronunciavit dignum esse, qui avulsis visceribus discerperetur"; Calvin, xiv, 614, Röhrich and Tollin doubt this, as being inconsistent with Butzer's kindly attitude to Servetus at the time; but under exasperation one sometimes acts inconsistently with his normal habit.

[67] Oecolampadius to Butzer, July 18, 1531, Calvin, viii, 866. Servetus's books were also suppressed at Ulm; Nov. 14, 1538; *Ulmer Religionsprotokollen*, 1537–1545, A 245, fol. 51b, 52a.

[68] cf. his report to the Council, Calvin, viii, 863–865. Contemporary Latin translation from the original German, Oecolampadius & Zwingli, *Epistolae* (1536), p. 18a; (1592), p. 83; also in Mosheim, *Versuch*, pp. 394–396.

[69] Oecolampadius to Butzer, Aug. 5, 1531, Calvin, viii, 867.

[70] As he had done, *De Trinitatis erroribus*, p. 82b.

Supper should now be further widened, and the Protestant movement be permanently split into two mutually hostile camps. Hence the request that Oecolampadius made to Butzer, that he write Luther in the name of the churches, disowning responsibility for the book. Finally, there was the ever-haunting fear that the Catholics, and especially the Emperor, might be stirred up by any extreme tendencies among the reformers to use strong measures to suppress the whole Protestant cause; though as a matter of fact Servetus's book seems not to have made any impression in France, nor to have attracted Catholic attention at the time, except in one instance to be mentioned a little later, nor was the book placed on the Index until many years afterwards.

Finding himself unwelcome, perhaps not even safe, at Strassburg, where he would have preferred to stay, Servetus returned to Basel where, as he thought, he still had friends. But Oecolampadius had various complaints to make of his teachings, and when Servetus called he received him in so much anger that he dared not approach him again uninvited. He therefore wrote a letter in humble spirit, asking two favors: that he be not hindered from sending to the autumn fair at Lyon the copies of his book which he had brought with him, and that his name and reputation be spared. He had not thought to give such offence by what he had said of the Lutheran doctrine of faith, as to which the leading reformers themselves were not agreed. At all events, it was a property of man to err, and it was a serious thing to put men to death for some mistake in their understanding of Scripture. If Oecolampadius thought it better that he should not stay here, he would of course leave, provided he were not deemed to be a fugitive from justice, for he had written all with clear conscience, even if crudely.[71] We know nothing further of Servetus at Basel.

In his opinion rendered to the Basel Council, Oecolampadius had recommended that the books either be wholly suppressed, or be permitted only to persons that would make no bad use of them; but that if the writer acknowledged and retracted his errors in writing, they should be overlooked as only human.[72] It is probable that this counsel was communicated to Servetus, and that chastened by the unexpected hostility

---

[71] Servetus to Oecolampadius, Calvin, viii, 861 f.; Fueslin, *Epistolae*, p. 77 f.

[72] 'Die Bücher wär gut das sy eintweder gantz undertruckt wurden, oder gelesen von denen die sich der nit miszbruchten. Wo der so jrsälig gschribben mit gschrifften sin jrsal bekante und widerfechte, wär jm als einem menschen, sin fall nit so hoch zuschetzen', Calvin, viii, 865. cf. Latin version in Mosheim, *Versuch*, p. 394.

that he had aroused, and by the grave danger to which he found that he had exposed himself, he determined to follow the advice given. At all events, early in 1532 there appeared from the same press as before [73] a little book [74] which may probably be regarded as an outgrowth of the retraction suggested by Oecolampadius, and accepted in lieu of the prosecution for heresy that had seemed to threaten, and which was at the same time Servetus's parting word to the reformers who had shown themselves so inhospitable to his well-meant arguments.

The Dialogues on the Trinity [75] were intended, according to the preface, to set forth a more perfect statement of the subject in place of the unsatisfactory one in the previous work which, Servetus confesses, was rude, confused, incorrect and carelessly printed, and hence likely to give offence. The contents and style show that while Servetus did not mean to retract anything of the substance of his position as to the main questions involved, yet alarmed by the danger he had so narrowly escaped, and instructed by the impression his work had made on the reformers and by the objections they had filed against it, he wished to express his views so as to give as little offence as possible. The attitude is therefore conciliatory, and the language comparatively restrained. Apart from the extremely irritating language he had used of his opponents and their views, the criticism of the book on the Errors had fallen into two main classes: one concerned the views he had expressed in relation to the Trinity, the other concerned the attacks he had made upon the teachings of Luther. As to the former, under the guise of a dialogue with a collocutor named Petrucius, he defends himself against some of the objections that have been made. The specific points most objected to were that the Holy Spirit is an angel, that Christ is divine not by nature but only by God's grace, and that the Word ceased to exist after the incarnation. He tries to restate or explain these points so as to make them acceptable; and in doing this he goes so far in adopting the current doctrinal phraseology as sometimes to seem quite orthodox. Nevertheless, his central contentions as to the Trinity and the nature of Christ are

[73] It was perhaps the last work to issue from Setzer's press, for he died suddenly at the beginning of February. Bullinger regarded his death as a divine retribution upon the wicked and blasphemous printer. cf. his anonymous *Ministrorum Tigurinae ecclesiae . . . apologia*, p. c4a; Stieff, *Setzer*, p. 313.

[74] *Dialogorum de Trinitate libri duo. De justicia regni Christi, capitula quatuor.*

[75] cf. Tollin, 'Michael Servets Dialoge von der Dreieinigkeit,' *Theologische Studien und Kritiken*, i (1877), 301–318.

not retracted. The offence given by his criticism of Luther's doctrine of justification by faith he softens in the four appended chapters. Here he holds the balance fairly even between the value of faith and of works, pleading for the merit of each. In conclusion, he states that he does not wholly agree with either the Lutheran or the Catholic view, each of which is partly right and partly wrong, and laments that the current leaders of the Church exercise a tyrannical power, and give newer views no chance to be heard.

The work bears evidences of haste, and was probably put through the press at Hagenau after Servetus had left Basel, and just before he removed from the country. He did not stay to see how it was received, but there is no evidence that the feeling against him was perceptibly softened. Berthold Haller wrote Butzer from Bern that his new apology was full of monstrous errors, which if Butzer did not oppose he would bring trouble upon the Church, and would himself be suspected of agreeing or conniving at them.[76]

The feeling aroused by Servetus's two books in Lutheran circles was less violent than that in the cities of the upper Rhine, but yet it was decidedly unfavorable. Melanchthon, being asked by his intimate friend Joachim Camerarius his opinion about Servetus, replied that he was keen and subtle enough in argument, but was too little serious; he seemed to be confused in his ideas, and not to have thought his subjects through, and was plainly off the track as to justification. He had always feared that questions about the Trinity, unprofitable as they were, would break out and lead to tragedies.[77] A few weeks later he wrote again that he was reading Servetus a good deal.[78] At the middle of the year he wrote Johann Brenz (Brentius), preacher at Hall, that he found many signs of fanaticism in Servetus, and that he misinterpreted the Fathers whom he quoted. No doubt after a little great controversies would arise on the subject. Though there was much to complain of in the scholastic doctrine, yet Servetus should have made Christ really Son of God by nature.[79] He was then preparing a new edition of his *Loci*

---

[76] March 16, 1532. "Michael Hispanum ferunt Apologiam priori libello dedisse plenam monstrorum ac errorum, quibus ubi tu, qui triados mysteria ex fomite hausisti, non occurres, non solum incommodabis Ecclesiam, sed te quoque suspectum reddes qui vel consentias vel conniveas." Quoted by Röhrich, *Reformation*, ii, 82, n.

[77] Melanchthon to Camerarius, Feb. 9, 1533, *Opera*, ii, 630.

[78] "Servetum multum lego." Melanchthon to Camerarius, March 15, 1533, *Opera*, ii, 640.   [79] Melanchthon to Brentius, July, 1533, *Opera*, ii, 660 f.

Communes. In the first edition of this (1521), the first attempt to put
the teaching of the reformers into some kind of system, he had said, 'It
were more fitting to adore the mysteries of the Godhead than to inquire
into them; for this can not be attempted without great peril, as holy
men have more than once found out. . . . There is no reason why we
should pay much attention to the profoundest subjects about God, his
unity, his trinity. What, pray, have scholastic theologians in all the
centuries gained by dealing with these subjects alone? When Paul
in his Epistle to the Romans drew up a short statement of Christian
doctrine, he did not philosophize on the mysteries of the Trinity, did
he?' [80]

The results of Melanchthon's study of Servetus are clearly seen in the
1535 edition of the *Loci Communes*.[81] These appear not only in the fact
that he now takes up the doctrines that he formerly avoided, giving the
persons of the Trinity full treatment, and undertaking to refute the
views of Servetus on this and other doctrines that he had attacked, but
also in his method of approach. He now insists that it is not enough to
entertain an opinion about faith and the knowledge of the will of God,
but that one must have a sure and firm opinion about the articles of
faith according to the Scriptures; for doubt begets wickedness and despair.[82] From now on Melanchthon becomes openly and aggressively
the opponent of Servetus. In the first chapters of his *Loci* he several
times singles Servetus out for special mention by name, and alludes to
him frequently. When a Venetian student brought to Wittenberg in
1539 a report of the alarming spread of Servetus's views in the Venetian
territory [83] a long letter was addressed to the Council at Venice over
Melanchthon's name, seriously warning against them, and confuting
them at length.[84] And when Servetus was finally put to death at Geneva
in 1553, no one was more hearty than Melanchthon in expressing his
approval. Luther, on the other hand, seems to have concerned himself

[80] Melanchthon, *Loci*, pp. 102–105.

[81] cf. Tollin, *Ph. Melanchthon und M. Servet*, (Berlin, 1876), especially chaps. iv.–vi.
for detailed evidence.

[82] Est et hoc sciendum de fide ac notitia voluntatis Dei, quod non satis est opinionem
aliquam in animo circumferre, sed contra habere certam et firmam sententiam de articulis
fidei ex scripturis. Nam dubitatio parit impietatem ac desperationem. *Opera*, xxi, 255.

[83] In the next chapter it will be seen more at length how widely such views spread in
northern Italy.

[84] Melanchthon, *Opera*, iii, 745–750. Melanchthon subsequently denied being author
of the letter, though approving of its message. *v. infra*, p. 79.

but little with Servetus or his heresies. In all his works Servetus is mentioned but thrice, and then only briefly and by the way.[85]

Calvin also was greatly disturbed at the spread of Servetus's views in Italy, and it was the hope of counteracting these that was one of the main reasons that led him to publish his *Defensio Orthodoxae Fidei* in 1554.[86] The influence of these early writings of Servetus long persisted. More than twenty years later Peter Martyr was reported to be writing at Strassburg a book (never published) in opposition to Servetus's *De Trinitatis erroribus*, and to be wishing to write against his other books if he had copies.[87]

Although Catholic writers at a later period cited the blasphemous errors of Servetus as a witness of what Protestantism could lead to, and joined with orthodox Protestants in the absurd conjecture that he had been in league with the Grand Turk in a conspiracy to undermine Christianity in western Europe and thus to pave the way for conquest by the Mohammedan power, which was then a seriously threatening danger, there is from the time of which we have been speaking no record of attention from Catholic quarters save in one instance. In April, 1532, while the diet was sitting at Ratisbon (Regensburg), Servetus's book on the Trinity was discovered on sale there by Johannes Cochlaeus, who at Augsburg had been the chief opponent of the reformers and the liberal Catholics. He brought it to the more tolerant Quintana, head of the board of censors, perhaps not without malicious pleasure that here was the work of a fellow-countryman of Quintana's. The latter was annoyed beyond measure both by the unheard-of heresies in the book, and by the fact that the author was a Spaniard. With prudent reserve he confessed that he knew the author by sight, and he had the sale of the book prohibited.[88] A copy of it was sent to the Bishop of Augsburg to see what

---

[85] *v. supra*, p. 56, n. 28, *fin.* Cf. Luther, *Opera*, ed. Walch, xxii, 377, 2367.

[86] cf. letter of Paolo Gaddi of Cremona to Calvin, July 23, 1553. "Multas inter eundum Italiae civitates invisi . . . multa ibi haeresum genera vigere sensi . . . sed quae inter omnes maxime viget, est superbissimi diabolicique Serveti opinio, quam ut scriptis impugnes multi te obsecrant fideles," Calvin, xiv, 577. "Multos esse in Italia tabe ista infectos . . . In Italis forte propter rarum acumen magis eminet . . . Hoc quum fidi et idonei testes quibusdam suis popularibus contigisse retulerint . . . quosdam scio ex diametro inter se dissidere, qui se tamen Serveti discipulos esse profitentur," *id. op.* viii, 459. Guillaume Postell also wrote in 1555 that Servetus had many followers in Italy. cf. Mosheim, *Versuch*, p. 474.

[87] cf. Gratarolo to Bullinger, Dec. 19, 1553, Jan. 5, 1554, Calvin, xiv, 707; xv, 3.

[88] cf. Johannes Cochlaeus, *Historia . . . de actis et scriptis Martini Lutheri* (Coloniae,

action he would take; [89] while Girolamo Aleandro, who had from the first been Luther's uncompromising opponent, and was now papal representative at the Emperor's court, wrote that if nothing else were done he would call together the theologians, especially the Spaniards, there present, and would have the book formally censured, and a letter written to Spain to have it proclaimed and burned, and the heretic dealt with in the Spanish manner, since it was said that he had perhaps made some impression there with his heresy and had already sent his book thither. Steps would be taken to have the heretic punished wherever found.[90]

Such steps evidently were taken; for on June 17 of that same year a decree of arrest was issued at Toulouse against forty fugitives, students, monks, etc., and among the first of these was Michel Serveto *alias* Reves.[91] A few weeks earlier than even this, measures against Servetus were instituted in Spain. Acting on information received from Germany, the Council of the Inquisition directed the Inquisitor of Aragón to make inquiries as to the origin, family and history of Servetus, and to have him summoned by the usual public notice to appear before the Inquisition. Instructions were given to try by any means to persuade him to return to Spain, but not to betray to him or his family what was really intended. Servetus's own brother, the priest Juan, at that time chaplain to the Archbishop of Santiago de Compostela, was deputed to undertake this mission, and apparently went to Germany for the purpose. Even if he acted in good faith he can not have succeeded in his undertaking, for Servetus had already left Germany and disappeared into thin air. When in 1538 the Council impatiently called for a report of progress on the case, though Juan had filed his deposition, no information was forthcoming as to the whereabouts of his brother Miguel. The records give no trace of further proceedings.[92]

1768), pp. 232–234; Laurentius Surius, *Commentarius brevis,* etc. (Coloniae, 1602), p. 223; Tollin, *Verfasser,* pp. 419–429.

[89] Letter of Aleander to Sanga, Ratisbon, April 17, 1532, in Laemmer, *Monumenta,* p. 109. 'Al presente lui ha mandato il libro al Vescovo di Augusta.' It is not clear from this whether the book was sent by Quintana or by Servetus, though the former would seem the more likely. Nor is it certain that Augusta is not meant as an abbreviated form of Caesaraugusta (Saragossa), though Servetus was not of that diocese.

[90] cf. Laemmer, *loc. cit.*

[91] cf. *Bulletin de la Société de l'histoire du Protestantisme Français,* liii (Mar.–Apr. 1904), 103.

[92] For the documented story of this interesting episode, but recently brought to light,

It was not in the nature of the case possible for Servetus, young as he was, and in all the circumstances of his life, to win a personal following of disciples to form a school and spread his views; and although the questions that his little books raised led many to carry their inquiries and speculations further than he had gone, yet hardly one came forward as his acknowledged follower. One person, however, deserves mention in this connection, Claude d'Aliod (Claudius Aliodus), commonly spoken of as Claude of Savoy.[93] He was a native of Moûtier in Savoy, and first comes to our attention when preacher at Neuchâtel as colleague of Farel. He was a restless, contentious, somewhat erratic figure, and he grew increasingly fanatical as time went on and persecution of him increased. The doctrines he preached at Neuchâtel gave offence, and as they were spreading, and it was feared that they were infecting Farel himself, the Bernese preachers called him to account and argued with him. As they could not convert him, they ordered him not to spread his views; and when he disobeyed the order the Bernese government banished him from its territory early in 1534.[94] He next lived for several months at Constanz, where similar trouble ensued. Being put on examination by the ministers of the city, he made no secret of his views, but presented a confession of them. Here he declared, as at Bern, that Jesus Christ was a mere man; but he later admitted that Christ was the natural Son of God and hence divine, though not eternally so, and he asserted that Farel agreed with him. He denied a Trinity of persons in both name and fact, and concluded: 'In short, I do not believe that three persons are the one God.'[95] He was therefore banished from Constanz. At Zürich, where he also appeared, Bullinger thought it necessary to counteract his influence, and to defend the reformers' reputation for orthodoxy by writing a book on the two natures in Christ.[96]

---

cf. Marcel Bataillon, 'Honneur et Inquisition: Michel Servet poursuivi par l'Inquisition espagnole' *Bulletin Hispanique*, t. xxviii. (Bordeaux, Jan.–Mar., 1925).

[93] cf. Trechsel, *Antitrinitarier*, i, 55–59; *id.*, 'War Servet bei Luther in Wittenberg?' *Theologische Studien und Kritiken*, liv (1881), 669–684; J. G. Schelhorn, *Dissertatio epistolaris de Mino Celso*, etc. (Ulmae, 1748), pp. 73–77; Dunin Borkowski, *Quellenstudien*, i, 116 f.

[94] cf. Haller to Bullinger, May 7, 1534, (A. L. Herminjard, *Correspondance des Réformateurs* (Genève, 1870), iii, 172–174, also in Fueslin, *Epistolae*, p. 139, f.

[95] cf. Johann Zwick to Vadian, Aug. 23, 1534 (Herminjard, *op. cit.*, iii, 173); J. H. Hottinger, *Bibliotheca Tigurina* (Zürich, 1664), p. 77; Frecht to Blarer, Aug. 28, 1534 (*Museum Helveticum*, pars xxviii, 672, 676).

[96] *Utriusque in Christo naturae*, Zürich, Oct. 1534.

Claude now determined to thresh the question out with Luther, but on his way north stopped for a conference with Myconius at Basel, where he was soon imprisoned and again banished, as also from Strassburg. He stayed at Wittenberg a month or so, but when it was discovered that he was stirring up trouble about the Trinity, he was again ordered to move on.[97] Undaunted, he returned to Switzerland and tried his fortunes at Lausanne, where he won so much favor among the more liberal spirits that a synod was convened over the matter, at which Butzer feared that they might carry the day.[98] He was voted down, however, and forced to recant,[99] presumably as an alternative to yet another banishment. A few years later he appeared at Augsburg, where he won a following and was again arrested and banished; then at Strassburg in 1542, where Schwenckfeld earnestly opposed him; then again for a considerable time at Constanz. His last reported activity was at Memmingen in 1550, where he assumed the rôle of a prophet, made fanatical claims, and won so many converts that even after he had once more been driven into banishment (from which he later stole back) it took five years of incessant work on the part of the ministers, assisted by a theologian imported from Ulm, to convert them from their errors. After this nothing further is known of him. The views reported as his, and expressed in his confession at Constanz, show distinctly the influence of Servetus, and he also anticipated some positions commonly credited to Socinus. But his experiences in trying to spread his views show how far the Protestant world had yet to go before realizing the ideals of freedom, reason and tolerance in religion.

Despite the assertions of some more recent writers to the contrary, there is no contemporary evidence that Servetus was forced to leave Basel; though he must have been haunted by a constant sense of danger in a country where he was known as the author of two such heretical works. But he knew not where to turn. Spain, Italy, Germany, Switzerland, France were all dangerous lands for one whom Protestants and Catholics equally considered heretical. Ten years or so later he writes with deep feeling of the terrors and lonesomeness of this period, when for years he felt divinely impelled to spread his views of Christian truth,

---

[97] cf. Melanchthon to Veit Dietrich, Aug. 5, 1537, Melanchthon, *Opera*, iii, 400. J. K. F. Knaake in *Theologische Studien und Kritiken*, liv (1881), 320.

[98] Melanchthon to Dietrich, *ut supra*.

[99] cf. Herminjard, *op. cit.*, iv, 196 f, 200, 235.

and yet humanly tempted to flee from his duty like Jonah, by going to sea or emigrating to the New Isles (America).[100] In his testimony at Geneva he stated that his reason for leaving Germany was that he was poor and did not understand the language,[101] but these can hardly have been the compelling reasons. He had had money enough to publish his books, and would scarcely be likely to have more in another country; and German is one of the modern languages with which he says in his preface to Ptolemy, published three years later, that he is to some extent acquainted.[102] At all events, he proceeded from Basel (perhaps stopping at Hagenau on the way to see his Dialogues through the press) to Lyon,[103] where he could find remunerative employment, and feel at home in the language that he had spoken at Toulouse. In order effectually to cut himself off from his past and so guard against discovery, he now concealed himself under the name Michel de Villeneuve (Michael Villanovanus), in allusion to his earlier home in Spain. He left no trace of his movements, and it was twenty-one years before he was again discovered to the world in his own person. Ignorance meanwhile opened the door to conjecture, and a few years later the rumor was current that he had perished mad in some old castle dungeon.[104]

With the first half of his life completed, we must now take our leave of Servetus for a time, in order to trace the working of the leaven of his thought and the progress of the struggle for freedom and reason in religion during the next twenty years, until he again appears upon our scene.

[100] Causa haec tua est . . . quae mihi adolescentulo annos vix nato viginti, impulso quodam divino tractandum sese obtulit . . . Testem te iterum invoco Deum ob eam rem me distulisse, et ob imminentem persecutionem, ut cum Jona in mare fugere potius cuperem, aut in insulam aliquam novam. The passage (lacking in the printed text) is on p. 3 of a Ms copy of what is apparently a first draft of the *prooemium* of his *Christianismi Restitutio*, which is bound in with the copy at Edinburgh. cf. Alexander Gordon, "Servetus and America," *Christian Life*, li, 360, Oct. 24, 1925; David Cuthbertson, *A Tragedy of the Reformation* (Edinburgh, 1912).

[101] cf. Calvin, viii, 767.

[102] Materna lingua tanquam faciliore plurima urbium vocabula explicuimus: ut Germanis Germanice, etc., quorum omnium linguas utcunque novimus. Preface to Ptolemy, 1535.

[103] At Geneva he testified, "De Agnouw el sen retournit a Basle, de Basle a Lyon," Calvin, viii, 767.

[104] cf. Frecht to Capito, Oct. 31, 1538. "Non ignoras ut sanctae memoriae Oecolampadius illum Michaelem Serveto confutarit. De quo olim accepi illum impietatis suae poenas meritas dedisse. Nunc furiosum in catenis misere obiisse istuc an sit certum cuperem ex tua humanitate cognoscere." Calvin, xxi, 238; cf. X, ii, 289. Tollin in *Jahrbücher für protestantische Theologie*, xvii (1891), 428, n.; iii (1877), 642, n.

CHAPTER VI

THE UNITARIAN ANABAPTIST MOVEMENT IN ITALY

IN THE PREVIOUS CHAPTERS have been traced the scattered outcroppings north of the Alps, in the wide-spread but incoherent body of those that were popularly classed together under the name of Anabaptists, of a marked tendency, during the first forty years or so of the Reformation, toward a more liberal type of Christianity than that which was rapidly becoming fixed among the followers of Luther, Zwingli and Calvin. We have seen that while the leaders of this tendency were in the main men of outstanding ability and ample learning, the rank and file of the whole movement were of the humbler classes in rank, wealth and education. Their primary interest in Christianity was not as a system of belief but as a way of life; and their main emphasis was laid not upon theological doctrines but upon the practical application of Christian principles to personal conduct and character, and to the Christianizing of human relations in organized society.

In contrast with the Roman Church and the existing Protestant confessions, with their insistence first of all upon strict compliance with fixed standards of orthodoxy, they had taken a long step forward toward the realization of full mental freedom in religion. They adopted no creed and imposed no confessions, and even if they accepted without question or qualification whatever seemed to them to be the teaching of Scripture, yet it had not occurred to any of them to regard the Bible as a limitation of the freedom of the Christian man, but rather as the charter of it. Again, as regards the fundamental principle of tolerance of differing religious views, they had taken an equally long step forward, and one indeed essentially involved in the idea of liberty, when the principle of religious tolerance which they practiced with one another became transformed, as applied to civil government, into the kindred policy of religious toleration, which they so steadily advocated and so seldom enjoyed. But as regards the third fundamental of liberal religion as here conceived, the full use of reason in religion as applied to religious doctrines, they left much to be realized. In fact, in doctrines themselves they had only a secondary interest, and that least of all in those of a speculative nature to which objection might be made on grounds of reason. In any case, their question would have been not, Is the doctrine reasonable? but, Is it scriptural?

A little later than the Anabaptist tendencies above noted, there also began to develop south of the Alps, out of the bosom of the Catholic Church, liberal tendencies in some respects similar to these, in some respects contrasted with them, and in some complementary to them. These were the outgrowth of quite different antecedents, rooted in the soil of the Renaissance. Soon after the middle of the fifteenth century, the writings of the Greek philosophers began to spread abroad, and to be widely read and discussed, in Italy. The intellectuals, therefore, were led to regard the traditional dogmas more in the light of philosophy than in that of theology; and while still maintaining an outward conformity to the Church, they were often, even in clerical circles, at heart more pagan than Christian. The consequence was that even before the Reformation the hold of various Christian doctrines upon many nominally Catholic minds had been decidedly weakened.[1] The supernatural birth and the divinity of Christ had already been denied by 1500, and it was said that half a century later, in the time of Pope Paul IV. (Caraffa), a man was deemed to be of little account unless he were tainted with heresy.[2] When the seeds of the Reformation spread from northern Europe into Italy they found, therefore, their most fertile soil not, as often north of the Alps, among the humbler classes, but among the educated middle class, especially in the cities, whose interest in the new movement centered largely upon the reform of Christian doctrines. Here it was inevitable that, while many would still hold the traditional doctrines unchanged, yet others would reject them as not acceptable to reason. It was these bolder and more radical thinkers, not very many in number, though notable for the extent of their influence, that furnished the stimulation that before the end of the century led to the separate existence of the movement with whose history we are here concerned. The first springs of the Socinian-Unitarian movement, therefore, regarded for the moment as a system of religious belief, are to be

[1] cf. Jacob Burckhardt, *The Civilization of the Renaissance in Italy* (London, 1929), pp. 479–481.

[2] cf. E. Rodocanachi, *La Réforme en Italie* (Paris, 1920), i. 26, citing Caraccioli, *Vita Pauli IV*.

found not in the Protestant lands of the North, but in Catholic Italy. The especial contribution of these Italian liberals was the recognition of the importance of reason in religion which, when added to the fundamental principles of freedom and tolerance which the liberal Anabaptists had already fully adopted, furnished the principle still needed to make their system complete by assuring it sane guidance. When these Italians, by that time exiled from Italy, came a generation later into connection with the Anabaptists who were multiplying in Poland, they thus brought to the movement there the intellectual stimulus and leadership that were needed to transform a loose aggregation into a coherent body, and to win it respect. From that time on, as will be later seen, this movement began to assume definite shape.

Before proceeding to speak of the leading pioneers of this movement south of the Alps, it will be well first to survey the beginnings of the Reformation there, and to tell of a transient movement in northern Italy which, while it was headed in the same direction, was yet largely independent of them. In no part of Italy did the Reformation take earlier or wider root than in the Republic of Venice,[3] whose active trade with the commercial cities of Germany drew many traveling merchants thither, many or most of whom would of course be Protestants. Venice had indeed had on its books since 1249 an undertaking to burn at the stake any found guilty of heresy,[4] but it had long been allowed to slumber, for the burning of Protestant heretics would have tended seriously to interfere with the German trade; and in practice, in the first half of the sixteenth century Venice enjoyed in Catholic Italy a reputation for toleration comparable to that which Holland later had among Protestant lands. For Venice long showed itself impatient of interference in its local concerns by the Roman curia, and resisted the increasing pressure to have the laws enforced, so that the Inquisition was not in full cry there until 1547.[5] Long before this Lutherans were known to be holding meetings (of course more or less in secret) in various parts of the city.[6] They were yet more numerous in Vicenza and other cities in the vicinity, where there are said to have been from 200 to 500, includ-

---

[3] Its territory at this time extended from the head of the Adriatic nearly to Milan, and included half a score of important cities in which the Reformation had groups of adherents.

[4] cf. Cesare Cantù, *Gli Eretici d'Italia* (Torino, 1867–'68), iii, 129.

[5] cf. Karl Benrath, *Geschichte der Reformation in Venedig* (Halle, 1886), p. 74.

[6] *id. op.*, p. 19.

ing some persons of importance, who used to meet, generally in the houses of patricians, to discuss religious subjects. The Pope, when informed of this, was much concerned, and put fresh pressure upon the local government to take severe measures for uprooting the heresy. Many prosecutions and trials for heresy ensued, and the Lutheran meetings were thus broken up by the Inquisition.[7] This was in 1546, the date which Socinian tradition later fixed as that of the origin of the Socinian movement, as will presently be seen.

Along with the views of Luther, those of the Anabaptists also early penetrated northern Italy, most likely coming from Zürich after the Anabaptists were driven thence in 1525,[8] and probably by way of the Grisons. It was among these northern Italian Anabaptists that a definite formulation of Unitarian doctrine was first adopted for purposes of propaganda; and this is apparently to be traced to the two books on the Trinity which Servetus had published in 1531-'32. The influence of Servetus in these parts was early noted with deep concern. In 1539 [9] an unknown person addressed to the Venetian Council a letter bearing the signature of Melanchthon, saying, 'I have learned that a book of Servetus is being circulated there, which has revived the error of Paul of Samosata condemned by the primitive Church. . . . I have thought that you should be warned and entreated to urge and encourage them to avoid, renounce and detest the wicked error of Servetus.' [10] Girolamo Zanchi, minister to the Protestant congregation at Chiavenna at a time when radical opinions were causing much disturbance there, traced them all to Servetus.[11] Guillaume Postel in 1553 published at Venice

---

[7] cf. Bernardo Morsolin, 'L'accademia de' Sociniani in Vicenza,' *Atti del Reale Istituto Veneto di Scienze, Lettere ed Arte* (Venezia, Nov. 1878–Oct. 1879), tomo v., serie v., pp. 473–475.

[8] cf. Karl Benrath, 'Wiedertäufer im Venetianischen um die Mitte des 16. Jahrhunderts' *Theologische Studien und Kritiken*, lviii (1885), 9–67.

[9] Not 1538, as Bock has it, *Antitrinitar.*, ii. 398. cf. Illgen, *ut infra*, p. 21, n. 18.

[10] *v. supra*, p. 70. cf. Melanchthon, *Opera*, iii, 745. Melanchthon two years later denied to Contarini, the Venetian ambassador to the German Emperor, that he was the author of this letter, but said that others had composed it over his name. cf. Giuseppe de Leva, *Storia documentata di Carlo V* (Venezia, 1860–'94) iii, 327, n. 2. It bears contemporary witness, however, to the essential fact. cf. K. Benrath, 'Notiz über Melanchthon's angeblichen Brief an den venetianischen Senat,' *Zeitschrift für Kirchengeschichte*, i (1877), 469; *id.*, *Wiedertäufer*, pp. 9–12; C. F. Illgen, *Symbolarum ad vitam et doctrinam Laelii Socini illustrandam*, Particula i (Lipsiae, 1826), p. 20 ff.

[11] Facile est divinare unde hoc malum et per quos fotum. Hispania gallinas peperit, Italia fovit ova, nos jam pipientes pullos audimus. Zanchi to Bullinger, Aug. 19, 1565,

an apology for Servetus in which it was declared that he had many
followers in Italy who denied the Trinity and the deity of Christ;[12]
and the wish to convert these from their errors was a large motive for
Calvin in the following year to write his refutation of the errors of
Servetus.[13] Again, Pierpaolo Vergerio, an Italian Protestant fugitive
living at Tübingen, writes on September 6, 1554 to Bullinger, leader
of the Reformation at Zürich: 'There is with me now Girolamo Don-
zelino, a physician lately driven from Italy for the Gospel's sake, a prudent man, who knows much of what is going on in Italy. He declares
that the Servetian plague is spreading a great deal more,' etc.[14] Finally,
Pope Paul IV. in a bull of August 7, 1555, refers to apostates who deny
the dogmas of the Trinity and the divinity of Christ.[15] Here are evidences enough of a smoldering fire in the north of Italy, ready under
favoring conditions to burst into a flame. How this took place, and
how the flame was speedily extinguished, only to burst out two decades
later in other lands, can now be related.

For two centuries and a half a legend has been current, and repeated
as authentic by successive generations of writers on this period, of a
certain heretical society at Vicenza, some forty miles northwest of Venice, which was the original source of that movement, and of its leaders,
which twenty years later came to the surface in Poland as a nascent
form of Socinianism. The story is so interesting, and has so often been
told and accepted as true, that it deserves to be told again here, if only
that it may be rejected as unhistorical, and then be replaced by the
authentic facts out of which it grew up to its current form. The legend
is given in three successive forms appearing within a few years of each
other. *A Brief Narrative of the Origin of the Unitarians in Poland*, by
Andrew Wiszowaty, grandson of Faustus Socinus, was first printed in
an appendix to the *Ecclesiastical History* [16] of Christopher Sandius, an
Arian living at Amsterdam. It was again given in 1684 in the same au-

---

H. Bullinger, *Korrespondenz mit den Graubündnern* (Basel, 1904–'06), ii, 627. cf. Hottinger, *Helvetische Kirchen-Geschichten*, iii, 874; Bock, *Antitrin.*, ii, 415.

[12] Reprinted in Mosheim, *Versuch*, pp. 466–499; and in Johann Kvačala, *Postelliana*
(Tartu, 1915); cf. Bock, *op. cit.*, ii, 542.

[13] cf. Calvin, viii, 459.

[14] cf. P. D. Rosius de Porta, *Historia Reformationis Ecclesiarum Raeticarum* (Curiae
Raetorum, 1772–'77), I, ii, 159.

[15] cf. Angelo Cherubini, *Bullarium Magnum Romanum* (Roma, 1638), i, 590, 599;
cited by C. F. Illgen, *Symbolae*, p. 76.

[16] Sandius, *Nucleus* (ed. 2, Coloniae, 1678), pp. 86–90 of Appendix.

thor's *Bibliotheca Antitrinitariorum*.[17] Finally, Stanislas Lubieniecki in his *History of the Polish Reformation*, published in 1685, but written some time before his death in 1675, and perhaps used in manuscript by Sand and Wiszowaty, gives a more extended version, citing as his authorities a manuscript history by Stanislas Budziński,[18] and a life of Laelius Socinus, neither of which is now extant. From the data transmitted in these three accounts, all of which appear to derive from a common source, the story can be made out as follows:

About the year 1546, in various cities in the territory of Venice, there were numerous persons who undertook to explore the truth, and to this end held religious meetings and conferences. Laelius Socinus, together with some Italian associates more than forty in number, held such conferences and meetings at Vicenza, in which they called in question especially the current dogmas about the Trinity, the satisfaction of Christ, and the like. Among the members of this society are said to have been an Abbot named Leonardo Buzzale (Busale), Lelio Sozini, Bernardino Ochino, Nicola Paruta, Valentino Gentile, Giulio di Treviso, Francesco di Ruego (Rovigo), Jacopo di Chieri, Francesco Negri, Dario Sozzino, Paolo Alciati and others.[19] When the matter became known, they fell under severe persecution, some were put to death, others saved their lives by scattering, leaving Italy, and going to various countries. The Abbot Buzzale together with forty others sought and found among the Turks a safety not to be enjoyed as Christians among Christians. Buzzale went at last to Damascus, where he lived the rest of his life as a tailor; the rest to Thessalonica, all but three, Giulio di Treviso and Francesco di Ruego, who were put to death by drowning at Venice, and Jacopo di Chieri, who died a natural death there. Those that did not go to Turkey took refuge in Switzerland, Moravia, and at length in Poland; of whom the chief was Lelio Sozini.

The version given by Lubieniecki adds a detailed statement of the main topics of Christian faith agreed upon in these meetings, which are found to anticipate all the main positions of the Socinianism later to

---

[17] Andreas Wissowatius, *Narratio compendiosa quomodo in Polonia, a Trinitariis Reformatis separati sint Christiani Unitarii* (in Sandius, *Bibliotheca Antitrinitariorum*, etc. (Freistadii-Amsterdam, 1684), pp. 207–217).

[18] Stanislaus Lubieniecius, *Historia Reformationis Polonicae* (Freistadii, 1685), pp. 38–40. Budziński had been secretary to Francesco Lismanino, an early leader of Antitrinitarianism in Poland, and both of them were intimate with Laelius Socinus.

[19] The names, garbled in the Latin text, are here restored to their proper Italian form.

arise in Poland. The conclusion is therefore drawn that these meetings were the primary source of the Socinian doctrine, and of the apostles that were to spread it north of the Alps. Not content with the story even as it is, the fancy of subsequent writers has sometimes seen in these *Collegia Vicentina*, as they have been called, one of those Academies that were so marked an element in the Italian culture of the sixteenth century, and has made out Laelius Socinus (a youth of twenty-one!) as the president of it.[20] Nothing else, however, is known of this alleged Academy, nor what its title was, nor where it met, nor what it discussed, nor of the decree that condemned it, except that unverifiable local tradition places the meetings in the Casa Pigafetta,[21] or in one of the splendid mansions in Lonedo in Lugo, a pleasant town on the left bank of the Astico, where the plain of Vicenza reaches the foot-hills of the Alps; and the road is shown by which the members escaped in their flight to Germany.[22]

The authenticity of this story, however, has long been under suspicion among historical scholars.[23] It is noted that there is no contemporary reference, either Catholic or Protestant, to these meetings, and that the first mention of them occurs only in 1676, a hundred and thirty years after the alleged date. Of the alleged participants in the conferences, at least three can not have been living at Vicenza at the time. Ochino, as we shall later see, had fled the country in 1542 in circumstances that would certainly have rendered his life a forfeit had he ever ventured to return to Italy; Negri was already living at Chiavenna across the border

[20] cf. Bock, *Antitrinitar.*, ii, 412.

[21] The house, still handsome even in decay, is in the Via Antonio Pigafetta, No. 5, a little to the rear of the splendid Palladian communal palace on the main Piazza. Pigafetta was a companion of Magellan in the circumnavigation of the globe. The house dates from 1481.

[22] cf. Cantù, *Eretici*, iii. 156; Morsolin, *Accademia*, p. 459.

[23] G. G. Zeltner, *Historia Crypto-Socinismi Altorfini* (Lipsiae, 1729), p. 321, n. b, was the first to raise the question. It was followed up successively by Mosheim, *Institutiones historiae Christianae recentioris* (Helmstedii, 1741), pp. 309–311; *id.*, *Institutes of Ecclesiastical History* (London, 1863), iii, 167 f; Wannfred von Camben, *Anmerckungen zu dem siebenten Band der Leipzigischen Universal-Chronick*, in J. C. Fueslin, *Beyträge zur Erläuterung der Kirchen-Reformations-Geschichten des Schweitzerlands* (Zürich, 1747), iii, 326–329; by the anonymous author of *Vier Sendschreiben an . . . Mosheim* (n. p., 1751), p. 8; Bock, *Antitrinitar.*, ii, 395–426; C. F. Illgen, *Symbolae*, part i.; and most fully by Trechsel, *Antitrinitarier*, ii, 391–408. The result of this thorough criticism is that while sound historical facts have been incorporated in the legend, yet oral and written tradition operating during the four generations between 1546 and our earliest extant source has added to them many details that, if true, belong in another setting.

in 1543, and too well known to have risked his life by residence near Vicenza;[24] and while Laelius Socinus did not leave Italy until 1547, he did not then do it as a suspected heretic fleeing for safety, and returned to Italy several times within the next eight years.[25] At least two other names seem out of place in the above list. Giulio di Treviso (Giulio Gherlandi) and Francesco di Ruego (Francesco della Saga of Rovigo) were indeed put to death at Venice as related, in 1562 and 1565 respectively; but Gherlandi was not baptized until 1549, after which he joined the Anabaptists in Moravia, whence he was sent back to Italy in 1559 to visit the brethren there, and especially to persuade them to abandon their radical views, and to promise them a welcome in Moravia; while Francesco di Ruego, who had also been sent from Moravia on a similar missionary journey, was in 1546 only a young lad.[26]

Again, the doctrinal points said to have been agreed upon at these conferences on the one hand make no mention of several points emphasized at the time by all the Italian reformers, while on the other hand the view of Christ is opposed to that later held by Gentile and Alciati, the views in general are much more positive and definite than those ever confessed by Laelius Socinus or Ochino, and they show a striking likeness, even to word and phrase, to those set forth sixty years later in the Racovian Catechism in Poland. The conclusion thus seems irresistible that the plastic tradition of four or five generations gradually cast together into one piece the authentic but hazy memory of a liberal Anabaptist movement at or near Vicenza about the middle of the sixteenth century, the conclusions of an Anabaptist council at Venice in 1550 (to be related below), the names of some of the most important Italian pioneers of Antitrinitarianism, and the developed system of doctrine that the Socinians eventually reached in Poland early in the seventeenth century; but that it unconsciously fell into glaring inconsistencies which put us in the way of discovering the historical truth.[27] That truth the researches of competent scholars now enable us to state.

The correct statement of the case, resting for the most part on records of the Inquisition brought to light at Venice fifty or sixty years

[24] cf. de Porta, *Historia*, I. i., 197.

[25] cf. J. H. Hottinger, *Historiae ecclesiasticae* (Tiguri, 1655–57), ix, 436; C. F. Illgen, *Vita Laelii Socini* (Lipsiae, 1814), p. 20; de Porta, *Historia*, I. ii, 86.

[26] cf. Benrath, *Reformation*, pp. 91–99; *id.*, *Wiedertäufer*, pp. 38–53; Emilio Comba, *I nostri Protestanti* (Firenze, 1895–'97), ii, chaps. xiv, xv.

[27] cf. Trechsel, *Antitrinitarier*, ii, 402–408.

ago, is as follows.[28] After Lutheranism had been uprooted at Vicenza,[29] Anabaptism began to spread with great rapidity through all that region. Its chief missionary was an ex-priest named Tiziano, of whose later history we shall speak in another connection in a later chapter. He is said to have been the first to spread Anabaptist doctrines in Italy, though he had the assistance of several others. By the middle of the century the movement had adherents in more than sixty places, and there were definitely known to be more than a thousand of them in Venice alone.[30] They were well organized, with ordained ministers, and under the oversight of ten or more 'apostolic bishops,' who went from congregation to congregation to preach, ordain, and give counsel. They were almost wholly of the humbler class, mainly artizans, and they held their meetings in private houses in great secrecy.[31] They seem to have been much more concerned with the doctrinal phase of the Reformation than were their northern brethren; and their beliefs, evidently influenced by the writings of Servetus, tended to be much less orthodox. For besides the usual Anabaptist views, there was more or less general denial of the Trinity, and difference of view as to the nature of Christ. This tendency was especially marked in the congregation at Vicenza, so that in order to determine these questions it was decided to call together a council of leaders of all the congregations in northern Italy. This was about the beginning of 1550.

Word was sent to each congregation to send two delegates to a formal council of Anabaptists to be held at Venice in September. About sixty delegates met, including some from two congregations in Switzerland,

[28] For the relation of the full story, properly documented, see Morsolin, *Accademia*; Benrath, *Wiedertäufer*; *id.*, *Reformation*; Emilio Comba, 'Un sinodo Anabattista a Venezia anno 1550' *Rivista Cristiana*, xiii, 21–24, 83–87 (Jan. and April, 1885); *id.*, *Protestanti*, ii, chap. xiii. The sources are in the records of heresy trials before the Inquisition, in the Frari Archives, Venice, which were explored by Morsolin and used in his writing already cited; and in the State Archives at Venice, Busta ix, *Processi del Sant' Uffizio*, explored by both Benrath and Comba and used in their works as cited above. Unless they are speaking of two different councils, which seems unlikely, there is some confusion between Morsolin and Benrath. Benrath places the council at Venice in September, 1550, adjourned from discussions at Vicenza earlier in the year (*Reformation*, p. 78); while Morsolin places it in 1551, adjourned from a meeting earlier in the year at Padua (*Accademia*, p. 486). In other respects the accounts are in substantial agreement. I follow here the account given by Benrath and Comba (who by an obvious slip gives the date as 1549) as apparently the more correct.

[29] *v. supra*, Ms p. 114.

[30] cf. Benrath, *Reformation*, pp. 77, 41; Comba, *Protestanti*, ii, 567 f.

[31] cf. Comba, *op. cit.*, ii, 506 f; Benrath, *op. cit.*, pp. 81, 83.

and several in the Grisons. It is noteworthy that of the names of those reported as attending the council only two bear any resemblance to those given in the tradition above quoted — the Abbot Girolamo (not Leonardo) Buzzale, and 'il Nero,' (perhaps Francesco Negri). The brethren were scattered about the city in lodgings, and their expenses were borne by the several congregations. They met almost daily and discussed all points freely in the light of Scripture. Meetings were opened with prayer, and the Lord's Supper was observed three times. Sessions continued for forty days, and at length agreement was reached on these ten points:

1. Christ is not God but man, born of Joseph and Mary, but filled with all the powers of God.

2. Mary had other sons and daughters after Christ.

3. There is no angelic being created by God, but where Scripture speaks of angels it means men appointed by God for a given purpose.

4. There is no other Devil than human prudence, for no creature of God is hostile to him but this.

5. The wicked do not rise at the last day, but only the elect, whose head is Christ.

6. There is no hell but the grave.

7. When the elect die, they sleep until the judgment day, when all will be raised.

8. The souls of the wicked perish with the body, as do all other animals.

9. The seed of man has from God the power of producing flesh and spirit.

10. The elect are justified by the eternal mercy and love of God without any outward work, that is, without the merits, the blood, or the death of Christ. Christ died to show forth the righteousness of God, that is, the sum of all the goodness and mercy of God and of his promises.

These ten points certainly show a refreshing independence of the doctrines hitherto received, and they were unanimously agreed to save by the delegates from the congregation at Cittadella, which was therefore excluded from further fellowship with the others. Two ministers were appointed to go about among the churches to instruct them in these doctrines, which marked by far the most radical pronouncement made in the Protestant world hitherto. An especially fertile field was reported [32] to lie in the Valtellina, and an echo of missionary activity there is perhaps to be found in a letter written to Bullinger of Zürich not long afterward.[33]

One of the two traveling preachers appointed was Pietro Manelfi of San Vito,[34] an ex-priest who had now been a Protestant for about ten years, and had of late been very active among the Anabaptists. He performed his new office for a little more than a year, during which persecution of Protestants in Italy was becoming ever more frequent. Whether or not moved by fear for himself, he returned to the Church, confessed his errors, and in depositions given before the inquisitors at Bologna and Rome related all he could recall regarding the Anabaptists, their council, their beliefs and organization, and the names and addresses of individuals.[35] Arrests and prosecutions speedily followed, and trials continued during the following year. Some suffered punishment, some recanted, some fled to Moravia or Turkey, while yet others succeeded in escaping observation, kept the faith, and continued to practice it in greater secrecy than ever. But although for some time these still kept up correspondence with their brethren elsewhere,[36] their congregations had been so thoroughly scattered that they could no longer carry on effective propaganda or exert an active influence. The traveling bishops, who went about among the congregations to instruct them in the new articles, soon discovered that beside the dissenting congregation at Cittadella, whose delegates kept the vote at the Venice council from being unanimous, there were also numerous individuals that were unwilling to accept them. This was true at Vicenza, at Verona, in the

[32] Perhaps by Tiziano. (See the following chapter.)

[33] Gallicius to Bullinger, Feb. 29, 1552, Bullinger, *Korrespondenz*, i, 244. Ex Italia auditur esse ibi, qui non vereantur dicere Christum ex Josephi semine natum esse, quae vero Matthaeus et Lucas tradant de conceptione Christi de spiritu sancto, aliunde infulta esse evangelio. Ambitiosa ingenia quiescere non possunt, nec eadem via cum aliis ingredi. cf. de Porta, *Historia*, I. ii, 167.

[34] cf. Comba, *Protestanti*, ii, 507, n. 2.

[35] These depositions and the testimony given in the trials following are the chief source of our knowledge of the Anabaptist movement in northern Italy. Manelfi has perhaps to share his dishonors with another. Morsolin, (*Accademia*, p. 467) also reports as follows: In 1553 the Abbot Busale di Nola was in the dungeons of the Inquisition at Rome. The Antitrinitarian historians (wrongly calling him not Matteo but Leonardo) accuse him of having first revealed the secret of the Academy of Vicenza.

[36] Thus in 1553 Gribaldi reported the trial of Servetus to the brethren at Vicenza. *v. infra*, p. 215.

Valtellina, and doubtless elsewhere.[37] These naturally fell away from the movement, or perhaps were excluded from membership in it. Under the persecution following, which fell on all Anabaptists alike, some of these found their way to Moravia where a conservative wing of the Anabaptist movement was enjoying comparative peace. Of these exiles in Moravia there were some thirty,[38] and it was from these that della Saga and Gherlandi were sent back, as we have seen, in 1559 to convert to more orthodox views the surviving radical brethren, of whom no further knowledge has been preserved to us.

The movement that flourished at Vicenza and held the council at Venice, which is so interesting in itself, and which had it been allowed to develop freely might have done much in Italy for the cause of mental freedom, reverent reason, and generous tolerance in religion, was therefore but a transient and tragic episode, which seems in fact to have had but slight connection with the movement that later arose in Poland, and little if any historical influence upon it.

[37] cf. Comba, *Protestanti*, ii, 497 f.
[38] cf. Johann Loserth, "Communismus der mährischen Wiedertäufer im 16. und 17. Jahrhundert," *Archiv für oesterreichische Geschichte*, lxxxi (1894), 168.

CHAPTER VII

PIONEERS OF LIBERAL PROTESTANTISM IN ITALY

THE LIBERAL MOVEMENT among the Anabaptists in the north of Italy, though it was modified by the Italian temper of mind enough to develop characteristics of its own, was not so much an Italian movement as an importation from north of the Alps. It was influenced in its doctrinal views by Servetus, and was primarily concerned with the outward fruits of the Christian religion in personal character and in the relations of men in society. Its adherents were of those that had quite withdrawn from the Catholic Church but, thanks to the diligence of the Inquisition, it left no enduring mark. During the same period, however, a liberal ferment was working in another quarter, in the south of Italy, which was to be transported into northern Europe and there to become firmly established. Its leaders had derived an impulse from Erasmus, and its deepest interest was in the effect of the Christian faith upon inner spiritual experience, and in the purification of life from an inner source. Its adherents were devout Catholics within the very bosom of the Church, who still conformed to its worship, practiced its rites, and at least passively accepted the general body of its doctrine. This movement first gathered about a Spanish gentleman at Naples whose name was Juan de Valdés.[1]

The family Valdés was of the important little city of Cuenca in eastern-central Spain, whose hereditary proprietor at the beginning of the sixteenth century was Hernando de Valdés, a man of large wealth and wide influence. To him were born about 1500 two sons, Alfonso and Juan, who were what are called identical twins, for even in mature life

---

[1] cf. Edward Boehmer, *Cenni biographichi su i fratelli Giovanni e Alfonso di Valdesso*, appended to G. Valdesso, *Le Cento e dieci divine Considerazioni* (Halle, 1860), pp. 477–598, also his *Lives of the Twin Brothers Juan and Alfonso de Valdés* (London, 1882); and his article on Valdés in the *Realencyklopädie*, xx, 380–390; B. B. Wiffen, *Life and Writings of Juan de Valdés* (London, 1865); Wilhelm Schlatter, *Die Brüder Alfonso und Juan Valdés* (Basel, 1901); Jacob Heep, *Juan de Valdés* (Leipzig, 1909). Valdés is the form of the name that he himself employed, but it is also given as Valdez, or (Italian) Valdesso.

they were so much alike not only in form and feature but also in voice, manners and mind that they were continually mistaken one for the other, and by some writers were thought to be but a single person.[2] Both were of delicate health and ascetic habit, handsome in appearance, and polished in manner. Their education was supervised by Pedro Martir de Angleria, a remarkable character of enlightened views and influential connections, and favorable to reform in the Church. After a career at the University of Alcalá, Alfonso devoted himself to Latin and jurisprudence, and Juan to Spanish and the study of the Bible, though without conventional theological training. The writings of Erasmus were, by their pointed criticisms of the Church, attracting much attention in Spain at this time, and arousing violent opposition in ecclesiastical circles. Alfonso was a disciple of Erasmus and his intimate friend, and when he became Latin Secretary to the Emperor Charles V. he won the favor of the latter for Erasmus in the face of attempts to ban his writings. He accompanied Charles at his coronation as German Emperor at Aix-la-Chapelle in 1520, was with him at the Diet of Worms, and again at Bologna in 1530 when Charles was crowned Roman Emperor by the Pope.[3] He followed the Emperor to Augsburg immediately after, where in the interest of peace with the Protestant party he had interviews with Melanchthon, and translated the Augsburg Confession into Spanish for the Emperor to read. He remained in his office until he was carried off by the plague at Vienna in 1532.

His brother Juan, after spending some ten years in frivolous life, and indulging an insatiable appetite for romances of chivalry, at length came to a serious mind and turned his thoughts to religion and its reformation. In the spirit of Erasmus he published a *Dialogue of Mercury and Charon* [4] which contained such sharp comments on political and religious affairs as to make it unsafe for him to remain within reach of the long arm of the Inquisition. He therefore bade his native land farewell, and came to Naples [5] about the end of 1529. In 1533 he received appoint-

---

[2] So, apparently, Bock, *Antitrinitar.*, ii, 315 f.

[3] A double coronation at Bologna is often spoken of; but the coronation with the iron crown of Lombardy was not, as is sometimes said, performed by the Pope, but by Cardinal Cinque Porte. cf. M. Young, *Life and Times of Paleario* (London, 1860), i, 53.

[4] Marcel Bataillon, *Alfonso de Valdés, auteur du "Dialogo de Mercurio y Carón,"* in *Homenaje a Menéndez Pidal* (Madrid, 1924), i, 403–415, holds that this was the work of his brother.

[5] Naples now belonged to Spain, but was governed by a separate Viceroy under the Emperor.

ment as Chamberlain (a sinecure, largely honorary) to Pope Clement VII. at Rome, but when the Pope died within a year Juan, now knighted by the Emperor, returned for the rest of his life to Naples, where he was appointed Secretary to the Viceroy, Don Pedro de Toledo.

It is not his public duties but his more private religious interests that claim our interest here. At this period he was evidently giving most serious attention to the questions of religion and the reformation of the Church which Luther had stirred up. Naples was experiencing an unusual interest in religion, and the eloquent sermons of Ochino at the crowded lenten services in San Giovanni Maggiore, avoiding the traditional refinements of scholastic theology, and preaching directly to the heart and on the faults of the age, chained the attention of all from the peasant to the Emperor himself. During several years in this period Valdés gathered about himself a small but select circle of persons interested in religious problems and in a deeper experience of personal religion. Of the number there were such eminent personages as Pietro Martire Vermigli, Bernardino Ochino, Pietro Carnesecchi, Galeazzo Caraccioli, Giulio da Milano, and the noble ladies Giulia Gonzaga and Vittoria Colonna, all outstanding names in the religious history of the time. They used to spend their Sundays in intimate religious discussion at Valdés's suburban home by the bay shore where the Chiaja now is. He would read a translation of a chosen passage of Scripture and comment upon it, with devotional application, and then the others would engage in discussion. Much freedom was used in the intimate circle, and some of the members were profoundly influenced in thought and life.

Out of these conferences grew the books of Valdés which, at first circulated only in Spanish manuscripts now lost, were after his death published in Italian translation. One of these was the *Alfabeto Cristiano*, a devotional work containing in dialogue form the sum of an evening's conversation with Giulia Gonzaga and constituting a primer of his teaching.[6] But his chief devotional work was *Le cento e dieci considerazioni*, which was translated into six languages, has been published in a dozen or more editions, and is still prized in the world's devotional literature.[7] Curioni wrote of it, 'Many persons have written on Christian

---

[6] First published 1546. Reprinted, with Spanish and English translations and introduction by Wiffen, London, 1861. (*Reformistas Antiguos Españoles*, tomo xv.)

[7] Brought to Basel by Vergerio in the Italian translation by Marcantonio Flaminio, it was there published in 1550 with a commendatory preface by Celio Secundo Curioni. An

subjects, but it would perhaps be difficult to find any one that has treated them more completely and divinely than Juan Valdés.' Valdés died of fever at Naples in the summer of 1541. His friend Jacopo Bonfadio wrote to Carnesecchi of him, 'He was one of the rare men of Europe. . . . He was without doubt in his actions, his speech, and in all his conduct a most perfect man.' [8]

Through his personal acquaintance and by his writings, which though banned in Italy and not published until after his death were eagerly and widely circulated by Protestants, Valdés in the few years of his activity exercised a lasting influence. Naples had already been infected with Lutheranism by the 8,000 German soldiers that had been quartered there in 1528, after the sack of Rome; but it was afterwards said that Valdés caused a far greater destruction of souls than they all.[9] The anonymous author of the *Trattato utilissimo del beneficio di Cristo crocifisso*, a work that had enormous popularity at first, but was considered so pernicious that the Inquisition destroyed it almost to the last copy, was a disciple of Valdés and inspired by him.[10] Ochino was intimate with Valdés, who it is said often suggested to him the themes for his sermons; and there is hardly a point of doctrine in the *Alfabeto Cristiano* that is not found, often in the same expressions, in Ochino's *Prediche*.[11] Ochino is the preacher frequently referred to in the *Alfabeto*. In fact, Valdés would seem to have started most of the Italian apostles of Protestantism on their way, or at least to have influenced their thinking. Only one of these fell a martyr to the Inquisition. Carnesecchi, who stood high in the Church and had much favored the reform of it, after having long been protected against the Inquisition, was in 1567 condemned as a stubborn, incorrigible heretic, beheaded and then burned. At his trial he stated that he had first been led into heresy by Valdés.

English translation by Nicholas Ferrar, with prefatory epistle by George Herbert, appeared at Oxford in 1638. Translations by John T. Betts of minor devotional works, and of Commentaries on the Psalms, Matthew, Romans, and Corinthians, were published in London, 1882–'94. [8] *Lettere* (1870), p. 33; cited by Boehmer, *Lives*, p. vii.

[9] By Carraciolo, *Vita Pauli IV.*, p. 239, quoted by Boehmer, *op. cit.*, p. vii.

[10] Published Rome, 1543. Long attributed to Paleario, but, according to the testimony of Carnesecchi, written by the Benedictine Don Benedetto of Mantua and revised by Marcantonio Flaminio. Reprinted from the unique copy at Cambridge, with English translation, London, 1855. cf. Karl Benrath, 'Chi fu l'autore del Benefizio di Cristo?' (*Rivista Cristiana*, iv, 3–10, 1876.)

[11] cf. Wiffen, in Valdés's *Alfabeto Cristiano* (London, 1861), p. lxxvii.

Sandius, who first compiled a brief dictionary of Antitrinitarians and their works, included Valdés among them,[12] and in this has been followed by other writers. However, in Valdés's extant works there is no evidence of antitrinitarian views. On the contrary, his statement of his view of Christ is entirely conventional.[13] It is true that he nowhere speaks of the Trinity; but this is quite consistent with his principle of not taking into consideration anything not based on religious experience. He did not leave the Church nor encourage others to do so, but went faithfully to mass, communicated, and kept the usual religious observances. He certainly was not Lutheran nor Calvinist, still less Anabaptist; nor is it easy to classify him theologically beyond saying that he may fairly be called a liberal Catholic, who accepted the usages of the Church as a well-proved medium of spiritual nurture, yet may have taken its doctrines symbolically and put his own interpretation upon them rather than agree to their literal sense. Such a view is supported by the testimony of Carnesecchi, who said at his trial that Valdés always maintained a certain reserve as to the ultimate consequences of his doctrines;[14] and of course he would not have ventured to put on paper any of the dangerous heresies later laid at his door. Moreover, he believed strongly in religious freedom and tolerance,[15] and his habitual appeal was to the authority of inner experience rather than to some external source. Thus in principle, if not on doctrinal grounds, he would seem to be entitled to honorable mention in the preliminary history of the general movement with which we are concerned.[16] But more positive evidence has come to light justifying Sand's inclusion of Valdés. In the trial of Lorenzo Tizzano (or Tizziano) before the Inquisition at Venice in 1550, evidence was given that in Valdés's circle at Naples there were heretics that denied the virgin birth, and held that Jesus was not the Messiah but only a prophet, and that Valdés himself held these views.[17] It is no wonder, then, that a sig-

---

[12] cf. Sandius, *Bibliotheca*, p. 2, citing as his authority Blandrata's *De falsa et vera unius Dei . . cognitione* (1567), p. E ii.a, which quotes an alleged writing of Valdés expressing a definitely Unitarian view. The passage does not occur in any work of Valdés now extant.

[13] cf. *Divine Considerations*, cix, xcv.

[14] cf. Richard Gibbings, ed., *Report of the trial and martyrdom of Pietro Carnesecchi*, etc. (Dublin and London, 1856.)   [15] cf. *Divine Considerations*, lxxvi.

[16] The Catholic Menéndez y Pelayo, *Heterodoxos* (ed. 2, Madrid, 1928), iv, 239–241, judges that in his christology Valdés was an Arian.

[17] cf. Domenico Berti, 'Di Giovanni Valdés e taluni di suoi discepoli secondo nuovi

nificant number of his disciples, when once beyond the reach of the Inquisition, came out more boldly in the avowal of doctrines as to which they had when in Italy maintained a discreet reserve. Such were Ochino, Francesco di Calabria, Camillo Renato, Giovanni Valentino Gentile, and Celio Secondo Curioni, who will appear later on in our history. Valdés therefore appears to have been if not a pioneer, at least a herald of our movement.

Of those in the company that gathered about Valdés at Naples and were influenced by him, none had a more conspicuous relation to our movement than the celebrated friar Bernardino Ochino, who has also been reckoned as perhaps the most influential propagator of the Protestant doctrine in Italy.[18] Ochino was born in 1487 at Siena, the son of an obscure citizen named Domenico Tomassini, who dwelt in the quarter of the city called la contrada dell' Oca, whence he acquired the cognomen Ochino. He had but a moderate education, but from early youth was deeply concerned for the salvation of his soul; and to that end he entered the branch of the Franciscan order called the Observants, whose rule seemed to him to be the strictest of all, and whose convent, the Osservanza, still stands outside the eastern gate at Siena. There is a tradition that after a time he left the order to study medicine at Perugia. If so, he later returned to it, and in due time was advanced to be General of the Observants. Finding their discipline too lax, he resigned his office and in 1534 sought greater peace of soul in the yet greater austerity of another branch of the Franciscans, the recently founded order of the Capuchins. During all these years he was by his extremely ascetic habits steadily gaining among all classes a great reputation for sanctity. Pale of face, barefoot and bareheaded, clad in coarsest garb, he went at all seasons and in all weather begging his way from door to

---

documenti tolti dall' Archivio Veneto,' *Atti della Reale Accademia dei Lincei anno cclxxv, 1877-'78*, serie terza, Memorie della classe di Scienze morale, storiche, e filosofiche (Roma, 1878), ii, 61–81.

[18] cf., *inter alia*, Bock, *Antitrinitar.*, ii, 483–532; Trechsel, *Antitrinitarier*, ii, 202–276; Karl Benrath, *Bernardino Ochino of Siena* (London and New York, 1877), excellently reviewed by Alexander Gordon in *Theological Review* (London), xiii. 532–561, Oct. 1876, and by C. A. Hase in *Jahrbücher für protestantische Theologie*, i (1875), 496–535; Paolo Negri, *Bernardino Ochino* (Torino, 1912); Daniel Bertrand-Barraud, *Les idées philosophiques de Bernardin Ochin de Sienne* (Paris, 1924); Roland H. Bainton, *Bernardino Ochino* (Firenze, 1940). Portraits in Benrath and in Étienne Desrochers, *Recueil de Portraits* (Paris, 1735).

door, and even when received in the palaces of the great he did not change his habit of life.[19] Vittoria Colonna, Marchioness of Pescara, was his devoted disciple. To her Pietro Bembo, later Cardinal, wrote in 1539, 'I have this morning conversed with the venerable father Fra Bernardino, to whom I have opened my whole heart and thought as I should have done to Jesus Christ. It seems to me that I have never talked to a holier man than he.' [20]

At the same time he was coming to be known as incomparably the best preacher in Italy. Preaching was done at this period not by the secular clergy but by friars of the preaching orders, principally the Franciscans, and especially in the lenten season. No one since Savonarola had equaled Ochino. The chief cities of Italy vied for his services, and competition between them was so great that the Pope, in order to prevent disputes, was forced to decide between them. Wherever he went, no church was large enough to hold the throngs that crowded to hear him, though he preached almost daily. When he preached at San Giovanni at Naples in 1536 the Emperor would often go with pleasure to hear him, and his eloquence was so moving that it was said that he made even the stones weep.[21] When he preached the first lenten sermons at Venice in 1538, Bembo wrote of him, 'I never heard any one preach more profitably or more devoutly than he'; and at the urgent request of many citizens he made early application for the coming year. In 1538 he was elected Vicar-General of his order by a nearly unanimous vote, ruled it with great wisdom, saw it extend rapidly, and against his will was re-elected in 1541 for, as the historian of the order wrote, it seemed as if nothing were wanting to make him a perfect General.[22] Of his preaching again in Venice in 1539 Bembo wrote, 'He is literally adored here. There is no one that does not praise him to the skies.' He also preached with great effect in Rome, and at Perugia, Lucca and Modena; while at Siena the Consistory urgently begged the Pope to let him stay longer, and sent repeated requests for his lenten preaching.

---

[19] cf. Benrath, *op. cit.*, p. 17 f.

[20] This and the following quotations are from Bembo's *Lettere* (Venezia, 1560), vol. iv.

[21] Predicava con ispirito grande che faceva piangere i sassi. The saying is often attributed to the Emperor himself, but is really the expression of the narrator. cf. Pietro Giannone, *Istoria civile del regno di Napoli* (La Haye, 1753), iv, 81 f.

[22] cf. Zaccaria Boverio, *Annales ordinis Minorum S. Francisci qui Cappuccini nuncupantur* (Lugduni, 1632–'76), vol. i.

It was while preaching at Naples in 1536, 1539 and 1540 that he came under the influence of Valdés, as we have seen; and he was already spied upon there in 1539 by zealous guardians of orthodoxy, though up to his re-election in 1541 no serious suspicion seems to have fallen upon him. His sermons avoided scholastic subtleties and the arguing of doctrinal theories, and were directly personal and practical in character.

But now he began to incline more and more to new ideas in religion, and away from the practices of the Church. He seriously criticized religious vows, fastings, indulgences and purgatory. Doubts about him began to arise, and while there was as yet no Inquisition, the Pope gave his nuncio orders to keep an eye on him when he went again to Venice in 1542 to preach in the Sant' Apostoli, then considered the finest church in the city. He was before long called on to explain certain expressions that sounded heretical, and easily did so. Soon after this the nuncio condemned for alleged heresy the preacher Giulio Terenziano at Milan, who had also been one of Valdés's circle at Naples.[23] Ochino boldly expressed his indignation at this act of ecclesiastical tyranny, whereupon the nuncio forbade him to preach any longer; but the uprising of the citizens in Ochino's favor was so strong that the nuncio yielded, and after three days Ochino resumed the pulpit, though now preaching with more restraint. But he had gone too far. The doctrines of the Reformation were spreading alarmingly in Italy, and something more effective must be done to check them. Acting upon advice given ten years before by Cardinal Caraffa but then rejected, the Pope issued on June 21 the bull 'Licet ab initio' establishing the Italian Inquisition. Ochino's teaching required looking into, and he was perhaps the very first to be summoned to appear before it. The summons was veiled under a polite note inviting him in the Pope's name to visit Rome 'on matters of importance.' It was whispered in Rome that he was soon to be made a Cardinal, and Ochino himself thought it might have been planned in this way to purchase his silence.[24] At all events, he was suspicious. However, he determined to obey the summons, and was ordered to appear forthwith, without waiting, as he had proposed, for the summer's heat to be over.

[23] After some years Giulio escaped from his dungeon, fled from the country, and was for more than thirty years minister of a Protestant congregation at Poschiavo in the Grisons, where he was known as Giulio da Milano.

[24] cf. Ochino, *Prediche*, i. 10; Boverio, *op. cit.*, an. 1542.

Ochino set out on foot at the middle of August, but he had not gone far before he learned what was really wanted of him. He had now to decide whether to face the Inquisition and renounce the views that had brought him under suspicion, or to remain steadfast to his convictions and suffer death, or to flee the country and thus save both his conscience and his life. When he had gone as far as Florence, he fell in with Vermigli, another member of the Valdés circle whose case was parallel to his own, and who had already determined to flee. He persuaded Ochino to do the same.[25] After proceeding to Siena to take leave of his family, Ochino then turned his steps northward. It was fortunate for him, for at a Capuchin convent just south of Siena guards were set to seize him when he should appear. Vermigli followed him two days later, traveling to Switzerland by another route. By the flight of these two advocates of reform in the Church the cause of reformation in Italy suffered a blow from which it never recovered. At Ferrara Ochino is said to have been given clothing and other assistance by the Duchess Renée,[26] Protestant in faith and friend of Calvin, to whom she doubtless gave him a letter of introduction. Proceeding by way of Chiavenna and Zürich he came in time to Geneva, where we shall later renew our acquaintance with him. He was now fifty-five years old.

When the flight of Ochino became known in Italy, it created the greatest sensation. Pope Paul III. was enraged, and at first threatened to suppress the Capuchins altogether as accomplices in the matter. The Inquisitor Caraffa, finding his prey escaped, wrote him a long letter of bitter reproaches, comparing his apostasy to the fall of Lucifer. A Sienese nobleman, Claudio Tolomei, wrote him at length beseeching him to return to the Church, while others heaped abuse upon him. He in turn wrote a long letter to the Council at Siena to justify his action; but he never showed any disposition to return to the obedience of the Church.[27] He was now, and for some time had been, Lutheran in the doctrine of justification, but his more serious heresies were not to appear until later.

[25] cf. Edmondo Solmi, 'La fuga di Bernardino Ochino' (*Bullettino di storia patria*, (Siena, 1898), xv, 23–98.

[26] Florimond de Raemond, *Histoire de . . . l'hérésie* (Rouen, 1647), p. 293.

[27] The above letters are quoted at length in Benrath, *Ochino*, chap. v.

CHAPTER VIII

ANTITRINITARIAN PIONEERS IN THE GRISONS

As soon as the Inquisition in Italy grew active, increasing numbers of those that were suspected of having accepted the new doctrines began to follow the example of Ochino and Vermigli and seek safety in flight. The greater number of these made for Switzerland, to which the nearest and most convenient way of escape was through the land known as the Grisons (Ger. Graubünden), which must now claim our attention. This district lies between ranges of the Alps about the headwaters of the Rhine and the Inn. In Roman times it had borne the name of Raetia, and it now forms the southeastern and largest of the Swiss cantons; but in the sixteenth century it was an independent and highly democratic republic, composed of three federated leagues which in the fifteenth century had won freedom from their former oppressors.[1] At the time of which we speak it also included some territory that now belongs to Italy, lying north and east of Lake Como — the counties of Chiavenna and Bormio and the populous Valtellina. Modern tourists know it for its profusion of the most beautiful Alpine scenery, and for such summer or winter resorts as Chur (Coire), Davos, St. Moritz and the Engadine. The population was of Italian origin, speaking in the Engadine a modification of the Latin tongue known as Ladin, and farther north, where it had been more mixed with German, a related dialect called Romansch.

The reformation at Zürich under Zwingli early spread among the churches in the Grisons, especially in the three valleys of Bregaglia, the Valtellina, and the Engadine. Despite the opposition of the priests it made such headway, and led to so much contention, that after a public discussion of matters in dispute, and in order to preserve domestic peace and prevent violence between the parties, the Diet of Ilanz in 1526, with the general consent of both sides, agreed to a decree granting equal liberty to each one to profess either the Catholic or the Reformed re-

[1] cf. de Porta, *Historia*; Ulrich Campell, *Historia Raetica* (Basel, 1887–'90); Trechsel, *Antitrinitarier*, ii; Thomas M'Crie, *Reformation in Italy* (Edinburgh, 1856).

ligion as he might choose, and strictly forbidding religious persecution by either side.[2] This decree of Ilanz occupies an honorable place in the history of religious liberty, for it is earlier than any similar legislation elsewhere. It should not, however, be regarded as an instance of general toleration, for that was not realized until long afterwards. It applied only to the two parties of Catholics and Reformed, and instead of resting on the broad principle of freedom of conscience, it was simply an expedient for preventing mutual oppression and strife between the two; while against Anabaptists or members of any other sect it was utterly intolerant. It did, however, open the way for the further spread of reformed views.

The toleration thus opened to Protestants naturally made the Grisons the nearest safe place of refuge for those fleeing from the Inquisition, and Chiavenna and the Valtellina offered them a home in a mild climate, and among people of kindred race and speech. Fugitives from religious persecution therefore began to pass this way as early as 1542, some to settle here, but more to pass on to the greater opportunities of Protestant towns in Switzerland or Germany. According to Vergerio, by 1550 two hundred had entered the Grisons, a quarter of them educated and well known; and ten years later there had been eight hundred.[3] The most of these held no heresies worse than those of Luther, and they were heartily welcomed by the rising Protestant churches in the Grisons, to which they furnished experienced and able preachers, not a few of them having been members of the preaching orders.

There were, however, also some that cherished unorthodox views about God and Christ, which they may have imbibed from the radical elements in the circle of Valdés at Naples, or from the reading of Servetus, or from contact with the radical Anabaptists of northern Italy.

[2] Singulis utriusque sexus, et cujuscunque conditionis, et ordinis hominibus, intra foederatorum Rhaetorum fines incolentibus, liberum stet ex his duabus Romana et Evangelica religionibus utram quis velit, aut spiritus boni instinctu admoneretur, eligere, amplecti, et profiteri religionem; adnexo severo interdicto, ne quis alterutrius dictarum religionum quenquam adversae partis, religionis nomine, neque publice, neque privatim odiosius insectetur, vel ullo contumeliae aut probri negere . . . afficiat. . . Quod vero ad Anabaptisticam, aut alias cujuscunque generis, vel nominis sectas, sunt, illae simul, semelque pro semper, eodem decreto interdictae, exilio iis sine discrimine indicto, qui lege insuper habita, post idoneam erroris confutationem et fidelem et sedulam adhibitam informationem, errorem praefracte retinere, vel malitiose etiam aliis affricare praesumpserint. De Porta, *op. cit.*, I, i, 146. Also in Trechsel, *op. cit.*, ii, 70, n. Campbell, *op. cit.*, ii, 161, gives a slightly different wording.

[3] cf. M'Crie, p. 188; de Porta, I, ii, 36.

With the native intellectual keenness of Italians they tended especially to question such dogmas as the Trinity, the deity of Christ, predestination, atonement, resurrection and the sacraments; and as they often shared the views of the Anabaptists as to infant baptism, they tended in the popular mind to be identified with them. Some of them used their new-found freedom to indulge in very free doctrinal speculations, and also to preach these before they were matured or carefully tested, some attacking one article of the traditional creed, others another. The first to attract attention in this way were two that claimed to be disciples of Ochino, and had presumably been Capuchin monks: Francesco of Calabria, and Girolamo Marliano (or Milano), who had offered their services to the vacant churches of Fetan and Lavin respectively, both in the Lower Engadine, and had been gladly received.[4] After about a year it was reported that these two, but especially Francesco, were beginning to teach some terribly wicked things. Girolamo, indeed, was soon forced to leave Lavin, and later went to Basel;[5] but at Fetan, where the congregation had lately abolished the mass and removed the images from their little church, which still dominates the charming Alpine village lying on a sloping bench of land over a thousand feet above the rushing Inn, and facing mountain scenery of incomparable beauty and grandeur, Francesco by his eloquence and learning had won the enthusiastic adherence of his congregation, and stood his ground.

It was a critical period for the young and as yet loosely organized and ill-disciplined Protestant congregations of the Engadine. No standard of doctrine had been adopted, and everything was in flux. The wildest and rashest speculations might be preached as well as the soundest and most sober. A contemporary writer who was witness of developments gives a picture of the doctrinal chaos prevailing, which may well serve to illustrate a similar stage of development in other countries with which we shall later be concerned:

Some were notable for their learning and sincere piety, sound in the faith, quiet and peaceable; but not a few were quite captious, and often gave much trouble to the more sober-minded ministers of the same synod in Raetia, and even to the rulers of the land. Nothing seemed to please them but to differ as widely as possible from the common practice and to utter the strangest doctrines of their own devising. These all professed, indeed, to believe whatever Holy Scripture taught,

---

[4] cf. Campell, ii, 297–307; de Porta, I, ii, 67–75; M'Crie, pp. 215–218.
[5] cf. Bonet-Maury, *Sources*, p. 188.

but when more closely examined they were found to be infected with the pestilent doctrines of the old heretics. Thus one would refuse to confess his belief in the holy Trinity; another would not venture to declare that Christ was God, equal with the Father; this one would declare that we are saved by the grace of God and hence that there was no need of Christ's descending to earth, nor of his body and blood, since the whole work of our salvation is to be ascribed to the grace of God. Another, discriminating more sharply, said that we are indeed saved by Christ, yet not by his body suffering for us, but by the pain that he suffered in that body. Some declared that good and evil are from God himself, the source of all things; and that God himself rejoices in wicked deeds not less than in good ones. Some talked of nothing but divine predestination: that a man is saved though all his deeds are wicked; but that another can not escape damnation, let him believe what he will, and even if all his deeds are good. Some said there is no hell even though punishment is appointed for the wicked.[6]

The teaching of such doctrines had a disastrous moral effect upon the people, and pressure came from all sides for the two congregations to dismiss their preachers. Lavin yielded to the pressure, but Fetan resisted it. As Francesco declared that he was prepared to defend his teaching publicly, a disputation was appointed in 1544 at Süss in the Middle Engadine, where he was cited to appear. The meeting was attended not only by the Protestant ministers of the Engadine, but by various persons of importance from neighboring regions, as well as by several Catholic priests. Proceedings lasted two days.[7] Francesco had already been examined by a synod of the Protestant preachers, and found unsound in the faith, and had failed of being duly admitted as an approved member. Further public examination now proved unsatisfactory to those conducting it, for though he gave a hesitating assent to the test questions asked, he evidently did not sincerely believe in the deity of Christ. The final vote was adverse: that Francesco should be required to leave the Engadine as a disturber of the peace of State and church, and be expelled from the whole jurisdiction of the Grisons and the Tyrol. The church at Fetan protested that it was no concern of the other congregations whom they had for preacher, or what he believed, and that they would keep him whether the others would or no. But when the decree was then referred to the civil authorities to enforce at the expense of the Fetan church, the opposition yielded. The further

---

[6] Campell, ii, 296 f. Campell reduces most of these views, together with others of Anabaptist origin, to six general heads, which he gives as the teaching of Francesco, p. 298 ff.

[7] An extended report is given by Campell, ii, 299–307; cf. de Porta, I, ii, 70–75.

history of Francesco is unknown, but it cost the preachers of the Enga-dine much labor to uproot the tares that he had sown in their field, and it was felt that had not this prompt action been taken, there would have been no hope of success; for, as will be seen, as much as twenty years later fire still remained in the ashes and threatened to burst into flame.

Four or five years after the affair of Francesco, there appeared in the Grisons at various places both south and north of the Alps an Italian Anabaptist missionary named Tiziano.[8] His first name is unknown, nor is there any trace of his early life or of his later career or end; but from the testimony of Manelfi before the Inquisition at Bologna in 1551 [9] we gather that he had been at the court of a Cardinal in Rome, and while there had begun to learn the doctrine of Luther, in which he was confirmed by Ochino. Probably in 1542 or soon afterwards he fled from Italy and went to Switzerland, and also formed a friendship with Renato and Negri and their circle at Chiavenna.[10] Thus he became an Anabaptist, and went about teaching this doctrine and making converts to it in the Italian churches, and here and there in the Grisons. He appears to have won a numerous following in many places, and thus to have caused considerable concern to the Protestant churches in their conflict with the Catholics. Wherever he went disputes sprang up which threatened the peace of both church and State. The church synod brought the matter to the attention of the authorities. The Council at Chur at length had Tiziano arrested; and fortunately for him, for the populace were so enraged that they threatened to put him to death, had he not been taken out of their hands. The civil authorities were not indisposed to inflict the extreme penalty; but the clergy, especially Gallicius (Saluz), deemed a milder punishment more expedient, lest his followers become more fanatical and dangerous than ever. Tiziano was put under examination as to his beliefs, but the answers he gave were evasive and unsatisfactory. Then a formal recantation was pre-pared, containing a specific denial of the offensive doctrines that he had

[8] One is tempted to identify him with the Lorenzo Tiziano (or Tizzano — the name is given in several different forms) of Naples, a brother of the order of Monte Oliveto, who embraced Lutheran opinions, left the order, studied medicine at Padua toward 1550, changed his name to Benedetto Florio for fear of being discovered, and finally confessed to the Inquisitor and figured in a trial before the Inquisition at Venice (cf. the work of Domenico Berti cited above); but the identification is difficult. Perhaps he was a brother of Lorenzo. cf. de Porta, I, ii, 76–81; Comba, *Protestanti*, ii, 477–517; Trechsel, ii, 82–84.

[9] *v. supra*, p. 86.

[10] Mainardo to Bullinger, Aug. 7, 1549, *Bullingers Korrespondenz*, i, 148.

been spreading. He hesitated, but as there appeared to be no choice but either to sign the recantation or to be put to death, he submitted. He was then sentenced by the magistrate to be flogged through the whole city, and forever banished from the Grisons, as were several of his followers.[11] This was in 1547 or 1549.[12] After this he returned to Italy and continued zealously to spread the Anabaptist doctrines, which some believe that he was the first to introduce into Italy.[13] In the course of his missionary journeys he met Manelfi at Florence in 1548 or 1549 and converted and baptized him; and they went together to Vicenza where the doctrinal discussions were in progress. He was a member of the Anabaptist council at Venice in 1550, to which he had summoned the delegates from the congregations in Switzerland where he had been well known; and he was (with Manelfi) one of the two Apostolic Bishops appointed to visit the churches after the council and instruct them in the beliefs there adopted. From then on he disappears from our sight.

From Tiziano's recantation at Chur we are enabled to learn precisely what his doctrines were.[14] He denied the Trinity, the eternal divinity of Christ, and the virgin birth. He held that the Scriptures had been falsified in many places. As an Anabaptist he opposed infant baptism, and held that no Christian might hold an office inflicting capital punishment. He was thus the most outspoken pioneer of our movement whom we have thus far encountered. He was evidently one of the leading spirits in shaping the conclusions of the council at Venice, and his activities form a connecting link between the development in Italy and that in the Grisons.

Francesco and Tiziano were but sporadic instances of a tendency that manifested itself in many widely scattered places in their generation. They appeared too early to be reckoned as adherents of a coherent movement, and their influence was ephemeral. But with Camillo Renato [15] we come at length to one who has a definite and influential historical relation to the stream whose origins we are trying to trace. He was a

---

[11] cf. de Porta, I, ii, 80.

[12] cf. de Porta, I, ii. 76 with *Bullingers Korrespondenz*, i, 148. Not 1554, as has sometimes been said through misunderstanding of the letter of Gallicius to Bullinger in that year. cf. *Bullingers Korrespondenz*, i, 374–376; de Porta, I, ii, 76–81, 134; Bullinger to Calvin, June 12, 1554, Calvin, xv, 158.

[13] So apparently Manelfi; cf. Comba, *Protestanti*, ii, 492.

[14] cf. de Porta, I, ii, 78 f; *Bullingers Korrespondenz*, i, 375 f.

[15] cf. de Porta, I, ii, chap. iv, pp. 81–138; Trechsel, ii, 85–107.

Sicilian scholar (hence sometimes called Camillus Siculus), who upon adopting the views of the Reformation dropped whatever may have been his original name, and substituted the significant one of Renato. He is said to have been one of the circle of Valdés at Naples. Soon after accepting the reformed religion he fell under suspicion, was imprisoned and tortured, and narrowly escaped life imprisonment or death.[16] Escaping, he came to the Valtellina in 1542 at about the same time with Celio Secondo Curioni, with whom he formed a life-long friendship; and for several years he supported himself by serving as tutor to the children of the nobleman Rafaello Paravicini at Caspano, and by teaching a school at Traona.[17] In 1545 he removed to Chiavenna, where opportunities for making a living were better.

Renato was a man of keen and fertile mind, of fine education, and of a shy and reserved nature which some interpreted as sly and crafty;[18] persuasive and adroit in discussion, and very tenacious of his opinions. He was looked upon as the prime author of the radical doctrinal tendencies in the Grisons, and is said to have caused the churches more trouble and to have disturbed their peace more than any other.[19] Tiziano was his disciple, and so probably was Francesco of Calabria. He was on intimate terms with Stancaro,[20] Negri, Laelius Socinus and other

[16] Non multo sane ante verum Deum ipsumque eius filium Jesum Christum agnovi et credidi, quam et in suspiciones Satanae, minas, insidias, carceres, dedecora, cruciatus atque id genus maximas calamitates incidi: nihil me certius aliquando manebat Antichristi jussu quam aut perpetuo in carcere agentem extrema solitudine et inedia absumi aut, . . . ad immaturam secreto mortem rapi. Sed tamen . . . Deus et Domini nostri Jesu Christi, et certe nostrum omnium pater, consuluit atque periculis liberavit. Camillus to Bullinger, Nov. 9, 1542, *Bullingers Korrespondenz*, i, 50. Trechsel, ii, 76, n. 1; de Porta, I, ii, 26 f.

[17] Camillus to Bullinger, May 10, 1545, *Bullingers Korrespondenz*, i, 75.

[18] Arbitror enim te non ignorare callidi et tortuosi Camilli ingenium et mores. . . Vix enim credi potest, quam flexibilis sit haeretici vafrificies et quam obliquo et volubili flexu iste anguis effugiat, nisi fortiter prematur. Giulio Milano to Bullinger, Nov. 4, 1555, *Bullingers Korrespondenz*, i, 421.

[19] cf. de Porta, I, ii, 81.

[20] Francesco Stancaro was born at Mantua about 1501 and became one of the most famous Hebrew scholars of his time. He was author of one of the first Hebrew grammars to be published after the Reformation. After teaching this language at Friuli he embraced the Reformation and left Italy in 1542, coming first to the Valtellina, where he taught for a time. After vainly trying to find a post in Switzerland he came to Chiavenna, where he sided with Camillo, Negri, and Laelius Socinus in the quarrel in the church; but after a few months he departed in 1548 for Zürich and Basel, and finally went to Poland and Transylvania where (as will be later seen) his persistent advocacy of a peculiar view of the atonement caused the churches much trouble. cf. de Porta, *op. cit.*, I, ii, 90; *Realencyk.*, xviii, 752; Pierre Bayle, *Dictionary*, *s. v.* Stancaro.

well-known heretics; and it was a common opinion in his time not only
that he was the leader of the Anabaptists in the Grisons, but that all
the Anabaptism in Italy could ultimately be traced back to him.[21] Escaped from Italy, he at once entered upon an active correspondence with
Bullinger, leader of the Reformation at Zürich, and although going
beyond the views of Zwingli, he sought to make himself acceptable to
the Swiss reformer. His theology, however, was cast in a different
mold, for he was by temperament a mystic, akin to the Anabaptists.

At Chiavenna he at first had cordial relations with the pastor, Agos-
tino Mainardo, an earnest but irritable and impatient spirit; but friction
soon arose over difference of opinion, and strained relations were followed by open hostility. The beginning of the trouble lay in their different views of the Lord's Supper, which Camillo regarded as only a commemorative meal in memory of the death of Christ; and he also held
that baptism had no sacramental value, but was useful only as an outward sign to distinguish Christians from non-Christians. This of course
involved opposition to infant baptism, as a meaningless or superstitious
ceremony. He also had his own views on almost all points of Christian
doctrine, although apart from the sacraments he would not state them
positively, but expressed them in the form of doubts or questions, or
proposed them as subjects for discussion. The doctrine of the Spirit was
much more prominent in his thought than that of the Father or the Son,
while the cardinal point was regeneration. In fact, he was essentially a
radical Anabaptist. He denied the vicarious suffering of Christ, and
he held that he had a nature corrupted by original sin, so that he might
have sinned even if he did not actually do so; hence he was not essentially divine. It was difficult to draw him into controversy, for when
hard pressed he became non-committal; but though such views and
doubts were not expressed openly, but only to intimate friends, yet they
gradually came to be more widely known.

Mainardo now began from the pulpit to preach against Camillo's
views, whereupon the latter abstained more and more from attending
church, and many of his sympathizers followed his example. Mainardo
then sought his end in another way. He composed a confession of
twenty articles, of which the tenth explicitly condemned twenty-one

---

[21] A repentant Italian Anabaptist at Chiavenna 'addit totum Italiae Anabaptismum
pendere ab illo utre venenato.' Vergerio to Bullinger, Jan. 10, 1553, *Bullingers Korrespondenz*, i, 280; de Porta, I, ii, 86, 97.

objectionable teachings of Camillo, though without naming him.[22] This he asked the members of the church individually to sign, but to his surprise many of them refused. Among these, taking the part of Camillo, were Negri and Stancaro; and the striking resemblance of his views to those later held by Laelius Socinus, who was at this very time living at Chiavenna, and was considered by his contemporaries to be an Anabaptist, strongly suggests that he was much influenced by Camillo.[23]

The ministers of the churches in the Grisons were much grieved over the schism in the flourishing church at Chiavenna, and the synod therefore intervened to compose the quarrel, requesting both Mainardo and Camillo to appear at Chur in order to explain their doctrine, and if possible come to agreement. Camillo did not obey the summons, nor send an excuse; but the confession which Mainardo presented was approved, and Camillo was ordered henceforth to keep the peace and to give Mainardo no further trouble. It was all to no purpose. The quarrel became more heated than ever; Mainardo was all but ready to resign his post, and Bullinger broke off relations with Camillo. Presently the tension was relaxed, Mainardo was persuaded to be more conciliatory, Stancaro had taken his departure, and the opposition for a time withdrew from the church. At length, acting upon a suggestion from Bullinger, four ministers were sent to Chiavenna in December, 1549 in the name of the synod to investigate the situation and discover a way of

---

[22] The confession has perished, but the tenth article was preserved in Italian translation in a little book by Pietro Leone published ten years later, itself also now lost, and from that retranslated into Latin for Bullinger by Gallicius. cf. de Porta, *op. cit.*, I, ii, 83–86. From this we learn what (besides the views above mentioned) were the peculiar teachings of Camillo. In condensed form the most striking are these: That the soul of man is by nature mortal, and dies with the body, to be raised at the last day in another form, though the souls of the wicked will perish; that man has no natural knowledge of good and evil, but that good men have no need of any other law than the Spirit; that the unregenerate are irrational like brutes. cf. Mainardo to Bullinger, Dec. 10, 1548, *Bullingers Korrespondenz*, i, 139 f. Comparison of these items with the shortly subsequent heads of doctrine adopted by the Venice council in 1550, especially numbers 7 and 8, is very suggestive of the influence of Camillo in the latter, perhaps mediated by Tiziano and Negri.

[23] cf. Giulio da Milano to Bullinger, Nov. 4, 1555, *Bullingers Korrespondenz*, i, 421; de Porta, I, ii, 87. According to Dunin Borkowski, (*Untersuchungen*, p. 113 f) Gregory Paulus, one of the early Antitrinitarians in Poland, in his *De Vera Morte*, took his view of the mortality of the soul from Camillo; and Francis Dávid in Transylvania was essentially influenced by his views in his 16 theses — in both cases doubtless through the mediation of Biandrata. cf. F. A. Lampe, *Historia Ecclesiae Reformatae in Hungaria et Transylvania* (Trajecti ad Rhenum, 1728), p. 306; *Defensio Francisci Davidis, ad finem* (p. B4b, ff.); Konrad Górski, *Grzegorz Paweł z Brzezin* (Kraków, 1929), p. 236.

settlement. Camillo shrank from the ordeal, though he did his best to make a good showing; but after two days' discussion the investigation resulted unfavorably for him. He was forbidden henceforth to preach in private or in public, and a declaration on the points in dispute was drawn up, mostly favoring Mainardo.[24] Camillo accepted it with the rest, but only *pro forma*, for he now gathered a congregation of Anabaptists, nor would he surrender his favorite beliefs. A few months later he was therefore excommunicated. Early the next year another attempt at reconciliation was made. Two visitors appointed by the synod came to Chiavenna and assisted Mainardo and the elders of the church in preparing a confession of faith, ostensibly based on Scripture authority, but directly rejecting Camillo's particular views, and adopting the Apostles', Nicene and Athanasian Creeds, and emphasizing the doctrine of the Trinity and of the deity of Christ.[25] Camillo subscribed it, but his sincerity was doubted, and the synod refused to admit him until better assured of his change of mind.[26] He had already removed from Chiavenna back to the Valtellina, where in spite of efforts to have him banished, he resumed his teaching at Sondrio in 1552. He found it fruitless to engage in further controversy. From Traona, in the year after the execution of Servetus at Geneva, he issued a long Latin poem denouncing Calvin for his part in the affair, and containing an eloquent plea for religious toleration.[27] The last we know of him is that early in the seventies he was still living at Caspano, long since blind.[28]

The most active and persistent of Camillo's followers in the controversy at Chiavenna, though they did not agree in all points of doctrine, was Francesco Negri.[29] He was learned in Greek, Hebrew and theology, and highly esteemed by the scholars of his time, especially north of the Alps. He also had reputation as a man of letters, through a Catechism in the spirit of Luther and Zwingli,[30] and his tragedy on Free Will, a dramatic treatment of theological questions, which had much

---

[24] cf. de Porta, I, ii, 101–103; Campell, ii, 333 f.

[25] Text of the confession in Trechsel, *Antitrinitarier*, ii, 409–414.

[26] cf. Trechsel, ii, 414 f.

[27] Text in Trechsel, i, 321–328; Calvin, xv, 239–245.

[28] *Bullingers Korrespondenz*, i, p. lxx.

[29] cf. Cantù, *Eretici*, iii. 153–156; Comba, *Protestanti*, ii, 297–322; G. B. Roberti, *Notizie storico-critiche della vita e delle opere di Francesco Negri*, etc., (Bassano, 1839).

[30] *Brevissima somma della dottrina Cristiana recitata da un fanciullo in domanda e risposta.*

reputation in its time.[31] Mainardo, however, characterized him as 'a good man, but easily influenced.' [32] He was born at Bassano about 1500, and was for a short time an Augustinian monk; but about 1525 he left the order, fled to Germany, embraced the Reformation, traveled widely, and made distinguished acquaintance among the reformers. After revisiting Italy he settled at Chiavenna as a teacher of Hebrew, and was there or in the Valtellina during most of the time from 1531 to 1550.

Negri took an active part in the schism in the church at Chiavenna (1547–1549), and took sides against Mainardo, though agreeing as to the sacraments now with Renato, now with Stancaro. He refused to sign the confession proposed by Mainardo, though in 1549 he signed that prepared in the name of the synod, and was thought to be quite orthodox as to the sacrament. But as he appears among the delegates from the Grisons at the Anabaptist council in Venice in 1550, and accepted the doctrines adopted there, it is clear that he was both Anabaptist and antitrinitarian at heart. After this he lived for a time at Tirano, and again at Chiavenna. In 1562 or 1563 he undertook the long journey to Poland, presumably to visit his son Giorgio, who had long lived at the court of Prince Nicholas Radziwiłł at Wilno.[33] In the latter year he was with Lismanino, preaching to the little Italian congregation at Pińczów; and in May of the next year, when on the point of returning to his family at Chiavenna, he died at Kraków.[34] In view of his

[31] *La libertá, o sia del Libero Arbitrio*, (Poschiavo, 1546, 1550); Latin edition, (Zürich, 1559), dedicated to Prince Nicholas Radziwiłł, Palatine of Wilno, a patron of early antitrinitarianism in Poland.

[32] Francesco Negro, viro bono, sed facili. Mainardo to Bullinger, Dec. 10, 1548, *Bullingers Korrespondenz*, i, 139.

[33] A dozen years earlier Giorgio had gone to Hungary and Poland with his father's close friend Stancaro, who had undertaken to see him educated. He was kindly received by the Pinczovian group in 1557, and was appointed domestic chaplain of the Italian Prosper Provanna the following year. He later learned Polish in order to minister to native churches. He gravitated to the liberal wing of the Reformed Church, and was chosen secretary of the famous colloquy at Piotrków in 1565, but was objected to as a foreigner under the ban of the edict of Parczów. His name often occurs in the minutes of the early synods of the Reformed Church, and he became minister of the Italian congregation at Pińczów following his father. cf. Hermann Dalton, *Lasciana* (Berlin, 1899), p. 451 *et passim; Reformacja w Polsce*, i, 222; v, 61; Theodor Wotschke, *Briefwechsel der Schweitzer mit den Polen* (Leipzig, 1908), p. 320; *id.,* 'Christoph Thretius' (*Altpreussische Monatsschrift*, xliv (1907), 69, n.)

[34] *Bullingers Korrespondenz*, i. p. lxii f; Wotschke, *Briefwechsel*, p. 177.

later career, he may justly be reckoned as one of the pioneers of our movement.

Camillo might be excommunicated and put to silence, but he still continued to make his influence felt by keeping up relations with his followers both at Chiavenna and elsewhere. Not a few of the ministers of the churches in Bregaglia, Chiavenna county, and the Valtellina, and even one or two in the lower Engadine together with many of the laity, still cherished his views, especially as to the providence of God, predestination, and the merits of Christ's death. Some held that as all things are subject to the plan and will of God, he is the author of both good and evil. These were commonly called Libertines. To guard against the spread of bad doctrines and hold speculation within due bounds, the synod of the Grisons in 1553 adopted the Raetian Confession,[35] which all preachers were bound to subscribe. It especially emphasized the doctrines of the Trinity, predestination and baptism, and incorporated the Apostles', Nicene and Athanasian Creeds. It was not acceptable to a considerable number of the Italian preachers, who were disposed in general to favor latitude of belief, and some of whom (especially Pierpaolo Vergerio and Celso Martinengo) were regarded as favoring the views of Servetus.[36] Several of them at first refused to subscribe the confession as being too strict, and proposed forming a separate Italian synod, but they finally signed, with reservations.[37]

Despite the new confession, the Italian ministers continued to think for themselves, though cautious in expression; especially Aurelio Scytarcha, pastor at Vicosoprano, Girolamo Turriano of Plurs, Michelangelo Florio of Soglio, Pietro Leone of Chiavenna and others who were unable to stomach the doctrines about God, the atonement and the like.[38] They were confirmed in their thoughts a few years later by Alciati and Biandrata, who represented the radical element in the Italian church at Geneva, visited churches in the Grisons,[39] and were ere

---

[35] cf. de Porta, I, ii, 193–224. Gallicius wrote to Bullinger from Chur, Sept. 12, 1553, De Serveti blasphemiis audieram ante; utinam non essent in Valle Tellina; *Bullingers Korrespondenz*, i, 325.

[36] cf. de Porta, I, ii, 63.

[37] *id. op.*, I, ii, 225 f.

[38] cf. de Porta, I, ii, 391.

[39] cf. de Porta, I, ii, 391, whose later statement (p. 632) that Alciati and Biandrata were going about confirming the brethren, and were ordered by decree of the Diet Jan. 11, 1579, to leave the country, on pain of arrest and prosecution, must be incorrect as to its date. This is perhaps an error for 1559, with reference to a tour that may have been made

long to emerge as promoters of an antitrinitarian movement in Poland. They were also encouraged by Ochino, now pastor of the Italian congregation at Zürich. Mainardo, fearing that the old controversy was about to break out again, resorted to his old expedient, and demanded that the ministers subscribe the confession of the Chiavenna church. Some refused to do this as superfluous, in view of previous subscriptions; others could bind their consciences to nothing beyond Scripture and the Apostles' Creed; and Leone, who had been a pupil of Camillo, wrote a book opposing subscription.[40] Mainardo then had the recalcitrant ministers cited before the synod at Chur in 1561, while they in turn sought to win the support of the reformed churches in Switzerland by submitting a series of twenty-six questions, of which the burden was to inquire whether members must be forced to assent to detailed and abstruse statements of often speculative doctrines in order to avoid the charge of heresy or the pain of excommunication.[41]

The reply of the Zürich ministers was moderate in spirit, but the mind of the synod was less tolerant. When the case was brought up, Lodovico Fieri, one of the two recalcitrants at Chiavenna, was examined and, to the surprise of all, he boldly stated that he disagreed with the church in three points: he did not believe that Jesus Christ is the eternal Son of God, nor equal to the Father, nor the creator of heaven and earth; and he proposed a discussion as to whether a man of blameless life should be considered a heretic for a simple error about the doctrine of the Trinity.[42] The synod condemned and excommunicated Leone, the Diet ordered him arrested and tried, and as no further mention of him occurs, he was probably banished.[43] Fieri suffered a milder form of discipline, but was to be kept under close observation. He soon went to join the tolerant community of the Anabaptists in Moravia. The rest of the accused took counsel of prudence, made their peace with the church, and were received back into fellowship. Within the next year or two in the Lower Engadine dissensions broke out which were be-

---

the previous summer, after their leaving Zürich (see below, chap. xv.) There is no evidence that either of them ever returned to Switzerland after going to Poland. cf. Heberle in *Tübinger Zeitschrift*, 1840, Heft 4, p. 127, n. 3. cf. *infra*, p. 225, n. 63.

[40] cf. *supra*. p. 105, n. 22.

[41] Text and reply in Trechsel, *Antitrinitarier*, ii, 417–428.

[42] An pro Haeretico sit habendus quispiam ob simplicem errorem in articula de Trinitate, quum alioquin esset probatissimis moribus ac maxima erga pauperes praeditus charitate? De Porta, I, ii, 396.

[43] cf. Hottinger, *Kirchen-Gesch.*, iii, 851.

lated echoes of the teaching of Francesco at Fetan twenty years earlier, but after a short time they were composed.

Mainardo, worn out by his long struggles, died at Chiavenna in 1563; but his successor, Girolamo Zanchi, inherited his troubles, as did the latter's successor, Scipione Lentulo. Fieri returned from Moravia in 1569, more ardent than ever in spreading his beliefs, and found sympathizers. Solomon of Plurs, who had been excommunicated for Arianism a little after Fieri, appeared on the scene, as did Francesco of Bagnocavallo, denying the deity of Christ.[44] Lentulo complained of all this to the synod, and of the Arians and Anabaptists in the Valtellina; and at the request of the synod the Diet passed (1570) a decree ordering that all residents of the country must adhere to one of the two legal religions and subscribe its confession, and that if after diligent search any were found infected with Arian or Anabaptist doctrines they should be declared heretics, and forever banished.[45]

The decree actually was not strictly enforced, for only one or two were banished;[46] but the ministers to whom it applied, headed by Turriano of Plurs, were outspoken in condemning it as unjust, infringing liberty of conscience, beyond the proper province of the secular power, and opening the door to a Protestant Inquisition as oppressive as the Roman. Several did not hesitate to write urging the abolishment of the decree.[47] At the diet in 1571 there was a sharp conflict between Egli and Gantner,[48] two ministers of Chur, over the punishment of heretics; and Celso, who was present at the debate, incorporated a large part of the acts of the synod into his *In haereticis coercendis*, 1577.[49] The debate was long and heated, and ended in victory for the conservatives, who thereupon removed from the ministry Gantner and the Arianizing

[44] cf. de Porta, I, ii, 497 f.

[45] *id. op.*, I, ii, 501.

[46] cf. Trechsel, ii, 135.

[47] Bartolomeo Sylvio, preacher at Traona, wrote thus, and was answered by Josias Simler, Professor at Zürich, in his *De una persona et duabus naturis in Christo* (1578), with the Arians in the Grisons in mind (cf. his second preface). Mino Celso of Siena, lately escaped from the Inquisition, was greatly disturbed to find the same persecuting spirit developing in a Protestant land, and was thus moved to write his work on the capital punishment of heretics, of which we shall hear in connection with Servetus. Marcello Squarcialupo, a physician, also wrote on the subject; and was later one of the early Antitrinitarians in Transylvania and Poland. cf. de Porta, I, ii, 502–508.

[48] cf. de Porta, I, ii, 507.

[49] Minutes in de Porta, I, ii, 517–557.

Italian ministers: namely, Camillo Sozini (brother of Lelio), Nicola Camulio, Turriano, and one Mario.[50]

Thus ended any organized effort to promote more liberal views, or even to tolerate them, in the Grisons; and any individuals still holding such views found it best to maintain a discreet reserve. The final recorded instance is that of Fabrizio Pestalozzi who, after seventeen years in exile, returned and was brought before the consistory at Chiavenna in 1595 and required either to renounce his opinions or else to leave the country.[51]

The slow process of time has brought its changes. Despite the horrible massacre of Protestants in the Valtellina in 1620 — the *sacro macello* — nine of the old Italian Protestant churches south of the Alps still exist, with a numerous membership. In 1867 acceptance of the Helvetic Confession ceased to be required of ministers in the Grisons churches, who were thenceforth required only to preach according to the Bible and the essential bases of the Protestant Church. The majority of the pastors are decidedly liberal, preaching a Christianity which no longer insists upon creeds or believes in miracles, and many of them do not accept the deity of Christ.[52] The influence of Camillo, while it was smothered in the Grisons before the end of his century, long survived him abroad, working through his disciples as they scattered to Switzerland, England, Poland and Transylvania, where we shall trace it later.

In concluding this chapter, it is time to take account of the progress thus far made toward realizing the three principles spoken of at the beginning of this work as characteristic of the whole movement. The pioneers thus far considered achieved a considerable degree of mental freedom in religion, in that they quite emancipated themselves from the binding authority of creeds, confessions and traditions in so far as these were found unsupported by Scripture or unacceptable in themselves. They still willingly acknowledged the supreme authority of Scripture, indeed, but they found in it emancipation rather than oppression. The appeal to reason as the final authority in matters of religious truth was not to be confidently made until later, although some ap-

[50] cf. Ferdinand Buisson, *Sébastien Castellion sa vie et son oeuvre* (Paris, 1892), ii, 305–308.

[51] cf. de Porta, I, ii, 632.

[52] Emilio Comba, *Ein Besuch im evangelischen italienischen Graubünden* (Hamburg, 1897), p. 183; Schaff, *History,* vii, 144.

proaches to it were made as those touched with the spirit of Italian Humanism undertook to reconstruct the fabric of Christian doctrine, and objected to certain doctrines as unreasonable or incomprehensible. Tolerance also, as a personal attitude of mind, was in its fulness a late achievement; but an approach to it was made in the struggle for toleration at the Diet at Chur in 1561, and in the series of questions at that time submitted to the ministers at Zürich. The council at Venice, on the other hand, insisted on the acceptance of the doctrines there agreed to, on pain of excommunication. In fact, so long as to all parties the holding of correct doctrines was a matter of the very first importance, tolerance of incorrect ones would be not a virtue, but well-nigh a crime; and so long as each side strenuously insisted on propagating its own views, and on violently quarreling with those holding conflicting ones, the interference of secular power in the interest of peace by repression or persecution of the minority was little less than inevitable. From the time of Constantine down to the age of enlightenment, the prime cause of persecutions by the civil power has been quarrels between Christians over doctrine; and it was only when governments tried to hold the reins even, refusing to persecute one party in the interest of another, that true religious liberty for all was secured.

CHAPTER IX

THE LATER LIFE OF SERVETUS, 1532–1546

WHEN SERVETUS mysteriously disappeared from the German-speaking world immediately after publishing his Dialogues in 1532, he took no one into his confidence; and, as we have seen, he effectually covered his tracks by dropping his old cognomen and adopting a new one from his boyhood home at Villanueva. When he appeared in France it was therefore as Michael Villanovanus (Michel de Villeneuve); and it was twenty-one years before it was discovered that the two names denoted one and the same person. The record of his life during this intervening period is obscure, for the extant data are scanty and more or less inconsistent, being largely his personal testimony given when he was on trial for his life at Vienne and Geneva, and had strong motives for withholding or misrepresenting important facts. He seems, however, to have gone from Basel (or Hagenau) to Paris, either directly or with an intermediate residence at Lyon.[1] From the character of the existing evidence it is impossible to speak positively, but it seems probable that before proceeding to Paris Servetus was for a year or two at Lyon,[2] and that he there entered into relations with the publishing trade, and was employed as corrector for the press. Lyon was at this time a seat of wealth, learning and culture. In publishing it was second only to Paris, and the brothers Melchior and Kaspar Trechsel were distinguished for the beauty of the books they printed. The office of corrector was one that called for knowledge of both ancient and modern languages, and was often followed by scholars,[3] and Servetus was well qualified to fill it. Erasmus himself had in his time been corrector for the celebrated press of Aldus Manutius at Venice. Whether

[1] At Vienne he declared, "de là (Allemagne) s'en vint à Paris"; at Geneva he said, "de Agnouw il sen retournit à Basle, de Basle à Lyon, là ou il demorit envyron 2 ou 3 ans . . . et de Lyon sen allit à Paris." cf. d'Artigny, *Mémoires*, ii, 102 f; Calvin, viii, 767.

[2] Mosheim (*Versuch*, p. 55) conjectures that soon after going to France Servetus must have visited Italy; but such a visit rests upon a mistaken assumption, as does also his inference of a visit to Rome.

[3] cf. J. C. Zeltner, *Correctorum in typographiis eruditorum centuria*, (Norimbergae, 1716).

he came from Lyon, or directly from Germany, we find Servetus in Paris as early as 1534, studying for some time at the Collège de Calvi,[4] though whether this marks the beginning of his medical studies is not quite clear. It will have been in this year that he saw Francis I. touch a great many for the cure of king's evil, or scrofula, of which he speaks in his edition of Ptolemy the following year.[5] In this year too, when Calvin had ventured secretly to return to Paris after having had to flee for safety, Servetus seems to have challenged him to meet him in debate over matters of doctrine. Calvin, as related by his biographer, accepted the challenge, though at the risk of his life, and an hour was appointed at a house in the rue St. Antoine, where Calvin hoped to convince Servetus of his errors; but Servetus, though long waited for, failed to appear — out of fear, it was later charged.[6]

Servetus now interrupted his studies and returned to Lyon, presumably to earn money with which to continue them.[7] His first occupation here was to see through the press for the brothers Trechsel, the most famous publishing house in Lyon,[8] a new edition of Ptolemy's Geography,[9] which they had employed him to edit and revise, and on which he had perhaps been occupied in Paris. Ever since the second Christian century this famous work had maintained its place as the standard one on the subject. It had been repeatedly reissued, but the editions now current were based on a very faulty translation of the original Greek,

[4] cf. d'Artigny, ii, 103.

[5] In the *Descriptio Galliae.*

[6] cf. Beza, *Vita Calvini,* in Calvin, xxi, 123 f; Colladon, *Vie de Calvin, id. op.,* xxi, 57; Calvin, *Refutatio errorum Serveti, id. op.,* viii, 460, 481. The *Histoire Ecclésiastique des Églises Reformées* (Paris, 1883), i, 25, wrongly places the meeting in 1533, when Calvin was not yet in danger; while Calvin (viii, 460) dates it *ante annos sexdecim,* i. e. 1538, when he was already at Geneva.

[7] Mosheim, *Versuch,* pp. 122–126, tries to prove that Servetus was only once at Lyon as corrector, but the development is clearer if two different periods are supposed. He also thinks (*Nachrichten,* p. 32) that in 1534 Servetus was for some time at Orleans, where the Rhenish physician, Johannes Weyer (cf. his *Opera,* Amsterdam, 1660, p. 422) mentions having formed a friendship in that year with a well-known physician named Michael Villanovanus. But Villanovanus was a fairly common name and Servetus had not yet come to fame under this name, so that the identification is extremely doubtful. cf. Henry, *Calvin,* ii, 173.

[8] cf. Julien Baudrier, *Michel Servet ses relations avec les libraires et les imprimeurs lyonnais* in *Mélanges offerts à M. Émile Picot* (Paris, 1913), i. 41–56.

[9] *Claudii Ptolomaei Alexandrini Geographicae Enarrationis Libri Octo, ex Bilibaldi Pirckhemeri tralatione . . . a Michaele Villanovano jam primum recogniti,* etc. (Lugduni, 1535).

they abounded in errors, and the explorations of the preceding half-century had made them quite out of date. Geography was now the subject of widest popular interest after theology, and a thorough revision was urgently wanted. By his attainments as a scholar and his observations as a traveler Servetus was well fitted for his task. For the basis of his revision he took the edition of Wilibald Pirckheimer (Strassburg, 1525), and he introduced it by an interesting preface.[10] He revised the text by comparison with manuscripts and earlier editions, corrected numberless errors as to the names and locations of places, added many notes drawn from his wide reading of authors both ancient and modern, and from his own observations as an extensive traveler, and added the modern names to the classical ones.

He contributed new accounts of the British Isles, as well as of the lands he himself had visited, Spain, Italy, France and Germany, and made penetrating comments upon the character and customs of their inhabitants, with a discriminating comparison and contrast between the Spaniards and the French. He took account of the most recent discoveries in the New World, and deemed it a gross mistake that it had not been named after Columbus.[11] As for other lands, he reprinted Pirckheimer's edition with little change, including, unfortunately for himself as it later proved, the remarks upon the Holy Land. For Pirckheimer himself had taken over without change a passage from an earlier edition (Strassburg, 1522) of the Dutchman Lorenz Friese (Phrisius) to the effect that upon the evidence of merchants and travelers, Palestine so far from being fertile was uncultivated, sterile, and wholly wanting in charm, and should be pronounced, though a 'promised' land, yet a land of no promise.[12] This passage, though Servetus denied being the author of it, was at his trial at Geneva made the basis of one of the items in his indictment, that in it he had defamed Moses.[13] One other passage betrayed a sceptical mind, and might have brought upon him a charge of lèse majesté. Speaking of the current rumor that the King

[10] Reprinted in Mosheim, *Versuch*, pp. 396–398.

[11] Toto aberrant coelo qui hanc continentem Americam nuncupari contendunt, cum Americus multo post Columbum eandem terram adierit.

[12] The Latin (Quare promissam terram pollicitam, et non vernacula lingua laudatam pronunties) hints at a play upon a word in the original German: *gelobtes* if a participle from *geloben* meaning promised, but if from *loben* meaning praised. cf. J. G. Schelhorn, *Amoenitates literariae* (Frankfurt, 1725–'31), xiv, 395 f; J. G. de Chauffepié, *Nouveau Dictionnaire historique et Critique* (Amsterdam, 1750–'56), iv, 223, n.

[13] cf. Calvin, viii, 727, 732, 738, 741, 745, 496; Mosheim, *op. cit.*, pp. 260–265.

of France was curing scrofula by a touch he remarks, 'I myself have seen the King touch a great many, but whether they were cured I did not see.' [14]

Ptolemy had been not only geographer but also astronomer and mathematician, and he had used both these sciences in the service of geography. As his editor Servetus had therefore to acquire some familiarity with both these fields of study, which were to bear fruit a little later. His Ptolemy, though still susceptible of much improvement, marked a substantial advance over any previous edition, and its excellence was at once recognized. The German geographer Sebastian Münster, in the dedication to his *Geographia Universalis* (Basel, 1540), credits the keen-eyed Michael Villanovanus with detecting many errors that had escaped the notice of Pirckheimer, restoring the text, explaining abstruse points, and elucidating obscure matters by his notes;[15] and in Montanus's edition of Ptolemy (Frankfurt, 1605), the preface acknowledges Servetus's contributions, as have many writers since. He has indeed even been eulogized as the founder of Comparative Geography and the forerunner of Ritter and von Humboldt in this field.[16]

Servetus seems to have been employed as corrector at Lyon from two to three years, and not only to have occupied himself here with his studies in geography, mathematics and astronomy, but also to have become deeply interested in medicine, probably enough through correcting the proof-sheets of medical works that were at the time passing through the press. Some of these were by Dr. Symphorien Champier (Campegius, 1472–1539), one of the most celebrated physicians of the time, and founder of the college of medicine at Lyon.[17] Servetus was

[14] Vidi ipse Regem plurimos hoc languore corruptos tangentem, an sanati fuerint non vidi.

[15] Multa fugerunt hunc bonum virum, quae post eum deprehendit oculatissimus Michael Villanovanus, qui non poenitendas vigilias locavit in Ptolomaeum, emendando corrupta, explicando retrusa, et scholiis illustrando obscuriora.

[16] cf. Tollin, 'Michael Servet als Geograph,' *Zeitschrift der Gesellschaft für Erdkunde zu Berlin*, x (1875), 182–222; *id.*, 'Michael Servet, ein Vorläufer K. Ritter's und Alex. v. Humboldt's,' *id. op.*, xiv, (1879), 356–368; Eloy Bullón y Fernández, *Miguel Servet y la Geografía del Renacimiento* (Madrid, 1929). Dr. Giulio Ceradini, on the other hand, along with opposing Servetus's claim to distinction as an anatomist, makes light of Servetus's contributions to geography, and treats his work with sarcastic contempt; cf. his *Opere* (Milano, 1906), i. 237, n., 256 ff, 293–437.

[17] cf. F. Allut, *Étude biographique et bibliographique sur Symphorien Champier* (Lyon, 1859); Tollin, 'Des Arztes Michael Servet Lehrer in Lyon, Dr. Symphorien Champier,' *Archiv für pathologische Anatomie und Physiologie*, lxi (1874), 377–382; *id.*, 'Trois

thus inspired to become a physician, and presently became his devoted pupil.[18] Dr. Champier was a free-thinking Catholic, and a man of broad culture, who in his time published over a hundred books or tracts on a wide variety of subjects. He was very proud of his attainments, and a man of great personal vanity. Contemporary with him was Dr. Leonhard Fuchs, professor at Tübingen, the most celebrated anatomist of the Protestant world, a botanist of note for whom the Fuchsia was named, also an author of numerous books, something of a theologian, and a rabid Protestant. Fuchs had published a work on the errors of recent physicians (*Errata recentiorum medicorum*, 1530), so carelessly done that it was itself full of errors. Thereupon Champier published a collection of tracts (1533), not all written by himself, animadverting upon these errors as well as criticizing the positions taken by Fuchs. Fuchs replied with a revised edition of his former work (reentitled *Paradoxa medicorum*, 1534), ridiculing Champier, and so severely wounding his vanity that the latter took his revenge by getting Fuchs's work condemned by the Sorbonne and publicly burned (1536); for in his work Fuchs had mingled Lutheran theology with medicine, and so laid himself open to attack from ecclesiastical authority.

It was at this juncture that Servetus entered the lists with an Apology addressed to Fuchs in defence of Champier,[19] his first work under his new name. He had a two-fold interest in publishing his tract, since by it he could both discharge a debt of gratitude to the master whose cause he had championed, and from a safe point of vantage attack an objectionable doctrine of the Protestant reformers. For Fuchsius in his work had gone out of his way to advocate Luther's cardinal doctrine of justification by faith, which Servetus had with such unhappy results already criticized in his first two books. After an introductory fling at

---

médecins du xvie siècle: Champier, Fuchs, Servet,' *Revue Scientifique*, xxii (May 16, 23, 1885), 613–620, 651–654.

[18] "Symphoriano Campegio, cui ut discipulus multa debeo"; (Servetus), *In Leonardum Fuchsium Apologia*, p. Aii. cf. Tollin, 'Wie Michael Servet ein Mediciner wurde,' *Deutsche Klinik*, xxvii (Feb. 20, 27, 1875), 57–59, 65–68.

[19] *In Leonardum Fuchsium Apologia, autore Michaele Villanovano,* (Lugduni, 1536), 15 pp. The tract had long been known only by title, and its very existence was doubted (cf. Mosheim, *Versuch*, p. 73), when Tollin in the winter of 1858–'59 discovered the first part of it reprinted in another work. The whole was later found, and a copy is in Dr. Williams's Library, London. cf. Tollin, 'Michael Servet's Brevissima Apologia pro Symphoriano Campegio in Leonardum Fuchsium,' *Deutsches Archiv für Geschichte der Medicin und medicinische Geographie*, vii, (1884), 409–442; van der Linde, *Servet*, pp. 41–52.

Fuchs, therefore, for the fierce petulance of his attack, Servetus devotes his first chapter to the subject of faith and works, refuting Fuchs in much the same vein that he had followed in his Dialogues of four years earlier. He repeats anew his earlier charge that Lutherans do not know very much about the meaning of justification; though it is arresting to note that he now speaks as a loyal son of the Catholic Church.[20] The remaining two chapters deal with two questions of medicine, but though they show considerable medical knowledge, they do not concern us here. To this tract Fuchs made no reply.

Before the middle of November Servetus was back in Paris,[21] and for something like a year and a half [22] or more he apparently occupied himself with private studies in the two fields that had lately engaged his interest; geography and related subjects, on which he was presently to be giving lectures, and medicine, which he was to make his chosen profession.

As a fruit of his studies during this interval, while as yet only an amateur student of the subject, he published in 1537 a contribution to a hotly disputed question in medicine, his famous little treatise on the use of syrups.[23] The medical world of the time was divided into two schools of theory and practice, the Galenists and the Arabists, and they stood in sharp critical antagonism to each other. A controversy had lately arisen between them as to the value of so-called syrups, sweetened infusions used to hasten the curative process. The Galenists held that these were useless; the Arabists used them extensively. Servetus in this

---

[20] "Justificationis vim non satis intelligunt," p. Aiii. "Pro ecclesia (Catholica), ut pro matre filius," p. Aii.

[21] A tradition has found its way into print that in 1535 (hence during the Lyon period) an ardent Protestant pastor named Michel Servet came to Saint-Étienne de St. Geoirs in Dauphiné and spread antitrinitarian teaching among numerous converts, but was driven from the commune in disgrace, to be put to death by his friend Calvin at Geneva two years later. The archives of Saint-Étienne yield no support for this tale, which bears obvious marks of being apocryphal. cf. A. P. Simian, *Saint-Étienne de St. Geoirs, village delphinal* (Grénoble, 1861), pp. 105–107; E. J. Savigné, *Le Savant Michel Servet* (Vienne, 1907), p. 13.

[22] The preface to the *Apologia* is dated 'Lutetiae Parisiorum, pridie Idus Novembris, 1536'; and his matriculation at the University, "Michael Villanueva Cesaraugustanens. dioec.," was March 24, 1537/8 (*Acta rectoria, sive juratorum registra*, cited by Tollin, 'Servet-Kritik,' p. 449). As under the old calendar this latter date was the very last day of the year, the interval will have been as stated.

[23] *Syruporum universa ratio, ad Galeni censuram diligenter expolita* (Paris, 1537), 71 pp. Also Venice, 1545; Lyon 1546, 1547, 1548.

work took independent ground, holding that syrups have a number of uses, which he enumerated, but that they ought not to be used indiscriminately. The book evinces deep acquaintance with the writings of Galen in the original Greek, and an original mind, and it became very popular, running through five editions in France and Italy. It soon won him the high praise of his preceptor, Professor Jean Guinter.[24]

At length Servetus enrolled himself at the College of the Lombards, where he studied (or lectured on [25]) mathematics, and as his chief subject pursued medicine under the professors Jacques Sylvius (du Bois), Jean Guinter of Andernach, and Jean Fernel.[26] He became a skilful dissector, and together with Andreas Vesalius, later to be recognized as the father of modern Anatomy, he served as pro-sector for Professor Guinter, who in a work published a little later praised him as a man highly accomplished in all departments of letters, and hardly second to any in his knowledge of Galen.[27]

Of the year, more or less,[28] during which Servetus was a medical student at the University of Paris, we have no record save concerning a single episode growing out of some public lectures that he gave. By the usage of the University one was supposed to have the Master of Arts degree before one might enter upon the study of Medicine or give public lectures;[29] but despite his testimony at Geneva,[30] no other evidence has been discovered that he was ever admitted to a degree.[31] The

[24] Or, in Latin form, Joannes Guinterus. The name is also incorrectly given as Günther, Winter, and Gonthier. See note below. cf. Édouard Turner, 'La circulation du sang,' *Progrès Médicale*, xiii, 365 (Paris, 1885).

[25] *S'en alla lire les Mathématiques.* d'Artigny, *Mémoires*, ii, 103.

[26] cf. Calvin, viii, 780.

[27] Auxiliarium habui, primum, Andream Vesalium, juvenem meherculem in Anatomia diligentissimum. Post hunc, Michael Villanovanus, familiariter mihi in consectationibus adhibitus est, vir omni literarum genere ornatissimus, in Galeni doctrina vix ulli secundus. Ioannis Guinteri *Anatomicarum Institutionum ex Galeni sententia libri iiii* (Basel, 1539), preface. Servetus's contribution to anatomy will be spoken of a little later.

[28] From his matriculation, March 24, 1536/7, to his trial before the Parlement, March 18, 1537/8, which must have been close to the end of his residence.

[29] cf. Tollin, 'Anleitung zum Studium der Medicin aus den Jahren 1533 und 1540,' *Archiv für pathologische Anatomie und Physiologie*, lxxx (1880), 47–78.

[30] "Respond quil est docteur en médicine, maistre es ars de Parys," Calvin, viii, 767.

[31] In the Paris trial he is spoken of only as a student of medicine (*scholasticus medicinae*). In the trial at Vienne, though he called himself *Docteur en Médecine*, he is spoken of only as *medecin juré*, *médecin*, and *medicus*, and is so addressed by a correspondent (cf. d'Artigny, ii, 101 f, 119, 123; Calvin, viii, 785, 835, 845, 851). On the other hand, in that same year another correspondent addressed him as *Docteur en Médecine* (Calvin,

rule, however, was not strictly enforced.[32] Taking advantage therefore of the existing laxity, and supported by the reputation he had deservedly won by both his Ptolemy and his two medical publications, Servetus lectured publicly on geography, mathematics and astronomy.[33] These three terms perhaps refer less to three distinct subjects of lectures than to three related branches treated under the comprehensive subject of geography, on which his Ptolemy had won him a reputation; for we have already seen that his studies for that work led him into the allied fields of astronomy and mathematics. No subject at that time excited wider popular interest than geography, which the age of discovery had done so much to bring to popular attention, and Servetus's lectures had a large and respectable hearing. Prominent among his auditors was Pierre Palmier (Paulmier), who had been an extensive traveler and was widely read in the subject, and standing high in royal favor had often been sent on missions by the King. He had ten years before been chosen Archbishop of Vienne, and was later to become Servetus's patron.

As geography led to astronomy and mathematics, so these in turn

---

viii, 835), and in an extant contract of 1540 he is described under that title (cf. Baudrier, *Servet*, p. 44.)

In a thorough search of University records at Montpellier, Tollin found no entry for Servetus, unless he had disguised himself as *Michael Navarrus, dioces. Caesar August.*, when matriculating in September, 1540; and even then there was no record of a degree. It was therefore inferred that if Servetus ever obtained a degree at all, it was probably by purchase (a common practice at the time), perhaps at Avignon, which he visited after leaving Paris (cf. d'Artigny, p. 103). cf. Tollin, 'Michael Servet in Charlieu' *Deutsches Archiv für die Geschichte der Medicin und medicinische Geographie*, viii. (1885), 90–94. The registers at Padua are no longer extant. Nor can Vesalius or Silvius be proved by records to have taken the Doctor's degree; cf. Tollin, 'Andreas Vesal,' *Biologisches Centralblatt*, v, (1885), 341 f.

[32] cf. van der Linde, *Servet*, p. 57.

[33] "Multis jam annis . . . Geographiam ipsam Ptolomaei a me sis dignatus audire" (Ptolemy, ed. of 1541, Dedication to Pierre Palmier). "S'en alla lire Mathématiques au Collège des Lombards" (d'Artigny, ii, 103). "A Paris la ou il a estudié en médecine et a leu publiquement en mathématique (Calvin, viii, 767). "Quil la (Ptolemy's Geography) leu à Parys" (*id. op.*, p. 738).

It is not to be taken for granted (as is often done) that the lectures were given at the University, or under its auspices. They may have been independent lectures elsewhere in the city. While the case of Servetus was under discussion, Dean Tagault called the attention of the faculty of arts (March 4) to the fact that very many who were not at all approved by the University were publicly teaching subjects in the liberal arts in the city of Paris, and that if this evil were not checked, it would bring the University to ruin. cf. *Commentarii facultatis artium*, quoted by Tollin, 'Michael Servet's Pariser Process' *Deutsches Archiv für Geschichte der Medicin und medicinische Geographie*, iii (1880), 212.

bordered on astrology. The line between astronomy and astrology was not yet strictly drawn, and astrologers liked to call themselves mathematicians.[34] Now astrology had from time immemorial been a recognized element in the culture of the western world, and in the first third of the sixteenth century it had only lately passed its zenith. Although it had been dealt a mortal blow by the humanist scholar Pico della Mirandola [35] toward the end of the preceding century, and being now forbidden as a capital crime was on the wane, it was still believed in and employed by eminent personages. Princes and free cities had their astrologers to be consulted when important enterprises were under consideration, and professors of astrology lectured at the universities.[36] The Emperor Charles V. and Francis I. had their astrologers. The Medicis and Richelieu were given to it; Melanchthon was addicted to it.[37] Two branches of astrology were recognized, the so-called natural astrology, and judiciary astrology.[38] The former was a descriptive science, treating of the heavenly bodies and their movements. It recognized that bodies here below are more or less influenced by those above, as for example tides and changes of weather; and it was held that there was a similar influence upon human bodies, from which light might be got as to the cause and treatment of bodily ailments. Its use in medical practice was still regarded as legitimate.[39] Judiciary astrology, on the other hand, was a predictive science. Holding that the whole fortunes and fate of men are determined in advance by the positions of stars and constellations at the hour of birth, it professed to be able by casting one's horoscope to foretell future events. It was a form of divination, mingled with superstition, appealing to credulity, widely accepted in popular belief, and extensively used by impostors as a means of livelihood. In short, it was fortune-telling by the stars; and it was so deeply involved

---

[34] cf. van der Linde, *Servet*, pp. 256, 258; Calvin, vii, 516; xxxvii, 123.

[35] *Disputationes adversus Astrologos* (in his *Opera omnia*, Venetiis, 1519).

[36] cf. Burckhardt, *Renaissance*, pp. 507–518.

[37] Laelius Socinus to Bullinger, Aug. 20, 1550: "Omnes ab uno Melanchthone, qui astrologiae judiciariae fuit addictus (pendent), et unus ille ab astrisne magis an ab astrorum conditore ac Domino pendeat, ignoro." Cited by Illgen, *Symbolae*, part. ii, p. 19. cf. Wilhelm Bernhardt, *Philipp Melanchthon als Mathematiker und Physiker* (Wittenberg, 1865).

[38] cf. Calvin, *Advertissement contre l'Astrologie qu'on appelle judiciaire* (1549), *Opera*, vii, 516.

[39] Dr. Champier employed it, and had published a work on the subject: *Pronosticon de presagiis Astrologorum*, etc. (Lyon, 1518.) cf. Lynn Thorndike, *History of Magic and Experimental Science* (New York, 1923), *s. v.* 'Astrology in Medicine.'

in gross superstition that the tide of intelligent opinion was now running strongly against it. Dr. Jean Tagault, Dean of the medical faculty,
was active in trying to stamp it out, and not long before this date Jean
Thibault, the King's regular physician and astrologer, had been haled
before the Parlement or chief judicial court, condemned, and expelled
from the medical profession for practicing without license from the faculty.[40] It was under such conditions that Servetus's lectures were delivered.

So long as the lectures were confined to geography, all went well
enough; but when they crossed the border into the field of astrology
they entered dangerous ground, and complaints arose. Servetus followed his master, Dr. Champier, in holding a firm belief in the value
of astrology in the practice of medicine; but it is by no means unlikely
that he had also privately engaged in the practice of judiciary astrology
as a ready source of income, and that a rumor of this had reached the
Dean's ears. Professional envy that an uppish young student should
have attained such popularity by his writings and his lectures may also
have been a factor in what followed.[41] By late in February, 1538 the
medical faculty of the University learned that Servetus had for some
time been publicly lecturing in Paris on judiciary astrology.[42] Some of
the faculty admonished him to cease from this, but he refused; and
when several of them remonstrated with him kindly several times, he
answered them disrespectfully. Thereupon the Dean, Dr. Tagault, interrupted him one day in the midst of a lecture, peremptorily telling
him that the doctors of the faculty had forbidden discussion of the subject either in lectures or in public disputations, and giving reasons for
rejecting it as a delusion. The lectures were therefore discontinued.

    [40] cf. Tollin, 'Johann Thibault, Michael Servet's Pariser Freund,' *Archiv für patholo-
gische Anatomie und Physiologie*, lxxxviii (1879), 302–318; *id.*, 'Zu Thibault's Prozess,
urkundlich dargestellt,' *Deutsches Archiv für Geschichte der Medican und medicinische
Geographie*, iii (1880), 332–347.
    [41] The sources for this episode were unearthed by Tollin in 1858–'59 in the *Archives
de France*, Matinées x, 4905, p. 581b ff; *Commentarii Facultatis Medicinae Parisiensis*, v,
97, 98; *Commentarii Facultatis Artium*, No. 18. Verbally reprinted by Tollin, 'Michael
Sarvet's Pariser Process,' *Deutsches Archiv für Geschichte der Medicin und medicinischer
Geographie*, iii. (1880), 183–221. cf. C. E. Bulaeus (du Boulay), *Historia Universitatis
Parisiensis*, (Paris, 1665–'73), vi, 311 f, 331–334; Mosheim, *Versuch*, pp. 399–404.
    [42] February 2, 1537/38. Quidam scholasticus medicinae, Michael Villanovanus, na-
tione Hispanus, aut, ut dicebat, Navarrus, sed Hispano patre progenitus, anno 1537 (i. e.,
1538, N. S.) professus fuerat aliquot dies judiciariam sue divinatricem astrologiam Parisiis.
cf. Tollin, *op. cit. supra*, p. 204.

Angered at this public humiliation, Servetus prepared to defend his cause
by a written apology, and put it to press. The Dean and two or three
of the other doctors quietly advised him not to publish it, as it would
cause him trouble. He disregarded their advice, and in the court-yard
of the college, before several students and teachers, made violent threats
against the Dean. The medical faculty then petitioned the Parlement
to forbid publication, and Servetus was ordered to appear in court the
next day, but the matter was adjourned from day to day. Meantime
the Dean sought the support of the other faculties and of the whole
University, which was readily agreed to on March 4. Some of the
doctors in their public lectures retaliated against Servetus by saying that
he was nothing but a fraud and an impostor. He began to be apprehensive, and sent his friends to try to get the trouble quieted, though
he refused to apologize to the faculty. Impatient at the court's delay
they then had Servetus cited before the Inquisitor as if for heresy.[43]
The latter really had no jurisdiction, but Servetus obeyed the summons,
was readily acquitted, and freely boasted that he would win against the
Dean and the doctors. Meantime, smarting at the treatment he had received in the public lectures of the professors, and wounded in his
honor, he paid the printers extra to hasten the printing of his Apology,[44]
before publication should be forbidden by the court, and had distributed a large number gratuitously, being aided in this by the King's
astrologer, Jean Thibault, who had already had his own affair with the
medical faculty.[45]

The Apology consists of two parts. In the first and much longer one
Servetus appeals to the teaching of ancient authorities of high repute
who testified to the influence of the heavenly bodies upon mundane
affairs: Plato, Aristotle, Hippocrates, Galen and others. If modern
teachers oppose astrology, then they have departed from the teachings
of their acknowledged masters, and shut their eyes to the light. He
ridicules them with the names of ape and sophist, and intimates that
they are the plague of their profession. As Galen in his day had against

---

[43] Ils le font citer par devant l'Inquisiteur de la Foy, comme sil eust este suspect de
mauvaise doctrine. cf. Tollin, *op. cit. supra*, p. 193.

[44] *Michaelis Villanovani in quendam medicum Apologetica disceptatio pro astrologia*
(Paris, 1538), 16 pp., small 8°. Bibliothèque Nationale, No. V. 2410. This unique copy
discovered by Tollin in 1858 was reprinted with introduction by him (Berlin, 1880).
Dutch translation by van der Linde, *Servet*, pp. 65–81.

[45] *v. supra*, p. 178.

his will and in the face of disapproval of his contemporaries discussed astrology when importuned by his friends, so he himself, when already deep in medical studies, has taken up the subject at the insistence of his friends. He has realized the risk he runs, and has counted the cost.[46] In the second part he briefly answers the objections that his opponent has offered: first, that astrologers do not tell the truth, since they do not proceed upon fixed and consistent principles, hence that astrology of this sort is not a science; and secondly, that the certain casting of a horoscope is impossible. To these objections he replies that his opponent does not reason logically, and that his objections betray stupid and intolerable ignorance. This Apology was addressed to the attendants at his lectures, which had been interrupted, and was intended to furnish them materials for defence if they should be attacked.

The trial finally took place on March 18, behind closed doors, the University, the medical faculty, and Servetus, being each represented by counsel. It was not, as is sometimes stated, a criminal trial of Servetus for a capital crime, but a hearing on the faculty's petition that his Apology be not placed on sale.[47] The attorney on behalf of the University pleaded that judiciary astrology was contrary to the laws of God and man, as the defendant well knew; that he had taught it publicly and privately in Paris, and had cast horoscopes for money, and had led several scholars astray; and that he had had an Apology printed which contained astrological predictions. It was therefore asked that he be forbidden henceforth to teach judiciary astrology publicly or privately, and to publish his Apology; and that he confess his wrong, and as far as possible withdraw all his printed Apologies and deposit them with the court. The attorney for the faculty set forth that Servetus had rejected their advice kindly given, and though but a student had charged them with incompetence and called them insulting names, and had published his Apology despite their request; and he asked that Servetus make due reparation for the insults he had offered the faculty,

[46] Galenus suo saeculo . . . jurat per deos immortales, se amicorum precibus coactum de astronomia disseruisse, nam id sponte facturus non erat, videns sui temporis medicis alia potius nugamenta placere, et haec esse illis invidiosa. . . Per deum immortalem cum Galeno juro, me non sponte, sed ab amicis adactum, ad mathemata divertisse, cum in medicina totus essem. Sciebam enim cum tot monstris mihi esse dimicandum. Sed postquam in arenam descendi, stabo viriliter. *Apologetica disceptatio*, pp. 37–39.

[47] The Dean's statement in bringing his case before the court was: "Porrigo supplicem libellum senatui, quo petimus, ut Apologiae illae venales non exponantur." cf. Tollin, *op. cit.*, p. 205.

and show them due honor and respect. The attorney for the defence acknowledged the mildness of the action taken by the faculty against Servetus, and explained away the offensive passages in the Apology. His students were called to witness that he had never said a word of judiciary astrology, but only of astrology as related to things in Nature. He had published his Apology only in self-defence against scandalous things said of him by some doctors in their lectures, and was willing to submit all that he had said to the judgment of the court and the theological professors, and to stand corrected if found in the wrong. He then retracted all that he had said or written, and promised not to defend judiciary astrology in future.[48] Upon recommendation of the Attorney General the court then pronounced judgment. Servetus was to do all in his power to withdraw the Apologies from circulation and deposit them with the court; and to show the faculty and doctors the respect and obedience due to teachers; and to say or write against them nothing abusive or insulting; and to behave peaceably and quietly. The faculty and doctors were also enjoined to treat Servetus gently and kindly, as parents their children. He was forbidden in any way public or private to profess judiciary astrology, but only, if he likes, astrology touching the influence of the heavenly bodies on the weather and other things in Nature; all on pain of exclusion from the University, and further at the discretion of the court. The whole episode does not show Servetus in a very attractive light, but manifests the characteristic faults of his impetuous nature, self-conceit, quickness of temper, and an apparent failure to realize clearly what he was doing and what it might involve. For in the very text of the Apology itself he boasts of having made astrological predictions, in which he shelters himself behind the authority of Galen and Hippocrates. In all the circumstances it is perhaps strange that the faculty did not seek more serious punishment, instead of contenting themselves with such formal discipline as is given to unruly students. For Servetus, however, this was enough, and as nothing further is heard of him in Paris it is likely that he at once left the University for a more congenial field.

If we may credit his testimony at Vienne,[49] Servetus after leaving

---

[48] cf. Tollin, *op. cit.*, p. 207.

[49] cf. d'Artigny, ii, 103; Calvin, viii, 767, 769. The view espoused for a time by Gordon (*v. Encyclopaedia Britannica*, ed. 11, xxiv, 685) that Servetus was enrolled at the University of Louvain, 1537–'38, as Michael Villanovanus, was later disproved and retracted.

Paris was for some time at Lyon, thence went to Avignon and back to
Lyon, and finally to Charlieu, a little town about forty miles northwest
of Lyon, where he practiced medicine for some three years.[50] Here he
lived at the mansion of the noble la Rivoire family,[51] with whose members he had had relations at Lyon. But two incidents are reported of
his life at Charlieu: that he contemplated marriage with a young woman
of the place, but abandoned the idea because he thought himself not
physically fit; and that while returning from a professional visit one
night he was set upon by friends of another physician who had a
grudge against him. A fight ensued in which both sides were wounded,
and he was under arrest for two or three days.[52] Soon after this (perhaps late in 1540)[53] he must have left Charlieu, returning to Lyon,[54]
where he met his sometime Paris auditor, Archbishop Palmier. He was
a scholar and lover of letters, who liked to have the society of scholars
about him and to show them favor, and in 1541 he had induced Gaspard
Trechsel to remove from Lyon and establish his press at Vienne, sixteen miles south.[55] He now urged Servetus also to take up his residence
there, and provided him with an apartment in the palace precincts.[56]
The society here was stimulating, and included several prelates who
were eager students of geography, as well as a fellow-student of Servetus at Paris, Dr. Jean Perrell, now the Archbishop's personal physician.[57]

Servetus had cordial relations with the Archbishop, with Guy de
Maugiron, Lieutenant General of Dauphiné, and with the aristocracy
in general. He engaged in the practice of medicine, and cured of grave
illness the only daughter of Antoine de la Court, the Vice-Bailiff and

[50] cf. Tollin, 'Michael Servet in Charlieu,' *Deutsches Archiv für die Geschichte der
Medicin und medicinische Geographie*, viii (1885), 76–96.

[51] cf. Hiérosme Bolsec, *Histoire de la vie . . . de Jean Calvin*, ed. Chastel (Lyon, 1875),
p. 18 f.

[52] cf. Calvin, viii, 769, 781.

[53] cf. Mosheim, *Nachrichten*, p. 40 f.

[54] cf. d'Artigny, *loc. cit.* Mosheim (*Versuch*, p. 83) conjectures that Servetus, being
thirty years old in 1539, must have followed the example of Jesus, and have received adult
baptism at that age (cf. *Christianismi Restitutio*, p. 412: *Triginta annorum Christus baptismum accepit, exemplum nobis dans*, etc.), hence from Anabaptists, either in Switzerland
during his Charlieu period, or (assuming birth in 1511) at Vienne in 1541; but there is
no positive evidence that he was ever re-baptized at all.

[55] cf. Baudrier, *Servet*, i, 50.

[56] cf. d'Artigny, ii, 65, 90.

[57] cf. Ptolemy (1541), dedication.

judge; and he showed great devotion to those ill of the plague in 1542.[58]

If the fifty letters might still be discovered that Servetus wrote from Vienne to Dr. Jean St. Vertunien de la Vau, Protestant physician at Poitiers, and which Scaliger saw a generation or two later,[59] we might have a clue to what was really passing in the restless mind of Servetus during this period of external calm. For though he had in his first books sharply criticized some of the teachings of the Church, he had never withdrawn from it, and he had recognized its authority,[60] while the Reformed churches had decisively repudiated him. In short, he was still nominally a Catholic, albeit a liberal one. He therefore continued to attend the church services regularly, and abstained from religious discussion. At the Geneva trial he confessed that he had sinned in doing this, but said that he had been forced to do so by his fear of death, and he cited the example of St. Paul in similar circumstances as his warrant.[61] His reputation was well established, and here he enjoyed twelve happy years.[62]

Apart from his medical practice, Servetus continued to act as corrector for the press. At about the time of his leaving Charlieu, he had contracted with the Compagnie des Libraires of Lyon to correct and edit a Bible in six volumes and index for a price of 400 livres tournois (about $80.), and the work extended over four years.[63] He also corrected another and very rare Latin Bible, printed by Trechsel at Vienne and published in 1542 by de la Porte at Lyon; and for the firm of Frellon, publishers at Lyon, he corrected, *inter alia*, the *Summa* of St. Thomas Aquinas in Spanish, and prepared summaries for it;[64] and he

[58] cf. Savigné, *Servet*, p. 19.

[59] cf. Tollin, 'Saint Vertunien de la Vau' *Archiv für pathologische Anatomie und Physiologie und für klinische Medicin*, ci (1885), 44–70; *Scaligerana* (Lugduni Batavorum, 1668), p. 197 f, "*J'ai veu ces lettres-la*"; *Naudaeana et Patiniana*, (Amsterdam, 1704). De la Vau appears in the Reformed church at Poitiers in 1555 as an opponent of Calvin, and at Geneva later on he was called to account for disapproving of the execution of Servetus and taking the side of Castellio in the controversy that followed. He was friendly with Castellio, Borrhäus and Curioni at Basel. Calvin called him "*ceste beste sauvage*." cf. Calvin to the church at Poitiers, Feb. 20, 1555, xv, 435–446. [60] v. *De Trin.*, p. 2a.

[61] v. Acts. xxi. 26; cf. Calvin, viii, 789; Servetus, *Restitutio*, p. 563 f.

[62] cf. d'Artigny, *op. cit.*, ii, 66, 113.

[63] cf. Baudrier, *Servet*, i. 44–46. *Biblia Sacra cum glossis*, etc., (Lugduni, G. Trechsel, 1545 and following). Unsigned preface by the corrector. This edition is little known. Part of it was perhaps printed at Vienne after Trechsel's removal thither.

[64] cf. d'Artigny, *op. cit.*, p. 68.

translated from Latin into Spanish several treatises on grammar, of which none has as yet been identified. He also saw through the press at Lyon three revised editions of his book on Syrups, 1546, 1547, 1548.[65] But by far his most important work while at Vienne was his editing of revised editions of his Ptolemy and of Pagnini's Latin Bible. Ever since his previous edition of Ptolemy he had been diligently preparing a more correct one, in which he might use a freer hand than his publisher had formerly allowed him. The Archbishop had pointed out some errors, and his new publisher was willing to spare no expense in bringing out a faultless edition. The work was difficult, had long been needed though never attempted, numberless errors had crept into the text, and the lapse of time, wars, and modern discoveries, had wrought many changes. Servetus therefore made so many betterments as now to offer not merely a revision but practically a new edition. Apart from such corrections and additions as were needed, the most striking changes were by way of removing objectionable passages. The passage about the promised land of Palestine was omitted on account of the offence it had given, and the whole page was left blank. The skeptical reference to cures of scrofula by the royal touch was rewritten to read, 'I have heard in various places that a great many were cured.'[66] The captious reference to Germany was softened down. The new work was printed at Vienne by Trechsel, but published at Lyon by de la Porte, with a dedication dated February 28, 1541/2. This edition was much handsomer than the previous one, and was introduced by a graceful and highly flattering dedication to Archbishop Palmier as a friend and patron of letters, an accomplished student of Geography, a wide traveler, and a generous friend of the editor.[67]

The other work of Servetus's Vienne period was in connection with a revised edition of Pagnino's translation of the Bible.[68] Sante Pagnino or Pagnini (Santes or Xantes Pagninus), 1470–1541, was a Dominican monk from Lucca, and had been a pupil of Savonarola. He was one of the company of liberal Catholic humanists in a brilliant intellectual circle at Lyon, where Servetus had undoubtedly known him. A very learned Hebraist, he had published a Hebrew lexicon, and an edition

[65] cf. Baudrier, *op. cit.*, i, 50–52.
[66] Pluresque sanatos passim audivi.
[67] The dedication is reprinted in Mosheim, *Versuch*, p. 404 f.
[68] *Biblia Sacra ex Santis Pagnini tralatione*, etc. Lugduni, 1542, Hugo à Porta (printed by Gaspard Trechsel).

of the Koran in Arabic,[69] and it was said that he had devoted twenty-five years of his life to making an accurate and scholarly translation of the Bible into Latin, which is said to have been the first Bible with chapter divisions. Such a work was much needed, for the current Vulgate version was known to have been made from a very faulty text, and to be full of errors. Pagnino's version had been first published at Lyon in 1527/8 (Servetus had often quoted texts from it in his first book on the Trinity), and already republished at Cologne in 1541; for it was highly esteemed by both Protestants and Catholics for its accuracy, especially in its translation from the Hebrew, and it had been recommended by two Popes, Adrian VI. and Clement VII. But when Pagnino died soon after, he left a large mass of notes, and many marginal corrections on a copy of the recent edition, as though he contemplated a further revision. This copy fell into the hands of the enterprising publisher de la Porte of Lyon, who seized the opportunity of publishing a new edition thoroughly revised in the light of these notes and corrections; and he engaged Servetus to be the editor.

Servetus wrote for this work a noteworthy preface,[70] in which, after urging that one should first learn Hebrew and familiarize himself with Hebrew history before undertaking to read the prophets, he sets forth his view of the interpretation of prophecy. It has, he says, two meanings. The first and literal meaning relates to the events and persons of the writer's own time, and has often been disregarded. But this also foreshadows the true meaning, which is the spiritual one, relating to the mysteries of Christ prefigured in the ancient history. In brief marginal notes which he here and there added to Pagnino's translation, Servetus applied this principle and pointed out the original historical meaning, in order that the mystical or spiritual meaning as applied to Christ might be the more clearly understood as the aim of it all; and he says that he has been at great pains to do this. In all this of course there was nothing heretical, unless to those who, overlooking the historical sense, had considered the mystical one to be the only one involved, and the work was at first well received. But the theologians at Louvain ere

---

[69] Venice, 1530. cf. J. M. Langius, *Dissertatio de prima Alcorani Arabici editione*. It was perhaps from this work or its Latin introduction that Servetus derived the references to the teaching of Mohammed which he makes in his *De Trinitatis erroribus*.

[70] Reprinted in Mosheim, *Versuch*, p. 404 f. English translation in *An Impartial History of Michael Servetus* (London, 1724), pp. 40–44.

long scented heresy in it;[71] and when the Council of Trent in 1546, despite the verdict of the best scholarship, adopted the Vulgate as the authentic text of Scripture to be accepted and used by the Church, Pagnino's superior version was doomed to general oblivion.

According to the publisher's laudatory preface, this edition had been so much changed and enlarged by incorporating the notes of Pagnino as to be practically a new work; but such does not seem to have been the fact, for comparison with the previous edition shows comparatively few changes, and those, being only verbal or stylistic, not important in character.[72] Servetus's actual contribution to the work has been considerably overestimated. In spite of his use of the historical principle in the interpretation of prophecy, it is going too far to herald him as in any serious sense a pioneer of the Higher Criticism two and a half centuries before Eichhorn. Apart from the preface, his work (which can not always be confidently distinguished from Pagnino's) concerns passages mostly in the Psalms and those Prophecies that had been interpreted as messianic, which he wished to show had originally a local and historical meaning, though they are also to be understood in a higher and spiritual sense as referring to Christ.[73] Calvin, who made these one of the items in his prosecution of Servetus at Geneva, declared that the 500 livres (about $100.) that Servetus received for his services was an extravagant charge for a trifling labor.[74]

The most important result of Servetus's work as editor of the Pagnino Bible was its effect upon Servetus himself. It may have had much to do with rekindling his interest in the questions of religion which had so deeply occupied him ten years before, but had since seemed to lie dormant. For henceforth we hear no more of his acting as corrector for the press.[75] When not occupied in his medical practice he was there-

---

[71] It was placed on the Louvain *Index librorum prohibitorum* of 1546 and 1550, reprinted at Rome in 1559. The Spanish Inquisitors were less severe, approving the translation as good enough, but on account of the marginal notes, which were deemed wicked and judaizing, the work was placed on the *Index expurgatorius* of Sotomaior (Madrid, 1567), and of Quiroga (Madrid, 1584). For a list of the passages to be expurgated, see Mosheim, *op. cit.*, pp. 410–414.

[72] So Mosheim declares, *op. cit.* (p. 89), who apparently had compared the two editions.

[73] Examples of the most interesting of these are given by Mosheim, pp. 407–410, and by Willis, *Servetus*, pp. 146–154.

[74] cf. Calvin, viii, 727, 745, 497.

[75] According to Sandius (*Bibliotheca*, p. 11), he is said to have been the author of a devotional book entitled *Desiderius Peregrinus*, originally written in Spanish, but afterwards translated into Latin, Italian, French, German and Dutch, and hence very popular;

fore probably brooding over his old plan of Christianity restored to its
original purity and simplicity by freeing it from the traditions of perverse philosophy and misunderstanding of the Bible. The issue of this
period of his life was his *magnum opus* on the Restoration of Christianity, which was in turn to bring him to a tragic and hideous death.

also known under the title, *Thesaurus Animae*. The style and spirit are totally unlike
Servetus, and there seems no good reason for attributing it to him.

CHAPTER X

SERVETUS: THE "CHRISTIANISMI RESTITUTIO"

EVER SINCE HIS ARRIVAL in France, Servetus had felt constrained to keep his own counsel as to the subject nearest his heart. Apart from the abortive attempt to have a debate about it with Calvin in Paris, there is no evidence that he ventured to discuss religious questions with any one. If they still concerned him, they had to all outward appearance lain dormant with him for ten long years. But in Jean Frellon, printer and publisher at Lyon, for whom, as mentioned in the previous chapter, he corrected several works, he seems to have found a sympathetic spirit. Frellon was nominally a Catholic, and he behaved so discreetly that he was supposed to have remained sound in the faith as long as he lived;[1] but he had in fact no little sympathy with the reforming movement, and he enjoyed the friendship and confidence of Calvin.[2] He was also an intimate friend of Servetus.[3] The latter, having his interest in the thorough reformation of Christian doctrine now rekindled by his editing of the Pagnino Bible, and by his work on the Bibles and other religious works corrected for Trechsel and Frellon, was apparently eager to see whether, even though he had failed with Oecolampadius and Butzer, he could not win Calvin over to a radical reformation of the doctrines of Christianity. For Calvin at Geneva was now leading the constructive thought of Protestantism.

Servetus secured (perhaps by way of Frellon) copies of Calvin's writings,[4] read them eagerly, and seemed to find in them endless points where Calvin had gone hopelessly wrong. With the aid of Frellon as confidential go-between, who would undertake to forward to each the letters of the other, he therefore opened correspondence with Calvin

---

[1] cf. Dominique de Colonia, S.J., *Histoire littéraire de la ville de Lyon* (Lyon, 1728–'30), ii, 611; cited by Mosheim, *Nachrichten*, p. 37.

[2] At the end of a cordial letter to Frellon, Calvin signs himself, "Votre serviteur et entier amy." Calvin, viii, 834.

[3] He addresses a letter to Servetus, "A mon bon frère et amy"; begins it, "Cher frère et amy"; and ends, "Vostre bon frère et amy." *ibid*.

[4] Ipse vero . . . quoscunque meos libros nancisci potuit, etc.; Calvin, viii, 481.

by sending him some of his own writings,[5] and submitting three questions for him to answer: 1, Whether the man Jesus, the crucified, is the Son of God; 2, Whether the kingdom of Christ is in men, when one enters it, and when one is born again; 3, Whether the baptism of Christ should be received in faith, as the Lord's Supper is, and to what purpose these were instituted under the new covenant.[6] Although in retrospect Calvin felt that Servetus had been only trifling with him,[7] for the present he took the questions seriously as those of a sincere seeker after light, and answered them calmly and at length,[8] giving a clear statement of the received doctrine, with supporting texts of Scripture. Since there was danger that heretics might betray themselves or their friends through their correspondence, Calvin wrote over the name of Charles Despeville which he had already often used to conceal his identity; while Servetus (now known in France as Villeneuve) seems to have adopted as pseudonym his true name of Servetus.[9]

Servetus was by no means satisfied with Calvin's answers, for his real purpose was not so much to seek enlightenment as to bring out the errors and inconsistencies in Calvin's position. This became clear in his second letter,[10] in which he took up Calvin's answers one by one, and tried to show that they led to inferences which it was impossible to accept. Calvin, he said, had cut his own throat, and left us with three sons of God instead of one; and his doctrine of regeneration and of baptism were both unsatisfactory, and landed one in inconsistencies. He ended by asking five further questions, at the same time begging Calvin to take the trouble to read what he had written about baptism, as he seemed not yet to have done. It was some time before Calvin found time to reply, and meantime Servetus grew impatient for an answer. Calvin saw little hope (so he wrote to Frellon)[11] of any good result

[5] This is implied in Calvin's answer: "Tu Christum fateris esse filium Dei . . . Tu illas miscendo utramque distruis" (*id. op.*, p. 482). In the light of Servetus's reply (p. 486, *fin.*), the writings were apparently a first recension of what was later published as *Christianismi Restitutio*. According to Bolsec (*Calvin*, p. 19), this was in 1546.

[6] cf. Calvin, viii, 482 ff.

[7] "Tres mihi quaestiones, quasi illudens, solvendas misit"; Calvin, viii, 481.

[8] Calvin, viii, 482–484.

[9] It was a characteristic act of daring, such as he later used in his last work, in which he several times gave clues to his identity which the uninitiated would pass over without recognizing them. The important thing now was that the writer of these letters should not be identified with Michel de Villeneuve of Vienne.   [10] cf. Calvin, viii, 484–486.

[11] Calvin to Frellon, Feb. 13, 1846, viii, 833 f. Translation in Richard Wright, *Apology for Servetus* (Wisbech, 1806), p. 119.

from correspondence with a man of such haughty spirit unless perchance God should give him a change of heart, though he was willing to try once more; but if Servetus were to continue as he was, he was too busy with other matters to be willing to waste time upon one whom he believed to be a Satan trying to tempt him from more useful work. Frellon forwarded the letter to Servetus at Vienne by special messenger.[12]

This second letter,[13] three times as long as the first, expanded and defended what had been said in the previous one, and was written on the whole in surprisingly good spirit; but as Calvin went on he became increasingly irritated at the arrogance and self-conceit of his correspondent, and by the time he was done with the original three questions his patience was exhausted. He was willing, he said, to answer the five new questions proposed, if he could make out what Servetus really wanted; but he was too busy to write whole books for one man. Moreover, Servetus might, if he would, find all the points discussed in his *Institutio*. He ended with asking pardon if he had spoken too strongly in his resentment at Servetus's rude attacks upon sound doctrine; then, having briefly answered the five questions, he referred Servetus once more to the *Institutio*. Servetus replied yet once again, criticizing Calvin's answers, and then concluded: 'Since you fear I am your Satan, I stop. So then return my writings, and farewell. If you really believe that the Pope is Antichrist, you will also believe that the Trinity and infant baptism according to the teaching of the Papacy are the doctrine of demons. Again farewell.'[14]

Calvin did not answer again, but on the same day on which he sent Frellon this letter for Servetus, he wrote another to Guillaume Farel, his fellow-reformer at Neuchâtel, saying that Servetus had lately sent him a letter together with a long volume of his boastful ravings, and offering to come to Calvin (for discussion) if he liked. Calvin however would give him no promise; on the contrary, if Servetus came and he had any authority, he would never let him get away alive.[15] From this

---

[12] cf. Calvin, viii, 833–835; Doumergue, *Calvin*, vi, 260; Mosheim, *Nachrichten*, p. 89 f.

[13] cf. Calvin, viii, 487–495.

[14] cf. Calvin, viii, *prolegomena*, p. xxx f.

[15] Calvin to Farel, Feb. 13, 1546/7, Calvin, xii, 283. Servetus nuper ad me scripsit ac literis adjunxit longum volumen suorum deliriorum cum thrasonica jactantia, me stupenda et hactenus inaudita visurum. Si mihi placeat, huc se venturum recipit. Sed nolo fidem

time on Calvin seems to have cherished implacable enmity to Servetus, and Servetus to have grown increasingly irritating and insulting to Calvin. The correspondence between them was now broken off, but Servetus did not yet abandon his efforts to keep it open, though Calvin would no longer reply, and paid no heed to Servetus's request that his writings be returned.[16] These remained in the possession of Calvin, and were afterwards made exhibits in the prosecution of Servetus at Geneva.[17] Servetus procured such books of Calvin as he could, made insulting notes on the margin, and sent them to Calvin, leaving, as Calvin remarked, not a page free from his vomit.[18] Calvin on his part, convinced by now that Servetus was incorrigibly wicked, and that he desired only to overthrow all traditional religion, held his peace, and paid no more attention than to the braying of an ass.[19]

Servetus next attempted to gain Calvin's attention by sending him a series of thirty letters,[20] in which he set forth his system of doctrine with

meam interponere. Nam si venerit, modo valeat mea auctoritas, vivum exire nunquam patiar.

Calvin's bitter enemy, Bolsec (Calvin, pp. 19–21, 61), mentions a letter of this very date, and to substantially the same effect, but addressed to Pierre Viret of Lausanne. Though it is of course possible that Calvin wrote to both on the same day and in similar terms, Bolsec seems more likely to have confused the names.

Calvin's apologists long denied the existence of such a letter as apocryphal (cf. Mosheim, *Versuch*, pp. 126–138), despite the assertions of Grotius (*Opera*, iv, 503d, Amsterdam, 1679) and Varillas (*Histoire des Révolutions*, etc., iv, 254, Paris, 1689–'90) that they had seen it. But it was rediscovered by Audin (*Histoire de la vie . . . de Calvin*, Paris, 1841, chap. xli), and is extant in Calvin's hand in the Bibliothèque Nationale in Paris (Collection Du Puy, No. 101, 102), and it is now included among Calvin's letters in the authorized edition of his works.

16 They seem for the time to have been passed on to Viret, who had not yet returned them. cf. Calvin, viii, 843.

17 cf. Calvin, viii, 734, n. 2. The writings in question were doubtless a first draft of the *Christianismi Restitutio*, of which a presumed copy is extant in the Bibliothèque Nationale, Paris.

18 cf. Calvin, viii, 748, 481. Quoscunque meos libros nancisci potuit, non destitit insulsis conviciis farcire, ut nullam paginam a suo vomitu relinqueret.

19 De eo homine . . . cui hoc unum fuisse propositum palam est, ut quidquid unquam de religione traditum fuit, nullo adhibito delectu convelleret . . . Mihi interea nihil melius visum fuit quam tacere. Sciunt etiam familiares mei, non magis quam asini ruditu me fuisse commotum. Calvin, viii, 495, 481.

20 These are in fact not so much thirty separate letters as thirty chapters of a more or less continuous work, though occasional endings suggest that they may originally have been composed as nine letters; but they may all have been sent at once. Some of them seem to imply answering letters of Calvin. The letters were appended to the *Restitutio*, and also published in Calvin, viii, 645–714. They are summarized in English in Willis, *Servetus*, pp. 172–190.

supporting scripture texts, much after the manner of his first two works, and with frequent comments on Calvin's views. Still Calvin made no sign. Servetus therefore turned to Calvin's fellow-reformers. He addressed three letters to Abel Pouppin, Calvin's colleague at Geneva; but he, doubtless advised by Calvin, made no reply, so that in his third letter Servetus burst out impatiently, exclaiming, 'Instead of one God you have a three-headed Cerberus, instead of faith you have a fatal dream, and you say that good works are nothing but empty pictures.' And then, as if in prophetic foreboding of his approaching fate, he added, 'That for this matter I must die, I know full well; but for all that I am not faint of heart, that I may become a disciple worthy of my Master. . . . Farewell, expect no further letter from me.' [21] Yet one more attempt Servetus made. In the summer of 1548 he wrote to Pierre Viret, the reformer at Lausanne, in much the same tone as to the others, and though the letter was unsigned Viret recognized the hand. Disposed to answer, but doubtful what to say, he sent the letter to Calvin and asked his advice. Calvin thought it a waste of time to have further words with so stubborn a man, and would have no more to do with him.[22]

Servetus had at last to realize that he could hope to make no impression upon the reformers in French Switzerland. With them he had failed as hopelessly as sixteen years before with Oecolampadius and Butzer. Now as then he was driven to the only course remaining, the use of the printing-press. During the next four years or so, therefore, in such leisure time as his profession left him, he gave himself to preparing for the press the text of his *magnum opus*, of which the main body

---

[21] Evangelium vestrum est sine uno deo, sine fide vera, sine bonis operibus. Pro uno deo habetis tricipitem cerberum, pro fide vera habetis fatale somnium, et opera bona dicitis esse inanas picturas . . . Mihi ob eam rem moriendum esse certe scio, sed non propterea animo deficior, ut fiam discipulus similis praeceptori. Vale, et a me non amplius literas exspecta. cf. Calvin, viii, 750 f; also in Mosheim, *Versuch*, p. 414 f.

[22] Viret to Calvin, August 25, 1548. Quum proximis diebus ad te scriberem, oblitus sum ad te mittere quae ad me Servetus scripsit. Quem hujus scripti autorem minime fuissem suspicatus, quia suum nomen suppressit, nisi ejus agnovissem manum, et ex argumento conjecturam fecissem. Ejus ad te scripta mitto per hunc tabellarium uxoris meae fratrum, super quibus tuam velim mihi sententiam significes, hoc est, num putes mihi esse respondendum, quid et quomodo, si modo id tibi non grave est nimis. . . Remitte scripta Serveti. Calvin, xiii, 33; cf. viii, 776, 780, No. 14.

Calvin to Viret, Sept. 1, 1548. Puto aliquando te legisse quae Serveto responderam. Tandem nolui cum desperata hominis haeretici pervicacia diutius certare. At sane Pauli monitioni obtemperandum erit. Nunc te aggreditur. Videbis quousque refellendis ejus deliriis insistere debeas. A me nihil posthac extorquebit. *ibid.*, xiii, 42.

was to consist of the work of which he had sent a first draft to Calvin
for his criticism and which Calvin had failed to return to him, and also
of the thirty letters that had followed that. He had of course retained
a copy of both. Dr. Jérôme Bolsec, who had fallen into bitter controversy with Calvin at Geneva in 1551 over the subject of predestination, and was consequently banished from Geneva, and who later returning to the Catholic Church spent much of the rest of his life in
open hostility to Calvin and his memory, declared in a life of Calvin
published in 1577 that Calvin (it must have been at this period) wrote
a letter to Cardinal de Tournon, then Viceroy in France, accusing Servetus of heresy, whereat the Cardinal broke out laughing that one
heretic should accuse another. He added that he and several others had
been shown this letter by the Cardinal's secretary.[23] Not too great
credence need be given this statement in itself; but Servetus apparently
believed that Calvin had taken some such action, for Calvin himself,
writing in 1554, complained that four years previously Servetus had
spread such a story in Venice and Padua.[24] It is perhaps not without
significance that Calvin, instead of denying the story strongly and categorically, as he could easily have done, contents himself — he had been
bred to the law — with dwelling upon the intrinsic improbability of the
charge being true.

Concerning Servetus's life during the four years after he broke off his
correspondence with the Swiss reformers, we have no direct information. His most absorbing interest, however, will have been in revising
and preparing for the press the text of the work that he had for some
years previously been composing. Early in 1552 it was at last finished;
and the question now arose as to where he should get it printed. He
first attempted to have this done in Switzerland; and since at this time
he had at Basel an intimate friend, about whom we know no more than

[23] Calvin . . . escrivit une letre au Reverendissime seigneur Cardinal de Tournon, pour
lors vice roy en France, et en icelle letre il accusoit Servet d'héresie dequoy ledict seigneur
Cardinal se print fort à rire disant qu'un héretique accusoit l'autre. Ceste letre me fut
monstrée et à plusieurs par monsieur du Gabre secrétaire du dict seigneur Cardinal. cf.
Bolsec, *Calvin*, p. 21 f.; also the "Historia de morte Serveti" in (Castellio's) *Contra libellum Calvini*, 1562, p. M ii.; Sunt qui dicunt Calvinum ipsum scripsisse ipsi Cardinali in
hanc sententiam, Si tam religionis studiosus esses, quam tu esse simulas, non patereris
Servetum qui est apud vos, etc. cf. also Mosheim, *Versuch*, pp. 234–237: "Ob Johann
Calvin den Serveto als einen Ketzer bey dem Kardinal von Tournon angegeben habe."

[24] Jam fluxerunt anni quatuor ex quo hanc de me fabulam commentus est Servetus
ipse, et spargendam Venetiis (et à Padoue) curavit; Calvin, viii, 479.

that his name was Marrinus, and that he was acquainted with Servetus's true name,[25] he sent him the manuscript to manage. Unfortunately Marrinus found it not safe, even if possible, to get it printed there, and he returned it by a trusty messenger whom Servetus had sent to fetch it. A printer was therefore sought in Vienne itself. Now there happened to be at Vienne a publisher named Balthazar Arnoullet, who had lately arrived from Lyon, and was secretly sympathetic with the Protestant movement, and was at least nominally a friend of Calvin.[26] The director of his press was his brother-in-law, Guillaume Guéroult, who had formerly lived at Geneva as a member of the liberal party opposed to Calvin, but for fear of punishment for his scandalous conduct there had fled and come to Vienne.[27] To these two Servetus addressed himself. He gave them to understand that though his book was against Calvin, Melanchthon and other heretics, he had strong reasons for having it printed without indication of author, publisher or place. As an inducement, he would himself bear the expense of printing, would correct the proof, and would pay them the generous bonus of one hundred *écus* each. This was agreed to.[28] Presses were set up in great secrecy in an abandoned house, and three printers, ignorant of the character of the book, were occupied with it from Michaelmas till early in January. The work was done so secretly that no one else at Vienne had the least suspicion of it;[29] and the manuscript was burned page by page as fast as printed.[30]

Throughout Christian history efforts to reform Christianity have commonly aimed at a return to the literal standards of primitive Christianity rather than at adaptation of its principles to changed conditions of thought or life. The idea of a restitution, or restoration, was thus popular in the Reformation period, especially in Anabaptist circles,[31]

[25] It has been guessed that he was perhaps brother to the Pierre Merrin to be mentioned below; and since he inscribed his letter to Michael Serveto, Medico, he may have been an old Basel friend of earlier days. cf. d'Artigny, ii, 73 f; Calvin, viii, 835. Others conjecture with much plausibility that d'Artigny, to whom we owe this detail, mistook, reading Marrinus instead of Martinus, i.e., Borrhäus, of Basel, to whom Castellio says Servetus sent the Ms of his work. cf. Calvin, xiv, 309; Buisson, *Castellion*, ii, 478.

[26] cf. Doumergue, *Calvin*, vi, 265 f; A. Rilliet, *Relation du procès criminel contre Michel Servet* (Genève, 1844), p. 146.

[27] cf. Calvin, xxi, 146; Doumergue, *op. cit.*, Guéroult would thus have had a personal motive for being willing to facilitate the publication of a work calculated to annoy Calvin.

[28] cf. d'Artigny, ii, 74.

[29] *id. op.*, ii, 116 f, 78.

[30] cf. Calvin, viii, 781.   [31] cf. Rembert, *Wiedertäufer*, pp. 242–246.

and it had already been accented by Johannes Campanus, Bernhard Rothmann, Urbanus Rhegius, David Joris and others. Hence it was natural enough for Servetus to entitle his work *Christianismi Restitutio*: and it has not escaped notice that this title stood in a sort of contrast to that of Calvin's *Institutio*. Of this work an edition of 1,000 copies [32] was printed. Servetus had all the copies sent to Lyon as soon as printed. Of these, five bales, said to contain only blank paper, were deposited with the type-founder Pierre Merrin to be held until called for that they might (so it was supposed) be sent to Italy; while Frellon undertook to send the rest to Frankfurt.[33] Of these latter a part was consigned to Jacques Bertet (a bookseller lately removed from Lyon to Geneva, who acted as agent for Arnoullet's publications) to be put on sale at the next Easter fair, where he had a stall.[34] Yet another lot seems to have been consigned to the well-known printer and bookseller, Robert Estienne (Stephanus), who had part of them held at Frankfurt for sale at the Easter and Michaelmas fairs, and the rest sent to his shop at Geneva, of course without being aware of their heretical nature, for he was a close friend of Calvin.[35]

Calvin not only had, as we have seen, the original draft of a large part of the *Restitutio*, but in some way unknown to us he early came into possession of a printed copy of it. It has generally been said [36] that Frellon took the liberty of forwarding one out of the quantity deposited with him, not foreseeing the possible danger to Servetus, since he had already forwarded the draft of the work without evil results. But Servetus may have sent Calvin a copy directly,[37] or perhaps a copy came by way of Estienne. At all events, Calvin had a copy several days before the end of February, hence only some six weeks from the time when the first copies had reached Lyon. Nothing was easier than for

---

[32] According to his testimony at Geneva (Calvin, viii, 749). D'Artigny (ii, 75), says 800, but not as a part of Servetus's testimony.

[33] cf. d'Artigny, ii, 78, 118.

[34] The Frankfurt fair in the sixteenth century was Europe's greatest book market. cf. Rilliet, *op. cit.*, p. 144; W. K. Tweedie, *Calvin and Servetus* (Edinburgh, 1846), p. 239; Doumergue, *Calvin*, vi, 265, n. 6; Calvin's letter to the Frankfurt pastors, Aug. 27, 1553, Calvin, xiv, 599 f.

[35] cf. Mosheim, *Versuch*, p. 261 ff.; Doumergue, vi, 269–271.

[36] Repeating d'Artigny's statement (ii, 78), which is perhaps as likely to have been an inference as to have been derived from Frellon's no longer extant deposition of May 23; *ibid.*, p. 68.

[37] cf. Doumergue, vi, 270–272; N. Weiss, in *Bull. Prot. Franç.*, lvii (1908), 395, 399.

him to identify the author of the book with his correspondent of a few years before, who again was already identified both with Servetus and with Villeneuve, since he had excused himself to Calvin for using an assumed name in France.[38]

At about the same time the name of the printer leaked out at Geneva, though through what channel is not known. But Guéroult had belonged to the party there opposed to Calvin, and had had to flee the city to escape prosecution. He would thus have had a motive for letting it be known that Arnoullet (supposed to be Calvin's friend) had published a book strongly attacking Calvin and his doctrine. This could have been done through Guéroult's nephew at Geneva, one Simon du Bosc; for Guéroult also had a falling-out with Arnoullet over business affairs, and soon afterwards, having returned to Geneva, brought suit against him there.[39] If Calvin still cherished in his heart the wish that Servetus's pernicious activities might be brought to an end, as those of an abandoned heretic infinitely dangerous to the souls of men, and aiming to overthrow the very foundations of the true Christian religion, the stage was now well set for the final act; for the flagrant crime had now been committed on Catholic soil at Vienne, though the evidence was all in Protestant hands at Geneva. But before going on to tell how Servetus was betrayed to the Inquisition at Vienne, and of the trial that followed, something should be said of the book itself.

In Servetus's final work he set forth, though by no means in systematic form, his whole plan for a thorough reformation of Christianity by restoring the doctrine and teaching of the Christian religion to their original form.[40] The whole work consists of six main parts. The first

[38] cf. the letter of de Trie to Arneys, March 31, 1553; En la dernière Epistre que vous avez receu vous trouverez ce qu'il déclare de son nom, lequel il avoit déguisé: car il s' excuse de ce qu'il s'est fait nommer Villeneufve, combien que son nom soit Servetus alias Reves, disant qu'il a pris son nom de la ville dont il est natif; d'Artigny, ii, 95; Calvin, viii, 843.

[39] cf. *supra*, p. 202, n. 3. cf. also Arnoullet's letter to Bertet, Calvin, viii, 752 ff.; Doumergue, vi, 265–268. De Trie in naming the printers (Calvin, viii, 843; d'Artigny, ii, 96) withholds the source of his information: Quant à l'imprimeur, je ne vous mande pas les indices par lequels nous avons entendu que c'estoit Balthasard Arnoullet et Guillaume Guéroult son beau frère mais tant y a que nous en sommes bien assure.

[40] *Christianismi Restitutio. Totius Ecclesiae Apostolicae est ad sua limina vocatio, in integrum restituta cognitione Dei, fidei Christi, justificationis nostrae, regenerationis baptismi et coenae domini manducationis. Restituto denique nobis regno caelesti, Babylonis impiae captivitate soluta, et Antichristo cum suis penitus destructo.* (Viennae), MDLIII. 734 pp., 8°. At the end of the book the initials M. S. V. (Michael Servetus Villanovanus).

part comprises seven books on the divine Trinity, of which the last two are two Dialogues on the divine Trinity. Although these have some-times been confounded with Servetus's first two works of 1531–'32, they are by no means identical with the earlier works or even revisions of them, of which Servetus apparently dared bring no copy into France. In a reverently expressed preface [41] Servetus declares his purpose to set forth that way of light without which no one can read the Holy Scrip-tures, nor know God, nor become a Christian, and says that having formerly treated this subject he now feels compelled out of regard to divine truth to treat of it again, being moved thereto by some divine impulse, since the time is fulfilled.[42] The five books on the Trinity in a broad sense cover the same ground as the seven books on the Errors of the Trinity (1531), and the essence of their teaching remains the same; but though Servetus sometimes repeats the very words or phrases as though remembered after over twenty years, there are many differ-ences of matter and order and expression, and many omissions and addi-tions. The two Dialogues have a closer resemblance to their prototype, which suggests that of this he may have retained a copy.

The second part of the work is made up of three books on Faith, the Righteousness of Christ's Kingdom, and Love. They are only a more detailed statement of the doctrine previously set forth in the four brief chapters following the Dialogues of 1532. The third part consists of four books on Regeneration from above, and on the Kingdom of Antichrist. Here Servetus leaves speculative doctrines behind and en-ters a new field in which he deals with the practical side of the Christian faith; especially with the means of grace, preaching, baptism and the Lord's Supper. The fourth part contains the thirty letters of Servetus to Calvin mentioned above; the fifth enumerates sixty signs of the king-dom of Antichrist; and the final part is an Apology in which he pas-sionately defends himself against the attacks which Melanchthon in the second edition of his *Loci Communes* has made upon his earlier works

---

Page-for-page (but not line-for-line) reprint, (Nürnberg, 1790). Partial reprint (edition suppressed while incomplete), (London, 1723). German translation by Bernhard Spiess, *Wiederherstellung des Christentums* (Wiesbaden, 1895–'96).

[41] The Edinburgh University copy has a Ms of what is apparently an earlier recension of this preface, in some interesting particulars differing from the printed copy.

[42] Causa haec tua est . . . quae divino quodam impulsu tractanda sese mihi obtulit, cum essem de tua veritate sollicitus, Tractando aliquando coepi, et nunc iterum tractare cogor, quia completum est vere tempus, p. 4.

on the Trinity, even turning his defence into a violent attack. This Apology is deemed the best part of the whole work, and an excellent compendium of Servetus's system of thought.

It would little serve the purpose of the present work, and it would be tedious in itself, to give anything like a detailed summary of the contents of this chief work of Servetus.[43] It will be enough briefly to sketch the most striking features of his proposed reformation of Christianity in its relation to his personal fate and to the development of religious thought. After more than twenty years of dwelling upon the subject, Servetus was more firmly convinced than ever that the Church wanted thorough reformation, and that the reforms introduced by Luther and Calvin had not gone nearly far enough, nor reached the heart of the matter. Of three fundamental points in Christian theology, Trinity, Incarnation, Redemption, the reformers had not ventured to revise the first two at all, and they had dealt with the third only in very unsatisfactory fashion. He felt that Christian theology urgently required to be reconstructed from bottom to top, both in its speculative doctrines and in its relation to practical life; and it was his distinction in this book to be the first to propose a thorough-going plan, however imperfect, for carrying out such a reconstruction. In doing this he took a position independent of both the Catholic and the Protestant systems, and in his new construction he aimed to reject the false and retain the true in each.

Servetus was the more impatient to see this work set on foot, because he was convinced that the fall of the kingdom of Antichrist (the Roman Church), and the consequent establishment of the millennial reign of Christ upon the earth, was at hand; and he had lost hope that a thorough restoration of pure Christianity might be expected from the reformers. He dated the beginning of the corruption of the Church and the rise of Antichrist from the time of the Emperor Constantine and Pope Sylvester in the fourth century, when the Emperor became a monk and Bishop Sylvester was transformed into a Pope-king [44] (i.e., when

---

[43] An excellent synopsis is given in Mosheim, *Versuch*, pp. 346–372. Servetus's doctrinal system as a whole is surveyed at length in Henri Tollin's *Das Lehrsystem Michael Servet's, genetisch dargestellt*; 4 vols. (Gütersloh, 1876–'78), and some of its more important phases are separately treated by the same author in articles to be cited below. cf. also G. C. B. Pünjer, *De Michaelis Serveti doctrina* (Jena, 1886); E. Doumergue, *Calvin*, vi, 224–253, 'La Théologie de Servet'.

[44] Quod totum plane a Constantini et Sylvestri tempore factum videmus . . . Constantino imperatore facto tunc monacho, et Sylvestro in Papam regem converso, necesse fuit faciem orbis inverti; *Restitutio*, p. 398.

the civil State began to interfere in the affairs of the Church, and the Papacy entered upon temporal power), and the world was thus turned upside down; when moreover at the Council of Nicaea the doctrine of three persons in the Godhead, invented by Satan to draw the minds of men away from the knowledge of the true Christ,[45] was imposed, and the practice of infant baptism began to prevail. Reckoning from the mystical number in Rev. xii. 6, he concluded that the 1260 years of the reign of Antichrist were nearly at an end. Though his ideas of the millennium were not gross and material like those of many of the Ana-baptists, yet he expected to live to see its advent. He thought that he saw many signs of the approaching fight between the archangel Michael and his hosts against Antichrist (Dan. xii. 1; Rev. xii. 7), in which he expected to take part as one of the first fighters.[46] He deemed both Catholic and Protestant Christianity hopelessly corrupted in doctrine and practice. He exhausted the vocabulary of epithets by which to ex-press the abomination of Antichrist (the Pope) and of Babylon (Rome), and outraged religious feeling by referring to the Trinity as a three-fold Geryon, a three-headed Cerberus, and a triple monster Chimaera.[47] Nor did he spare the reformers, heaping upon them the names of ancient heretics, and calling Calvin a thief and a robber.[48] His attitude toward them grew increasingly violent as his indignation continued to grow, and he concluded one section of his work with this reproach of the re-formers for their halting attitude toward a thorough reform: 'Whoever truly believes that the Pope is Antichrist will also truly believe that the papistical Trinity, infant baptism, and the other sacraments of the Papacy, are the doctrines of demons.' [49]

When we come to the constructive part of Servetus's system as shown in his *Restitutio*, we see that his teaching here, although it shows ma-turer thought, is not so much new as it is a fuller development of that in his early works. His proposed reconstitution of Christianity springs largely from two roots, the one the speculative doctrine of God, the other the more nearly practical doctrine of baptism. He firmly believed

---

[45] *id. op.*, p. 22.

[46] In his twentieth letter to Calvin, *id. op.*, p. 628: In hujus ecclesiae restitutione jugiter laboro . . . quod pugnae illi Michaelis me immisceam, et pios omnes misceri desiderem.

[47] cf. *Restitutio*, pp. 456 f, 466 f, 700; Tollin, 'Der Antichrist Michael Servet's' *Zeit-schrift für wissenschaftliche Theologie*, xxii (1879), 351–374.

[48] cf. *Restitutio*, pp. 700 f, 614.

[49] *id. op.*, p. 670; cf. *supra*, p. 70.

that thorough reconstruction of Christianity must begin with a reform of its teaching about God, as expressed in the doctrine of the Trinity. His objections to this doctrine in the form then current in the Church have been stated in a previous chapter in connection with his first book. His treatment of it now shows that in the meantime his thinking has been much influenced by the Platonic philosophy into which he had been initiated years before by Dr. Champier, and by reading of Hermetic literature, from both of which sources he frequently quotes. One that would well understand Servetus's latest thought of God must first familiarize himself with these sources. His doctrine of God is very noble: the mind fails when thinking of him, for he is incomprehensible, invisible, inaudible, intangible, ineffable, immeasurable, transcending all things, above all light, being, spirit or any object of thought.[50] Hence he can be known only through the ways in which he has chosen to manifest himself to us, through eternal wisdom, through the word that he has uttered, through Christ, through created things.[51] For he fills all things, on earth and even in hell. It is his presence in them that gives them their existence. God creates nothing to which he does not present and communicate himself. He is everywhere, the complete essence of all things. He so contains in himself the essence of all things that by his own essence alone, without another creature, he can here manifest himself as fire, as air, as stone, as amber, as a twig, as a flower, as whatever else you will.[52]

Small wonder that in view of such teachings Servetus should have been set down as a pantheist; for though he does not indeed identify God with the created universe, but rather makes the universe a manifestation of God dwelling within it, yet pantheism is the nearest system of thought to which most would incline to assign it.[53] Of course in such a doctrine of God there was no room for anything like the accepted doctrine of the Trinity. In his former works, as we have seen in a previous chapter, Servetus still accepted belief in a Trinity, not in the traditional sense, indeed, but as a threefold manifestation of divinity in three won-

[50] *Restitutio*, p. 110 f.

[51] *id. op.*, pp. 111, 588.

[52] *id. op.*, pp. 240, 278, 588 f; cf. Calvin, viii, 496.

[53] cf. Tollin, 'Servet's Pantheismus,' *Zeitschrift für wissenschaftliche Theologie*, xix (1876), 241–263; Émile Saisset, 'Doctrine philosophique et religieuse de Michel Servet,' *Revue des Deux Mondes*, xviii (Feb. 15, 1848), 585–618; reprinted in his *Mélanges d' histoire* (Paris, 1859).

derful 'dispositions.' Here, however, even this view has faded away before the grander conception of a God who is manifested in everything.
His previous views of the Holy Spirit and of Christ are retained in
somewhat expanded form, but actually they stand in the shadow of the
all-embracing doctrine of God. The God-man of the theologians has
disappeared from the plan; though as an object of religious worship in
mystical devotion Christ continues to be the centre of Servetus's personal religious experience.

Turning from speculative doctrine to practical, Servetus finds in baptism the second cardinal doctrine calling for reformation. In the practice of infant baptism he sees the source of all the corruption in the life
of the Church; for as it is baptism that is supposed to regenerate one
and introduce him into the kingdom of heaven, infant baptism is a
delusion, formally admitting into the Church those that in the nature
of the case are not yet capable of regeneration; since one can not really
be regenerated unless he is guilty of sin, and he can not sin without
knowledge of good and evil, which is not attained before the twentieth
year.[54] Baptism must be preceded by faith and repentance, which are
inconceivable for children; and baptism itself, if the example of Jesus
be followed, will not be sought before the thirtieth year.[55] At length,
after canvassing through many pages the harm that comes to individuals, and the corruption to the Church, through this practice, Servetus's indignation breaks its bonds as he concludes this topic with the
main part of his work thus: 'I call infant baptism a detestable abomination, a quenching of the Holy Spirit, a laying waste of the Church of
God, a confounding of the whole Christian profession, an annulling of
the renewal made by Christ, and a trampling under foot of his whole
kingdom.' [56] As a natural consequence of his view of baptism, the effort was made in his trial at Geneva to prove Servetus an Anabaptist,
and thus to fasten upon him the stigma generally attaching to that sect.
However, he need not necessarily have got this view from Anabaptist
sources, and he did not adopt the most conspicuous and objectionable
doctrines of their movement. As has been said, he did not hold their
fanatical view of the millennium; and in the present dispensation he

[54] cf. Tollin, 'Michael Servet über den Geist der Wiedergeburt,' *Zeitschrift für wissenschaftliche Theologie*, xxv (1882), 310–327.

[55] cf. *Restitutio*, pp. 500, 363, 564 f, 472, 512.

[56] *id. op.*, p. 576.

approved of one's acting as judge and holding high office, of bearing the sword to preserve order, though not of killing except as a last resort; and of bearing witness under oath, though not of taking vows for the future.[57]

It is a surprising circumstance that though Servetus put into his *magnum opus* the results of a lifetime's serious reflection on religious subjects, and produced a work which, despite all its eccentricities and shortcomings, showed marked independence of thought in its proposals for a radical reformation of Christian theology, and might, had it not been at once so completely suppressed, have exercised a marked influence in modifying Christian thought, yet his fame in the world to-day rests hardly at all upon this work, but upon two things relatively incidental: that under Calvin he was burned at the stake for denying the doctrine of the Trinity, and that he was the reputed discoverer of the pulmonary circulation of the blood. Indeed a competent medical writer has declared that the few pages in which he treated of this latter subject have done more for his reputation than all the rest of his work put together.[58] This phase of his work therefore deserves passing mention here.

In the fifth book of the *Restitutio*, while treating of the Holy Spirit, Servetus reaches a point where he thinks the matter may be made plainer by an illustration from anatomy (p. 169). In order to understand how the divine spirit is communicated to man, one must understand how its real complement, the human spirit, is produced in the human body; and the human spirit, as Scripture teaches (Gen. ix. 3; Lev. xvii. 11; Deut. xii. 23, though not so obviously in the English version) has its seat in the blood. Now the living spirit, he says, is produced by a mixture in the lungs of inspired air with blood which the right ventricle of the heart communicates to the left; *but this communication does not take place through the middle partition of the heart, as is commonly believed, but by a grand device the blood is driven from the right ven-*

---

[57] *id. op.*, pp. 665 f, 430. For studies of Servetus's view of doctrines not detailed here, cf. Tollin, 'Die Zeugung Jesu in Servet's *Restitutio Christianismi*,' *Zeitschrift für wissenschaftliche Theologie*, xxiv (1881), 68–88; 'Servet's Lehre von der Gotteskindschaft,' *Jahrbücher für protestantische Theologie*, ii, (1876), 422–450; 'Servet's Anthropologie und Soteriologie,' *Zeitschrift für wissenschaftliche Theologie*, xxiii (1880), 323–343; 'Michael Servet's Teufelslehre,' *ibid.*, xix (1876), 371–388; 'Servet's Lehre von der Welt', *ibid.*, xxii (1879), 239–249.

[58] Albert Dastre, 'Les trois époques d'une découverte scientifique,' *Revue des deux Mondes*, lxiv (Aug. 1, 1884), 647.

tricle of the heart by a long course through the lungs.[59] This brief and clear statement, made only by the way, in order to illustrate a theological point, marks a revolutionary step in the development of the anatomy of the human body.

It was well known that the blood in some way passes from the right ventricle to the left. But Galen, the father of physiology, had taught in the second century that the blood passes from the one ventricle to the other through minute orifices in the middle partition which, though not discernible in a dead body, are open in a living one. This teaching, to be sure, was not based on experiment, but it seemed a necessity of the case, since no other explanation could be discovered to account for the facts. So completely, in fact, did Galen dominate medical opinion that for fourteen centuries this view was blindly accepted on his authority, and until Servetus no one had ventured to challenge it. Servetus's statement contained two important new contributions to human knowledge: that the middle partition of the heart is not permeable as formerly believed, and that the blood passes from one side of the heart to the other through the lungs by the network of the pulmonary arteries and the pulmonary veins. This did not indeed mark the discovery of the general circulation of the blood — that distinction was reserved for William Harvey in his *De circulatione sanguinis*, published seventy-five years later, in 1628 — but it did establish the fact of the lesser or pulmonary circulation, which was an important step toward Harvey's discovery.

Epoch-making in anatomy as was the doctrine here stated by Servetus, it was lost to contemporary thought since, as we shall see, the book in which it was published was so soon and so thoroughly suppressed; and it was not until 1694 that the passage on the circulation was brought to light and reprinted in England.[60] Meantime, in 1559,

---

[59] *Restitutio*, p. 170. Vitalis spiritus ex aere inspirato et subtilissimo sanguine componitur et nutritur. Vitalis spiritus in sinistro cordis ventriculo suam originem habet, juvantibus maxime pulmonibus ad ipsius generationem . . . Generatur ex facta in pulmonibus mixtione inspirati aeris cum elaborato subtili sanguine, quem dexter ventriculus cordis sinistro communicat. Fit autem communicatio haec non per parietem cordis medium, ut vulgo creditur, sed magno artificio a dextro cordis ventriculo, longo per pulmones ductu, agitatur sanguis subtilis. The passage is given at length in Mosheim, *op. cit.*, p. 499; and (in facsimile) in William Osler, *Michael Servetus* (London, 1909), p. 28 f.; also in translation in the same work, p. 26 f.; Robert Willis, *Servetus*, pp. 206–210; and Alexander Gordon, in *Theological Review*, xv (1878), 419 f.

[60] By William Wotton (Chaplain to the Earl of Nottingham), in his *Reflections upon*

six years after the publication of Servetus's work, Matteo Realdo Colombo, who had in 1554 succeeded Vesalius in the chair of anatomy at Padua, published (posthumously) an account of the pulmonary circulation in terms which in some respects resemble those used by Servetus;[61] and in this he declares that no one hitherto has noticed or written of the obvious facts.[62] Colombo states that he had begun his work many years before.[63] What is thought to have been perhaps a copy of a first draft of Servetus's work, dating from as early as 1546, is also extant.[64]

Hence a heated controversy has long been rife between those that would credit the discovery of the pulmonary circulation to Servetus who first published it, and those maintaining that he discovered nothing, but was simply the first to print, without suggesting the slightest claim to originality, a reference to a discovery made by Colombo or some other. Three competing views of the question are put forth. First, that Servetus made the discovery, and that some printed or manuscript copy of the *Restitutio* reaching Italy fell into the hands of Colombo, who a few years later, relying on the fact that Servetus's book had never become known to the world, published the discovery as his own. This view rests upon assumptions of which there is no proof. Second, that Servetus had either been at Padua in the forties, and had there heard Colombo lecture on the subject (of this also there is no proof, since the

---

Ancient and Modern Learning (London, 1694), pp. 211–213 (also 1697 and 1705). One or two copies of the *Restitutio* were at that time in England, and in one of these the passage was seen by Dr. Charles Bernard, surgeon at St. Bartholomew's Hospital, London, who brought it to Wotton's attention. Mosheim, (*Versuch*, p. 254), was in error in crediting the first discovery of the passage to the Danish anatomist, Thomas Bartholin. Reference to the passage in Bartholin cited by him (*Anatomia Reformata*, p. 594, Leiden, 1673, also 1694 with same paging) shows that Mosheim hastily mistook P. Paulus Servita Venetus (Fra Paolo Sarpi, a Servite monk, who had also made some contributions to anatomy) for Servetus.

[61] For the parallels, cf. Tollin, 'Ueber Colombo's Antheil an der Entdeckung des Blutkreislaufs,' *Archiv für pathologische Anatomie*, xci (1888), 57–61.

[62] Quod nemo hactenus aut animadvertit, aut scriptum reliquit; licet maxime ab omnibus animadvertendum. *De re anatomica* (Venetiis, 1559), p. 177.

[63] Quod abhinc multos annos inchoaveram. *id. op.* (Paris, 1562), preface.

[64] In the Bibliothèque Nationale, Paris, Ms No. Fonds Latins, 18.212. For collation of this passage with the printed text, cf. Gordon, *loc. cit.* That this Ms can certainly be dated as early as 1546, and that it is really a copy of a first draft, instead of an inaccurate copy of the printed text, are points not wholly beyond debate. cf. Doumergue, *Calvin*, vi, 214; Tollin, 'Die Franzosen und die Entdeckung des Blutkreislaufs,' *Archiv für pathologische Anatomie*, xciv (1883), 106 f.

matriculation records for Padua before 1600 are no longer extant),[65] or else had learned of the new view from students that brought it from Padua to Paris (of which again no proof is extant), and so published it incidentally as an established though not yet generally recognized truth. Finally, that Servetus and Colombo each made the discovery independently of the other, as has more than once been the case in the history of science. Plausible arguments are made for each of these views, though each is open to objections that make acceptance of it more or less difficult. In the absence of positive and decisive evidence it is not likely that the question can ever be settled beyond controversy. The one fact placed beyond all dispute is that, whoever first made the discovery, and whatever its importance, the first to publish it in print was Servetus.[66]

[65] cf. Dardier's Appendix to Tollin's *Michel Servet Portrait-caractère* (Paris, 1879), p. 69.

[66] Recent researches seem to show that Servetus's views were anticipated early in the thirteenth century by Ibn An-Nafîs, an Arabian anatomist of Damascus and Cairo, and recorded in a Ms first unearthed some seven centuries later, and published in 1935. cf. Bayon, *op. cit. infra*, iii (1938), 497 f.

The literature on the circulation controversy is very extensive. The most important items in it are the following: Giulio Ceradini, *Qualche appunto storico-critico intorno alla scoperta della circolazione del sangue* (Genova, 1875), opposing Servetus's claim; Henri Tollin, *Die Entdeckung des Blutkreislaufs durch Michael Servet* (Jena, 1876), defending Servetus; Ceradini, *Difesa della mia memoria intorno alla scoperta*, etc. (Milano, 1876), answering Tollin — both Ceradini's works reprinted in his *Opere* (2 vols., Milano, 1906); Achille Chéreau, *Michel Servet et la circulation pulmonaire* (Paris, 1879), critical of Tollin; Charles Dardier, appendix to Tollin's *Michel Servet Portrait-Caractère* (Paris, 1879), answering Chéreau; Édouard Turner, 'Remarques au sujet de la lecture . . . par M. Chéreau,' *Progrès Médical*, vii (Aug. 9, 16, 1879), 631 f, 651 f, supporting Servetus's claim; Emmanuel Orientin Douen, 'Une polémique récente,' *Revue Politique et Littéraire*, xviii (1880), 801, reviewing the controversy; Tollin, 'Ueber Colombo's Antheil an der Entdeckung des Blutkreislaufs,' *Archiv für pathologische Anatomie und Physiologie*, xvi (Jan. 2, 1883), 39–66; H. P. Bayon, 'William Harvey, Physician and Biologist: his precursors, opponents and successors,' *Annals of Science*, iv (1939), 65–106.

CHAPTER XI

THE DENUNCIATION AND TRIAL OF
SERVETUS AT VIENNE

WITH HIS MAGNUM OPUS, the fruit of a quarter of a century of prayerful reflection upon the reformation of a long corrupted Christian religion, at last off the press and secretly stored until the Easter fair should begin to spread it through the world, Servetus doubtless felt no small measure of happiness as he went on his rounds among his patients at Vienne. He can not have dreamed what trouble was brewing for him over the border at Geneva. He knew indeed that Calvin was in the secret of the assumed name that he bore in France, and knew that as soon as Calvin should see his new book he would recognize its authorship. He had also long had a presentiment that if he once came within Calvin's reach his life would not be safe.[1] But he was safe on French soil, where he had done nothing openly to compromise himself, he had a circle of very distinguished friends, and he was to all appearance an irreproachable Catholic. It can hardly have entered into his calculations that he might be betrayed into Catholic hands by Protestants themselves. Yet so it was to happen.

At just this time there was living at Geneva a young merchant named Guillaume de Trie.[2] He was of a distinguished family of the French nobility, and had been sheriff at Lyon, but having accepted the Protestant faith he had fled to Geneva in 1549, where in 1555 he became a citizen, and eventually a member of the Council of 200. He was one of the most distinguished of the many Protestant refugees at Geneva. He was son-in-law of Guillaume de Budé, the noted French humanist and founder of the Collège de France. At Geneva he was one of Calvin's close friends, and his near neighbor, and when he died in 1561 he made Calvin guardian of his children, who found in him a second father.[3]

[1] *v. supra*, p. 136, n. 21.
[2] cf. Aymon Galiffe, *Notices Généalogiques sur les familles Génevoises* (ed. 2, Genève, 1908), iv, 248 ff.
[3] cf. *Bull. Prot. Franç.*, x (1861), 216.

He was a fanatical Protestant, and his relatives at Lyon much lamented his departure from the Catholic faith. His cousin, Antoine Arneys, therefore wrote him a letter of friendly remonstrance which, as may be inferred from his reply, criticized the lack of church discipline and order at Geneva, and the general abuse of liberty among Protestants. De Trie replied that moral standards were better maintained at Geneva than at Lyon; and that as for doctrine, blasphemies and heresies were repressed at Geneva which existed at Lyon without restraint. To support this grave charge he cited the case of a heretic who in blasphemous terms denied the Trinity and the deity of Christ, and was allowed even to print books to spread his heresies, and yet was unpunished, while orthodox Protestants were being put to cruel death at the stake for maintaining the simple doctrines of the Gospel. He added that this man was properly named Michael Servetus, though he now passed under the name of Villeneuve, a practicing physician at Vienne, and that his book had been printed by Arnoullet. As proof he inclosed the first sheet of sixteen pages of the printed book. Having shot this bolt, de Trie excused himself from taking up Arney's charges in detail.[4]

At this period the diocese of Lyon was especially exposed to infection from the Protestant influences ruling at Geneva; and to check this, Cardinal François de Tournon, Archbishop of Lyon, had as early as 1535 had a trained Inquisitor sent from Rome in the person of a Dominican friar named Matthieu Ory, who set up in Paris the *chambre ardente* for the trial of heretics,[5] and for over twenty years was famous as the vigilant Inquisitor-General for all France.[6] Arneys therefore at once communicated the letter to the Inquisitor who, together with the Archbishop's Vicar-General, examined it and the printed pages. They in turn laid the matter before the Cardinal in his palace at Roussillon, and it was decided to commence proceedings against Servetus. The next day they went to Vienne, and put Servetus under examination. He met them with engaging frankness, and when they searched his

---

[4] De Trie's letter, dated Feb. 26, 1553, and those following it, though already referred to in the so-called *Historia de morte Serveti* (see below, and in chapter xiv.), circulated in Ms in 1554, was first published in full from the Archives at Vienne by d'Artigny, *Mémoires*, ii, 79–97. Also in Calvin, viii, 835–838, 840–844; and in Mosheim, *Nachrichten*, pp. 90–95. English translation in Wright, *Apology*, pp. 132–143; and in Willis, *Servetus*, pp. 236 ff, 246 f, 249 f.

[5] cf. Nathanael Weiss, *La chambre ardente*, (Paris, 1889).

[6] cf. Jacobus Echard, *Scriptores ordinis praedicatorum* (Paris, 1719–1721), ii, 162 f.

lodgings for incriminating evidence they could find none. They also questioned the printers, their employees, families and servants, and searched their houses, papers and printing office, again without success.[7]

Since it was agreed that there was as yet no evidence on which Servetus could fairly be held, it was decided that Arneys be asked to write de Trie for the entire book, of which only one sheet had been sent. Arneys therefore wrote to this effect a letter dictated by the Inquisitor. De Trie responded with alacrity, doing even better than had been asked. He could not indeed at once furnish the desired book, which was not then in his hands, and which in any case Servetus could disown; but he sent instead two dozen more or less heretical pieces in handwriting which Servetus could not disown. These he had obtained from Calvin, though only, he said, with great difficulty, since Calvin was at first unwilling to play into the hands of a Catholic prosecution for heresy. However, he finally yielded to de Trie's importunity in order to spare him the embarrassment of being charged with trifling in making charges that he was unable to substantiate. The writings he sent would be more than enough to furnish a basis for prosecution, though he hoped a little later to furnish the rest of the printed book.

Five days later de Trie sent another letter, calling attention to the fact that in one of the letters already sent Servetus had acknowledged his true name; and renewing his promise to send if necessary the other printed writings, manuscripts and letters, which for two years past had been at Lausanne in the hands of others to whom they were addressed. He added some other data that might aid in the prosecution.[8]

Sufficient evidence being now in hand to ensure successful prosecution, the arrest, trial, conviction and sentence of Servetus followed in due course. As to the part that de Trie played in the development of this drama, there has been no difference of judgment. That one should, in the performance of official duty, have to serve as executioner, prosecutor or Inquisitor is itself bad enough. But that one should voluntarily assume the rôle of informer, betraying a fellow-man in another country, in a matter in which he had no personal concern, and helping to com-

---

[7] Almost the only source for these and the following proceedings at Vienne is d'Artigny's often cited work. Mosheim (*Nachrichten*, pp. 89–101) published a year later substantially the same account, which had been communicated to him by a correspondent in France as taken from archives at Vienne; but it had perhaps simply been taken from d'Artigny's printed article.

[8] These last two letters were dated March 26 and 31, 1553.

pass his death simply to gain a point in debate with an adherent of a rival religion, is too contemptible for words. By the unanimous verdict of Catholics and Protestants alike, de Trie stands pilloried as guilty of the wanton and shameless act of a fanatical bigot, who covered up his odious conduct by pious phrases and a professed concern for religion.

As to Calvin's share in the transaction, opinions have been more divided, being naturally somewhat colored by prepossessions. Upon the surface of the record he would seem to have done no more than to give de Trie the first pages of Servetus's book, and later reluctantly yielding to de Trie's importunity, to furnish him with writings or letters in Servetus's own hand. But from the first there were those that discerned behind the hands of Esau the voice of Jacob, believing or suspecting that the letters signed by de Trie had been dictated, or at least suggested, by Calvin. This view was apparently held by the judges that condemned Servetus at Vienne, who in their sentence recited as ground of their action the letters and other writings addressed by him to Calvin.[9] When the records of the trial were first published two centuries later, the editor did not hesitate to entitle them as from him, saying outright (though this was of course only his own opinion)[10] that Calvin dictated the letters. This view Servetus himself plainly adopted, and he made the most of it in his trial at Geneva, pressing the point four successive times with increasing definiteness;[11] but as it was Servetus that was on trial, and not Calvin, the latter was not bound to reply, and discreetly held his peace.

[9] Veu par nous les pieces justificatives des dictes heresies, mesmes les Epistres & Escriptures de la main du dict Villeneufve, addressees a M⁶ Jehan Calvin Prescheur de Genefve & par le dit de Villeneufve recogneues. cf. d'Artigny, ii, 119; Calvin, viii, 785; Mosheim, *Versuch*, p. 415 f.

The so-called *Historia de morte Serveti* appended to the *Contra libellum Calvini* (see below, chapter xiv.) is more explicit, saying that the authorities at Vienne, in a communication addressed to those at Geneva, added that 'Servetum, judicio summi Genaevensium concionatoris, venisse in manus Viennensium' (p. Mii b). This interesting item was not incorporated in the official records of the Geneva trial. cf. Calvin, viii, 783.

[10] *Lettre de Calvin sous le nom de Guillaume Trie*. . . "Calvin lui dictoit les reponses." cf. d'Artigny, ii, 79.

[11] Respond quil est vray quil fut prisonnier a Vienne a la poursuicte de Mons. Calvin et Guilliel. Trie (Calvin, viii, 732). Et que Monsieur Calvin le poursuyvi tellement quil na tenu audict Calvin quil nayt este brusle tout vifz (p. 738). Quil fut constitue prisonnier pour certaines lettres quil Servet dict que Guillaume Trie avoit escriptes a linstance de Calvin (p. 789). Servetus demande que Jehan Calvin soit interroge, Si le mois de Mars dernier passe fit escrire par Guillaume Trie a Lyon, disant tout plein de choses de Michel Villanovanus, dict Servetus (p. 805).

Not long after the death of Servetus an anonymous tract was circulated in manuscript giving an account of the last months of his life.[12]
This quoted the pertinent part of de Trie's letter and added, 'Those
that have seen this letter suspect that it was written by Calvin, on account of a similarity in style, and they do not believe that (de Trie)
had a good enough use of the language to be able to write so clearly;
though he said that he wrote it himself. Moreover, care was taken to
send it so that it should fall into the hands of the Magistrate, and so of
Cardinal Tournon himself. Some say that Calvin himself wrote to the
Cardinal himself.' [13] Calvin was sorely pricked as this view gained increasing currency among his opponents, and when a little later he issued
his apologetic work, defending the capital punishment of heretics in
general and his treatment of Servetus in particular,[14] he did his best to
turn the point of the criticism. He felt it a heavy charge that many
were laying against him, that he had done a most shameful thing in
betraying Servetus to the acknowledged enemies of Christ as though
he were throwing him to wild beasts, and declaring that it was through
his agency that Servetus had been imprisoned at Vienne. His answer
deserves close examination for the adroit way by which, instead of
making a straightforward and unequivocal denial of any responsibility
in the case, he evades the crucial issue by means of a rhetorical question,
and in the end really denies no more than that he himself had had any
direct correspondence with the authorities at Vienne.[15]

[12] The so-called *Historia de morte Serveti*. Incorporated in (Castellio's) *Contra libellum
Calvini* (see below, chapter xiv), pp. Mii.–Mvi. Reprinted in Mosheim, *Versuch*, pp.
446–451.

[13] Has literas qui viderunt putant scriptas fuisse a Calvino, ob stylum similem; nec
tantam Lugdunensis illius eloquentiam, ut potuerit tam diserte scribere. Ipse quidem Lugdunensis dixit a se fuisse factas. Fuerunt autem de industria ita missae (sicut nobis nar-
rarunt qui ipsi has literas viderunt) ut venirent in manus Magistratus, atque adeo ipsius
Cardinalis Turnoy. Sunt qui dicunt Calvinum ipsum scripsisse ipsi Cardinali, etc.; *loc. cit.*
The last sentence gives in germ the legend referred to above on p. 137.

[14] *Defensio orthodoxae fidei*, etc. (Geneva, 1554); French version, *Déclaration pour
maintenir la vraye foi*, etc. (Genève, 1554).

[15] Verum quidquid de jure magistratuum probatum sit, me propria invidia, qua gravor
apud multos, non levat. Nihil minus decuisse aiunt, quam ut Servetum professis Christi
hostibus quasi immanibus bestiis objicerem. Mea enim opera factum fuisse affirmant, ut
Viennae in provincia Lugdunensi captus fuerit. Sed unde mihi tanta cum papae satellitio
repente familiaritas? unde etiam tanta gratia? Scilicet credibile erit literas inter eos ultro
citroque volitare, quibus non minus est inter se dissidium quam Christo cum Belial. Quare
pluribus verbis tam futilem calumniam refellere nihil attinet, quae simplici negatione fracta
concidit. Calvin, viii, 479.

The French version ends a little more strongly: Quand j'auray dict, en un mot, qu'il

The blot upon his reputation was not so easily removed, but rather tended to deepen with time. In 1577 Bolsec, continuing his campaign of hostility to Calvin and all his works, renewed the charges against him, duly embellished.[16] Thus the case rested, between the charges of Calvin's enemies on the one hand and his own somewhat equivocal denial on the other, until 1749, when the Abbé d'Artigny discovered in the archives at Vienne and brought to light for the first time the actual letters of de Trie, unpublished at the time of Calvin's denial and so compromising to him. These were on the whole convincing to Mosheim, orthodox Protestant as he was.[17] Criticism was brought to its height a few years later by the trenchant pen of Voltaire.[18] Since then discussion has proceeded with diminishing heat between loyal disciples of Calvin who make as good an apology as possible for his action, and his critics or enemies whose interest it is to make his action odious and his character unattractive. In the long perspective of history, however, and in the calm light of the available evidence, the judgment of scholars tends to converge upon the view that (1) while it can not be proved, and probably is not likely, that the letters were written by de Trie at Calvin's dictation, or perhaps even at his instigation, yet he certainly had knowledge of them; that (2) from contents, arrangement and style it is highly probable that Calvin furnished de Trie at least with material, and very likely with suggestions, for them; that (3) he certainly supplied de Trie (even if with professed reluctance) with the first printed sheet of the *Restitutio*, and with four pages of Calvin's *Institutio* bearing marginal annotations in Servetus's hand,[19] also with two dozen manuscripts of Servetus which had been sent to Calvin in confidence,[20] and was willing, if needed, to send yet more of the printed sheets, and

---

n'en est rien. The author of *Contra libellum Calvini*, indeed, says, *à propos* of this oblique denial, Enimvero Calvinus hoc crimen sic negat, ut propemodum fateatur. p. Kiv b.

[16] Sed eodem quoque tempore a Calvino instigatus Guilielmus Trie de eadem re Lugdunum atque Viennam litteras misit; factumque hinc est, ut in carcerem Servetus abriperetur. *Histoire de Jean Calvin*, chap. iii.

[17] Ich gestehe, es sei sehr wahrscheinlich, dass Kalvin diesen Handel regiert und des Trie Briefe selbst abgefasset habe. *Nachrichten*, p. 48.

[18] *Essai sur les moeurs et l'esprit des nations* (Stoutgart, 1756), chap. cxxxiv., "De Calvin et de Servet."

[19] cf. d'Artigny, ii, 103–105. This latter was identified by Weiss, cf. *Bull. Prot. Franç.*, lvii (1908), 400, n.; Mosheim, *Nachrichten*, p. 65.

[20] Luy escripvit le pryant que cella fust entre luy & moy seulement sub sigillo secreti. v. d'Artigny, ii, 107; Calvin, viii, 848.

other manuscripts as well as the epistles;[21] and that (4) he did all this knowing full well that he was putting into the hands of the Inquisitor evidence on which Servetus was likely to be put to death. This page in the life of Calvin, therefore, is one that those that admire him for his great gifts, revere him for his general character, and feel forever grateful to him for his incalculable service to the cause of Protestantism would, were it possible, most gladly see cancelled from the record.[22]

De Trie's last letter was dated March 31, and on April 4 a considerable number of high ecclesiastics met at the Cardinal's palace at Roussillon and examined the evidence with the greatest care.[23] Proof being considered complete, it was unanimously voted to have Servetus and Arnoullet arrested forthwith. The Archbishop returned to Vienne that afternoon, and to prevent any collusion had the two simultaneously arrested the same evening and committed to separate prisons. Servetus was found in attendance at the sick bed of the royal Governor, Guy de Maugiron, and was summoned thence to attend some sick and wounded prisoners at the royal prison, where upon arrival he was told of the charges against him and was placed under arrest, with orders that he be strictly guarded, but treated with a consideration befitting his rank. He was allowed to keep his young body-servant, and to receive visits that day from his friends. The next day the Cardinal was early informed, and the Inquisitor came in hot haste to assume charge of the case.

In the afternoon Servetus was placed under examination by the Inquisitor and three assistants,[24] and being duly sworn testified as to his name, place and date of birth, the course of his life hitherto, and the books he had published. His answers were a little vague, and of course he did not mention his two early books on the Trinity. He was then shown some printed leaves of Calvin's *Institutio*, on the margins of

---

[21] cf. d'Artigny, ii, 95; Calvin, viii, 843.

[22] For typical treatments of this episode from different points of view, cf. Mosheim, *Versuch*, pp. 237–247; Amedée Roget, *Histoire du peuple de Genève* (Genève, 1877–'83), iv, 17–34; Doumergue, *Calvin*, vi, 276–301; Theodor Schneider, *Calvin und wir* (Wiesbaden, 1909), pp. 19–32; N. Weiss, 'Calvin, Servet, G. de Trie et le Tribunal de Vienne,' *Bull. Prot. Franç.*, lvii (1908), 387–404, also separately. The theory that Calvin hoped, by putting Servetus into the power of Cardinal Tournon, to secure his influence in favor of five French Protestant students then on trial at Lyon, is not supported by any extrinsic evidence. cf. Roget, *op. cit.*, iv, 29.

[23] cf. d'Artigny, ii, 98 f.

[24] cf. d'Artigny, ii, 101–105; Calvin, viii, 844–847; Mosheim, *Nachrichten*, p. 96 f.

which he had written some compromising remarks about baptism, and was asked to explain the meaning of them. He reluctantly admitted having written the notes, explained them as well as he could, and declared his willingness, if they were found contrary to the faith, to submit to the judgment of the Church and to correct them. The examination was then adjourned. On resuming, the next day,[25] he was shown the manuscript of some epistles he had written to Calvin; but he soon found himself cornered as to signing himself Servetus. At the second letter he broke into tears, and declaring that he was about to tell the judges the truth, he fabricated a story in which truth was mingled with an elaborate invention, and by which he strove to explain how he had come to sign himself as he did; and he ended by saying that he had never meant to spread doctrines (*dogmatiser*) nor to support anything contrary to the Church or the Christian religion. The examination continued through the afternoon,[26] during which he was shown more epistles, nineteen in all. As to the suspicious doctrines expressed in these, he said that he had written them not as respresenting his own beliefs, but as a debater's challenges, to draw Calvin out. The judges can hardly have been favorably impressed by his answers, but as he professed willingness to reply upon any and all points, the examination was adjourned to be continued the following day.[27]

Servetus by now must have realized that his situation was one of critical danger, and he evidently considered plans (perhaps with the assistance of friends that had been allowed to see him) for making his escape. After the second examination he sent his body-servant to the monastery of St. Pierre for a sum of 300 *écus* owing to him, which the Prior had lately collected for him.[28] He was barely in time, for Ory too was alert, and within an hour had given the jailer orders that Servetus should be allowed to speak to no one without his permission. The next morning (April 7) he rose at dawn, and asked the jailer for the key that he might enter the garden, as he had done the evening before. As Servetus appeared to be only in his night clothes, the jailer suspected nothing, gave him the key, and went about his work. Servetus then threw off his nightcap and *robe de chambre*, jumped down upon a roof and thence

---

[25] cf. d'Artigny, ii, 106–109; Calvin, viii, 847–849; Mosheim, *op. cit.*, p. 98 f.
[26] cf. d'Artigny, ii, 109–111; Calvin, viii, 849 f; Mosheim, *op. cit.*, p. 99.
[27] cf. d'Artigny, ii, 149 f.
[28] cf. d'Artigny, ii, 111.

into the court, and was soon across the Rhône and out into the country.[29] It was more than two hours before his escape was discovered and reported to the jailer's wife, who in her vexation behaved like one gone mad. The city gates were ordered closed, and were guarded for several nights; the houses of Vienne and suburbs were searched; the governments of other cities were notified; and Servetus's effects were seized, but all to no purpose.[30]

It was commonly believed at Vienne that his escape had been facilitated by Antoine de la Court, Vice-Bailiff of the bailiwick of Vienne, who was one of the judges at the examinations of Servetus, but had also been his intimate friend, since Servetus had cured his only daughter of a dangerous illness. This, however, was only a suspicion, and was denied by Servetus in his testimony at Geneva.[31] At the beginning of May the Inquisitor found out where Arnoullet's secret presses had been set up, though the latter had not mentioned them. He visited them and found the three journeyman printers who, trembling for fear of death, made a clean breast of all: that the printing had taken from Michaelmas (September 29) to January 3; that Servetus had borne all the expense and corrected the proofs; and that ten days after the printing five bales of the books had been sent to Pierre Merrin at Lyon. The Inquisitor at once had these seized and brought back to Vienne, where they were all destroyed later.[32] Also a priest of Vienne, one Jacques Charmier, who had borne a message from Servetus to Merrin about the bales (though he stedfastly denied all knowledge of their character), and had been known to be a close friend of Servetus, was so strongly suspected of complicity with him that he was later sentenced to three years in prison.[33]

Arnoullet languished in prison for four months, charged with complicity in the printing; but he finally persuaded the judges that he had been misled by Guéroult as to the character of the book, and having been set free returned to Geneva so as to be beyond further reach of the Inquisition. While his case was still pending, as he feared to become

---

[29] This account of his imprisonment and escape as given by d'Artigny is supplemented and somewhat altered by Servetus's testimony at Geneva. cf. Calvin, viii, 732, 746, 749, 788.

[30] cf. d'Artigny, ii, 111–113.

[31] cf. d'Artigny, ii, 113 f; Calvin, viii, 749, 789.

[32] cf. d'Artigny, ii, 118–122.

[33] cf. d'Artigny, ii, 117; Calvin, viii, 853, n.

further incriminated, he wrote from prison to his agent Bertet [34] (then staying at Châtillon, about twenty-five miles west of Geneva), urging him to go to Frankfurt and destroy to the last leaf the books consigned to him there.[35] This was duly done, whereupon Bertet won praise from Calvin as a pious and upright man.[36] When Estienne on his part learned of the nature of the book and reported it to his friend Calvin, he will of course have destroyed whatever copies he still had at Geneva. Moreover he sent his servant Thomas to Frankfurt with instructions to burn the copies still held there for the autumn fair; bearing also a letter from Calvin to the pastors of the Frankfurt church to make sure that this was faithfully done.[37] It is not known how many copies (if any) had been sold at the Easter fair at Frankfurt, or by Estienne at Geneva; and more copies may have gone into circulation than has been generally supposed;[38] but save for the few copies retained by the authorities, the work was so thoroughly suppressed that at the present day only three copies are known to be in existence.[39]

The trial of Servetus went on for ten weeks after his escape, and the rest of April was spent in examining the documents in the case.[40] The Inquisitor drew up an abstract of the principal errors in the *Restitutio*, and the case having been duly prepared and no defence offered, sen-

[34] cf. *supra*, p. 139.

[35] cf. letter from Arnoullet to Bertet, July 14, 1553, in Calvin, viii., 752–757; Doumergue, vi, 259; Rilliet, *Relation*, p. 142; Tweedie, *Calvin*, p. 237.

[36] Instar typographi, vir pius et integer, quum admonitus foret, nihil illic praeter immensam errorem contineri, suppressit quicquid habebat. Calvin to the Frankfurt pastors, xiv, 599.

[37] cf. *Contra libellum Calvini* (1612), p. Mii. b, f; also quoted in Mosheim, *Versuch*, p. 449; and Calvin's letter just cited.

[38] Tollin's calculation that over thirty definite copies can thus be accounted for is almost certainly an overestimate. cf. Tollin, 'Ein Italienisches Urtheil über den ersten Entdecker des Blutkreislaufs,' *Archiv für die gesamte Physiologie*, xxiii (1884), 484–486.

[39] One in the Bibliothèque Nationale, Paris, where there is also an important Ms copy of what has been thought to be an earlier recension of pp. 92–247 of the printed work (copies at Manchester College, Oxford, and the Starr King School for the Ministry, Berkeley); a second in the National-Bibliothek, Vienna; a third (in which the first 16 pp. are missing, and are replaced by a corresponding but variant Ms of what is supposed to have been the first draft) in the Edinburgh University Library. A copy existing at Vienne was destroyed by fire in 1854 (cf. Savigné, *Servet*, p. 30). For the interesting history of the Paris and Vienna copies, cf. Tollin, 'Die Franzosen und die Entdeckung des Blutkreislaufs,' *Archiv für pathologische Anatomie und Physiologie*, xciv (1883), 99 f. A page-for-page (but not line-for-line) reprint was published at Nürnberg in 1790, and is also very rare. A few copies exist of a partial reprint made in London in 1723, which was interrupted and suppressed by ecclesiastical authority. Various Ms copies are extant.

[40] cf. d'Artigny, ii, 115.

tence was pronounced on June 17.[41] After reciting the evidence offered, and the flight of the accused, the sentence pronounced Servetus guilty by default, and fined him 1,000 *livres tournois*.[42] It was further ordered that as soon as he was arrested he should be taken with his books on a tumbril on the next market day to the place called Charnève,[43] and there be burned alive by slow fire; and meanwhile the sentence was to be executed on his effigy. His goods were confiscated, and eventually given to a Bishop, son of the Governor de Maugiron.[44] On the day appointed, therefore, his effigy and the five bales of books were taken as directed, the effigy was hanged on a gallows specially erected, and all was reduced to ashes.[45] The secular arm, seeing that Servetus had defaulted in the case, had not waited for an opinion from the ecclesiastical authorities, to whom it was customary in such cases to refer the question whether the accused were guilty of heresy. But the ecclesiastical judges continued their investigation, which was prolonged until late in December. Two days before Christmas they were ready with their verdict: that in view of all his writings that had been submitted for their examination, it was evident that Villanovanus [46] was a very great heretic; and they declared his goods confiscated, and that any of his books yet found were to be burned.[47] Eight weeks before this, Servetus had already been burned at the stake at Geneva.

[41] Servetus had apparently already been excommunicated. cf. the sentence of the Ecclesiastical Judges in d'Artigny, ii, 123 f: Visis . . . ternis litteris citatoriis & excommunicatoriis per eundem R. Dominum Inquisitorem & nos Vicarium generalem . . . concessis & debitis executis.

[42] cf. d'Artigny, ii, 118–121; Calvin, viii, 784–787; Mosheim, p. 415 f; Rilliet, *Relation*, p. 150 ff; Tweedie, *Calvin*, p. 289 ff.

[43] Le Charnève was an open place on the north bank of the Gère near St. Martin's church and the Place St. Martin.

[44] cf. Calvin, viii, 791; H. de Terrebasse, *Histoire et généalogie de la famille de Maugiron en Viennois* (Lyon, 1905), p. 35.

[45] cf. d'Artigny, ii, 121 f.

[46] Throughout the whole proceedings he had been called Villeneuve and not Servetus.

[47] cf. d'Artigny, ii, 122–127; Mosheim, *Nachrichten*, p. 100 f.

CHAPTER XII

THE TRIAL AND DEATH OF SERVETUS

AFTER HIS ESCAPE from the prison at Vienne, the world completely lost track of Servetus during more than four months. Legends naturally sprang up, and within less than a month the rumor was accepted at Wittenberg that he had already died in Paris in a state of horrible insanity.[1] Calvin, however, drawing a mistaken inference from a correspondent lately returned to Zürich from Italy, and greatly concerned over the wide spread of Servetus's views there, wrote to another friend that Servetus after his escape had been wandering in Italy for almost four months.[2] Again, a Geneva historian writing nearly two centuries later, though without giving any authority, stated that Servetus lay hidden at Geneva a month before he was discovered.[3] Neither of these views was well founded. On the contrary, the earliest evidence states that Servetus was discovered and arrested on the very day of his arrival at Geneva.[4]

Not knowing which way to turn, he had spent over eighteen weeks as a man without a country, skulking in out-of-the-way France, before

---

[1] The Lutheran Tilemann Hesshusen, in a disputation at Wittenberg May 5, 1553, referred to Servetus, "qui furens Lutetiae mortuus est" (cf. Melanchthon, *Opera*, xii, 591); while Melanchthon in the same year, in the 1553 edition of the German translation of his *Loci Theologici* (*Heubtartikel Christlicher Lere*), also spoke of Servetus "der zu Paris neulich rasend in grausamer Unsinnigkeit gestorben ist." (*id. op.*, xxii, 77, n. 48).

[2] Gaddi to Calvin, July 23, 1553: Multa etenim ibi haeresum genera vigere sensi . . . sed quae inter omnes maxime viget, est superbissimi diabolicique Serveti opinio, quam ut scriptis impugnes multi te obsecrant fideles, quum praecipue jactet neminem unquam fuisse qui in eam scribere ausus sit (Calvin, xiv, 577). Translation in Willis, *Servetus*, p. 302. cf. Calvin to Sulzer, Sept. 9, 1553: in carcerem est conjectus. Unde nescio quomodo elapsus, per Italiam erravit fere quatuor menses; xiv, 614.

[3] Servet arriva à Genève, ou il se tint caché pendant un mois en attendant une commodité pour partir: J. A. Gautier, in his notes to Spon's *Histoire de Genève* (nouvelle ed., Genève, 1730), ii. 61, n. This statement is apparently only a conjecture made to account for a supposed collusion between Servetus and the party opposed to Calvin. It was literally copied by d'Artigny (p. 127), and has been blindly accepted and repeated as fact by many subsequent writers. It has no support in contemporary evidence.

[4] Cum ex vinculis clam elapsus esset, venit Genevam, & eodem die, videlicet Dominico, audivit conciones post prandium. *Contra libellum Calvini*, p. Mii.

he ventured to cross its borders into another land.[5] He had at first
started to go into Spain, but he turned back for fear of the gendarmes,[6]
and as he dared not return to the Rhine cities whence he had fled
twenty-one years before and where he might still be recognized, he
finally decided to go to the Kingdom of Naples where there were many
of his countrymen, and to practice his profession among them.[7] Two
routes thither were possible: either that through Piedmont which,
though the more direct, offered greater danger of arrest while still on
French soil; or the more roundabout way through Geneva, Zürich and
the Grisons into northern Italy where, as he perhaps knew, he had many
disciples. This was the favorite route for Protestant refugees from
Italy, and was taken this very summer by Gribaldi returning from
Geneva to Padua;[8] and it would bring him at once into relatively safe
Protestant territory. Thus it was that, having spent the night at the
little Savoy village of l'Éluiset, a few miles west of town, and disposed
of his horse, he arrived at Geneva on foot and alone on August 13, and
turned in at the Rose d'Or, at the corner of the place du Molard and
the rue du Rhône, at that time the most comfortable hotel at Geneva.[9]
He did not intend to stay at Geneva, and he had already requested his
host to procure him a boat for conveyance up the lake on the way to
Zürich. In order not to be recognized, he kept out of sight as well as
he could, and had no communication with any one.[10] Unfortunately
the day was Sunday, when even a stranger might not absent himself
from church without inviting trouble. He therefore attended afternoon
worship (at the Madeleine, it is said), and there he was recognized by
persons who went forthwith to report him to Calvin.[11]

[5] Respond . . . que dempuis quil sortoit de prison il ne sortit jamais de France. Calvin,
viii, 782.

[6] *op. cit.*, viii, 749.

[7] *op. cit.*, viii, 770.

[8] Gallicius to Bullinger, Oct. 19, 1553; *Bullingers Korrespondenz*, i, 332; Calvin, xiv,
649.

[9] cf. Calvin, viii, 782, 770; E. Doumergue, *Guide historique et pittoresque de l'étranger
à Genève* (Genève, n. d.), p. 20.

[10] cf. Calvin, viii, 770.

[11] Rumor had it that while standing in church, concealed by his cloak and cap, as he
listened to the preacher, he was recognized by some whom he had once attended as physician at Vienne (cf. *Lyncurii Apologia*, in Calvin, xv, 54); *Renati Carmen*, line 52 f, (*ibid.*,
p. 240).

Agnitus est a quibusdam (*Contra libellum Calvini*, p. Mii). Recogneu par quelques
freres (*Registre de la Compagnie des pasteurs*, Calvin, viii, 725). Recognu par aucuns qui
l'avoyent veu ailleurs (*Vie de Calvin par Colladon, id. op.*, xxi, 76). Statim agnoscitur a

Calvin had no idea why Servetus had come to Geneva,[12] but lest the contagion of his heresy spread further, he thought it his duty to have him taken into custody as one that, in obstinate contempt of all warnings, had for over twenty years been spreading the poison of his prodigious errors.[13] He therefore at once had Servetus denounced to the magistrate that he might be arrested on the charge of heresy. The magistrate replied that this might not be done legally unless some one at the same time submitted to imprisonment as accuser.[14] For the laws of the republic provided, as a bar to malicious or unwarranted accusation of crime subject to corporal punishment, that the accuser should be held together with the accused until a case had been made out, and that if it were not established he should himself suffer the penalty for the crime charged — the so-called *poena talionis*.[15] As it would have been impracticable for the chief of the company of the city's pastors to meet this condition, he got one Nicolas de la Fontaine, a servant in his employ,[16] to stand as nominal accuser in his stead. Servetus was then called out of church and lodged in the city prison, where he was held *incomunicado* (save to those friendly to Calvin), and he never left it except to be led to the stake.[17] Although Calvin had shrunk from

---

quodam (Beza to Bullinger, Aug. 27, 1553, *id. op.*, xiv, 602). There may easily have been among the refugees at Geneva some from Lyon or Vienne who had known his face in his long residence there. The statement attributed to Beza (*Life of Calvin*, Eng. trans., Philadelphia, 1909, p. 61; Williston Walker, *John Calvin*, New York, 1906, p. 332), that he was providentially recognized by Calvin himself, rests upon a misunderstanding of the original Latin. cf. Beza, *Calvin*, Calvin, xxi, 146.

[12] Necdum enim scitur quo consilio venerit. Calvin to Farel, Aug. 20, Calvin, xiv, 589.

[13] Calvin to Sulzer, Sept. 9, 1553, xiv, 614 f.

[14] *Contra libellum Calvini*, p. Mii.

[15] cf. Édits du 12. Nov., 1542; Ordonnance de 1529, No. 8; text cited in Rilliet, *Relation*, p. 28, n. 1; Tweedie, *Calvin*, p. 94 f; Calvin, viii, 461, 479; Doumergue, *Calvin*, vi, 311 f.

[16] *Contra libellum Calvini*, p. Mii. b. As a Protestant refugee from France he had come to Geneva in 1548 as cook for another refugee, Jacques de Bourgogne, Seigneur de Falais, who lodged for a time in Calvin's house, until they had a serious falling out. Nicolas then remained in the service of Calvin, whose enemies referred to him as Calvin's cook (*op. cit.*, p. Kvi). It is more likely that he was now performing the various duties of a famulus, especially as amanuensis. For his services to Calvin he was received into citizenship in 1555. cf. Mosheim, *Versuch*, p. 155 f; Doumergue, *Calvin*, vi, 312 f.

[17] Though this statement comes from a source unfriendly to Calvin, there is no evidence at all to support the conflicting statement that the arrest was made not in church but at the hotel. cf. *Contra libellum Calvini*, p. Mii. b, Diii. b.

When Geneva accepted the Reformation in 1535, the Bishop's palace in the rue de l'Évêché was converted into a prison, which served until 1849, when it was demolished to make room for the present one. cf. Doumergue, *Guide*, p. 56.

acknowledging any responsibility for the arrest of Servetus at Vienne, he repeatedly avowed that he had caused that at Geneva,[18] being fully persuaded that thereby he had done God service.

Before proceeding to an account of the trial of Servetus, it is important to have a clear understanding of the situation existing at Geneva in the summer of 1553, since political and religious factors furnish the background against which the trial must be seen. Geneva had become Protestant in 1535; but the reform was at first less a religious movement than a political revolution, in which Geneva threw off the oppressive yoke of the Duke of Savoy and the Bishop. The religious leadership of Farel had been accepted as a means to this end, and the form of worship was changed and the Protestant faith adopted. But many citizens were still Catholic at heart, and many more interpreted the Reformation as a guarantee of the largest personal freedom in conduct, no less than of freedom from political oppression. The reformed pastors, however, took the movement with the utmost seriousness, and in their efforts to make Geneva a model of what a Christian city should be, they adopted and enforced ordinances applying to the last details of social and private life.[19] As the Genevans had long been a gay and pleasure-loving people, with rather loose standards of private morals, they regarded the new régime as an encroachment on personal liberty. A powerful party, including many of the most prominent families as well as a large number from the humbler classes, took form against the strict discipline enforced by the pastors. They called themselves Patriots, but by the stricter party were called Libertines. In 1538 they succeeded in gaining control of the government, and banished both Farel and Calvin who had come in 1536 to assist him. After two years and a half of civil and moral chaos, when there was grave danger that the Catholics would regain control, the government of the city asked Calvin to return. After a year of urging he reluctantly did so in 1541. His church discipline was adopted as law, and henceforth, though in name only one of the city's pastors, he was in effect dictator in both the religious and the civil life of Geneva.

Opposition to Calvin's strict form of government did not cease, how-

---

[18] Nec sane dissimulo . . .; Qui non dissimulo . . . me autore factum esse ut in hoc urbe deprehensus . . . ego libenter fateor . . . ex me prodiisse accusatorem; Neque enim dissimulo. cf. Calvin, viii, 461, 479; xiv, 615.

[19] Municipal interference in private life was no invention of Calvin's. It but continued a practice that had been common in the Middle Ages.

ever, despite many fines, imprisonments, banishments and even executions of recalcitrants, and it had never been more active and determined than in the summer of 1553. Calvin was doubtless the best hated man in Geneva. Four new members of the Council had lately been elected who were opposed to him, and his leading opponent was made Chief Syndic. Dr. Jerome Bolsec, who had been banished for persistent opposition to Calvin's doctrine, was attempting to get reinstated, and bid fair to succeed. A distinguished citizen named Philibert Berthelier, who had been excluded from the Lord's Supper by the Consistory, won the support of the Council, which reversed the sentence of excommunication. The pastors were excluded from participation in the general assembly of citizens. The rights of citizens of alien origin, who sided with Calvin, were abridged. Anabaptists were troublesome to public order. Calvin was all but ready to confess himself defeated and his cause lost, had he not been encouraged by leaders of the Reformation in the other Swiss cities.

It was at just this juncture, when the contest between Calvin and the Libertines was culminating, and the very fate of the Reformation at Geneva seemed to be at stake, that Servetus unexpectedly appeared on the scene. There is no ground for thinking (although it has often been assumed) that during the past four months Servetus had been in communication with the Libertines, or indeed that he had any knowledge of how things were going. So far as can be known, his coming at this critical time was a pure co-incidence. But Calvin did not know this, nor that Servetus meant to pass on as soon as possible; and there was at least the possibility that if Servetus learned of the situation he might seize the opportunity to stay and spread his heresies here, relying upon protection from the Libertines. This indeed they actually gave during his trial in a small and ineffectual way, not indeed to favor him, but to undermine the power of Calvin. Beside the known fact of Servetus's long-continued activity as a persistent heretic, Calvin therefore had additional reason to cause his arrest as soon as he was discovered; and a further spur to his action had been furnished only a few days before in Gaddi's letter reporting the alarming spread of Servetus's heresies in northern Italy, and begging him in the name of the faithful there to write against him.[20] The trial of Servetus must therefore be regarded in two distinct though related aspects: the trial of an individual for

---

[20] Gaddi to Calvin, July 23, 1853, Calvin, xiv, 577. *v. supra*, p. 161, n. 2.

grave and persistent heresy, and a phase of the struggle between those that would enforce a high and strict standard of doctrine and morals as an essential part of the Reformation at Geneva, and those that opposed such a movement.

The law required that within twenty-four hours after arrest the charges against the accused should be given him to answer.[21] Calvin therefore proceeded to extract from the writings of Servetus a list of incriminating passages for de la Fontaine to present.[22] The complaint thus drawn up by Calvin was on the following day (August 14) preferred by de la Fontaine in thirty-eight articles,[23] based upon heretical teachings found in the manuscript draft of the *Christianismi Restitutio* sent to Calvin by Servetus several years before.[24] This was read to Servetus in prison at a preliminary examination conducted by the assistant prosecuting attorney. After reciting the long heretical career of Servetus and his wicked publications, the complaint set forth in detail his denial of the doctrines of the Trinity, the eternal divinity of Christ, and infant baptism, and also his defamation of Calvin and his doctrine. Servetus then answered the charges one by one, admitting some, denying some, making qualified answers to others. They were, in fact, so stated that he could not in justice to himself answer them with a simple yes or no, as had been demanded. It was significant, however, that in two of his answers he made a rather spirited attack upon Calvin. This gives support to the conjecture that even in the short time since his arrival he had, at the hotel or elsewhere, learned of the political situation at Geneva, and was willing in this way to make a bid for support from Calvin's enemies in the Council before which he was to be tried. De la Fontaine then refuted Servetus's answers, offered from his writings proof of the charges made, and asked to be discharged from custody. The two were then remanded, and Servetus's money and valuables were taken in charge by the jailer.[25]

---

[21] Édits du 28 Janvier, 1543, quoted in Rilliet, *Relation*, p. 27, n. 1; Tweedie, *Calvin*, p. 95, n.   [22] Nec infitior meo consilio dictatam esse formulam; Calvin, viii, 479.

[23] The documents and records of the trial are given in full in Calvin, viii, 725–832; also, after an early copy, abridged, in Trechsel, *Antitrinitarier*, i, 285–320. Well summarized in Rilliet and Tweedie, *opp. citt.* Important additional data are found in Calvin's *Defensio orthodoxae fidei*; viii, 457 ff.

[24] References to volume and page were given, but none to the two early works on the Trinity, for Calvin could lay his hands on no copy of these. He wrote to Viret for one, and had hopes of receiving one through him. cf. Viret to Calvin, Aug. 22, 1553, Calvin, xiv, 591.   [25] 97 *écus soleil*, 6 gold rings, 1 gold chain. cf. Calvin, viii, 735, 831.

On the following day the attorney reported to the Little Council [26] the result of the examination, and it was voted to proceed with the case. That same afternoon the Council met in the hall of the old Bishop's palace, now the prison. Servetus was again put under oath and examined on the same points as before, and answered more fully and definitely than previously. About half of the charges he denied outright, and of the rest he admitted about half, while he made it clear that in the others his meaning had been misunderstood or misrepresented. He expressed belief in three persons in the Godhead, but showed that the form of his belief in the Trinity was not the one currently held. He also declared his belief in Jesus Christ as the Son of God, supernaturally born, though he differed in details from the received doctrine. He stoutly rejected the practice of infant baptism; and he repeated and confirmed his previous charge that Calvin had sought to bring about his death at Vienne. He declared that Calvin had been the first to use insulting language toward him in their correspondence, which he had repaid only in self-defence. He challenged Calvin to meet him in public debate of the questions at issue between them, apparently thinking that thus he might gain public support from Calvin's opponents. Calvin declared that he should like nothing better,[27] but the Council did not consent to the proposal. The result of the session satisfied the Council that there was a case. De la Fontaine was released from custody, with Calvin's brother Antoine as his surety, and was directed to present evidence in support of his cause. The Council then adjourned.

At the next day's session two new figures appeared at the trial, Germain Colladon, confidential friend of Calvin, to represent de la Fontaine as prosecutor in the case, and Philibert Berthelier as attorney representing the State. Berthelier embodied better than any one else in Geneva the Libertine opposition to Calvin, for the struggle was just then on to remove the ban of excommunication which Calvin had laid upon him, in which Calvin said he would die a hundred times sooner than yield.[28] His intervention in the case therefore brought into relief the fact that

---

[26] This Council of 25 members, including the four Syndics, the prosecuting attorney and the treasurer, constituted the criminal court of Geneva. Édits de 28 Janvier, 1543. cf. Rilliet, p. 32, n. 2; Tweedie, p. 103.

[27] Respondi . . . nihil mihi fore gratius quam si in templo et toto populo audiente disceptaretur. cf. Calvin, viii, 500.

[28] cf. Beza, *Calvin*, Calvin, xxi, 147; Calvin to Viret, Sept. 4, 1553, xiv, 606; Calvin to Bullinger, Oct. 25, 1553; xiv, 655.

this was to be not merely the trial of an individual for heresy, but a contest for supremacy in the government of Geneva between Calvin's party and the Libertines. The session was brief and stormy, and before it had proceeded far it was interrupted and the case put over to the next day.

Seeing the critical turn the case was assuming, Calvin now came forward and asked permission to fill the rôle of prosecutor, and was allowed whatever assistance he might wish. The proceedings were resumed, and the examination continued, now directed by Calvin. It went into further detail, as evidence was introduced from Servetus's writings to sustain the charges. His notes on the Bible and on Ptolemy were examined, and especially his attack upon belief in the doctrine of the Trinity. He countered this by saying that what he attacked was a distorted doctrine, which destroyed the unity of God by making a division in his being. Those that did this he called Trinitarians [29] and atheists; and it was such an idea of God that he had called a three-headed Cerberus.[30] In the course of the examination he revealed that the printer had sent some of his books to Frankfurt, and it was upon this clue that Calvin, as previously related, sent a messenger with a letter to the ministers there and had the books destroyed. Calvin had pursued the examination with unrelaxing severity, giving Servetus no quarter,[31] and he was evidently well satisfied with the result; for at the end of the session it was judged that the preliminary examination had sufficiently established the items in the charge to warrant a formal trial, and de la Fontaine and his surety were therefore discharged from further responsibility. This was on August 17. Three days later Calvin, writing to Farel, his fellow-reformer at Neuchâtel, reported progress to date, and added, 'I hope that he will at least be sentenced to death,

[29] To this epithet Calvin strenuously objected, and made it the basis of one of his items in the indictment. To a modern ear this seems a singular ground for a charge of heresy; but the term *Trinitarius* has an interesting history. Apart from a non-theological use in the name of a monastic order founded in the twelfth century, the term seems to have been first employed by Servetus in his *De Trinitatis erroribus*, p. 35a, as a term of reproach, to designate those that worship an abstract philosophical notion called Trinity rather than the living God. This was the ground of Calvin's objection to it. Later transformations in the meaning of the term will be noted in another chapter.

[30] cf. Servetus to Pouppin, "Pro uno Deo habetis tricipitem Cerberum"; Calvin, viii, 750. *v. supra*, p. 136.

[31] For some details not included in the summary records of the trial, cf. Calvin's *Defensio orthodoxae fidei*; viii, 496–499.

though it is my wish that he be spared needless cruelty.'[32] Farel replied
that this would be showing friendship to his bitterest enemy,[33] since
Servetus was a most obstinate and dangerous heretic. Calvin later insisted that he had never thirsted for Servetus's blood, and that his life
might have been spared had he only showed some modesty.[34]

Now that de la Fontaine as complainant had been excused from taking further part in the case, it fell to the Attorney-General Rigot to
prosecute it in the name of the State, and Calvin henceforth took no
further active hand in the prosecution. Ten days intervened before
Rigot appeared in court to conduct the trial. Meantime a session
was held, given over to discussion of the theological questions involved,
in which Calvin and his brother ministers undertook to refute the
citations from the early Fathers of the Church to whom Servetus had
appealed as his authorities. The records of this discussion are scanty.
Calvin afterwards wrote of it that he and his colleagues were ready to
discuss the points at issue quietly, and even took a defensive position,
offering to answer any objections that Servetus might propose; but that
Servetus at once heaped so many insults upon him that the judges
themselves were ashamed and disgusted, and he refrained from making
any reply. He declared, moreover, that Servetus was in no danger of
serious punishment had he only shown some sign of amendment; but
that, far from doing this, he showed himself so boastful and fierce as
to scorn any sound or helpful advice.[35] The appearance of Berthelier
at the trial the previous week, as in some sense Servetus's champion,
had evidently quite gone to his head, and led him to the mad conclusion
that his case was already as good as won. At the close of this session it
was ordered that he be provided with the books he required to use in
defence, and with ink and a sheet of paper on which to write a petition
to the Council; and that he be held in strict confinement — evidently
to cut him off from any communication with sympathizers in the Libertine party opposed to Calvin.[36]

[32] Calvin to Farel, Aug. 20, 1553. Spero capitale saltem fore judicium; poenae vero
atrocitatem remitti cupio. Calvin, xiv, 590.

[33] Farel to Calvin, Sept. 8, 1553. Quod poenae atrocitatem leniri cupis, facis amici
officium in inimicissimum tibi hominem. Calvin, xiv, 613.

[34] Hoc tantum in praesentia testatum volo, me non ita capitaliter fuisse infestum, quin
licitum fuerit vel sola modestia, nisi mentis privatus foret, vitam redimere. In his *Defensio*,
viii, 480.   [35] In his *Defensio*, viii, 479 f.

[36] After this even his windows were nailed up: On lui avoit cloué les fenestres. cf.
Calvin, viii, 789.

On the following day (August 22) two new steps were taken. The Council addressed a letter to the court that had tried Servetus at Vienne, asking that a copy be furnished them of the evidence and other documents in the recent trial of Servetus there;[37] and on the same day Servetus on his part addressed to the Council a petition that further indicates how confident he was as to the outcome of his trial. He requested, first, that he be set free from any criminal charge, on the ground that both in the Apostolic Age and in the early Church religious questions were not determined in criminal courts, but only by the churches themselves; and that in any case the punishment of heresy was only banishment. Secondly, that as he had not created any sedition or disturbed the peace at Geneva or elsewhere, had never discussed doctrinal questions save with theologians, and had always condemned the Anabaptists for their views on civil government, he should no longer be charged with crime on these grounds. Thirdly, that as he was a foreigner, and ignorant of the customs of the country, he might be granted legal counsel.[38]

This petition was filed with the other documents in the case; but the prosecution had by now proceeded too far for the case to be thrown out of court as Servetus had requested. Three days later the Attorney-General answered his petition and its arguments at length. He refuted in detail the points that Servetus had drawn from history, and charged him with wilful misrepresentation of facts in order to predispose the judges in his favor. He called him one of the boldest, most rash and dangerous heretics that had ever lived, and a conscious and deliberate liar who showed not the least trace of being innocent and of therefore deserving counsel.[39] The refusal to grant him legal counsel seems by the standards of to-day to be the height of injustice; but under the law as it then stood at Geneva (and also in various other lands until long afterwards) the accused was not allowed to plead in defence except by special permission; and it was not until 1734 that he could legally claim the right to be represented by counsel.[40]

Meanwhile the Attorney-General had prepared new articles of impeachment to take the place of the preliminary ones of de la Fontaine,

[37] cf. Calvin, viii, 761.

[38] cf. Calvin, viii, 762 f.

[39] cf. Calvin, viii, 771–775.

[40] cf. Ordonnance de 1543, quoted by Rilliet, p. 62, n.; Tweedie, p. 143, n.; Doumergue, vi, 326, n. 4.

as a basis for the formal trial. They were thirty in number, and very different in content from the former ones. Those had dealt largely with points in speculative theology, and were designed to show that Servetus's doctrines were calculated to undermine the Christian religion. The new ones paid no attention to these matters, which might not impress the members of the Council nearly so much as they had Calvin, but were devoted to the more practical purpose of showing the dangerous effects of such heresies in leading him into a criminal and dissolute life, encouraging the young in crime and immorality, favoring the teaching of Jews and Turks, and reviving ancient heresies long since condemned by the Church. As is often the case in criminal prosecutions, they took the guilt of the accused for granted as undoubted, and sought to set his case in the worst possible light. The contents of the articles suggest that Calvin may have assisted in the framing of them, though no reference is made to attacks on him or his doctrine. Calvin on his part was not disposed to neglect any opportunity to counteract any sympathy for Servetus that might be taking place in the popular mind; and on the next Sunday, before a crowded congregation, he exposed the errors of Servetus and treated them at length.[41]

The new examination brought out many new and interesting details in his life, which on the whole agree well with what we know of it from other sources. His answers seemed for the most part to be straightforward, and they were made with great skill, conciliatory in tone, and calculated to create a good impression upon unprejudiced minds, and to show that he had tried to live as a sincere and virtuous Christian,[42] desiring only to correct some long-standing errors in which the faith and practice of the Church had departed from the standards of its early ages. The persistent attempts of the prosecution to discredit his character were crowned with little success.

After about a week a reply was received from the court at Vienne, begging in politest terms to be excused from furnishing the documents asked for, to be used in the prosecution of one whom they had already sentenced to death, and requesting that he be returned to them to suffer

---

[41] Quodam die Dominico frequentissima congregatione Serveti (qui tum recens erat in carcere) opiniones populo exposuisti & concione tractasti. cf. *Contra libellum Calvini*, p. Bii. b. (Calvinus) ipse eum in carcere absentem quotidianis concionibus populum invidiosissime traduxit. *id. op*, p. Avii. b.

[42] Respond quil a este estudieux de la saincte escripture, ayant zele de verite, et pense avoir vescu comme ung chretien. cf. Calvin, viii, 769.

his penalty. A copy of the sentence was enclosed.[43] The Council, having read these communications, after a due exchange of compliments, regretted their inability to comply with the request made, but gave assurance that justice should be done to the prisoner. Before this, Servetus had been faced and identified by the jailer who had come from Vienne; and when asked whether he would rather remain here or be sent back there, he begged on his knees that he might stay here and be dealt with as seemed best. He also furnished a written statement relieving the jailer of any responsibility for his escape. Yet another communication followed from Vienne, from the royal Governor de Maugiron, from attendance at whose sick-bed Servetus had been haled away to prison, expressing much pleasure that he had been captured, and the hope that he would not again escape punishment (perhaps hoping thus to allay the well-grounded suspicion that he had facilitated his escape). He also reported that the King had awarded the property of Servetus to his (Maugiron's) son, amounting, it was said, to 3,000 or 4,000 écus, and requesting that a list of his debtors and the sums owing be obtained from Servetus and forwarded, that collections might be made.[44] Servetus declined to furnish the information, saying that it had nothing to do with his case, and that it might embarrass many poor people that were indebted to him.

Servetus was now called in again to continue the discussion with Calvin that had been broken off ten days before; but he professed to feel too sad and troubled in mind,[45] and the oral discussion promised to be tedious to the Council. It was therefore voted that instead it be conducted in writing and in Latin.[46] This last condition was doubtless made in view of the vote passed early in the trial, that when the data were all in hand a full report should be furnished the Councils and churches of other Swiss cities, where Latin would be better understood than the French used at Geneva.[47]

In opening this written discussion, Calvin submitted in quotations from Servetus's book, with page references given, thirty-eight 'State-

---

[43] cf. Calvin, viii, 783–787.

[44] cf. Calvin, viii, 791.

[45] Quum post octo dies iterum esset productus, et libera conferendi nobiscum illi daretur facultas, se tristitia et curis impediri praetextuit. Calvin in his *Defensio*, viii, 480.

[46] Pource que seroit trop long douyr ycy le discours et que ce seroit chose trop confuse, est este advise, etc. cf. Calvin, viii, 793, also p. 500.

[47] Aug. 21. cf. Calvin, viii, 752.

ments or propositions extracted from the books of Michael Servetus, which the ministers of the Geneva church assert are in part wicked and blasphemous toward God, in part full of impious errors and madness, and all wholly foreign to the Word of God and the generally accepted teaching of the orthodox Church.'[48] It would be tedious to the reader to rehearse these in detail, further than to say that they covered in general substantially the same ground as the articles originally offered by de la Fontaine, and that they were submitted without comment or argument. Servetus in return submitted passages from Tertullian, Irenaeus and the Clementines supporting the passages complained of, and besides made some further comments, in terms of which some were insulting to Calvin.[49] Calvin rejoined, still in writing, with a 'Brief Refutation of Servetus's Errors.'[50] This was composed with much skill, and was carried out, with few exceptions, in the dignified tone of serious discussion; and it concludes with the statement, calculated to be extremely prejudicial to Servetus: 'Any one therefore that really and seriously reflects upon the matter will acknowledge that it was his purpose to extinguish the light of sound doctrine, and overthrow all religion.'[51] A more utter distortion of Servetus's purpose than these last three words express it would be impossible to make.

Calvin's affairs at Geneva now came to a critical turn. On the morning of the very day on which the written discussion was ordered, the Libertines scored a conspicuous triumph over him, when despite the utmost opposition from Calvin the Council voted to annul the excommunication under which the Consistory had long held Berthelier, and he had again appeared at the session of the Council at which Servetus was to debate with Calvin. In some way unknown to us,[52] Servetus must soon have learned of the turn things had taken, and have leaped to the conclusion that now his case was as good as won. For when, some ten days later, he made his final rejoinder to Calvin's Refutation, it was only in the form of brief comments noted on the margin or be-

---

[48] Calvin, viii, 501–508.

[49] *ibid.*, viii, 507–518.

[50] cf. Calvin, viii, 519–553.

[51] Quisquis ergo vere et prudenter reputabit, hunc illi scopum agnoscit, ut luce sanae doctrinae extincta totam religionem everteret. Calvin, viii, 553.

[52] Most probably through the jailer, who was of the Libertine party (cf. Rilliet, p. 90; Tweedie, p. 182), for an additional guard was later ordered, as though he were not fully trusted. cf. Calvin, viii, 824.

tween the lines.[53] In these he abandoned all attempt at serious argument, and apparently in mad elation over the victory that he felt sure was to be his, he heaped upon Calvin a torrent of abuse and invective that could not but have a damaging effect upon his case in the minds of those that were bound to judge it upon the basis of the arguments submitted. He passes the lie direct some sixty times, calls Calvin Simon Magus [54] nearly a score of times, and repeatedly assails him as impudent, ignorant, know-nothing, ridiculous, sophist, crazy, sycophant, rascal, beast, monster, criminal, murderer.[55] Calvin was wise enough to say nothing in reply, but let the case rest here.[56]

Twelve days had passed since Servetus wrote his reply to the articles presented by Calvin, and he had had no response. The reply and Calvin's Refutation had in fact lain for ten days in the hands of the Council,[57] which was at the time too much preoccupied with the major struggle now at its height between the Libertines and Calvin to have any attention left for the minor one between Calvin and Servetus. All this time Servetus lay impatiently in prison. Having received no reply, he concluded that Calvin was at the end of his rope and had none to give. He therefore addressed to the Council on September 15 a second petition,[58] complaining of the long delay. He was being eaten alive by vermin, his shoes were ragged, he had but one poor shirt and no change. For five weeks Calvin had kept him in prison without proving a single point. He renewed his demand for legal counsel, which had been allowed to his opponent who had now been set free. He appealed his case to the Council of 200, and if his appeal were granted he invoked the *poena talionis* against both de la Fontaine and Calvin. The Council

[53] Intercalated with the relevant paragraphs of the Refutation; Calvin, viii, 519–553.

[54] In allusion to the famous sorcerer and impostor referred to in Acts viii. 9–11; and more fully in Irenaeus, *Heresies*, I. xviii, 1–4, and in the *Clementine Recognitions, passim.*

[55] It is to be remembered that at this period such use of language was often made even in religious controversy. Calvin himself was well practiced in it. It was said by a contemporary that a dictionary of terms of abuse could be compiled out of his writings: Si quid intemperantius dixit Servetus cum homine intemperantissimo confligens, nactus fuit Calvinus hominem se dignum . . . cum ipse Calvinus convitiis sic abundet, ut sint qui dicant ex ejus scriptis confici posse dictionarium convitiorum. *Contra libellum Calvini,* p. Kvii.

[56] Ne conqueri posset Servetus se multiplici concertatione a nobis obrui, ultimas ejus calumnias relinquere intactas maluimus, quam nobis sumere quod jure nostro licebat. Calvin, viii, 554.

[57] cf. Calvin, viii, 795, n. 2.

[58] cf. Calvin, viii, 797.

took notice, gave order that his wants be supplied, at his own cost (though the order was not obeyed), and that Calvin's Refutation be communicated to him for any final reply he chose to make.

A week later, the items in the written discussion now being all in hand, the Council despatched them, as had been voted a month before, to the ministers and the Council at Zürich, Bern, Basel, and Schaffhausen, with a letter to each, a copy of Servetus's book, and a request for their advice. Two years before, when a similar step had been taken in similar conditions in the trial of Bolsec for heresy, and Calvin was rumored to have desired Bolsec's death,[59] the advice of the churches consulted had been disappointing to him. Though without expressing approval of Bolsec's views, Zürich advised trying to come to a better understanding, and using greater moderation, and Bern recommended attempting conciliation.[60] Consequently Bolsec was punished only with banishment. Calvin was therefore opposed to the present step,[61] and for the same reason the councillors unfriendly to him will have favored it. He therefore took the prudent step of prepossessing the minds of the judges before the documents in the case reached them. Early in the written discussion he wrote to Bullinger, leader of the Reformation at Zürich, and two days later he wrote an adroitly composed letter to Sulzer at Basel;[62] later yet to Haller of Bern that they should treat Servetus as a blasphemer deserved. At the same time there was no one to say a word in extenuation of Servetus,[63] so that the verdict of the churches was a foregone conclusion.

Bullinger needed no persuading. Three weeks previously he had written to Beza that if the Geneva Council knew and did its duty, it would put Servetus to death. He also wrote Calvin in great concern, encouraging him, and urging him not to yield to his enemies, but to

---

[59] Nos vero sic ecclesiam nostram cupimus hac peste purgari, ne inde fugata vicinis noceat. Letter of the ministers of Geneva to those of Basel, Bern, and Zürich, Nov. 14, 1551. cf. Calvin, viii, 207. Calvin denied the charge: viii, 254.

[60] cf. Calvin, viii, 230, 238.

[61] Propediem senatus noster dogmata Serveti istuc mittet, ut judicium de illis vestrum intelligat. Nobis quidem reclamantibus vobis facessunt hanc molestiam. Calvin to Bullinger, Sept. 7, 1553, xiv, 611. A few months later, when his victory had been won, he remembered differently, saying that when Servetus appealed to the other churches, he gladly agreed to it: Deinde quum ille provocaret ad alias ecclesias, libenter a me haec quoque conditio suscepta fuit. cf. his *Defensio*, viii, 500.

[62] cf. Calvin, xiv, 610, 614.

[63] David Joris's eloquent plea for toleration excepted, to be spoken of below, p. 188.

remain at Geneva.[64] His answer and Sulzer's showed that they both could be depended upon to support Calvin's cause. Bullinger also exchanged letters on the subject with Haller and Musculus of Bern and Sulzer of Basel, and all manifested the liveliest interest in the case.

The letters to the four Swiss churches were sent by special messenger on September 21. On the following day Servetus presented to the Council another petition in which, on entirely new ground, he assumed a vigorous offensive against Calvin. He had evidently been persuaded, or persuaded himself, that his victory was assured; and he now came forward as the accuser of Calvin for the crime of making false charges against him. He demanded therefore that Calvin should be imprisoned along with him until the case should be decided, with death to one or the other under the *poena talionis*; and as de la Fontaine had done with him, he presented articles on which Calvin should stand examination. To this petition the Council paid no attention. It would indeed hardly have done so until replies had come from the churches, and these were not received for three weeks. All this time the condition of Servetus was growing more pitiable. His earlier petition for the plainest comforts and decencies of life had brought no response, and he was more wretched than ever, shivering with the cold, and tortured by physical infirmities. In a new petition [65] he besought the Council for the love of God to grant him some relief. This was at length done.

In another week the messenger returned with the answers from the four churches.[66] In each case the Councils of the cities had referred the matter to their ministers as the more competent judges in such matters. Zürich took the lead, and the correspondence between the various ministers shows that the other churches looked to Bullinger for guidance before expressing their own judgment.[67] There was therefore a noticeable similarity in the answers given. In slightly differing words they all spoke with the voice of Bullinger. The ministers of Zürich noted Servetus's wicked and horrible blasphemies against the Trinity and the Son of God, and his insulting impudence to Calvin; and Schaffhausen briefly subscribed to their whole judgment. Bern received a copy of

---

[64] Bullinger to Beza, Aug. 30, 1553; Bullinger to Calvin, Sept. 14, 1553, Calvin, xiv, 604–621.

[65] cf. Calvin, viii, 806 f.

[66] cf. Calvin, viii, 555–558, 808–823. Translated in Richard Wright, *Apology*, p. 216 ff.

[67] cf. the correspondence of Bullinger with Haller and Sulzer, Calvin, xiv, 623–648.

Zürich's reply and agreed with it wholly; while Haller wrote Bullinger that when the Bern Council heard what errors Servetus had tried to spread, they were all so enraged that, had he been their prisoner, he would undoubtedly have been burned.[68] The Bern ministers made a digest of Servetus's heresies, noting that many of them were simply old ones revived, and that he put them forth without showing due modesty; and Basel echoed the same opinion. None of those consulted committed the impropriety of suggesting to the Geneva Council what sentence should be imposed; though it was not difficult to divine what they had in mind. Zürich concluded, 'How your Excellencies are to restrain this man, we leave to your wisdom to determine,' but they called especial attention to the evil reputation the Swiss churches were getting abroad for their indulgence to heresy and heretics, and to the providential opportunity now offered for clearing them from such a suspicion.[69] Schaffhausen had no doubt that Servetus's efforts would be repressed lest his blasphemies spread further like a cancer. Bern wrote, 'We pray the Lord to grant you a spirit of prudence, understanding and firmness to remove this plague from both your own churches and others, and also at the same time to let nothing be done that can be deemed unbecoming in a Christian magistrate.'[70] Basel urged that all diligence be used to cure him if curable, but if not, and he remains perverse, then to employ whatever power the Lord has granted to keep him from giving the Church further trouble.[71]

Now that their replies had been sent to Geneva, the leaders in the other churches were on a tiptoe of suspense to know what action would be taken at Geneva. Vergerio at Chur, indeed, who like many of his fellow-countrymen had lately fled before the terrors of the Italian Inquisition, had already written Bullinger [72] that though he held Servetus and his sort in abhorrence he did not think that fire or sword ought to be used against them; and he now wrote again: 'I have seen the letter that you wrote to the Senate of Geneva. You do not say in so many words that the heretic should be put to death, but you so state the case that the reader can easily see that that is your opinion. I wrote you what I thought.' [73] But Sulzer wrote to Bullinger expressing the hope that no ill-timed mercy would be shown,[74] and Bullinger begged

[68] cf. Calvin, xiv, 647; Oct. 19.
[69] cf. Calvin, viii, 558.
[70] cf. Calvin, viii, 819.
[71] cf. Calvin, viii, 823.

[72] Oct. 3, 1553, Calvin, xiv, 633.
[73] October 8, Calvin, xiv, 635.
[74] Oct. 16, Calvin, xiv, 645.

Calvin to relieve his anxiety by writing him what had been done in the case.[75] Calvin was well content with the answers, especially with the decisive ones from Zürich and Bern.[76]

The Council proceeded with all due deliberation, no doubt reluctant to take the fateful step. The replies from the churches were in hand for at least a week before sentence was passed, and in the meantime it was voted to look into the matter more fully. The advice of the churches was read and the evidence in the case reviewed. The Libertine Syndic Amied Perrin appeared in Council after an absence of several days, and attempted at least to delay action by having the case transferred to the Council of 200; but the Little Council were in no mood at this late day to relinquish jurisdiction.[77] The records of proceedings in the Council at this juncture are scanty, but from another source [78] it is related that Perrin, seeing that a death sentence was evidently to be passed, was unwilling to be present, saying that he refused to be a partaker of his blood,[79] and that some others followed him; while of the rest some favored banishment, and some life imprisonment, though the majority were for the stake unless he would recant. Calvin and the other ministers tried to have the form of death changed, but to no purpose.[80] A phrase in the sentence indicates that before passing it the Council sought the advice of other citizens, perhaps of the Council of 60.[81] Whatever difference of opinion there may have been about the manner of punishment, there could, in face of the consenting views of the churches to which appeal had been made, hardly have been any question of acquittal, and the sentence was passed without debate [82] on October 26.

After formally reciting at length the false and heretical doctrines that Servetus, despite warning and correction, had for many years been

75 Oct. 28, Calvin, xiv, 659.

76 cf. Calvin to Farel, Oct. 26, Calvin, xiv, 657.

77 Calvin to Farel, Oct. 26, 1553, cf. Calvin, xiv, 657.

78 The *Historia de morte Serveti*, in *Contra libellum Calvini*, p. Mii. Reprinted in Allwoerden, *Servetus*, pp. 156–161; Mosheim, *Versuch*, pp. 446–451.

79 Rilliet, *Relation*, p. 107, states, evidently on the authority of an authentic source, that Perrin was present nevertheless when sentence was passed. cf. Tweedie, *Calvin*, p. 203.

80 Genus mortis conati sumus mutare, sed frustra; Calvin to Farel *ut supra*. cf. Calvin to Farel, Aug. 20, 1553; xiv, 590; ix, 315. Death by fire was too suggestive of the punishments of the Inquisition.

81 Ayans heu bonne participation de conseil avec nos citoyens; Calvin, viii, 829.

82 Sine controversia tamen damnatus est; Calvin to Farel *ut supra*. Not necessarily by unanimous vote as has usually been said.

spreading, to the ruin of many souls thus infected by their poison, it condemned him to be bound and taken to the place called Champel, there fastened to a stake and burned alive together with his written and printed book.[83] Although the orthodox writers of the time habitually insisted on speaking of Servetus not as a mere heretic, but as a blasphemer, the sentence was not for the odious crime of blasphemy (of which it makes no mention), nor for holding heretical views, but for *spreading* heresy;[84] and the heresies most emphasized in the preamble related to the Trinity, the eternal deity of Christ, and infant baptism. Servetus had of late been in a state of elation, having been misled into expecting, if not acquittal, at least a light punishment. When now informed that he must die, so Calvin relates, he stood like one stunned, drew deep sighs, wailed like a madman, and at length recovering himself kept beating his breast and moaning in Spanish (or was it not in Latin?), *Misericordia, misericordia.*[85] Farel, whom Calvin had desired to have at his side for moral support at so critical a juncture,[86] opportunely arrived on the very day on which the sentence was passed by the Council, and he was with Servetus constantly from seven the next morning until the execution at noon, endeavoring to bring him to a state of repentance.[87] Together with some ministers that had come in from the country, Farel urged him that on his last day on earth he should acknowledge his errors and confess the truth. He replied by asking to be shown a single passage proving the eternal sonship of Christ, and could not be shaken. They then persuaded him

---

[83] cf. Calvin, viii, 827–829; also in Mosheim, *Versuch*, p. 444 ff. Burning had for centuries been the punishment for heresy under the law of the Empire, and the law had not been changed under the new régime at Geneva.

[84] Musculus early called attention to this as inviting criticism from good men. cf. Musculus to Blaurer, Feb. 27, 1554; Calvin, xv, 47.

[85] cf. Calvin, viii, 498, 826, n. 3.

[86] Calvin to Farel, Oct. 14, 1553, xiv, 640.

[87] Ab hora septima paene ad meridiem. Farel to Blaurer, Dec. 10, 1553, Calvin xiv, 694. The sources for Servetus's last hours are in the above letter; also in *Contra libellum Calvini*, p. Miii ff., reprinted in Mosheim, *Versuch*, pp. 448–451; Calvin's *Defensio*, viii, 460, cf. p. 826 and n. 3, p. 498 f. The details given in a Ms history of his death by Peter Hyperphrogenus of Ghent, quoted by Sandius, *Bibliotheca* (1684), p. 8, can not be accepted as authentic; still less can a dying speech attributed to Servetus and given in Lubieniecius, *Historia* (1685), pp. 99–105, also in Allwoerden, *Servetus*, pp. 131–138, and Mosheim, *op. cit.*, pp. 451–455 (English trans. in Wright, *Apology for Servetus*, pp. 244–255). Internal evidence shows that this speech was written and put into the mouth of Servetus for propaganda purposes by some Socinian, ignorant of Servetus's real views, and using a style totally unlike his.

to ask Calvin for an interview, that he might become reconciled to him.[88] Calvin dared not go without the Council's leave, but when this was given, he went to the prison accompanied by two councilmen. Servetus asked his forgiveness. Calvin replied that he had never persecuted him for any personal wrong, but had for many years warned him as kindly as he could, and had been answered only with rage. He ought rather to ask God's forgiveness, whom he had so outrageously insulted. Seeing that he was accomplishing nothing by his admonitions, Calvin then withdrew, two hours before Servetus's death, and left him to his fate.[89] Farel and the other ministers stayed with him to the end. When brought to the Hôtel de Ville to hear his sentence formally pronounced, he begged the magistrate for death by the sword, lest the great suffering of death by fire should lead him in desperation to retract what he believed to be true, and so to lose his soul; and he said that if he had sinned it was in ignorance, for he had meant and tried to promote the glory of God. Farel interceded for him, but the magistrate was inexorable, and he was therefore led away crying, 'O God, save my soul; O Jesus, Son of the eternal God, have mercy on me.' [90]

The *via dolorosa* led from the Hôtel de Ville out through the city gates to about three quarters of a mile south.[91] On the way they kept urging him to confess his fault and disavow his errors, but he replied that he was suffering unjustly, and prayed for God's mercy on his accusers. Upon this, Farel threatened to leave him if he went on thus. He desired forgiveness of his mistakes and ignorance and sins, though he could never be got to confess Christ as the eternal Son of God; and to the end he held true to his convictions. Arrived at the place of execution he fell upon his face and continued long in prayer, while Farel seized the opportunity to make an edifying address to the spectators. Again exhorted to say something, he cried, 'O God, O God; what else can I speak of but God.' Then he asked the people to pray

[88] Farel to Blaurer, *ut supra*. cf. Calvin's report of the interview, viii, 460; and the Council's consent, p. 826.

[89] 'Duabus ante mortem suam horis'; Calvin, viii, 460.

[90] *Contra libellum Calvini*, p. Miii.

[91] The precise place of execution was on the west side of the present chemin de Beau-Sejour, where the new clinic now stands, and on the terrace in front of the house and overlooking the chemin de la Roseraie. The expiatory monument erected in 1903 was placed as near this spot as possible, near the bottom of the rue Michel Servet. cf. E. Doumergue, 'L'emplacement du Bûcher de Michel Servet,' *Bulletin de la Société d'Archéologie de Genève*, ii (May, 1908), 856–863; *id., Guide*, p. 108.

for him. Being led to a pile of wood made up of small sticks and bundles of green oak with the leaves still on,[92] he was seated on a log with his feet touching the ground, his body chained to a stake, and his neck bound to it by a coarse rope; his head covered with straw or leaves sprinkled with sulphur, and his book tied to his thigh. He besought the executioner not to prolong his torture; and when the torch met his sight he uttered a terrible shriek, while the horrified people threw on more wood and he cried out, 'O Jesus, Son of the eternal God, have mercy on me.' After about half an hour life was extinct. He had died and made no sign.[93]

The fact of the execution of the sentence was duly entered on the records of the Council, and Servetus's valuables were delivered over to the public treasurer.[94] Farel also rendered his report of the event, and requested that the facts be published. It was voted to reimburse Calvin from Servetus's money for the expenses he had incurred in the case. Two weeks later, on Calvin's motion, it was voted that he prepare and have printed an account of Servetus's opinions, as requested by the cities of Germany. With this the case was officially concluded.[95]

Writers on this subject have made much of a supposed collusion between Servetus and the Libertine opponents of Calvin, to explain the great bitterness that Calvin showed in the prosecution of the case. Calvin thought it reasonable to suspect that Servetus was buoyed up from some source by a vain assurance; Farel wrote Blaurer that some led him to hope there was no danger; Beza in his life of Calvin says that one of his opponents was believed to have whispered something in Servetus's ear that gave him courage; Bullinger heard (probably from Calvin) that the Libertines were supporting Servetus out of hatred of Calvin; Calvin wrote the ministers of Zürich that the friends of Berthelier vociferously supported the cause of Servetus; and four years later the Council wrote

---

[92] This is usually cited as an item of gratuitous cruelty, designed to retard the burning. It was perhaps rather an act of mercy, as the denser smoke from the green leaves and wood would be the more suffocating and thus abridge conscious suffering. The sulphur would have the same tendency.

[93] Mino Celso, *In haereticis coercendis* (1577), p. 109, reports hearing from trustworthy sources that many of the orthodox bystanders were persuaded by Servetus's constancy that this must be due to the spirit of God, and believing therefore that he was clearly a martyr, embraced his heresy as the truth.

[94] 97 *écus soleil*, 1 florin, 3 deniers; 6 gold rings, 1 gold chain weighing about 18 *écus*. cf. Calvin, viii, 831.

[95] *ibid.*, p. 832.

to the Swiss churches that the then banished Libertines had given protection and favor to Servetus at his trial.[96] Evidently all these testimonies rest only upon more or less probable conjecture, or upon mere suspicion. The only indication appearing above the surface was the appearance of Berthelier in the earlier proceedings, and of Perrin at the end of them.[97] On the other hand, Jean Trollier, repentant Libertine formerly Perrin's closest confidant, testified in 1558 that so far as he knew, the leading Libertines had never supported Servetus and other heretics in opposing 'our religion' and the ministers.[98] The whole truth, therefore, seems to be no more than this: that the Libertines had no interest in Servetus or his doctrines as such, but that they simply made a tool of him, secretly encouraging his defiant attitude as a means of annoying Calvin, while another case was pending in which they were much concerned; but that though they had a majority in the Council, they were entirely unwilling to come out into the open and bear the burden of his heresies, and actually took not a single effective step in his behalf. Even if some of them voted against conviction, at all events none of them had the hardihood to speak against it.[99]

It is well-nigh impossible to remain impartial in considering the case between Servetus and Calvin. When two persons are pitted against each other in mortal combat, each having such strongly marked and sharply contrasted characters, each uniting in a single individual outstanding abilities and admirable qualities together with lamentable defects, and each shamelessly displaying his worst side, one's sympathies can hardly remain quite neutral. Writers dealing with these two can nearly all be labeled according to their ill-concealed bias; by which those whose prime office as historians should be simply to present and interpret the facts, are yet irresistibly drawn to pronounce judgments of praise or blame. Moreover, the difficulty of coming to a just judgment is immensely increased since also it is so nearly impossible for one now to attain, and to retain for any length of time, a firm grasp of the mental

[96] Itaque probabilis suspicio est, alicunde vana fiducia inflatum fuisse, quae illum perdiderit. cf. Calvin, viii, 480; xiv, 693; xxi, 146; xiv, 624, 675; xx, 438.

[97] cf. Calvin, viii, 741; xiv, 657. The rumor reported by the author of *Contra libellum Calvini* (p. Dii.), that Servetus would have been put to the rack but for the intercession of Pierre Vandel, Calvin's enemy, seems highly incredible. The records of the trial show that it did not move in that plane.

[98] cf. Roget, *Genève*, iv, 337.

[99] Sine controversia damnatus est. Calvin, viii, 657. cf. Roland H. Bainton, 'Servetus and the Geneva Libertines,' *Church History*, v (1936), 140–149.

and spiritual background of the age in which this tragedy was enacted: its presuppositions, its prejudices, its intensity of convictions, its scale of values, all taken for granted, and all so different from those of the modern man.

Servetus shows himself at heart, and when not engaged in controversy, a devout and profoundly religious man, as deeply concerned as Calvin himself to have the Christian religion firmly grounded in the teachings of the Bible, and conformed to the 'uncorrupted' practice of the Ante-Nicene Church; and he was far more ready than Calvin to forsake even the most cherished doctrines and customs if they were found to lack scriptural support. But he had an eager, impetuous, almost fanatical temperament, in which feeling and passion played a much larger part than calm reason. When speaking from strong conviction of truth, he could show himself intolerably conceited toward an antagonist; and when impatient or irritated that others could not or would not see what seemed to him as clear as daylight, he displayed a mastery of the language of abuse which, in an age when courteous controversy was unknown, equaled if it did not surpass even that of Calvin himself.

Calvin, on the other hand, while a man of deep personal affections, and boundless in kindness to those that went his way, was in another aspect a cold-blooded logician, who never shrank from carrying out to the farthest limits whatever consequences followed from the premises he had adopted. In such a case, any feelings or sympathy he may normally have had were sternly repressed, and he acted with the relentless precision of a machine. It has been well said of him that as a man he was not cruel, but as a theologian he was merciless;[100] and it was as a theologian that he dealt with Servetus. In his *Institutes* he had wrought out with logical precision a systematic statement of Christian doctrine as he saw it, buttressed at every point by scripture authority. Any deviation from this he regarded not as a difference from him on a mere matter of personal opinion, but as a repudiation of the word of God, of which he was only the transmitter. Hence denial of the doctrines of Christianity as he taught them was not merely heresy, it was no less than blasphemy against God. To speak against these doctrines as Servetus did was to contradict God himself as well as to defame his messenger. When Servetus denied the accepted form of the doctrine of

[100] A. Bossert, *Calvin* (Paris, 1914), p. 171.

the Trinity and the deity of Christ, and rejected the hitherto universal practice of infant baptism, and sought to spread abroad his own views on these subjects, Calvin therefore looked upon him as committing the greatest conceivable crime, endangering the eternal welfare of countless souls. When to his denials Servetus added an exasperating manner in controversy and a profusion of insulting language, when he spoke of Calvin's God as a three-headed Cerberus, and of those that believe in him as atheists, and of infant baptism as an invention of the Devil, it can excite no wonder that Calvin, temperamentally irritable, bigoted in mind, and nervously worn to the point of exhaustion from his incessant struggle with the Libertines, should have declared war to the death with one who, as he believed, was at once attempting to undermine man's hope of eternal salvation, and apparently plotting for the overthrow of the Reformation at Geneva.

Nevertheless Calvin was, in theory, for toleration in religion. In his annotations to Seneca's work on Clemency, published when he was but twenty-three, as a warning against religious persecution, he said, 'It belongs to the nature of the merciful man that he not only uses opportunities of vengeance with moderation, but does not avail himself of even the most tempting occasions to take revenge.' [101] Again, in the first edition of his *Institutes of the Christian Religion* (1536), in his dedicatory epistle he addressed to King Francis I. of France brave words against persecution for differences of religious belief and practice; and in the treatise itself he says of the excommunicate 'We are bound to try in every possible way, whether by entreaty and instruction, or by mercy and kindness, or by our prayers to God, to bring them to a better life ... nor are the means to be anywise approved which many have employed hitherto, forbidding them water and fire and the common necessities of life, refusing them all acts of kindness, and pursuing them with the sword and arms.' [102] Also in the very year before the death of Servetus, addressing King Christian III. of Denmark, he wrote that 'wisdom is driven from among us, and the holy harmony of Christ's kingdom is compromised, when violence is pressed into the service of religion.' [103] Calvin had thus in theory long believed in the use of reasonable persua-

---

[101] Book II, chap. iii (Calvin, v, 152), as translated by Willis, *Servetus*, p. 300.

[102] cap. ii; *Calvin*, i, 77.

[103] Dedicatory epistle prefixed to Commentary on Acts, Feb. 29, 1552 (xiv, 294), as paraphrased by Willis, *op. cit.*, p. 512.

sion rather than force as a general policy in religion.[104] But when confronted with an actual and critical situation in which he believed that the eternal welfare of many souls was at stake, and the fate of the Reformation was threatened, he threw theory to the winds, and sought the shortest way to compass his ends.

It was thus inevitable that, if ever these two antipathetic characters, after their earlier approaches, came into personal contact, there would be a conflict without compromise or concession, or even any effort at mutual understanding. At any time before the passing of the sentence, Servetus might have escaped serious punishment by retracting, as Gentile did five years later. But unfortunately misled by hope of support from Calvin's opponents, and wholly overestimating the extent of it, he assumed an attitude increasingly defiant and insulting to Calvin, and thus threw away whatever chance of mercy he might have had. As Coleridge wrote of him: 'If ever a poor fanatic thrust himself into the fire, it was Michael Servetus. He was a rabid enthusiast, and did everything he could in the way of insult to provoke the feeling of the Christian Church.' [105] On the other hand, Calvin, wholly convinced that the system of Christian theology as he had stated it was ultimate truth, seems never seriously to have tried, perhaps would have been quite unable, fairly to understand Servetus's purpose as being, not to undermine Christian faith, but to place it on firmer foundations of Scripture, uncorrupted by hair-splitting philosophical speculation. Servetus, therefore, working single-handed at his project of reform, and in his impatience often resorting to weapons of the crudest and most offensive sort, was from the outset foredoomed to defeat. Whatever transformation Christian theology was to experience was to come about far more gradually and slowly, and under the mellowing influence of long periods of time.

[104] Luther, at the outset of his career as reformer, had said, 'The burning of heretics is contrary to the will of the Holy Spirit.' *Resolutio de Indulgentiis*, Conclusio lxxx., 1518.

[105] *Table Talk*, January 3, 1834.

CHAPTER XIII

AFTER DEATH, THE JUDGMENT:
CALVIN ON THE DEFENSIVE

THE BURNING OF SERVETUS settled only one of the questions raised by his appearance on the stage at Geneva. He himself was indeed now removed from the stage, and could no longer spread his ideas in person. But the burning of the man, as Calvin and other champions of the faith soon discovered, by no means put an end to his ideas; while it did bring to the front a much broader, more important and more vital question, that of religious toleration. Calvin's critics, in centering their attention on his responsibility for this tragedy, have largely overlooked the fact that in this case he was but the conspicuous embodiment of a policy toward heretics that was at the time universally accepted in principle by Protestants no less than by Catholics. It ought therefore to cause no surprise that from the most influential leaders of the Reformation this shocking occurrence called forth an all but unanimous response of approval. All this, however, was solely on an *ex parte* presentation of the case by Calvin, who had drawn the terms of the indictment of Servetus which formed the basis of the prosecution and sentence, and had taken the pains to prepare their minds for it. This approval was given by men not one of whom had had a fair opportunity to read and judge the book on which his conviction had been founded, if indeed they had even seen it, but who nevertheless endorsed all that was done, without apparent hesitation or further inquiry.[1]

Bullinger not only had approved of the death of Servetus in advance, but two years later he wrote that he was persuaded that if Satan were to return from hell and preach to the world as he pleased, he would

---

[1] Though a copy of the *Christianismi Restitutio* was indeed forwarded to the Swiss churches together with the various documents in the case, yet the two or three days during which the matter was under consideration at each place allowed for no proper study of the work or just judgment on it. Bullinger therefore requested that a copy be sent him for fuller examination, but he did not receive it until a month after Servetus's death. cf. Bullinger to Calvin and Calvin to Bullinger, in Calvin, xiv, 659, 671, 684.

employ many of Servetus's expressions.[2] Years afterwards he still firmly held that the Geneva Council had done its duty in this case.[3] Peter Martyr wrote in 1556, 'I have nothing to say of the Spaniard Servetus except that he was a veritable son of the Devil, whose poisonous and detestable doctrine should everywhere be hunted down; and the magistrate that condemned him to death should not be blamed, seeing that there was no hope of his amendment, and that his blasphemies were quite intolerable.'[4] Gallicius at Chur commended the deed;[5] Walther at Zürich saw the hand of God in it;[6] Musculus at Bern broke into verse over it;[7] Dr. Gratarolo at Basel, though doubtful as to the death by fire, believed that Servetus deserved two deaths rather than only one;[8] while Sulzer at Basel, Haller at Bern, and Farel at Neuchâtel had all spoken unmistakably in the course of the trial.

At a greater distance, despite theological differences between Calvinists and Lutherans, the approval of Melanchthon was no less pronounced. He wrote to Calvin, 'I maintain that your magistrates did right in putting a blasphemer to death by regular judicial process.'[9] A year later he expressed the formal opinion that the Geneva council did right in putting Servetus to death for reviving the heresy of Paul of Samosata and denying the deity of Christ and the worship of the Son of God.[10] At almost the same time and in the same tone he wrote to Bullinger, expressing surprise that any disapproved so severe a punishment.[11] Yet two years later, in an admonition about the case of Thamer,

---

[2] Persuadeo mihi, Si Sathanas ex inferis rediret, & pro libidine sua orbi praedicaret, usurum multis Serveti Hispani loquutionibus. 'Epistola ad Polonos,' in Fueslin, *Epistolae*, p. 371.

[3] Quod cum applissimus Genevensis Senatus fecit, pro pio suo officio, quod debuit, fecit. Unde eius factum judiciumve sanctum, nunquam accusavimus, neque nunc quoque accusamus. In preface to Josias Simler, *Libri IV. de aeterna Dei Filio* (Tiguri, 1570).

[4] Letter to the Nobles of Poland, Feb. 14, 1556; quoted by Doumergue, *Calvin*, vi, 387.

[5] Gallicius to Bullinger, Nov. 20, 1553; Calvin, xiv, 668.

[6] Gualtherus to Haller, Nov. 26, 1553; *ibid.*, 683.

[7] Musculus to Blaurer, Dec. 22, 1553, *ibid.*, 708 f. Various other poems called forth by the execution of Servetus are reprinted by Allwoerden, *Servetus*, pp. 116–129 f; Mosheim, *Versuch*, p. 276 ff; Michel de la Roche, 'Historical account of the life and trial of Michael Servetus,' *Memoirs of Literature* (ed. 2, London, 1717), iv, 320–333.

[8] Gratarolus to Bullinger, Nov. 16, 1553, Calvin, xiv, 666.

[9] Affirmo etiam vestros magistratus juste fecisse, quod hominem blasphemum re ordine judicata interfecerint. Melanchthon to Calvin, Oct. 14, 1554; Melanchthon, *Opera*, viii, 362; Calvin, xv, 268.

[10] Melanchthon, viii, 520.

[11] Melanchthon to Bullinger, Aug. 20, 1555, *Opera*, viii, 523; also in Calvin, xv, 734.

who was disturbing the peace of the church at Minden, he held up the course pursued at Geneva in the treatment of incorrigible blasphemy as a good example, and one deserving to be remembered to all posterity.[12] In short, down to the end of the sixteenth century the chief spokesmen of Lutheranism in Germany expressly approved of Servetus's death.[13]

Even at the time, however, and even among those whose orthodoxy was not under suspicion, the sentence pronounced against Servetus was not unanimously approved. It has already been noted that Vergerio was opposed to a capital sentence.[14] Also, while the case was under consideration by the churches, David Joris, then living in the full odor of sanctity at Basel, addressed to the magistrates of the Swiss cities an anonymous epistle containing an earnest plea for Servetus, urging them that as disciples of Christ they should not put one to death for his teaching, but rather give him kindly warning, and at most only banish him.[15] Basel, indeed, as the chief centre of liberal thought and tolerant sentiment in Switzerland, was naturally the focus of reaction against the measures that Calvin had taken at Geneva. The influence of Erasmus still survived here; Borrhäus (Cellarius), Castellio and Curioni were professors at the University, and Ochino, Laelius Socinus, Joris, and later Acontius were sojourners. Borrhäus had been a secret correspondent of Servetus,[16] and it was reported that he had not favored his death, and that he and some of the lesser ministers of the city who agreed with him had therefore not been invited to join in the reply that the rest sent to Geneva.[17] Within a month of Servetus's death Vergerio,

---

[12] Dedit vere et Genevensis Reip. Magistratus ante annos quatuor punitae insanabilis blasphemiae adversus Filium Dei, sublato Serveto Arragone pium et memorabile ad omnem posteritatem exemplum. Melanchthon, *Opera*, ix, 133. He repeatedly reaffirmed the judgment subsequently. cf. *Opera*, ix, 1003; x, 851; xii, 143; xxiv, 501.

[13] C. H. Barckhusen, *Historica Narratio de Johanne Calvino* (Berlin, 1721), pp. 147–150, lists nearly forty Lutheran and Reformed theologians that approved, and quotes from many of them. cf. N. Paulus, 'Servet's Hinrichtung im Lutherischen Urteil,' *Historisch-politische Blätter für das katholische Deutschland*, cxxxvi, 2er Band (1905), 175.

[14] cf. Calvin, xiv, 633.

[15] Original in Joris's *Sendbrieven*, Boek i., Deel 4, Brief 9; reproduced in Allwoerden, *op. cit.*, pp. 87–93; Mosheim, *op. cit.*, pp. 421–425; English translation in Roland H. Bainton, *Concerning Heretics* (New York, 1935), pp. 305–309. The letter bears the date, July 1, 1553, which is obviously a slip for Oct. 1. It admits of doubt whether the letter was ever actually sent; nevertheless it bears witness to a current sentiment.

[16] Miserat enim librum manuscriptum Servetus Borrae, ut de eo judicaret, antequam imprimeretur. From an unpublished Ms fragment of *Contra libellum Calvini*, quoted by Buisson, *Castellion*, ii, 478.

[17] Cellarum (sic!) etiam eius urbis summum Professorem Theologiae, affirmant

Gallicius, Dr. Gratarolo and Calvin all wrote Bullinger from different quarters complaining of this sympathy with Servetus, or at least of this tolerant attitude, in high quarters,[18] and Bullinger begged Calvin not to mention in his projected defence the attitude of these Basileans. Calvin complied with the request.[19]

To stem this apparently rising tide of discontent, which might fall in all too well with any designs the Libertines at Geneva might still have on foot, it seemed important that Calvin should issue some convincing defence of what had been done, by submitting to the judgment of the world all the facts, of which they had hitherto had only scattered fragments or distorted rumors. Something of this sort had been authorized by the Council at the close of the trial; and as requests had come from the 'German cities,' (i.e., those in German Switzerland) for information as to Servetus's opinions, Calvin was voted leave to print a book on the subject.[20] He took up the project with due zeal, having already written Bullinger that as soon as he was somewhat rested he would show in a short book what a monster Servetus was, in order to stop the mouths of slanderers like those at Basel, as well as the complaints of the uninformed.[21] Bullinger gave his hearty encouragement, saying that a history of the whole affair would be highly useful, not to say necessary, and reminding him to point out that blasphemers like Servetus were justly put to death, and to give a full description of Servetus and his end, that all men might abhor the beast.[22] Viret at Lausanne and Musculus at Bern also anxiously awaited it.[23]

The work appeared about the beginning of February, 1554,[24] and a

---

nuncquam nec in Serveti, nec in illius haeretici mortem consensisse. Idemque putant de quibusdam eius urbis ministris inferioribus, qui ad dicendam de Serveto sententiam, propterea non fuerunt vocati. *Contra libellum Calvini*, p. Miii.

[18] cf. Vergerio to Bullinger, Oct. 14; Gallicius to Bullinger, Oct. 19; Gratarolus to Bullinger, Oct. 28, Nov. 16; Calvin to Bullinger, Nov. 22, 1553. Calvin, xiv, 642, 649, 658, 666, 671.

[19] Bullinger to Calvin, Nov. 28, 1553; Calvin to Bullinger, Dec. 31, 1553; Calvin, xiv, 684, 723.   [20] Dec. 11, 1553, Calvin, viii, 832.

[21] Calvin to Bullinger, Nov. 22, 1553, xiv, 671.

[22] Bullinger to Calvin, Nov. 28, Dec. 13, 1553; Calvin, xiv, 684, 698.

[23] Calvin, xiv, 690, 708.

[24] Calvin, viii, p. xxviii. *Defensio orthodoxae fidei, contra prodigiosos errores Michaelis Serveti Hispani: ubi ostenditur haereticos jure gladii coercendos esse, et nominatim de homine hoc tam impie juste et merito sumptum Genevae fuisse supplicium.* The work is often cited under one of the sub-titles: *Fidelis expositio errorum Michaelis Serveti*; or, *Refutatio errorum Michaelis Serveti*; or, *Brevis refutatio*; or, by the title of the French version (*infra*). Printed in Calvin, viii, 453–644.

French version late in the same month.[25] Calvin thought that though it was hurriedly written it was better than nothing.[26] It was, he admitted, perhaps too condensed in style for clearness, for almost his sole purpose was to show all men the detestable irreverence of Servetus, so that even the plain man might without much trouble find the involved subtleties of Servetus straightened out and made clear. But if it were seen that he had sincerely defended sound doctrine, he was content.[27] Copies were at once despatched to the leading reformers.[28]

The *Defensio* is not a literary unity. Upon a brief and very loose thread of narrative, in which however are found various interesting data not elsewhere reported, there are strung: a closely-knit argument defending the rightfulness of putting heretics to death (pp. 461–479); a discussion of three questions proposed to Calvin by Servetus in his Vienne period [29] (pp. 482–495); the propositions drawn up by Calvin as a basis for the written discussion in the course of the trial, together with Servetus's replies, the refutation of the ministers, and Servetus's brief rejoinders (pp. 501–553); the response of the Zürich ministers (pp. 555–558); a fuller exposition by Calvin of the errors of Servetus (pp. 559–588); and a refutation in the name of the Geneva ministers of the calumnies that he had heaped upon Calvin in the written discussion (pp. 587–644). The whole therefore offered both a general and a specific defence of the execution of Servetus.

Calvin, though otherwise disinclined to treat of this matter, felt called upon to do so, he said, since the teachings of Servetus were spreading, and many were in danger of being misled unless put on their guard against so serious a danger. Moreover, since the death of Servetus, new discussions had been stirred up which required answer. He would be untrue to his faith if he kept silent while souls were being lost. He first

---

[25] *Declaration pour maintenir la vraye foi que tiennent tous Chrestiens de la Trinite des personnes en un seul Dieu. Contre les erreurs detestables de Michel Servet Espaignol. Ou il est aussi monstre, qu'il est licite de punir les heretiques; et qu'a bon droit ce meschant a este execute par justice en la ville de Genève.* This version does not strictly follow the Latin version, but has many longer or shorter omissions, additions, or changes rather freely made, doubtless by Calvin himself. Mosheim (*Versuch*, p. 237) and Trechsel (*Antitrinitarier*, i, 264) are in error in making the French version precede the Latin. cf. Calvin, viii, p. xxxiii.

[26] Calvin to Bullinger, Feb. 23, 1554; xv, 40.

[27] Calvin to Bullinger, Apr. 29, 1554; xv, 124.

[28] Calvin, xv, 19 ff.

[29] *v. supra*, p. 133.

refutes some current objections to the use of the sword in religious matters, and the argument that kindness should be used rather than force, and says it would be no kindness to expose the sheep to attack while sparing the wolves.[30] Coming to the positive side of the argument he shows by ample scripture instances that punishment of false teaching is divinely sanctioned; and that while minor errors may be patiently dealt with, and moderate ones may have moderate punishment, blasphemous attempts to overthrow the very foundations of religion deserve the extreme penalty. The milder policy had long been used with Servetus and had failed. Every chance had been given him to escape death; but as he had shown himself invincibly stubborn and intolerably irreverent, there was no other way. Finally, evidence of Calvin's patient treatment, and of Servetus's shocking language, was offered in detail. Calvin nowhere expresses the least regret at what has been done, and throughout shows the utmost loathing and contempt for Servetus as a very monster of iniquity, applying to him the foulest epithets. Seldom if ever in religious history has posthumous insult been more violent or odious, or more self-righteously used as in the service of God.[31]

Sulzer approved the work as holy and accurate, and strongly calculated to profit the churches and confound and refute those that oppose the punishment of heretics.[32] Musculus, in answer to Blaurer, who had withheld his own opinion, spoke with more reserve. While not disapproving the death of Servetus, he thought that if the charge had been blasphemy instead of heresy, less offence would have been given to those that had disagreed about the burning of heretics, and less occasion would have been given to the Papists to continue their cruel treatment of heretics.[33] For at this very period Protestants were being burned by the scores in France, and the Catholic reaction under 'bloody Mary' was

[30] Calvin considered heresy worse than murder or poisoning, and a treason against God. cf. xxiv, 362; xxvii, 244 f; xxix, 337 f; xliv, 347 f.

[31] For examples, among many, cf. detestabilis impietas; rabies magis quam bilem effudit; pestiferum; vomitu . . asini ruditum . . rabies; obscoenus canis; belluina stupiditas; haec bestiae ferocitas. Calvin, viii, 452, 460, 480 f, 498, 589.

[32] Sulzer to Bullinger, Feb. 26, 1554, Calvin, xv, 44; cf. Sulzer to Blaurer, Mar. 9, 1554, *ibid.*, xv, 74.

[33] Musculus to Blaurer, Feb. 27, 1554. De Serveto, quod flammis est absumptus, non improbo factum senatus Genevensis. Existimo autem potuisse illud rectius et convenientius defendi titulo blasphemiae quam titulo haereseos, et minus offensi boni viri, qui de haereticis comburendis diversum sentiunt, et scripserunt, denique non fuisset et furori et crudelitati papistarum objecta occasio in saevitia sua pertinacius quam antea pergendi. Calvin, xv, 47.

beginning in England. The statement of the Catholic Varillas, that Calvin's defence of exterminating heretics was not well received by the Calvinists in France, is credible enough.[84] Dr. Gratarolo praised the excellent and powerful book, and wondered that any could have disapproved the death of such a sink and sewer of all heresies, or could even adhere to his doctrine, though in secret.[35] Farel was enraptured with the work, and exhausted his vocabulary of adjectives in reproach of Servetus, who was now exposed as the prince of heretics, and whose power to harm was at length destroyed. All good Christians would be Calvin's debtors.[36] Bullinger thought the treatment too brief for clearness, and the argument too heavy for the common mind to grasp, yet all good men would be very grateful for it, most of all the more learned. Viret was of the same mind.[37] Melanchthon wrote Calvin that the Church would be forever grateful to him, and Calvin was greatly pleased at this 'splendid testimonial.'[38] In the Lutheran world the outstanding confutation of the *Restitutio* of Servetus was by Professor Alexander Alesius of Leipzig in four academic disputations.[39]

Even among Calvin's followers, however, there was division of judgment, though those that dissented from him were naturally not too outspoken, lest they be set down as sympathizing with the views of Servetus. The carefully guarded criticism of Vergerio and Musculus has been noted above; and even before the death of Servetus was known at Basel, Gratarolo wrote to Bullinger that there were some there, especially those that would be deemed the most learned and distinguished (referring to academic circles), who sympathized with Servetus, and who stigmatized Calvin as an executioner.[40] Nicholas Zurkinden also, Secretary of State and one of the most honored and cultivated citizens of Bern, as well as a broad-minded friend of Calvin, had seen and heard too much of the cruelty of the sword as used against Anabaptists, and freely confessed that he would have it very rarely used in defence of

[34] cf. Varillas, *Révolutions*, iv, 255.

[35] Gratarolus to Bullinger, Feb. 21, 1554, Calvin, xv, 45.

[36] Farel to Calvin, Mar. 8, 1554, Calvin, xv, 71.

[37] Bullinger to Calvin, Mar. 26, 1554; Calvin, xv, 90. Viret to Calvin, May 15, 1554; Calvin, xv, 139 f.

[38] Melanchthon to Calvin, Oct. 14, 1554; Calvin, xv, 268. Calvin to Melanchthon, Mar. 5, 1555; Calvin, xv, 488.

[39] Alexander Alesius (Praeses), *Contra horrendas Serveti blasphemias*, etc. (Lipsiae, 1554–'55). The whole four parts are extremely rare, but are to be found at Berlin and Munich. cf. also Johannes Wigand, *De Servetianismo* (Regiomonti, 1575).

[40] Gratarolus to Bullinger, Oct. 28, 1553, Calvin, xiv, 658.

faith. Better results had been obtained by milder treatment, so Musculus had reported to him. While he did not disapprove the death of wicked blasphemers like Servetus, the onus of which must in any case lie upon the Council, yet he did not approve such punishment for heretics and dissidents in general.[41] Calvin complained that some censured him harshly as a master of cruelty and atrocity in attacking with his pen a dead man whose death he himself had caused;[42] while others though well-disposed to him wished he had never taken up the subject of the punishment of heretics. So Bullinger assured him.[43] Frecht of Ulm questioned whether life imprisonment would not have been better, and desired to know what Negelin and Sulzer thought about it.[44] Toussain of Montbéliard confessed that as he was by nature disposed to mildness he should have preferred to have Servetus given longer time for repentance.[45]

Above the undertone of these guarded murmurs, however, there now rose a loud and clear voice squarely protesting against the principle advocated and defended in Calvin's apologetical work. Not much more than a month after the *Defensio* there appeared at Basel a secretly printed anonymous book on the punishment of heretics which, as almost the earliest [46] and one of the most eloquent pamphlets against intolerance in matters of religion, marked the rise of a new spirit in Protestantism.[47] The body of the work consisted of extracts on toleration

[41] Zerchintes to Calvin, Feb. 10, Apr. 7, 1554, Calvin, xv, 20 f, 115 f.

[42] Referring to the so-called *Historia de morte Serveti* in the *Contra libellum Calvini*, p. Miv.b.

[43] Calvin to Bullinger, Apr. 29, 1554, Bullinger to Calvin, June 12, 1554, Calvin, xv, 124, 158.

[44] Frecht to Negelin, June 12, 1554, Calvin, xv, 155 f.

[45] Tossanus to Calvin, Oct. 9, 1554, Calvin, xv, 262.

[46] Not forgetting the mediaeval Marsiglio of Padua, nor the Anabaptist Hubmaier's *Von Ketzeren und ihren Verbrennern*, 1524.

[47] *De haereticis, an sint persequendi, & omnino quomodo sit cum eis agendum, doctorum virorum tum veterum, tum recentiorum sententiae. Liber hoc tam turbulento tempore pernecessarius, & cum omnibus, tum potissimum principibus & magistratibus utilissimus, ad discendum, quodnam sit eorum in re tam controversa, tamque periculosa, officium.* (Magdeburgi, 1554, mense Martio). A few weeks later appeared (probably at Lyon) a French edition: *Traicté des heretiques, a savoir, si on les doit persecuter*, etc. (Reprint, Genève, 1913). German translation, undated, *Von Kaetzern, ob man auch die verfolgen*, etc. Dutch translation, *Van ketteren*, etc., c. 1620; again, *Het gevoelen van verscheyden zo oude als nieuwe schrijvers aeng. de ketters*, etc. (Amsterdam, 1663). English translation with introduction and notes by Roland H. Bainton, *Concerning Heretics* (New York, 1935). The work was published at the expense of a wealthy Italian refugee, Bernardino Bonifazio, Marquis d'Oria. cf. Buisson, *Castellion*, ii, 14–18; Francesco Ruffini, 'Il giureconsulto chierese Matteo Gribaldi Mofa e Calvino,' *Rivista di Storia del diritto*

taken from some twenty-five Christian writers ancient and modern, including Calvin himself and Luther; but the most significant parts of the work were a dedication to Duke Christoph of Württemberg by 'Martin Bellius' (preceded in the French edition by 'the translator's' dedication to Duke Christoph's son-in-law, Count Wilhelm of Hesse), and a refutation of the reasons usually given for persecution, by 'Basil Montfort.' Beza, who was then teaching at Lausanne, and was daily growing more devoted to Calvin and his cause, early took note of the new work, and at once saw in the 'Magdeburg' of the title-page only a cover for Basel. He also strongly suspected that Castellio lay concealed under the assumed name of Bellius, and that Laelius Socinus and Coelius Secundus Curioni (Lat., Curio)[48] had a share in the author-ship.[49] Calvin entertained a similar suspicion. Curioni strenuously

Italiano, i (1928), 224; Frederick C. Church, *The Italian Reformers*, 1534–1564 (New York, 1932), chap. xi.

[48] Curioni (as he himself wrote his name) was born at Cirie in the province of Turin in 1503. After several narrow escapes from the Inquisition he fled to Switzerland (meeting Renato on the way), became Rector of the newly founded university at Lausanne in 1542, and four years later went to Basel where as Professor of Eloquence he taught the ancient classics with great distinction till his death in 1569, and attracted many students from Poland and other foreign lands. His great reputation won him flattering invitations to go elsewhere: from the Pope to come to Rome, from the Duke of Savoy to Turin, from the Emperor to the university in Vienna, and from the Prince of Transylvania to the new college he was establishing at Alba Julia. He declined them all. Though not a professed theologian he wrote *Christianae religionis institutio*, 1549, from which he omitted any mention of the Trinity or the deity of Christ as doctrines necessary to salvation. In 1550 he attended the Anabaptist council at Venice (Benrath, *Reformation*, p. 79). In 1554 he published a work *De amplitudine beati regni Dei* (with a noteworthy dedication to King Sigismund Augustus of Poland), in which he opposed Calvin's doctrine of predestination, proving from Scripture and reason that the great majority of mankind will ultimately be saved. In 1559 indications appeared that he was infected with the heresies of Gribaldi (see chapter xv.), and the meddlesome trouble-maker Vergerio of Strassburg accused him of heresy, but the university at Basel exonerated him (cf. Trechsel, *Antitrinitarier*, i, 216 f; Church, *Reformers*, p. 288 f). Though he was cautious about committing himself to compromising doctrinal positions, his latitudinarian tendencies and his intimacy with Castellio, Ochino, Laelius Socinus and others at Basel and elsewhere fairly entitle him to be counted as one of the precursors of the Socinian-Unitarian movement.

cf. J. G. Schelhorn, 'C. Secundi Curionis ejusque familiae historia,' *Amoenitates*, xiv, 325–402; *id.*, 'Historia Dialogorum . . . de amplitudine,' *ibid.*, xii (1730), 592–627; *id.*, *Amoenitates historiae ecclesiasticae*, i, 759–776 (Frankfurt, 1737); W. G. Streuber, 'Celio S. Curioni und seine Familie,' *Basler Taschenbuch*, iv, 45–95 (Basel, 1853). Carl Schmidt, 'Celio Secondo Curioni,' *Zeitschrift für die historische Theologie*, xxx (1860), 571–634; Robert Wallace, *Antitrinitarian Biography* (London, 1850), ii, 19–44; Stanisław Kot, 'Polacy w Bazylei za czasów Zygmunta Augusta' (Poles at Basel in the time of Sigismund Augustus), *Reformacja w Polsce*, i (1921), 108–119.

[49] cf. Beza to Bullinger, Mar. 28, May 7, June 14, 1554, Calvin, xv, 97, 134 f, 165–168; Calvin to Bullinger, Mar. 28, 1554, *ibid.*, xv, 95.

denied having had any hand in it,[50] and nothing was ever proved of Socinus; enough that the group of liberal spirits then living or sojourning at Basel (Borrhäus, Castellio, Curioni, Joris, Ochino, Laelius Socinus) may all in some measure have collaborated in the work. But it is now conclusively demonstrated that Castellio disguised himself under the names of Bellius and Montfort, and possibly also under that of Georg Kleinberg, and that he was the responsible guiding spirit of the whole.[51]

Sebastian Castellio [52] was born in 1515 at Saint-Martin-du-Fresne, a village of Bresse, about thirty-five miles west of Geneva. He was educated at Lyon, where he established a reputation as a classical scholar and teacher. Having adopted the views of the Reformation, he went to Strassburg at the time of Calvin's exile there from Geneva. Calvin gave him friendship, and after his recall to Geneva he invited Castellio thither in 1541 to be Rector of the reorganized college. Finding after a year or two that his salary here was quite inadequate, he sought admission to the company of the city's pastors. But though he was admitted to be otherwise admirably fitted for such an office, yet he showed a mind too independent and a spirit too little docile to fit well into Calvin's régime; for upon examination it transpired that he could not with good conscience accept the Song of Solomon as a sacred book worthy to be included in the Bible, and that he did not accept the article of the creed about Christ's descent into hell.[53] He was therefore refused admission to the ministry, and not long afterwards resigning his office he left Ge-

---

[50] Bullinger to Calvin, Apr. 22, 1554, Calvin, xv, 119.

[51] Beza's statement that Castellio was reported to have disowned the work (*aiunt ab eo esse ejuratum*) may be disregarded as a mere rumor quoted by a notoriously inaccurate historian. cf. Calvin, xxi, 149. He was not certain about it in 1563. cf. Beza to Gratarolus, Aug. 11, 1563, Calvin, xx, 132. *v.* review of a recently discovered Ms in *Church History*, ix (1940), 271.

[52] The Latin form of his name, and the one most frequently used (Fr., Castellion). The native French form was Châteillon or Châtillon; while for a time he was pleased to adopt the form Castalio (Fr., Castalion). For his life cf. Buisson, *Castellion;* Étienne Giran, *Sébastien Castellion et la Réforme Calviniste* (Haarlem, 1913); Jakob Maehly, *Sebastian Castellio* (Basel, 1863); J. C. Fuesslin, *Sebastian Castellio* (Frankfurt, 1775); (also in N. Barkey's *Bibliotheca Hagana* (Amsterdam, 1771) iii, 441–486; *Athenae Rauricae* (Basel, 1778), pp. 354–360; Jules Bonnet, 'Sébastian Castalion ou la tolérance au xviᵉ siècle,' *Bulletin du Protestantisme Français*, xvi, xvii. (1867–'68); Rufus M. Jones, 'Sebastian Castellio: a forgotten prophet' (in his *Spiritual Reformers*); Roland H. Bainton, *Sebastian Castellio and the toleration controversy of the sixteenth century*, in the volume, "Persecution and Liberty" (New York, 1931); Stefan Zweig, *The right to heresy: Castellio against Calvin* (New York, 1936).

[53] cf. Calvin, xi, 673–676; xxi, 328 f, 336–340.

neva disappointed and resentful against the pastors and especially against Calvin, and sought employment elsewhere.[54] Calvin was at first disposed to treat him kindly, but relations between them soon became strained, and thenceforth to the end of his days Calvin treated him with that bitter and implacable hatred which he displayed toward those that opposed or disagreed with him. Castellio, embittered in turn by Calvin's persistent attacks, received them in anything but a spirit of Christian meekness. From Geneva he went to Basel, and here for eight long years he dragged out a miserable existence in extreme poverty, earning for himself and his numerous family a precarious living by correcting proof, a little teaching, fishing, and manual labor of the most menial sort. Meantime every spare hour was given to what had become the great project of his life, a new and improved translation of the whole Bible from the original tongues. He hoped thus to make it more acceptable to the educated by rendering it into correct and simple Latin in place of the debased Latin of the current Vulgate; and also to the common people by dressing it in vivid current French. By this he designed to do for France what Luther's Bible had done for Germany; and his work reminds one of recent attempts to render the Bible into modern colloquial English. At length, in the very year of Servetus's death, he was made Professor of Greek at the University of Basel. Here he was greatly beloved by his students, while on the other hand Calvin and Beza for years kept urging the Basel authorities to prosecute him as a dangerous enemy of religion as they conceived it. In 1561 their attacks almost drove him to leave Basel and seek refuge in Poland.[55] It was while such a prosecution was on hand that, worn out by all that he had long suffered in body and mind, he at last weakened and died in 1563 at the early age of forty-eight. Beza and Bullinger rejoiced at his death.[56]

[54] In the face of the record, Beza's statement (*Vita Calvini*, Calvin, xxi, 135), often repeated by later writers, that he was forced to leave the city, is destitute of truth. He resigned voluntarily, and bore a testimonial from the pastors, including Calvin.

[55] cf. Church, *Reformers*, pp. 340–342. He had been present at the posthumous execution of Joris in 1558. cf. Buisson, *op. cit.*, ii, 156.

[56] cf. Calvin, xx, 242, 256; Giran, *op. cit.*, p. 432 f. He was buried in the tomb of the illustrious Grynaeus family, in the west cloister of the Münster, and three young Polish noblemen who had been his grateful students marked his burial place with an inscribed stone (cf. Calvin, xx, 240). When the tomb was later opened for another internment, the fragile stone was unfortunately broken and is no longer extant, though the epitaph has been preserved. The legend, current since Scaliger (*Scaligerana*, Amsterdam, 1740, ii, 360), that the body was removed as that of a heretic and interred elsewhere, is exploded. cf. Maehly, *op. cit.*, p. 80 ff; Buisson, *op. cit.*, ii, 264, 500.

CHAPTER XIV

CASTELLIO AND THE STRUGGLE FOR TOLERATION: SERVETUS IN RETROSPECT

WHEN the Reformation brought a conflict of new ideas into Christian Europe, it was at first uncertain how they would be met. After a brief hesitation, the Church decided to repress them by force, if necessary, through the civil power guided by the Inquisition, whether by the stake as in Spain and France, by massacre as in the Vaudois valleys, or by mass executions as in the Low Countries. The early reformers had suffered too much by this method to be willing to approve it, and at first Luther and Calvin wrote in condemnation of it. The Protestant extermination of Anabaptists was more on political and social than on religious grounds. The new church had not formally pronounced itself on this subject and, until the case of Servetus, persecution purely for heresy had been as rare among Protestants as it was usual among Catholics. Even after the leaders of the Reformation had generally approved the death of Servetus there was a significant if timid minority that stood for the principle that there should be no persecution for religion; that conscience should be free since faith was given by God rather than to be imposed by man, and hence should not be subject to force. Even before the publication of *De Haereticis*, or of Calvin's *Defensio*, Castellio had prefixed to his Latin translation of the Bible (1551) a dedication to Edward VI., the young Protestant King of England, in which he made what has been called the first manifesto in favor of toleration.[1] In this he urges that true religion makes slow progress because we engage in endless disputes, which issue only in bloodshed,

[1] cf. Doumergue, *Calvin*, vi, 434. In contrast to this Calvin had a little more than two years before (Oct. 22, 1548) urged upon the Duke of Somerset, Lord Protector, the opposite policy to be followed in establishing the Protestant faith in England. Speaking of enemies to the Reformation: "les ungs sont gens fantastiques, qui soubs couleur de l'Evangile vouldroient mettre tout en confusion. Les autres sont gens obstinez aux superstitions de lantechrist de Rome. Tous ensemble meritent bien destre reprimez par le glaive qui vous est commis"; Calvin, xiii, 68. Castellio's preface is reprinted in *Contra libellum Calvini*, pp. Oiii.–Pb; and in Bainton's *Heretics*, pp. 212–216. It is well summarized, with extracts, in Buisson, *op. cit.*, i, 303–308.

while we condemn those that differ from us, and pretend to do it in the name of Christ. But it is absurd to use earthly weapons in spiritual warfare, in which the enemies of Christians, which are vices, are to be overcome by virtues. If we tolerate among us Turks, Jews, and sinners in general, how much more should we suffer those that confess the name of Christ, but would rather die than violate their consciences. In the three years that followed, Castellio evidently pursued this subject further, with especial attention to what others had said on the subject, so that when the death of Servetus had forced the question of toleration into public notice, and Calvin had with all his ability defended the principle of persecution, the ground was well prepared for *De Haereticis*.

Calvin's argument for the capital punishment of heretics was based upon the assumption, at the time almost universally accepted without question or examination, that one's eternal salvation depended upon one's acceptance of the central dogmas of the Trinity, the eternal divinity of Christ, and the like. Castellio did not make a direct personal attack upon Calvin, but he sought to shatter the force of this argument by boldly challenging the truth of this major premise. In his dedication to Duke Christoph,[2] which bears a striking resemblance to that to Edward VI., he says that the cultivation of Christian character is neglected while Christians spend their time in disputes about speculative questions, such as the nature of Christ, the Trinity, predestination, free will, also about the eucharist and baptism, which are not necessary to salvation, and do not make a man better; while they condone moral offences, and condemn as heretics those with whom they disagree. He hates heretics, but the name is often misapplied, and the offence is too severely punished, whereas the extreme punishment should be banishment.

Castellio's book, with the persuasive reasoning of its dedication amply reinforced by extensive quotations from so many honored Christian writers, produced a profound impression in the Swiss churches. Beza, now thoroughly aroused as Calvin's champion, at once saw what a critical challenge was offered to the whole orthodox system by this revolutionary book. He wrote in alarm to Bullinger: 'If what he has spewed out in his preface is to be endured, what, pray, have we left of the Christian religion? The doctrines of the office of Christ, the Trinity, the Lord's Supper, baptism, justification, free will, the state of souls after death, are either useless or at least not necessary to salvation. No

---

[2] Translation in Bainton, *op. cit.*, pp. 121–135.

one is to be condemned as a heretic. You see what this leads to. I have
therefore decided to reply.' [3] In order to spare Calvin the trouble, who
was busily occupied in writing his commentary on Genesis,[4] and to
counteract and correct the impression created by Castellio's book, Beza
undertook to prepare a reply. He went at his self-imposed task *con
amore*, and published his work early in September.[5] Regarding Servetus as a monster, 'of all men that have ever lived the most wicked and
blasphemous,' and those that condemned his death as 'emissaries of
Satan,' [6] and the liberty of conscience for which Castellio had pleaded
as a simply diabolical doctrine,[7] he went on with all the wrath of intense
conviction to controvert Castellio's positions point by point, and on
historical and scriptural grounds to argue successively, on the contrary,
that heretics are to be punished, that they are to be punished by the civil
magistrate, and that in extreme cases they are to be put to death.[8]

Beza had early in life studied law, and with great skill he presented
a clear, methodical, consistent and eloquent argument, which must have
seemed conclusive for those that accepted his (and Calvin's) premise,
that belief in the Trinity is the very foundation of the Christian religion,
and absolutely necessary to salvation — the point with which Castellio
squarely took issue in contending that this and the related doctrines not
only are unscriptural, speculative and in controversy, but are in any
case of subordinate importance. Beza argued this point at length.[9] He
declared that to make religion consist, as Castellio did, in a pure heart,
and in the correction and reformation of life, is blasphemy, impiety,
sacrilege; [10] for the chief aim of society is to maintain religion, and at
the centre of this lies doctrine, so that one who attacks this undermines
society. Society therefore must defend itself by force, even unto death

---

[3] Beza to Bullinger, Mar. 29, cf. May 7, 1554, Calvin, xv, 97, 134 f.

[4] cf. *Vita Calvini*, Calvin, xxi, 149.

[5] *De haereticis a civili magistratu puniendis libellus, adversus Martini Bellii farraginem,
& novorum Academicorum sectam.* (Geneva, 1554). French translation, *Traité de l'au-
thorité du Magistrat en la punition des hérétiques*, etc. (Genève, 1560). Dutch translation, *Van het ketterstraffen* (Franeker, 1601). Also in his *Opuscula*, (Geneva, 1568), pp.
85–169. cf. Buisson, *op. cit.*, ii, 18, 27.

[6] cf. *Vita Calvini*, Calvin, xxi, 146; *De haereticis*, p. 3 f.

[7] *Est enim hoc vere diabolicum dogma*; Letter to Dudith, June 18, 1570, in Beza,
Epistolae theologicae, (ed. 2, Genevae, 1575), p. 20.

[8] The argument is well summarized by Henry M. Baird, *Theodore Beza* (New York,
1899), pp. 59–69; and by Buisson, *op. cit.*, ii, 18–28.

[9] cf. *De haereticis*, pp. 29–63.

[10] *ibid.*, pp. 41, 52.

if necessary, since no greater crime is conceivable than blasphemy, which leads souls to eternal death. Zanchi at Strassburg was also moved to write a treatise on the same subject, though after seeing what Beza had written he felt that his own work might be superfluous; while some dissuaded him lest it make the case of Protestants in Catholic lands worse rather than better. It is not known to have been published.[11] While Beza's work was calculated to confirm Calvin's supporters in their views, it does not seem otherwise to have made any notable impression, unless by supporting Catholics in continuing their policy against Protestants, which eighteen years later culminated in the St. Bartholomew's day massacre in France.

There was, however, a significant minority to whom this defence of the criminal prosecution of heretics did not in the least appeal. It was natural that feeling on this subject should be strongest among the Italian and French refugees in Switzerland who had themselves fled their native lands to escape the very fate that had overtaken Servetus, and now began to be disillusioned as they found a Protestant Inquisition threatening to take the place of the Catholic one. Several of these were persons of no little distinction, who might have added lustre to the Protestant cause. Thus in the course of Servetus's trial, Professor Matteo Gribaldi, a celebrated jurist from Padua, who will be further spoken of in the next chapter, happened to come to Geneva; and when told of Servetus he said he had never felt that one should die for one's opinions, however heretical, gave reasons for his view, and unsuccessfully sought an interview with Calvin on the subject.[12] Laelius Socinus wrote to a friend in Geneva that the blood of Abel was crying to God, and that Cain would find no peace on earth. Ochino returning from England reached Geneva the very day after the execution of Servetus, and when it was reported to him he expressed his disapproval, and was disliked for it.[13] Some liberal Protestants in the Grisons sent a poem [14] in which it was said that if Calvin had put one Servetus to death, countless others had come to life; that though his body was burned his spirit was uninjured; that if Christ himself came to Geneva he would be crucified;

[11] Gratarolo to Bullinger, May 26, 1554; Zanchi to Bullinger, Sept. 24, 1554, Calvin, xv, 142, 237.

[12] cf. *Contra libellum Calvini*, p. A5b.

[13] *id. op.*, p. A5b, f.

[14] Possibly the one that Curioni strenuously denied having written. cf. Curio to Bullinger, April, 1555, Calvin, xv, 102 f.

that one must not go there to find Christian liberty, for there was another Pope there, only one that burned men alive, whereas the Roman one strangled them first.

In fact, nearly all the Italians at Geneva, even those that had no quarrel with Calvin's doctrines, were said to have been greatly shocked by his cruelty, and so for the most part were the Protestants in France.[15] At Zürich also, so Walther wrote Haller, Servetus had more sympathizers among the Italians and the French than one would have thought.[16] Camillo Renato, whose influence in the churches of the Grisons has already been noted, addressed to Calvin a long poem in elegant Latin hexameters, reproaching him for his cruel and unchristian act in burning Servetus.[17] Under the name of Alfonso Lincurio of Tarragona, otherwise unknown to us, there appeared early in 1555, not long after Calvin's *Defensio*, an Apology for Servetus, containing an eloquent defence of him, with mordant irony attacking his persecutors for their cruel, unjust and unchristian treatment.[18] Finally, mention should be made of Guillaume Postel, that extraordinary and enigmatical character, famed for his marvelous learning, who, without ever having heard of Servetus until after his death, saw in Italy a manuscript of what may have been a first draft of the *Christianismi Restitutio*, and found in it such a resemblance to his own views of the World-soul and the Trinity, that he regarded him as his pupil. Having been informed in Paris that Calvin accused him of agreeing with Servetus in various doctrines, he composed an Apology for Servetus,[19] in which he bore witness to the large number of Servetus's followers in Italy, and boldly pleaded for freedom of conscience and speech in religion as against the repressive policy of Calvin.

[15] *Contra libellum Calvini*, p. Avi.

[16] Gualtherus to Haller, Nov. 26, 1553, Calvin, xiv, 683.

[17] Dated at Traona, Sept. 1554. Text in Calvin, xv, 239–245; also in Trechsel, *Antitrinitarier*, i, 321–328.

[18] Text (said in the margin of the Ms to have been corrected by the hand of Curioni) in Calvin, xv, 52–63. It bears the appearance of being a product of the academic circle at Basel, whose thought it closely resembles. It may well have been written by either Curioni or Castellio. Despite Sandius's note (*Bibliotheca*, p. 40), one must suspect that the name is fictitious. Menéndez-Pelayo (*Heterodoxos*, ii, 313) says that the name does not sound Spanish. Delio Cantimori, 'Serveto e Lelio Sozzini,' *Religio*, xii (1936), 414–438, with much plausibility attributes it to Laelius Socinus.

[19] *Apologia pro Serveto Villanovano, de anima mundi*, etc. Dated Venice, Aug. 15, 1555. Reprinted, with introduction, in Mosheim, *Versuch*, pp. 455–499, from the original Ms in the Basel University library. cf. Bock, *Antitrinitar.*, ii, 532–546.

The *De Haereticis* of Castellio was written not as an answer to Calvin's *Defensio*, but contemporary with it as a part of a campaign of the Basel liberals in favor of toleration and against the policy of Calvin at Geneva, which was threatening to spread further. It was understood, according to Vergerio, that there was at Basel an organized movement of natives and Italians to this end; and he reported recent information from Venice that the Servetian plague was spreading there a great deal too much (*plus nimis*).[20] Calvin saw in Castellio as the centre of this 'conspiracy' a beast as poisonous as he was wild and stubborn.[21] Undismayed by Beza's reply, Castellio now composed another book which, ignoring Beza, attacked Calvin directly and unsparingly. This new work, *Contra libellum Calvini*,[22] apparently could not find a publisher that dared print it at the time when it was written in 1554, so that it circulated only in manuscript copies. It was not until a half-century later that it first saw the light in Holland, as part of the struggle for toleration then being waged by the Arminians against the Calvinists there.[23]

After an introduction by the Dutch editor, the author in a brief preface states it as his purpose to undertake an examination of Calvin's book (the *Defensio*). He is not a disciple of Servetus, and has not even seen his books. He is not defending his doctrine, but attacking Calvin's; hence he will not discuss the Trinity, baptism or other difficult ques-

---

[20] Res certa conspirationem esse aliquorum Basiliensium cum nonnullis Italis, qui nisi comprimatur, pariet nobis magnum malum. Vergerio to Bullinger, Sept. 8, 1554. cf. de Porta, *Historia*, i, ii, 159; Calvin, xv, 246 n.

[21] Castalio, mihi crede, non minus virulenta est bestia quam indomita et pervicax. Calvin to Sulzer, Aug. 7, 1555, Calvin, xv, 209.

[22] *Contra libellum Calvini in quo ostendere conatur Haereticos jure gladii coercendos esse*. Though anonymous, the authorship by Castellio is made certain by the discovery of the unpublished last sheet of the original Ms in Castellio's hand in the University library at Basel. cf. Buisson, *Castellion*, ii. 32, n. 5, 477–499; *Le Lien*, Genève, Nov. 7, 1868. What was apparently a remainder of the same sheets was (according to a practice then common) also published with a different title, *Dissertatio qua disputatur quo jure, quove fructu, haeretici sint coercendi gladio vel igne*.

[23] The place of publication was doubtless Amsterdam. The puzzling date on the titlepage, M. D. LC. XII., was perhaps deliberate and intended to suggest a typographical error for either 1562 or 1612. Internal evidence shows that it was written in 1554 (p. Aii.) and that it was not published earlier than 1602 (p. Nii.) It was evidently intended to counteract the impression made by a Dutch translation of Beza's *De Haereticis* published at Franeker in 1601. 1612 may be taken for the probable date, for a Dutch translation (*Corte ende duydelijcke Wederlegghinghe*, etc.) was published in 1613. Despite frequent citations of a first edition in 1554, there is no evidence that there actually was such an edition.

tions. He will take up passages of Calvin in his very words, and then comment upon them so as to show how false they are and how blood-thirsty Calvin is (p. Aii.b). The rest of the book assumes the form of a Dialogue between Calvinus and Vaticanus, and is often cited as though this were its proper title. It is in fact not a dialogue at all, but a running commentary on Calvin's book, passage by passage, as bearing on the question of the rightfulness of putting heretics to death. It is Castellio himself that speaks under the name of Vaticanus. The theological part of Calvin's argument is passed without notice, and the criticism is confined to the question of the right to punish heretics, and the facts of the trial and death of Servetus. Castellio chooses his passages for criticism with great skill, overlooking no vulnerable point. His criticisms are alert, biting, often bitter and full of sarcasm. He handles Calvin without gloves, turning an unsparing light on his inconsistencies, his self-contradictions, his forced interpretations of Scripture in his own interest, his preference for the rigid Old Testament law over the Christian law of love, his total lack of the Christian spirit of gentleness, kindness, mercy and forgiveness. It is shown that he surpasses even the Papists in cruelty (pp. Db–Diii.)

Out of scores of telling passages that invite quotation, three must suffice as samples.

If it is not blind rage to torture in the flames a man who is calling on the name of Christ, and not only is not convicted but is not even accused of any crime, then there is no such thing as blind rage. (p. Cviii.)

To kill a man is not to protect a doctrine, but it is to kill a man. When the Genevans killed Servetus, they did not defend a doctrine, but they killed a man. To protect a doctrine is not the Magistrate's affair (what has the sword to do with doctrine?) but the teacher's. But it is the Magistrate's affair to protect the teacher, as it is to protect the farmer, and the smith, and the physician and others against injury. Thus if Servetus had wished to kill Calvin, the Magistrate would properly have defended Calvin. But when Servetus fought with reasons and writings, he should have been repulsed by reasons and writings. (p. Eb)

In reply to Calvin's argument that the sword is put into the hand of the Magistrate for him to defend sound doctrine, Castellio replies:

Paul calls sound doctrine that which renders men sound, i.e., endowed with charity and faith unfeigned and a good conscience; but unsound, that which renders them meddlesome, quarrelsome, insolent, ungodly, unholy, profane, murderers of fathers, etc. (I. Tim. i. 5, 9 f), and whatever else is contrary to sound doctrine. But they observe another law; for they take for sound those that think with them about Baptism, about the Supper, about Predestination, etc. Such men, though they be covetous, envious, slanderers, hypocrites, liars, buffoons, usurers, and whatever else is opposed to sound doctrine, are easily endured, nor is any one killed for men's vices, unless one has committed murder or theft or some atrocious crime of this sort, or has displeased the preachers; for this with them is just like a sin against the Holy Spirit, as is now said in a proverb everywhere common. But if one disagrees with them about Baptism, or the Supper, Justification, Faith, etc., he is a Heretic, he is a Devil, he must be opposed by all men on land or sea, as an eternal enemy of the Church, and a wicked destroyer of sound doctrine, even though his life be otherwise blameless, yea gentle, patient, kind, merciful, generous, and indeed religious and god-fearing, so that in his conduct neither friends nor enemies have anything to complain of. All these virtues, and this innocence of life (which Paul did not think it unseemly to approve in himself) can not with them protect a man from being regarded as wicked and blasphemous, if he disagrees with them in any point of religion. (p. Iiv, b–v.)

Appended to this 'Dialogue' is the brief *Historia de morte Serveti*, which has already been mentioned,[24] together with several other brief items relevant to the subject.

The rising tide of criticism against him and his persecution of Servetus gave Calvin much concern. 'If you knew only a tenth part of how distressed I am by violent abuse,' he wrote to the minister at Montbéliard, 'your human feeling would make you groan at the afflictions to which I have had to harden myself. The dogs are yelping at me from every quarter. On all sides I am being called a heretic. Every slander that can be invented is being heaped upon me. Envious and spiteful men even of our own flock are attacking me more outrageously than our open enemies among the Papists.'[25] Many were now more eager than ever to read Servetus's books; and at Basel, so Gratarolo wrote Bullinger, they were much incensed that they had been burned, and were willing to pay a high price for them. He complained that he himself had almost no friends there, as he was neither Servetian, Coelian, Castalionian, or Lutheran.[26] Zebédée, pastor at Noyon, declared in veiled terms that while the fires of the Spanish Inquisition were outdone by those in France, those at Geneva outdid them both.[27] Nearly two

[24] This, as well as most of the items following it, is probably by Castellio, though perhaps composed earlier than the 'Dialogue.' cf. the parallelism between the six points on p. Aii. and p. Miv, f.

[25] Calvin to Tossanus, Oct. 15, 1554, Calvin, xv. 271.

[26] Gratarolus to Bullinger, Dec. 24, 1554, Calvin, xv, 354.

[27] Ignis Gallicus vicit ignem Hispanicum, sed ignis Dei vincit ignem Gallicum. Reported to Bullinger by Haller, April, 1555, Calvin, xv, 565. cf. Calvin's version of the saying, xv, 603.

years after the death of Servetus, the jurist Hotoman wrote to Bullinger
from Basel that most people there were devoted to Castellio, while
Calvin was in no better odor there than in Paris; and that if one re-
proved a man for profane or lewd speech, he would be called a Calvinist
as a name of insult. On all sides the dogs were barking violently and
savagely.[28] All this did not swerve Calvin from his course. But at the
very end of 1563 Castellio died, hounded till his death by persistent
persecutions initiated from Geneva; and five months later Calvin also
died.[29]

The views that Calvin and Beza had defended long remained dominant, but those of Castellio also survived and gradually spread far and
wide. In 1557 or 1558 an Italian scholar named Acontius (Aconzio,
Contio), whom we shall later find in England preparing the way for
our movement, feeling himself no longer safe in Italy, crossed the Alps
and appeared at Basel, where he published his first work. He will certainly have known Castellio at this time, and was evidently influenced
by him. For in 1564 he returned from England to Basel and published
a fresh manifesto in favor of liberty of conscience and tolerance, which
occupied the same standpoint and in part expressed the same line of
thought as Castellio's *De Haereticis*. It continued in print for over a
century, and by its broad spirit and temperate manner had an incalculable influence in promoting a tolerant spirit throughout Europe.[30]

The sharp struggle for generous freedom of conscience in the reformed churches of the Grisons has already been briefly spoken of.[31] It
finally culminated in 1571 in a drawn battle between Egli and Gantner,
two ministers of Chur, with the issue drawn on the question of punishment of heretics. The two champions drew for their materials in argument on the two works by Castellio, and Beza's *De Haereticis*, and thus
the influence of the former was powerfully employed on the side of
toleration in that part of Switzerland.[32]

[28] Hotoman to Bullinger, Sept. 29, 1555, Calvin, xv, 803 f.

[29] A little book of Castellio's *Dialogues*, published posthumously, was edited by Faustus
Socinus, whose *Praelectiones Theologicae* show striking resemblance to Castellio in their
leading thoughts. cf. Alexander Schweitzer, *Die protestantischen Centraldogmen* (Zürich,
1854), i, 376.

[30] *Satanae Stratagemata*. Published at the end of 1564, and with a corrected edition
and a French translation in 1565. cf. Buisson, *op. cit.*, ii, 291–295. English translation,
edited by Charles D. O'Malley (San Francisco, 1940).

[31] *v. supra*, chapter VIII., p. 110 f.

[32] cf. Buisson, *op. cit.*, ii, 295–305; *Historia*, de Porta, ii, ii, 517–557.

At the very time in which this trouble was brewing in the Grisons, there appeared another Italian refugee, one Mino Celso of Siena,[33] a man of distinguished family and mature age, and reputed for his scholarship. He had perhaps been converted to the Reformation by his fellow-townsman Ochino. Fleeing before the Inquisition under Pope Paul IV. he came to the Grisons in 1569. Here he was greatly disappointed to find so many doctrinal dissensions among the reformed, and that corporal or even capital punishment of heretics was defended by the majority.[34] The controversy between Egli and Gantner about the punishment of heretics, at which he was an observer, disturbed him so much that he determined to write in Italian a book on the subject for his fellow-countrymen there, who largely espoused the liberal view. His personal circumstances hindered him from printing it at the time, and he soon afterwards removed to Basel, where he engaged in literary work. Among other things he edited a new edition of Castellio's Latin and French New Testament. At Basel the lively interest in freedom of conscience revived his own interest in the subject, and moved him to translate his work into Latin and publish it. Before the revision was quite finished he died, probably between 1575 and 1577.[35]

Celso's work was published soon after,[36] under the care of one of his friends. The original Italian draft doubtless used many of the arguments of Castellio's treatise, which had been freely drawn upon in the debate at Chur, and the present work obviously took the *Traité des Hérétiques* as a basis, enlarging, completing and paraphrasing it. It also used generous extracts from Castellio's other writings and from Acontius's recent work, and quoted from a much larger number of

---

[33] It was long doubted whether a person of this name had actually existed at this time, and the name was thought to be only a pseudonym for Castellio, or for Faustus or Laelius Socinus. The question was settled by the discovery of a letter addressed to him in 1548. Cf. Schelhorn, *Amoenitates*, vii, 86. For studies of his life, cf. Schelhorn, *Dissertatio epistolaris de Mino Celso Senensi* (Ulm, 1748); Mosheim, *Versuch*, pp. 293–302; de Porta, *op. cit.*, I, ii, 504–508; Wallace, *Antitrin.*, iii, 552–554; Buisson, *op. cit.*, ii, 308–313.

[34] cf. his *In haereticis coercendis*, pp. Av b, f.; 9a, b.

[35] cf. Buisson, *op. cit.*, ii, 309.

[36] *In haereticis coercendis quatenus progredi liceat: Mini Celsi Senensis disputatio. Ubi nominatim eos ultimo supplicio affici non debere aperte demonstratur.* (Christlingae, 1577). Christlingen was a fictitious name, indicating that the book was published without due authority. The unsold sheets of the issue seem to have been worked off a few years later under a fresh title (*Mini Celsi Senensis De Haereticis capitali supplicio non afficiendis.* s. l., 1584), with what was ostensibly a new preface, with the last sheet reset, and the addition of an epistle of Beza to Dudith and *vice versa*.

writers ancient and modern, some sixty in all. The work does not in fact contain much that is new on the subject; but the material is better arranged, being grouped under four main heads: Scripture testimonies in favor of toleration; Testimonies of various writers; Answers to various arguments against toleration; Duty of the Magistrate not to use force in opposing error. Beza meant to write a refutation, but lacked leisure to do so; and the work long served to extend and prolong the influence of Castellio, by furnishing a practical manual for those that would defend freedom of conscience.[37]

It was in Holland, however, that Castellio's advocacy of religious toleration was exerted to greatest effect.[38] Here, after the struggle with the Catholics had been won and the Republic proclaimed in 1578, a form of Calvinism succeeded to power more strict, if possible, than that of Geneva, and a new battle for religious freedom had to be fought. The pioneer in this struggle was the Secretary of State, Dirk Volkertsz. Coornhert (1522–1590), who had had ample experience of the troubles that come of religious intolerance. He opposed obligatory confessions of faith, though here the chief stumbling-block was not the doctrine of the Trinity but that of predestination. He translated two of Castellio's tracts (1581, 1582), and did much to make his thought known. He thus became the advance herald of the liberalizing movement in Dutch Protestantism that came in the next generation to be known as Arminianism. A conservative reaction followed, and Beza's De Haereticis was published in Dutch translation in 1601. This was answered by Castellio's Contra libellum Calvini in 1612, and by a complete edition of his minor works a year later. How much Castellio had influenced the early thought of the Remonstrants is seen by the fact that of the five articles that they opposed to the objectionable five points of Calvinism in 1610, the first four are almost literally the conclusions of the four

37 Daniel Zwicker, the Socinian controversialist in Holland nearly a century later, published a brief condensation of Celso's work in Dutch at Amsterdam in 1661: *Vereenings-Schrift der Christenen*; and the following year a Latin translation of it: *Henoticum Christianum, seu disputationis Mini Celsi Senensis, Quatenus in haereticis coercendis progredi liceat? lemmata potissima.* Another link of Castellio with the beginnings of Socinianism is found in the fact that Faustus Socinus was sojourning at Basel from 1574 to 1577, and that he became familiar with Castellio's writings and (under the pseudonym of Felix Turpio) contributed a preface to Castellio's posthumous *Dialogi Quatuor*, published in 1578. Examination of his early writings shows that he was considerably influenced by Castellio's thought. cf. Buisson, *op. cit.*, ii, 313–319. *v. supra*, p. 205, n. 29.

38 cf. Buisson, *op. cit.*, ii, 319–328; Giran, *Castellion*, chap. xi.

Dialogues of Castellio, and the fifth the conclusion of another tract of his.[39] Castellio was thus, after his death, the inspiration and effective source of the liberal development in Holland whose intimate relation with our movement will later be considered in detail.

This whole movement with which we are concerned may be regarded in two associated but yet distinct aspects. The one that has most often been emphasized is the theological, concerning the development of the *doctrines* that it has favored. The other and more significant aspect concerns the fundamental *principles* of freedom, reason and tolerance that have evolved in its history and been ever increasingly realized as the necessary conditions of the fullest development of religious thought and life. As regards the former aspect, the figure of Servetus stands out above all others in the beginnings of the movement. As regards the latter, Sebastian Castellio deserves more ample recognition than he has as yet received from more than a very few. In this respect he is entitled to be considered, even more than Servetus, as the real founder of liberal Christianity; for the first and most essential of its three controlling principles named above is that of generous tolerance of differing views. This is, at bottom, the outgrowth of an entirely new conception of religion as centered not in dogma but in life and character; and it is of the very essence of this conception of religion to regard freedom and reason not as incidental, but as fundamental conditions of a thoroughly wholesome existence of religion. At a time of extreme dogmatism, Castellio was the first in Protestant history to emphasize and place on firm and enduring foundations this principle of tolerance. It is therefore but just to honor him as one of the prime founders of liberal Protestantism. The succeeding chapters of this work will trace the widening spread and increasing prevalence of this element which had its source in him.

It remains to speak of the especial contribution made to our movement by Servetus. It runs in two widely different lines. As to the first of these, his great hope and purpose was to reform the doctrinal system of Christianity before it became hardened into dogma. In his earlier works this reform extended little beyond the doctrine of the Trinity; but in the end his larger design was to reform the whole body of Christian theology. His method of treating the subject is poorly ordered, and

[39] cf. Buisson, *op. cit.*, ii, 326.

the presentation of it is piecemeal and marred by grave defects. It still waits for some one to rearrange it and present it in clear and logical order, shorn of excrescences. If this could once be done, and the whole set forth in comparison with the old scholastic theology and the newer systems of the reformers, Servetus's proposed reconstruction of Christianity would be found to present some very attractive features, and regret might be aroused that some at least of his reforms were not adopted. His own conviction was that if it could only be once fairly considered on its merits along with competing systems, it would be enthusiastically adopted by those whom the Roman system failed to satisfy. But his work fell still-born; and he perished without having formed a school or left even a professed disciple to adopt and carry on his system as a whole.

The influence of Servetus upon the development of Protestant theology, therefore, was simply this: that by his criticism of the traditional doctrine of the Trinity he led many to reconsider the foundations of this doctrine for themselves. Yet from this time on, the doctrine of the Trinity, which at the beginning of the Reformation had stood in the background of the Protestant faith, suspected, disliked, ignored or lightly passed over by the reformers (as we have seen in chapter ii.) was brought to the front and acknowledged, even as by the Catholics, as the central dogma of Christianity, and all the creeds and confessions of the period adopted and defended it. But Servetus himself was not in any sense a Unitarian, nor even a Socinian. Though he disliked the traditional terminology of the doctrine, he too was a Trinitarian of a sort, if not an Athanasian. Thus though he has often been regarded as the first Unitarian martyr, the most that can be fairly claimed for him in this connection is that, in a negative way, he started an influential number in his generation on a path that was to issue first in Socinianism, and eventually in Unitarianism. It was chiefly Italian humanists that carried on this line of thought and, instead of ending where he did, wrought out a new doctrine which in the end went far beyond anything that he would have been at all likely to approve. Many of those whom his writings had stirred up to examine this doctrine for themselves presently became active opponents of it in any form; first in northern Italy, then among the Italian dispersion in the Grisons and in their congregation at Geneva, and finally in Poland where Servetus was much read, and in Transylvania where in later chapters we shall find clear traces of his influence.[40] From that point on, the movement outgrew him and pursued an independent course.

The other line of Servetus's contribution to our history is one that he can not in the least have designed or foreseen: it is in the impulse that his tragic death gave to the growth of toleration in religion. We have seen how this movement rose and gained momentum under Castellio and his associates at Basel. Emancipated souls who knew Servetus's doctrines, if at all, only as they were stated by his enemies and persecutors, and who felt no sympathy with his heresies, yet totally disapproved of his having been put to such a cruel death. His execution came to stand as a symbol of religious persecution at its worst, and his name as a symbol of martyrdom for freedom of conscience, even with those that knew or cared little for him as an individual. He thus not only gave, as we have seen, an indirect stimulus to the rise of Unitarian doctrines, but had a vastly more important influence in stimulating the rise of religious toleration as a general policy, and the spread of tolerance in religious thought as an attitude of individual minds.[41]

One other evidence of Servetus's lasting impression upon religious history deserves to be remarked. It is in the gradual but complete reversal of the verdict of history upon him. When he died, there was none so poor to do him reverence, and few even to pity. It was generally accepted without question that he had been an abandoned and blasphemous heretic; and this view was for a hundred and seventy-five years repeated by historians as a matter of course. It was not until 1730 that Gautier, who as Secretary of State had been the first to examine the records of the trial, while editing a new edition of Spon's *Histoire de Genève* ventured in a foot-note to correct Spon's unfavorable view of Servetus and to say that his views were not so detestable as they had been represented.[42] Even before this the English littérateur de la Roche

[40] For example, 166 out of 734 pages of his *Christianismi Restitutio* were reprinted in Transylvania by early Unitarians. cf. (Georgius Blandrata) *De regno Christi. . . . De regno Antichristi, etc.* (Albae Juliae, 1569).

[41] Heresy was for a long time still punished as a capital crime in Protestant countries — in England till 1612, at Geneva till 1632, in Germany till 1687, in Scotland till 1697 — but this penalty received its death-blow in the execution of Servetus, and from that time on became increasingly disapproved. Only Anabaptists and Socinians from the beginning defended toleration on principle and without wavering.

[42] cf. Jacques Spon, *Histoire de Genève, rectifiée et augmentée, etc.* (Genève, 1730) ii, 64, n. z.

had been at Geneva and been permitted to see the records, from which
he had made copious extracts, which he published with a running commentary often favorable to Servetus.[43] A copy of the long lost *Christianismi Restitutio* had also come to light in London and increased interest in its author, which was heightened yet more by the elaborate
study of his life by Mosheim in 1748, and the records of the Vienne trial
published the following year by the Abbé d'Artigny. The more the
actual facts about the life and views of Servetus came to be known, the
more there were to give sympathy to him and to withdraw it from
Calvin. The change in opinion reached its climax of feeling when
Voltaire published at Geneva in 1756 his *Essai sur les moeurs*, in which
he sharply attacked Calvin, and later said of him that he *avoit une âme
atroce, aussi bien qu'un esprit éclairé.*[44] The essay produced a prodigious sensation throughout Europe. The city pastors at Geneva sprang
to the rescue of Calvin, and appointed one of their number to reply to
the calumny; but when he sought access to the records of the trial for
materials in defence, his request was refused.[45] The Council took the
ground that the less said on the subject the better, and that the whole
affair should as far as possible be buried in oblivion. For nearly a century the records were supposed to have been destroyed. By the middle
of the nineteenth century the warmth of feeling had much abated on
both sides. All the documents in the case were at length made public.
Many scholars have studied the question from every angle, though few
have succeeded in maintaining a perfectly judicial attitude throughout;
but at length a certain state of equilibrium has been reached, and the
great merits and the striking defects in the characters of both Servetus
and Calvin can be calmly weighed. As far as posterity could succeed in
doing so, the professed followers of Calvin made expiation for the
tragedy of Champel on its 350th anniversary, by erecting an expiatory
monument [46] as nearly as possible on the spot where it occurred. In

---

[43] In his *Memoirs of Literature*, vol. iv.; also republished in his *Bibliothèque Angloise*
(Amsterdam, 1717–'28), tom. ii, part i.

[44] Essai, chap. cxxxiv., *De Calvin et de Servet*; cf. his letter in the *Mercure de France*,
Mai, 1757, pp. 35–38.

[45] See the interesting correspondence on the subject published by Galiffe, *Notices*, iii,
441–444; also in his *D'un siècle à l'autre* (Genève, 1877), i, 86–97. cf. Roget, *Genève*,
iv, 126–129.

[46] On the suggestion of Calvin's biographer, Professor E. Doumergue; following an
early suggestion by Henry, *Calvin*, ii, 231, that such a monument be erected on the 300th
anniversary.

four or more other cities of Europe admirers of Servetus have erected monuments in his honor.[47]

[47] In Madrid, in front of the Anthropological Museum, 1870; at Annemasse, Savoy, near Geneva, statue by Clotilde Roch, 1908, after being denied a public site by the municipal authorities at Geneva; in Paris, Place de Montrouge, statue by Jean Baffier, 1908; at Vienne, in the Jardin Publique, statue by Joseph Bernard, 1911; at Zaragoza, at the entrance to the Medical Faculty. A statue was also planned or authorized at Barcelona, 1911, to be placed on the summit of the Tibidabo, but whether it was actually erected is not known. There is a sculptured medallion of Servetus in the court-yard of the Medical Faculty, Calle Atocha, Madrid; and streets are named for him at Geneva, Madrid, and Vienne.

CHAPTER XV

FOLLOWERS OF SERVETUS IN SWITZERLAND:
GRIBALDI, BIANDRATA

TOWARD THE END of the preceding chapter it was observed that though the great hope and purpose of Servetus was to reform the doctrinal system of Christianity, yet he died without having formed a school or leaving even a professed disciple to carry out his plan as a whole. He was, however, survived by a number of individuals who, though they had never known him in person, were in some respect influenced by his writings, especially as to the doctrines of the Trinity and the deity of Christ. Taking up his criticism of these doctrines they carried it further, first in Switzerland and later in the more tolerant atmosphere of Poland and Transylvania. They thus form the connecting link between Servetus as precursor and the fully developed Socinian and Unitarian movements in those countries. They were all Italian Humanists who under the influence of the early Reformation had abandoned the dogmas of the Roman Church, and who, especially in the north of Italy where the influence of Servetus was wide-spread, proceeded, independently of the guidance of Luther and Calvin, to think out for themselves a liberal biblical theology. We have already traced the beginnings of their movement in Italy and the Grisons before the death of Servetus. It remains in this chapter to follow the fortunes of those who after that prolonged and extended his influence in Switzerland. Apart from the work of the liberal circle at Basel, which bore more on freedom of conscience and toleration than on doctrinal reform, this development in Switzerland centered chiefly at Calvin's own city of Geneva, and secondly at Zürich, in both cases in the congregations of Italian refugees.

Geneva was a convenient and attractive city of refuge for those that fled from Italy after the establishment of the Inquisition, and not a few were admitted to citizenship and established their permanent home there. A nucleus of an Italian Protestant church was formed there in 1542, when Ochino, just escaped from Italy, became their preacher, and they were assigned a chapel of their own. After three years Ochino left Geneva, and the movement lay dormant until 1552 when it was revived and regularly organized as a church after the Geneva model, with not only Sunday worship, but week-day meetings in which there was free discussion of religious questions.[1] As the Italian mind was very keen for debates over doctrines, these meetings afforded a ready ground for bringing forward heretical views; and as all was done in Italian, Calvin was unable to have his usual close oversight of proceedings. It was among these Geneva Italians, with whom the doctrines of Servetus had been quietly smoldering during the year since his death, that a revival of something like them took place in the summer of 1554. It was occasioned, strangely enough, not by one of the members of the church, but by a passing visitor, to whom Calvin ascribed all the trouble that ensued during the next few years.[2] This visitor was Professor Matteo Gribaldi Mofa of the University of Padua.[3]

Gribaldi was born early in the sixteenth century of a patrician family at Chieri near Turin.[4] Giving his attention to legal studies he became one of the most famous jurists of his age, and is said to have taught jurisprudence in some ten different universities in France, Italy and Germany, which eagerly sought his services. Meantime, by his marriage with a French lady who had inherited the property,[5] he became owner of an estate at Farges about twenty miles west of Geneva in Bernese territory, and thus a citizen of Bern.[6] He used every summer to come to Farges for his holidays. In 1548 he became professor at Padua, where students came to his lectures in such crowds as to rouse envious hate in

---

[1] cf. Oscar Grosheintz, *L'Église italienne à Genève au temps de Calvin* (Lausanne, 1904).

[2] Calvin to Vermigli, May 22, 1858, Calvin, xvii, 176.

[3] The Italian pharmacist Girolamo Varro testified that at Geneva it was said that the Devil had begotten Servetus, and Servetus Farges (Gribaldi), and Farges Giorgio (Biandrata), and Giorgio Paul (Alciati), and Paul several more. *v.* Arturo Pascal, 'Gli Antitrinitari in Piemonte (G. Paolo Alciati),' *Bollettino Storico-Bibliografico Subalpino*, xxiii (1921), 39.

[4] cf. Francesco Ruffini, 'Il giureconsulto chierese Matteo Gribaldi Mofa e Calvino,' *Rivista di Storia del Diritto Italiano*, i (1928), 205–268, 417–432; Cesare Nanni, 'Di un libro di Matteo Gribaldi Mofa, giureconsulto chierese del secolo xvi,' *Memorie della Reale Accademia di Scienze di Torino*, Serie ii, vol. xxxv, parte ii (1884), 131–161; François Naef, 'Un Unitaire au seizième siècle,' *Étrennes Chrétiennes par une réunion de Pasteurs et de Laiques*, i (1874), 147–175; Church, *Reformers, passim*; Trechsel, *Antitrinitarier*, ii, 54–60, 277–302.

[5] cf. Church, *op. cit.*, p. 110.

[6] cf. Ruffini, *op. cit.*, p. 213.

his colleagues. As a rationalistic humanist he inclined to the Reformation; but though he maintained correspondence with refugees in Protestant quarters,[7] he was so circumspect as long to escape the notice of the Inquisition. At length he became known as author of a narrative of which the Protestants were making much use,[8] and he was thenceforth narrowly watched by the spies of the Church. These brought such pressure to bear upon the university authorities that he had to choose between outward conformity and conscience. He therefore resigned his professorship in April, 1555, and crossed the Alps, not knowing whither he went. He had, however, an influential friend there in Pierpaolo Vergerio, who six years before had resigned his bishop's mitre in Italy and fled the country, and to whom Gribaldi had then given a letter of warm recommendation to Calvin.[9] Vergerio, advised of what had taken place, met Gribaldi at Zürich with an invitation that he had procured from the Duke of Württemberg to accept a chair at his University at Tübingen.[10]

Trouble, however, was also lying in wait for him, and all unwitting he at once exposed himself to it. It had happened that while Servetus was on trial in 1553 Gribaldi, returning from Farges to Padua, passed through Geneva; and being told of the case he said that he had never thought that one should be put to death for his opinions, however heretical. When unwillingly dragged into discussion of the unity of God before a large congregation, he gave reasons for his view, also adding that he had nothing against Servetus's view of the nature of Christ, for he had held the same view from boyhood. Offence was taken at this, and as feeling ran high he suggested a meeting for open discussion of the subject, though nothing came of it, nor of his effort to get an audience with Calvin, which the latter haughtily refused. Greatly disturbed at this, he went his way and wrote the brethren at Vicenza a letter about it.[11] On his return journey to Padua he talked with Bul-

---

[7] He was a friend of Curioni and of the jurist Amerbach at Basel, whose sons lodged with him when students at Padua; Laelius Socinus was his guest for two months at the time of Servetus's death (cf. Trechsel, *op. cit.*, ii, 55 f, 164); and he was intimate with Vergerio.

[8] The story of Francesco Spiera, who after renouncing his new faith died in horrible torments of conscience. Written 1549, and often reprinted.

[9] Gribaldi to Calvin, Nov. 9, 1549, Calvin, *Opera*, xiii, 448.

[10] The jurist Bonifacius Amerbach had previously brought him to the Duke's attention in 1552. cf. Nanni, *op. cit.*, p. 134, n. 4; Ruffini, *op. cit.*, p. 231 f.

[11] "Superbe repudiatus" (*Contra libellum Calvini*, p. Dii, A5b, f), because Calvin had

linger at Zürich, and with Gallicius and Vergerio at Chur, apparently
not concealing from them his sympathy with Servetus.[12] This sympathy
was much increased the following winter when he was given a copy of
Servetus's *De Trinitatis erroribus*, without which he afterwards declared
that he should never have known Christ.[13] In the autumn of the following year Gribaldi was again at Geneva, and was present at a general
meeting of the Italian congregation, where he was against his will again
dragged into a discussion of the still burning question about the Trinity.
The views he expressed were taken for heretical, and gave great offence,
though the scripture proofs he brought forward were not refuted, and
his saying that he believed that the Father and the Son were one only
in the scriptural sense — 'I and the Father are one' — was misunderstood. It was therefore left for him to write on the subject rather than
continue an oral debate; and to correct the misunderstanding he wrote
the next day a brief and clear statement [14] of how he understood the
unity of God. Gribaldi promised to send from Padua the Scripture
passages and citations from the Fathers in support of his view, though
whether he did so is not known. It is clear from this statement that in
making a layman's attempt to explain the doctrine of the Trinity in
terms that might be acceptable to the lay mind while also agreeable to
Scripture and reason, he laid himself open to the charge that he believed
in three Gods. Rumor of his unsoundness spread rapidly. Vergerio
wrote Bullinger [15] in close confidence that Gribaldi had certainly deserted the cause, and was on the point of introducing Servetus to others,
as he knew for certain.

In the course of the winter, Vergerio's confidence in Gribaldi must
have been restored, as his recommendation of him to Duke Christoph
of Württemberg [16] indicates. Before proceeding to take his chair at
Tübingen, Gribaldi went to visit his estate at Farges, and on the way he

---

learned of his sympathy with Servetus, so he later declared. cf. Calvin to Count George,
May 2, 1557, Calvin to Zerchintes, July 4, 1558, Calvin, xvi, 464, xvii, 237.

[12] cf. Vergerio to Bullinger, Oct. 3, 1553, Calvin, xiv, 633, cf. 635; Gallicius to Bullinger, Oct. 19, 1553, *ibid.*, p. 649.

[13] cf. Church, *op. cit.*, p. 206.

[14] cf. Gribaldi to the Fratres Itali, Calvin, xv, 246 ff; Trechsel, *op. cit.*, ii, 460 f.

[15] From Tübingen, Sept. 6, 1554: Certum est Gribaldum prorsus descivisse, et totum
in eo esse ut aliis Servetum insinuet. Non affirmarem . . . nisi certe scirem; de Porta,
Historia, i, ii, 159.

[16] The same to whom Castellio dedicated his *De Haereticis*. cf. also Vergerio to Bullinger, Sept. 14, 1555, Calvin, xv, 767.

had the unfortunate thought to visit his friends at Geneva. Calvin learned of his presence there, and this time it was he that proposed a conference about the doctrines that Gribaldi held.[17] Calvin refused to meet him alone in his own house, but proposed a meeting in the presence of witnesses. He was therefore invited to meet with members of the church Consistory, at which the ministers hoped to convert him from his errors. He accepted the invitation and came, accompanied by several Italian friends; but when Calvin declined to take the hand he offered, until they had reached agreement in doctrine, Gribaldi at once said, 'Adieu, messieurs,' and left the room in anger.[18] Calvin was not to be put off, and then had him summoned for examination at the Hôtel de Ville before members of the Council. Here, assuming a bold and confident air, he complained of Calvin's rudeness to him, and of being persecuted for a difference of opinion; while when questioned he evaded and evidently tried to conceal his beliefs. After a little he inadvertently let fall some expressions that indicated serious error; but the Council, finding it impossible to accomplish his conversion, and seeing that he was a foreigner, let him go. He soon afterwards left the city, although his surviving influence there was long a source of trouble.

On his way from Farges to Tübingen, Gribaldi passed through Zürich, and complained bitterly to Bullinger of the treatment he had received at Geneva.[19] Bullinger counseled him to beware of spreading heresy. Apparently taking serious warning from the danger he had just escaped at Geneva, he wrote out a confession that Bullinger could not but approve; for he not only professed the Nicene Creed, but also expressed his abhorrence of Servetus. He proceeded to Tübingen, where he was cordially received, was made one of the Duke's counselors, and consulted in affairs of great importance.[20] Vergerio, who had had misgivings, and had had from Beza a letter severely reproaching him for taking Gribaldi's part,[21] was reassured, and wrote Bullinger not to be concerned about him.[22] Beza, however, still continued to exert pressure,

[17] Calvin to Count George, May 2, 1557, Calvin, xvi, 464 f; Calvin to Zerchintes, July 4, 1558, id. op., xvii, 237, cf. xxi, 79 f, 151, 610.

[18] cf. Colladon, Vie de Calvin, Calvin, xxi, 80, cf. 610.

[19] Beza to Bullinger, Oct. 22, 1555, Calvin, xv, 838; Trechsel, op. cit., ii, 289, n. 1. Bullinger to Beza, Dec. 3, 1555; Trechsel, op. cit., ii, 287, n. 2.

[20] cf. Ruffini, op. cit., p. 239.

[21] cf. Vergerio to Bullinger, Aug. 22, 1555, Trechsel, op. cit., ii, 288, n. 2.

[22] Vergerio to Bullinger, Sept. 14, 1555, Calvin, xv, 767.

and wrote Vergerio expressing great surprise that he cared for, and was even willing to be intimate with, the most impious man he had ever heard of,[23] and repeating in detail the offensive views he had expressed about the person of God and Christ. He had no faith that Gribaldi had renounced the errors of Servetus and returned to orthodox beliefs, and he would do all in his power to expose him to the churches.[24] Even before Gribaldi's arrival at Tübingen, Calvin had written Wolmar there, warning him against Gribaldi for his insinuating ways, his vanity, his boastfulness, and his swaggering airs, as well as for his heretical views.[25]

Gribaldi on his part now sought to conciliate favor at Geneva. In response to an urgent request from a former pupil of his there that he clear his name from the increasing rumors against him, he sent from Backnang, whither the University had temporarily removed to avoid the plague raging at Tübingen, a carefully prepared statement of his faith, to be presented to Martinengo, minister of the Italian church at Geneva. It is expressed in the terms of the Nicene Creed, and covers the articles concerning God, Christ, and the Holy Spirit, 'according to their true and evangelical sense.' [26] This qualifying phrase left the way open to considerable latitude in intepretation within the limits of sincerity; but it may be seen on close examination of his statement that Gribaldi, while employing accepted orthodox phraseology, took care not to deny the views that he had hitherto expressed. It may be offered in his defense that perhaps he meant to accept the Nicene Creed as a traditional and conventionally accepted summary of Christian faith as a whole, without meaning to assent to its statements in detail — a usage that has enjoyed long and wide currency, even in high quarters, in the Christian Church.

All through Gribaldi's first year at Tübingen, rumors kept coming from various quarters that he was not orthodox, until the confidence of even his friends began to be shaken. Musculus of Bern still believed in him in April,[27] and Zanchi suspended judgment;[28] but Vergerio, hitherto his prime sponsor, began again to be disquieted, and to suspect that

---

[23] Beza to Bullinger, Oct. 22, 1555, Calvin, xv, 838; Trechsel, ii, 289, n. 1.

[24] Beza to Bullinger, Jan. 1, 1556, Calvin, xvi, 1 f; cf. Beza to Zanchi, Sept. 1, 1562, Calvin, xx, 490.

[25] Calvin to Wolmar, undated, Calvin, xv, 644; Trechsel, ii, 288, n. 1.

[26] cf. Calvin, xv, 856; Trechsel, ii, 461–463. The date given is Nov. 7, 1555.

[27] Musculus to Zanchi, Apr. 7, 1556, Trechsel, ii, 290, n. 2.

[28] Zanchi to Beza, July 6, 1556, id. ii, 290, n. 3.

he had been misled by a man of slippery character;[29] while Bullinger
warned Sulzer of Basel against him,[30] as one that attacked the doctrine
of the Trinity. For the Easter vacation in 1557 Gribaldi went as usual
to Farges; but he passed through Zürich without calling on his fellow-
countryman Vermigli, by whom he had heard that his doctrines were
detested.[31] While he was thus absent, Vergerio confided to the Duke
that Gribaldi was said to entertain some very bad opinions; and a few
weeks later, on his return from a mission to Switzerland, where he had
got much new information about him, he wrote the Duke strongly
confirming all he had previously said.[32] It was a hard thing to do to
one that had been his trusted friend, and he has been much blamed for
it; but conscience urged it as a duty to the Duke, even had no self-interest
been involved. The Duke's uncle, Count George, now wrote to Geneva
(doubtless at the Duke's request) for further information; and the answers soon received from both the Geneva Council and Calvin gave an
accurate account of their experience of Gribaldi two years before.[33]

The Duke had previously questioned Gribaldi privately as to his
belief about the Trinity, and had received satisfactory answers; but now
the charges had become too definite to be ignored, and in view of the
information received from Geneva he felt bound to make further investigation. He therefore had Gribaldi summoned to appear before
him and the University Senate to answer to charges of heresy.[34] The
discussion was amicable and lasted for two days. Gribaldi was faced
with a manuscript in his own hand, and had to acknowledge the doctrine it contained as his own. He was asked to make a frank and clear
confession about the doctrine of the Trinity, which should disprove the
rumors current about him. He sought to parry by making evasive statements; but a mere profession of accepting the Apostles' and Nicene

[29] Vergerio to Bullinger, Apr. 11, 1556, Calvin, xvi, 104; ditto, Apr. 27, 1556, ibid.,
xvi, 121.
[30] Sulzer to Bullinger, May 19, 1556, Calvin, xvi, 148.
[31] Vermigli to Calvin, Apr. 8, 1857, Calvin, xvi, 444.
[32] Vergerio to Duke Christoph, June 17, 1557, Calvin, xvi, 513.
[33] Council to Count George, May, 1557, Calvin, xx, 451. Calvin to same, May 2, 1557,
ibid., xvi, 463.
[34] cf. Delio Cantimori, 'Matteo Gribaldi Chierese e l' Università di Tubinga,' Bollettino Storico-Bibliografico Subalpino, xxxv (Dec., 1933), 4 f; Haller to Bullinger, Aug. 23,
1557, in Trechsel, ii, 295, n. 3; Bock, Antitrinitar., ii, 461, quotes from M. Fischlinus,
Memoria theologorum Württ., i, 109, that the investigation opened June 6, which in view
of the date of Vergerio's letter cited above must be an error for July 6.

Creeds was not now enough to dispel doubts. The Athanasian Creed had been expressly designed to define the Trinity in terms that could be neither evaded nor explained away. He was therefore ordered to state simply whether or not he accepted this creed and the corresponding section of the Theodosian Code. He again sought to evade the issue, saying that it was only a difference in words, as to which they might easily come to agree if a little time were only given. He was therefore granted a space of three weeks to prepare his answer. Efforts to arrive at a settlement continued, but just as the period was about to expire, Gribaldi, without having given his answer, quietly slipped away on foot, bound for his estate at Farges.[35] A few days later he sent back from Zürich a letter of apology to the Rector and Senate.[36] He had felt, he said, that he had become a constant burden to them, and he had also received an intimation from friends at court that the Duke would be pleased if he should leave the country as soon as possible. It was doubtless the easiest way out of a situation embarrassing to all concerned. The Duke, however, felt it his duty to inform the Council at Bern of these events involving one of their subjects. He also had Gribaldi's library searched, and forwarded to Bern some writings found in it, together with an account of what had taken place, and a warning to keep watch of him.[37]

Had he learned prudence from his experiences, Gribaldi might now have been left unmolested at Farges; but his eagerness for propaganda was insatiable. Unaware that orders had issued from Bern that he be watched, he at once began circulating his writings. In much less than a month, therefore, he found himself arrested and taken to Bern for trial. He was lodged in prison, and his books were given to the ministers for examination. From these it was clear that the heresies with which he had been charged two years before had grown only more pronounced and definite with time. The examination lasted nine days. Some were for burning him, others for banishment. The latter punishment was decided on and the banishment was to end and his estate to be restored to him only when he had returned to the Duke and obtained a due acquittal.[38] But Gribaldi was so reluctant to return to Tübingen that

---

[35] cf. Haller to Bullinger, as cited above.

[36] Dated Aug. 8. Given by Cantimori, *op. cit.*, p. 11 f.

[37] cf. Haller to Bullinger as above, Trechsel, ii, 296, n. 1; Haller, 'Ephemerides', *Museum Helveticum*, ii (1747), 114; also Calvin, xvi, 624, n.

[38] cf. Calvin, xvi, 623 f, and n.

he declared he would sooner return with his whole family to the Papacy;[39] and he begged the Council rather to send him back to the ministers, promising to submit to whatever they decreed. His request was granted. The conference between them lasted long. Finally the ministers drew up a confession that explicitly affirmed the Athanasian doctrine, and as explicitly denied the doctrines he had been spreading. They asked him to subscribe it. He turned and squirmed, but they were inexorable. As he was not prepared to face martyrdom, he renounced his errors and signed. The ministers were satisfied; but the Council (as well they might) evidently doubted his sincerity, and banished him nevertheless.[40] He was granted a few months in which to try to sell his estate,[41] and then withdrew to Langres in France, only to hear in a few months of the death of his wife. The heart-broken man now appealed anew to Bern for permission to return to his home with his seven motherless children.[42] Through the intervention of Zurkinden, the noblest friend of toleration among the public men of his age,[43] the request was granted; and henceforth he kept his heresies to himself. The magnanimous Duke offered him his old chair at the University if he would submit a confession of faith, and this he did in 1558; but the Senate at Tübingen would not accept it as satisfactory.[44] The following year he was recalled to his former chair at the University of Grenoble, which had declined ever since he left it fourteen years before,[45] but here also troubles lay in his path. He had taught but a few months when internal

---

[39] cf. Trechsel, ii, 299, n. 4.

[40] Haller to Bullinger, Sept. 17, 20, 1557, Calvin, xvi, 635 f. Haller, *Ephemerides*, p. 115. Gribaldi's confession in Calvin, xvi, 636–638. cf. Zerchintes to Calvin, June 13, 1558, Calvin, xvii, 207. Trechsel, ii, 299–302.

[41] In this he was not successful. The Marquis d'Oria of Naples (who had financed the publication of Castellio's *De Haereticis*) would have bought it, had he not been dissuaded by Zurkinden on account of impending political changes involving it. cf. Castellio to Zurkinden and *vice versa*, Oct. 22, Nov. 3, 1557, in Buisson, *Castellion*, ii, 390 f. Also Church, *op. cit.*, chap. xi.

[42] cf. Ruffini, *op. cit.*, p. 254. Gribaldi to Haller, April 24; 1558, Trechsel, ii, 301, n. 3.

[43] Zerchintes to Calvin, June 13, 1558, Calvin, xvii, 207. cf. August von Gonzenbach, 'Nicolaus Zurkinden,' *Basler Taschenbuch*, 1877; Eduard Bähler, 'Nikolaus Zurkinden von Bern (1506–1588), ein Vertreter der Toleranz im Jahrhundert der Reformation' *Jahrbuch für Schweizerische Geschichte*, xxxvi, xxxvii (1911–'12). Zurkinden had no sympathy whatever with Gribaldi's heretical opinions, and his exertions in Gribaldi's behalf brought upon him no little criticism and ill-will. cf. Calvin to Viret, Sept. 1557, Calvin, xvi, 609; Zerchintes to Calvin, Jan. 13, 1558, *id.*, xvii, 208.

[44] cf. Church, *Reformers*, p. 240.

[45] cf. Ruffini, *op. cit.*, p. 264 ff.

strife broke out in the University, arising from a quarrel between partisans of Gribaldi and those of another professor. The friends of his rival dragged Gribaldi's doubtful orthodoxy into the question, with the result that the authorities of the University were forced by the government, against their will, to dismiss him, or else see the University suspended.[46] Nothing further is known of him, save that he died of the plague at Farges in September, 1564 (four months later than Calvin), deserted by all his friends, of whom hardly one could be found to give him burial;[47] nor of his seven children, save that fifteen years later one of his sons came to Tübingen to settle some outstanding matters relating to his father's property.[48]

The doctrines that Gribaldi held and tried to spread are not to be learned from the several confessions that he composed for Bullinger and Martinengo, or subscribed at Bern; for in these he was trying as far as possible to accommodate his language to that of the accepted creeds, or was subscribing reluctantly and under no little stress. The true source is found in the statement that he first prepared for the brethren at Geneva, and in his discussions at Bern.[49] From these his beliefs may be condensed and briefly stated as follows. Father, Son and Holy Spirit are really three distinct beings, each of them very God. The Father is self-existent, a sort of supreme being like Jove, chief of the Gods; while the Son and the Holy Spirit are derived from him, and subordinate. Taken concretely, the persons are distinct; taken abstractly, they are one and the same divinity, as manifesting one power and wisdom. Thus taken, the mind easily understands their unity; but the usual notion of a triune God is an incomprehensible scholastic dream. The *communicatio idiomatum* in Christ is also denied. It is clear from this that Gribaldi was only an amateur theologian who, in trying to avoid certain difficulties in the orthodox doctrine, incurred others no less serious. In themselves his doctrines have no great significance. Their importance in history lies in the fact that he was the only person of distinction in his own time who attempted to set forth a doctrine of God and Christ that should be

[46] cf. Ruffini, *op. cit.*, pp. 264–268.

[47] Gribaldus peste correptus, fugientibus illum omnibus, vix a quo sepeliretur invenit. Letter of Beza, Aug. 5, 1567, in his *Epistolae Theologicae*, p. 338. cf. Calvin, xxi, 151.

[48] cf. Cantimori, *op. cit.*, p. 10.

[49] Gribaldus Fratribus Italis, Sept., 1554, Calvin, xv, 247 f, also in Trechsel, ii, 460 f. cf. Beza to Bullinger, Oct. 22, 1555, Calvin, xv, 838 f. Haller to Bullinger, Sept. 14, 1557, *ibid.*, xvi, 623 f; Haller, *Ephemerides*, p. 114.

more scriptural and more reasonable than the current one, and who also gained some currency for his views. This currency was almost entirely limited to Italians, and the tritheism that he launched in 1554 lasted hardly longer than a dozen years; but it served as a bridge between Servetus and the beginnings of what was soon to develop into the Socinian movement in Poland. Gonesius, the first to advocate anti-trinitarian views in Poland, had probably come under Gribaldi's influence when a student at Padua, and been there introduced to the doctrine of Servetus. In 1562 Sylvius wrote Calvin that Lismanino had drawn a whole nest of Gribaldines from Switzerland to Poland, where they were causing the churches great trouble; and he especially named Biandrata, Gentile, and Alciati.[50] We must therefore follow the story of these as Gribaldi's best known disciples.

Of the three just named, Dr. Giorgio Biandrata [51] (Lat., Blandrata) was in our history quite the most important. He was born of a noble family at Saluzzo in Piedmont, about thirty miles south of Turin, in 1516.[52] He had his early education in Piedmont, and took his degree at the University of Montpellier in 1533. He applied himself very diligently to the study of medicine, specializing in the diseases of women. On this subject he wrote several works, and acquired so wide a reputation that by 1540 he had been called to the court of King Sigismund of Poland, to be the personal physician of the Queen, the Milanese Bona Sforza. Later on, as we shall see in due course, he was to have marked influence on the development of our movement in Poland and Transylvania. After serving the Queen, and her daughter Isabella, wife of the King of Hungary, for something like a dozen years, he returned to Italy, where we find him first at Mestre in 1553,[53] and later practicing his profession at Pavia. Here he became acquainted with the views of the reformers, and at length falling under the eye of the Inquisition he made his escape to Geneva in 1556, where he joined the Italian congregation, was elected

[50] Sylvius to Calvin, Oct. 20, 1562, Calvin, xix, 560.

[51] cf. Vincenzo Malacarne, *Commentario delle opere e delle vicende di Giorgio Biandrata* (with portrait) (Padova, 1814.) W. Heberle, 'Aus dem Leben von G. Blandrata,' *Tübinger Zeitschrift für Theologie*, 1840, 4es Heft, 116–185. Trechsel, ii, 303–316.

[52] cf. Michael Burian, *Dissertatio historico-critica de duplici ingressu in Transsilvaniam Georgii Blandratae* (Albae Carolinae, 1806), p. 271. cf. Frédéric de Gingins-la-Sarraz, Documents pour servir à l'histoire des Comtes de Biandrate' etc., *Memorie della Reale Accademia delle Scienze di Torino*, Serie seconda, Tom. x (1849), 123–187.

[53] cf. Malacarne, *op. cit.*, p. 40.

one of the four Elders of the church early that year,[54] and was received as a resident in November, 1557.[55] For a time he lived quietly in the practice of his profession, but later on he began cautiously to raise questions with others as to the deity of Christ, and to put such questions to the minister, who became so offended by them that he refused longer to employ Biandrata as his family physician. He also repeatedly came to Calvin with his questions, going away apparently satisfied, yet returning the next day with the same ones in another form.[56] He wished to know to whom the name of God may justly be applied; what is the meaning of the terms person, essence, substance, subsistence, property, divinity, deity, as used in the creeds, and what is the difference between them; to whom prayer is to be addressed; and how the incarnation of the Word is to be understood.[57] If these and similar questions were sincerely put, they seem to indicate a mind trying to frame for itself a clear, intelligible, scriptural and reasonable statement of the central Christian doctrines, yet persistently puzzled by the theological terms used to explain them. Calvin at first treated him patiently, and at length wrote out an extended answer to his questions;[58] but at last he concluded that Biandrata's real purpose was to stir up dissension in the church.

Complaints also arose in the Italian church itself that the common people were being secretly perverted by false doctrines.[59] Biandrata was therefore called before the Consistory with some others and admonished, but assured that they should not be punished for what was past. He must, however, have had a bad conscience, for sometime later, while attending a lecture of Calvin's, he felt a presentiment that he was about to be arrested, and suddenly fled the city, nor dared he return until his intimate friend Alciati had begged a safe conduct for him. The late minister of the Italian church, Martinengo, had already when on his death-bed in the summer of 1557 most urgently besought Calvin and his colleagues to undertake to cure the evil of the doctrinal discussions that had been set on foot by Gribaldi.[60] As the evil was spreading, the

---

[54] cf. Ernst von Moeller, 'Der Antitrinitarier Johann Paul Alciat,' *Historische Vierteljahrsschrift,* ix (1908), 469.

[55] Galiffe, *Notices,* iv, 55.

[56] cf. Calvin, xix, 39 f.   [57] cf. Calvin, xvii, 169 ff; cf. Trechsel, ii, 467–470.

[58] Calvin, ix, 325–332.

[59] The several references to the following episode are fragmentary and somewhat disordered, but it is believed that the arrangement here given presents them in proper sequence. cf. Calvin, xxi, 691–695; xvii, 168 f, 236 f, 258 f; xix, 40 f; xxi, 85.

[60] Calvin to Vermigli, May 22, 1558, Calvin, xvii, 176.

CHAPTER XVI

FOLLOWERS OF SERVETUS (CONTINUED):
ALCIATI AND GENTILE

BIANDRATA'S COMPANION in refusing to sign Calvin's test confession of faith imposed on the members of the Italian church at Geneva, and in consequently going into exile for the sake of his convictions, was Gianpaolo Alciati de la Motta,[1] a nobleman of Piedmont, born perhaps about 1515–1520 at Savigliano, just east of Saluzzo.[2] He was evidently an educated man, but he followed a military career until somewhere near the middle of the century, when he embraced the reformed religion and removed to Geneva. Here his rank and wealth gained him consideration, and he is recorded as a member of the Italian church in 1552.[3] In 1554 Calvin addresses him as a 'dearly beloved brother,' answering an inquiry about the baptism of an infant;[4] in 1555 he is received as a citizen of Geneva,[5] in the same year he is elected Deacon, and in the following year Elder of the church. It was at the very period when the doctrinal discussions above referred to were beginning, and in these Alciati was drawn to the liberal side. In the discussion that preceded the signing, Alciati shocked many by the sacrilegious statement that in the Trinity 'we worship three devils, worse than all the idols of the Papacy, because we make it three persons.'[6] It is therefore no wonder that Beza a few years later referred to him as a person that was evidently mad and unbalanced.[7]

[1] cf. Moeller, *Alciat.*; Arturo Pascal, 'La vita e le dottrine di G. Paolo Alciati,' *Bollettino storicobibliografico Subalpino*, xxii (1920), 29.

[2] Hence not a Milanese as said by Beza and many following him. cf. Moeller, *op. cit.*, p. 463 f. Nor is there any basis for adopting Bock's tempting conjecture (*Antitrinitar.*, ii, 465 f), likewise often repeated, that he was related to the celebrated jurist, Andrea Alciati, 1492–1550, the founder of modern jurisprudence. *ibid.*, p. 460 f.

[3] Bock's statement (*op. cit.*, ii, 466), citing as authority an irrelevant passage in Hottinger, that in 1553 he made a missionary tour of the Grisons with Biandrata, is probably an error for 1558. cf. note on p. 108, *supra*.

[4] Calvin to Alciati, Oct. 11, 1554, Calvin, xv, 265.

[5] cf. J. B. G. Galiffe, *Refuge italien de Genève* (Genève, 1881), p. 114; Moeller, *op. cit.*, p. 469.   [6] cf. Calvin, xix, 40.

[7] Paulus quidem Alciatus Mediolanensis, homo jam antea plane phreneticus et vertiginosus. Beza, *Valentini Gentilis teterrimi haeretici*, etc. (Geneva, 1567), pref. p. 14.

Not long after parting from Biandrata at Zürich, Alciati returned to the vicinity of Geneva, hoping to save some of his business interests there. He apparently made his headquarters at St. Julien, six miles south. Here he kept in communication with his friends, who used to meet him at the pont d'Arve until the Council taking notice of it formally declared him an enemy of the Geneva church, and forbade all communciation with him, under penalty of banishment, and sequestered his property.[8] Being thus cut off from his friends at Geneva, Alciati now went to Basel and was enrolled at the University for the winter semester.[9] Meanwhile history had been making at Geneva. Gentile, one of the six recalcitrant liberals who finally signed the confession, soon relapsed into his old heresies, was arrested, tried, found guilty and sentenced to death, which he narrowly escaped by performing a humiliating penance. Soon after this he fled to Gribaldi at Farges, as will be told a little later on in this chapter. Caterina Coppa of Ferrara, who had come to Geneva to seek her fugitive son, found things here so different from what she had expected that it was hard for her to keep to herself her impressions of Calvin's *régime*. The ever-present spies informed against her, and she was tried on the charge of having said, among other things, that Servetus died a martyr of Jesus Christ; that Gribaldi, Alciati and Biandrata had good doctrine and were wrongly persecuted; that she did not like the Italian church; that the magistrate did wrong to punish any kind of heretic; and that Calvin was jealous of Gribaldi's superior wisdom. She was found guilty, condemned to make a solemn retractation, and banished within twenty-four hours, on pain of being beheaded.[10]

After having visited Turin in the spring, and created serious doctrinal trouble in the reformed congregation there,[11] Alciati returned to Farges, and from there wrote a letter to the Geneva government resigning his citizenship, with some skilfully veiled reflections on Calvin and his oppressive rule. A little later a suit was filed against him and another, and they were cited to appear.[12] He replied that he would not set foot in

[8] cf. Calvin, xxi, 704, 708; Nov. 14, 1558.

[9] cf. Church, *Reformers*, p. 306.

[10] May 3, 1559. cf. Trechsel, *Antitrinitarier*, ii, 330 f; Galiffe, *Notices*, iii, 541 f; Ruffini, *Gribaldi*, p. 261 f.

[11] cf. letter of Martinius to Calvin, Turin, May 13, 1559, Calvin, xvii, 516 f; Beza, *Histoire ecclésiastique* (Paris, 1883–'89), iii, 475.

[12] cf. Pascal, *op. cit.*

Geneva so long as Calvin lived, since he had no mind to suffer like Gentile;[13] and he was consequently banished from Geneva territory forever, on pain of being beheaded. The charge against him was that he had broken his oath of citizenship in introducing confusion into the church. His property was not restored to him.[14]

While this trial was in process Alciati wrote a second letter, from St. Julien, declaring himself innocent of any ground for prosecution, unless possibly on account of his religious views. To avoid any misunderstanding as to these he submitted a carefully drawn confession of faith for their inspection.[15] This confession is very different in matter and tone from the things that witnesses declared that he had said the previous autumn, which were certainly far from being orthodox;[16] but as it was not written under stress, nor with any hope of reconciliation, it may be accepted as sincere for the time when it was written. He squarely denies the things he has been accused of saying, and he confesses that in the quiet atmosphere of the University he has become better instructed as to the meaning of the term *person*, to which he formerly so strongly objected. Yet though this confession is essentially orthodox, Alciati's career in Poland, to which we shall return in a later chapter, shows that he did not long remain so. His was apparently a mind that did not so much think for itself as reflect the thoughts of those with whom he closely associated; but in the history of religious liberty he deserves to be remembered for the fearless ardor and persistence with which he defended his convictions, even in the very face of Calvin. For in the field of religious controversy he showed the same courage that he will have displayed as a soldier on the field of battle.[17]

As we have already seen, not a few of the reforming Italians of the sixteenth century manifested, as sons of the Renaissance, a much freer spirit of inquiry than was common among the reformers north of the Alps. Their primary interest in the reformation seems to have lain in the intellectual field, and their first effort was to have its new system of doctrine not only more scriptural but also more reasonable. It was independent and daring thinkers moved by this spirit that were giving Calvin much trouble in the Italian church at Geneva. Gribaldi was the

---

[13] cf. Jean Gaberel, *Histoire de l'Église de Genève* (Genève, 1855–'62), ii, 334.

[14] cf. Moeller, *op. cit.*, p. 476 ff.

[15] cf. Moeller, *op. cit.*, p. 478 ff.

[16] cf. Trechsel, ii, 311, n. 2.

[17] cf. Pascal, *op. cit.*, p. 44.

first there to give public expression to this tendency; Biandrata by his questions secretly promoted it at Geneva, and in Poland and Transylvania was later able to do most to propagate its radical views until they became well rooted there. But the one to advocate them most boldly in Switzerland was Gentile, whose conspicuous trial at Geneva, adventurous experiences elsewhere, and heroic death at last at Bern, make him a figure second only to Servetus in dramatic interest. Beza [18] regarded him as the author of the antitrinitarian views that so seriously infected the Italian congregation, and he was certainly their most conspicuous advocate. But Calvin called him a man of no account, and a mere mouther of Gribaldi's lines,[19] though he thought it worth his while to devote an octavo book of over a hundred pages to refuting his teachings.

Giovanni Valentino Gentile [20] was born at Cosenza in Calabria, presumably in the first quarter of the sixteenth century. He made great progress in his studies, and going to Naples soon established a reputation as a teacher of *grammatica*, i.e. Latin.[21] He had a keen and subtle mind, inclined to speculation,[22] presently embraced the Reformation, and attracted by the reputation of Calvin [23] came to Geneva in 1556. It is evident that his closest associations there were with the liberal circle, for when the members of the Italian congregation were asked in May, 1558 to subscribe a confession of faith, he was one of those that at first refused to do so. After five days, however, and conference with Calvin, he professed to be convinced, and submitted to the inevitable;[24] though he was evidently unsatisfied, for he later returned for further conference on the subject.[25] As Biandrata and Alciati, who had hitherto been the

---

[18] Hominis monstrum Valentinus Gentilis, Gribaldi illius socius, Serveti · discipulus, Blandratae et Alciati collega, omnium istorum malorum vel praecipuus autor. Beza to Haller, June 19, 1566, in Trechsel, ii, 488; *Vita Calvini* in Calvin, xxi, 153 f.

[19] "Homo nihili," Calvin, ix. 365; "Gribaldus, cujus Valentinus est histrio," *ibid.*, ix. 379.

[20] cf. Trechsel, ii, 316–344, 355–380; Beza, *Valentini Gentilis teterrimi haeretici*, etc. (Genevae, 1567); Henri Fazy, 'Procès de Valentin Gentilis,' *Mémoires de l'Institut National Génevois*, xxv (1879), 1–103; Benedictus Aretius, *Valentini Gentilis . . . brevis historia* (Genevae, 1567); Eng. trans., *Short History of Valentinus Gentilis the Tritheist* (London, 1696); Emilio Comba, 'Valentino Gentile un nuovo Serveto?' *Rivista Cristiana*, N. S. i (Jan., Feb., 1899), 20–25, 41–52; Calvin, ix, 389.

[21] cf. Salvatore Spiriti, *Scrittori Cosentini* (Napoli, 1750), p. 66, cited by Trechsel, ii, 317, n. 4.

[22] Beza, *Vita Calvini*, Calvin, xxi, 154.

[23] Calvin, ix, 390.

[24] Calvin, xxi, 694 f.

[25] Fazy, *op. cit.*, p. 37.

leaders of the liberal group, had now left Geneva, there was promise of quiet in the church, had not the minister of it continued to attack as Arians and Servetians some of those that had subscribed,[26] and thus kept the matter stirred up. Calvin's spies were also on the watch, and one of them, engaging Gentile in what he supposed to be a private conversation on theological subjects, drew out of him several expressions interpreted as heretical, made a note of them, and reported them to Calvin,[27] denouncing Gentile as a heretic. He was therefore arrested and put under examination.[28] In the first examination before the Council, based upon the confession he had signed, the attempt was made to fix on him the charges of perjury, mutiny and sedition in violating his promise there given. But he declared that since signing he had observed the faith and agreed with the view of Calvin, and had always believed in the Trinity as well as in the Unity. At the next examination he was faced with his accusers, whose testimony he flatly contradicted. Calvin also appeared and tried to prove him in error in saying that in the Old Testament the name God is used only of God the Father.

In the meantime he had, at the command of the Council, prepared a confession of his own faith.[29] In this, while he confessed belief in the one God, and in Jesus Christ his only Son, he did not scruple to say that Calvin's view of the Trinity was sophistical, and involved not a Trinity but a Quaternity; and he appended a list of citations from the early Fathers in support of his view. At the same time he addressed a letter [30] to the ministers of the church, defending himself against the charges made, raising several questions the answers to which he felt would confirm his view, and promising to abide by their judgment. At these writings Calvin took great offence, and at the following examination he heaped all possible abuse upon Gentile, and threatened him with a capital charge.[31] To refute his arguments the ministers, or Calvin in their name, made a lengthy reply, bitter in spirit and filled with invectives.[32] At the next session he was again asked whether he adhered to

<hr/>

[26] Calvin, ix, 391.

[27] cf. Fazy, pp. 7, 35.

[28] July 11. The full report of the successive examinations is given in Fazy, p. 31 ff; cf. Calvin. xxi, 698–703, *passim*.

[29] cf. Fazy, p. 64 f; Calvin, ix, 389 f.

[30] Fazy, pp. 65–71; Calvin, ix, 390–399.

[31] cf. Fazy, p. 83; Calvin, ix, 411, "Minatus est hoc in caput meum esse vertendum."

[32] cf. Fazy, pp. 71–82; Calvin, ix, 399–410.

the confession he had first made, and he replied that since signing he had come to a different view, as he had recently written, and that he should hold this until otherwise taught by Scripture; though he was ready to accept Calvin's formula, provided it asserted a Trinity and not a real Quaternity. He also asked for counsel to represent him; but this was refused to him as it had been to Servetus.

Gentile now began to realize that he was at the mercy of civil and ecclesiastical judges whose attitude toward him was entirely hostile, with Calvin's enmity against him especially pronounced; and he was even threatened with torture if he should attempt to evade direct answers. He therefore asked an opportunity to write out his views and the grounds for them. Proceedings were now suspended for more than two weeks, during which Gentile came to adopt a different attitude. Seeing that the ministers to whose judgment he had appealed unanimously condemned his view as erroneous,[33] he acquiesced with them as he had promised, asking their pardon, especially that of Calvin. The following day he retracted more explicitly and confessed his broken oath; but his accusers were not satisfied until they had also introduced witnesses to assail his private character.[34] At each of the successive sessions he continued humbly to confess his errors, and to declare his repentance and ask for pardon and mercy. The committee of five lawyers, however, to whom the Council had referred the case, pronounced him worthy of death for his perjury and heresies, ignored his recantation as feigned, declared him unworthy to be pardoned, and called attention to the mischief he might do if set at liberty. They added, however, that although under the law he deserved death by fire, yet in view of his recantation there might be ground for mitigating his punishment to mere beheading.[35] It was voted that he be executed the following day. When the next day came, however, it was voted to postpone matters for further light as to his guilt. At the same time a letter arrived from an influential Italian gentleman then at Lyon, powerfully interceding for Gentile.[36] He threw the whole blame upon the influence of Biandrata, and declared that Gentile was the victim of transient mental disturbances; but also that he had rare talents, which might be of great service

---

[33] Quum tot sapientissimi viri . . . meam opinionem uno ore erroneam ostentur; Fazy, p. 85; Calvin, ix, 412.

[34] cf. Fazy, pp. 59–62.

[35] cf. Fazy, pp. 22, 90–92.

[36] Nicola Liena to the Council, Aug. 13, 1558; Fazy, pp. 88–90; Calvin, xvii, 286 ff.

to the cause of the Reformation; and that clemency would attract more converts among the Italians. The letter was referred to Calvin. Two weeks passed. More Italians asked for clemency, and the sentence pronounced against Gentile was seen to have aroused general indignation. Meanwhile he was again examined as to the sincerity of his repentance, and presented a new confession of faith, in which he more definitely than ever abjured his errors, even that concerning a Quaternity.[37] The Council again took up the case, and finally commuted the death sentence to a performance of an *amende honorable*.[38] By this sentence he was required to appear at the Hôtel de Ville clad only in his shirt, with head and feet bare, a lighted torch in hand; to kneel before his judges and beg God and them for mercy, confessing the wickedness of what he had done and written; then to throw his writings into the fire; and finally to be led through the streets and squares to the sound of a trumpet, and to be forbidden to go from the city without permission.[39] Gentile performed this public penance the next day,[40] almost joyfully according to one account,[41] so glad was he to have made his narrow escape. He can no longer have felt at ease at Geneva. Two weeks after this he was granted permission to go beyond the city limits. Apparently he never returned. Whether he fled, or whether the authorities were glad to be rid of his presence, and so winked at his absence, is not quite clear.[42] At all events, he at once went to join his friends Gribaldi and Alciati at Farges, where his recently suppressed views were naturally revived and confirmed.

After a short time he went on to Lyon,[43] where many Italians then resided, inclined to the Reformation. There being assisted in his studies he compiled the teachings of the Fathers, and composed a considerable book, entitled *Antidota*.[44] In this work he made a sharp attack on Cal-

[37] cf. Fazy, p. 86 f; Calvin, ix, 414 f.

[38] cf. Fazy, pp. 93–95; Calvin, ix, 415–418. This humiliating punishment was more or less common in western Europe until near the end of the eighteenth century, and was occasionally employed far into the nineteenth.

[39] In view of his poverty he was exempted from depositing the security at first decreed.

[40] Sept. 3. He had been in prison since July 9, only two weeks less than Servetus, of whose trial Roget (*Genève*, v, 165) has called this a pale but faithful copy.

[41] cf. Trechsel, ii, 330.

[42] cf. Calvin, xxi, 703. The inaccurate Beza does not mention the permission granted (*Vita Calvini*, Calvin, xxi, 155), and represents it as flight *before* Biandrata and Alciati.

[43] The main authority for the rest of Gentile's life is Aretius, *op. cit.*

[44] The work is not known to have been printed, nor is any manuscript of it now known; but its contents are given in part in the work of Aretius above cited.

vin's doctrine of the Trinity as set forth in his *Institutes*, set forth his own statement of the true doctrine of the Trinity and related doctrines, and vindicated himself against his enemies at Geneva. The state of his health and fortunes ere long led him to Grenoble, where Gribaldi had just established himself. While he was here recovering his health, his doctrines fell under suspicion, and he was ordered to present a confession; but he succeeded in expressing himself so skilfully that, while avoiding the main point, it was accepted by the Catholics as directed against only the Protestants, and especially against Calvin. Returning now to Farges he found that the account of his trial at Geneva had become well known there, so that the local governor had him arrested and imprisoned at Gex. After a few days he was released,[45] upon promising to cause no disturbance, and to submit a confession that might be sent to Bern for examination. This done, he returned to Lyon. There his confession presently appeared in print in the form of a letter to the governor at Gex, together with some theological propositions, and some notes on the Athanasian Creed, which set forth his beliefs and criticisms in the boldest and baldest form.[46] Gentile later declared that the publication was made without his knowledge or consent, after a copy that he had given to Alciati, which had apparently fallen into the hands of a printer.[47] Copies of the book soon reached Poland, and shocked leaders of the reformed church there by its apparent belief in a plurality of Gods. Calvin wrote to them that Gentile was a second Biandrata.[48] In Lyon the unfortunate man was again soon imprisoned on suspicion, but again he succeeded in clearing himself just as he had done at Grenoble,[49] and after fifty days he was released. He realized, however, that he could no longer feel safe there, and he therefore gladly accepted an invitation from Biandrata, and went to Poland in the summer of 1562, accompanied by Alciati.[50] His part in the growing antitrinitarian movement there will be related in its due place; but after somewhat less than two years a royal edict was issued against foreign heretics, and Gentile was forced

---

[45] It is said that Alciati secured his release by depositing caution-money. cf. Sandius, *Bibliotheca*, p. 26; Lubieniecius, *Historia*, p. 107. Aretius, cited by Bayle, denies this.

[46] Printed at "Antwerp" (=Lyon), 1561. No extant copy is known; but the Bern Stadtbibliothek has a Ms copy, Cod. 122, p. 98 ff., which Trechsel reprinted, *op. cit.*, ii, 471–488. cf. Calvin, ix, p. xxxviii.   [47] cf. Trechsel, ii, 336, 360.

[48] Sarnicki to Calvin, Sept. 1, 1561, Calvin to Sarnicki, Sept. 10, Calvin, xviii, 672 f; xix, 35.   [49] Beza to Haller, June 19, 1566, Trechsel, ii, 488.

[50] cf. Trechsel, ii, 344, following Lubieniecius, *Historia*, p. 107, who wrongly gives the date as 1563.

to depart. He then spent some time in the Anabaptist colony in Moravia,[51] whence he went to Vienna; but finding no rest for the sole of his foot he decided to return to Savoy.[52] For he knew that Calvin had now died, and he supposed that Gribaldi was still alive; though he too had been carried off by the plague, which had cost Switzerland 38,000 lives.

Gentile found the same governor still in office at Gex, though he little suspected how much he had been angered that his own name should have been involved in Gentile's published confession. Being full of almost fanatical confidence in his cause he therefore ventured to go at once to the governor with a proposal for a theological disputation to be held under his auspices. He would challenge all the Protestant divines of neighboring France and Savoy to debate with him three theses about God and Christ, the vanquished party to suffer death as a teacher of false religion.[53] The governor's only answer was to have him at once lodged in prison, pending instructions from the capital at Bern. Gentile's arrest aroused the liveliest interest at Geneva, whence Beza at once wrote Haller at Bern, calling it providential that Gentile had again fallen into their hands, reminding him of his shamefully wicked record, rehearsing his heresies, telling how near he had recently come to ruining the reformed cause in Poland, and praying above all that they might not let him escape at Bern as he had done at Geneva.[54] He also urged Bullinger to exert upon Haller what pressure he could.[55] After five weeks' detention at Gex, he was taken to Bern, where he had still to wait two weeks before his trial could begin.[56] While some espoused his cause, as one that had been persecuted by Calvin, his case was not a little prejudiced because of his supposed sympathy with the Anabaptists, who had of late been causing much scandal in that vicinity, as well as by several attacks that well-known theologians had recently published against his doctrines.[57]

[51] Several of the persecuted Antitrinitarians referred to above in chapters vi. and vii. found refuge in this community at this period: Negri, Leone, Fieri, Paruta, Alciati, Ochino, Darius Socinus, Rizzetto, della Sega.   [52] cf. Aretius, *op. cit.*, p. 10.

[53] cf. Aretius, *op. cit.*, p. 47 f; Trechsel, ii, 358 f.

[54] Beza to Haller, June 19, July 16, 1566, Trechsel, ii, 488 f, 490 f.

[55] cf. Trechsel, ii, 364, n. 3.

[56] The best report of the trial is in Trechsel, ii, 365–373.

[57] cf. Trechsel, ii, 366, 374. Especially Alexander Alesius, *Assertio doctrinae Ecclesiae catholicae de S. Trinitate cum confutatione erroris Valentini Gentilis* (Lipsiae, 1564) (reprinted in Beza, *Valentini Gentilis*, pp. 101–128, together with other similar contemporary writings).

After examination of his books and papers, Gentile was charged with seven specific errors about the Trinity, and also with making false accusations against the Church, and repeatedly practicing cheats and deceptions in order to evade due punishment.[58] He did not deny that he held the views charged, but defended them as true. Beza returning from Zürich to Geneva went to talk with him, but could make no impression.[59] The clergy strove to get him to recant and subscribe the confession that Gribaldi signed nine years before; but he only replied that Gribaldi had committed a grievous sin in doing this. Finally, after a month's fruitless effort for his conversion, the Council sentenced him to death by the sword. The grounds stated were his errors about the Trinity and other doctrines that he had abjured at Geneva but later defended again, his shocking blasphemies against the Son of God and the mystery of the Trinity, and the stubbornness with which he had resisted all instruction to the contrary.[60] His execution followed on the next day. Unlike his master Gribaldi, and unlike his former self at Geneva, he now remained true to his convictions, continually declaring on his way to the block that he died as a martyr to the honor of the most high God, and reproaching the attendant clergy as Sabellians. For a single moment he wavered, then went stedfastly to his death.

Gentile had formed his characteristic beliefs after coming to Geneva, and under the influence of Gribaldi, though in time he moved away from Gribaldi's position. Aside from the usual objections to the doctrine of the Trinity, its want of clear support from Scripture, and the unscriptural terms used to explain it, and the further objection (derived from Servetus) to the *communicatio idiomatum* as an explanation of the union of the two natures in Christ, he held that only the Father is self-existent, while the Son and the Holy Spirit are derived from him and subordinate. In the Godhead he asserted the existence of three distinct eternal spirits, equally divine, yet differing in rank, dignity and character; while (again like Servetus) he condemned Calvin's view of the Trinity as one that led to a Quaternity. While rejecting the current orthodox doctrine, therefore, and trying to take a middle course between Sabellianism and Arianism, he laid himself open to the yet more serious charge of Tritheism. This Tritheism was only a brief passing episode

---

[58] cf. Aretius, *op. cit.*, vi, xix, xx; Trechsel, ii, 369–372.
[59] Haller to Bullinger, Aug. 22, 1566, Trechsel, ii, 369, n. 1.
[60] Sentence in Aretius, *op. cit.*, p. 49.

in the history of reformation theology. It began in Geneva with Gribaldi, reached its climax in Gentile, and for a few years had an alarming spread in the new reformed church in Poland, giving the Swiss reformers the deepest concern as they watched it from afar. But in hardly more than a dozen years it had dissolved, or been transformed into Arianism and then shortly into the more rational and consistent doctrine of humanitarianism, as framed into a system by Socinus, on its way to fully developed Unitarianism. In its time, however, it was taken seriously into account by theologians, and beside the controversial works already mentioned, it was elaborately answered and opposed in the theological work of Zanchi at Heidelberg.[61]

In view of the reaction following the death of Servetus, it is interesting to note that hardly a voice was now raised in protest at the death of Gentile save at Basel. Even there it was perhaps more because of the strained relations existing with the rest of Switzerland than because of any strong sentiment for religious toleration. For it will be remembered that it was there that the body of Joris had seven years before been taken from its grave and burnt. In fact, in the thirteen years since the death of Servetus, all open sympathy with any criticism of the doctrine of the Trinity had been thoroughly suppressed. So great had been the fear, both at Geneva and elsewhere, that the tritheistic views of which Gentile had been the most conspicuous advocate might spread, and bring confusion and division in the reformed churches in Switzerland, as they were already doing in those in Poland, that the greatest efforts were put forth to exterminate the heresy. In this very year most of the Swiss churches adopted the Helvetic Confession, which ere long was to be adopted also by the reformed churches of France, Hungary and Poland. Calvin's refutation of Gentile's doctrine, which together with a summary account of his trial, recantation and sentence at Geneva [62] had been published immediately after the publication of Gentile's confession at Lyon in 1561, was now republished by Beza with a long preface of his own and considerable other matter, and a most urgent appeal to the kings of Poland and Transylvania and the leaders of the churches there to check the spread of this heresy.[63] Finally Aretius, professor at Bern,

---

[61] Hieronymus Zanchi, *De Tribus Elohim*, in his *Opera* (Heidelberg, 1572), vol. 1, pars ii, liber v, pp. 515–564. The whole of liber v is concerned with Tritheism.

[62] *Impietas Valentini Gentilis detecta, et palam traducta, qui Christum non sine sacrilega blasphemia Deum essentiatum esse fingit* (Geneva, 1561). In Calvin, ix, 361–420.

[63] *Valentini Gentilis teterrimi haeretici*, etc.

published in the same year a brief history of Gentile with a lengthy refutation of his teachings,[64] which was to be translated and published in England toward the end of the following century as a contribution to a similar controversy then arising there. Thus not only the heresies of which we have spoken, but also freedom of conscience and of speech in religion, were as effectually suppressed in western Switzerland under Calvin's stern régime and powerful reasoning as they had been in Italy twenty years before by the Inquisition.

[64] *Benedictus Aretius, Valentini Gentilis justo capitis supplicio Bernae affecti brevis historia, & contra ejusdem blasphemias orthodoxa defensio articuli de sancta Trinitate.* (Genevae, 1567.)

CHAPTER XVII

FOLLOWERS OF SERVETUS AT ZÜRICH: LAELIUS SOCINUS AND OCHINO

URING THE SAME PERIOD at which the effort for greater freedom
of conscience and more liberty in speech in religion of which
this chapter has spoken was going on at Geneva and Bern, a
similar movement was taking place at Zürich, though attracting less
attention because it went on much more privately and quietly. The two
most conspicuous figures in it were first Sozini and then Ochino. Laelius Socinus (Lelio Sozini)[1] is of particular interest to us in this work
because he has been called 'the patriarch of Socinianism', the movement
whose history we are soon to follow. Laelius was born March 25, 1525
at Siena,[2] of one of the most distinguished families in the city. His ancestors for several generations had been celebrated jurists whose fame
extended over Europe. His father, Mariano Jr., was called *princeps
jurisconsultorum*, and taught jurisprudence successively in the universities at Pisa, Siena, Padua and Bologna.[3] Laelius passed his childhood
at Padua whither his father had now been called, and here he studied
at the University, expecting to follow the family tradition of the law.
Conceiving that he ought to trace the laws of men to the law of God as
their source,[4] he was led to a diligent study of the Scriptures. Thus he

---

[1] Unlike most other members of the family, Lelio uniformly spelled his name with one
z. For fullest accounts of his life, cf. Bock, *Antitrinitar.*, ii, 567–664; Illgen, *L. Socinus*;
id., *Symbolae*; Trechsel, *Antitrinitarier*, zweites Buch, *Lelio Sozini und die Antitrinitarier
seiner Zeit*, pp. 137–201, 431–459; Eugène Burnat, *Lelio Socin* (Vevey, 1894). Delio
Cantimori, 'Serveto e Lelio Sozzini,' *Religio*, xii (1936), 414–438.

[2] In the palazzo at the southwest corner of the via di Pantaneto (formerly Ricasoli),
No. 9, and the via di Follonica, still standing and bearing a commemorative tablet at the
corner of the building. Both he and his more famous nephew Faustus are commemorated
by sculptured medallions in the loggia in the Piazza dell' Indipendenza.

[3] His tomb is in the choir of San Domenico at Bologna. A recumbent bronze statue of
Laelius's great-grandfather, Mariano, Sr., by Vecchietta, is one of the ornaments of the
Bargello in Florence.

[4] Humanarum legum scientiam ex ipsis divini juris fontibus hauriendum sibi putavit.
(Przipcovius), *Vita Socini*, p. **, prefixed to *Fausti Socini Opera*, i (*Bibliotheca Fratrum
Polonorum*.) Qui juris humani studium familiae suae haereditarium aggressus, dum id e

soon discovered that many of the commonly received dogmas of the Church were plainly opposed to the teaching of the Bible as well as inconsistent with reason. Consequently he became interested in the efforts for the reform of the Church that were then coming to the front in Italy. At the age of twenty-one, therefore, he abandoned the study of the law and went to Venice, under whose freer government the reform movement was further advanced, and where the writings of Servetus were already known. Tradition connects his name, as we have seen, with the more or less legendary meetings of free reforming spirits at Vicenza in 1546.

Whether for fear of the Inquisition or for other reason, Socinus left the Venetian territory in 1547 and went among the refugee communities in the Grisons. He was for some time at Chiavenna, at the very time when the heated controversy over the sacrament was at its height between Mainardo and Camillo; and though he did not take sides, but kept friendship with both, there are strong indications that his thought and method were much influenced by Camillo.[5] As he was amply supplied with funds from his father, he now improved his opportunity for extensive travel in the lands where the Reformation was taking root, and for forming acquaintance with many of the reformers. He seems first to have gone to Geneva and to have had interviews with Calvin, next to Basel, thence to the court of the Protestant Marguerite of Navarre for some time, and on to England early in 1548. There he will have found Vermigli as Professor at Oxford, and Ochino who had arrived at London with him late in the preceding year. By the end of the year he was back in Switzerland, at Geneva where Calvin received him kindly, and at Zürich where the way had been prepared for him by a letter addressed to the Swiss churches by Nikolaus Maier, ambassador in Italy from the Prince of Württemberg,[6] and where, having now surveyed the Protestant world so widely, and become acquainted with so many of its leaders, he settled and found henceforth his second home.

---

juris divini fontibus hauriendum ratus. Wissowatius, *Narratio compendiosa*, in Sandius, *Bibliotheca*, p. 210. Hic Laelius, cum ad paternum studium se praepararet, ut prius fontes cognosceret, scilicet jus divinum, studiose legit libros Propheticos et Apostolicos. Melanchthon to Sigismund Augustus, Dec. 1, 1557, Melanchthon, *Opera*, ix, 380. cf. Melanchthon to Maximilian II., *ibid.*, p. 381.

[5] cf. *supra*, p. 103 ff.

[6] cf. Hottinger, *Hist. Eccl.*, ix, 436 f; Illgen, *Symbolae*, part iii, p. 4; Bock, *Antitrinitar.*, ii, 585.

He lodged with Pellikan, Professor of Hebrew, and applied himself
with great diligence to Hebrew and Greek that he might understand
the Scriptures more perfectly, and he even attempted Arabic. At the
same time he contracted warm friendships with the reformers there,
above all with Bullinger, who became to him as a father to whom he
could confide his doubts and with whom he could discuss his problems.
Wherever he went, Socinus inevitably won friends by his courtly manners, his breadth and depth of culture, his frank and attractive character, crowned by irreproachable morals and a deep and sincere piety.
At the same time he was a lawyer turned theologian, and in his intellectual approach to the problems of religion he was by temperament a
reverent skeptic, always looking for the fundamental reasons of doctrines before he could accept them as his own. Modest and undogmatic
in his spirit, he would seldom express his convictions save to his intimate
and trusted friends; while to others he was the eager and unwearied
inquirer, veiling his doubts under the form of questions. It was not
until later that others chose to interpret his habitual reserve as deliberate hypocrisy by which he concealed his heresies while secretly trying
to spread them among others.[7] It is quite as likely that it sprang from
an instinctive caution about expressing tentative views while still trying
to construct a doctrinal system satisfactory to himself.

During the following year (1549), Socinus was in correspondence
with Calvin on various doctrinal questions. He inquired about whether
one might marry a Catholic woman, whether Catholic baptism of infants were valid, whether one might be present at the Mass, whether
one must believe in the literal resurrection of the flesh.[8] Calvin at first
answered patiently and fully, but afterwards, when Socinus pressed his
questions too insistently, Calvin, busy man that he was, began to suspect
idle intellectual curiosity about speculative details of minor importance,
and broke off the correspondence in impatience,[9] though their friendship continued. Meanwhile Socinus had spent the summer semester at
Basel, where he met many important persons, and pursued his Hebrew
studies under Münster with whom he lodged. Having now for the
present exhausted the resources in Calvin's quarter, Socinus was desirous

---

[7] cf. Beza, *Vita Calvini*; Calvin, xxi, 142, 149.

[8] Socinus to Calvin, May 14, July 25, 1549, Calvin, xiii, 272 ff, 336 ff.

[9] Calvin to Socinus, June, Dec. 7, 1549, Socinus to Calvin, Feb. 1, 1550, Calvin, xiii,
307 ff, 464 ff, 517.

of knowing the other great Protestant leader, Melanchthon at Wittenberg. He therefore left Zürich at midsummer, 1550 and arrived at Wittenberg a month later, bearing flattering introductions from his friends at Zürich, Nürnberg and Basel. He was received cordially by Melanchthon, and lodged with Professor Forster, with whom he continued his studies in Hebrew. In the autumn he regularly matriculated at the University, and he remained there until the next summer,[10] making hosts of friends, enjoying intimacy with Melanchthon,[11] and keeping up a constant correspondence with Bullinger and other friends in Switzerland. While here he formed acquaintance with numerous Polish students at Wittenberg, and thus his attention was drawn to that country and the promising outlook for reformation there. His *wanderlust* therefore next led him in that direction, and after just less than a year he departed *via* Prague and Breslau for Kraków. He bore with him a general testimonial from Melanchthon to all and several, commending him as his intimate friend, learned, honest, discreet, a lover of public peace, faithful and upright in every respect, and commending him to the hospitality of good men everywhere.[12] The Polish capital had long been a seat of Italian culture, and Socinus found old friends among his countrymen there, especially the Queen's confessor, Lismanino, who was destined a decade later to be prominent in the early antitrinitarian movement. Socinus's stay in Poland was comparatively brief, and he returned through Moravia, where there were already Italian Anabaptist refugees, to Zürich where he arrived toward the end of the year.

He found Geneva wrought up over the doctrine of predestination, and Bolsec in prison for opposing it, and he felt called upon to urge Calvin to use milder measures.[13] Concerning his questions about predestination, Calvin in reply admonished him not to waste his time in early spec-

---

[10] He arrived July 18, 1550, and left June 23, 1551. cf. Melanchthon to Baumgärtner, July 18, 1550; Melanchthon to Chytraeus, June 24, 1551; Melanchthon, *Opera*, vii, 632, 802. Melanchthon or his amanuensis therefore made a slip in the three letters of recommendation dated Dec. 1, 1557 (*Opera* vii, 380–382) in which he speaks of Socinus's stay as "amplius triennio" — a statement that has led many later writers astray. cf. Illgen, *Symbolae*, part. ii, "Quo tempore Laelius Socinus Vitebergae vixerit."

[11] In summa, nemo Vitebergae est, qui Laelii amicitiam non ambiat, nemo, qui non libenter cum homine conversetur; inprimis autem Philippus omnia sua cum illo communicat. Statuit etiam videre Poloniam. Mącziński to Pellican, Aug. 24, 1550, in Illgen, part. ii, p. 20; also in Wotschke, *Briefwechsel*, p. 28. Illgen misspells the Polish name Mącziński as Macfinsky.

[12] *Melanchthon omnibus lecturis*, June 20, 1551, *Opera*, vii, 798 f.

[13] Melanchthon to Camerarius, Feb. 1, 1552; *Opera*, vii, 930.

ulations about questions of no importance, and concluded by warning him as a friend that unless he soon cured his itch for questionings, he was likely to bring serious trouble upon himself.[14] Socinus now turned his questions upon Bullinger, asking for a written answer, which Bullinger obligingly gave at some length,[15] adding however his own counsels against indulging his curiosity in season and out. He then turned to Bullinger's colleague Walther with a series of anxious questions about repentance, and received another extended answer.[16] In the spring of 1552 Socinus undertook a journey after five years' absence to visit his father who had just been called to a chair at Bologna. On the way he visited Vergerio in the Grisons for several weeks, and they traversed the whole of the Valtellina together.[17] Socinus then continued on his perilous journey alone,[18] having failed to receive in time a warning letter from his father.[19] He dared not pass the winter at Bologna as he had hoped, for fear of the Inquisition, but he spent considerable time at his native Siena. The next autumn he revisited Padua, the home of his youth, where he was for two months the guest of Gribaldi, but lately returned from Geneva.[20] He did not reach Zürich until the very end of the year.[21]

During the year after Socinus returned to Zürich the air of all Switzerland was tense over the case of Servetus. The letters exchanged between the reformers during this period constantly recur to it. Socinus had not yet fallen under suspicion of heresy, but though declaring that he did not share Servetus's opinions, he freely expressed disapproval of his execution. He soon went to Basel for some time, lodged with Castellio, and was on such intimate relations with the liberal circle there that Beza, who by now had come to regard him as a dangerous heretic,

[14] Nisi hunc quaerendi pruritum mature corrigas, metuendum est ne tibi gravia tormenta accersas. Calvin to Socinus, Jan. 1552, xiv, 229.

[15] Bullinger to Socinus, Feb. 21, 1552, Trechsel, ii, 447–452.

[16] Socinus to Gualther, undated, and Gualther to Socinus, May 18, 1552, Trechsel, ii, 452–458.

[17] Vergerio to Bullinger, June 20, 1552, *Bullingers Korrespondenz*, i, 253.

[18] Giulio Milanese was mistaken in saying that Vergerio secretly went to Bologna with him. Milanese to Bullinger, June 23, 1552, *Bullingers Korrespondenz*, i, 255.

[19] Vergerio to Bullinger, July 10, 1552, *Bullingers Korrespondenz*, i, 256.

[20] cf. Trechsel, ii, 164, n. 4.

[21] He was therefore not (as is sometimes stated) a witness of the execution of Servetus, being then at Padua. But he wrote a letter to a friend at Geneva in which he said that the blood of Abel was crying out to God, and that the time would come when Cain would find no peace on the earth. *Contra libellum Calvini*, p. A6.

charged him with having been in large measure responsible for the work *De Haereticis*.[22] His relations with Calvin, who had also grown suspicious, became strained, though they were never quite broken off.[23] To Bullinger Vergerio wrote from Tübingen, Gallicius from Chur, and Martinengo from Geneva, all complaining of Socinus's heresies, especially as to the Trinity.[24] Yet Bullinger's confidence remained unshaken. Socinus carried on an extensive correspondence with the leaders of the Reformation, and continued to prosecute his inquiries about grace, predestination, the sacraments, and above all the Trinity. Besides the letters just mentioned, further suspicion was aroused by a letter from Giulio Milanese, minister at Poschiavo in the Valtellina, to Bullinger, warning him to guard lest Socinus spread Arian or Servetian doctrines. Bullinger reported to Socinus the rumors that were repeatedly coming to him. Socinus felt aggrieved by this backbiting, and denied having said anything that should be construed as heresy, unless perhaps that he had not liked it that Servetus was put to death so soon, and that he would rather have had him set right than burned; but as for the Trinity, etc., he felt and professed the doctrine taught in Scripture and the Apostles' Creed. Bullinger, after questioning a little further, professed himself satisfied, and asked only that Socinus should put his faith in writing, to make it a matter of record.[25]

The confession of faith that Socinus accordingly composed and presented to Bullinger is an exceedingly interesting document.[26] Bullinger, reading it from the standpoint of confidence in Socinus and faith in his essential soundness of belief, accepted it without suspicion as a convincing answer to the charges that had been made against Socinus. But one reading it with close attention to precisely what it says, and also what it avoids saying, discovers that while making generous use of orthodox

---

[22] Beza to Bullinger, June 14, 1554, Calvin, xv, 166.

[23] Calvin to Bullinger, Aug. 7, 1554, Bullinger to Calvin, Sept. 9, 1554, Calvin, xv, 208, 230.

[24] Vergerio to Bullinger, Sept. 6, 1554, in de Porta, *Historia*, i, ii, 156; Trechsel, ii, 182, n. 1; Gallicius to Bullinger, Sept. 17, 1554, *Bullingers Korrespondenz* i, 388; Martinengo to Bullinger, Nov. 14, 1554, Calvin, xv, 310.

[25] Bullinger to Julius von Mailand, July, 1555, *Bullingers Korrespondenz*, i, 411 f. Hottinger, *Hist. Eccl.*, ix, 417–421; Bock, *op. cit.*, ii, 597–599.

[26] Dated July 15, 1555. cf. Hottinger, *op. cit.*, ix, 421–426; Bullinger's reply, *ibid.*, pp. 427–436; Bock, *Antitrinitar.*, ii, 599–602; Illgen, *L. Socinus*, pp. 49–52. Eng. trans. by Edward M. Hulme, 'Lelio Sozzini's Confession of Faith,' in *Persecution and Liberty*, essays in honor of George Lincoln Burr (New York, 1931), pp. 211–225.

phraseology it is one of the most remarkable documents on record for the skill with which, while giving the casual reader the impression of its being free of all heresy, it yet leaves the door open to a wide range of heretical views.[27] He does not declare his belief in either of the three great creeds, but only says that he honors them as far as he ought. He does not express belief in the Trinity, though allowing that the doctrine has been current for many centuries. He says he avoids the errors of the Catabaptists (Anabaptists), but does not say what those are. Finally he says he accepts all the things necessary for salvation, but does not name one of them. In short, while veiling the subject in vague and equivocal phrases, he studiously refrains from revealing either what he believes or what he disbelieves on any of the disputed points. But the unsuspecting Bullinger was reassured, and he begged Giulio to absolve Socinus from further suspicion. Giulio accepted his judgment, and promised to comply with his wish, though it was with evident misgivings.[28]

Henceforth we hear no more of Socinus's heresies. He heeded the cautions given him, and was reserved in his questionings. When the church of Protestants exiled from Locarno in 1555, for whom he had expressed deep sympathy in their afflictions,[29] settled at Zürich, he found in its members and their minister opportunities for the intimacy he craved. Midway of the next year, however, his father died at Bologna, and his worldly affairs were thrown into confusion. For his father had disinherited him, and the Inquisition had sequestered the fugitive heretic's share of his father's estate, and left him without means of support. He therefore determined to return to Italy in order if possible to recover his patrimony. That he might be safe from arrest while doing this, he must go as the representative of a foreign power. He therefore went first to Melanchthon to seek his intervention, and from him received letters commending him to the King of Poland, the King of Bohemia, and the latter's court preacher.[30] Returning to Switzerland, and supported by Bullinger's request, he got from Calvin a strong letter to Prince Nicholas Radziwiłł, after the King the most important person in Poland, and an influential supporter of the reform movement in the

[27] cf. the searching examination of it by Hulme in the article above cited.

[28] Julius von Mailand to Bullinger, Nov. 4, 1555, *Bullingers Korrespondenz*, i, 419–422.

[29] cf. his letter to the congregation, Jan. 13, 1555, Trechsel, ii, 459.

[30] cf. the three letters of Melanchthon to Maximilian II., Sigismund Augustus, and Pfauser, all dated Worms, Dec. 1, 1557; Melanchthon, *Opera*, ix, 379–383; Illgen, *Symbolae*, part. ii, 24–27.

Church.[31] Bullinger also recommended him heartily to Łaski (à Lasco),
who was then at the head of the Reformation in Poland.[32] Thus armed
with these and other credentials Socinus set out for Poland, where the
Reformation had made great progress since his previous visit. He was
received with honor in the houses of magnates, was the guest and became the intimate friend of Radziwiłł, had frequent private conversations with the King and most kind treatment from him,[33] and will
undoubtedly have met Biandrata and Alciati and have quietly encouraged the beginnings of the antitrinitarian movement. Returning to
Vienna he had conversation with King Maximilian,[34] and thence, bearing the desired commissions from both kings, proceeded to Venice and
Florence. The Doge Luigi Priuli at Venice and the Duke Cosimo
de' Medici at Florence failed to accomplish anything for him; and his
patrimony remained in the hands of the Inquisition. Worst of all, the
Socinus family had fallen under persecution, two of his brothers and
his nephew had fled the country, others lay long in prisons, and only
the letters he bore saved him from a like fate. His long mission had
utterly failed, and he returned to Zürich, whence he wrote Calvin interesting accounts of the progress of the Reformation in Poland.[35] In
the autumn he had the opportunity of returning to Italy to live in safety
under the protection of Cosimo,[36] but he finally decided not to embrace
it. He continued at Zürich to live a life more and more withdrawn
within itself. A brother and a nephew shared his exile there,[37] and on
May 14, 1562, he died, at the early age of thirty-seven. His nephew
Faustus, who a year before had removed from Siena to Lyon, was informed of his uncle's death by one of Socinus's Italian friends at Zürich,
and came at once and took possession of his books and manuscripts, of
which he was to make fruitful use, as will be later seen.

During the last quiet years of Socinus at Zürich, in which he was
more and more withdrawn from association with others, he seems to
have given himself increasingly to reducing to form the results of his

[31] Bullinger to Calvin, May 8, 1558, Calvin to Bullinger, May 22, Calvin to Radziwiłł,
May 24, Calvin, xvii, 160, 173, 181.

[32] Bullinger to à Lasco, June 24, 1558, Fueslin, *Epistolae*, p. 413 f.

[33] Socinus to Bullinger, Jan. 29, 1559; Trechsel, ii, 197, n. 4.

[34] Socinus to Bullinger, May 10, 1559, Trechsel, ii, 198, n. 1.

[35] Socinus to Calvin, Aug. 22, Oct. 2, 1559, Calvin, xvii, 604, 650.

[36] cf. letter of Oct. 2, *supra*.

[37] Trechsel, ii, 199, n. 4; Ferdinand Meyer, *Die evangelische Gemeinde in Locarno*
(Zürich, 1836), Theil ii, 152.

years of reading, inquiry and thought. He was at length beginning to
yield to the entreaties of his friends to give them, at least in brief compass, some fruit of his studies,[38] when his premature death occurred.
Little of what he wrote therefore ever appeared in print,[39] but his manuscripts that fell to his nephew Faustus seem to have given direction to
the latter's thought,[40] and thus to have laid a foundation for the system
of Socinian doctrine in Poland, where we shall follow it in the chapters
immediately following.

Socinus was too reserved in his communications, and left too little in
published form, for us to speak definitely of his doctrines; while the
verdict of contemporary opponents was too much colored by theological
prejudice, and that of his friends and followers too much warmed by
admiration, to be relied upon. But it may at least be said that as he
attempted by incessant inquiry to frame for himself a new system of
doctrine in place of that which he had discarded, he relied upon the
verdict of reason equally with the teaching of Scripture; and in this he
brought into prominence an element hitherto largely neglected. When
this principle was applied to the restatement of such doctrines as the
Trinity, the nature of Christ, redemption, the sacraments and others,
the effect was bound to be revolutionary. But he was not fitted by temperament to be a constructive theologian; and with his method of cautious inquiry, and his reluctance to offend the weak, there was lacking
that strong and positive conviction which gives vitality to a system of
doctrine. This was to be supplied later when the seed-thoughts that
Laelius had planted came to fruitage in the fully developed system of
his more famous nephew Faustus.

During the latter part of the period just spoken of, there was at
Zürich another Italian who had an interesting and influential relation

[38] F. Socinus to Dudith, Mar. 20, 1583, Socinus, *Opera*, i, 508.

[39] Besides his confession of faith above mentioned, and a few extant letters (several in
Trechsel, ii, 431–459, and Burnat, pp. 89–92), it is doubtful whether any other writing of
his survives, save two brief dissertations, *De sacramentis*, and *De resurrectione corporum*,
both included in a tiny *Tractatus aliquot theologici* published secretly at Amsterdam in
1654, also reprinted in Trechsel, *op. cit.*, ii, 438–446. Other writings mentioned are no
longer extant; but cf. Delio Cantimori e Elizabeth Feist, *Per la Storia degli Eretici Italiani*
(Roma, 1937). His relation to writings against Calvin published by Castellio has already
been mentioned.

[40] Faustus was influenced by Laelius even at an early age: Cum adhuc adolescens ac
paene puer essem, Laelio praecipue Socino patruo meo monitore, etc.; *Opera*, ii, 118. cf.
i, p. **b f. His obligations to his uncle, and his unbounded admiration for him, are recorded in his *Opera*, i, 362, 423, 433, 476, 508, 782; ii, 505, 625, 640.

to our movement. This was Bernardino Ochino, whose earlier career in Italy has been related in a previous chapter.[41] In his flight from Italy he crossed the Alps by the usual route of the refugees through the Grisons, coming first to Zürich,[42] and thence passing on to Geneva, where a numerous company of Italians had been gathering since persecutions began to thicken in Italy. He reached Geneva about the twentieth of September. Calvin was well impressed by the venerable old man,[43] declared that the better he knew him the more he liked him, and hoped that if he could learn the language he would in time be of great service; while all that knew him thought him a great accession to the cause of the Reformation. His old friends made great efforts to get him back, but he remained stedfast, and burned the bridges behind him by publishing a volume of sermons in which he openly professed his unqualified adherence to the new religion. He was supported by gifts from his noble friend Ascanio Colonna at Ferrara, and in his three years at Geneva he published five volumes of sermons in Italian for circulation among his fellow-countrymen, as his contribution to reform in the land he had had to leave.[44] After a month the Council granted him the chapel of the Cardinal of Ostia (chapel of the Maccabees) adjoining the cathedral of St. Peter, for services in Italian, and voted him a modest stipend and a colleague.[45] The churches in the Venetian territory wrote the ministers of Geneva to express their gratitude for the kindness shown the refugee.[46] Early the next year Paleario wrote Calvin highly recommending Ochino, and Calvin wrote Melanchthon of him as a great and famous man who had stirred Italy not a little by his departure. One of the friars of Ochino's order tried to rouse Calvin's suspicion of Ochino as heretical concerning the Trinity and the nature of Christ; but after searching doctrinal conversation his confidence remained unshaken.[47]

[41] Chapter vii, pp. 93–96, *supra*. For the literature on him, cf. p. 93, n. 18. See also Struve, 'De vita, religione et fatis Barnardini Ochini Senensis,' *Observationes Selectae*, iv (1701), 406–440.   [42] Bullinger to Vadian, Dec. 19, 1652, Calvin, xi, 478 ff.

[43] Vir magnus omnibus modis. Magnum et praeclarum virum. Calvin to Farel, Dec. 15, 1542, Calvin, xi, 475.

[44] Bullinger to Vadian, *ut supra*; Calvin to Viret, Oct. 1542, Calvin, xi, 447, 458.

[45] Registres du Conseil, Oct. 23, 1542, Calvin, xxi, 304.

[46] Dated Dec. 8, 1542, Calvin, xi, 472 ff.

[47] Paleario to Calvin, Calvin, xi, 509; also in Schelhorn, *Amoenitates historiae ecclesiasticae et literariae* (Lipsiae, 1737–'40), i, 448–462; Calvin to Melanchthon, Feb. 16, 1543, to Pellikan, Apr. 17, xi, 518, 528.

After two years and a half the Council assigned Ochino a residence [48] as recognized pastor of the Italian congregation; but at midsummer he left Geneva for Basel, bearing a cordial letter to Myconius,[49] the pastor there. Here he stayed with Castellio, whom he had doubtless known before the latter left Geneva, and who may perhaps have stimulated the course of his thought. Henceforth they were intimate friends, and Castellio translated most of his writings from Italian into Latin. Thence he proceeded by way of Strassburg, where he visited his old friend Vermigli, to Augsburg. There he soon received from the Council an appointment as preacher in St. Anne's church to the numerous Italian congregation, at a handsome stipend, and remained for between one and two years (1545-1547), very happy in his work, which included the publishing of several volumes of sermons and of commentaries;[50] but here a bare year and a quarter was permitted him. The Emperor won the Schmalkaldic war, and Augsburg was forced to surrender. One of his conditions was that Ochino should be delivered over to him; but timely warning was given, and before the Emperor arrived Ochino had fled late in January to Zürich, Basel and Strassburg. Butzer tried again to secure a post for him at Geneva, but at that time none was available.[51]

Fortunately for Ochino, he had not many months to wait with his friend Vermigli at Strassburg; for Archbishop Cranmer in England, whose scheme for the Reformation then in progress there included bringing foreign theologians to England, ere long invited Vermigli to a chair at Oxford, and Ochino to accompany him. They arrived at London in December, 1547. Ochino seems to have been Cranmer's guest at Lambeth palace until his wife arrived four months later, when he took a house in London. He devoted himself more actively than ever to writing, being supported by a pension from the crown and a non-resident prebend at Canterbury; though he was not appointed preacher to the Italian congregation in the Strangers' Church, as is often said on the basis of a mistaken inference.[52] He enjoyed over five years of busy life here, and published several more volumes of sermons in

[48] Registres du Conseil, Apr. 7, 1545, Calvin, xxi, 350.

[49] Calvin to Myconius, Aug. 15, 1545, Calvin, xii, 136.

[50] cf. J. G. Schelhorn, *Ergötzlichkeiten* (Ulm, 1764), iii, 1141 ff. Viret to Calvin, Apr. 2, 1547, Calvin, xx, 382.

[51] Calvin to Viret, Apr. 6, 1547, Calvin, xii, 508.

[52] cf. C. H. Smyth, *Cranmer and the Reformation under Edward VI* (Cambridge, 1926), p. 115 f.

English, and a polemic of unusual dramatic power against the Papacy, entitled *Tragoedie*, which he dedicated to the young King. The Princess Elizabeth read his sermons, and sought his counsel in her religious doubts; and when she later ascended the throne he dedicated to her his important work, the *Labyrinthi*. Edward VI. unexpectedly died in the middle of 1553, and was succeeded by the reactionary Catholic Mary. All foreign Protestants were driven from the country, and for the third time Ochino, now sixty-six years old, was forced into exile. He returned to Strassburg, made visits to Chiavenna and Zürich, and arrived at Geneva the day after Servetus's death,[53] waiting there long enough to publish a volume of *Apologhi*, an anecdotal attack on the abuses of the Papacy. But the atmosphere of Geneva, in the tense period following the burning of Servetus, can not have been congenial to Ochino. He therefore returned to Basel, where he occupied himself with literary work for something more than a year, when an unexpected opportunity offered for him to take an interesting post at Zürich, as pastor of a newly-arrived congregation of Italian exiles, to whom reference has already been made.

There had for some ten years been a Protestant congregation at Locarno on Lago Maggiore, but the opposition on the part of the Catholic government had grown so severe that early in 1555 the members were forced to choose between renouncing their faith and going into exile.[54] They chose the latter, and having been assured of a welcome at Zürich they emigrated in a body, and early in the spring, before the passes were free of deep snow, they crossed the Alps. Some stopped on the way, but about sixty families reached Zürich where they were welcomed and assigned a place of worship in St. Peter's church. As their pastor did not think himself competent in comparison with the pastors of the Zürich church, he made way for another, and the choice easily fell upon Ochino.[55] Socinus was one of those sent to Basel to bear him the invitation. He gladly accepted, and began his new labors in June. His salary was paid by the city, and as the demands of his little congregation were light he continued to publish sermons and controversial writings more industriously than ever. Of these the most noteworthy were a *Dialogue*

---

[53] cf. Meyer, *Locarno*, i, 297, n. 79; *Contra libellum Calvini*, p. A6.

[54] cf. Meyer, *op. cit.*; H. E. Benrath, *Vertreibung der Evangelischen aus Locarno* Barmen, 1889); Josias Simler, *Narratio de vita H. Bullingeri* (Tiguri, 1575), p. 28b; *id.*, *De aeterno Dei Filio* (Tiguri, 1570), pref.

[55] Bullinger to Calvin, June 14, 1555, Calvin, xv, 655.

on Purgatory, which by its manner of treatment gave offence even to some of the Protestants; *Labyrinthi*, an acutely reasoned treatise on the freedom of the will, predestination, and related themes;[56] and a *Catechism* in Italian which, being now near the end of life, he meant to bequeath to his flock for their instruction and guidance after he should be taken from them. He was happy in his associations with his young friend Socinus, and with his old friend Vermigli, who had succeeded to Pellikan's chair at Zürich, and he is said to have led Francesco Lismanino to forsake the Roman Church, who had lately been confessor to the Queen of Poland, and was soon to be active in promoting the liberal movement among the reforming party in that country. Ochino himself seems to have made a brief visit to Poland in 1559, and to have associated with Biandrata in the growing liberal circle there.[57] Thus far, however, his orthodoxy had been entirely free from suspicion. Bullinger had stood sponsor for his child, and Ochino had written affectionately to Calvin after coming to Zürich.[58] Several of his works had, indeed, been unfavorably criticized in Protestant circles,[59] though not as being seriously heretical; but although the Blandratists in Poland were already boasting of his adherence to their view, the orthodox denied this as a slander.[60] Nevertheless, a certain measure of distrust was more and more felt toward the Italian refugees in general, and some of this will naturally have attached also to him. It was reported that there was a plot of the Pope to send assassins against the Italian religious exiles, and some Spaniards were said to have tried to poison Ochino.[61]

Like the Italian reformers in general, Ochino was less disposed than most of the northern reformers to accept the traditional dogmas without criticism, and more inclined to subject them to free inquiry. This tendency had already aroused some misgiving, but now came a book

---

[56] cf. Bertrand-Barraud, *Les Idées philosophiques de Bernardin Ochin*, chap. iii, for a full summary of the work.

[57] cf. G. Schomann, *Testamentum*, in Sandius, *Bibliotheca*, p. 193. Anno 1559 . . . Pinczoviae, ubi ego cum Petro Statorio . . . D. Francesco Lismanino, D. Georgio Blandrata Medico, Bernardino Ochino, familiariter vixi, & evidenter didici, errorem esse non fidem Christianam, Trinitatis personarum omnimodam aequalitatem, sed unum esse Deum Patrem, unum Dei Filium, unum Spiritum Sanctum, licet adhuc multa non intelligeremus ad hoc pertinentia.

[58] Ochino to Calvin, Dec. 4, 1555, Calvin, xv, 880 f.

[59] cf. Haller to Bullinger, Mar. 15, 1556, Calvin, xvi, 73.

[60] Sarnicki to Tretius, Nov. 1562, Calvin, xix, 577.

[61] Gratarolo to Calvin, Apr. 22, 1559, Calvin, xvii, 502.

in which he laid himself more than ever open to criticism. In his two volumes of *Dialogues*,[62] he employed the then popular method of presenting both sides of the questions under discussion, and this so successfully that it was not always clear which side he himself espoused. The first volume treated in the main of Jesus as Messiah, the second of the Trinity, polygamy and other topics. The work was published in the spring of 1563, and for six months or so attracted no marked attention. Beza indeed early heard evil reports of it, and wrote Bullinger that it was said to favor the heresies of Servetus and his followers; but though Bullinger had had no time to read it, he did not in the least believe the charge.[63] It was not until November that the storm suddenly burst. At the public table of an inn at Basel at the time of the fair,[64] it was stated that a book had been printed at Basel, by a Zürich minister, which justified polygamy and thus put Zürich to open shame. Some Zürichers present resented the statement and challenged it. Proof was soon forthcoming. The matter was at once reported to the Council at Zürich, and an investigation was ordered. A copy of the *Dialogues* was obtained and examined by the ministers and professors, and report was made to the Council that in the dialogue on polygamy Ochino had indeed attacked the practice, but with obviously weak arguments; and had put far stronger ones into the mouth of the defence, at the end practically confessing defeat. The book had been published without passing the censors,[65] despite the fact that Ochino had two years before been admonished for not regarding the ordinance in this respect. Public and private remonstrances had been received, and the good name of the Zürich church was suffering reproach. Polygamy had in fact been a sore subject with Protestants, and the object of heavy reproaches by Catholics, ever since Philip of Hesse had in 1539 contracted a polygamous marriage and been defended in it by Luther himself.

The Council acted without hesitation or delay. The very suspicion of heresy or of questionable morals was feared, like the plague, no less

---

[62] Bernardini Ochini Senensis, *Dialogi xxx, in duos libros divisi*, etc. (Basileae, 1563). cf. Struve, 'De Barnardini Ochini Dialogorum libris,' *Observationes Selectae*, v (1702), 1–63; Simler, *op. cit.*, p. 38–40a.

[63] Bullinger to Beza, June 12, 1663, Calvin, xx, 41.

[64] cf. Meyer, *Locarno*, ii, 168 ff; Hottinger, *Kirchen-Gesch.*, ii, 869 ff.

[65] The regulations of the Zürich church (1559) prescribed: Non liberum est cuivis, quidquid velit, in lucem edere; sed constituti sunt librorum censores ex senatoribus et ministris, qui curent ne edantur libelli famosi, aut cum vera fide ac honestate pugnantes. cf. Trechsel, ii, 261, n. 2.

by churches and communities than by individuals. Without even grant-ing Ochino a hearing they removed him from office and banished him from their territory.[66] They also wrote to Basel, urging that further sale of the *Dialogues* be stopped, though it was too late, as the last copy had been sold. The sentence was based on two grounds: that the book had been published without legal permission, and that its teaching as to polygamy was scandalous. There was no reference to theological heresy. The Council must have had misgivings for having taken such hasty action, for they now went through the empty form of giving Ochino a hearing, in which he declared that his book had been duly passed by the censor at Basel, and defended its teachings as sound. They only confirmed their sentence; but to make their case the stronger they now directed the ministers to examine all the dialogues in search of offensive matter. It was not until now that the taint of theological heresy was discovered, for thus far the complaint had been solely on civil and moral grounds. Now they discovered errors as to justification, the atonement, baptism, and above all the Trinity. He begged that, as it was now winter, he and his four small children [67] might be allowed to stay the winter out. The Council were inexorable, and granted him a respite of only two, or at the most three, weeks.[68] Bullinger refused his request for a letter of recommendation.[69] In severe weather at the beginning of December the old pilgrim of seventy-six set forth with his young children on his fourth exile, again not knowing whither he went. Fearing he might venture the attempt to cross the Alps in winter with his children, Bullinger at once wrote to Chur to prevent his doing so.[70] But Ochino turned rather toward Basel.[71] The ministers there

[66] Bullinger to Beza, Nov. 28, 1563, Calvin, xx, 195.

[67] His wife had not long before been killed by a fall down stairs. cf. Wolf to Dudith, Sept. 7, 1570, in Dudith, *Quaestio ubi vera*, etc. (Hanoviae, 1610), p. 38; Calvin, xx, 41, and n. 9.

[68] Bullinger to Beza, Nov. 28, 1560, Calvin, xx, 195.

[69] cf. Meyer, *Locarno*, ii, 176 f.

[70] Bullinger to Fabritius, Dec. 27, 1563, Fabritius to Bullinger, Jan. 3, 1564; *Bullingers Korrespondenz*, ii, 476, 479; Meyer, *op. cit.*, ii, 179 f, nn. 208, 209; Bullinger to Beza, Jan. 6, 1564, Calvin, xx, 228 f, nn. 8, 9.

[71] The rumor that after leaving Zürich Ochino accidentally met his old acquaintance, the Cardinal of Lorraine, at an inn near Schaffhausen, complained to him of the treatment he had received, and offered to return to the Catholic Church, though it is vouched for by Beza as authentic (Beza to Dudith, June 18, 1570, in Beza, *Epistolae*, p. 11) was categori-cally denied by Ochino, and must be dismissed either as pure myth or as a gross exag-geration. cf. Bullinger to Beza, Jan. 6, 1564, Calvin, xx, 228; Rüger to Bullinger, Jan. 9,

were willing to intercede for him,[72] if he would give a written explanation of what he had written; but the Council had been beset by bitter letters of reproach from Strassburg, felt that he had disgraced their city, and would not listen to him.[73] Leaving his children here he sought Mühlhausen, only to be repulsed, but finally found shelter at Nürnberg, where he lay hidden until spring.[74]

While at Nürnberg Ochino wrote his final work, a dialogue entitled *La Prudenza Humana e Ochino*, in which he defended himself against the charges on which he had been banished from Zürich.[75] The writing begins in a lofty tone, but it later falls into bitter invective and unfair charges against the Council and the ministers, especially Bullinger. The final impression left is unfavorable. This apology was intended for circulation among the Italians in the Grisons, but a copy soon found its way into Bullinger's hands,[76] who had it translated into Latin. The ministers at Zürich at once prepared a reply, answering Ochino's charges and justifying the action taken against him.[77] The answer was temperate in manner, and placed the action of Zürich in strong light, even if it did not justify the passionate haste in which it was taken. Bullinger and Beza were more than ever convinced that justice had been done. After examining the *Dialogues*, the former wrote to Beza that the whole book was nothing but wicked perverseness; while Beza wondered that so much was made of the dialogue on polygamy, when there was scarcely a page in the book that did not swarm with foul errors.[78] But Andreas Dudith, who after having been councilor to three Emperors, and bishop of three successive sees, had gone over to the Reformation as perhaps its most distinguished convert, criticized the severity of Ochino's punishment as not at all Christian, and a serious blot on the

---

1564, *ibid.*, xx, 234 f; Fueslin, *Epistolae*, p. 463 f; Benrath, *Ochino*, pp. 277–279; Hottinger, *Kirchen-Gesch.*, iii, 875; Bainton, *Ochino*, p. 193 f.

[72] Bullinger to Fabritius, Mar. 17, 1564, *Bullingers Korrespondenz*, ii, 496.

[73] Weissenburg to Bullinger, Dec. 18, 1563, Hottinger, *op. cit.*, iii, 874; *ditto*, Nov. 25, Calvin, xx, 194; Bainton, *loc. cit.*

[74] Bullinger to Fabritius, Mar. 17, 1564, *Bullingers Korrespondenz*, ii, 496.

[75] The work was circulated only in manuscript, and was first printed in Schelhorn, *Ergötz.*, iii, 2009–2035.

[76] Fabritius to Bullinger, Mar. 20, 1564, Bullinger to Fabritius, Mar. 24, *ditto* Apr. 7; *Bullingers Korrespondenz*, ii, 497 f.

[77] *Spongia adversus aspergines Bernardini Ochini*, etc. Reprinted in Hottinger, *Hist. Eccl.*, ix, 475–510, and in Schelhorn, *Ergötz.*, iii, 2157–2194.

[78] Bullinger to Beza, Nov. 28, 1563, Beza to Bullinger, Dec. 4, Calvin, xx, 195, 205.

character of the reformed religion.[79] At the very time of Ochino's banishment the implacable Beza was pressing charges against Castellio before the Basel Council, as being a Libertine, Pelagian, defender of all vicious, heretical, adulterous, thievish men, a Papist and blasphemer, a skeptic and Anabaptist, adding to all the rest that he had translated the *Dialogues* for Ochino from the original Italian into Latin. The last charge he frankly admitted, as translating was one of his means of livelihood, though he had not passed judgment on the work.[80] Before the case was determined, at the very end of the year, death rescued Castellio from the hand of his accusers.

Early in the spring Ochino went to Frankfurt to get his children, and set out with them for Poland. At Lismanino's request [81] he had dedicated the second volume of his *Dialogues* to Prince Nicholas Radziwiłł,[82] and doubtless hoped for a friendly reception. Of course he would find friends among the liberal Italians already there. But the Catholics had been keeping track of Ochino, and while he was still at Nürnberg Cardinal Borromeo wrote from Rome to Cardinal Commendone, the papal nuncio in Poland, that Ochino was proposing to seek refuge there, and urged in the Pope's name that the King be informed and measures be taken to prevent his spreading his heresies.[83] Commendone took the matter in hand, and Cardinal Hosius addressed to the Diet a letter on the subject,[84] so that at the Diet at Parczów in August the King was induced to issue an edict banishing from the kingdom within four months all foreign Protestant refugees who were in any way venturing to spread their doctrines.[85] Ochino had mean-

---

[79] Dudith to Beza, in Beza, *Opera*, iii, 390; Beza to Dudith, June 17, 1570, in Beza, *Epistolae*, p. 10 f. Also Dudith to Wolf, 1569, in Dudith, *Quaestio ubi vera*, etc., p. 13; Wolf to Dudith, Sept. 7, 1570, *ibid.*, pp. 37–39; Beza, June 18, 1570, *ibid.*, pp. 93–95.

[80] Weissenburg to Bullinger, Nov. 25, 1563, Calvin, xx, 194. Castellio to the Basel Council, Nov. 24, 1563, *ibid.*, xx, 190 ff.

[81] Theodor Wotschke, *Geschichte der Reformation in Polen* (Leipzig, 1911), p. 211.

[82] Radziwiłł thought highly of Ochino, but had not read nor even received the copy sent him. He suspected it had been intercepted in Germany. Radziwiłł to Calvin, July 6, 1564, Calvin, xx, 336.

[83] Borromeo to Hosius, Feb. 5, 1564, quoted by Bock, Antitrinitar., ii, 507 f. cf. Trechsel, ii, 269, n. 2; Schelhorn, *Ergötz.*, iii, 2001 ff.

[84] In this he called Ochino "non bipedum solum, sed etiam quadrupedum omnium impurissimum . . . quod non tantum Christi deitatem inficietur, sed etiam ambigat, an Deus existat, ipsique curae sint homines." Quoted in Bock, *loc. cit.*

[85] Text of the edict in Raynaldus, *Annales ecclesiasticae* (Cologne, 1727), xxi, pars ii, 551 f; cf. *infra*, p. 320, n. 54.

while for some time been preaching in the capital to the Italians residing at Kraków, and a nobleman had given him a small estate at
Alexandrowice, near Kraków.[86] Several of the nobles sought permission from the King for him to stay in the country, and offered him
hospitality and protection on their estates, but in vain. To all their
entreaties he himself replied that he must and would obey the magistrate, even if he must die on the road or be devoured by wolves in the
forest.[87] Before he could leave, he was smitten by the plague, which
carried off two sons and a daughter. He was faithfully cared for by
his noble host Filipowski at Pińczów, and when recovered, toward
Christmas, he made his way with his daughter to Moravia, where he
found refuge with Nicola Paruta [88] in the Anabaptist colony at Slavkov
(Austerlitz), where after three weeks he too died. His daughter Au-
relia survived him, married Lorenzo Venturini, an Italian of Lucca,
and died a widow at Geneva in 1624.[89] His refugee church at Zürich
did not long survive his departure from it. The members petitioned
for another preacher, but enthusiasm over Italian Protestants had somewhat cooled, and their request was denied, on the ground that by now
most of them knew German well enough to join in the worship of the
other city churches.[90]

It is difficult to say with any approach to definiteness what Ochino's
doctrinal system was.[91] His heresies were slow in developing, and were
cautiously expressed. Like most of the liberal spirits of his generation
he employed conventional terminology which appeared to be orthodox,
but was susceptible of considerable latitude of meaning, unless one
carefully observed what he omitted to say. But in the *Catechism* published near the end of his life he used language to which any Socinian

[86] cf. the document of gift in *Reformacja w Polsce*, ii, (1922), 129.

[87] cf. Lubieniecius, *Historia*, p. 110.

[88] A nobleman of Lucca, and one of the Venetian Anabaptists. He came from Venice
to Geneva in 1560, and was also in Poland and Moravia. In 1558 he had assisted Biandrata
in preparing a catechism at Radnoth in Transylvania. Returning finally to Venice he was
seized and put to death in 1567. cf. Bertrand-Barraud, *Idées*, p. 31 f; Benrath, *Wiedertäufer*, p. 55; do., *Reformation*, p. 59. For some account of Ochino's last days, cf. Barotto's
testimony before the Inquisition at Venice, quoted in Bainton, *Ochino*, p. 159 f.

[89] Benrath in Hauck, *Realencyklopädie*, xiv, 260. The story related in Boverio, *Annales
Minorum Capucinorum*, that Ochino abjured his errors and became reconciled to the Roman Church, and that he was consequently put to death by Protestants at Geneva in 1557
is pure invention.

[90] cf. Meyer, *op. cit.*, ii, 182 ff.

[91] cf. Dunin Borkowski, *Quellenstudien*, pp. 118–121.

could subscribe. The early Antitrinitarians of his age laid claim to him;[92] and Giorgio Negri is said to have brought to Italy the report that Ochino had openly declared himself a Servetian and Anabaptist.[93] His two dialogues on the Trinity, though they ostensibly defend the doctrine as both true and necessary for salvation, furnish a complete arsenal of arguments against it drawn from both Scripture and reason, which were later adopted by the Socinians with little change or addition. His influence on the doctrinal development of our movement was therefore marked; and it was felt a full century later, even in England.[94] Apart from particular doctrines, however, as to which some doubt might be felt, in his general temper of mind, his readiness to conduct free inquiry into religious questions, and his tolerance of competing views, Ochino was perhaps better entitled than any other that we have mentioned, to be regarded as a pioneer of the movement whose history we are following.

[92] e.g., Biandrata in *De falsa et vera unius Dei cognitione* (Albae Juliae, 1567), p. Eii. Schomann, in Sandius, *Bibliotheca*, p. 193. Faustus Socinus frankly admits that he derived his doctrine of redemption from Ochino's *Dialogues* (Letter to Vadovita, *Opera*, i, 475).

[93] cf. Zanchi to Bullinger, Oct. 7, 1566, in Wotschke, *Briefwechsel*, p. 274.

[94] cf. Louis A. Wood, *The form and origin of Milton's antitrinitarian conception* (London, Ontario, 1911), who contends that Milton, besides other respects, derived from Ochino the semi-Arianism of his posthumous *De doctrina Christiana*. Martin A. Larson, however, in his "Milton and Servetus," *Publications of the Modern Language Association of America*, xli (1926), 891–934, dissents, and favors Servetus as the source of Milton's heretical views.

CHAPTER XVIII

A SPORADIC OUTBREAK OF ANTITRINITARIANISM AT HEIDELBERG

WE HAVE NOW FINISHED our survey of those that may fairly be reckoned as pioneers of our movement by virtue of their more or less direct relation to its later stages; but there remains an isolated and sporadic case of superficially similar character which deserves record. The pioneers we have thus far considered were all Latins, and their field of activity was Italy or Switzerland. The group now to be mentioned were all Germans, and their theater of action was at Heidelberg. The Palatinate had accepted the Reformation under the form prevalent in Switzerland; and about 1570 Olevian, leader of the church at Heidelberg, was strenuously urging the adoption of a strict discipline like that of Calvin at Geneva. This step was violently opposed by several persons of influence, among them Adam Neuser, first preacher at St. Peter's church, a man of marked ability, eloquent and popular, but of unstable temperament.[1] He at length became so quarrelsome that the Elector was forced to remove him from his conspicuous office and assign him to nominal service at an obscure post. Deeply humiliated and embittered, he now became alienated from the prevailing religion, and began to nourish doubts of its doctrines. He declared that this change in him was not caused by anything that he had read outside the Bible,[2] though it would be strange if he had not already learned something of the views of Antitrinitarians from Poland who were at the University.[3]

---

[1] The main authorities for this episode are *Monumenta pietatis et literarum variorum*, etc. (Frankfurt, 1701); Heinrich Alting, *Historia de ecclesiis Palatinis* (Groningen, 1728); Stephan Gerlach, *Tage-buch*, etc. (Frankfurt, 1674); G. E. Lessing, 'Von Adam Neusern,' in his *Beyträge zur Geschichte und Literatur*: Sämmtliche Schriften (Leipzig, 1897), xii, 205–254; Daniel L. Wundt, 'Versuch einer Geschichte des Arianismus . . . im Kurfürstentum Pfalz,' *Magazin für die Kirchen- und Gelahrten-geschichte des Kurfürstentums Pfalz*, i (1789), 88–154. cf. also (M. V. de La Croze), *Dissertations historiques sur différents sujets* (Rotterdam, 1707), i, 102–125.

[2] *Monumenta pietatis*, p. 339.

[3] Stanislas Farnowski, soon to become leader of an Arian party in Poland, was at

Neuser won to his views three other preachers of the vicinity, who were discontented with recent tendencies in the church: Johannes Sylvan [4] of Ladenburg, Jakob Suter of Weinheim, and Matthias Vehe of Lautern. He told them of the new Unitarian Church in Transylvania under the patronage of the Prince, where they might hope to exercize their ministry under congenial conditions and with ample support from the State. A considerable number of laymen also shared their views. Both Sylvan and Neuser wrote essays sharply attacking the Trinity, and Neuser also drafted a letter to the Sultan, with whose religious views he expressed warm sympathy; and he assured him of wide support in Germany if he should push his conquests so far. His new theological views appear to have been crude and superficial, while his political scheme was too fantastic to deserve serious attention.

The Emperor Maximilian II. was about to hold a Diet at Speyer in June, 1570. Gáspár Békés (of whom we shall hear in connection with our history in Transylvania) was in attendance, as envoy from the Unitarian Prince of Transylvania; and Neuser, Sylvan and Vehe went to seek an interview with him there. Sylvan handed him a letter for Biandrata, who was now directing the Unitarian movement in Transylvania; and Neuser one for the Sultan, though he added later instructions not to forward it. They offered their services to the new church.[5] In order to gain a point in his mission to the Emperor,[6] Békés unfortunately gave him these letters to read. He reported their contents to the Elector, who was greatly disturbed, and at once gave orders that the four preachers be arrested, and their books and papers seized;

Heidelberg shortly before this time, and had to leave the University on account of his heretical views. There were also at Heidelberg several Italians who were later to be associated with the movement. cf. Wundt, *op. cit.*, pp. 116–119; Hans Rott, *Neue Quellen für die Geschichte der Stadt Heidelberg*, etc. (Heidelberg, 1910–'11), viii, 184–259; ix, 1–70.

[4] A letter from the Polish Calvinist Lasicki to Wolph of Zürich, dated Heidelberg, May 10, 1570, makes it very probable that both Neuser and Sylvan were influenced by the Transylvanian Unitarian Biandrata's purely Servetian *De regno Anti-Christi*, 1569, which had just reached Heidelberg. cf. Wotschke, *Briefwechsel*, p. 327; Bullinger to Egli, Sept. 1, 1570, *Bullingers Korrespondenz*, iii, 21. On Sylvan, cf. Schelhorn, *Ergötz.*, i (1761), 571–606, 'Anmerkung von Johann Sylvano.'

[5] For these letters, cf. *Monumenta pietatis*, pp. 318–344.

[6] An important part of Békés's mission was if possible to contract a marriage for his Prince with some German princess. The Emperor objected to such a union on the ground that the Prince was not an orthodox Christian. Békés would try to dull the point of this objection by pointing out similar heresies among the German clergy.

though Neuser, having been forewarned, made his escape and set out for Transylvania. The case of the other three was referred to the theologians, who in turn sought counsel in other countries. They judged Neuser and Sylvan guilty of holding and spreading heresies, and of conspiring with the Sultan against the Emperor, and hence worthy of death. The secular councilors were mostly opposed to capital punishment, and delayed action so long that the Elector, growing impatient, and encouraged by the Elector Augustus of Saxony whom he had consulted, took the matter into his own hands, and passed sentence in April, 1572. As Suter and Vehe had evidently been led astray by the other two, they were simply removed from office and banished from the country. Sylvan had now lain in prison at Mannheim well toward two years, and had meantime repented and retracted his errors; but he was nevertheless sentenced to death. The Elector was apparently still reluctant to put to death one that had been his tutor, and it was not until late in December that Sylvan was beheaded in the market-place at Heidelberg. The Elector then salved his conscience by pensioning the wife and son, who had shared his imprisonment.

Of Suter's later fortunes nothing is known. Vehe, after being released from imprisonment at Speyer, went to East Friesland, and at length, after Latinizing his name as Glirius,[7] made his way to Transylvania, where he became Rector of the Unitarian college at Kolozsvár.[8] The fortunes of Neuser were more dramatic. After evading arrest with the others he wandered for some weeks, meaning to join the Unitarians in Transylvania, but in Hungary he found his further progress barred. He therefore returned to the Palatinate and gave himself up, counting upon indulgence.[9] Instead, he was at once lodged in prison, whence after six weeks he found means to escape.[10] He now fled to Poland, in the spring of 1571, and soon appeared at Śmigiel (Schmiegel), where there was an 'Arian' church. Here and at the neighboring town of Kościan (Kosten) a few miles south-west of Poznań (Posen) his eloquence won him a large following; but when in the spring of 1572 the Parczów edict of 1564 against foreign heretics was invoked against him, he fled in haste, going first to Kraków, and

---

[7] This is the brilliant and very plausible conjecture adopted by Lessing, *op. cit.*, p. 247, which seems, however, to have been derived from Zeltner, *Crypto-Socin.*, p. 353, n. b.

[8] Wundt, *op. cit.*, p. 147.

[9] cf. Lessing, *op. cit.*, p. 214.

[10] *Monumenta pietatis*, p. 209; cf. also Lubieniecius, *Historia*, pp. 198–200.

soon afterwards to Koloszvár in Transylvania,[11] where again he would have been acceptable as a preacher, but that he did not agree with the preachers in some points of doctrine,[12] and that rumors also came that the Elector had taken measures to have him seized and taken back to Heidelberg. He was therefore advised to go to Hungary for safety. There he was detained as a suspicious character; but upon declaring his religious views he was sent to the Sultan at Constantinople, where he formally embraced the Mohammedan faith. Here, if there be any truth at the heart of the legend that rapidly grew up about his last years, he fell into the irregular habits that so easily beset one torn away from family, friends and all wholesome traditions, whose hopes in life have all been frustrated. After some four years he died a wretched death in 1576. The Unitarians in Transylvania are said to have bought his writings for a handsome sum.[13] Gerlach, who had conversation with him, reports that Neuser made this statement to him in writing: 'no one known to me in our time has become an Arian who was not first a Calvinist; ... therefore if any one fears he may fall into Arianism, he should avoid Calvinism.' When this report spread, the Lutherans exulted; and Osiander said in triumph that Calvin had been Neuser's first step on the way to hell. To clear the Calvinistic churches of this charge, the Elector had his theologians publish in 1574 their famous confession as to the Trinity and the person of Christ.[14]

Although the episode of Neuser and his companions lies outside the direct stream of the movement we are following, yet it is an added instance of a tendency to burst through the barriers of conventional orthodoxy in an effort to achieve a more complete spiritual freedom and a broader tolerance. First and last there were many other such

[11] cf. Theodor Wotschke, 'Die Reformation in Kosten' *Correspondenzblatt des Vereins für Geschichte der evangelischen Kirche Schlesiens* (Liegnitz, 1905), ix, 174 f.

[12] cf. Lessing, *op. cit.*, p. 207 f. He claimed to have originated the doctrine that Christ is not to be worshiped, and to have persuaded Francis Dávid of it, who was then at the head of the Unitarian Church in Transylvania; *id. op.*, p. 245; letter of Samuel Crellius to La Croze in *Thesaurus Epistolicus Lacrozianus* (Lipsiae, 1742), i, 111.

[13] cf. Gerlach, *op. cit.*, p. 254. Gerlach was a Tübingen theologian who was envoy with the Imperial Ambassador at Constantinople at the time of Neuser's death and for some time before. He relates in his diary that Neuser planned a self-propelled vehicle that would run at high speed, and that the small model was successful, and though the larger one needed perfecting he had great hopes of it. *id. op.*, p. 285.

[14] cf. *Monumenta pietatis*, p. 211; Conrad Schlüsselburg, *Haereticorum Catalogus* (Frankfurt, 1597), i, 4; Ludwig Häusser, *Geschichte der Rheinischen Pfalz*, ed. 2 (Heidelberg, 1856), ii, 50.

attempts, which were too obscure in themselves or were too soon checked to leave more than a ripple on the stream of history.[15]

We have thus far been engaged with a period of our movement in which it embraced only individuals acting separately, or at most a few small and unrelated groups. Save for the single council in 1550, we have recorded no attempt at concerted action. The reason for this fact has been obvious. Any considerable variation from the received standard in religious belief and practice was by Catholics and Protestants alike regarded with grave suspicion, and doubt or denial of any of the fundamental doctrines of the creeds was supposed to endanger the eternal welfare of immortal souls. The spreading of such heresies was, in theory, deemed to be as much worse than murder as the soul is of more value than the body; and there were all too many in religious or civil authority that accepted this view literally and were willing to follow it out to its logical practical consequences. In such circumstances, only brave and daring spirits would venture to risk all manner of punishment, even unto death, in vindication of freedom of belief and conscience; and those that valued their lives or their freedom were driven to ways of secrecy, and to equivocations in language, for practicing which there is little excuse or justification to-day, but for which they in their time have been unfairly reproached, seeing what alternative lay before them.

These hardy pioneers were, with one or two exceptions, Italians, sons of the enlightened Humanism of the Renaissance. They were a small company in all, strong by the acuteness, boldness and independence of their thinking, their refined culture, their individual prestige; but they did not appeal to the popular ear, nor, save in the case of Ochino, did they succeed in attracting the masses. They were, it has been well said, generals without an army. There was no acknowledged leader of their thought, still less of their action. Servetus, Gribaldi and Ochino were strong and independent thinkers, but they left no well wrought system

---

[15] It will be enough merely to mention one or two other such isolated cases. First, that of an abortive antitrinitarian movement in Moravia; cf. Norbert F. Čapek, *Úryvky z dějin kacéřovaných křestanu* (Sketches from the history of Christian heretics) (Brno, 1901). Second, Lukas Sternberger's antitrinitarian heresy at Olomouc (Olmutz), Moravia in 1561; cf. Fridericus Staphylus, *Apologie* (Antwerp, 1565), p. 17 f, 112 f; Gilbertus Genebrardus, *Chronographia* (Paris, 1585), p. 740; Laurentius Surius, *Commentarius* (Coloniae, 1602), p. 569; Sandius, *Nucleus*, p. 429; Schelhorn, *Amoenitates*, xi, 7; Stanislaus Rescius, *De atheismis et phalarismis Evangelicorum* (Neapoli, 1596), pp. 111, 401.

of doctrine; and though each of them influenced a few followers, none of them left a school to develop and carry on his teaching. Before their embryonic efforts could develop into a mature and permanent movement in religious history, two conditions were required that had hitherto been lacking. There must be tolerant laws, which would guarantee full freedom of thought and conscience, and reasonable liberty in speech and teaching; and there must be competent intellectual leadership by some one that could state their religious thought in a consistent and well-rounded system of doctrine, strong for both defence and attack, which could enter the lists in competition with the systems of Melanchthon and Calvin. These two conditions were to be met at about the same time in Poland under Faustus Socinus, and in Transylvania under Francis Dávid. The further development of the movement under these conditions and in these two lands will occupy the two following divisions of this history.

A point has now been reached where it is appropriate to estimate the progress thus far achieved. In the introductory chapter the movement whose development we are following was defined as fundamentally characterized by its steadily increasing adherence to three leading principles in religion: entire freedom from bondage to traditional creeds or confessions, confident reliance upon reason as the ultimate seat of authority, and an attitude of generous tolerance of differing views. How far did the pioneers of whom we have spoken conform to these three principles? To the first they were conspicuously true. Indeed, their most striking superficial characteristic was their refusal to acknowledge the authority of existing creeds and their denial of some of their leading doctrines. This constituted the formal offence that brought prosecution and punishment upon them. If when hard pressed they sometimes conformed so far as to seem to accept the phraseology of the creeds, they still asserted their independence of mind by placing on them interpretations that were by no means the accepted ones.

To the second principle they showed a more wavering adherence. They still accepted Scripture and its teachings as the word of God, and hence of supreme authority; but they interpreted it in accordance with reason, even at the cost of constructions that at times seem strangely forced. The question whether the Scriptures when fairly interpreted could ever conflict with reason had hardly arisen, and would certainly have received a negative answer. If doctrines of the creeds were rejected, it was on the ground that they were not scriptural, or not reasonable, or both. It remained for a later period squarely to accept reason, in any case of conflict, as of higher authority than even Scripture.

It was the principle of tolerance that was slowest in developing. Both the orthodox and the heretical considered right beliefs as a matter of highest importance. Neither could look with indifference on what they regarded as errors in doctrine. Both Servetus and Gentile seem to have regarded the death penalty as allowable for punishing those whose doctrines are demonstrably false. It was long before it was generally accepted that false doctrine is best overcome not by force but by calm reasoning; and it was not until men had ceased seriously to believe that the salvation of their souls really depended upon their acceptance of certain doctrinal statements, that they could with clear conscience feel tolerant of beliefs in others that they considered to be untrue. The body of this history will have its main significance from tracing the steps by which, under the principle of perfect spiritual freedom, men have come more clearly to appreciate the value of the guiding light of reason in the search for religious truth, and more generously to practice that tolerance of spirit which allows that as each man is by nature fallible, so each must struggle for truth in his own way and by his own lights and learn by his own mistakes, no less than by the help of others in his search.

CHAPTER XIX

POLAND: THE EARLY REFORMATION

IF WE MAY now pause for a moment at the threshold of a new division of the history whose course we are following, and make a brief survey of the ground thus far traversed, and if we inquire what progress has been achieved from a condition in which freedom of thought and of teaching in religion was narrowly limited by ossified traditions from the past, the use of reason in religion was avoided and opposed as tending to undermine religious faith, and mutual tolerance of different views or practices in religion was dreaded as opening the door to infinite error, toward a condition in which men should enjoy entire freedom of thought and teaching in religion, should be at liberty to make full use of reason as perhaps the best available criterion of religious truth, and should exercize generous tolerance of differences as the best guarantee of progress in religion, it must be confessed that little solid ground has thus far been won. For we have been concerned not with a coherent and organized movement, but only with individuals more or less independent of one another, and widely separated in time and space. Each of these, as a pioneer explorer of new fields, of course made his own contribution to the movement, and had his own limited sphere of influence, as he questioned or criticized accepted modes of thought and traditions of practice, in the effort to arrive at a purer, truer and more acceptable system of the Christian religion; but each had to face almost alone the resistance of the consolidated forces of a hostile world, Catholic or Protestant, already firmly committed to a system assumed and sincerely believed to be divinely ordained, infinitely important, and scarcely susceptible of improvement or of any change save for the worse.

Of the daring spirits that, in the first generation of the Protestant reformation, ventured thus to transgress the established limits of Christian thought and usage, some, like Servetus, Gentile and Sylvan, forfeited their lives rather than be untrue to their honest convictions by denying what they felt to be the truth; others, like Campanus and

Neuser, had trial of bonds and imprisonment; yet others, like Kautz and Ochino, being banished were forced to go out, not knowing whither they went; some, like Denck, Gribaldi and Castellio, were chased from pillar to post or hounded to their death; some, like Biandrata and Alciati, anticipating the trouble that was sure to overtake them, fled from it before the storm could burst; while others, like Cellarius, Laelius Socinus and Curioni, taking better counsel of worldly prudence, cautiously either concealed their thoughts or veiled them under language vague and equivocal, thus managing to save intact their liberty of person at the expense of freedom of speech and influence. It is thus easy to see that there was little better hope in Protestant lands than in Catholic for the development of a more liberal type of religion. Switzerland, Germany and France were effectively closed to it; and the cry of heretic raised against any innovator was in itself enough to make his cause be by most prejudged and condemned unheard. The liberal movement in Protestantism, whose course we have set out to explore, would have been smothered in its infancy had there not happened to be two lands remote from the western centres of the Reformation, in which comparatively tolerant governments for a time allowed it something like an even chance to survive and spread alongside the more conservative following of Luther, Calvin and Hus. These two lands were Poland and Transylvania. The movement in each of these rose in the same generation, and for its first century the two ran parallel in their development and mutual interests. That in Transylvania has had an unbroken though somewhat isolated history down to the present day, while that in Poland was persecuted out of existence at the end of a century; but the latter has had so significant an influence on the course of religious thought and life in Europe and America that it claims our first attention. We are therefore about to follow the rise, spread, decline and tragic end in Poland of the religious movement that eventually came to be best known as Socinianism.

Poland in the sixteenth century, when our history first becomes concerned with it, was one of the principal States of Europe, ranking next after France, the German Empire, and England. A third larger than France, and a little larger than the American State of Texas, it then stood at its greatest geographical extent and at the summit of its power and prosperity. Its population of some twenty millions was predominantly of that great Slavic stock which pressing from the East has for centuries disputed the possession of eastern central Europe with the peoples farther west. Directly or indirectly they were mostly devoted to agriculture; for the native gentry deemed it undignified to engage in crafts or trade, though in the larger towns there was a strong infiltration of German, Dutch or Scotch origin, engaged as artisans or merchants.

The dominant class were the nobility (*szlachta*), a body of country gentry, hereditary land-owners, numbering all together about a million,[1] and usually living on their landed estates, though the more wealthy often also had town houses in the provincial capitals. While theoretically they all held land, lived on their own estates, and were equal in rank and privileges, yet actually half of them had become impoverished, and either worked their own little farms like peasants, or quite landless stood in the service of the wealthy, and forfeited some of the privileges of their order.[2] A few possessed vast domains of which they were autocratic lords, and were known as magnates. The nobles were exempt from taxation, though in time of national danger they were bound to give military service, in token of which they usually wore spurs and went girt with a sword; and only they might hold public office or sit in the local diets. Their houses were inviolable, a circumstance which at this period of our history was of importance, for on the estate of a sympathetic noble a heretic might remain safe from arrest. They were inclined to be turbulent individualists, extremely jealous of their traditional privileges, and more studious to retain or extend these in the face of encroachments by the Crown or the Bishops than to subordinate them to the interests of State or Church. The Polish nobility in the sixteenth century were perhaps the best educated and most highly cultivated of any similar class in Europe. At the first congress of Vienna in 1515 the Emperor Maximilian was astonished to find in his rival, King Sigismund I. of Poland, a humanist as distinguished as himself, and in his entourage a company of highly cultivated gentlemen; and when envoys of Poland in 1573 went to Paris to offer their crown to Henry of Valois, they are said to have excited general admiration for their learning and accomplishments and for the elegance of their manners.[3]

[1] cf. Siegfried Hüppe, *Verfassung der Republik Polen* (Berlin, 1867), p. 79.

[2] *op. cit.*, p. 74.

[3] J. A. Thuanus, *Historiae sui temporis* (Genevae, 1626–'30), lib., lvi, cited by Valerian Krasinski, *Historical Sketch of the Reformation in Poland* (London, 1840), ii, 29.

By the middle of the sixteenth century the culture of the nobility was becoming Latin rather than Slavic or Teutonic. A strong current of Italian influence was experienced after the marriage (1519) of King Sigismund I. with Bona, daughter of Giovanni Galeazzo Sforza, Duke of Milan, noted for her beauty and accomplishments. A crowd of Italian courtiers, scholars and artists followed in her train, and the capital at Kraków (Cracow) was adorned with noble specimens of architecture in the style of the Italian Renaissance.

At the other end of the social scale from the nobles were the peasants, who had no privileges, were bound to the soil on which they lived, and might not leave it without permission of the lord of the estate, who even held over them the power of life and death. Bound to do forced labor several days each week, they might not own land themselves, and were virtually slaves.[4]

The country in its greatest extent consisted of the old Kingdom of Poland (made up of the two major geographical divisions of Great Poland in the west and Little Poland in the southeast) and the Grand Duchy of Lithuania in the northeast. These two, after a series of approaches (following 1386, when Jagiełło, Grand Duke of Lithuania, married a Polish princess and became King of Poland), were finally united as a common republic under one crown and with one Diet by the Union of Lublin in 1569. These three larger divisions were divided for administrative purposes into more than thirty subdivisions known as palatinates (*województwa*), each administered by a hereditary chief called Palatine (*wojewoda*, or vaivode), and the palatinates again into over eighty castellanies administered by Castellans. The traditional form of society in Poland was feudal, but the government was a limited constitutional monarchy of mixed character.[5] In theory a democracy of land-holders, it was actually an aristocracy of the higher nobility. The State was administered as a federation of palatinates with a King at the head of all; and since after 1572 the King was elected, the later Poles often liked to call their nation a republic.

Next to the King in the administration came the Senate. This was not, as the name might seem to suggest, the upper house of the national

---

[4] For their miserable condition, cf. A. Berga, *Un prédicateur de la Cour de Pologne* . . . *Pierre Skarga* (Paris, 1916), pp. 36–41.

[5] cf. Gottfried Lengnich, *Jus publicum Regni Poloniae* (Gedani, 1742–'46); Hüppe, *op. cit.*

legislature, but rather a sort of large Privy Council which the King consulted, and whose approval he required, on all important matters. As constituted by the Union of Lublin it was composed of 139 members (later enlarged), appointed by the King for life. Besides ten of the highest ministers of state, it consisted of fifteen Archbishops and Bishops, 32 Palatines and 82 Castellans. The Archbishop of Gniezno (Gnesen) presided, and in all proceedings the Bishops took precedence of the lay Senators. Though it could not veto or annul the acts of the Diet, from which it sat separate, the Senate freely used its advisory power, and it had great influence in the affairs of the realm. As the higher clergy in it were always Catholic, the Senate could be relied upon to give the cause of the Church weighty support even when, as in 1572, there were only two Catholics among the lay Senators.

By far the most important and influential branch of the national government, and its effective legislative arm, was the Diet (*sejm*). This was a representative body roughly corresponding to the Chamber of Deputies in western parliamentary governments. It ordinarily numbered 200, with a prescribed representation from each Palatinate; and the members were chosen by the provincial diets (*sejmiki*) from the great body of the lesser nobility, those of the 'equestrian order' as distinguished from the nobles of senatorial rank. The Diet met when summoned by the King, most often in the autumn or the winter of each year, and its sessions normally lasted six weeks. Before the Union of Lublin sessions were held at various places, oftenest at Piotrków, but afterwards generally at the new capital, Warsaw. At the end of the session the Senators and Deputies met jointly for final consultation; and when the body of laws passed had been collectively agreed to, they were subscribed by all the members and the King, and were then known as the Constitution. Such was the country and such were its institutions as far as they need be known in order to furnish the background required for a clear understanding of the history we are next to follow.[6]

Although missionaries had already preached the Christian religion in Poland for nearly a century, Poland itself first formally accepted Christianity upon the conversion of King Mieszko (Mieczysław) I. in

[6] For general works on the Reformation in Poland, cf. Krasinski, *Reformation*, ii; G. W. Th. Fischer, *Versuch einer Geschichte der Reformation in Polen* (Grätz, 1855–'56); Wincenty Zakrzewski, *Powstanie i wzrost reformacyi w Polsce* (Rise and growth of the Reformation in Poland) (Leipzig, 1870); Theodor Wotschke, *Geschichte der Reformation in Polen* (Leipzig, 1911); Karl Völker, *Kirchengeschichte Polens* (Berlin, 1930).

965, while Lithuania did so upon its union with Poland in 1386. The inhabitants of the land, however, long clung to remnants of their old pagan religion, and it was longer yet before the authority of the Roman Church was fully accepted. Contests between the clergy and the secular power, between the Pope and the Crown, were frequent, as the King insisted on his right to name his own Bishops. Worship in the Polish tongue instead of the Church's Latin was common to the end of the fifteenth century, and marriage of priests was practiced in Poland long after it had been successfully forbidden elsewhere. With old heresy laws [7] slumbering on the statute books, the heretical doctrines of the Waldenses became current from the twelfth century on, while the teachings of Jan Hus were wide-spread in the fifteenth and the first half of the sixteenth century. An Inquisition had been established in the fourteenth century to stamp out heresy, yet only one conspicuous *auto da fe* took place, when five Hussite preachers were publicly burned in 1439; and though severe repressive laws against heresy were passed by church synods and by the national Diet, they remained for the most part dead letters. By the middle of the fifteenth century serious opposition to the increasing claims and aggressions of the Church had arisen among the nobles; and at the Diet of 1459 Jan Ostroróg, a noble of great learning and high rank, presented a remarkable series of proposals asserting the sovereignty of the State as not subject to Rome, and protesting against the abuses and exactions of the Church, and the gross corruptions of the clergy.

Thus even before Luther the stage was well set for reforming the Church whenever a favorable juncture should present itself. The very temper and native character of the people were calculated to foster such a movement; for the spirit of the Polish noble was restless and adventurous, alert to catch at new ideas and curious to try new experiments. By inherited tradition he was a pronounced individualist, jealous of his liberties and watchful against encroachments on his rights. Even in religion he did not take kindly to acknowledging the supremacy of a foreign authority; and for him to be summoned for trial and sentence before a church court deriving its powers from a foreign source in Rome seemed to him a gross violation of his traditional freedom. Under these conditions the Catholic Church had by the end of the fifteenth century largely lost its real hold in Poland. Indeed, doubtless from

[7] cf. *Volumina Legum* (Petersburg, 1859–'60), i, 38, 63.

geographical reasons, the Catholic clergy had never succeeded in gaining such power and independence there as in the western countries of
Europe.

In the revolt from the Church a variety of distinct factors co-operated.
One of the most conspicuous of these was its alarming growth in wealth
and secular power, for this inevitably resulted in a growing conflict between the Bishops and the nobility. The Church in Poland had grown
enormously wealthy by gifts from the Crown and from pious individuals. After the King's estates, the largest ones were those of the Bishops
and the monasteries. It has been estimated that in the sixteenth century
one third of the entire landed property of the country was in the hands
of the Church.[8] Besides all this, church estates were exempt from public
burdens, while on the other hand the clergy were entitled to one tenth
of the nobles' income from their estates, and to one tenth also from the
peasantry. In the sixteenth century they are estimated to have absorbed
half of the total national income.[9] In this way the Bishops had not only
greatly encroached on the power and privileges of the nobles, but had
themselves become almost completely secularized, and generally indifferent to the spiritual welfare of the Church. The remark attributed
to Bishop Zebrzydowski of Kraków, 'Believe even in a goat if you like,
provided you only pay me my tithes,'[10] was regarded as typical.

Along with this extreme worldliness and luxury, the moral life of
many of both the higher and the lower clergy was notoriously corrupt,
uncorrected and unrebuked by those in authority; and from the coming
of Queen Bona, and with her encouragement, simony was freely employed in securing ecclesiastical preferments. Such a condition in the
Church religiously and morally, added to the conflicts economic and
social that were steadily growing more aggravated, provided fertile soil
for the seeds of the Protestant Reformation, by which the Bohemian
and German population dwelling in the west of Poland were already
influenced. With the University at Kraków at a low ebb in the early
sixteenth century, the young nobles that could afford it went abroad
for their higher studies, and in the Protestant universities at Wittenberg,
Marburg, Heidelberg, Strassburg, Basel and Zürich became acquainted

[8] Ludwik Kubala, *Stanisław Orzechowski* (Warszawa, 1906), p. 20; cited by Paul Fox,
Reformation in Poland (Baltimore, 1924), p. 95.

[9] Kubala, *op. cit.*, p. 21.

[10] Aleksander Brückner, *Różnowiercy Polscy* (The Polish Dissidents) Warszawa, 1905,
p. 143.

with the new religious doctrines of the Protestants; while those that resorted to such Italian centres of learning as Padua became saturated with the emancipating spirit of Italian Humanism. Returning home they helped bring to the surface the latent wide-spread desire for a new religion, insisting less on dogma and ceremonial and more on the fundamentals of Christian life and character, more clearly founded on Scripture, independent of Rome and its Bishops with their worldliness and luxury — in short, a Polish national church, worshiping in the national language, granting communion in both kinds, inclusive of both Roman and Greek Catholics, and with the King at its head.

The desire for a national Synod or council of the Church, which should in earnest take up the work of reform, was strong and wide-spread; but the King hesitated to take so decisive a step, which might cause serious division among his people, while Rome, fearing lest such a movement might end in alienating Poland from the Church, as had lately happened in England, strove to delay action by vague promises of a general reforming council of the whole Church in all Europe. The result was that before anything effective could be accomplished for reform from within, the Protestant Reformation entered Poland from without. The new faith was introduced in the several parts of Poland in several different forms: the Evangelical Church (followers of Luther), the Bohemian Brethren (followers of Jan Hus), and the Reformed Church (followers of Calvin). The earliest Protestant movements were in Polish Prussia which, with a population strongly German, became overwhelmingly Lutheran. For a time Lutheranism spread rapidly also in Lithuania, though in the next generation it became instead thoroughly Calvinistic, under the influence of Prince Nicholas Radziwiłł, who while studying abroad had accepted Protestant views, and was followed by the great majority of the gentry. It also won many followers in Great Poland, where Calvinists on the other hand were few. The Bohemian Brethren had their greatest strength in Great Poland. Besides its conquest of Lithuania, as just mentioned, Calvinism so fully won Żmudź (Samogitia) that only seven priests were left in the principality;[11] but the Reformed Church flourished most of all in Little Poland, where there were but few Lutherans, and where its democratic organization, granting a large voice to the laity, appealed most to the nobles.

[11] Stanisław Załęski, *Jesuici w Polsce* (The Jesuits in Poland), Lwów, 1900–'06, i, 183.

With the steady growth of abuses in the Church on the one hand, and on the other the steady stream of students returning from abroad, the wide circulation of the writings of Luther and other Protestants, and a divided and feeble resistance on the part of the Church, the Reformation had quietly spread so far that by the middle of the sixteenth century the nobles of Poland found themselves very largely Protestant. To satisfy the authorities of the Church who saw their cause now in danger, King Sigismund I. indeed half-heartedly forbade the nobles to send their sons to Germany to study, and prohibited the importation of heretical books, though neither order was much regarded. But when in 1526 Luther's celebrated adversary, Johann Eck, in dedicating to the King a work against Luther, urged him to imitate Henry VIII. of England in opposing the reformer, the easy-going King replied that Henry might do so, but as for him he begged leave to be king of both sheep and goats.[12]

The Protestants had as yet no public houses of worship, but like the early Christians worshiped in private houses, generally in the spacious halls of nobles, where they were secure from molestation. One of the most important of such early Protestant congregations was at Kraków, where large numbers inclined to the doctrines of the Reformation. A place for their worship here was provided for them first in the manor-house at the village of Wola Justowska, about five miles west of town, and later by Jan Bonar, Governor of the castle, in the garden of his home just outside the city wall. Well before this priests here and there, when assured of the protection of noble patrons, abandoned the old ceremonies, preached the new doctrines, married and openly attacked the Church, counting on the indulgence of sympathetic or at least indifferent Bishops, or even setting their discipline at defiance. But the boldest attack on the Roman Church hitherto was when Nicholas Oleśnicki, owner of the town of Pińczów,[13] an important centre some forty miles north-east of Kraków, encouraged thereto by Stancaro,[14] drove the monks from their monastery on his domain (1550),

---

[12] Scribat rex Henricus contra Martinum. Permittas mihi fieri ovium et hircorum regem. Cited by Krasinski, *Reformation in Poland*, i, 134.

[13] In 1552 Oleśnicki established here in the old monastery the first Protestant school in Poland, which ere long became distinguished for its excellence. As the progressive wing of the Reformed Church predominated here for a time, its adherents were often designated as Pinczovians. After Oleśnicki's death in 1585 the town was bought by the Bishop of Kraków who restored the Catholic worship, and Protestantism here then became extinct.

[14] Francesco Stancaro, whose acquaintance we have already made in the Grisons (p.

removed the images from the church and set up reformed worship there.

Within a few weeks after Oleśnicki's daring act the King issued an edict against the reformers, and the Bishop of Kraków cited Oleśnicki to appear before the Senate and answer for violating the old heresy law of 1424; but he was so stoutly defended by high officials that nothing of importance resulted except Stancaro's temporary banishment. For a year or two now the Bishops exerted themselves to stamp out heresy by force, and for a time the ministers went into hiding for fear,[15] but the nobles were only roused to more determined resistance.

Coincident with the steadily spreading revolt of priests and nobles on religious grounds, a closely related political struggle was daily gathering force as the nobles sought to secure themselves from criminal prosecution at the hands of the Bishops. For besides the usual courts of the State, the Bishops also had courts of their own. These had originally existed to handle cases of church discipline, but they had with time gradually extended their scope so as to cover various secular matters as well. They exercized what was called 'ecclesiastical jurisdiction,' and it fell to the starosts or civil authorities to execute the punishments that the Bishops' courts decreed. These were often so arbitrary and severe as to arouse intense indignation among the nobles, who felt their rights unjustly invaded. After the death of King Sigismund I. in 1548, the new King Sigismund Augustus, whom the reformers had fondly been hoping to win to their side, began instead to favor their opponents. Thus encouraged, the church synod at Piotrków in 1552 resolved to extirpate heresy by severe persecution. At least one priest was put to

---

103, n. 20), having failed to find employment for his talents there, went at length to Transylvania, whence in 1549 he came to Kraków, bearing strong recommendations from the King's sister, Queen Isabella of Hungary. Bishop Maciejowski having therefore no suspicion of his heretical tendencies, appointed him Professor of Hebrew at the University, which he was then trying to strengthen as a weapon against the Reformation. Heresies in his teachings were soon complained of, whereupon the Bishop removed him from his chair and imprisoned him in the episcopal castle at Lipowiec, some twenty-five miles west of Kraków. He had evidently already made friends among the reforming nobles, for they now espoused his cause and made him their hero. After eight months they managed to bribe the guards and procure his escape. He soon found safe refuge at Pińczów, and assumed leadership of the reform movement going on there, but before the end of the year he was banished by royal edict. Returning later to Poland he became, as we shall see, the storm-centre of a fierce controversy in the Reformed Church, unintentionally paving the way for the antitrinitarian movement to follow. cf. Theodor Wotschke, 'Francesco Stancaro,' *Altpreussische Monatsschrift*, xlvii (1910), 465–498, 570–613.

[15] Dalton, *Lasciana*, p. 398.

death, and other vigorous measures were undertaken; but the nobles united in determined opposition, and public resentment was so strong that the Bishops' efforts proved largely futile. For as Catholic and Protestant nobles alike were rising in revolt, civil magistrates were little inclined to execute the decrees of the church courts. In the Diet of that same year, the Protestant interest had an overwhelming majority; and while they still left to the Bishops the right to pronounce upon heresy, they succeeded in getting ecclesiastical jurisdiction suspended for a year, so that the decrees of the spiritual courts could no longer be put into effect.

From this time on, the growth of the reformed congregations went on apace. Though the Bishops renewed their efforts at repression it was to little purpose. In 1553 various Lithuanian magnates accepted the Reformation, following Nicholas (the Black) Radziwiłł, Palatine of Wilno, the most powerful and wealthy man in the Grand Duchy, who had imbibed the reformed doctrines while traveling abroad, and now opened many churches in his territory to reformed worship.[16] The temporary arrangement of 1552 was followed at the Diet of 1555 by an Interim which was to remain in force until a national council should be called. By this, religious freedom was insured to commoners and peasants as well as to nobles, ecclesiastical jurisdiction was virtually abolished, and it was among other things provided that each noble might have a clergyman of his own choice, and choose his own form of worship. The Bishops in the Senate would indeed not consent to this arrangement, but the decision of the Diet stood fast and became effective, so that Poland was henceforth for a good while a land of wide

[16] It must be kept in mind that in Poland at this time the churches on a nobleman's estate, or on the broad domains of a magnate, depended upon the will of the lord. If he changed his religion, he might require the congregations subject to him to change theirs, and might turn out priests and install reformed ministers, or *vice versa*. Thus one or other of the confessions might at a single stroke either gain or lose a considerable number of churches.

Nicholas (the Black) Radziwiłł, so called in distinction from his cousin Nicholas (the Red) whose sister Barbara was second wife of King Sigismund Augustus, was quite the most powerful and important lay adherent of the Polish Reformation in its first period. He was Calvinist rather than Lutheran, and his sympathies were evidently with the liberal wing which in the very year of his death was separated from the orthodox majority. He gave the hospitality of his court at Wilno to several of those most influential in leading the liberal tendencies. He was a generous patron of the Reformation, and at the personal cost of 10,000 gulden bore the expense of publishing the first Protestant Bible in Polish, the so-called Bible of Brest, 1563. After his death in 1565 his sons became fanatical Catholics, and did all possible to undo the work of their father.

religious liberty. The old heresy laws were indeed not repealed; but as they could now no longer be enforced, Protestantism was in practice treated as legal, and enjoyed full freedom of worship.

The reformers, feeling at last secure from serious persecution, now became more active than ever, and energetically set about consolidating and organizing their forces. Their first meeting looking toward organization had been when seven reforming pastors, on Stancaro's motion, met with him at Pińczów in October, 1550, soon after his escape from the Bishop's prison, and discussed a reformed order of worship.[17] Affairs now progressed rapidly. In November, 1554, they held a formal synod at Słomniki, some fifteen miles northeast of Kraków, which was attended by a large concourse of ministers and nobles.[18] There was general discussion as to joining forces with some church already organized, especially that of the Bohemian Brethren, whose doctrine, worship and discipline were much praised. In March, 1555, at Chrzczęcice [19] Felix Cruciger (Krzyżak) was appointed Superintendent of the churches, and several ministers were ordained; and in August of the same year, at a synod at Koźminek [20] in Great Poland, a formal union of the two bodies was entered into, and the worship, doctrine and discipline of the Bohemian Brethren were approved.

The heartiness with which these measures of union were at first adopted ere long gave way to more or less dissatisfaction; and in the end the harmonious arrangement reached at Koźminek proved to be not a union of two churches in one, but a federation of two independent bodies. The reformers had no experience to guide them in shaping their new church, and they were free to adopt whatever standard of faith and practice might commend itself to them. They found themselves, however, disposed to follow the Geneva model, on which the Pińczów church had already been formed.[21] But what they just now

[17] This has been called the first reformed synod. It was hardly that, in any proper sense of the term, but simply an informal meeting of a few individuals on their own responsibility. The first proper synod was at Słomniki in 1554.

[18] Very interesting records of the early synods of the Reformed Church in Little Poland from 1554 to 1561 were fortunately discovered in 1873, and published in Dalton's *Lasciana*, pp. 396 ff, and are the main authority for what here follows.

[19] *Lasciana*, p. 399 f.

[20] *op. cit.*, p. 400.

[21] cf. Józef Łukaszewicz, *Dzieje kościołów wyznania Helweckiego w dawney Małej Polsce* (History of the churches of the Helvetian Confession in ancient Little Poland), Poznań, 1853, p. 162 f.

most acutely needed was experienced and competent leadership; and a month later, at a synod at Pińczów,[22] they eagerly seized an opportunity to elect a second Superintendent in the person of Dr. Francesco Lismanino.[23]

Lismanino was born on the island of Corfu in 1504 of Greek parents who brought him as a boy to Kraków. He finished his studies in Italy, and entered the Franciscan order. Italian friends of his at Queen Bona's court invited him to return to Kraków, where he soon became popular for his courtly manners and his eloquence as a preacher. His rise was rapid. Appointed Italian preacher at the royal court, he became the Queen's confessor, and by her influence he was in 1538 made Provincial of his order in Poland. The Queen gave him Ochino's sermons to read, and procured for him many Protestant books from abroad. In 1550 he succeeded in bringing about a reconciliation of the Queen Mother to the King's new wife, Barbara Radziwiłł, in gratitude for which the King promised him the first vacant see in his gift. In 1551, when Laelius Socinus first visited Poland, Lismanino formed an intimate acquaintance with him, made him his guest, and may thus have been influenced in the direction of the Reformation;[24] at all events, he enjoyed the King's close confidence, and used his influence to interest him in a reform of the Church. Thus during three years he used twice a week after dinner to read to him privately from Calvin's *Institutes*,[25] and to discuss points of doctrine with him with great freedom. The King therefore determined to send him abroad as his agent in collecting a royal library, but with private instructions also to visit foreign theologians, observe various churches in their organization, worship and administration, and on his return to report all to him personally, apparently with a view to introducing reforms in the Church in Poland. He left Poland in 1553, and made purchases of books and studied religious life in northern Italy, Switzerland, France and Germany. While in Switzerland he was much drawn to the reformed theologians at Zürich, who persuaded him to become an intermediary for furthering

[22] *Lasciana*, p. 400; Calvin, xv, 868.

[23] On Lismanino, cf. Theodor Wotschke, 'Francesco Lismanino', *Zeitschrift der Historischen Gesellschaft für den Provinz Posen*, xviii (1903), 213–332; Lubieniecius, *Historia*, lib. ii, *passim*.

[24] So says Andrew Wiszowaty, *Narratio compendiosa*, in Sandius, *Bibliotheca*, p. 210. cf. C. G. von Friese, *Kirchen-geschichte des Konigsreichs Polen*, etc. (Breslau, 1786), ii, 249.

[25] Lubieniecius, *Historia*, p. 41.

the Reformation in Poland. They in turn warmly recommended him
to Calvin, who at his suggestion wrote the King (Calvin had already
five years before dedicated to him his Commentary on Hebrews, which
strongly attacked the Catholic doctrine of the Mass), urging him now
to prosecute the work of the Reformation in earnest, and at the same
time speaking in high terms of Lismanino.[26] Calvin now procured the
doctor's degree for him at the University, and encouraged him to leave
the Roman Church, throw off his cowl, and marry a French lady of
Geneva. Lismanino sent the King the books he had bought, and rendered his accounts, but did not return as expected to report in person
on his observations. Instead he prepared to stay in Switzerland.

At the same time he wrote Cruciger, reporting what he had done.
Cruciger must have taken it as an intervention of Providence, for when
he broke the glad news to the brethren at Pińczów in September, 1555,
they at once elected Lismanino his co-Superintendent, as above related.
Cruciger wrote him in the name of the ministers, urging his acceptance
of the call, and asking that they might be recommended to the pious
interest of the Swiss ministers, and have their counsel and aid.[27] Several of the nobles wrote him in the same vein, and Alexander Witrelin
(Vitrelinus), minister at Pińczów, had also written him of the state of
affairs in the new churches.[28]

Lismanino accepted the invitation with alacrity, little foreboding
what disappointments were to follow for him, and what troubles for
the Church; for he was to be an unwitting agent in the outbreak of
Antitrinitarianism in it, as we shall see in the next chapter. To pave
the way for his return, he urged Calvin to write again to the King,
and to nearly a score of influential nobles and clergy.[29] He revisited
the Swiss churches to inform himself better as to their doctrine and
worship, and setting out for Poland in midwinter, bearing the letters
that Calvin had written, he reached his destination at the end of
March, 1556.

Lismanino now began to experience the first results of the step he
had so rashly taken. For he had quite too confidently counted on the
King's approval, and had aroused his anger instead, as a confidential
agent who had broken faith with him. The King in disgust now aban-

---

[26] Calvin, xv, 329–336, Dec. 5, 1554.
[27] Wotschke, *Lismanino*, pp. 223–225 for his letter.
[28] Wotschke, *op. cit.*, p. 226; Calvin, xv, 869.
[29] cf. Calvin, xv, 892–895, 900–913.

doned any plan he may have entertained for reforming the Church in Poland, and never admitted him to his presence again. The leaders of the new church for their part had expected that Lismanino, by his deep learning and wide experience, through his influential acquaintance, and with his fluency in the language and familiarity with the customs of the Poles, would at once prove a great addition to their cause. They were doomed to disappointment. For he had returned to a country where he no longer had any public standing, since he had already been excommunicated by the Catholic Church, and he was soon to be outlawed by an edict issued in the name of the King, though not by his express direction. Hence he had at once to go into hiding under the protection of a friendly noble and old friend, Ivan Karniński of Alexandrowice, some five miles west of Kraków.[30] It was not safe for him to appear at synods of the young Church, nor could he enter upon his office as its Superintendent, though by correspondence from a distance or by private conferences he did give valued help. Catholic opposition to him as an apostate was so bitter that for a time he was almost on the point of fleeing before it.[31] It was more than a year before the intercession of powerful nobles with the King could get his ban lifted. He actually was already in Great Poland on his way back to Switzerland, when the unexpected news reached him that the ban against him was suspended.

While impatiently waiting for Lismanino, the brethren also sought leadership in a yet more important personage. At the Pińczów synod in April, 1556, after general discussion it was enthusiastically voted to call Dr. Jan Łaski[32] (John à Lasco) to return from Germany and direct their churches in the work of reformation. Łaski was born in 1499 of a very distinguished noble family, and was nephew of the Archbishop of Gniezno, Primate and Grand Chancelor of Poland. After finishing his education in Italy, he entered the priesthood and was rapidly advanced in the honors of the Church. Had he been willing to accept the

---

[30] He stayed here for several months, then with the Palatine Jan Bonar, with the lady Agnes Dłuska at Iwanowice whose sons he had lately had under his oversight at Zürich, and with Stanislas Lasocki at Pełsznica.

[31] v. Utenhove's letter of June 23, 1557, Calvin, xvi, 526.

[32] cf. Hermann Dalton, *John a Lasco: his earlier life and labors* (London, 1886); *idem, Lasciana*; Georges Pascal, *Jean de Lasco, Baron de Pologne, Évêque Catholique, Réformateur Protestant* (Paris, 1894); Krasinski, *Reformation in Poland*, i, chap. 5; Abraham Kuyper, *Johannis a Lasco opera*, 2 vols. (Amsterdam, 1866).

dignity, he might have been Bishop of Kujawy (Cujavia); but he had early become dissatisfied with the condition of the Church. He therefore went abroad and spent several years at Basel with Erasmus, whose intimate friend he became, whose hope that the Church might be reformed from within he shared, and whose library he ultimately acquired. Returning to Poland he labored for ten years for reform, and then gave up, resigned his offices, left the country, and gave himself to the Reformation elsewhere. For three years he labored successfully in organizing the reformed churches in East Friesland. Another three years he spent in London as Superintendent of a church embracing all the foreign Protestants there, the so-called Strangers' Church, of which we shall hear something in a later division of this history. Driven from England in the Catholic reaction under Mary, he was for yet another three years a wanderer on the Continent, everywhere trying to aid the Reformation and to persuade Protestants of every name to unite against their common Roman foe. He was in fact the only Pole to play an important part in the Reformation outside his own land. It was at this juncture in his life that the reformers at Pińczów called on him to return to Poland, as above related, and assist and direct their movement. He did so, after nearly twenty years' absence, and arrived at the very end of 1556.

A better man to undertake his difficult task could not have been found. The Catholics exerted themselves with the utmost bitterness to have this 'butcher of the Church,' as they called him, outlawed; but the King granted him audience and assured him protection. Though now broken in health by all he had endured, he gave himself unweariedly for a final three years to his critical work, as center and head of the Reformation in Poland. He preached, held synods, forwarded the important project of a Protestant translation of the Bible into Polish (the Bible of Brest, not published until 1563, after his death), developed at Pińczów an academy for the youth of the new church, strove to strengthen the church's organization and give its doctrines acceptable form, and above all else labored unceasingly at his great design of bringing the three divided sects of Protestants into one united national Polish Reformed Church. Too many obstacles hindered, so that this design was not finally realized until ten years after Łaski's death, when Calvinists, Lutherans and Bohemian Brethren, under the growing pressure of the Catholic reaction, tardily and reluctantly consented to

submerge their differences in the Union of Sandomir (Sandomierz) —
the *consensus Sendomiriensis*, 1570. But before his lamented death in
1560 Łaski could already count some 160 congregations united by an
efficient organization, using a common form of rites and worship, and
broadly agreeing in their doctrinal point of view if not in the details
of their faith. As the first period of its history came to an end with
Łaski's death, the future of the Reformed Church in Poland looked
bright, even if not quite cloudless. It was questions of further reform
in doctrine, which he had left still unsettled, that were soon, long and
sorely to disturb its peace and hamper its progress; and it is these that ,
are to claim our attention in the next stage of our history.

CHAPTER XX

BEGINNINGS OF ANTITRINITARIANISM IN POLAND

THUS FAR we have been concerned only with the earliest stages of Protestantism in Poland, and that only in the type represented by the Calvinism of the Reformed Church. For the movement whose history we are following never, save in a few isolated instances, produced any impression upon Lutheran circles. The Reformed Church of Poland, however, was scarcely organized before symptoms began to appear of a tendency to carry the reform of Christian doctrines much further than the churches in Switzerland under the influence of Calvin had ventured to carry it. For the Protestants of the West, however disposed they may at first have been to be more thorough and more scriptural in framing a new system of doctrine, dared not, in the existing political situation in Europe, risk all they had so hardly won, by giving further and greater doctrinal offence. It was doubtless the part of wisdom in them to stop where they were, and to devote themselves now to fortifying the positions they had taken.

Of the Italian Humanists, however, who sought refuge in Switzerland, not a few, as we have seen, were dissatisfied that the Swiss Reformation had not more thoroughly broken with the Papacy and formed for itself a body of doctrine purely and strictly scriptural. They were desirous of carrying reform further than merely to correct abuses in outward organization and form of worship. The more notable of these, as we shall see, therefore took advantage of the comparatively generous religious liberty that had recently been secured in Poland, to go thither and work for the realization of their ideals. No other country in Europe could have been so hospitable to them. Whatever may have been the attitude of the Catholic Church itself toward differences in religious belief, the Pole before the Reformation had not been a religious bigot. He had for generations been used to seeing Roman Catholic, Greek Orthodox, Jew and Mohammedan live side by side in Poland in comparative peace and friendship. And now that the nobles had won their struggle for liberty to choose their own form of Christianity, the field must have seemed promising for such a reform as they hoped to see.

Even before the Reformation the Catholic Church in Poland gave some signs of criticism of traditional dogmas. Early in the sixteenth century there had been published the so-called Kraków Missal, with a commentary by Cardinal Hugo,[1] in which it was explained that any prayer should be directed to the Father or the Son, but never to the Holy Spirit, which is only a gift. This is of course inconsistent with the doctrine of the Trinity, and strangely like the teaching of Servetus and several of his early followers.

But what has often been spoken of as the first instance of Antitrinitarianism in Poland [2] is the tragic case of Katharine Weigel.[3] She was wife of Melchior Weigel, a wealthy goldsmith and member of the Kraków Council, and offspring of a noble Polish family. At the age of seventy she had been accused of apostasy to the Jewish religion, but after being convicted and facing punishment she finally recanted and was received back into the Church. Ten years later she was again accused at the instance of Bishop Gamrat of Kraków, recently elevated to his see through the influence of Queen Bona, a man who was compensating for his notorious immoralities by his zeal in hunting heretics. She made a clear confession of an intelligent faith in God, but would not say she believed in Christ as his Son. She defended herself with great ability, but as she could not be brought to change her confession she was judged guilty of blasphemy, and on April 19, 1539, the white-haired old lady of eighty was burned at the stake in the small market-place (Mały Rynek) at Kraków, going to her death in a spirit worthy of the first Christian martyrs, boldly and cheerfully, as the old historian relates, as though it had been to her wedding. Though her faith was clearly not trinitarian, it is doubtful that she really belongs in the historical stream we are following. For in the chaos of religious thought

---

[1] *Missale Cracoviense . . . una cum expositione misse Hugonis Cardinalis* (Argentorati, 1510). Copy in the University library, Kraków. cf. Czartoryski Ms no. 369; Lubieniecius, *Historia*, p. 213.

[2] Following the evident opinion of Budziński, the earliest historian of Socinianism, as cited by Lubieniecius, *op cit.*, p. 17.

[3] Her name is variously given: as wife of Weigel (Waygel, Vogel), Waiglowa or Wayglowa; as wife of Melchior, Melcherowa, Malcherowa, Melchierowa; and from her name before marriage, Zalaszowska or Zalassovia. The sources for the narrative are Łukasz Górnicki, *Dzieje w Koronie Polskiej* (Happenings in the Kingdom of Poland), Kraków, 1637, p. 5; Marcin Bielski, *Kronika* (Sanok, 1856), ii, 1031; Julian Bukowski, *Dzieje Reformacyi w Polsce* (History of the Reformation in Poland) Kraków, 1883–'88, i, 176–179.

that was wide-spread in Russia and Poland at the end of the fifteenth and in the first half of the sixteenth century, the Jews were carrying on an active propaganda for their faith, and making so many converts to it that repressive measures were at just this time instituted to check it. It seems most likely that Katharine Weigel was simply a convert to this faith, as at first charged; and this is the more credible since her husband is known to have had active business relations with Jews.[4]

A closer and more direct approach to our subject is found in an occurrence of a different sort reported from Kraków in the year 1546, and revealing a significant undercurrent of secret but daring thought in influential Catholic circles at the capital. There was at this time a group of a dozen or more Humanists, learned and distinguished in Church and State, who used to meet privately for discussion of theological matters and of reforms desirable in the Church, often with Lismanino, who seems to have been their leading spirit, or at the houses of members. One evening the company met for dinner at the house of Jan Trzycieski, a learned bookseller and pupil of Erasmus, who had a famous library. Among the guests was a stranger from Holland, who passed under the name of Spiritus.[5] While waiting for dinner they amused themselves by examining their host's books. Spiritus thus fell upon a book of prayers, in which he observed that some were addressed to God the Father, some to God the Son, and some to God the Holy Spirit. What, said he, have you three Gods? To their reply that they had one God in three persons he rejoined with some thought-provoking criticisms, and discussion continued until the subject was changed as they went in to dinner.

The member of the company who left us the report of this incident [6]

---

[4] cf. Wacław Sobieski, 'Propaganda Żydowska w 1530-'40' (Jewish propaganda in 1539-'40), *Przegląd Narodowy*, xxi (1921), 24–42; Ignacy Schipper, *Studya nad stosunkami gospodarczymi Żydów w Polsce* (Studies on the economic relations of the Jews in Poland), Lwów, 1911, p. 275.

[5] The bearer of this evidently assumed name has not been identified. Wiszowaty assumed that he might have been Adam Pastor (cf. his *Narratio compendiosa* in Sandius, *Bibliotheca*, p. 217); but modern Dutch scholars deny this (cf. W. J. Kühler, *Socinianisme in Nederland*, Leiden, 1912, p. 5). G. G. Zeltner, *Martini Ruari Epistolae* (appended to his *Crypto-Socin.*), p. 503, n., perhaps influenced by the etymology (*spiritus=geest*) conjectures Everhard Geesterans. Similarly (L. A. Guichard), *Histoire du Socinianisme* (Paris, 1723), p. 14, makes Spiritus the equivalent of de Witt; while van Slee, *Socinianisme*, pp. 27–29, n., suggests Peter Nannius of Lyon. The riddle remains unsolved.

[6] Andreas Frycz Modrzewski (Modrevius), in his *Sylvae quatuor* (Racoviae, 1590), p. 81 f, reprinted by Lubieniecius, *Historia*, p. 19 f; by Wiszowaty in Sandius, *Bibliotheca*,

relates that he was deeply impressed by it, and that there were some present in whose minds the question stuck like a barb, and troubled them until it later came to the surface in Poland. The Socinians for their part looked back upon this episode as the historical beginning of their movement in Poland; and as Lismanino and Modrzewski both came to play influential parts in that movement, there would seem to be some ground for such a judgment. However that may be, we here have evidence that the soil in influential Catholic circles was becoming receptive for the seeds of the movement soon to come. The main current of development, however, is to be most clearly traced in the heart of the Reformed Church, as its leaders addressed themselves to questions of organization and doctrine.

In the letter that, as we have seen,[7] Witrelin of Pińczów wrote to Lismanino, relating the condition of the churches that he was asked to aid in their work of reformation, he reported that so far as doctrine and worship were concerned everything was thus far satisfactory; but he added that some troublesome questions had arisen of late as to the mediatorial suffering of Christ, that some were denying that Christ was really the Son of God, and some were holding the erroneous doctrine of Servetus. He therefore desired to know what the brethren in Switzerland thought on these questions; for the Polish churches had as yet adopted no standard of doctrine to which they might be referred. He was evidently speaking of the first appearance of controversial questions that were soon sorely to vex the church in the persons of Gonesius and Stancaro.

At the important synod of Secemin the following January (1556) the matter came sharply to the front. One Peter Giezek of Goniądz, known in history by his latinized name of Gonesius,[8] had come to the synod from Lithuania, bearing credentials from Radziwiłł, and apparently seeking admission to its membership. To this end he gave a full ac-

---

p. 216 f, with additions from Budziński; reprinted in turn by J. M. Ossoliński, *Wiadomości historyczno-krytyczne* (Historico-critical notices), Lwów, 1852, iv, 477 f. Modrzewski became the trusted Secretary of the King, and at length was prominent in the antitrinitarian movement, as were one or two others of those present at the above meeting. Prof. Aleksander Brückner, *Reformacja w Polsce*, i (1921), '12, is of opinion that Modrzewski here used a fictitious narrative as a vehicle for views of his own that it was not prudent to express openly; and Prof. Stanisław Kot, *Andrzej Frycz Modrzewski* (Kraków, 1923), pp. 247–249, is inclined to agree.

[7] *v. supra*, p. 278; Calvin, xv, 869.
[8] The forms Goniądz, Gonedzius, Conyza also occur.

count of his life, and presented a written confession of his reformed faith.[9] This was found unsound to the point of blasphemy. For he held that there is no Trinity, and that the very word is an invention; he wholly rejected the Athanasian Creed as a fiction of men; he said that the only God is God the Father, proving this from the words of Christ himself, and that Christ was less than the Father; and he denied that Christ was of one substance with the Father. These points he argued at length, and in support of them quoted Scripture and cited Irenaeus. The next day he was called back and admonished of his error, and as he stubbornly persisted in it he was bidden go to Wittenberg and discuss his confession with Melanchthon, and submit it to the judgment of the scholars there, and after that return if he wished, and show due evidence of repentance. Prayers were offered for him, a contribution was made toward the expenses of his journey, and agitated in spirit he bade them a tearful farewell. Sandius rightly records this as the first public denial of the doctrine of the Trinity in Poland.[10]

Gonesius[11] was born about 1530 at Goniądz in northern Podlasie (Podlachia). Of his ancestry and early life nothing is known. Evidently he was not a congenital heretic, for the first notice we have of him is in 1550 when Stancaro interpreting one of the Psalms to his pupils at the University at Kraków said something against the invocation of the saints, and Gonesius is reported as one of those that joined in the uproar against him which led to his imprisonment.[12] A year later he was sent by the Bishop of Wilno (Vilna), at whose court he may have been living, to Padua for further studies. Here he won the doctor's degree and in 1554 lectured for a short time on some subject in philosophy.[13] His studies at Padua fell toward the end of Gribaldi's residence there, and it is possible that they may have met;[14] and this was also in the

---

[9] cf. Lubieniecius, pp. 111–115; *Lasciana*, p. 403 f.

[10] Primus fuit qui palam Trinitatis dogma in Polonia oppugnavit. Sandius, *Bibliotheca*, p. 41.

[11] cf. the sketch in Ossoliński, *Wiadomości*, iv, 465–483; and the monograph of Józef Jasnowski, 'Piotr z Goniądza' (Peter of Goniądz), *Przegląd Historyczny*, xxxi (1935), 1–58.

[12] *v. supra*, p. 273, n. 14. cf. Andreas Wengerscius, *Libri Quatuor Slavoniae Reformatae* (Amstelodami, 1679), p. 125; quoted also in Sandius, *Bibliotheca*, p. 40 f.

[13] cf. Antonio Riccoboni, *De Gymnasio Patavino Commentariorum libri sex* (Patavii, 1598), p. 28, cited by Ossoliński, *op. cit.*, iv, 466 and by Bock, *Antitrinitar.*, 1079 f.

[14] Wotschke apparently goes beyond the record in making Gonesius Gribaldi's pupil, and in suggesting that he probably followed him to Tübingen (cf. Wotschke, *Reforma-*

period of Servetus's trial and death at Geneva. It is therefore not strange that he should have become familiar with the views of Servetus while abroad. At all events, when he returned to Poland, probably in the summer of 1555, he was a radically changed man, in both his religious and his social views; for on his return journey he had sojourned among the Anabaptist communists in Moravia long enough to imbibe their sentiments on social questions in general and on pacifism in particular, in token of which he henceforth went girt with a wooden sword in place of the instrument of war that Polish gentlemen commonly wore.

It did not lie in the nature of Gonesius to keep to himself the revolutionary new views that thrilled him. He came home to Poland an ardent propagandist for them. His return coincided with the time when Radziwiłł was most zealously promoting the spread of the reformed religion in Lithuania, and he will naturally have turned thither when seeking a field of work. Apparently Radziwiłł at once received him into the number of his ministers, without inquiry into his particular views. The rest of the story we can easily construct. He will have made converts to his opinions, and it will undoubtedly have been these that Witrelin mentioned to Lismanino in his letter of September, 1555, saying that some also hold the erroneous doctrines of Servetus. This will explain why Radziwiłł sent him to submit his confession of faith to the judgment of the synod at Secemin. These views Lismanino evidently communicated to the ministers in Switzerland, and of them Beza wrote to Bullinger that for the most part they so closely agreed with Gribaldi's confession that they might almost seem to have been copied from him.[15] Whether they were in fact derived from Gribaldi, or instead from the writings of Servetus plus independent study of the New Testament and the early Fathers, can not be confidently determined.

Though the impression made upon the members of the synod at Secemin by Gonesius's statement was on the whole distinctly unfavorable, yet some were set seriously to thinking. One of these was a minister named Gregory Paulus, who a decade later was to be for some time the head of the antitrinitarian cause in Little Poland. In fact, of the sixteen ministers there present seven, including Witrelin himself, were later found in the antitrinitarian camp, as were several of the noble

---

tion, pp. 194, 297). Gonesius's studies were not in the faculty of Law, and he was apparently back in Poland before Gribaldi reached Tübingen in the late autumn of 1555.

[15] Beza to Bullinger, Jan. 1, 1556; Calvin, xvi, 2.

laymen.[16] Meanwhile Gonesius's journey to Wittenberg proved fruitless for him. From a writing that he submitted, Melanchthon at once
discovered that he was infected by the Arian or antitrinitarian heresy,
refused to have anything to say to him, and denied his insistent request
for a public disputation. Had not Gonesius voluntarily withdrawn he
would have sent him from the town forthwith lest he spread his heresy
among the students by private discussion. Melanchthon also warned
the students against such discussions,[17] and for some time he entertained the design [18] (never fulfilled) of writing a controversial work
against Gonesius and the large book on the *communicatio idiomatum*
which he had brought with him to Wittenberg. The judgment on
Gonesius's doctrine which he several months later wrote to the Polish
brethren is not extant.[19]

Gonesius went from Wittenberg to Frankfurt on the Oder, where
his doctrine found no better favor, and thence to Poznań (Posen) with
like result. Like Servetus before him he therefore determined to have
recourse to print, and published a little Latin work containing the
marrow of his doctrine, especially as to the divinity of Christ. It created
an instant sensation. Within a month (April 23, 1556) a joint synod of
the Little Poland Calvinists and the Bohemian Brethren met at Pińczów,
and Gonesius attended it. Lismanino also ventured from his hiding to
be present. He was exasperated at what Gonesius had done, and on his
motion it was almost unanimously voted that he be excluded from the
synod [20] as an Arian, that his book be refuted, and that two gentlemen
be sent to the Bishop of Kraków to inform him that this heretic was not
one of them, and had never been.[21]

[16] Lubieniecius, *Historia*, p. 115; Jasnowski, *op. cit.*, p. 11 f.

[17] cf. Gothardus Arthusius, *Mercurii Gallo-Belgici Sleidano succenturiati*, etc. (Franco-
furti, 1609), i, 25; *Apologia oder Verantwortung des Christlichen Concordien Buchs*
(Dresden, 1584), p. 174; both cited by Ossoliński, *Wiadomości*, iv, 479 f. and Bock,
Antitrinitar., i, 1080.

[18] Melanchthon, *Opera*, viii, 845 f, 858.

[19] Melanchthon, *Opera*, viii, 677 f; *Apologia, loc. cit. supra.*

[20] Hardly excommunicated (in the sense of expulsion from membership), since he had
never yet been admitted as an acknowledged member of the synod.

[21] cf. Józef Łukaszewicz, *Dzieje kościołów wyznania helweckiego w Litwie* (History
of the churches of the Helvetian Confession in Lithuania), Poznań, 1842, p. 108; German
trans., ii, 70; *idem, w dawnej Małej Polsce* (ditto, in ancient Little Poland), p. 161; Jasnowski, *op. cit.*, p. 15.

No copy of the book has survived, though its title was perhaps, *De Filio Dei homine
Christo Jesu* (cf. *Briefwechsel zwischen Christoph, Herzog von Württemberg und Petrus
Paulus Vergerius*, ed. von Kausler und Schott, Tübingen, 1875, p. 136). It seems to have

Thus shut out from the fellowship of the reformed churches in Little Poland, and denounced to a Bishop who might at any time turn his prosecutor in court, Gonesius could no longer expect protection there. Undaunted he therefore turned to his earlier home in Podlasie,[22] where he was not long in winning to his views Piekarski the minister at Biała, and his deacon Falconius (Sokolowski). Upon learning of this, the Superintendent of the churches of the district accused these two to the synod at Włodzisław in 1558 of holding the views of Arius, Servetus and Gonesius. Fearful of consequences, they stoutly denied the charge, subscribed an orthodox confession of faith, and promised henceforth faithfully to avoid such scandals.[23] Succeeding synods kept sharper watch against the spreading of these heresies; and in the following year it was decreed that on beginning their ministry ministers should submit to a special examination as to their belief in God and the Trinity.[24] However, as there was no close union of the Little Poland churches with those of Lithuania, the movement begun by Gonesius grew stronger every year in the latter country, both among the ministers and with the nobles that gave him their aid and patronage.

Henceforth Gonesius ceased trying to attend the synods in Little Poland. He turned instead to more friendly territory, and in December, 1558, he appeared at a synod at Brześć (Brest) in Lithuania, where he again freely expressed his favorite view about Christ and God, and also brought before the churches for the first time an attack upon infant baptism, a subject that was to engross their attention for many years to come. Although he won some converts, these views gave general offence, and only Piekarski, who now again appeared as his follower, ventured to speak in favor of them.[25] But he defended his cause so ably, and his personal character was so exemplary, as to win the favor of the Lady Anna Kiszka,[26] sister of Radziwiłł and mother of Jan

---

been published at Kraków, perhaps under the patronage of Radziwiłł, for upon learning of the action of the synod he had the whole edition withdrawn and banned from sale or destroyed. cf. Melanchthon, *Opera*, viii, 858; ix, 763 f.

[22] Though Podlasie was properly a part of Little Poland, its churches seem to have been more closely connected with their nearer neighbors in Lithuania, cf. *Lasciana*, pp. 469, 500 f.

[23] *Lasciana*, pp. 452 f, 468 f.

[24] *Lasciana*, p. 472 f; Lubieniecius, *Historia*, p. 148; Sandius, *Bibliotheca*, p. 184 f.

[25] cf. Lubieniecius, pp. 118, 144–147; Sandius, pp. 184, 211.

[26] cf. Lubieniecius, *loc. cit.;* Ossoliński, *op. cit.*, iv, 469 f; *Monumenta Reformationis Polonicae et Lithuanicae* (Wilno, 1911), Serja I, Zeszyt i, p. 29.

Kiszka of Ciechanowiec, who was soon to show himself a powerful patron of antitrinitarian churches in Lithuania. Under her patronage he was made minister of the Reformed congregation at Węgrów, where he continued to live until his death. Already at Wilno in 1557 the first Lithuanian synod had taken note of heretical movements of Servetus and Gonesius, modern Arians, whose writings made them anxious;[27] and at the synod of Pińczów in 1559 it was complained that men evidently Arian were occupying pulpits though not ordained by the Superintendent and without his leave.[28] Hence the Pińczów synod in May, 1560, with Kiszka evidently in mind, admonished the Lithuanian nobles 'who were promoting this fanatic' to combat the heretics and expel Gonesius from their churches.[29]

The influence of Gonesius thus far had enlisted no organized support, but had been only sporadic, and from now on for some years his share in the development of antitrinitarianism in Little Poland seems to have been negligible, save in so far as it operated through those whose minds he had set in motion by his addresses at the synods, or through his book. In fact, his interest was now more and more centered in the question of baptism, which he had brought forward at Brześć, and in that of Christianizing society through social reform after the principles of the Moravian Anabaptists. It was not until after the definite split between the orthodox Calvinists and the liberal wing in the Reformed Church had taken place in 1565 that Gonesius again took part in the synods of the latter. In the disputes that then arose, as the liberals tried to arrive at their own doctrine as to God and Christ, he became, along with Farnowski, one of the chief spokesmen of the conservative so-called Arian party, whose position he defended with particular heat;[30] for most of the Antitrinitarians had by this time already moved on quite beyond the position with which he so much shocked the synod at Secemin in 1556. In an attempt to stem this rising tide, he therefore once more resorted to print; and in 1570, near the end of his life, on a press that Kiszka had placed at his service at Węgrów, he published four little works [31] as his final legacy to the world. He probably died in the following year.

[27] *Monumenta, ut supra*, Serja x, Zeszyt i, p. 5.

[28] *op. cit.*, p. vi; *Lasciana*, p. 482 f.   [29] *Lasciana*, pp. 501, 504.

[30] cf. Lubieniecius, *Historia*, p. 214 f; Stanisław Zachorowski, 'Najstarsze synody Arjan Polskich' (The earliest synods of the Polish Arians), *Reformacja w Polsce*, i (1921), 232 f.

[31] The titles were: (1) *Doctrina pura et clara* (unique copy in the Bibliothèque Na-

Postponing for the present any account of Gonesius's part in the protracted controversy over the subject of baptism, and in that over the application of Christianity to social and civic relations, in both of which he took the initiative in the Reformed Church, even if he did not become leader, we may here summarize his contribution to the revolutionary doctrinal changes in Polish Protestantism, of which he was the first herald.[32] To begin with, he accepts Scripture as the perfect standard of faith, containing everything necessary for salvation. One of its chief teachings is that the Father of Christ is the only and Most High God; and whoever recognizes him as the true God is not far from the kingdom of God, be he Jew or Turk. God the Father is not the first person of the one God, but is himself the only true God. His Son is quite another being than God the Father. There is no difference between his essence and his person, for his essence is at the same time his person. It is to God as supreme Being and source of all that we must give highest honor.

The dogma of the Trinity is the chief cause of schisms and sects in the Church. It is a conception that has no support in Scripture, but is a mere invention of men. It is the foundation of all other errors in matters of faith. Neither Christ nor the Apostles taught it, as they would have done had it been true. God in his essence is simple, and a Trinity can not be made by dividing the one substance of God into three parts. If one takes it as three separate substances, three real beings, and then joins them into one common essence, he commits the same error as Sabellius.

Christ (it is here that Gonesius opposes the new Unitarians of his time) existed before the creation of the world which, as John's Gospel teaches, God created through him as his agent. But in this Gonesius is not properly Arian, for Arius taught that God created his Son out of

---

tionale, Paris, catalogued under the name of Conedzius, — no. D². 1425); (2) *O Synu Bożym* (Of the Son of God); (3) *O Trzech, to iest, o Bogu, o Syna iego, y o Duchu S. przeciwko Troycy Sabellianskiey* (Of the Three, that is, of God, of his Son, and of the Holy Spirit, against the Sabellian Trinity); (4) *O ponurzaniu Chrystyanskym* (of Christian immersion) — the last three, all but unique, in libraries at Kraków, Warsaw, or Kórnik.

[32] cf. Jasnowski, *op. cit.*, Rozdział vii. A concise summary of his doctrine, composed near the end of his life, as a corrective of the more radical unitarian doctrine that was already rapidly spreading among the Antitrinitarians of the newly formed Minor Reformed Church, and which he much deplored, is found in his *Doctrina pura et clara*, and more at large in the other works mentioned in the preceding foot-note.

nothing, whereas he teaches that Christ was created out of the very substance of God.

Neither in the teaching of the Apostles nor in the belief of the first Christians have we any proof that the Holy Spirit of which Scripture speaks was God. It is distinct from the Father not only in its substance but in its whole person. It is through the Holy Spirit that God regenerates and renews those that are to become members of Christ's Church. The way to salvation is through faith, of which the sacraments are only a confirmation. The necessary sacrament, and the one commanded by God, is immersion, a sign of the forgiveness of sins.

Such, in very brief summary, is the primitive and original form of the doctrine out of which eventually developed the movement whose history we are following. In the little group of new Protestant churches that it immediately concerned it aroused grave controversy; and in wider circles it was deemed of enough consequence to call forth a formal refutation from the Heidelberg theologian Zanchi, and to attract the attention of the Zürich theologian Simler, who characterized Gonesius as the Servetus of Poland.[33] His particular form of doctrine was destined soon to be outgrown and left behind; while that which succeeded it did not in fact develop out of Gonesius's teaching so much as run parallel to it and largely independent of it, as we shall see. Yet most of his followers eventually adopted it. More memorable than his distinction as a pioneer in doctrinal change is the fact that Gonesius was the first in Poland to connect religion with vital social problems, aiming through a reform in religious conceptions to bring about changes in personal life and reforms in men's social relations and in the organization of society. This aim, which he was the first to advocate, a programme of radical social change through the application of religious teachings to the functioning of the social organism, was to become one of the most noteworthy marks of the antitrinitarian movement in Poland.

In an age when religious controversy was often rude and abusive, Gonesius was grave and dignified in manner, speaking from the level of thorough scholarship, and with a straightforward use of logic and an appeal to reason that raised him well above the usual level of re-

---

[33] Hieronymus Zanchius, *Adversus blasphemum Petri Gonedzii libellum Responsio*; in his *Opera* (Heidelberg, 1613), viii, 533–551; cf. Bock, *Antitrinitar.*, i, 108–110; Josias Simler, *De aeterni Dei Filio*, etc. (Tiguri, 1570), pp. 5, 7.

ligious debate. It is one of the ironies of history that though he was the first outspoken pioneer in Poland of our movement, yet he never became in any sense one of its leaders, and never won an organized following. He was one of those seed-sowers that are already forgotten before their harvest is ripe, a man a decade or two ahead of his time. It has remained for recent generations to recognize his services and to give his name such honor as it deserves. We have now to take leave of him for a time, and to trace the progress of events through which others carried on to permanent results the changes that he did not live to see come to full fruition.

CHAPTER XXI

GROWTH OF LIBERAL THOUGHT IN THE
REFORMED CHURCH IN POLAND

NOT LONG AFTER Oleśnicki had defied the authority of Rome and removed the images from the church and the monks from the monastery in his town of Pińczów (1550), he took steps to establish a school in the abandoned cloister; for education was then at a low ebb in Poland. The University at Kraków, poorly endowed and thoroughly scholastic in spirit, no longer attracted able scholars to its faculty, nor could it long hold active-minded students; while the numerous local schools had such inferior teachers that the sons of the nobility were forced to resort to foreign lands for a satisfactory education. Especially was this the case with those that favored the Reformation.[1] Hence, not only for the education of the young nobles, but also for the training of their own ministers, it became a matter of much importance to them to have schools of their own to take the place of those of the Church on which they had hitherto depended.[2] Thus a gymnasium was established at Pińczów as early as 1551; and as soon as the Reformed Church had completed its own organization its development was rapid and its fame spread. Pińczów became a centre of learning, and religious exiles from Italy, taking advantage of the generous privileges offered those that were suffering for conscience' sake,[3] flocked thither in such numbers that an Italian church was ere long organized, with Giorgio Negri as its minister.[4] It was here that the scholars gathered who made the first Protestant translation of the Bible into Polish, here that the first Protestant press in Poland was set up in 1558, and here that the early synods of the Reformed Church were most often held. Thus Pińczów, besides being for some twenty

[1] cf. Stanisław Kot, 'Pierwsza Szkoła Protestancka w Polsce' (The first Protestant school in Poland), *Reformacja w Polsce*, i (1921), 15–34.

[2] cf. *Lasciana*, p. 234.

[3] cf. Theodor Wotschke, *Briefwechsel*, p. 97.

[4] cf. *Lasciana*, p. 474. Giorgio was son of the Francesco Negri whom we have met in the Grisons. cf. p. 106 f, *supra*.

years the metropolis of the Polish Reformation, presently came to be called 'the Sarmatian Athens.'[5]

Not long after his return to Poland, Lismanino wrote Calvin urging him as soon as possible to send Peter Statorius to assist in the work of the new school.[6] Statorius was a zealous French Protestant of marked ability, who had been a pupil of Beza at Lausanne, and was well known to Lismanino at Zürich. He arrived in Poland later in the year, going first to Kraków as minister, and not long afterwards to Pińczów as assistant teacher in the new gymnasium. Results were soon apparent, and the growth of the school was so striking as to alarm the Catholics, so that in two successive years their synods demanded of the King to close it.[7] A second French scholar was added to its teachers in 1558, in the person of Jean Thénaud of Bourges, and Statorius soon set about reforming the plan of the school, upon the model of that at Lausanne.[8] It thus became the first humanistic gymnasium in Poland, and its fame spread abroad. Statorius, who in due time acquired so fluent a knowledge of the language that he became one of the translators of the Bible into Polish,[9] and even published the first Polish grammar,[10] was made Rector of the school in 1561, and gave his name a Polish turn as Stojeński (Stoiński — Stoinius).

The Pińczów school existed for about twenty years, and under Statorius's influence became the first 'Arian' school in Poland, while Pińczów itself was for a time the focus of the antitrinitarian movement in the Reformed Church. Statorius is said to have been already secretly

---

[5] Lubieniecius, *Historia*, p. 33.

[6] Lismanino to Calvin, April 15, 1556, Calvin, xvi, 108. He describes himself as "Petrus Statorius Gallus ... Tonvillanus ... e Sequanis," but these data furnish a puzzle as yet unsolved, as is also the vernacular form of his name. The latest guess is that his original name was Pfoertner (Latinized as Statorius), and that his place of origin was Thionville in northern Lorraine; but this is not in the country of the Sequani, nor is there in their country any such place as Thionville or Thonville. cf. Kot, *op. cit.*, p. 28; André Mazon, 'Pierre Pfoertner = Petrus Statorius Gallus,' *Revue des Études Slaves*, xiv (1934), 82–84.

[7] Bukowski, *Reformacya*, ii, 404, 457.

[8] cf. his *Gymnasii Pinczoviensis Institutio*, c. 1560; also Kraków 1912, ed. A. Karbowiak; Józef Łukaszewicz, *Historya Szkół w Koronie i w Księstwie Litewskiem* (History of schools in the Kingdom and in the Duchy of Lithuania), Poznań, 1849–'51.

[9] Statorius to Calvin, Feb. 1, 1559, Calvin, xvii, 426.

[10] P. Stojeński, *Polonicae grammatices institutio*, (Cracoviae, 1568,) written in Latin for the use of immigrants. It is interesting to note also that the first Polish dictionary also was the work of one of the early adherents of the 'Arian' movement: Jan Mączyński, *Lexicon latino-polonicum*, (Regiomonti, 1563).

a follower of Servetus when he came to Poland, and to have brought Servetus's works with him,[11] though some time elapsed before heresy was suspected of him; but at the Pińczów synod in September, 1559, he was by some accused of opposing the invocation of the Holy Spirit.[12] He replied that he had only opposed the order of the prayers, in which it was customary at the opening of public worship to invoke the Holy Spirit before the Father, in the hymn, *Veni, Creator Spiritus*. To clear himself he declared that he had not opposed the divinity of the Holy Spirit, that he held that the three persons of the Trinity ought to be equally worshiped, and that he detested all Arian or Servetian heresy as blasphemy. Two months later, however, there was presented to the synod at Pińczów an unsigned letter from one of the nobles, Remigjan Chełmski (supposedly inspired by Statorius with whom he was intimate), calling the worship of the Holy Spirit in doubt.[13] This disturbed many, and the Synod's reply did not satisfy the writer. Statorius was instructed to answer him as the spirit moved, and did so in evasive terms;[14] but being now promoted to be Rector of the Pińczów school, he not only broached his view in private to Chełmski, but even taught in the school that invocation of the Holy Spirit is idolatrous, and totally unwarranted by Scripture.

A discussion on the subject ensued between Statorius and some of the ministers,[15] in which he argued with great learning and eloquence, and at much length, that the Holy Spirit is not a third person in the Deity, nor God, but a power and gift of God which he awakens in the hearts of the faithful, dividing to each one severally even as he will. By his arguments he persuaded a good many, who even surpassed him in zeal for the new view, which however, as we have seen, had already been set forth a half-century before by the Catholic Cardinal Hugo.[16] Statorius, however, showed himself to be either of unstable convictions or else unfaithful in his acknowledgment of them. Under the pressure of repeated appeals from his old teacher Beza to return to the true faith,[17] and faced by fear that enemies might deprive him of his em-

---

[11] Lubieniecius, *Historia*, p. 148.

[12] cf. *Lasciana*, p. 384.

[13] cf. Lubieniecius, p. 148; Stoinius, *Epitome*, in Sandius, *Bibliotheca*, p. 185.

[14] cf. Stanislas Zachorowski, 'Najstarszy Synody Arjan Polskich' (the Earliest Synods of the Polish Arians), *Reformacja w Polsce*, i (1921), p. 201 f.

[15] cf. Lubieniecius, pp. 149–151, 209–213.   [16] *v. supra*, p. 283.

[17] cf. Beza, *Epistolae*, pp. 109–115, 243; Wotschke, *Briefwechsel*, pp. 258, 282, 306.

ployment, in a long discussion of the subject at a synod at Łańcut in 1567 he changed sides and denied ever having taught such doctrines, though his old pupil Alexius Rodecki who was present contradicted him to his face. In view of the repeated fickleness that we have recorded, the contemporary historian Budziński branded him as a Proteus,[18] and relates that not long afterwards he died.[19]

Despite his recantation of the views he had formerly urged, the seed that Statorius had sowed could not be recalled, and contributed not a little toward undermining the doctrine of the Trinity in the Reformed Church. More powerful and lasting factors in this development, however, came from another quarter, and had already begun to operate. The development we are now to trace heads back to Francesco Stancaro, whom Wotschke calls 'the most disagreeable theologian known to history':[20] a man of great learning and attractive eloquence, but withal ambitious, self-conceited, arrogant, aggressive, quarrelsome, intolerant, insolent, abusive, violent, obstinate. Soon after being, as we have already seen, banished from Poland by royal decree late in 1550, he repaired to Prussia, where under the patronage of the Protestant Duke Albrecht he became Professor of Hebrew at the new Protestant University of Königsberg. A sharp controversy was already in progress with Professor Osiander over Luther's doctrine of justification by faith, and the Duke invited him to assist in composing it. He sadly mistook his man, for Stancaro plunged into the matter with such violent partisanship that within less than three months he was obliged to leave the city.[21] The greater part of the next two years he spent in various places in Germany, by controversy everywhere making himself offensive. Then, as the King's edict against him had now been annulled, he

---

[18] So called perhaps in allusion to his recently published poem with that title. cf. Tadeusz Grabowski, *Literatura Aryańska w Polsce* (Arian Literature in Poland), Kraków, 1908, p. 32.

[19] cf. Lubieniecius, p. 213 f; *Reformacja w Polsce*, v (1928), 47 and n. 2. His son Peter, however, became a distinguished minister and writer in the Minor Church, pastor at Lucławice, and beloved disciple of Faustus Socinus. For bravery in war two of the children of the elder Statorius were ennobled by Sigismund III. in 1591 with the cognomen Stojeński (Stoiński, Stoinius). cf. Kot, *Szkoła*, p. 34, n. 4.

[20] cf. Theodor Wotschke, 'Francesco Stancaro,' *Altpreussische Monatsschrift*, xlvii (1910), pp. 465–498, 570–613; Francesco Ruffini, 'Francesco Stancaro,' *Ricerche Religiose*, viii, ix (1932, 1933). An excellent account of the following controversy is given by Heberle, 'Aus dem Leben von G. Blandrata', *Tübinger Zeitschrift für Theologie* (1840), 4es Heft, pp. 142–159.

[21] cf. Johannes Wigand, *De Stancarismo* (Lipsiae, 1585), pp. 63–65.

returned to his old friends among the nobles of Little Poland. His efforts here to promote the Reformation now met with little success, and after yet another year he went late in 1554 to Hungary. Here again he fell into doctrinal quarrels, in which his maligning of Melanchthon,[22] whom he called 'the Arian of the North,' gave great offence, so that he was forced to move on to Transylvania. At Kolozsvár he promptly fell out with the ministers of the city and was excluded from their synod; at Hermannstadt he broke his promise to keep the peace and had to leave town; wherever he went he raised a storm in the churches, and finally after nearly five years of constant quarreling, his patron having died, he came to Poland for the third time in May, 1559, and at once began to stir up dissension in the churches which Łaski was just getting fairly organized.[23]

By this time his attitude on theological questions had become almost pathological. His hatred of Melanchthon passed all bounds, and he published a little tract in which he flatly said that it was evident that the doctrine of Melanchthon, and of his own recent adversaries in Transylvania, about the Son of God, was Arian.[24] The ministers from Łaski down, most of whom had been Melanchthon's pupils at Wittenberg, were scandalized, all copies of the tract that could be found were burned, and the printer was called to account. Łaski and most of the ministers and the nobles in the church opposed him, while he in turn fiercely maligned them. Hence a synod was convened at Pińczów (1559) to sit in judgment on Stancaro and his doctrine, and Lismanino was directed to draw up a confession on the subject, to be published in the name of the Synod. Revision and correction of this confession was Łaski's last work before his death. Some of the younger partisans of Stancaro complained that he had been unfairly treated, and he himself demanded a public debate on the subject. Though this was refused, he was allowed to defend his view before a congregation in the Pińczów church.[25] This he did with intolerable insolence and bitterness, calling

[22] Melanchthon had already in 1553 written a *Responsio de controversiis Stancari* (Pinczoviae, 1559); cf. Melanchthon, *Opera*, xxiii, 87.

[23] cf. Statorius to Calvin, Aug. 20, 1559, Calvin, xvii, 600 ff; Wotschke, *Reformation*, pp. 179–193.

[24] Ex hac collatione manifestum evadit Ph. Melanchthonis . . . cum complicibus doctrinam de filio dei arrianam esse. Stancaro, *Collatio doctrinae Arrii et Philippi Melanchthonis* (Pińczów, 1559), p. 12. cf. Calvin to Stancaro, xix, 230.

[25] cf. *Lasciana*, p. 482 f; 487 f; Statorius to Calvin, Aug. 20, 1559, Calvin, xvii, 1600.

all that disagreed with him Arians, while they in turn accused him of Sabellianism.

The particular doctrine which had by now become a fixation with Stancaro concerned the mediatorial office of Christ.[26] In the attempt to interpret the scripture texts on this subject,[27] in connection with the orthodox doctrine of the two natures in the person of Christ, the teaching generally accepted was that as Mediator between God and man, Christ acted in both natures. Stancaro, however, held that it would be absurd to say that Christ mediated with himself, and that since a mediator must always be subordinate to the one with whom he mediates, Christ could not be Mediator in his divine nature without being inferior to the Father.[28] He insisted therefore that Christ could be Mediator only in his human nature; and declared that the generally accepted doctrine involved an Arian view of Christ.

With Łaski's firm hand now removed, the schism widened; and although Stancaro's doctrine had been consistently disapproved by synods at Pińczów in 1559, his followers continued to agitate the matter and to disturb the synods with it during the two years following, though with no change of result. The issue of the whole controversy was that the synod at length voted to sever all relations with him, to burn his writings, and to remove from office in the churches all the ministers that followed him.[29] Meantime the synods solicited the aid of the Swiss theologians in combating the heresy that was working such havoc. Various letters from them were circulated, including two careful refutations by Calvin, sent in the name of the theologians at Geneva,[30] though Stancaro refused to believe that these were other than forgeries by his enemies. He restated his doctrine in a new work, which was refuted in turn by Simler of Zürich,[31] not to mention several other Re-

---

[26] He seems to have derived it from Peter Lombard, *Sententiae*, lib. iii, cap. 7, dist. 19; and in the course of the controversy he declared that one Lombard was worth more than 100 Luthers, 200 Melanchthons, or 500 Calvins. cf. Christophorus Hartknoch, *Preussische Kirchen-Historia* (Franckfurt, 1686), p. 341.   [27] I. Tim. ii. 5; Gal. iii. 20.

[28] cf. Wotschke, *Briefwechsel*, p. 102; Cruciger to the Zürich ministers, March 17, 1560, Calvin, ix, 338; xviii, 371 ff; Conrad Schlüsselburg, *Catalogus Haereticorum* (Francofurti, 1599), lib. ix, 36–375, *De haeresi Stancaristarum*.

[29] *Lasciana*, pp. 507–510, 536–538.

[30] *Responsum ad Fratres Polonos*, 1560, and *Responsio ad Nobiles Polonos*, 1561; Calvin, ix, 333–358. Also, *Epistolae duae ad ecclesias Polonicas* (by the Zürich ministers), Tiguri, 1561.

[31] Stancaro, *De Trinitate et Mediatore Domini Nostri Jesu Christi* (Cracoviae, 1562); Josias Simler, *Responsio ad maledicum Francisci Stancari Mantuani librum* (Tiguri, 1563).

formed theologians who saw in Stancaro a dangerous enemy to the cause of the Reformation; while the Polish man of letters, Stanisław Orzechowski (Orichovius), from having been an ardent Protestant now again become Catholic, turned his sharp pen against him in a famous work.[32] Nevertheless a considerable number of nobles and of the younger ministers, carried away by his eloquence and his skill in argument, and by his hostility to Arianism, took Stancaro's part, and Modrzewski even wrote a book in his defence, though in it he appealed for harmony.[33] His disciples ministered to congregations in a dozen or more places,[34] and he and his family found refuge with the noble Stadnicki at Dubiecko in Red Russia. Here, as long as his patron lived, he continued to seek adherents, and he also conducted a gymnasium with five teachers and some 300 scholars, mostly young nobles.[35]

Despite all the attacks made upon him, and his being in the later years of his life driven from pillar to post, Stancaro remained unyielding and defiant, even calling the Reformed Church worse than the Catholic.[36] That he had influence in high quarters may be judged from the fact that in 1569 at the Diet of Lublin Sigismund Augustus made him a Polish citizen with standing as a noble.[37] In his last important work [38] he defended the doctrine of the Trinity against the then rising tide of antitrinitarianism of Paulus and Gentile, which will soon claim our attention. At length his followers came to realize that the whole cause of the reformers was being weakened and distracted by a futile quarrel over a merely speculative doctrine of no religious value, which threatened to separate them from all the reformed churches in the West. At the synod of Kraków in 1567, as he would still yield nothing, they began to fall away from him; and when at the Union of Sandomir (*Consensus Sendomiriensis*) in 1570 the three Protestant confessions at length drew together, the last seven ministers of Stancaro's little sect returned to the fold. Finally he himself, at the end of his life, after having disturbed the peace of the churches for nearly twenty years,

---

[32] *Chimaera: sive de Stancari funesta Regno Poloniae secta* (Cracoviae, 1563).

[33] *De Mediatore libri tres* (Basileae, 1562).

[34] cf. Wengerscius, *Slavonia*, p. 126.

[35] Wengerscius, *ibid.*

[36] Papistica ecclesia mala est, peior lutherana, omnium pessima helvetica at sabaudica. Reported to Calvin by Sebastian Pech; Calvin, xviii, 183.

[37] Wengerscius, *op. cit.*, p. 413 f; Szymon Okolski, *Orbis Polonus* (Cracoviae, 1641), iii, 108.

[38] *De Trinitate et Unitate Dei* (Cracoviae, 1567).

renounced his doctrine and became reconciled to the church. He died in 1570.[39]

The significance of Stancaro in the history of our movement does not lie in the fact that he was in any sense a pioneer of Antitrinitarianism, for he was an unwavering and passionate defender of the trinitarian doctrine throughout, insomuch that even the chief leaders of the Reformation were not orthodox enough to win his approval. It was rather that his view about the mediatorship of Christ was so extreme that those defending the traditional view against him were led unwarily to lean toward a form of tritheism. Calvin early anticipated this danger, and warned the brethren in Poland to assert mediation in both natures, lest in following Stancaro they find themselves asserting more Gods than one;[40] while Stancaro himself, writing to Calvin at the end of 1560, declared that Arians (meaning his Calvinistic opponents) in Poland were teaching that Father, Son and Holy Spirit were not one but three, as separate from one another as three different men,[41] and that the Son of God was subordinate to the Father.

So long as Łaski lived he was able to hold Stancaro's movement successfully in check, but after his death the defence of the faith fell to the less able and experienced hands of Lismanino, whose career with the Reformed Church had been disappointing.[42] Called to be its leader, with high expectations from his learning, experience and influence in high quarters, he found himself, upon returning from his long sojourn abroad, at once an excommunicate from the Church and an outlaw from the State; and it was more than a year before his friends succeeded by strenuous exertions in getting the King to annul his banishment so that he dared appear in public. Meantime Łaski had returned, and had assumed leadership of the church with so much greater prestige that Lismanino was quite overshadowed. There was, moreover, a growing resentment among the ministers that so important a part in the Polish Reformation should be taken by foreign refugees, especially Italians, of whom many had flocked to Pińczów.[43] Lismanino therefore seemed to some almost superfluous, and when provision for his support was repeatedly pressed upon the synods, some of the nobles impatiently

---

[39] Wengerscius, *op. cit.*, p. 84.
[40] Calvin, vol. ix, p. xxxiv.
[41] Stancaro to Calvin, Dec. 4, 1560, Calvin, xviii, 260 f.
[42] cf. Wotschke, *Lismanino*, p. 279 ff.
[43] cf. *Lasciana*, p. 528.

inquired by whose authority he had been invited to come at all. Although in order to do so he had incurred large personal expense, and had become seriously involved in debts, repayment was grudgingly voted and tardily made.[44] It was more than three years after his return to Poland before he was given any definite appointment in the church, with oversight of churches in the Pińczów district and of the Pińczów gymnasium, yet another before he was made assistant Superintendent, and over five years before the church voted him a definite stipend.[45] Meantime he was forced to suffer the humiliation of depending on the bounty of generous patrons among the nobility.

Lismanino could not but feel sorely wounded by such an ill return for all the sacrifices he had made for the cause, and he requested to be relieved of his office, that he might make provision for his personal needs.[46] But several critical situations now conspired to thrust him into the breach, where he could ill be spared. Hence though not well fitted, and not at all inclined, to the task, he took up the burden of the controversy with Stancaro. Whereas Stancaro held a doctrine of God that verged on Sabellianism, hardly recognizing any distinctive qualities in the three persons, but almost dissolving them in the divine Unity, Lismanino sought to avoid this error by emphasizing a real difference of the persons in God. Agreeing to Stancaro's contention that mediation implies a sort of inferiority (as the Swiss theologians had been unwilling to do), he undertook, while still adhering to the Nicene doctrine, and holding that the three persons were equal in rank,[47] to maintain on scriptural grounds (John xiv. 28) a certain pre-eminence of the Father. This in itself was not necessarily heretical, but Lismanino was not acute enough as a theologian to foresee that it might easily end in emphasizing the three persons more than the unity of the one God. This further development was to be promoted by influences of Italian origin.

For in 1558, at the very time when the controversy with Stancaro was at its height, Laelius Socinus and Biandrata had lately arrived in Poland from Switzerland, the former for the winter, the latter to stay. Lismanino had known Socinus on his first visit to Poland in 1551, when he is said to have been Lismanino's guest and to have influenced him in

44 cf. *Lasciana*, pp. 426 f, 431, 495, 523 f, 541 ff, 551–553.
45 cf. *Lasciana*, pp. 481, 515, 553.
46 cf. Wotschke, *Lismanino*, p. 281 f.
47 Lismanino, *Brevis explicatio doctrinae de sanctissima Trinitate*, (1565).

favor of the Reformation,[48] and the acquaintance will have been renewed more recently at Zürich. Lismanino will also certainly have known Biandrata when they were both at Queen Bona's court before the middle of the century, the one as her physician, the other as her confessor. Both Socinus and Biandrata were again now welcomed at court. Socinus had been warmly commended to Łaski by Bullinger, and by Calvin to Radziwiłł,[49] and in intimate conversation with Lismanino he may, with his customary caution, have fostered unorthodox views; while the influence of Biandrata on Lismanino is evident from a comparison of Biandrata's already known opinions with those that Lismanino ere long espoused. Biandrata did not at first attempt any open propaganda, and he so well satisfied Łaski and Lismanino of his substantial orthodoxy, and of his desire to be on good terms with Calvin, that Statorius wrote Calvin at Lismanino's suggestion urging a reconciliation; and when after six months he had received no reply, he wrote a second time to the same effect.[50] Calvin's opinion of Biandrata's character and purposes, however, was not to be shaken, and he took offence at the suggestion, calling Biandrata a treacherous trouble-maker, a barbarian or rather a beast, and a dirty dog.[51] He had already written Lismanino to warn the brethren to beware of the monster,[52] though

[48] Sandius, *Bibliotheca*, p. 34 f.

[49] cf. Wotschke, *Briefwechsel*, p. 79; Calvin, xvii, 181.

[50] cf. Statorius to Calvin, Feb. 1, Aug. 20, 1559, Calvin, xvii, 424 f, 600.

[51] Calvin to Statorius, Nov. 15, 1559, June 9, 1560, Calvin, xvii, 676, xviii, 102.

[52] Quale monstrum sit Georgius Blandrata, imo quot monstra alat, antequam experiantur pii fratres admone ut sibi mature caveant. Calvin to Lismanino, Nov. 19, 1558, Calvin, xvii, 378.

Some allowance may be made for the characteristic violence of Calvin's feeling toward Biandrata. For he was fixed in the judgment, from which henceforth he never wavered, that Biandrata was a deliberate hypocrite who, while professing to seek only the scriptural truth, was all the while trying, as a disciple of Servetus, to undermine the orthodox doctrine of God and Christ, and to replace it by a non-Athanasian doctrine which he had already fully formed and wished to impose. This judgment was adopted by his colleagues in Switzerland at the time, and by their followers since. But another view is possible: that as an attentive student of Scripture, though but a lay theologian, he was sincerely desirous of arriving at a Christian doctrine both more scriptural and more reasonable than the current one, and that instead of trying to propagate a preconceived doctrine, as Calvin assumed, he was cautiously feeling his way to one that should not be open to the objections raised by Servetus. In this process, considering the treatment then everywhere meted out to heretics, he would naturally adhere as closely as possible to the accepted formulas, even when giving them an altered interpretation, and would thus incur the charge of deceit; even though it was not until later that he felt sure enough of his position, and secure enough in himself, to proclaim boldly the doctrine at which he at length arrived.

apparently to little purpose, for Vermigli reported to Calvin in the
spring that Biandrata was said to have wormed his way into friendship
with Lismanino, under the pretence of curing the chronic disease from
which he had suffered from his youth;[53] and he urged that further
warning be given him.

Meantime Biandrata was away in Transylvania for nearly a year,
whither the King had requested him to go to attend his sister, the
Queen Isabella, in what proved to be her last illness. She died at the
end of the year, but he did not return to Poland until the spring of
1560. The influence and favor which his medical skill and his blameless
conduct had won him survived his absence, however, and at the synod
at Pińczów in May he was cordially received for his great practical
.experience, was invited to join in their counsels, and was also requested
to go to Radziwiłł in Lithuania to solicit his aid for Lismanino.[54] At a
large synod at Xiąż (Książ) later in the year he and Lismanino took
an influential part in settling the organization of the church, and were
both appointed coadjutors to Cruciger, the Superintendent. Biandrata
modestly declined the honor, as one whose duties he as a foreigner and
an active physician could not well discharge, but the nobles persuaded
him to accept it for the time being.[55] Calvin on his part was not idle.
In August he issued a new edition of his Commentary on the Acts,
with an enlarged dedication to Radziwiłł, in which he took occasion
to attack Biandrata for being 'as much worse than Stancaro as the error
with which he is infected is more detestable, and as the poison that he
cherishes in his heart is more carefully concealed.' [56]

At the synod at Pińczów at the beginning of 1561 the matter broke
out into the open. A letter from Radziwiłł was read complaining that
Calvin had been hasty and unjust in accusing Biandrata of being a
Servetian. Biandrata challenged any accuser to come forward, demanded a public examination, presented a confession of faith that was
unexceptionably orthodox, and expressed abhorrence of the doctrine of
Servetus. He was then examined by a select committee, who found

---

[53] Said to have been epilepsy; cf. Sandius, *Bibliotheca*, p. 35; Vermilius to Calvin,
April 16, 1559, Calvin, xvii, 498.

[54] *Lasciana*, p. 498.

[55] *id. op.*, pp. 513–515, 524 f.

[56] Ecce ex altera parte medicus quidam, Georgius Blandrata, Stancaro deterior, quo
magis detestabili errore imbutus est, et plus occultae virulentiae in animo alit. Calvin,
xviii, 158.

nothing amiss in him, and voted that both Calvin and Radziwiłł be written to, clearing Biandrata from any suspicion of being a Servetian.[57] Cruciger therefore wrote Radziwiłł reporting what had been done, while Radziwiłł in turn wrote Calvin and Bullinger at length,[58] sending his personal messenger Martin Czechowicz, minister at Wilno, of whom we shall hear much in a later chapter. Radziwiłł, strongly vindicating Biandrata from suspicion, declared that his orthodoxy was approved by the churches, and asked Calvin to be reconciled to him. The ministers of Wilno added their testimony in his defence.[59] Calvin replied to all these appeals, but he remained unmoved.[60]

Whether Biandrata now felt that he had become too much the storm-centre of a controversy that bid fair to distract the churches as much as Stancaro's had, or for some other reason, he reported to the synod of Włodzisław in September that he had lately resigned the office of Elder which he had reluctantly accepted a year before, and he asked for an honorable discharge;[61] but the nobles begged him to retain his office, and he continued to hold it as long as he remained in Poland. The centre of attack now shifted in another direction. A little book by Gentile had just made its appearance,[62] advocating what came dangerously near to being tritheism, and strongly attacking the Athanasian Creed. Fear of the spread of heresy was now intensified, and suspicion began to turn toward Lismanino, who as now the recognized theological leader of the church was trying to turn the edge of Stancaro's doctrine, and whose intimacy with Biandrata was well known. A whispering campaign against him had already been noted and quieted at the Pińczów synod in January, and at the Włodzisław synod in September there was a rather sharp expostulation by one of the nobles against the writer of an anonymous letter intimating that Lismanino was tampering with the doctrine of the Trinity.[63] Hereupon Lismanino asked

[57] *Lasciana*, pp. 538–541.

[58] cf. Cruciger to Radziwiłł, March 13, 1561, Radziwiłł to Calvin, and to Bullinger, July 14, 1561, Calvin, xviii, 402, 556, 559.

[59] Wilno ministers to Calvin, July 23, 1561, Cruciger to the Swiss ministers, Sept. 3, Polish ministers and the Kraków synod to the same, Dec. 13, Calvin, xviii, 571, 675; xix, 166, 168.

[60] Letters of Oct. 9, 1561, xix, 35–45. Bullinger to Radziwiłł, Sept. 30, Calvin to same, Oct. 9, xviii, 753; xix, 43.

[61] *Lasciana*, p. 549; cf. Zachorowski, *Synody*, p. 218.

[62] Probably his *Confessio evangelica*; *v. supra*, p. 234. Sarnicki to Calvin, Sept. 1, 1561, Bullinger to Cruciger, Sept. 30, Calvin, xviii, 672, 757.

[63] cf. *Lasciana*, pp. 528, 549. One may well suspect that the unnamed author was

leave to read and explain a letter that he had lately written to his friend the noble Ivan Karniński of Alexandrowice.[64] The letter was intended as a contribution to the Stancaro controversy, and sought to oppose his Sabellianism by setting forth the true doctrine held by the early Fathers, which, along with the equal deity of both, recognized a certain inferiority of the Son to the Father. Consideration of so grave a matter was postponed to a later meeting of the ministers and Elders, which was held at Kraków in December. In the discussion that followed, Biandrata spoke in conciliatory fashion, urging that the matter be considered in a patient and tolerant spirit, and not objecting to phrases in the creeds, provided they harmonized with Scripture. Lismanino also was willing for the present to tolerate unscriptural terms if they were not made compulsory and urged against conscience. While opinions differed, moderation prevailed, and it was unanimously voted that Lismanino compose his confession of faith and maintain his innocence. The proceedings of the synod were reported to Calvin and Bullinger.[65]

Sarnicki, who was soon to come forward as the self-appointed guardian of the traditional doctrine.

[64] Karniński, now one of the Elders of the Kraków district, had been one of the circle of liberal Humanists at Kraków twenty years before, and one of the first of the nobles to join the Reformation. It was with him that Lismanino first found shelter for several months after his return to Poland, when under the ban of the King. The letter is given in full in Lubieniecius, *Historia*, pp. 119–126, but wrongly dated December instead of September. cf. also *id. op.*, pp. 23–28.

[65] cf. *Lasciana*, pp. 550, 554, Lubieniecius, p. 126 ff.

CHAPTER XXII

THE CALVINISTIC REACTION IN THE
REFORMED CHURCH IN POLAND

HAD THE SPIRIT of conciliation and mutual tolerance generally prevailed which characterized the proceedings of the synod at Kraków in December, 1561, consciences might have been left free as to the speculative questions on which there was difference of opinion, and all could have joined harmoniously and effectively in promoting the practical ends of the church. Had all been willing to deal patiently, the way seemed open for avoiding serious division. Some, however, were determined to force the issue, and to treat these speculative matters not as incidental but as central and primary in the life of the church. The leader in keeping the breach open and making it wider was Stanislas Sarnicki, a minister of no mean ability and energy, and of insatiable ambition, who had long aspired to leadership in the Reformed Church, and was not too scrupulous as to the means he employed or the associates with whom he joined to attain his ends. Even his ablest colleague in the cause of orthodoxy at length pronounced him a miserable hypocrite, who was willing to sacrifice the good of the church to his personal ambition.[1] He had early attached himself to the Reformed cause, and had for a time been chaplain to Jan Bonar, its most prominent patron in Little Poland. Later, while minister at Niedźwieź, twenty miles north of Kraków, he had alienated his patron Stadnicki by aggressively taking sides against Stancaro, and had therefore been forcibly ejected from his pulpit in 1560. He bitterly complained of this to the synod, and sought their aid and comfort. His ambition for leadership in the church had already led him to oppose

[1] Sarnicius, ille hypocritulus, qui ambitione sua conturbat ordinem bonum et ecclesias, etc. Thretius to Bullinger, Feb. 21, 1570, Wotschke, *Briefwechsel*, p. 314. Lismanino had years before said of him, Ambitione corruptus turbat ecclesias. Lismanino to Wolph, Apr. 28, 1563, Wotschke, *op. cit.*, p. 180. But while in the controversy that follows, factors of ambition, jealousy and rivalry are conspicuous on the surface, it was fundamentally a conflict of radically different theological principles involving questions of freedom, reason and tolerance in religion.

the vote by which Lismanino was invited to come from Switzerland.[2] He continued to be jealous of Lismanino's superior influence in the church,[3] and when in the summer of 1561 Czechowicz was sent by Radziwiłł to Switzerland, Sarnicki sent by him a letter opening correspondence with Bullinger; and he not long afterwards wrote one currying favor with Calvin, and a second one to Bullinger, in the rôle of a champion of orthodoxy against Biandrata and Lismanino, unjustly blaming the latter for introducing Biandrata to the Polish churches.[4] He also enlisted the cooperation of Jakob Silvius (Leśniowolski), a minister of kindred nature with his own,[5] who had already been compelled before the synod to retract, as unfounded, charges that he had made against Lismanino; and these two now induced two others to join them in signing a letter to Calvin containing, as though in the name of the synod, a confession that did not at all represent the views of the majority.[6] Hearing of this, the lawful officers of the Kraków synod wrote Calvin asserting their orthodoxy, and warning him against unauthorized letters of private persons;[7] while Lismanino wrote at length to allay the suspicions with which his enemies had sought to poison Calvin's mind.[8] 'Errare possum,' he humbly wrote Wolph, 'haereticus esse non possum.'[9]

In the meantime, while Biandrata's standing in the church was pending, Sarnicki was busier than ever. Instead of attending the synod at Kraków in December, 1561, at which the alleged heresies of Lismanino and Biandrata were to be examined, he went on a journey, ostensibly to his old home in Red Russia, but really on a hurried visit to Italy in order to enlist the aid of Christopher Tretius (Trecy) in the interest of the orthodox cause in Poland. Tretius[10] was a young scholar of

[2] *Lasciana*, pp. 413, 523. Lubieniecius, *Historia*, p. 58.

[3] *Lasciana*, p. 552.

[4] Sarnicki to Calvin, Sept. 1, 1561, to Bullinger, Sept. 28, Lismanino to Calvin, Dec. 14, to Wolph, Dec. 28, Calvin, xviii, 672; Wotschke, *Briefwechsel*, p. 129; Calvin, xix, 173; Wotschke, *Briefwechsel*, p. 142.

[5] Ambitiosi et turbulenti ingenii homine, Lismanino to Bullinger, Dec. 14, 1561, Wotschke, *Briefwechsel*, p. 142.

[6] Lismanino to Wolph, Nov. 23, 1563, Calvin, xx, 189; same to Calvin, Dec. 14, 1561, Calvin, xix, 171. Lismanino accused Sarnicki of usurping the title of pastor of the Kraków church, Lismanino to Bullinger, Dec. 14, 1561, Wotschke, *Briefwechsel*, p. 141.

[7] cf. letters of Dec. 13, 1561, Calvin, xix, 166–170.

[8] Lismanino to Calvin, Dec. 14, 1561, Calvin, xix, 171.

[9] Lismanino to Wolph, Dec. 28, 1561, Wotschke, *Briefwechsel*, p. 145.

[10] cf. Wotschke, *Thretius*.

great promise who had been sent abroad for two years of advanced study in preparation for a career as leader of education in the Reformed Church in Poland.[11] He was then at Padua, but he readily joined in Sarnicki's plan for inducing the Swiss theologians to work on the Polish nobles, through letters, to counteract the threatening heresy.

While these moves were being made in the background, Biandrata prepared his confession as previously voted,[12] and presented it to the next synod at Xiąż in March, 1562. It was held over nearly a month for consideration; for though some looked upon it as insincere, yet it was so scriptural and plain that they could find nothing to lay hold on, and after long discussion even they were forced reluctantly to accept it.[13] Biandrata was thus officially exonerated from suspicion. The synod promised to try to reconcile Calvin, while Biandrata on his part promised to consent to all that Calvin and the Polish churches should agree upon, if only permitted to confess that Christ is the Son of God most high and eternal, and if Calvin himself would speak of the one God simply and without any explanation; but if this did not seem good to Calvin, let him at least promise him this: that he would adhere to the simple word of God and the Apostles' Creed, and would retract his recently published letter to the Palatine of Wilno, prefixed to his Commentary on the Acts.[14] All this was agreed to; and that Biandrata thus demanded of Calvin concessions implying that they were treating on even ground eloquently shows how sure he felt of overwhelming support from the churches. Of no less significance is the resolution also

---

[11] He became founder and only Rector of the Calvinist school at Kraków, and was very influential in bringing about the Union of Sandomir in 1570. cf. Jan Czubek, 'Krzysztof Trecy,' *Reformacja w Polsce*, i (1921), 35–42. He was ennobled in 1580, and died in 1590.

[12] Lubieniecius, *Historia*, p. 129.

[13] At the synod of Pińczów, April 2, 1562. The confession was identical with the one presented at Pińczów in January, 1561. cf. *Lasciana*, p. 539; Lubieniecius, *op. cit.*, p. 130; Zachorowski, *Synody*, p. 215. For the text of the confession, with a confutation by Flacius, cf. H. P. C. Henke, *Georgii Blandratae Confessio Antitrinitaria*, etc. (Helmstadii, 1794). But Heberle doubts that the confession published by Henke is the same as that presented at Pińczów. cf. his article in *Tübinger Zeitschrift für Theologie*, 1840, 4es Heft, p. 176, n. 2.

[14] Pollicitus est in omnia consentire, quae a Calvino et Ecclesiis Dei fuerint conclusa: dummodo Calvinus ei permittat, ut confiteatur Illum esse Filium Dei altissimi et aeterni, et ipse de Uno Deo simpliciter loquatur sine aliqua interpretatione; quod si haec Calvino non placuerint, saltem ei hoc polliceatur, mansurum se in simplice verbo Dei et Symbolo Apostolico: et revocet epistolam suam tunc recens editam, praefixam Actis Apostolorum ad Palatinum Vilnensem. Lubieniecius, p. 130; Zachorowski, *Synody*, p. 215.

adopted at this synod: that none of the ministers in his teaching should use philosophical terms about the Trinity, essence, generation, or the method of proceeding, which are all foreign to the word of God; but that each should confine himself to the terms used by the Prophets and Apostles, and the Apostles' Creed.[15]

With this complete vindication of Biandrata by the Synod, and with the adoption of this direction for the ministers, the church was apparently committed to a position granting practically all that he desired, on a platform of simple, undogmatic, scriptural and apostolic Christianity, with generous tolerance of differences of view as to non-essential and speculative details, and primary emphasis on the cultivation of truly Christian life and character.[16] Had this fair regulation been complied with in good faith, a long step would have been taken toward the goal of full tolerance in religion, and all might have enjoyed freedom of conscience while pursuing the main end of the church as 'a national society for the promotion of goodness'; and the fatal division, which was first to weaken the Protestant movement in Poland just as its success seemed all but secured, and was eventually to bring it to the verge of complete ruin, might have been avoided.

But Sarnicki had other designs in mind. He had by now been elected an Elder in the church, and having no regular post, and being disappointed in a plan for a position as teacher at Kraków, he cast covetous eyes on the pulpit of the large congregation there, which worshiped in the suburban garden of Jan Bonar,[17] Governor of the castle, and of which Gregory Paulus,[18] also an Elder in the church, was now the minister.

[15] ibid.

[16] The letter that Biandrata, as Elder of the church, addressed immediately after this synod to the Lublin church upon the settlement of a new minister, makes no reference to controversial doctrines, but lays stress upon unselfish devotion to the church, the maintenance of strict discipline in the lives of members, and the avoidance of controversy. Zachorowski, op. cit., p. 213 f.

[17] cf. Zachorowski, op. cit., p. 219. Bonar's residence was just outside the Mikołaj gate, where the Carmelite cloister now stands. Lubieniecius (p. 131) is mistaken in placing meetings of the congregation in the castle itself.

[18] On Paulus, cf. Józef Maxymilian Ossoliński, Wiadomości, iv, 484–511; Theodor Wotschke, 'Gregorius Pauli', Zeitschrift für Brüdergeschichte, xiv (1920), 1–32; Konrad Górski, Paweł. His proper name in the vernacular is as given by Górski, latinized as Paulus. The geographical cognomen Zagrobelny is sometimes added. Brzeziny, his birthplace, was a little town some 75 miles southwest of Warsaw. An early misunderstanding led to the use of the incorrect form Pauli, which was widely used until within a generation; and this in turn led to the assumption that he was an Italian, and that the sometimes

Paulus scrupulously observed the regulation adopted at the Pińczów synod in April, avoiding scholastic terms in his sermons, and preaching simply of one God the Father, his Son Jesus Christ, and his Holy Spirit. But Sarnicki, taking advantage of his office as Elder, and of the credit that his rank as a nobleman gave him, began to spread rumors that Paulus was not sound in the faith, and to blame Lismanino for the fact.[19] Not content with this, he went to Bonar and other nobles of great influence in the church with charges of heresy against Paulus. Bonar, desiring to avoid public scandal, arranged a friendly conference between the two at his house at Balice,[20] and when this achieved nothing, yet other meetings to the number of four in seven weeks were held in July and August. The most important of these was at Rogów, July 20, which both ministers and nobles from the vicinity of Kraków attended in considerable numbers. At a synod at Pińczów August 18 Paulus defended his teaching eloquently on purely scriptural grounds, while Sarnicki appealed to ecclesiastical tradition, and pressed his charges that Paulus was heretical as to the Trinity, and maneuvered him into a clear assertion of the strict unity of God. The result of the debate was inconclusive; but the sympathies of the company were plain, from the unanimous vote still to observe the rule adopted at Pińczów in April: that scholastic terms be avoided in preaching. The synod also adopted a brief confession to be sent to the Swiss and the Strassburg churches as a witness of their orthodoxy.[21] Sarnicki protested in vain, but at

---

added adjective Brzezinensis or Bressinensis meant that he was of Bressana or perhaps Brescia. cf. Ossoliński, *Wiadomości*, iv, 484 n. He was born about 1525 of humble family (Sarnicki taunts him as being *aliquis obscuri nominis vir* — Lubieniecius, p. 138), and during seven years' study at Kraków proved himself an able scholar. His letter to Calvin (xviii, 209–211) gives interesting details of his life. After a short period of further study at Königsberg, and of teaching at Poznań, and a brief stay at Wittenberg, he returned to lead a reform movement in his native town. From the first organization of the Reformed churches in Little Poland he was one of their most active and trusted leaders. He was chosen Elder in 1556 and 1561, and in 1557 he became the first minister of the large Reformed congregation at Kraków. His evolution in the direction of liberal theology began with the impression made on him by Gonesius in 1556, and he was undoubtedly much influenced by Biandrata. From the departure of Biandrata and Lismanino in 1563 to the advent of Faustus Socinus in 1579, he was the most influential figure in the Minor Reformed Church.

[19] The main source for this controversy is Lubieniecius, lib. ii, cap. 7, briefly supplemented by reports of synods in Zachorowski, *Synody*, pp. 216–218, and by Sarnicki's letter to Tretius, Calvin, xix, 572–580; also well digested by Górski, *op. cit.*, pp. 88–106.

[20] For the doctrinal views which the followers of Biandrata defended here, cf. Calvin, xix, 573 f.   [21] cf. Wotschke, *Briefwechsel*, p. 153 f.

length yielded and promised to keep the peace, though he soon persuaded Bonar to put Paulus under examination for heresy. In what
followed, Sarnicki grew more aggressive and abusive until it was
obvious that his real purpose was to bring about a division in the church.
To put an end to the disorder a general synod was called at Pińczów
in August. Sarnicki promised to be present, but evidently realizing
how strong was the sentiment against him, he failed to appear, and
instead took up plans for a new movement. Nor would he attend a
later synod at Pińczów in November, where however Biandrata, Alciati
and Gentile were all in attendance.[22]

While this controversy was at its height an event took place which
created a profound sensation. Lightning struck the ball at the top of
the steeple of Trinity church at Kraków. Those opposing the doctrine
of the Trinity were disposed to take this as a sign that Heaven had set
the seal of approval on their cause; the Catholics, however, interpreted
it as a sign of divine anger at the current blasphemies.[23]

Less than a month after the August synod at Pińczów, Bonar suddenly died. He had already become so disgusted over the quarrel in
the church that three days previously he had refused to provide it
longer with a place of worship, and ordered the benches removed.
Hereupon Sarnicki, seeing that a large number had come to town for
Bonar's funeral,[24] seized the occasion to gather a few ministers and

---

[22] Zachorowski, op. cit., p. 218 f; Lubieniecius, p. 144.

[23] cf. the contemporary account in its apparently primitive form in Zachorowski, op.
cit., p. 218. The event furnished fertile soil for the growth of legend. A little later it was
said that the lightning threw down the ball into the street at noon of the very day on
which the final schism took place (ibid., p. 234). Later yet it was added that this took
place on Trinity Sunday, 1562, while Paulus was preaching against the dogma of the
Trinity (Sandius, Bibliotheca, pp. 43, 187, 213). Later still the legend runs that this took
place while Paulus was preaching in Trinity church, Kraków, at noon of Trinity Sunday
(S. F. Lauterbach, Ariano-Socinismus olim in Polonia, etc., Franckfurt, 1725, p. 123 f);
id., Fraustädtisches Zion (Leipzig, 1711), p. 51, citing Hottinger, Helvetische Kirchen-
Gesch. iii, 92. But Trinity Sunday, 1562, fell on May 26, some time before the controversy
broke out; and Paulus can never have preached in Trinity church, which was always in
the hands of the Dominican fathers. cf. Max. Ossoliński, Rozmaitości Naukowe, (Kraków, 1831), i, 30 and n. It is noteworthy that a similar omen is reported to have taken
place in Transylvania, cf. Fontes Rerum Transylvanicarum (Budapest, 1913), ii, 163; and
that, at a time when the question of the Trinity was under discussion between Calvinists
and 'Arians', Trinity church at Lublin was also struck by lightning on Trinity Sunday and
burned down just as it was being dedicated (Lauterbach, op. cit., p. 124; Sandius,
Bibliotheca, p. 188). One is tempted to wonder whether all these tales do not embody
much more myth than fact.

[24] Oct. 16; he had died Sept. 17; Calvin, xix, 575.

others of his faction, and with them to form an opposition synod of his own, at which he persuaded some of them to sign a confession that he had prepared. Paulus, though in town, was not invited to the meeting, was declared a heretic, and was deprived of his pulpit without a hearing, while Sarnicki was put in his place as minister of a new congregation of seceders. Those present subscribed a confession affirming the three ancient creeds, and expressly condemning the doctrine of Servetus, Gribaldi, Gonesius, Gentile and Alciati.[25] It is evident that in this high-handed proceeding Sarnicki felt confident that though he might be outvoted in the regular synod, yet he might count on the support of a majority of the local congregation, for Paulus offered no resistance. Instead, a new place of worship was at once offered his followers in the residence of the noble Stanislas Cikowski,[26] and his ministry continued without interruption. Sarnicki had his new confession distributed from house to house in Kraków, and even had it sold before the very door of Paulus's new meeting-place, thus seeking to win further adherents. Of the few ministers that took his side, the chief was a somewhat notorious Lawrence Discordia, who had previously been suspended from the ministry for his scandalous life.[27] Besides him, Sarnicki called to his side two other ministers of tarnished reputation, Silvius who, like Sarnicki, had formerly been chosen Elder but had not been retained in office, and Gilowski.

While these things were going on in the opposing synods of the two factions, other things were being done behind the scenes. On the one hand, while the seceders were writing full details to the leaders of the churches in Switzerland, to whom they looked for aid in their fight against the rising heresy, Paulus also wrote stating and defending the views he was maintaining against Stancaro.[28] On the other hand,

---

[25] Calvin, xix, 578–580.

[26] The site was at the southwest corner of Spitalna and St. Thomas Streets, where St. Thomas's church now stands.

[27] His vernacular name was Wawrzyniec Niezgoda z Przasnysza. The Latin equivalent of Niezgoda is Discordia, by which name he was generally called, as descriptive of his trouble-making disposition. He had once been court preacher, distinguished for his eloquence, but was undisciplined in mind and will. As an insubordinate minister he had brought much confusion among the churches in Lithuania, defaming ministers and breaking promises, and for this he was called to account at synods in 1560, and was judged unworthy of the ministry. cf. *Lasciana*, pp. 497, 505 f; Zachorowski, *op. cit.*, p. 219.

[28] Sarnicki to Calvin, Oct. 6, 1562, Silvius to Calvin, Oct. 20, Calvin, xix, 570, 558; Paulus to the Zürich brethren, Sept. 24, Nov. 17, *id. op.*, xix, 540, 581. See also the important letter of Sarnicki to Tretius, (Nov.) 1562, *id. op.*, xix, 572–580.

Paulus, conscious of the sympathy of the great majority of the ministers, came out in print in November with a little book, *Tabula de Trinitate*,[29] the best known of his early works. It was intended as his contribution to the controversy with Stancaro, but it marked a turning-point in the controversy over the doctrine of the Trinity, for it offended the orthodox by emphasizing the three persons at the expense of the unity in the Divine Being, and it furnished Sarnicki with demonstrable proof of Paulus's doctrine. When Tretius besought Calvin to reply to this work, Calvin, vexed that the Polish churches had paid so little heed to his warnings against Biandrata, at first refused to comply with the request.[30] But early in the year he yielded to importunity and came out with a *Brevis Admonitio ad Fratres Polonos*, which he confirmed a little later by an *Epistola ad Polonos*.[31] Calvin saw in the *Tabula* a worse heresy than that of Stancaro, a revival of the tritheism of Gribaldo and Gentile which he had lately put down at Geneva.[32]

At just this time fuel was added to the flame by the arrival of Alciati, who at Biandrata's invitation had come from Switzerland late in 1562 and joined the other Italians at Pińczów. He was a man of great talents, learning and piety,[33] but was a much more open propagandist than Biandrata. He had drawn up some twenty theses on the Triune God, and had loaned them in confidence to his fellow-countryman Prosper Provana; but unauthorized copies were made and circulated, and precipitated fresh controversy.[34] In the course of the following year (1563), Gentile also arrived to join Biandrata and Alciati.[35] Gentile had evidently hoped that his doctrine might be acceptable in Poland, for he had already dedicated his *Antidota* to Sigismund Augustus; and as in controversy he was much more modest than Stancaro, he was a welcome ally in the struggle against him. But he had sharply attacked the

---

[29] The work is not extant, but its contents are to be inferred from the replies to it.

[30] Calvin to Tretius, xix, 607.

[31] Calvin, ix, 629–638, 641–650.

[32] See chapters xv, xvi, *supra*.

[33] So judged by Andreas Dudith, quoted in *Schicksale der polnischen Dissidenten* (Hamburg, 1768–'70), ii, 137.

[34] cf. Lubieniecius, *Historia*, p. 156 f. Ruar relates that when Alciati was staying at Kraków during this controversy he was in imminent danger of his life, being set upon by lawless students for being, as they said, an Arian. He declared that he was rather a Marian, and being asked what he meant by that he replied that he believed in Jesus Christ the Son of the living God and of Mary; and upon hearing that revered name they let him go. *v.* Martinus Ruar, *Epistolae Selectae*, p. 185, appended to Zeltner, *Crypto-Socin*.

[35] Trechsel, *Antitrinitarier*, ii, 344, errs in making him come with Alciati.

Athanasian Creed (which he ridiculed by calling it Satan-asian),[36] and his explanation of the Trinity made of it three eternal and distinct spirits, hence obvious tritheism. He made many converts, and had numerous followers in both Poland and Lithuania,[37] but before the end of the year it became unsafe for him to remain at Kraków, and he removed to Pińczów at the invitation of the liberal group there. Both Alciati and Gentile at once entered into the controversy with Stancaro, but like Biandrata, Lismanino and Paulus, controverted him only with a doctrine more heretical than his.

At the time of the Diet in 1563, at which the reformers were in the saddle, and ecclesiastical jurisdiction of the Bishops' courts was annulled,[38] Sarnicki went to Piotrków and won over several of the ministers that had gone thither with their patrons, and also took advantage of the opportunity to force the hand of the other side by means of a joint debate.[39] In this the cause of Paulus was so strongly maintained by several distinguished nobles and ministers, of whom some came out against the Trinity, that it was more than ever clear that the two parties must separate.[40] Sarnicki therefore proceeded to organize synods for Great Poland, and chose Discordia, despite his unsavory record, as Superintendent. He also urged the King to execute against Antitrinitarians the death penalty prescribed by a long obsolete decree of 1424.[41] During the winter and early spring the schism was industriously promoted, and when the Superintendent Cruciger suddenly died after preaching a farewell sermon at Secemin on Easter,[42] Sarnicki seized the occasion to make a coup. In greatest secrecy he joined with Discordia and others to call at Kraków a synod of his faction, not inviting any of the opposition, and secured the support of some of the noble patrons. The synod when held proved to be a fiasco,[43] but Lutomirski, as lawful Elder of the church, when he learned of the plan for

---

[36] cf. Gilbertus Genebrardus, *De S. Trinitate libri tres* (Paris, 1569), pref., p. vi.

[37] He was confuted at length, at Tretius's request, by Simler, *De aeterni Dei Filio*, as also by Aretius and Zanchi.

[38] Nov. 21, 1562 to March 23, 1563; cf. *Volumina Legum*, ii, 19.

[39] This debate should not be confused, as it sometimes is, with the more important one at Piotrków in 1565.

[40] cf. Lubieniecius, *Historia*, p. 152; Friese, *Kirchengesch.*, ii, 1, 348; Schomann's *Testamentum* in Sandius, *Bibliotheca*, p. 194; *Starożytności Polskie* (Poznań, 1852), ii, 182; Sarnicki to Bullinger, Jan. 23, 1863, in Wotschke, *Briefwechsel*, p. 164 and n.

[41] cf. *Volumina legum*, i, 38.

[42] April 11, 1563; cf. Lubieniecius, pp. 159-161.

[43] In ventum abiit nihil in ea actum est. Lubieniecius, p. 165.

it, at once called a synod of the whole church to extinguish the spreading fire, and denounced the so-called synods held by Sarnicki as spurious and unauthorized. The call was signed by the Elders and twenty-one other ministers, and was also sent to the brethren in Lithuania.[44]

Much as they might differ in opinion, the brethren that received the letters of Lutomirski were generally desirous of harmony in the church, and those in Lithuania and Podlasie were so indignant at what had been done that instead of waiting for the synod appointed for September they at once got permission from Radziwiłł to hold a synod in his town of Mordy in Podlasie on June 6. Despite its being the busy season in the fields, forty-two were present, many of whom vigorously opposed the doctrine of the Trinity, while others, less clear in their opinions, wished longer time for consideration. The following resolution was adopted and reported to Radziwiłł: 'Although we have been unable, on account of some weaker brethren, wholly to reject the word Trinity, yet we have for the most part abandoned the present misuse of it, so that now, being man's word and not God's, it is by many less valued than formerly.'[45] In striking contrast with the inflexible rule of orthodoxy to which it was opposed, this will be noted as another distinct step toward freedom of conscience and tolerance in expression in religion.

Though the liberal wing had thus far had an overwhelming majority in the regular synods, and the conservatives following Sarnicki had from the first been pitifully weak, unable to count on more than the smallest handful of ministers of influence,[46] yet the rift was steadily growing wider, and the conservatives were slowly gaining strength. Some of the ministers who, after wavering, had gone with the majority, were now returning to the safety of the fold, and Sarnicki had won influential support among the nobles living near Kraków. Lismanino made one last feeble attempt to stem a tide of doctrine which had now swept beyond his control, and at the same time to justify himself, by publishing a *Brevis explicatio doctrinae de sanctissima Trinitate* early

44 Lubieniecius, pp. 161–166.

45 "Vocabulum Trinitatis, et si non omnino rejicere potuimus propter aliquos infirmiores, maxima tamen ex parte praesenti abusu illud purgavimus, ut nunc, utpote verbum hominis et non divinum, minus valoris quam antea apud multos obtinuerit." cf. Lubieniecius, p. 167; Zachorowski, *op. cit.*, p. 220.

46 Sarnicki in November, 1562 can name only four; and Thénaud writes Calvin July 21, 1563, that all the best educated ministers are going over to Paulus. cf. Calvin, xix, 574; xx, 71.

in the year. But he had lost his influence, was broken in health and spirit, burdened with debt, and with stipend unpaid. After wavering about accepting an invitation from Heraklides, an adventurer who with Polish aid had lately overthrown the government of Moldavia and was establishing the reformed religion there, and about returning to Switzerland to vindicate his orthodoxy, he finally took his leave of the brethren at the synod at Mordy, and sought and found shelter and a pension at the court of Duke Albrecht at Königsberg, where his life ere long reached its tragic end.[47]

Ever since his vindication in the spring of 1561, Biandrata had been content to stand in the background. Though attending synods, he seems to have taken no active part. He apparently realized that in Paulus a skilful and aggressive leader had now arisen who could be trusted to do the work and take the blows. Moreover, as the influence of Calvin in Poland was on the increase, he may have felt danger threatening him for that reason. At all events, when Prince John Sigismund invited him early in 1563 to come to Transylvania as his personal physician, as he had been that of his Queen mother Isabella, he at once accepted a position where he might feel secure from attack, and might through the young Prince at the same time influence the development of the Reformation in that country. How effectively he did this we shall see in the next division of this history. Meantime, though Lutomirski was soon elected to succeed Cruciger as Superintendent of the church, Paulus became in effect its real spiritual leader. A new synod was held at Pińczów in September. The attendance was larger than ever before. The liberals were in the majority, and a confession acceptable to them was adopted.[48] Paulus now became ever more active in propaganda, publishing in the course of the following months several works in Latin for circulation abroad, and several in Polish from Radziwiłł's press at Nieśwież in Lithuania for missionary purposes at home.[49] To these Sarnicki replied in three sermons preached at War-

[47] He fell into an open well in the night and was drowned, probably in April, 1566 (not 1563, as Sandius and others following him say), perhaps during an epileptic seizure, to which he had long been subject. Legends about the event soon arose, but the gossipy account given in Wotschke, *Briefwechsel*, p. 269 f, is suspicious (cf. *id. op.*, p. 272). The statement of Sandius, *Bibliotheca*, p. 35, that the unfaithfulness of his wife was said to be a contributory factor, may have some basis.

[48] Text in Calvin, xx, 349 f.

[49] The most important of these were *Turris Babel* (only a fragment extant in Polish translation in Sarnicki's reply to it); *De Antichristi Deo* (unique copy at Dresden); *Carmen*

saw at the time of the Diet there in April, 1564, to which Paulus rejoined with an *Antidotum* no longer extant.

The year 1564 was a critical one in the history of our movement in
Poland. Those that had hitherto directed it were gone: Cruciger, who
as Superintendent had at least not opposed it, had died, Biandrata had
gone to Transylvania, and Lismanino had retired to Königsberg.
Paulus, now its most conspicuous figure, was arousing increasing hostility by the boldness of his attacks on the received doctrine, while the
theologians of Switzerland were making a wide impression by their
writings in defence of the orthodox faith. A Calvinist reaction was
beginning to gather force, in which Tretius, at last returned from
Switzerland furnished for the fight, was showing himself an able
leader, while Sarnicki retiring into the background was to be henceforth active chiefly with his pen.

Coincidently with this, a powerful Catholic reaction against the whole
Reformation was also beginning. Cardinal Commendone, an ecclesiastical statesman of great ability and practical wisdom, had come as Papal
nuncio to present the decrees of the lately adjourned Council of Trent
for the acceptance of the King, and to represent the Roman Church at
court. In close connection with him, Cardinal Hosius [50] was beginning
a long campaign to undermine Protestantism by bringing Jesuit fathers
into the country to establish schools and colleges which should form the
minds of the nobles of the next generation. Finally the King, who had
hitherto shown himself more or less favorable to the Reformation, was
under the influence of the Calvinists becoming increasingly hostile to
Antitrinitarians as foes to any form of Christianity. Already on Christmas day in 1563 there had been an outbreak of hostilities between Cal-

---

ad Johannem Calvin (reprinted in Trechsel, *Antitrinitarier*, ii, 492–496); *Krótkie wypi-
sanie*, etc. (Brief account of the action taken about a true confession of faith, etc., at
Kraków and Pińczów in 1563); *O różnicach terazniejszich*, etc. (Of the present differences, i.e., what we are to understand, according to Holy Scripture, about the one God
the Father, etc.).

[50] Stanislas Hosius, born at Kraków 1504 of German parents from Baden named
Hosen, became Bishop of Ermland (Warmia) in East Prussia 1551, and Cardinal 1561.
He was twice President of the Council of Trent, and very high in favor at Rome, a man
of profound learning and lofty personal character, unqualified in his devotion to the
Church and in his fanatical zeal against all heretics, among whom he regarded Calvinists
as less pardonable than even Antitrinitarians. Under him Protestantism sensibly declined
in Poland. He died 1579. cf. Stanislaus Rescius, *D. Stanislai Hosii Vita* (Romae, 1587,
Kraków, 1879); Anton Eichhorn, *Der Ermländische Bischof und Cardinal Stanislaus
Hosius* (Mainz, 1854–'55); Hosius, *Opera*, (Coloniae, 1584).

vinists and their opponents at Warsaw so sharp that when the former complained to the King, he took their side and had Paulus's *Tabula* burned in the market-place, and forbade the printing of any Arian book at Kraków.[51]

Events that now followed in the struggle of the orthodox Calvinists against the Pinczovians were not a little influenced by political factors. For while a large majority of the lesser nobility, and nearly all the ministers, had gone over to Paulus, leaving Sarnicki but a very small and weak following among the clergy, most of the powerful nobles in Little Poland remained orthodox and were strongly represented in the Senate, in which there now remained only one or two lay Catholics, and no Antitrinitarians at all. The way therefore seemed clear for the orthodox to get their opponents suppressed by the secular power, even if they could not be overcome by argument; and in this plan they counted on the support of the Catholics, whom they would be glad to have held responsible for any persecutions that might follow. At the Diet at Warsaw (April, 1564) Tretius had indeed already got a promise from the King that he would banish the heretics, as he called them, or at least the foreign ones; though his plan had been thwarted by Hosius.[52] Of late, however, Paulus had grown increasingly aggressive, and it was even reported that a Calvinistic official at Kraków planned his arrest, but had been unable to lay hands on him.[53] When the next Diet met at Parczów in midsummer, 1564, therefore, Tretius was stirred up to renew his efforts to get all Antitrinitarians proscribed from the realm. The King was willing enough, but Commendone and Hosius, more far-sighted, brought to his attention that this would not only strengthen the Calvinists (whom Hosius considered more guilty than their opponents) by disposing of their chief rivals, but would also imply that since only Antitrinitarians were proscribed all other Protestants were approved. They strongly urged that all the sects should be proscribed without exception, but if not, that they should all be left to waste their strength in mutual quarrels rather than spend it in opposing Rome, according to the proverb, *Bellum haereticorum pax est Ecclesiae.* The

---

[51] cf. Zemlinus to Bullinger, March 19, 1564, in Wotschke, *Briefwechsel*, p. 220; *id.*, *Thretius*, pp. 31–33.

[52] In 1563 the King had refused to issue a decree against foreign heretics as urged by the Catholic synod. cf. Zakrzewski, *Powstanie i wzrost*, p. 186.

[53] cf. G. F. Commendone, *Pamiętniki o dawnej Polsce* (Memoirs of ancient Poland), Wilno, 1847, i, 164.

King saw great danger to the State if he attempted to banish all Protestants, numerous as they now were. A compromise measure was therefore arrived at, and the so-called Edict of Parczów was issued on August 7, decreeing that all foreign apostates from the Catholic faith who
had taken refuge in Poland and were in any way spreading any new
doctrine should be proscribed from the realm by October 1, and if found
thereafter should be taken and treated as criminals. A second edict was
appended to this, forbidding natives of inferior status to let themselves
be led astray by any strange doctrine, especially the antitrinitarian.[54]

When the attempt was made at Poznań to enforce the edict against
the Bohemian Brethren as foreigners, of whom there was a large number in Great Poland, such great opposition was made that the King
weakened, and having not long before accepted their confession as
sufficiently orthodox, he issued a declaration that the edict was meant
to apply only to Antitrinitarians.[55] At Kraków the Castellan Myszkowski was too fanatical a Calvinist to enforce the decree against any
of his own brethren. The Antitrinitarians planned also to protest, but
since they themselves as natives did not fall under the edict, they decided to wait. Now that Biandrata and Lismanino had already left the
country, the only persons actually to feel the force of the edict were
Alciati and Gentile, who had been in the country a year or two, and
Ochino who had but recently arrived.[56] Gentile returned to Switzerland

---

[54] . . . mandamus ut omnes extranei, qui propter religionem ex aliis regnis vel dominiis,
huc ad nos profugerunt, et qui ab universali Christiana fide separati, novam qualemcunque
doctrinam circa fidem, qua privatim, qua publice, in suis caetibus, et qua verbo, qua
scriptis tradunt, hi omnes ad summum post festum S. Michaelis tertio die, ex omnibus
nostris dominiis excedant. Quos nos jam vigore hujus decreti nostri ex nostris terris
proscribimus, et proscriptos esse volumus, denuntiantes id unicuique illorum, quod ubi-
cunque quispiam illorum visus abhinc, aut inventus fuerit, is ubique ab officio nostro
capitaneali capi et judicari, aeque ac alius malefactor puniri debet. Latin version in G. C.
Ancuta, *Jus plenum religionis Catholicae* (Vilnae, 1719), pp. 71–77; Polish original
(*ibid.*) pp. 65–71; also in *Braterskie napomnienie ad Dissidentes in religione* (a fraternal
admonition, etc.) (1546), pp. 8–10; Friese, *Kirchengesch.*, ii, 352. On the edict, cf. also
Commendone, *op. cit.*, ii, 101; Stanisław Karnkowski, *Epistolae virorum illustrium* (Cracoviae, 1578), p. 12 f, 28–30; Zakrzewski, *Powstanie*, pp. 186–188, 271–273; Eichhorn,
Hosius, ii, 221 f; Teodor Wierzbowski, *Jakób Uchański, arcybiskup Gnieźnieński* (J. U.,
Archbishop of Gniezno) Warszawa, 1895, p. 408 f.

[55] cf. Hosius, *Opera, ep.* 72, p. 219.

[56] For whatever reason, Giorgio Negri remained in the country (unless indeed he was
now in Lithuania), and was present at the debate at Piotrków the following year, where
he was objected to for Secretary as being under the ban by the Edict of Parczów; nor was
Statorius disturbed. cf. Zachorowski, *Synody*, p. 222.

to suffer death for his faith, as we have seen in a previous chapter.[57] Alciati went at first to Moravia [58] but ere long to Danzig, where he lived, probably practicing as a physician, until 1573 or later.[59] Ochino, who had been in Poland since May, preaching to the Italians at Kraków, retired to Pińczów for a time, but could not be persuaded to accept the shelter offered by noble friends. Obeying the edict, he went to Moravia, where he very soon died. No other person is known to have been immediately affected by the Edict of Parczów; but nearly eight years later, when the vigilant Tretius discovered that Adam Neuser, a religious fugitive from Heidelberg, was preaching to the antitrinitarian congregation at Śmigiel, he invoked the edict against him, and Neuser sought safety in immediate flight.[60]

Though concrete results of the edict were thus not serious, yet the Antitrinitarians apparently felt that it suggested caution, for they dared hold no further synod that year.[61] Yet they were not broken in spirit. Paulus's pen was more active than ever, and his writings were supplemented by those of others;[62] while Sarnicki replied to these in a work which, adopting a term recklessly employed in controversy by Stancaro, established the name Arian as the designation of any that were heretical in their doctrine of God and Christ, however wide the difference between their view and that of Arius himself.[63] The name was not fairly given, but it served its purpose of identifying its objects with the most

[57] cf. p. 235 f, *supra*.

[58] Pascal, *Alciati*, p. 41 f.

[59] cf. Ruar, *Epistolae*, p. 185. The legend that he went to Turkey and became a Mohammedan probably rests on a mistaken interpretation of a statement attributed to Gentile during his trial at Bern, relating to Alciati's Unitarian beliefs, which had gone beyond Gentile's tritheism. cf. Wigand, *Servetianismus*, p. 89 a; Beza, *Epistolae*, p. 332; Marek Wajsblum, 'Dyteiści Małopolscy' (The Ditheists of Little Poland), *Reformacja w Polsce*, v (1928), 41 n.

[60] *v. supra*, p. 260 f. The banishment of Christian Francken in 1585 as a foreigner publishing a book against the Trinity should also be charged to this edict.

[61] In face of the contemporary record to this effect (cf. Zachorowski, *op. cit.*, p. 221), Wotschke's unsupported reference to a large synod on November 11 (*Reformation*, p. 211) must be regarded with suspicion. It may be a confusion with some synod of the Calvinists.

[62] cf. Wawrzyniec Krzyszkowski, *Świętego Justyna Filozofa Rozmowa z Tryfonem Żydem* (Dialogue of St. Justin the Philosopher with the Jew Trypho) (Nieśwież, 1564); Jan Kazanowski, *Na upominanie Jana Kalwina do braciey Polskiey . . . krótka odpowiedź* (Brief reply to John Calvin's Admonition to the Polish Brethren), Nieśwież, 1564.

[63] Sarnicki, *Collatio in qua aperte demonstratur blasphemias Gregorii Bresinensis, quondam Cracoviensis ministri, adeo conformes esse in triginta nempe articulis doctrinae Arii, ut ovum ovo non sit similius* (1565).

hated heretics of the early Church, and in Poland it is to-day still applied to those that later were better known as Socinians.

The quarrel in the Reformed Church had thus far been one promoted by theologians, and it related chiefly to more or less disputable theological questions, having little enough bearing on Christian character or Christian civilization. It was coming, however, to have other bearings, which those prominent in the State could appreciate even if the spiritual leaders of the Church did not. There were among the Protestant nobles not a few whose old friendship with one another, notwithstanding their differences in matters of religious belief, remained unimpaired, and who realized the importance at this time of maintaining the Protestant ranks unweakened by internal quarrels. It was expected that at the next Diet the decrees of the Council of Trent, which at Parczów had been presented to the King, would be offered for the acceptance of the Diet, and the question thus be settled whether or not the long desired national council should be held, to undertake a thorough reform of abuses in the Church in Poland. In the hope of creating a solidly united Protestant front, therefore, to oppose the lately reviving power of the Catholics, some of these, following the initiative of a leading Antitrinitarian, Jerome Filipowski, and with the approval of the King who, in the face of an impending war with Russia, also was anxious to see harmony restored among his subjects, arranged for a debate of outstanding questions, to be held at the time of the coming Diet, in the hope that differences might be adjusted.[64] This was in no proper sense a synod of the church, as it is often called, but simply a carefully arranged debate between members chosen from each side, who had come together at Piotrków for the annual Diet, January 1 to April 30, 1565.

The meetings were held at the residence of Jan Firley, Palatine of

---

[64] The sources for this debate are *Colloquium Piotrkowskie* (Kraków, 1566), edited by the four disputants on the Calvinist side; an account by an Arian writer, first published by Zachorowski, *Synody*, pp. 221–229, reprinted in *Humanizm i Reformacja w Polsce* (Humanism and Reformation in Poland), ed. Chrzanowski i Kot (Lwów, 1927), pp. 419–423; Lubieniecius, *op. cit.*, pp. 201–207. Briefer account in Gilbertus Genebrardus, *De Trin.*, 8 pp. in preface; slightly condensed reprint in Antonius Possevinus, *Atheismi Lutheri, Melanchthonis . . . Arianorum et aliorum nostri temporis haereticorum* (Vilnae, 1586), pp. 55–60; and in his (same work under another title) *De sectariorum nostri temporis atheismis* (Coloniae, 1586), pp. 47–51; Stanislaus Rescius, *De atheismis et phalarismis Evangelicorum* (Neapoli, 1596), pp. 146 f. English account in Wallace, *Antitrin.*, ii, 184–187.

Lublin, and leader of the Protestants.[65] The debates occupied five sessions, held intermittently during two weeks in March, mostly in the afternoon or late evening, when the Diet was not sitting. Each side chose three or four disputants, a secretary, and four prominent noblemen as umpires, of whom one was to act as Moderator, to preside on alternate days. Rules of procedure were drawn up with great care, in the interest of peace and good order. All points to be discussed were to be presented in writing; speakers were bound to express themselves clearly, without rhetorical flourishes; and all was to be done in love, not in tumult. Any infraction of rules might after due warning be punished by exclusion from the meeting at the discretion of the Moderator. All was well meant, but trouble began almost at the start, when a Calvinist umpire proposed to open the debate with a prayer in the name of the Trinity, to which the spokesman for the other side objected as something in which they could not join. After a squabble the item was omitted, and the debate duly began.

It would not be greatly to the purpose to give a detailed report; indeed, the two earliest accounts are incomplete, and are more or less colored by the sympathies of the writers. The discussion followed three stages. The first concerned the Scriptures, which the Arians regarded as the only authentic source of Christian teaching; in the second, the appeal was to the early Fathers of the Church; in the third, it was to the testimony of Christian history. Each side tried to prove that its views were supported by these three witnesses, and to confute the interpretations and arguments of the other; and, radical as was the difference between the two in point of view and method of approach, each apparently began fully confident of being able to confute the other. The Calvinists seem to have taken the aggressive throughout, trying to expose their opponents as perverse heretics; while the latter tried to prove that the Calvinists laid their main emphasis on doctrines that had no support in the Scriptures nor in the writers of the early Church. The discussion ran at first on a calm and dignified plane as had been intended; but as it proceeded it became more angry, hot words were spoken, and there was increasing evidence of impatience and irritation. The Calvinists, emboldened perhaps by the strong support they had among the lay members of the Diet, held toward their opponents an overbearing attitude, which showed itself in terms of disrespect that

65 Commendone, *Pamiętniki,* ii, 122.

made the debate appear more like a conflict between sworn enemies than a conference of parties in the same camp seeking conciliation and willing to make mutual concessions. After various insulting expressions in the course of debate one of the Calvinist debaters so far forgot himself in the last session as to call his opponents Satans, blasphemers, and traitors to the country. They tried to get a verdict condemning the Arians, and inciting the nobles against them as enemies of the Christian religion, and were far more bitter against them than the Catholics themselves had been. At last the Calvinists, having made no headway in their attempt to convert their opponents, abruptly broke off the debate without giving notice,[66] and refused to have any further dealings with them.

What makes this debate significant in our history is the fact that it was the last serious attempt at harmony between the two wings of the Reformed Church. The schism had in fact already taken place when Sarnicki formed his first dissenting synod at Kraków three years before; but now it was recognized as final and complete, and the party led by Paulus from now on maintained its organization and held its synods without regard to the orthodox Calvinists. Henceforth no union of all Protestants was to be hoped for, still less a union of Protestants with Catholics in one reformed national Catholic Church. Hosius who, with the other Bishops, had done all in his power to prevent holding this debate at all, and had left Piotrków rather than be a witness to its heresies, now rejoiced at the issue of it. He perceived that Protestantism was beginning to disintegrate, and said with satisfaction, 'Now we shall hear no more of a national synod.' A more sinister result was not at once perceived. The Calvinist majority were now to use their influence for persecuting and suppressing their opponents through the power of the State, little anticipating that in two generations more the same weapon would be used against them. At the critical hour when the reformers needed all their forces united in the struggle with Rome, their blind, suicidal zeal against their brethren of more liberal beliefs alienated them, made them enemies, denied them the Christian name, and in the next year even all but secured for a time an edict of banishment against them, thus taking the first step toward digging their own grave.

[66] . . . lege lata non amplius de his controversiis faciendos sermones. Quin, ne quid injuriae deesset, nec conclusum illud ab se parti adversae communicarunt. Lubieniecius, *Historia*, p. 205.

The outcome of the debate was duly reported to the King, with whose consent it had been held, and he declared the case closed. Yet he seems even now not entirely to have abandoned hope of church union. For soon after the Diet at Piotrków he commanded his trusted Secretary Modrzewski [67] (Modrevius), who had long advocated measures of compromise, to collect all the various views as to the doctrine of the Trinity, and see if the warring parties could not be brought together. The result of his investigations fell into four extended theological tracts, which were presented to the King as written, and were at length published under the title of *Sylvae*. The manuscript when completed was sent to a Basel publisher to print. Tretius being at Basel and hearing of this, and knowing the liberal tendencies of the author, persuaded the printer to loan it to him for examination. He forthwith handed it over to the Zürich theologians that they might answer its arguments; but, being unwilling that such a book should ever see the light, he never returned the manuscript. When Tretius returned to Kraków, Modrzewski meeting him asked if he had seen the printer at Basel or knew anything of the book; whereupon Tretius shamelessly declared that he had seen neither book nor printer. The printer himself later revealed what had taken place. Fortunately Modrzewski had retained his draft and notes, and was thus able to reconstruct the work. It was then circulated widely in manuscript, but it was not until after the author's death that it was printed by the Antitrinitarians on their press at Raków as a valuable document in their cause.[68] Those that had the reading of the manuscript found it a book of great weight, and it called forth a careful controversial reply in Simler's work mentioned above,[69] the reply, singularly enough, for the reason explained in the preceding paragraph, being published more than twenty years earlier than the book replied to.

[67] He was born about 1503, and was elaborately educated abroad, a pupil and life-long friend of Melanchthon, and a man of the broadest humanistic culture. Though not an avowed Protestant, his sympathies were evidently with the liberal party in that camp. He had considerable influence on the early stages of the Reformation. cf. Ossoliński, *Wiadomości*, iv, 67–136; Kot, *Modrzewski*.

[68] In 1590. cf. Lubieniecius, *Historia*, p. 221 f; Sandius, *Bibliotheca*, pp. 36–38; Ossoliński, *Wiadomości*, iv, 112 f; Kot, *op. cit.*, p. 267 f.

[69] cf. *supra*, p. 315, n. 37.

CHAPTER XXIII

THE MINOR REFORMED CHURCH: ITS EARLY HISTORY; THE QUESTION OF BAPTISM

THE FRUITLESS CONFERENCE at Piotrków in 1565 between the two wings of the Reformed Church marked an important turning-point in the history of both the Polish Reformation and the antitrinitarian movement. It brought to completion that schism in the Reformed Church which began when Sarnicki in 1562 and 1563 formed seceding orthodox synods. With this, the orthodox reaction, against the liberal spirit that had been steadily spreading ever since the outbreak of the controversy with Stancaro, now came full circle. Henceforth the Calvinists steadily refused to have further association in synods with those of the liberal wing; nor would they from this time on give ear to any of the conciliatory approaches that continued for more than a generation to be made by them. For the reformation movement as a whole in Poland the schism was eventually to prove fatal; for at the very hour when its ultimate fate hung trembling in the balance, and when it needed its whole united forces in the struggle against the reviving power of Rome, the Protestants in their blind folly deliberately divided their camp and fell to fighting against each other. By demanding the acceptance of certain speculative dogmas as the thing of first and greatest importance in religion, they sacrificed upon the altar of dogma the chance of success for their whole cause. From this time on the history of Protestantism in Poland is therefore a record of progressive weakness, gradual decline, slow strangulation, and ultimate practical extinction at the hands of Rome.[1]

To the development of the Antitrinitarian movement, on the other hand, the separation from the orthodox Calvinists made a significant contribution. Emphasis was now transferred from criticism of traditional doctrines to the gradual formation of a new doctrinal system on a basis largely independent of tradition. Along with the freedom of thought and its expression in religion which the past few years had

[1] cf. Wotschke, *Reformation*, p. 213 ff.

asserted and so largely won, came a growing recognition of the claims of reason in religion and an ever wider and more broad-minded practice of tolerance between those that held conflicting views. It was this tolerance that in the years next following saved the movement from wreckage under striking differences of view within until, with the cultivation of Christian patience, harmony could be attained by the process of free discussion. Finally, when the strictly doctrinal questions that seemed most urgent had been brought to a state of comfortable equilibrium, the attention of the young church was largely transferred from Christianity as a doctrine to Christianity as a way of practical life, with main emphasis upon the application of the teachings of the New Testament, and especially of the Sermon on the Mount, to matters of personal character and conduct, and to the wider social problems arising in the State. The present chapter and those following will trace the development of this process in its various phases.

After Piotrków nothing remained for the liberal congregations in the Reformed body but to go their way alone. It can hardly be said that they seceded from the Calvinists, for they did not sever relations voluntarily. Indeed, they would have much preferred to continue in one undivided church in which room was allowed for differing doctrinal views to be held in a spirit of generous mutual tolerance, while all devoted themselves to promoting the ends that they had in common. Nor can they be said to have been excluded from the parent church by a dominant majority; for they formed in some respects the most important and influential element in it, and in the synods of the church in the years preceding the schism, the liberal contingent had steadily grown until they were themselves a very decisive majority.

The new church at first had no distinctive name. At their first synod after Piotrków the members are described in the extant records as 'the brethren in Poland and Lithuania who have rejected the Trinity.' [2] Their opponents, both Protestant and Catholic, usually called them (however inaccurately) Arians, and this name is the one still most commonly given them in Polish usage to this day; but they themselves preferred to be called simply Christians.[3] However, the official title of the church was the Minor Reformed Church of Poland. This title seems to imply that the Reformed Church from which they were now

[2] cf. Zachorowski, *Synody*, p. 229.
[3] cf. Brückner, *Różnowiercy*, p. 142, citing Czechowicz, *Rozmowy Christiańskie*, p. 13.

separated retained the larger number of members or of congregations;
though in effective strength and efficient leadership it was markedly
inferior to the Minor Church. Already two years before, Jean Thénaud, whom Calvin had sent to aid the reformed cause as teacher in
the academy at Pińczów, had written to his master that all the best
educated ministers in the church were going after Paulus;[4] and six
months after the schism at Piotrków Tretius wrote to Simler that the
affairs of the church were in no wise improved, and that its life was
quite demoralized.[5] Indeed, he wrote to Bullinger, the Arians continued so vigorous, and they had led so many of the ministers astray,
that the church was impoverished of superior ministers. However, the
orthodox excelled in numbers, and they had a great many of the nobles,
while the Arians had not a single member in the Senate, in which all
the (lay) members favored the orthodox. Yet the Arian opposition was
so strong and bitter than one must weep that the Christian cause, which
had seemed so prosperous, had come to such a wretched pass that one
knew not whether to have any hope of it.[6]

In such circumstances the orthodox, having failed to overcome their
opponents by methods of reasoning or persuasion, and seeing them on
the contrary steadily gain in strength and influence, resorted to methods
of force. Taking advantage of their predominance in the Diet and their
influence with high officials, they entered on a policy of persecution by
the civil power. From now on they sought with implacable bitterness
to crush 'Arianism' by every means within reach, and to this end
willingly joined with the Catholics or instigated them against their
opponents, little dreaming that the weapons now employed against
their enemies would next be used equally against themselves. The
members of the Minor Church on their part, finding themselves disappointed in their hopes that the whole reform movement would soon
be converted to 'the pure religion' as they understood it, devoted themselves intensively in their now restricted field to investigating the pure
truth of Christianity. They continued as before the schism to hold
synods, appoint ministers and general church officers, clear up any
unsettled questions of belief or practice, and in general to attend to
whatever matters concerned the welfare of their cause. Their con-

---

[4] Thénaud to Calvin, July 21, 1563, Calvin, xx, 71; cf. Sarnicki to Tretius, Nov. 1562, xix, 572.

[5] cf. Wotschke, *Briefwechsel*, pp. 245, 249.

[6] Tretius to Bullinger, Aug. 1, 1565, Wotschke, *Briefwechsel*, p. 248.

stituency included, besides a relatively large number of the ablest ministers that had sided with them in the Reformed Church before the schism, a large number of the lesser nobility, a few holders of high public offices, and a considerable contingent of commoners as well as not a few in humble life.

The one powerful magnate, who by his support and influence could have contributed incalculably to the progress of their cause, Prince Nicholas Radziwiłł, Palatine of Wilno and Chancellor of Lithuania, unfortunately for them died less than a month after the Diet at Piotrków. From early in the Reformation he had been its most active and powerful supporter in Lithuania. He had been a friend of Laelius Socinus, and patron of Biandrata and others in the liberal wing of the Reformed Church, and though he unmistakably favored the liberal tendencies in it, he had hoped to see the church remain an undivided body. But already in 1563 he was said to have driven from his large estates those clergy that did not agree with his views of the Trinity;[7] and upon his death Tretius declared that Radziwiłł had been infected with the Arian heresy, and by his patronage had in every way promoted the Arian cause.[8] Thus by the time of the schism at Piotrków the yoke of Calvinism had been largely shaken off among the Lithuanian churches, though it was still strong at Wilno, and there were ministers of both kinds both there and elsewhere.

It will be convenient at this point to interrupt our main narrative in order to carry through to the end the brief history of Antitrinitarianism in Lithuania. After Radziwiłł's death half the Calvinist ministers in the country, with Czechowicz at their head, are said to have gone openly over to 'Arianism,'[9] and his young nephew, Jan Kiszka,[10] soon did the same. Fifty ministers and 100 nobles followed his example.[11]

---

[7] cf. Commendone, *Pamiętniki* (July 6, 1563), i, 164; Seweryn Gołębiowski, *Czasy Zygmunta Augusta* (Times of Sigismund Augustus), Wilno, 1851, i, 171.

[8] cf. Tretius to Bullinger, Aug. 1, 1565, Wotschke, *Briefwechsel*, p. 248.

[9] Załęski, *Jesuici*, i, 183.

[10] Jan Kiszka of Ciechanowiec was son of the Lady Anna, sister of Radziwiłł (cf. Wotschke, *Briefwechsel*, p. 323, n. 2). As a youth he showed distinguished talents and fine character, and in 1563 he was sent to continue his studies at Basel (*id. op.*, p. 210), where he was a favorite pupil of Curioni and Castellio, for the latter of whom he erected a monument (*v. supra*, p. 196, n. 56), and was confirmed in the liberal spirit, from which his later residence at Zürich did not move him.

[11] Joseph Łukaszewicz, *Geschichte der reformirten Kirchen in Lithauen* (Leipzig, 1848), i, 20 f; cf. Grabowski, *Literatura*, p. 41.

Kiszka was proprietor of 70 cities and towns and some 400 villages,[12] and he transferred the Calvinist churches on his estates (in accordance with the custom of the time and land) to the 'Arians', or built them new ones, and provided them with a press at Łosk for publishing their works. He was already a patron and disciple of Gonesius at Węgrów.[13] The churches he patronized were especially numerous in the palatinates of Nowogródek and Brześć.[14] The Lithuanian churches in general, partly because of their remoteness and isolation from the churches in Poland, partly from factors in their local environment, became, as we shall see, extremely radical theologically, but remained correspondingly conservative as to social and political questions, though these too were much agitated by a strong minority. So long as Kiszka lived, they flourished; but when he died childless in 1592 the churches on his estates followed the fortunes of the estates themselves, and fell to his nearest relatives, his cousins the sons of Radziwiłł who since their father's death had become fanatical Catholics, and they were thus lost to Protestantism or had embraced Calvinism. A few of the antitrinitarian churches in the larger towns survived for a time, but many of the churches in Lithuania became extinct early in the seventeenth century, and the last of them perished in the Cossack war in 1654.[15]

We return now to the history of the Minor Church in Poland proper. Now that the vexed question of the Trinity had been largely disposed of, the members of the Minor Church were the more free to attend to other matters inviting discussion, and they therefore continued to meet in synods as though nothing had happened. Indeed, their Superintendent, Lutomirski, continued to be the same that they had had in the Reformed Church before the schism. Their first separate meeting was held June 10, 1565, at Brzeziny.[16] Though it might be difficult or im-

---

[12] cf. Sandius, *Bibliotheca*, p. 82; Łukaszewicz, *op. cit.*, i, 18, n. 27, mistakenly says 700 villages and towns.

[13] cf. Tretius to Wolph, Sept. 1, 1571, Wotschke, *Briefwechsel*, p. 346.

[14] cf. A. W. Koiałowicz, *Miscellanea rerum* (Wilno, 1550), p. 72.

[15] Skarga's complaint, cited from his *Synod Brzeski* (Synod of Brześć), Kraków, 1597, by Orest Lewicki, 'Socynjanie na Rusi' (Socinians in Red Russia), *Reformacja w Polsce*, ii (1922), 205, that there had been 800 congregations of the Arians in Lithuania, must be regarded as a gross overestimate.

[16] The sources are in Lubieniecius, *Historia*, lib. iii, cap. 3; Zachorowski, *Synody*, p. 229. There seems to be some uncertainty about the place. Lubieniecius, (p. 177), and Zachorowski (p. 229) both say Brzeziny in Kujawy; but Brzeziny is not in Kujawy, but in Łęczyca. Wotschke (*Thretius*, p. 48) takes Lubieniecius's term (Braesinia) to mean Brześć in Lithuania; but he later changes (*Reformation*, p. 221) to Brześć in Kujawy. Intrinsic

possible to pronounce which of the reformed congregations was the first definitely to adopt the new views, it may be confidently said that the synod of Brzeziny was the first assembly in which antitrinitarian congregations met as a separate body to consult for their common ends. This date may therefore be taken as that of the historical beginning of organized Unitarianism.

The occasion of the meeting was the pressing need of settling a disputed question as to baptism. To most persons to-day this subject may seem to be of trifling importance, but in the early Reformation it was almost universally considered vital. On the basis of New Testament teaching it was regarded as being, along with belief, essential to salvation, and a condition of the forgiveness of sins.[17] Moreover, the usage and tradition of centuries had made it the outward sign and seal of membership in the Christian community, without which one was regarded as virtually a pagan. Yet when the more liberal reformers began to examine the subject, it seemed to many of them that baptism implied previous repentance; and that infants, being as yet incapable of repentance, could not be said to have been really baptized at all; and that their eternal salvation was thus jeopardized. This was the general view of the Anabaptists, who therefore insisted that true baptism could be given only to regenerate adults; and that any that had been baptized in infancy should be rebaptized in mature life.

The origin of the Anabaptist movement in Poland is somewhat obscure. When it began to attract attention it was but natural to assume its connection with the fanatical and revolutionary Anabaptism of Münster and elsewhere in western Europe. Despite some superficial similarities of practice, however, there is no evidence of historical connection. Synods of previous years had repeatedly condemned the western type of Anabaptism, with its revolutionary tendencies and its loose moral practices; and the Polish Anabaptists regarded the term, when applied to themselves, as hostile and offensive,[18] and indignantly denied any association with the radical social movements in Germany and Holland. The movement that came to a head in 1565 seems therefore

---

probability would seem to favor the former, since the occasion of the synod especially concerned the Lithuanian brethren.

[17] v. Mark xvi. 16; Acts ii. 38.

[18] Lutomirski, Superintendent of the Minor Church, writing at the end of 1565 to the brethren at Wilno, deprecated the use of the name. cf. Lubieniecius, *op. cit.*, p. 179; Zachorowski, *loc. cit.*

rather to have come chiefly from independent study of the New Testament by ministers who were concerned to have the doctrines and usages of their churches conform as closely as possible to the New Testament standard; and it appears to have received its original impulse from Gonesius who, as we have seen,[19] at the synod of Brześć in 1558, attacked infant baptism as sanctioned by neither Scripture, the earliest Christian practice, nor reason.[20] His views were at the time almost universally condemned, but upon some they apparently made a lasting impression, and they quietly spread in both Lithuania and Little Poland; for within the next few years sporadic appearances of Anabaptist doctrines occurred in various places in both countries.[21] The movement now spread rapidly, and debates on the subject occupied nearly every synod, while even before the schism local synods at Wilno, Xiąż and Kościelec had voted not to baptize infants.[22] Thus after seven years of increasing discussion since Gonesius first brought the subject forward, infant baptism had in 1565 become the most prominent issue in the churches.

In the church at Wilno, Simon Żak (Zacius), the first Superintendent of the Lithuanian churches,[23] had already in 1559 sought to forestall trouble by publishing for the church a confession defending infant baptism; but now, after Radziwiłł's death, a fresh controversy on the subject arose between two ministers of the church, Martin Czechowicz [24] and Nicholas Wędrogowski, which became so aggravated that

[19] v. supra, p. 289.

[20] cf. Lubieniecius, op. cit., p. 144.

[21] As the hardy pioneers of this movement history has preserved (besides Gonesius and Piekarski in 1558, already mentioned) the names of Matthias Albin, minister at Iwanowice near Kraków; his friend, Jan Siekerzyński at Koryto, said to have been the first of those immersed in Poland; Stanislas Paklepka, minister at Lublin; Peter Pulchranin, Rector of a school at Bychawa, whom a noble, outraged at his administering immersion, attacked and had thrown into a pond, where he narrowly escaped drowning; Georg Schomann, minister at Xiąż, and its ablest champion, Martin Czechowicz, minister at Wilno. cf. Lubieniecius, op. cit., p. 176; Wengerscius, Slavonia, p. 537; Wajsblum, Dyteiści, p. 50.

[22] cf. Górski, Paweł, p. 185, citing Colloquium Piotrkowskie, p. E1.

[23] cf. Włodzimierz Budka, 'Szymon Zacius pierwszy Superintendent zborów Litewskich' (S. Z., first Superintendent of the Lithuanian Churches), Reformacja w Polsce, ii (1922), 288–295.

[24] Czechowicz, born of humble parents in 1532 at Zbąszyn on the western border of Poland, and originally designed for the Catholic priesthood, joined the Reformation while studying at Leipzig, and was accepted by Radziwiłł as one of the new Reformed ministers at Wilno, where he was so highly esteemed that Radziwiłł in 1561 sent him as his personal agent to investigate and report on the organization and workings of the Protestant churches in Switzerland (v. supra, p. 305). On his return journey he fell in with Gonesius, and was by him converted to Anabaptist views, of which he became an ardent

a new schism was threatened, this time among the Antitrinitarians themselves. To prevent such a misfortune, the synod above mentioned was convened at Brzeziny.[25] 32 of the ministers and 18 of the gentry were present. There was much discussion of baptism, but as many of the ministers felt as yet unprepared or not authorized to decide the question, action upon it was deferred for further consideration at a larger synod to be held at the end of the year. An outward form of reconciliation, however, was effected between the two ministers, both of whom had been shown to be at fault, as they were contritely to confess before their own church. As to baptism itself, it was resolved that they should be guided by the Holy Spirit, and that no one on either side should be forced against his conscience, but that they should dwell together in peace, refrain from using such invidious names as Anabaptist, and continue in fervent prayers to God until the next synod, when God of his mercy should show them the way.[26] Thus the leaders of the Minor Church had already come to realize the value of harmony in the church, and they henceforth emphasized the necessity for settling disputed questions in love and mutual respect. It was a long step toward that tolerance in religion which was to become one of the distinctive marks of their movement.

The interval before the adjourned synod was filled with preparations for it on both sides, and letters of propaganda flew back and forth, for it was realized that a crucial decision was to be made. The Lithuanians had complained of having so often to go to Poland to attend synods, whereas the Poles would not come to them. In order to accommodate them, therefore, the synod was appointed to meet at Węgrów, a town in Podlasie some forty miles northeast of Warsaw. The attendance

---

and lifelong advocate. Though disputes ensued with his Wilno colleagues, he retained Radziwiłł's confidence, and shortly before the latter's death dedicated to him a book on the subject, *Trzech dni rozmowa*, etc. (A three-days' discussion on infant baptism), first published in 1578. He was a thorough scholar, and besides a Polish translation of the New Testament published several books of importance in the history of our movement. He was, after Paulus, the most influential figure in the Minor Church until Socinus. cf. Bock, *Antitrinitar.*, i, 217–237; Łukaszewicz, *Geschichte*, ii, 95 ff; Brückner, *Różnowiercy*, pp. 239–280.

[25] Łukaszewicz, *op. cit.*, i, 19, follows the earlier authorities in placing it at Brzeziny in Kujawy, but differs from them in giving the date as Dec. 10, 1564 instead of June 10, 1565.

[26] Tretius, writing to Bullinger, Aug. 1, 1565 (Wotschke, *Briefwechsel*, p. 251), was in error in reporting: Conclusum est apud eos idque firmiter, ne pueri eorum baptizarentur, et quaedam alia fortasse et de rebaptizatione.

was large, with 47 ministers and 14 of the leading men and gentry present, besides commoners. The eminent Jerome Filipowski, Treasurer of the Palatinate of Kraków, who had been the leader of his party in the debate at Piotrków, was chosen to preside. A letter to the synod was read from the most noble Lady Anna Kiszka,[27] wife of the Palatine of Witebsk, mother of Jan Kiszka, and sister of Prince Nicholas Radziwiłł lately deceased; also from various other private members of the church unable to attend in person, as well as from churches and Elders of various districts. All manifested deep interest, and all earnestly begged that nothing be done contrary to Scripture, and that all care be taken to preserve harmony and charity, and to avoid quarrels and divisions.

The meetings began on Christmas day and lasted for six days, sessions continuing through the entire day without intermission.[28] The daily sessions opened with morning prayer, and the rest of the day was given over to discussion of the question of baptism: whether infant baptism were sanctioned by Scripture or not. Each one present gave his vote in turn as the Spirit moved him, and then discussion pro and con followed. The one side argued that baptism of believing adults is an ordinance commanded by Christ, and cited many passages from the Acts and the Epistles supporting their view, and added that there is nowhere in Scripture either command or example of infant baptism. If one looked to early Christian tradition, history and the writings of the early Fathers prove that in the Apostolic Age and the one next following infants were not baptized. The other side presented many arguments from modern writers defending their opinion, holding their ground and asking leave to baptize their little ones nevertheless. A few were undecided. Debate was long and warm, but at length it was agreed that since in matters of faith no one in the true church of God may lord it over another, nor be forced, each should enjoy freedom of conscience and be allowed to publish writings on the subject, provided nothing was said or written calculated to anger another or openly contrary to Christ's command. Thus (says the chronicler) they kept love inviolate by stipulating only that no one should do anything against

---

[27] Lubieniecius, op. cit., p. 179, seems to consider the Lady Kiszka and Anna Radziwiłł two different persons.

[28] For the sources, cf. Lubieniecius, Historia, pp. 179–189; Zachorowski, Synody, pp. 229–231.

the honor of God or burdening to conscience. Thus the practical question was harmoniously disposed of under the principle of mutual tolerance, although at the end only a small minority of eight continued to favor infant baptism.[29]

It was pointed out in course of the discussion that those that had been baptized in infancy could not regard themselves as really baptized. When on the other hand it was insinuated that opponents of infant baptism were followers of the revolutionary Anabaptists of Münster, they solemnly affirmed that as they had hitherto been sincerely obedient to the powers ordained of God, so they would in future, as a matter of conscience, take yet greater pains to this end. Despite their heated discussion, at the end they made mutual apologies for offence given or taken, and having forgiven one another they separated in love. This custom became almost a tradition, so often is it reported of later synods where sharp differences of opinion had been manifested.

The temperate conclusion reached at Węgrów may have been influenced by a letter from the Antitrinitarian churches in Transylvania written to those in Poland, doubtless at the instigation of Biandrata, who from a distance was watching with close attention the progress of the movement that he had done so much to guide in its first period, and who evidently cherished a plan for union between the churches that rejected the doctrine of the Trinity in the two countries; as well as also by a letter that he himself wrote to Paulus, largely on the doctrinal aspect of the desired union, but incidentally expressing concern lest a squabble over a subordinate matter like baptism should stand in the way of firmly establishing the primary article about the being of God.[30] Biandrata urged the churches not to split over baptism, which was not necessary to salvation, though it might be retained if it were found helpful, and which was practiced in ancient times only in the case of converts from Judaism or paganism.

A full and conciliatory account of the proceedings and conclusion of the synod, written by Lutomirski, who before the schism had succeeded

---

[29] cf. Żytno to Wędrogowski, Dec. 29, 1565, Wotschke, *Briefwechsel*, p. 251, n. 2. It is obvious that this conclusion did not, as historians have often stated, condemn infant baptism, but merely allowed the minority generous freedom of conscience, practice and speech in the matter.

[30] The former letter is summarized in Zachorowski, *op. cit.*, p. 281 (cf. Lubieniecius, *op. cit.*, p. 189 f); the latter, Biandrata to Paulus, Nov. 30, 1565, is given in full by Wotschke, *Reformation*, pp. 263–268.

Cruciger as Superintendent, and had continued in office in the Minor Church, was sent to the Wilno brethren in the name of the synod. Budny and Falconius, two ministers well known at Wilno, were also sent in order if possible to pacify the brethren there.[31] Their mission was unsuccessful, for the spirit of Lutomirski's letter was not reciprocated. A sharp reply to it was sent, calling Anabaptism a plague imperiling the souls of men, and its teachers false prophets. To this a rejoinder was made in defence against the insinuation that the Anabaptists of Poland were akin to those of Münster. Whether Gonesius, who had been the first to attack infant baptism at the synod at Brześć in 1558, and was now apparently living at Węgrów, was an interested listener or perhaps a participant in the discussions of the synod is not known, as names are not given. But at all events, though he had been excluded from the Little Poland synod at Pińczów in 1556, the ban against him seems now to have been lifted, and he appears to have taken active part in later synods.[32]

While disapproval of infant baptism had been all but unanimous at Węgrów and had already flooded Lithuania,[33] at Wilno its defenders were in the saddle, and now that Radziwiłł was no more, Czechowicz, their strongest opponent, had to leave. Henceforth he made his home in Poland, where it was largely through his able advocacy that the practice of infant baptism rapidly declined in the Minor Church, and adult baptism by immersion was at length accepted as the only form acknowledged by Scripture.[34] He went first to Kujawy, where he made a notable convert to his views on baptism and social reform in the person of Jan Niemojewski,[35] district judge of Inowrocław, learned and

31 cf. Żytno to Wędrogowski, *ut supra.*
32 *v. supra*, pp. 288–290; cf. Zachorowski, *op. cit.*, p. 222 f.
33 cf. Żytno, *loc. cit.*
34 In the earliest catechism to be published by a local congregation of the Minor Church, that at Kraków, which was frankly Anabaptist in its teaching (*Catechesis et confessio fidei*, etc., 1574, ascribed to its minister, Georg Schomann, perhaps with the assistance of his predecessor Paulus — *v. infra*, p. 342, n. 8), baptism is defined (p. i 6 a) as "hominis Evangelio credentis at poenitentiam agentis . . . in aquam immersio et emersio." Infant baptism is not even mentioned. But in the first catechism issued in the name of all the churches, the so-called Racovian Catechism, (*Catechesis ecclesiarum*, etc., Racoviae, 1609, p. 195 f), infant baptism was in the early editions declared unscriptural; though baptism by immersion was not prescribed until a half-century later, in the much enlarged and revised edition published in Holland (*Catechesis Ecclesiarum Polonicarum*, etc., Irenopoli, "1659," p. 221 f).
35 cf. Ossoliński, *Wiadomości*, iv, 32–57; Józefat Płokarz, 'Jan Niemojewski,' *Reformacja w Polsce*, ii (1922), 71–117.

eloquent, who had been member of several Diets. Born between 1526 and 1530, himself son of a judge, he had studied in Germany, had been active in promoting the Reformation, had adhered to the liberal wing and spread his views among the neighboring nobles, and had taken part on the liberal side of the debate at Piotrków. Following the teaching of Czechowicz, he now received immersion, and with several of his neighbors undertook to live a life strictly conformed to the precepts of the Sermon on the Mount; and he formed at Niemojówka a little antitrinitarian Anabaptist church. Though the wealthy proprietor of over twenty villages, he freed his serfs, and resigned his office as Judge, because in it he might have to sentence a fellow-man to death. He sold his property and distributed to the poor, and when a member of the Diet at Lublin in 1566 soon after his baptism, he appeared among the splendid throng of handsomely dressed and sword-girt nobles meanly dressed and without sword or retinue.[36] The rest of his life he spent in the unpaid service of the church, loyally supporting Czechowicz, earning his living with his own hands, and eloquently and unweariedly championing his cause in debate or in print against Jesuits, or fellow-'Arians' of another stripe: a mystical idealist, whose dignified and gentle character won the sincere respect of his opponents.

After several years of activity in Kujawy, Czechowicz with Niemojewski and several others removed to the newly-founded town of Raków, of which we shall soon have much to say, where a new religious community was gathering that promised to satisfy their ideal of a city of God on earth. But conditions here ere long became so chaotic religiously and socially that, discontented with the arbitrary and extreme leadership of Paulus, they went on in 1570 to Lublin, where Czechowicz heeded the Macedonian cry of a congregation that had for five years been without responsible leadership, and was threatening to fall to pieces.[37] Lublin was a populous, wealthy and cultivated town, and the two labored here with much success for nearly thirty years in building up what was for a considerable time the most influential congregation in the Minor Church. Czechowicz insisted upon immersion as a condition of joining the church, and persuaded many to receive it;[38]

---

[36] For the impression made upon a distinguished ecclesiastic there present, cf. Rescius, *De Atheismis*, p. 255.

[37] cf. Zachorowski, *op. cit.*, p. 232.

[38] cf. Lubieniecius, *op. cit.*, p. 192.

and here he published an important work against infant baptism,[39] which became a recognized classic on the subject, and which a critic over two centuries later pronounced to be still unequaled in its treatment of the question.[40] The church at Kraków, guided by its most influential lay member, Simon Ronemberg, had already taken the same ground; Georg Schomann, sometime teacher at Pińczów, had been immersed at the age of 42 while minister at Chmielnik in 1572, and when he became minister of Paulus's old congregation at Kraków in the following year his wife and mother there received the rite,[41] while the other congregations rapidly fell into line.

Czechowicz remained minister at Lublin until 1598 when, his patron and colleague Niemojewski having now died, he was retired from his ministry in favor of able younger men who laid less stress upon baptism, and had fallen under the more liberal influence of a new leader in Faustus Socinus. He died in 1613 at the age of 81, and his parting admonition to the group that still adhered to him was, in spite of all differences, not to abandon the Minor Church.[42]

[39] Known to us only in its Latin translation, *De Paedobaptistarum errorum origine*, Lublin, 1575. (cf. Brückner, *Różnowiercy*, p. 245, n.). It was dedicated to his patron, Jan Kiszka, and was designed to prepare him for his contemplated baptism. cf. the preface: "Quia baptizari cupis, et Deum assidue invocas, ut te per baptismum Christo consepeliatur, . . . necesse est te, quem maximis periculis et tentationibus eo magis exponendum video, undique armari," etc.; cited in Robert Robinson, *Ecclesiastical Researches* (Cambridge, 1792), p. 580, n. 6. Niemojewski, Paulus and others collaborated in the work (cf. Lubieniecius, p. 192).

[40] cf. J. F. Kiessling, *Das Lehrgebäude der Wiedertäuffer* (Leipzig, 1776), p. xiii f.

[41] cf. his *Testamentum* in Sandius, *Bibliotheca*, p. 195.

[42] cf. Lubieniecius, p. 192.

CHAPTER XXIV

EFFORTS AT CIVIL PERSECUTION OF THE ANTI-TRINITARIANS. DEVELOPMENT OF THEIR DOCTRINE OF THE PERSON OF CHRIST

WHILE THE DEVELOPMENTS spoken of in the previous chapter were taking place in the bosom of the Minor Church, tending to promote its inner harmony and strength, in other quarters hostile measures were being considered designed to bring about its destruction. The situation among the Calvinists had become desperate, since their most able and competent leaders had for the most part adhered to the Minor Church; and Tretius and others were writing to Switzerland pessimistic letters about their prospects.[1] There seemed little hope for their cause until the 'Arians' were put out of competition with them. They therefore entered upon a deliberate campaign of accusation. The 'Arians' were blasphemers or atheists; they were revolutionary Anabaptists; their teachings undermined social order and loyalty to the State. There was scarcely any reproach, religious, moral or political that was not launched against them; and when all had been done to poison the public mind and to arouse popular prejudice, they resorted to means of political persecution.

The Diet at Lublin in 1566 furnished them an opportunity. A large antitrinitarian Anabaptist congregation had arisen here, and held its worship under the very walls of the castle. Its patrons, besides being unorthodox in both their religious and their social doctrines, were numerous and wealthy, and its members were confident and aggressive. They took advantage of the presence of a large number of people during the session of the Diet to carry on a vigorous propaganda for their doctrines, holding many meetings in town and in the suburbs. They were reported to declare that Christians need recognize only Christ as their King, and to be opposed to the power of the State.[2] Whether these rumors were true or not, they were believed by many, aroused

---

[1] cf. Wotschke, *Briefwechsel*, pp. 246–274.

[2] cf. Krajewski to Hosius, Lublin, May 31, 1566, in Wotschke, *op. cit.*, p. 272, n. 1.

intense feeling, and led to a wide-spread demand that those holding such views should be outlawed as dangerous to the State. The Calvinists and Lutherans eagerly seized upon this ground for attack on their common enemy, and urged the Catholics to join them in demanding of the King an edict of expulsion from the country. The King was inclined to comply, and the draft of an edict was preparing when the Bishops unexpectedly demurred, as they had done at Parczów two years before for like reason, on the ground that though such a decree might ruin the 'Arians,' it would be taken as confirming the other Protestants. Strong opposition also arose in the Chamber of Deputies, where many of the nobles saw that their own rights might eventually be jeopardized by the proposed measure, while yet others pleaded for unimpaired freedom of conscience. Meantime Ruggieri, the new papal Nuncio, arrived and threw his weight together with that of Cardinal Hosius and the Primate against the proposed action. The result was that no decree was enacted, and the laws remained in statu quo.[3]

Though the proposed decree fell to the ground and no one suffered banishment, the members of the Minor Church had been thoroughly alarmed. While the subject was so long pending in the Diet, much hostile feeling was aroused against Filipowski as the most prominent layman in the Minor Church, and against Schomann as the most active debater among its ministers, and they both felt bound for a time to leave the city for their personal safety. Indeed, from this time on, the ministers, in order to avoid exciting persecution, left off accompanying their patrons to the Diets, where they had hitherto used to seize the

---

[3] The statement of Lubieniecius (*Historia*, p. 194), repeated by many historians during all the generations since, that at the Diet of Lublin in 1566 a decree was promulgated by the Senate by which all Trideists and Anabaptists were proscribed, and required to leave the country within a month, must be definitely denied. The earliest sources until recently accessible are scanty and confused. The written *draft* of a decree, discussed in the Senate and acceptable to the King, has been mistaken for a valid decree, but it was never adopted. The term Trideists here applied to the Antitrinitarians refers to a view that had an early but short-lived currency among them, which held to the essential deity of Father, Son, and Holy Spirit as three distinct persons, without also asserting their hypostatical unity. Hence Catholic writers of this period called them (strangely enough) *Trinitarii*. The earliest printed sources for the 'Decree of Lublin' are in Schomann's *Testamentum* (in Sandius, *Bibliotheca*, p. 194), and Lubieniecius, *op. cit.*, p. 194. Passing by many mistaken accounts of it, cf. the correct account in Teodor Wierzbowski, *Uchańsciana* (Warszawa, 1890), iii, 132, 134; *id.*, *Uchański*, p. 445 f; and the very conclusive review of the subject by Stanisław Bodniak, 'Sprawa wygnania Arjan w r. 1566' (The matter of the banishment of Arians in 1566), *Reformacja w Polsce*, v (1928), 52–59.

chance to spread their views; and some of the more timid patrons were frightened into giving up their chaplains altogether. At this time also large numbers of the Antitrinitarians of Poland removed to Lithuania, where Kiszka offered them room on his wide domains.[4]

After their narrow escape at Lublin, the Minor Church seems to have thought it safest for the present to attract little attention to itself until hostility had somewhat subsided; but at Kraków Filipowski, from the high position that he held in the State, as well as from his prominence in the church, could not escape notice. The Calvinists were especially embittered that one that had formerly been their patron should now be giving his active and powerful support to heretics, and he thus became the especial object of expressions of ill-will of unprecedented bitterness. The enmity already felt on religious grounds was aggravated by a family quarrel because of his marriage with the widow of one of the Myszkowskis, very wealthy and noble Calvinists, whose brother Stanislas was Palatine of Kraków, and in his jurisdiction surpassed all others in his fierce hatred of the Anabaptists. There were also those that envied him his office of provincial Treasurer. A malicious plot was therefore formed against him, by which he was made to seem disloyal to the King and concerned in a conspiracy against him. His enemies were on the point of succeeding in their infamous design, when two or three faithful friends who had the ear of the King outwitted them and demonstrated his innocence. Even then the Calvinist minister at Kraków allowed himself publicly to spread a scandalous rumor connecting him with Anabaptist practices of a sensational sort.[5]

All this reacted upon the oppressed congregation of the Minor Church at Kraków, strongly Anabaptist as it was; and its minister, Gregory Paulus, aware of the bitter hatred of the Palatine against him, and fearing to fall into his hands, again sought safety in flight,[6] and did not return. He seems to have remained in hiding for a year or two, but at length in 1569 he found refuge and a further field of influence in the newly-founded colony at Raków, where a new Anabaptist congregation gathered about him. His little flock at Kraków scattered like sheep

---

[4] cf. Schomann, *Testamentum*, in Sandius, *Bibliotheca*, p. 194; Sandius, *id. op.*, p. 82; Lauterbach, *Socinismus*, p. 28; Łukaszewicz, *Geschichte*, p. 18, n. 27; Friese, *Kirchengesch.*, ii, 243.

[5] For the above episodes, cf. Lubieniecius, *op. cit.*, pp. 194–197.

[6] cf. Lubieniecius, *op. cit.*, p. 198. Already in 1563 Myszkowski had sought to imprison Paulus, but could not then lay hands on him. cf. Commendone, *Pamiętniki*, i, 164.

before wolves, some removing into the country, but Matthias Albin, a neighboring minister at Iwanowice, got them together again; and under the conciliatory policy of Paulus's successor, Albert Kościeński, and especially by the influence of the Superintendent, Lutomirski, the hatred of the Calvinists was greatly moderated.[7]

The long and conservative pastorate of Georg Schomann, 1573-'86, seems to have been marked by internal peace and growth, and the Catechism published at this time in the name of the church [8] must have done not a little to soften the former animosity. This Catechism forms a notable landmark in the development of Unitarian doctrine, being the earliest attempt of the Antitrinitarians in Poland to state their position in detail.[9] It was designed to correct the existing prejudice against 'the little and afflicted company of those in Poland who were known by the disreputable and hated name of Anabaptists.' [10] In the form of simple question and answer it treats the subjects of God, Christ, the Holy Spirit, Justification, Church Discipline, Prayer, Baptism, and the Lord's Supper; and it is followed by a manual of directions and prayers to be used in daily family worship. All the teachings are supported by plain texts of Scripture. The distinctive doctrines are that God is one; that the Son is subject to the Father, is a man, and was *made* Christ and Lord; that his offices are those of Prophet, Priest, and King; that he is to be adored and invoked; that due obedience is to be given to civil authorities; and that baptism is by immersion. The Catechism is free from the spirit of religious controversy, and it contains no radical social doctrines.

---

[7] cf. Lubieniecius, *op. cit.*, pp. 198, 193.

[8] *Catechesis et confessio fidei, coetus per Poloniam congregati, in nomine Jesu Christi, Domini nostri crucifixi et resuscitati* (Cracoviae, 1574) unnumbered pp. 172, 32°; anonymous, but undoubtedly by Schomann, cf. his *Testamentum*, p. 196. Joint authorship of Paulus (cf. Sandius, *Bibliotheca*, p. 44) seems unlikely; his dominant interest at this period was in social questions rather than doctrinal. For an account of this catechism, cf. Jo. Adam Müller, 'De Unitariorum Catechesi et Confessione fidei typis expressa omnium prima,' *Fortgesetzte nützliche Anmerkungen* (Weimar, 1746), 21. Sammlung, pp. 758–779. For a rather unsympathetic summary in English, cf. Mosheim, *Institutes*, iii, 171, n. 2. The Lutheran theologian Ursinus deemed Schomann's Catechism important enough to deserve a refutation, and was engaged on it at the time of his death.

[9] Earlier than this, however, is the *Catechismus Ecclesiarum in natione Hungarica per Transylvaniam*, etc., issued by the Unitarians at Kolozsvár in 1566, which must stand as the earliest published Unitarian catechism.

[10] It was in this year that the first attack was made on their place of worship. cf. *Reformacja w Polsce*, iv (1926), 167.

During Schomann's ministry the Catholic opposition to the Protestants at Kraków grew steadily more intense. It was chiefly aimed at the Calvinists, as being the more numerous and the more aggressive, but the Anabaptist congregation also felt its force. Nearly every year on Ascension Day the students at the University would break loose in a riot, under a long-standing usage by which they were permitted as zealous Catholics to restrain the growing heresy by plundering the property of heretics,[11] and little serious effort was made to prevent or punish them. Thrice in seventeen years the Calvinist place of worship was destroyed by a wild mob. In 1586 Schomann was promoted to the important church at Lucławice, and two years later his old meeting-place at Kraków [12] was sacked by a mob. The place was restored, but in the great riot of Ascension Day, May 23, 1591, both the Calvinist church and the meeting-place of the 'Arians' were destroyed,[13] and for some time no further attempt was made to hold public Protestant worship at Kraków. The members of the congregation of the Minor Church dispersed, and presumably the most devoted of them went to join the now flourishing Anabaptist community at Raków, which had already come to be recognized as the centre of this movement in Poland.

From the account of the long persecution of the Anabaptist congregations up to this final point in the history of the Kraków congregation, we must now turn back more than a score of years to trace the inner development of thought in the antitrinitarian congregations as a body. After the vexed question of baptism had at Węgrów been left free from constraint, little further trouble was experienced in connection with that subject. As tradition loosened its hold, the practice of infant baptism rapidly fell into disuse, though the practice of baptizing adults did not at once establish itself. Indeed, at the synod of Pełsznica in 1568, there was no little mirth at the expense of the brethren in Little Poland who for several years had had a good deal to say about immersion, while thus far none of them had followed the example of the disciples

---

[11] cf. *Scriptores Rerum Polonicarum* (Kraków, 1897), xvi, 22.

[12] Where St. Thomas's church now stands, at the southwest corner of Spitalna and S. Tomasza Streets.

[13] cf. *Scriptores Polon.* (1881), vii, 117, 142; Kazimierz Dobrowolski, 'Nieznana Kronika Arjańska' (An unknown Arian chronicle) *Reformacja w Polsce*, iv (1926), 167 f; Wacław Sobieski, *Nienawiść wyznaniowa tłumów za rządów Zygmunta IIIgo* (The confessional hatred of the crowds in the reign of Sigismund III.), Warszawa, 1902, pp. 55–58.

of Czechowicz in Kujawy and submitted to it, though they now promised faithfully to introduce it.[14] Other questions, however, now claimed the attention of the Minor Church. While the Antitrinitarians had totally rejected the Athanasian doctrine of the Trinity as quite unsupported by Scripture, yet in searching for a new expression of their beliefs about God and Christ they had not as yet reached any generally satisfactory doctrine. In the midst of this uncertainty as to what they believed, not a few were beginning to waver, and to return to the Reformed or even the Catholic Church.[15] As soon, therefore, as their churches had somewhat recovered from the alarm that the Diet of Lublin had caused in them, their synods undertook to settle more carefully their beliefs as to the person of Christ and his relation to the Father.

The first stage in the development of their thought on this subject had proved to be but a temporary and unsatisfactory one.[16] Following the general line of thought of the Italians Gribaldi, Gentile and Alciati, Paulus in his *Tabula de Trinitate* [17] held that Father, Son and Holy Spirit are three divine beings, equally eternal; but he did not make them one except in all having one nature. Thus the unity of the Divine Being was sacrificed, and the resulting doctrine was virtually tritheism. Hence the Catholics gave his followers the name *Trinitarii*, thereby meaning worshipers of the three, rather than of the three in one. This first attempt to improve upon the alleged Sabellianism of the traditional doctrine was soon abandoned as unsuccessful, for it lasted hardly longer than from 1562 to 1565, after which those that had held it either went back to the orthodox view, or else went on to depart yet further from it.

Belief in the Holy Spirit as the third person in a Trinity of divine beings was indeed early abandoned as unscriptural; and the Spirit was instead held to be not a person but only a divine gift or power of God

---

[14] cf. Zachorowski, *Synody*, p. 233. Even the radical Budny and his followers decided to be rebaptized. cf. Stanisław Szczotka, 'Synody Arjan Polskich' (Synods of the Polish Arians), *Reformacja w Polsce*, vii (1936), 29.

[15] The papal Nuncio Ruggieri (1566–'68) reported that in the two years of his mission in Poland about 10,000 persons returned to the Catholic faith, and none abandoned it. cf. *Relacye Nuncyuszów Apostolskich*, etc. (Relations of the Apostolic Ambassadors), Berlin, 1864, i, 192.

[16] The discrimination of three distinct currents among them was first made by the Calvinist Paul Gilowski in a letter to Bullinger, May 16, 1568; cf. Wotschke, *Briefwechsel*, pp. 290–293.

[17] cf. *supra*, p. 314.

working in the hearts of men. But among those that had thus given up belief in any sort of Trinity, a new conflict for supremacy had now to be waged between two competing views of the person of Christ. There were some that still ascribed to Christ a certain deity, as having existed before the creation of the world, though even as yet subordinate in rank to the Father. Those holding this rank were consequently called Ditheists by the orthodox,[18] and although they did not hold with the ancient Arians that Christ was a created being, they were also called Arians. These were most numerous in Lithuania, and also at Lublin under the leadership of Czechowicz, and they long persisted in the Piedmont district of Little Poland under Stanislas Farnowski, an able and learned theologian who had a few years before achieved notoriety as a heretic at Heidelberg, where he had championed antitrinitarian opinions, and had been so presumptuous as to challenge all the professors to debate the question with him, whence he was required to leave the University.[19] His followers were called Farnovians. They existed in steadily diminishing but ever unyielding numbers for nearly a half-century; but when Farnowski, the last Ditheist, died in 1615, his following soon dispersed. Some returned to the Reformed Church, while the rest went over to their opponents, the Unitarians. It was these latter whose doctrinal views were to survive in the movement whose history we are following, and who achieved the third and ultimate stage in the development of antitrinitarian theology. They denied outright the pre-existence of Christ, and hence any sort of deity in him, regarding him as strictly a human being, having only a human nature. It now remains to be seen how within a few years at this period of our history this view, under the moderate and wise leadership of its advocates, came to possess the field that the other groups had gradually yielded.

The Ditheists or Arians first came into open collision with those holding the unitarian view at a synod held at Łańcut,[20] in the spring of 1567. Controversy on this point is said to have been first stirred up by Gonesius and Farnowski who, in defending the pre-existence of Christ, had said and written many severe things against their brethren who

---

[18] cf. Wajsblum, *Dyteiści*, 32–97.

[19] cf. Wajsblum, *op. cit.*, rozdział ii; Wotschke, *Thretius*, p. 27, n. 2; *id.*, 'Polnische Studenten in Heidelberg,' *Jahrbücher für Kultur und Geschichte der Sklaven*, ii (1926), 48.

[20] In Red Russia, c. 100 miles east of Kraków. cf. Lubieniecius, *Historia*, pp. 215–217.

held the other view, putting upon them the names of ancient heretics. Four leading men from the Kraków congregation, and two ministers, having heard of what was to be done, came to the distant synod, though uninvited and not wanted. The peace-loving Filipowski presided, but the meeting was stormy, the ministers behaving in the debate worse than the laymen. The noble Ivan Karniński,[21] however, became so angry at what he regarded as the blasphemies of the other party that he withdrew from the Antitrinitarians altogether, and henceforth became a violent Calvinist again; while Statorius, his early comrade in the antitrinitarian camp, shamelessly declared that he had never denied the divinity of the Holy Spirit.[22] He died not long afterwards. On the other hand, Lutomirski, the Superintendent, who hitherto had long wavered in his views, now came over to the Unitarians. The visiting brethren from Kraków were, for whatever reason, excluded from participation in the deliberations. The debate grew violent, and when the judges saw it going too far they put an end to it, and in order to let heated minds grow cool they adjourned the synod until June 24, at Skrzynno, a town some seventy-five miles southwest of Warsaw. This done, the record reads as usual: that 'all separated with love unimpaired, mutually promising that they would cultivate harmony and would observe moderation until the next synod.'

The synod at Skrzynno [23] had the very large attendance of 110 nobles and ministers, from all parts of Poland and Lithuania, besides a crowd of residents from the immediate vicinity. Filipowski, who seems more clearly than any one else to have seen the danger to the whole reformed cause if the Protestants allowed themselves to be split up into sects, and was still hoping for union of all parties among them, had the invitation to the synod addressed not simply to the members of the Minor Church, but to 'all that seek their own salvation and the glory of God.' He was again unanimously chosen to preside — a token of the reliance that all placed upon his discretion, justice and moderation. Every precaution was taken to prevent angry disputes and to observe due restraint in the discussion, in which seven or eight speakers were chosen to represent each side. To mention only the leading speakers, the pre-existence of Christ was supported by Farnowski, Niemojewski, and Czechowicz;

---

[21] cf. *supra*, p. 306, n. 64.
[22] cf. *supra*, p. 296 f. Biandrata had long suspected his sincerity.
[23] cf. Lubieniecius, *op. cit.*, pp. 217–220; Wajsblum, *op. cit.*, p. 66 f.

the opposite view by Schomann, Paulus, and Budny. Both sides rested their arguments solely on texts of Scripture, which was explored with the most exhaustive thoroughness in search of proofs. The discussion lasted five days, and was dignified and orderly; but no agreement as to doctrine was found possible. The Unitarians were evidently strongly in the majority, and at last they declared to their opponents that they would acknowledge no one as Son of God and Savior of the world but the Christ of the gospel history. Farnowski on his part would agree to no compromise statement.

Filipowski then, with the unanimous consent of the synod and in its name, prepared a statement of the conclusions reached. It was very skilfully expressed in broad terms, so as to some extent to meet the wishes of both parties, yet without infringing conscience, and with a recommendation of generous mutual tolerance. It declared (briefly summarized) that the term Trinity is to be reverently retained, on condition that brotherly love is to continue as Christ commanded; that the brethren should bear with one another's infirmities, and should on no account abuse one another; they might discuss their differences in writing, but without invective or condemning one another privately or in public; they might listen to one another's prayers and sermons so far as these followed the traditional form, but if not, they might without offence do as conscience bid, even to leaving the place of worship. Likewise as to infant baptism and the Lord's Supper the lead of conscience must be followed, with the fervent prayer that the ordinance may serve for the amendment of personal life, the glory of God, and mutual comfort; no one wishing to impose his faith upon another, since this is the gift of God; and until he sends his angels to separate the tares from the wheat they are not to exclude nor wound one another.

Having accepted this statement, the members of the synod, however differing in opinion, separated bearing no bitterness — except Farnowski, who proceeded henceforth to attack the other party in stinging writings; while the latter contented themselves with simply publishing an account of the whole proceedings with the arguments on both sides. Within the next year took place the so-called 'agreement of Lucławice,' whereby an important centre of the Arian movement, with a group of eight leading congregations, went over to the Unitarian camp.[24] Meanwhile, Farnowski found a zealous partizan and new patron in Stanislas

[24] cf. Wajsblum, *op. cit.*, p. 85.

Mężyk, Starost of Sącz on the border of Hungary, withdrew from the Minor Church and removed thither, where he built up a flourishing congregation of his own, and later set up a press and established a famous school, and thus continued for many years to lead a scattered group of Arian churches, or Farnovians as his sect came to be called.[25]

Doctrinal differences in the Minor Church were not wholly settled even with the withdrawal of Farnowski and his followers from the rest. At a local synod meeting at Kraków in September of the same year (1567),[26] to take notice of some complaints against the doctrines being taught there by the new minister, Kościeński, the delegates also took up a more serious question. The church at Lublin, which had been without a regular minister since Stanislas Paklepka (Paclesius) had died of the plague in 1565 (and which so remained until Czechowicz and Niemojewski came thither from Raków in 1570, and devoted themselves to restoring order and building up a strong and influential congregation), was reported as being led astray by two 'false prophets.' One of these was Esaias of Moskow, a refugee Russian priest, a convert from the Greek Church. He had been infected by Valentine Krawiec, a wealthy merchant of Lublin, whose business often took him to Hungary. He had there imbibed the teachings of a 'new Judaism' which was then (as we shall see at length in the next division of our history) spreading in that country the view that Christ should not be invoked in prayer; that the seventh day should be observed as the sabbath; and that various other Jewish usages should be honored. These two were said to have led astray some in the Lublin church. The school there had removed to Bełżyce, and the church was moribund. The synod at Kraków tried to counteract the new errors through a long letter admonishing the brethren not to be led astray from true Christianity by these falsifiers of it.

This seems to have been the first emergence in the Polish churches of views that were for a time to cause a further division of the now dominant Unitarians, headed by Paulus and Schomann, and holding that though Christ had a purely human nature, yet he became at his baptism divine by adoption, and was therefore entitled to worship as a subordinate divine being; and on the other hand, the consistently

[25] cf. Jan Sygański, *Historya Nowego Sącza* (History of Nowy Sącz) Lwów, 1901–'02, ii, 142–144.
[26] cf. Zachorowski, *Synody*, p. 231 f.

radical wing, holding that Christ, being purely human, should not be worshiped at all. As the latter party were inclined to esteem the Old Testament and its teachings as of greater authority than the New, they were called Judaizers, or Semi-Judaizers; as they opposed the worship of Christ, they were called Non-adorants; and as their most influential leader was Simon Budny, they were also called Budnaeans. They had comparatively few adherents in Little Poland, but were very numerous in Lithuania. The contest for survival between these two wings was the last doctrinal controversy of any importance before the system of thought in the Minor Church was given shape by Faustus Socinus; but as it falls for the most part a little later than the period of which we have just been speaking, it will be considered in a later chapter.

Meanwhile, at the next synod at Pełsznica in October, 1568,[27] controversy on the doctrinal matters previously discussed was already subsiding, and the debate ended as usual with expressions of mutual love and respect. On the other hand a new group of questions now appeared on the horizon, which were during the next thirty years or so to become very prominent in the life of the Minor Church, and to give it a marked distinction in Christian history, as a church many of whose leaders and members honestly and earnestly tried to put the literal moral and social teachings of Jesus into actual practice both in personal relations and in the discharge of their duties as citizens. The development of this phase too will claim our attention in the following chapter.

[27] cf. Zachorowski, *op. cit.*, p. 233.

CHAPTER XXV

THE MINOR CHURCH EXCLUDED FROM THE UNION OF PROTESTANTS. EFFORTS AT UNION WITH THE MORAVIAN BRETHREN

THE CONFERENCE between the two wings of the Reformed Church at Piotrków in 1565 was, as we have seen, largely due to the initiative of Filipowski who, with keen political foresight, saw the crucial importance at the present juncture of all the forces of reformation keeping a united front against the reviving Catholicism. Undiscouraged at the failure of this effort, he presented himself together with several other eminent men at a large gathering of Calvinists meeting in the hall of the Palatine at Kraków in 1568, where he was commissioned by the brethren of the Minor Church to speak on their behalf.[1] His address was marked by mildness and a conciliatory spirit, and showed an earnest desire for union on any basis consistent with adherence to the authority of Scripture as supreme; but his eloquent appeal for peace and harmony fell on deaf ears, and was received only with angry and insulting language.

An unexpected result followed, however, in the impression made upon a distinguished churchman present. The celebrated Andreas Dudith (Dudicz), one of the most eminent figures of his generation, had been Catholic Bishop of three sees in succession,[2] had had a prominent part at the Council of Trent, and was the trusted Councilor of three Emperors, a man of profound learning, great eloquence, and unblemished character.[3] Having been sent by the Emperor Maximilian to Poland in 1565 as permanent ambassador to the Polish court, he there embraced Protestantism out of disgust at what he had seen of the inner

---

[1] cf. Lubieniecius, *Historia*, p. 223 ff.

[2] Knin (Tinia) in Dalmatia, Csánad, and Pécs (Fünfkirchen) in Hungary; cf. Lubieniecius, *op. cit.*, pp. 222, 225 f.

[3] cf. Lorandus Samuelfy, *De vita et scriptis Dudith*, appended to Dudith's *Orationes Quinque* (Halae, 1743); Carl Benjamin Stieff . . . *Geschichte von Leben und Glaubens-Meynungen Andreas Dudiths* (Breslau, 1756); Bock, *Antitrinitar.*, i, 252–322; Pierre Costil, *André Dudith, Humaniste Hongrois* (Paris, 1935).

workings of the Catholic Church at Trent, resigned his see, married a lady of the court, and became a Polish citizen. At Rome he was presently excommunicated and burnt in effigy. At Kraków he attended worship with the Calvinists, and Tretius as their leader made every endeavor through letters from the leading theologians in the west to influence him to join their movement. But when he observed the bitter and dogmatic spirit in which they met the friendly advances of the Minor Church, he gave his sympathy instead to the latter. Though he never formally became a member of the Minor Church, remaining to his death nominally a Lutheran, yet when he not long afterwards became proprietor of the town of Śmigiel (Schmiegel) in Great Poland, he became patron of the antitrinitarian church there, for which he erected a house of worship and a school.[4] The Calvinists were greatly disgusted.

Even yet Filipowski, unwearied, did not cease his efforts to bring the two wings of the church once more together upon some acceptable basis, even though they did not agree in details of doctrine. It was doubtless largely due to him, seconded by many on both sides who desired union, that the synod at Bełżyce in March, 1569,[5] was attended not only by a large number of Unitarians, but also by an equally large number of Trinitarians, tritheists and ditheists, including both Sarnicki and Farnowski. The order of the day listed nearly two score topics for discussion. Some were doctrinal, yet more were social in their nature. Though discussion was had, the result was disappointing. The extant record breaks off incomplete, but it shows that opprobrious names were soon called, and that since the one side accepted only Scripture as authority, while the other insisted also upon the traditions of the Fathers and Councils, no agreement was to be expected. While for a good many years yet there were to be occasional half-hearted approaches

---

[4] De hinc partes amplexus melioris ecclesiae quidem ut minori ita et veriori nomen non dedit, ejus tamen fautor, et Smiglae, Majoris Poloniae oppido, patronus imo fundator fuerat. Lubieniecius, *op. cit.*, p. 226; Sandius, *Bibliotheca*, p. 61. But the church at Śmigiel had already existed for more than a decade when Dudith became proprietor and its patron in 1586.

The last ten years of his life, 1579–'89, Dudith spent in scholarly retirement at Breslau, where his tombstone may be seen at the head of the south aisle in the Elisabeth-Kirche. His religious views and sympathies may be gathered from the correspondence published in *Bibliotheca Fratrum Polonorum*, i, 495–534. His preference was for the more radical wing of the Minor Church, but he was too broad and free a spirit to commit himself unreservedly to any sect.   [5] cf. Zachorowski, *Synody*, p. 233 f.

toward healing the breach, yet this was the last attempt that showed the least promise of success; for within the next year two events took place that were profoundly to affect the future of both churches. In 1570 the three existing orthodox sects were to form at Sandomierz (Sandomir) a Protestant federation from which the Minor Church was deliberately and decisively excluded; and in 1569 came the foundation of Raków, to which large numbers of Antitrinitarians were to flock from all quarters, and which was to become, after an initial period of chaos, the capital of a united and vigorously active church. Henceforth the two bodies were to develop separately, and the course of the history of the Minor Church will be a simpler one to follow. We have now to speak in turn of these two events.

When the King, by accepting the decrees of the Council of Trent at the Diet of Lublin in 1564, dispelled any lingering hope of a Polish national synod which should arrive at some form of united national church, it became more than ever clear to the Protestant sects that if they were to maintain their existence against a now aggressive Catholicism they must come together in some sort of union; and this feeling was confirmed when, by the Union of Lublin in 1569 Poland and Lithuania became united in one kingdom, the largest west of Russia. After several preliminary meetings, therefore, to prepare the way, representatives of the three older Protestant bodies — Calvinists, Lutherans, and Bohemian Brethren — gathered at Sandomierz in April, 1570,[6] with a view to forming a national Protestant church, in the hope that it might acquire full legal status along with the Catholic Church, and have equal rights with it. Such a union had long since been advocated by Łaski, and had been repeatedly talked of at various synods in the ten years since his death in 1560.

The synod that thus gathered attracted an attendance of several thousand, but the official delegates were only from the members of the three orthodox sects. Several ministers and lay members of the Minor Church also presented themselves, and there was even a debate on the doctrine of the Trinity between their spokesman Witrelin and the Calvinists Tretius and Thénaud;[7] but they were not permitted to join in the general discussion nor to sign the resulting agreement. It was

---

[6] cf. Daniel Ernst Jabłoński, *Historia Consensus Sendomiriensis* (Berlin, 1731); Oskar Halecki, *Zgoda Sandomierska 1570 r.* (The Sandomir Agreement of 1570), Warszawa, 1915; Wotschke, *Reformation*, pp. 242–251.

[7] cf. Łukaszewicz, *Kościół helwecki*, n. 3, pp. 249–251; Halecki, *op. cit.*, pp. 221 f, 237, 249, 251.

not easy even for the three churches to arrive at a common doctrinal basis of union, for the Lutherans insisted on keeping their Augsburg Confession, the Calvinists were committed to the Helvetic Confession of the Swiss churches which they had adopted in Polish translation in 1566, and the Bohemian Brethren were naturally attached to their own statement. The chief obstacle was difference as to the doctrine of the Lord's Supper. Each of the three bodies, however, at last agreed to recognize the doctrines of the two others as scriptural, though the forming of a common body of doctrine was never accomplished. The Union of Sandomir (*Consensus Sendomiriensis*) was finally subscribed April 14, 1570,[8] and the surviving remnant of Stancaro's followers, seven in all, were then taken back into the church and included among the signers.

The Union, however, proved to be a disappointment. Two years later the King died without having given it legal recognition. Its chief purpose therefore was not accomplished; and though it was later repeatedly ratified by various synods, by the end of the century the Union began to break up, and by 1645 it had ceased to exist. So far as concerns the present history, however, the significance of the Union of Sandomir lies in the fact that, though tentative efforts continued to be made at intervals to have the Minor Church recognized as belonging to the whole body of Protestants, it was steadily treated henceforth as without the pale of common Christianity, and had more than ever to go its way alone. Thus at a period when the Protestant forces in Poland urgently needed the united support of every possible adherent, they deliberately lessened their strength by excluding from their ranks a vital and important contingent; blindly insisting, as the thing of first importance in religion, upon the acceptance of speculative dogmas, instead of tolerantly allowing for differences of belief so far as these were consistent with the practical end of cultivating Christian character in individuals and applying Christian principles to the life of society and the government of the State. Time brought its inevitable revenge. Protestantism in Poland had already reached its culmination in the period 1563-'65, and this was also the period when schism among its adherents began.

---

[8] For the Latin text of the *Consensus* with English translation, cf. Krasinski, *Reformation*, i, 383-392. At a joint synod of the three churches at Kraków in 1573 it was voted, after serious consideration, "that the Arrianabaptist preachers and laymen present be denied opportunity to debate their doctrine there; and if they stubbornly persist in their errors we will have nothing more to do with them, but shun them and their children as blasphemers, at war with the glory of God." cf. Johann Jakob Scheidemantel, *Acta conventuum et synodorum in Majori Polonia a Dissidentibus celebratorum* (Breslau, 1776), p. 17.

From this time on its strength steadily declined; and in 100 years from the Union of Sandomir its power in Poland was practically crushed. Thereafter it never had more than a feeble existence in Polish lands.

Excluded as they now were from fellowship with the other religious bodies in Poland, the Minor Church longed for sympathetic relations in other quarters; and the communities of Anabaptists in Moravia seemed to offer them the best promise. They had indeed already been somewhat influenced from this quarter through Gonesius and Czechowicz. There was not a little to draw them together. The Anabaptists had early won a reputation for greater strictness in church discipline, higher standards of personal morals, and more fervent piety than the other Protestants, and had a greater following among the common people.[9] Less concerned than were the others to insist on the traditional dogmas of mediaeval Christianity, they were the more in earnest about reviving the practices of the Apostolic Church in living a simple life, avoiding luxury, worldly pleasures, display in dress, and extravagance in food and drink, and in practicing community of goods and regarding private property as a sin, while treating all members as brothers and sisters on the same level, with no distinction of class or rank, master or servant. In Moravia at this period they were flourishing, and had perhaps 1,000 communities. At the same time, while the dominant Protestant churches in Poland, largely aristocratic in their cast, being composed of the higher nobility, were making little effort to bring their peasants to the Protestant faith or to better their condition, and were growing ever more worldly, the Minor Church on the other hand counted comparatively few of the wealthier nobles, but attracted large numbers of the artisan class in the towns, and not a few of the commoners and peasants in the country; and they were tending increasingly to encourage the homely virtues and simple standards of the early Christian Church. In broad terms, the Reformed and Lutheran churches were aristocratic, while the Minor Church, especially in its main centres at Kraków and Lublin, was democratic.

At the synod of Pełsznica in October, 1568 there appeared one Lukas Mundius, who had been a member of the City Council at Wilno, but had left his office and been traveling through various countries with religious interests in view.[10] He had just spent several weeks among

[9] cf. Johannes Loserth, *Communismus der Mährischen Wiedertäuffer im 16. und 17. Jahrhundert* (Wien, 1894), p. 222.

[10] cf. Zachorowski, *Synody*, p. 233; Lubieniecius, *Historia*, p. 227.

the Anabaptists in Moravia, and was full of praise of their moral discipline and singular piety. He announced that a delegation was coming to visit the brethren in Poland, of whose progress they had heard with much interest. Four of them soon came, and before returning home also visited the new settlement at Raków. Mutual impressions were evidently favorable, for three young students were at once sent to Moravia to learn some trade, since it was at the time felt at Raków that all ministers should support themselves by some trade rather than live by the sweat of others. They spent the winter there, though none too happily. Meantime they were followed by a delegation consisting of Filipowski, Schomann the minister at Chmielnik, Simon Ronemberg the apothecary,[11] a leading layman of Kraków, and several others, to confer with the Moravian brethren about their doctrine and moral standards.[12] They found the discipline and piety of the Moravians to be all that had been said, but in other respects they were disillusioned. The Moravians proved to be uncompromising trinitarians, who did not scruple at calling their guests pagans for rejecting this doctrine. Moreover, along with agreement in various respects, grave differences were discovered between them. The cultural level of the Poles was radically different from that of the Moravians, their educational standards were very unlike, and the general social arrangements of the Moravian community were quite unacceptable to the brethren from Kraków. Besides, when closely examined, the Christian brotherhood that the Moravians were supposed to practice in their community life seemed to fall far short of the professed ideal. So that although half-hearted efforts were still made, and at least one more large deputation was sent from Poland and Lithuania, nothing came of it, and relations were broken off, not without some reproachful expressions on both sides.[13]

[11] Ronemberg was a highly respected citizen of Kraków, and perhaps the most devoted and influential member of the congregation. It was through his wisdom and tact shortly after this that the chaotic congregation at Raków was rescued from dissolution. His place of business at Kraków was at No. 8 on the Rynek, in the building still standing and known as *Pod Jaszczurami* ('under the lizards,' from the sculptured figures over the doorway). The vaulted room on the street floor is said to have been a meeting-place for the congregation. His son became a Catholic, and his grandson a Jesuit.

[12] cf. Dobrowolski, *Kronika*, p. 166; Schomann, *Testamentum*, p. 195.

[13] cf. Stanisław Kot, *Ideologja polityczna i społeczna Polskich zwanych Arjanami* (Political and social ideology of the Polish Brethren called Arians) (Warszawa, 1932), chap. iv.; 'Traktat przeciwko "komunistom" morawskim z roku około 1569' (Treatise against the Moravian "Communists" from about 1569), *Roczniky Towarzystwa Przyjaciół Nauk w Poznaniu*, xv (1887), 59–80.

CHAPTER XXVI

RAKÓW AS CENTER OF THE MINOR CHURCH. THE WARSAW CONFEDERATION

THOUGH THE CONTACT with the Moravians did not issue as had been hoped, it was not without influence on the development of the Minor Church, which as yet was rather formless and undisciplined. For the envoys to Moravia evidently brought back with them some ideals of applied Christianity that they were soon to see tried in their own community. Meantime the members and leaders of the church were growing restive under the conditions of their church life. Those at Kraków were living in constant fear of severe persecution, and Paulus had some time since felt obliged to flee and seek safety in obscurity.[1] The hostility of the orthodox sects had increased since Piotrków and Sandomir, and many of the brethren were longing for some quiet retreat from the world's quarrels and alarms, where they might enjoy security and peace, and devote themselves to religious meditation and cultivation of the Christian virtues and graces. It was at this juncture that their prayers seemed to be answered in the foundation of Raków.

Jan Sieniński (Sienieński), a tolerant Calvinist magnate who was Castellan of Żarnów (later Palatine of Podole), had a wife who was a zealous 'Arian.'[2] She had evidently laid to heart the troubles of her fellow-believers, and meditated plans for their relief. To gratify her he determined to found a new town, and to incorporate in its charter provisions of wide religious toleration. This town, which was given the name of Raków (Lat., Racovia), from the fact that the founder's wife bore on her coat of arms a *rak* (i.e., crab),[3] lay about fifty miles west of Sandomir, and was pleasantly situated on the little river Czarna,

[1] Perhaps at Pełsznica, where he had been minister some fifteen years earlier, and where he again appears at a synod in 1568.

[2] cf. Henryk Biegeleisen, 'Aryanie Polscy' (The Polish Arians), *Krytyka* (Kraków, 1908), x, 271.

[3] cf. Lubieniecius, *op. cit.*, p. 239 f; Kasper Niesiecki, *Herbarz Polski* (Polish Armorial), Leipzig, 1839–'46, ix, 250.

in the midst of a wide, sandy plain, surrounded by forests and fertile meadows, with numerous ponds and a mild and healthful climate.[4] The generous provisions of its foundation [5] induced many from all parts of the country, who felt themselves alienated from the rest by their religious views, to emigrate to Raków. Although there were enough of the Reformed Church to form a small congregation, the great majority of the settlers seem to have been radicals, both socially and in doctrine. The brethren flocked thither in large numbers from all quarters far and near, and from its very foundation the town grew rapidly.[6] Besides Paulus, Schomann, Czechowicz, and a number of other ministers, there were Mundius from Wilno and others from Lithuania, there were nobles like Niemojewski and his friends from Kujawy who had sold their estates to distribute to the poor, there were learned men, commoners and artisans, all enthusiastically dreaming of a New Jerusalem to come into being at Raków, where all should dwell together in love and peace as members of one great family living again as the first Christians had lived. As all the brethren in such a community should be on an equality, nobles and commoners alike worked daily with their own hands, building their dwellings and tilling their fields. A flourishing industrial community arose, with manufacture of cloth, paper and pottery. The leading spirit was evidently Paulus, who at the synod at Pełsznica had already urged, with the sympathy of Czechowicz and his followers, that nobles should no longer live from the labor of their serfs, and that even ministers should lay aside their profession and earn their bread with their own hands. Indeed, all but Czechowicz and Schomann now did so.[7]

For a time all went smoothly, and the brethren occupied all their

[4] cf. Jan Wiśniewski, *Dekanat Opatowski* (The Deanery of Opatów), Radom, 1907, pp. 374–383.

[5] Extract from the charter: I, Jan Sieniński of Sienno, Castellan of Żarnów, have founded the said town . . . and make known to all personally, and particularly to those that have and shall have to do with it, that I will not rule over the religion of any of the aforesaid Racovians in which they differ from one another, nor of any of their successors or subjects, nor will I permit any agents to rule over the same, but each of them, as the Lord gives him grace, and as his knowledge of the truth leads him, shall cherish his religion in peace with himself and his descendants. (dated) March 27, 1567.

Jan Sieniński died 1597. The charter was renewed by his son Jakob, June 1, 1607. cf. Jan Wiśniewski, *Dekanat Iłżecki* (The Deanery of Iłża), Radom, 1910, pp. 111–129.

[6] Lubieniecius, *op. cit.*, p. 239, says the town was founded 1569; but the charter (see previous note) is dated two years earlier than that.

[7] cf. Zachorowski, *Synody*, p. 233; Schomann, *Testamentum*, p. 195.

vacant time in diligently investigating and discussing religious questions. Visitors of various sorts came to join in the discussions, some for a time, and some to stay. But among such various elements sharp dissensions inevitably arose, and extreme views were advanced or opposed, of asceticism, community of goods, and the like, so that for three whole years of uninterrupted debating there was no peace day or night, in what was something like a perpetual synod.[8] With no longer any regular minister to lead their worship and give competent religious instruction, their meetings became chaotic, in which any one might take part that felt moved to do so, and these often the rudest and most ignorant, speaking rather out of shallow feeling than out of wide knowledge or deep experience. Better minds found this profitless and hard to endure.[9] Disgusted with the religious chaos that prevailed, Czechowicz and his Kujavian followers removed to Lublin to build up a saner movement; while at Raków the influence of Paulus waned, some of the discordant elements left the community and some new adherents joined it, until at length comparative quiet and order ensued. At this juncture, when the whole project seemed, humanly speaking, to have collapsed, the Kraków apothecary Ronemberg, 'like a new Ezra,' leaped into the breach, supplied the leadership that was lacking, and in 1572 reorganized the church with a regular ministry again, and a membership composed of those that had received adult baptism. Biandrata also wrote from Transylvania to Filipowski, calling on them to abandon their superstition, live as men among men, and furnish a living example of true and godly life.[10]

From now on affairs went better. More than a score of ministers resumed their office and were appointed to congregations in all parts of the Republic, Kiszka taking ten to his estates in Lithuania and Podlasie.[11] Henceforth for more than sixty years Raków had a succession of ministers of the highest distinction, and came to be the acknowledged capital of Polish Unitarianism. A press was established here, which

---

[8] cf. Wotschke, *Briefwechsel*, p. 319; Andreas Lubieniecki, *Poloneutychia*, Czartoryski Ms 1370, pp. 72–78, reprinted in *Humanizm i Reform.*, pp. 419–423; Lubieniecius, *op. cit.*, p. 240.

[9] cf. Kaspar Wilkowski, *Przyczyny nawrócenia do wiary Powszechny od sekt Nowokrzczeńców Samosateńskich* (Reasons for my conversion from the Samosatenian Anabaptist sects to the Catholic faith), Wilno, 1583, p. 153; cited by Kot, *Ideologja*, p. 36 f.

[10] Cf. Schomann, *Testamentum*, p. 195; Lubieniecius, *op. cit.*, p. 240.

[11] cf. Lubieniecki, *Poloneutychia*, Ms, *ut supra*, p. 422.

Catholic came to the throne he might employ his power to oppress them and ruin their cause. For the old law against heretics [23] had never been repealed, but simply lay dormant; and while the Diet had not long since suspended ecclesiastical jurisdiction, it might by the same authority again be enforced. To guard against such a misfortune, the Protestant nobles, who were still very powerful and on political grounds could count on considerable support from even the Catholics, sought what measures they might take to ensure themselves against persecution. They desired guarantees of wide religious freedom and full civil equality. With this not a few Catholics sympathized, being willing to see the clergy curbed in power. The Protestants were the more concerned for their safety under a new king, in view of the recent massacre of St. Bartholomew in France, in which no fewer than 50,000 Protestants had fallen victims to the Catholic party. The Protestants declared that they would never let a Diet be held for the election of a king until they had been given assurance that they could live in safety in their own country,[24] and they had a plan ready.

After the death of the King, the Senate and the Chamber of Deputies, following a precedent already set at Korczyn in 1438, came together in a joint meeting at Warsaw in January, 1573 to make preliminary arrangements as to the time, place, and conditions of a new election.[25] When, therefore, the Confederation of Warsaw [26] was drawn up, it included a clause (article 3) on religious liberty, elaborated by a committee whose members had been half from the Protestants and half from the Catholics and clergy, as follows:

Since there is in our Republic no little disagreement on the subject of religion, in order to prevent any such hurtful strife from beginning among our people on this account as we plainly see in other realms, we mutually promise for ourselves and our successors forever, under the bond of our oath, faith, honor and conscience, that we who differ with regard to religion (*dissidentes de religione*) will keep the peace with one another, and will not for a different faith or a change of churches shed blood nor punish one another by confiscation of property, infamy,

[23] cf. *Volumina Legum*, i, 38.

[24] cf. A. M. Gratiani, *La vie du Cardinal Jean François Commendon* (ed. 2, Paris, 1680), p. 568.

[25] cf. Thaddäus von Piliński, *Das polnische Interregnum von 1572–1573* (Heidelberg, 1881).

[26] Confederation is the name given to the comprehensive preliminary basis of action with regard to the election of the King, agreed upon by the joint assembly at Warsaw, January 28, 1573.

imprisonment or banishment, and will not in any way assist any magistrate or officer in such an act.[27]

In conformity with this article, the form of oath to be taken at the coronation of the new King included this promise:

I promise and solemnly swear by almighty God that . . . I will preserve and maintain peace and quiet among those that differ with regard to religion (*dissidentes de religione*), and will not in any way, whether by our jurisdiction or by authority of any of our officers and institutions whatsoever, suffer any one to be influenced or oppressed by reason of his religion, nor will I myself influence or oppress him.[28]

The Confederation was somewhat modeled upon the Augsburg Peace of 1555 which had brought religious peace to Germany, and it was at first supposed to be acceptable to all parties. Almost all the Senators lay and clerical had fully approved it, and almost all the Deputies had signed it. But when it was presented to the Senate for final ratification, unexpected opposition was met. Archbishop Uchański made a violent speech against it, declaring that it would tend to overthrow Christianity and open the door to false religions. All the Bishops but Bishop Krasiński of Kraków withdrew their names, but it was nevertheless signed by a very large majority of the nobles.[29]

There were a half-dozen aspirants for the throne, and each was represented at the Diet by influential advocates (Dudith was active in promoting the interests of the Austrian candidate); but after a long and spirited contest, and certain concessions on the part of the Protestants, the choice finally fell upon the French candidate, Henry of Valois, an ardent Catholic, and the Confederation and oath were signed on his part by his representatives. Yet when it came to concluding negotiations with Henry in person three months later in Paris, new obstacles were encountered. A protest against the article about the *pax dissidentium*

---

[27] *Volumina Legum*, ii, 124.

[28] *Volumina Legum*, ii, 135. This oath was a part of the so-called *Pacta Conventa*, that is, the treaty or articles of agreement between the Senate and Orders of Poland and Lithuania on the one hand, and the King-elect on the other, which he was required to sign and to assent to orally before receiving his crown. The particular article of the Confederation assuring peace between the religious parties, and the corresponding part of the coronation oath, are commonly spoken of as the *pax dissidentium*.

[29] Out of 98 subscribers, 41 were Catholics. cf. Edmund Bursche, 'Z dziejów nazwy "Dysidenci"' (from the history of the name "Dissidents"), *Przegląd Historyczny*, xxvi (1926), p. 25.

was entered in the name of the clergy and the objecting Senators or Deputies, and Henry himself appeared to be disposed not to accept the article concerned. But when he was firmly told by Zborowski, the leader of the Protestants, *Nisi id feceris, Rex in Polonia non eris*, the Bishops yielded and agreed to abide by the articles, and Henry signed the articles and took the oath in Notre-Dame, though again in the face of protest. Finally at the coronation in the Cathedral at Kraków, February 20, 1574, the Archbishop attempted to substitute the ancient traditional coronation oath in place of the one agreed upon safeguarding the rights of the Dissidents. The substitution was noticed, and the Grand Marshal, a Protestant, insisted upon the form agreed upon, saying, *Jurabis, Rex, promisisti*, and the crown was seized and withheld until he had complied.[30]

From this time on the Protestants in Poland appealed to the Warsaw Confederation as the charter of their liberties, and its oath was required of succeeding kings; but the foundation of it was none too stable. From the first the Bishops refused to acknowledge it, and denied its legality, and in the following period they persistently and successfully opposed all efforts to get the Diet to enact a legal method of procedure [31] in prosecuting violations of the Confederation or evasion of its purpose. The history of Protestantism in Poland during the next century is in no small measure the history of efforts on the part of the Catholic powers by one means or another to annul the provisions of the Confederation and thus deprive Protestants of the equal rights and full religious freedom that they had hoped to secure. The first to feel the effect of these efforts were the members of the Minor Church. The 'Arians' in the Diet had borne their part in securing the Confederation and believed that they were included in its guarantees, and for some time no objection was raised against them. But the term Dissidents, which in 1573 comprehended all citizens of the Republic, Catholics and Protestants of every shade alike, and even adherents of other religions, in the course of time gradually shifted its meaning.[32] Before the end of

---

[30] The often repeated story that on this occasion the King was told, *Si non jurabis, non regnabis*, has been shown to be legendary. *v.* the searching discussion of the whole episode by Wacław Sobieski, 'Si non jurabis, non regnabis,' *Reformacja w Polsce*, ii (1922), 54–70; cf. Marquis E. H. V. de Noailles, *Henri de Valois* (Paris, 1867), ii, 213–417.

[31] The so-called *proces Konfoederaciey*.

[32] cf. Bursche, *op. cit.*, pp. 22–41.

the century it was coming to be used as meaning simply non-Catholic, hence Dissenters from the Catholic religion, and thus to imply no longer mutual tolerance of bodies on an equal footing, but toleration of inferior sects by a ruling Catholic power. Later still we shall see the effort made (with the willing co-operation of Calvinists and Lutherans) not to recognize 'Arians' as among the Dissidents at all, nor to extend to them the security guaranteed by the Confederation.[33] For the present, however, the field of our history will be more clear and distinct, since the relations of the Minor Church to the other Protestant sects on the one hand and to the civil government on the other have now been well defined.

[33] cf. Lengnich, *Jus publicum*, ii, 649.

CHAPTER XXVII

THE MINOR CHURCH: THE STRUGGLE WITH RADICALISM, DOCTRINAL AND SOCIAL

IN AN EARLIER CHAPTER it was noted that at a synod at Kraków in 1567 serious notice was taken of certain quasi-Jewish views imported from Hungary, and especially of the view that Christ should not be invoked in prayer.[1] This view of the non-adorants or Judaizers (as they were called) had by now made much headway among the Unitarians of Transylvania, where it was warmly espoused by their Bishop, Francis Dávid, as will be seen at length in the next division of this history. The question had led to serious controversy in the churches there, and Socinus, who had been summoned thither for the purpose, had been unable to settle it. The Catholic Prince had taken note of the matter, and had caused Dávid to be prosecuted for innovation in doctrine, with the result that he was condemned to prison, where he died in 1579. At Biandrata's suggestion the Transylvanian churches, which then enjoyed close relations with those in Poland, asked them for an expression of opinion as to Dávid's doctrine. This question was considered at a synod at Bełżyce near Lublin in 1579, where Dávid's view seems to have been unanimously disapproved.[2] This sentence, when published the following year, was at once answered by a defence of Dávid's view from Jacob Palaeologus.[3] Dávid's view continued how-

---

[1] *v. supra*, p. 348 f.

[2] cf. Szczotka, *Synody*, p. 30 f; Henryk Merczyng, *Szymon Budny jako krytyk tekstów biblijnych* (S. B. as critic of biblical texts), Kraków, 1913, pp. 94–96. *v. infra*, p. 369 f.

[3] cf. *Defensio Francisci Davidis* (Claudiopoli, 1582), pp. 121–236. Palaeologus, a scion of the Imperial family of Constantinople, born a Greek on the island of Chios, fled to Italy after the fall of Constantinople, and entered the Dominican order at Rome, but leaving it fled from the Inquisition in 1559 and joined the Protestants in Germany. He came to Poland in 1571, where he associated with the 'Arians' (cf. Lubieniecius, *Historia*, p. 200), as also later with the Unitarians in Transylvania, where he was Rector of their college at Kolozsvár, 1573–'74. Incessantly hunted by the Inquisition, he fled thence, was finally seized in Moravia, 1582, and after long imprisonment in Rome was burned at the stake, 1585. He agreed with Dávid and Budny as to the worship of Christ, and with Budny in opposing the radical social views of the Racovians. cf. Karl Landsteiner, *Jacobus Palaeologus* (Wien, 1873).

ever to spread in Poland, and in 1580, at a synod at Raków, it came to the surface in the case of Jan Krotowski, first minister of the church at Śmigiel. He inclined to Judaism, used only the Old Testament in the pulpit, and did not acknowledge the worship of Christ. It was only after long argument that he was brought to a better mind.[4]

It was in Lithuania, however, that the seeds of non-adorantism fell upon most fertile soil. From the middle of the sixteenth century a liberal religious movement fusing Judaism with rationalistic tendencies in the Russian Church had spread from northern Russia into Lithuania, opposing the Trinity and the deity of Christ, and also teaching radical social doctrines.[5] The Jews there were numerous, wealthy and influential, had famous scholars, and carried on an aggressive propaganda.[6] Not a few Christians were thus influenced to regard the Old Testament more highly than the New, to keep the Jewish sabbath, to abstain from pork and blood, and even to accept circumcision, also holding that Jesus was not the Messiah nor the Redeemer. To a Christian like Czechowicz, who considered only the New Testament as authoritative Scripture, those that held such views as these were anathema. It was these extreme free-thinkers, who ignored most of the distinctively Christian traditions in religion, and also anticipated most of the commonplaces of modern liberal biblical criticism, that were the 'Pagan Jews' or Epicureans, whom he so strongly opposed in his so-called 'Dialogues' already published in 1575.[7] However, these seem not to have had a very wide or deep influence. The trouble came rather from those who, without going so far as to discard Christian traditions and beliefs in favor of Jewish ones, yet held that since Christ was purely human he should not be regarded as in any sense divine, and hence should not be invoked in prayers. This subject seemed to be of the more crucial importance since,

---

[4] This was the first synod at which Socinus appeared. cf. Bock, *Antitrinitar.*, i, 425 f; Szczotka, *op. cit.*, p. 31; Sandius, *Bibliotheca*, p. 214.

[5] cf. Lewicki. *Socynjanie*, pp. 204–234, condensed and translated from the author's 'Socianstwo w Polsce i Jugozapadnoj Rusi' (Socinianism in Poland and southwestern Red Russia), *Kijewskaja Starina* (1862).

[6] cf. Wacław Sobieski, 'Propaganda Żydowska, 1530–1540' (Jewish propaganda), *Przegląd Narodowy*, xxi (1921), pp. 24–42.

[7] Marcin Czechowicz, *Rozmowy Christiańskie*, ktore z Greckiego nazwiska Dialogami zowią, etc. (Christian conversations, which they call by the Greek name Dialogues), Raków, 1575, chaps. 6, 8–10. cf. Henryk Merczyng, 'Polscy Deiści i wolnomyślicieli za Jagiellonów' (Polish deists and free-thinkers under the Jagellons), *Przegląd Historyczny*, xii (1911), No. 3.

rightly or wrongly, it was regarded as marking the fundamental distinction between Christianity and Judaism; and the majority of the leaders of the Minor Church feared that if they were thought to be in effect Jews, then they might be deprived of whatever rights they might otherwise have under the Warsaw Confederation.

For the reason given in the preceding paragraph, the view of the non-adorants was found most congenial among the churches in Lithuania, and it there had an able and active champion in the person of Simon Budny, whose acquaintance and sympathy with Palaeologus in Transylvania had kept him informed of the development taking place there. Budny deserves notice as one of the most significant characters in the history of Polish Unitarianism, being head of its most radical wing.[8] Born the son of a poor Polish country squire about 1533, he spent most of his active life in Lithuania. Well educated in the ancient languages, he was also fluent in both Polish and Russian. About 1559 Radziwiłł appointed him minister of the newly-founded Reformed church at Kleck in the Palatinate of Nowogródek, where he made converts among the Russian members of the Greek Church, and published a large *Katechisis* in Russian, which showed originality of view. Though he opposed infant baptism, he had no sympathy with the radical social views of the Anabaptists. He early became antitrinitarian, and openly denied the supernatural birth of Jesus. As the Bible of Brest had proved unsatisfactory to the churches, he was asked to undertake a revision, but in the end was led instead to make an entirely new translation from the original tongues. His translation of the Old Testament (1572) was highly praised by Jewish scholars for its correctness; while for that of the New Testament (1574) he used a critically revised text, and appended critical notes in which he pointed out many corruptions and interpolations in the received text, thus anticipating by nearly two centuries many of the findings of modern textual criticism. His critical biblical studies confirmed the radical doctrinal views to which he had already tended, and brought him into controversy with western theologians,[9] as well as occasioned attacks from the Unitarian camp, where Czechowicz opposed his views in his *Dialogues*, and also published for

---

[8] cf. Merczyng, *Budny*: Stanisław Kot, art. 'Budny,' *Polski Słownik Biograficzny* (Kraków, 1937), iii, 96–99.

[9] cf. Josias Simler, *Assertio orthodoxae doctrinae de duabus naturis Christi . . . opposita blasphemiis et sophismatibus Simonis Budnaei nuper ab ipso in Lituania evulgatis* (Tiguri, 1575); Johannes Wigand, *De Jesu Christo Deo et Homine* (Regiomonti, 1575).

use in the churches a rival translation of the New Testament (1577) to forestall the evil influence of Budny's work. Budny also sought to commend his view to the famous English Protestant martyrologist, John Foxe.[10]

His negative view of the divinity of Christ seemed so extreme that even some of the Antitrinitarians in Little Poland charged him with having accepted the 'Jewish atheism,' and he was attacked by Gonesius, Czechowicz and Farnowski. To these Budny finally replied in an extensive work on the Christian faith,[11] which was approved by the Lithuanian Antitrinitarians who under his leadership inclined to non-adorantism. This work has been called the most radical doctrinal work published in Europe in the sixteenth century, and it called forth controversy from Catholic writers [12] as well as from Protestants.

When in 1582 a synod was called at Lubecz in deep Lithuania to consider some urgent social questions, so much feeling on the subject had arisen that the Polish delegates refused to consider these until they had first come to terms as to the adoration of Christ. Budny's party had to yield the point, though there was vigorous discussion, in which they seemed to have the stronger arguments; but a compromise formula was agreed to: 'We have one God, whom we invoke as God; but we pray to and invoke the Lord Jesus as mediator in intercession with God.' [13]

Harmony was short-lived however, for only two months later at a synod at Lucławice, the excommunication of Budny, which had for some years been threatened, was carried through by the Lublin brethren led by Czechowicz and Niemojewski. He was judged unworthy the title of both minister and brother, 'on account of his wicked opinions and acts.' [14] This judgment was reaffirmed at Węgrów in 1584.[15] This

---

[10] cf. *Reformacja w Polsce*, vii (1936), 316–323; Ms in Bodleian Library, Oxford, Rawlinson Letters 107, pp. 97–100; Stanisław Kot, 'Anglo Polonica,' *Nauka Polska*, xx (1935), 105 ff.

[11] *O przedniejszych wiary Christiańskiej artikulech*, etc. (On the principal articles of the Christian faith), Łosk, 1576.

[12] cf. Stanisław Ostrowski, *O prawdziwym Bóstwie Jezu Chrysta Pana*, etc. (Of the true divinity of Jesus Christ the Lord), Poznań, 1588; *id.*, *De Trinitate . . . contra impia scripta Simonis Budnaei*, etc. (Posnaniae, 1591).

[13] cf. Szymon Budny, *O urzędzie miecza używającem* (On the office employing the sword), 1583; ed. Stanisław Kot (Warszawa, 1932), p. 27 f; Szczotka, *op. cit.*, p. 36.

[14] Ob impia placita et facta. cf. Bock, *op. cit.*, i, 81; Szczotka, *op. cit.*, p. 39; Sandius, *op. cit.*, p. 54, wrongly gives the date as 1584 instead of 1582.

[15] cf. Szczotka, *op. cit.*, p. 41 f. The excommunication of Budny does not seem, as has generally been assumed, to have been chiefly, if at all, on account of his views as to the

latter action seems to have been incidental to a condemnation of the views of Christian Francken,[16] a learned German ex-Jesuit who had recently taken a position as Rector of the 'Arian' school at Chmielnik, where he ere long declared that it was not necessary to worship Christ. He was challenged to debate the question with Socinus, and the debate took place in the manor-house of Socinus's host at Pawlikowice near Kraków,[17] and was wholly on logical rather than scriptural grounds. The tradition is that Francken, full of self-assurance, and wishing to overwhelm his auditors by his learning, proposed no fewer than fifty separate arguments in support of his thesis against the adoration of Christ. The defence had been entrusted to Socinus, but the brethren, fearing that he might forget some important point, urged him to take notes. This he did not do, but simply listened attentively; when, to the admiration of all, he took up the points in just the same order and answered each of them so fully that Francken had nothing to answer, and withdrew in confusion.[18]

worship of Christ, objectionable as these were, but rather for his conservative views on social questions, which were so strongly at variance with those then dominant at Lublin and Raków. It was these latter, with regard to the rightfulness of office-holding and of war for a Christian, that had been most prominent in discussions at synods for more than a decade.

[16] Christian Francken was a restless spirit, and moved rapidly from the most conservative Catholicism through the various stages until he arrived at the extreme left wing of Antitrinitarianism, whence his unstable nature turned back again to his starting point. At each stage he registered his state of mind at the time by some outspoken publication. He was one of those personalities that must gratify their craving for complete self-expression at whatever cost to the cause to which they are attached. Thus he allowed himself at Kraków to be persuaded to put into print views which, however little they may startle us to-day, were, as a little reflection should have shown him, so wide a departure from anything hitherto uttered, and were expressed in a spirit so little regardful of the convictions of others, and withal so rude in statement, that instead of winning adherents to his doctrine he caused men to shrink from it in horror. Even the tolerant King Stephen found him intolerable, and caused the Edict of Parczów (1564) to be enforced against him as a foreign heretic. cf. Maurycy Dzieduszycki, *Piotr Skarga i jego wiek* (Peter Skarga and his times), Kraków, 1850, i, 426.

[17] Not at a synod at Chmielnik as Socinus's biographer states, writing a half-century later, and perhaps hastily catching the name from the title of the *Disputatio* published in 1618. Socinus was not present at the Chmielnik synod, which followed that at Węgrów. cf. (Samuel Przypcovius), *Vita authoris*, prefixed to *Socini Opera* (*Bibliotheca Fratrum Polonorum*), i, p. **3b; Szczotka, *op. cit.*, p. 42. For a report of the debate, as later revised by Francken, cf. Socinus, *Opera*, ii, 767 ff.

[18] Przypcovius, *loc. cit.* In the same year Francken published at Kraków a work against the Trinity that aroused the Catholics to such hot anger against him that he was forced to flee the country, lest he be punished under the Edict of Parczów, and his book was publicly burned at Kraków, the first such case in Poland. cf. Henryk Merczyng,

Despite his excommunication, Budny seems to have continued in the confidence of the Lithuanians as long as he lived. His important relation to the social questions at issue in the church will be spoken of a few pages further on. After his death his form of doctrine seems to have declined; but in 1599 a report reached the synod at Lublin that a good many in Lithuania were still saying that Christ ought not to be invoked. Two leading ministers were therefore sent to warn them to repent, else they would be excommunicated. The mission was successful. The leader of the non-adorants, Fabian [19] Domanowski, having failed to appear, was excommunicated, and his followers voluntarily returned to the fold, after which we hear no more of non-adorantism except in Transylvania, as we shall later see.

In so far as Budny's excommunication from the Minor Church was for a difference of opinion on a matter of doctrine, it stands in striking contrast with the spirit of tolerance that had come generally to prevail in the Minor Church hitherto. But the feeling seems to have been strong that at whatever cost the church must not now lay itself open to the charge of having left the Christian religion in favor of Judaism; and the matter of the invocation of Christ in prayers was taken as the decisive test. This instance, however, is not quite unique. At the synod of Lublin in 1585 a certain Piekarski, a wealthy nobleman who had formerly been a Reformed minister, was excommunicated for favoring Judaism, though for seven years previously he had been left undisturbed in holding such sentiments.[20] Also in 1588 Stanislas Budziński was restored to the communion of the church after having been under excommunication for several years for sharing Budny's views, though whether it was his doctrinal or his social ones is not stated.[21] A fourth instance, and the final one, was that of Domanowski just now men-

---

'Domniemanie pierwsza w Polsce książka spalana przez kata' (Presumably the first book in Poland burned by the executioner), *Przegląd Historyczny*, xvi (1913), 187–199. The printer, Rodecki, was imprisoned; cf. *supra*, p. 359, n. 12. Francken fled to Transylvania where he was for several years professor in the Unitarian college at Kolozsvár; but he at length returned to the Roman Church and died at Prague at the end of the century. cf. Jacobus Gorscius, *Pro tremenda et veneranda Trinitate, adversus quendam apostatam Francken, falso appellatum Christianum* (Coloniae, 1585); *id., Praemunitio adversus insanum dogma Christiani Francken* (Cracoviae, 1584).

[19] Not Joseph, as Bock wrongly has it (*op. cit.*, i. 250), apparently confusing him with one that may have been his son. cf. the epigram prefixed to Budny's *O Urzędzie*. cf. Smalcius, *Diary*, p. 1172; Dobrowolski, *Kronika*, p. 170.

[20] cf. Bock, *op. cit.*, i, 631.

[21] cf. Sandius, *Bibliotheca*, p. 55.

tioned. So far as the present writer recalls, these are the only instances in the whole history of the movement we are following in which members were excluded from the church on the ground of their doctrinal opinions.

More or less parallel with the doctrinal question of which we have just spoken, in time and in persons concerned, is that of the application of the teachings of Jesus to social and political situations. In the young reformed churches this began to arise soon after the more urgent questions of doctrine. It was the bold pioneer Gonesius that first brought it forward. During his ministry at Węgrów [22] he expressed views that he had evidently imbibed when among the Moravian communists, and these spread more or less widely in Lithuania. For when in 1562 Budny, still a Calvinist preacher, published his *Katechisis*, he opposed the Anabaptist view of such questions as whether a Christian might hold public office, or own property, or use force in self-defence, or engage in war; and such views were evidently attracting wide attention.[23] For in a work published by Budny some twenty years later,[24] he speaks of Gonesius as the first to write on these subjects in a book entitled *De Primatu*, now no longer extant. This book evidently took the social teachings of Jesus in the Sermon on the Mount as commands which Christians are bound literally to obey; but while it convinced some, it aroused opposition in many others, for there was apprehension lest a radical social movement be stirred up like that at Münster. Nevertheless these radical social views made a strong appeal to those that meant conscientiously to apply the teachings of the New Testament in the practical affairs of daily life. Thus at a Lithuanian synod at Iwie as early as 1568 [25] it was debated whether a Christian may hold serfs or slaves, or own landed property when other brethren have none. Such questions now came to be discussed at almost every synod, and the radical social views dominant at both Raków and Lublin were warmly advocated by such leaders as Paulus, Schomann, Czechowicz, Gonesius and others, though as warmly opposed by Budny and a few more. As we have already seen, Niemojewski gave up high office and sold his estates in Kujawy and took to manual labor, and others of the gentry

---

[22] From about 1560 on; *v. supra*, p. 290.
[23] cf. Kot, *Ideologja*, p. 15 f.
[24] cf. Budny, *O urzędzie*, pp. 14, 18 f, 219; cf. Jasnowski, *Piotr z Goniądza*, p. 31.
[25] cf. Budny, *op. cit.*, pp. 180–216.

followed his example, dividing the proceeds among the poorer brethren, or putting them into a common fund as the first Christians had done in Apostolic times. In a similar spirit the noble Ożarowski at Lublin gave his landed estates back to the King, since he could not with good conscience enjoy an inheritance that his ancestors had gained by shedding blood in war, and that carried with it obligation to render military service.[26] Another classic case, and by no means an isolated one, was that of Jan Przypkowski in freeing his serfs.[27]

[26] cf. Lubieniecki, *Poloneutychia*, p. 75 f.

[27] 'Jan Przypkowski . . . freely and expressly recognizing that his subjects residing in (the five villages named) are along with him creatures of one Creator, and not being willing therefore further to hold the said his peasants and subjects and their sons and daughters in the villages aforesaid in bondage, . . .' sets the said his peasants and subjects aforesaid and their posterity free from all servitude, and he also gives the said his peasants and their children permission to leave his lands and remain and dwell wherever they please, nor will he prosecute them for so doing or ever try to recover them . . . but grants them and their children leave to enjoy the said liberty perpetually.' Original in the court records at Kraków, vol. 108, p. 134 (1572); reprinted in Grabowski, *Literatura*, p. 67, n; and, in free Polish translation, in Kot, *Ideologja*, p. 22, n.

CHAPTER XXVIII

THE MINOR CHURCH AND THE STATE: NON-RESISTANCE, PACIFISM. EFFORTS AT UNION WITH THE CALVINISTS. A DEMOCRATIC CHURCH

As has been seen, the attempt was made for several years to have the whole community at Raków live strictly according to the gospel rule, as brothers and sisters in one great family. These experiments were for a time considered by the people at large as the vagaries of fanatics who had gone harmlessly mad, and they were looked on at the worst with contempt or disgust. But when the King died in 1572, and the Senate ordered the whole nation under arms in the face of threatened attacks from hostile neighbors, the situation assumed a more serious aspect. For in antitrinitarian circles the use of weapons had for some time been strongly condemned, and many of the gentry were refusing to bear arms lest they disobey the plain command of Christ. The question was therefore seriously debated whether it were really true that obedience to Christ required his followers to be disloyal to the State; for in that case obedient Christians might be in danger of incurring the extreme penalty as traitors. The debate centered mainly about two questions: whether a Christian might engage in warfare, and whether he might hold a judicial or other office which was authorized to impose a capital sentence.[1] Minor questions were also involved, as to the rightfulness of holding estates, taking oaths, paying taxes that might be used in war, resorting to courts for obtaining justice or redress of injuries, and the like.

These questions were publicly discussed at a meeting at Kraków in 1572. Palaeologus happened at the time to be the guest of Dudith, and being present at the meeting he was invited to give his opinion as a

[1] 'The office of the sword,' as it was called. There is no equivalent English term. The Racovians insisted that no Christian might hold an office having the *jus gladii*, since that would involve breaking the command, 'Thou shalt not kill.' cf. Stanisław Estreicher, 'Pacyfizm w Polsce XVI stulecia' (Pacifism in 16th century Poland), *Ruch Prawniczy, ekonomiczny i socjologiczny* (Poznań, 1930).

foreigner. In doing so he defended the rightfulness of bearing arms in war. He was then requested to write out his argument for use a little later at a synod at Raków; and many there were found to agree with him.[2] He supported his position from the New Testament, but pursued his argument in a very sarcastic and even insulting manner. In defence of the Racovian view, therefore, Paulus composed a reply[3] which, however, was more like a sermon than like an argument, and appealed with much feeling to Christ's spirit and teaching of unconditional love toward one's enemies; for he was uncompromisingly non-resistant and pacific. Though he wrote in the name of the whole Raków church, there was outspoken opposition, and at the synod at Lutomirsko late in the same year Budziński protested against the intolerant spirit of the Racovians, which would allow for no difference of opinion, but would condemn to eternal punishment any one seen with a sword at his side.[4] The brethren took this reproach ill, and charged Czechowicz to reply. On his own part, Palaeologus, returning from a visit to Constantinople, found a copy of Paulus's reply in Transylvania and at once prepared an answer to it, presenting a complete and thorough discussion of the whole question at issue.[5] He paid especial attention to the 'office of the sword,' and held that not to resist evil or punish evil-doers would be madness. In contrast to the literal, unqualified idealism of Paulus, he showed himself a sober realist, and argued with great force, though in a spirit of supercilious contempt, concerning the practical consequences of the position defended by Paulus.

Paulus himself, grown old and weary of controversy, remained silent, but Czechowicz complied with the request of the synod and published an extensive Polish catechism, the *Dialogues* to which reference has already been made.[6] It was written in lively style, and instead of avoiding the thorny questions of the day, it wholly supported the Racovian views, though it was careful not to use expressions that might give offence to the government. This was well, for King Stephen Batory

[2] This writing was in the following year published in Lithuania by Budny: *Liber de magistratu politico* (Losci, 1573). cf. Jacobus Palaeologus, *Defensio verae sententiae de magistratu*, etc. (Losci, 1580), dedicatio; Szczotka, *op. cit.*, p. 27; Kot, *Ideologja*, p. 38 f., where the arguments of Palaeologus are summarized.

[3] *Coetus Racoviensis nomine adversus Jacobi Palaeologi scriptum quo docuit, Christum non sustulisse Magistratum politicum*, 1573. cf. Kot, *Ideologja*, pp. 39–44.

[4] cf. Budny, *O urzędzie*, pp. 172–179.

[5] *Defensio verae sententiae de magistratu politico*, etc.; cf. Kot, *Ideologja*, pp. 44–47.

[6] *v. supra*, p. 368, n. 7.

now came to the throne [7] (1576), a great soldier, who at once devoted himself to strengthening the authority of the State at home and abroad, in a series of important wars. It was no time for pacifists to urge their views. Though the official view of the church continued to be that stated by Czechowicz, public controversy was not in order.

In Lithuania, however, where war with Moscow was a constant menace, a passive attitude toward the State and its concerns seemed hardly loyal. An active movement against the gospel according to Raków therefore arose, with Budny at the head of it, who though he had at length accepted the Anabaptists' view of baptism at Łosk in 1578, did not at all agree to their extreme social and political doctrines. Many of the Lithuanian nobles also were not willing as yet to give up their estates as Czechowicz and Witrelin demanded, nor would the ministers surrender their glebes unless convinced from the word of God, holding that these and other things objected to by the brethren from Poland were not contrary to the Gospel.[8] When, therefore, Budny and Domanowski later in the year came as delegates to a synod at Lucławice in Little Poland with letters from the Lithuanian gentry asking for a sober discussion of the question and a written report on it, the brethren refused to discuss it with them at all, declaring that with them the matter had been definitely settled ('*ratum, gratum, et firmissimum*'), that a Christian might hold no office in the Republic. This they wrote in brief to the Lithuanian brethren, referring them further to the twelfth dialogue ('of the Christian Life') in Czechowicz's book.[9] Nor when a request was also made by the Lithuanians for the loan of Palaeologus's recent reply to Paulus was it granted. It was evidently suspected that Budny wished to publish it as he had the previous one; for at the next synod, at Lublin, 1579, it was voted that henceforth no book might be published without ecclesiastical censure, although to this the Lithuanian delegates did not give their consent. Budny, however, had no mind to see the question smothered in this fashion, and he soon obtained the desired manuscript from Palaeologus himself, then in Moravia; and in the following year he published the whole controversy.[10] When the Lithuanian brethren wished not long after to offer

---

[7] King Henry had abdicated after only a few months, in order to accept the crown of France.

[8] cf. Szczotka, *op. cit.*, p. 29.

[9] cf. Budny, *O urzędzie*, p. 23; Szczotka, *op. cit.*, p. 29 f.

[10] Jacobus Palaeologus, *Defensio*. The volume comprises the three items above spoken

a copy of the new book to the brethren at Lublin, Niemojewski refused to accept it and thus be drawn into further discussion of a subject already closed; [11] and he sharply reproached Budny for publishing it without leave from the synod. The book evidently found favor in Lithuania, however, for at a synod at Łosk in the next year, which was attended only by Lithuanians, all but two voted for the conservative view as to office-holding.[12] Still the question would not down; and as the brethren in Little Poland were unwilling to let Palaeologus go unanswered, they urged Socinus to reply to him. An account of his reply will be given in the next chapter.

The subject was still debated at a synod at Lubecz in Lithuania in the spring of 1582, but no agreement was reached and two months later, as we have seen above, apparently in despair of harmony, Budny was excommunicated in Little Poland as incorrigible. It is likely that as a result of this action Kiszka removed Budny from his pulpit. Yet he continued on good relations with the brethren in Lithuania, where he died probably between 1590 and 1595. Although in 1583 he published an important work reviewing the whole subject of the 'office of the sword,' [13] and defending his point of view against the radicalism of the Polish brethren, especially Czechowicz, they made no reply, and Budny's career in the Minor Church was evidently closed. Despite vague rumors to the contrary, there is no good evidence that he ever received, or sought, reinstatement in the church or its ministry. Budny was perhaps the ablest, as he was the most fearless and consistent, of the thinkers that our movement produced in Polish lands. He early reached and announced positions in both biblical criticism and doctrine that were not overtaken until three centuries after his time; and of all the religious leaders of his period, he is the one that would feel most at home in the Unitarian movement of the twentieth century.

Those that had long been the influential leaders of the church were now passing from the stage. Paulus at Raków, who in his time had been an active and able propagandist, and once had not hesitated to consider himself the logical successor of Luther and Zwingli in the reformation of the Church, was aging and fast losing influence in the

---

of: the author's first book now reprinted, Paulus's reply, and the author's long rejoinder. all with a suitable introduction prefixed.

[11] cf. Szczotka, *op. cit.*, p. 33.

[12] cf. Budny, *O urzędzie*, p. 25 f.

[13] *O urzędzie miecza używającem; v. supra*, p. 370, n. 13.

movement of which he had long been the leading spirit, and was absorbed in dreams of the millennial reign of Christ on earth, which was the subject of his last work.[14] He died in 1591, a month after his long-time co-laborer Schomann. Gonesius had long since gone from the scene, and Budny had been ejected. Only Czechowicz remained to lead the thought and shape the policy of the church, and his extreme views as to the duty of Christians to the State marked him as one whose star was declining. The newer members of his congregation were becoming restive, and as soon as Niemojewski, his powerful patron and colleague in the work of the church, had died in 1598, he was forced to retire from the ministry of the congregation he had served so long and so efficiently, and to yield it to younger men more *en rapport* with the spirit of the time. Yet his work, the *Rozmowy*,[15] was for nearly a generation the standard exposition of the faith and practice of the church. His last years were spent in quiet retirement until his death in 1613 at the advanced age of 81. His parting message to his followers, as he neared death, was that they should persevere in the Minor Church, despite its departure from his teaching on baptism.[16] In talents, knowledge and sobriety he surpassed all the other leaders in the first generation of the Minor Church. Besides his early work against infant baptism, and his translation of the New Testament in 1577 which became standard for the congregations of the Minor Chuch, and the work just mentioned, he engaged in several important controversies in print: with the Calvinist Paul Gilowski, over an exposition of the church Catechism;[17] with the Jewish rabbi Jakob of Bełżyce (near Lublin) who had vigorously attacked the Christian doctrine as it was set forth in Czechowicz's *Rozmowy* in opposition to the then active anti-Christian propaganda of the Jews;[18] and most important of all with Canon Hieronim Powodowski of Poznań, of which some account will be given in the next chapter.

[14] *Tractatus de regno Christi millenario*, c. 1590 (unpublished). cf. *Sandius, op. cit.,* p. 45. [15] *v. supra,* p. 368, n. 7.

[16] cf. Lubieniecius, *Historia,* p. 192.

[17] cf. Paweł Gilowski, *Wykład Katechizmu Kościoła Krześcijańskiego,* etc. (Exposition of the Catechism of the Christian Church) (Kraków, 1579; ed. 3, 1605); Czechowicz, *Rozsądek na Wykład katechyzmu . . . Gilowskiego* (a critique of Gilowski's Exposition), ·Kraków, 1581.

[18] cf. Czechowicz, *Odpis Jakoba Żyda z Bełżyc, na Dyalogi Marcina Czechowicza; na ktory zaś odpowieda . . . Marcin Czechowicz* (Reply of Jacob the Jew of Bełżyce to the Dialogue of M. C., with M. C's rejoinder), Raków, 1581; Brückner, *Różnowiercy,* pp. 250–253.

While the Lublin church was thus earnestly striving to strengthen its position, it received a severe blow in the apostasy of one of its prominent members. Kasper Wilkowski,[19] son of one of the Elders of the church, and himself a physician of note, having with the approval of his friends gone to Italy for study, there became impressed by the dignity and good order of the Catholic worship, in contrast with the heterogeneous, ill-organized and disunited little congregation in which he had been reared at home. Questionings were aroused in him that were not allayed when he returned, and seeking religious stability he at length sought conference with the rector of the Catholic church at Lublin, and in consequence became a convert. Being now treated by his old associates as a renegade, he was led to publish an *apologia* for the step he had taken.[20] The book was ably written, and excited much attention among both Protestants and Catholics, of whom the latter made much use of it in winning converts among the Protestants. After relating his religious experience, Wilkowski in twenty-five chapters sets forth his reasons for making the change, which briefly stated are these: Dissension is rife not only among the ministers, but also in private quarrels of the ministers and the poor with the gentry; there is uncertainty and much contention as to the right form of baptism; the churches are greatly declining in membership, the leading men and the more important nobles have died, and the whole church depends on two or three; the leading ministers are dead, others have gone over to Judaism or the Calvinists, or given up their ministry, and no successors are being trained up; fathers are negligent in training their sons in their own faith. In fact, Wilkowski touched upon some of the weakest spots in the life of the Minor Church, and it winced; but he was ably answered.[21]

In 1580 a half-hearted effort was again made to close the breach be-

---

[19] cf. Ossoliński, *Wiadomości*, iv, 512–520; Płokarz, 'Jan Niemojewski,' *Reformacja w Polsce*, ii (1922), pp. 84, 92 f; Brückner, *Różnowiercy*, pp. 219–234.

[20] *Przyczyny nawrocenia*, etc.: *supra*, p. 358, n. 9.

[21] By Niemojewski, *Okazanie, iż kościół Rzymski Papieski nie jest Apostolski, ani święty, ani jeden, ani powszechny* (Proofs that the Popish Roman Church is not Apostolic, nor holy, nor one, nor Catholic), 1583. From the Calvinist side by Grzegorz Żarnowec, *Antidotum, albo lekarstwo na odtręt od Ewanyelików Pana Kaspra Wilkowskiego*, etc. (An Antidote or medicine for Mr. K. W's aversion to the Evangelicals), no date. Wilkowski rejoined by translating into Polish the Latin work of an English Jesuit, Edmund Campion, *Dziesięc mocnych dowodów aż Adwersarze Kościoła Powszechnego w porządny o wierze Dysputaciey upaść muszą* (Ten strong reasons why the adversaries of the Catholic Church must fail in any proper discussion of the faith), Wilno, 1584.

tween the Calvinists and the Minor Church. This time the initiative was taken by the Calvinists. The proprietor of Lewartów, Nicholas Firlej, was the instigator of a joint synod at that town. Both sides prepared for a debate, and about 130 ministers of the different confessions were present, with the Calvinists stronger in numbers, but weak in able theologians. They had therefore sought help from abroad, and asked the University of Königsberg to send an accomplished theologian to assist them.[22] He arrived too late, and even Sarnicki was reluctant to face Czechowicz and Niemojewski in debate on scripture grounds only. After a skirmish therefore the Calvinist ministers declared that it was a sin for them to have a debate or anything to do with those Ebionites, Arians and Samosatenians, long ago excommunicated from the Church; and they withdrew from the scene, while the Unitarians went to Lublin in triumph. Nearly a generation later, if we may anticipate, the Socinians, feeling the need of allies in the face of growing persecution, sent a request to the district synod of the Calvinists, meeting at Lublin in 1611, that they might be permitted to present their cause in person. The Calvinists complied, on condition that not more than two or three persons should attend. Disregarding this limitation nearly twenty appeared, and were courteously received. The Socinians desired religious and political union, but after consultation they were told that in view of such a great difference in the chief articles of faith, religious union between them could not be considered, although in political and secular affairs they desired to live in harmony. Nevertheless the Socinians still sought religious union, and at the local synod the next year they begged leave to submit their requests in writing. The conference between the committees appointed came to nothing, for neither side would yield a hair in regard to doctrines, and they separated more estranged than ever. Undaunted still, the Socinians renewed their efforts once more at a synod at Bełżyce in 1613. This time the Calvinists lost patience, and appointed one of their ministers to show in a special writing the impossibility of any religious union between the two sects. The work when accepted by the synod was put to print,[23] and no further attempt at union was made.

[22] cf. Daniel H. Arnoldt, *Historie der Königsbergischen Universität* (Königsberg, 1746–69), ii, 460 f, *Beilage*, pp. 87–97; Andreas Wissowatius, *Narratio Compendiosa*, p. 214, in Sandius, *Bibliotheca*; Szczotka, *op. cit.*, pp. 31–33.

[23] Jakób Zaborowski, *Ogień z woda*, etc. (Fire with water: that is, a little book about union, in which reason is given why those that call themselves Christians of the Minor

We have now reached a point in the history of the Minor Church where it may be said to have developed its leading characteristics and measurably to have fixed its type. Before we proceed to the period of its middle life it may be well, therefore, after having traced the threads of its development separately, to survey the whole of the progress thus far made. By 1585, twenty years after the Minor Church began its separate existence after the schism at Piotrków, it probably had several score congregations with settled ministers. Many of these were hardly more than domestic chaplaincies on the estates of the gentry, but there were also meetings in perhaps a dozen of the larger towns, of which the most important were at Kraków, Lublin, Raków and Lucławice, all in Little Poland, and Śmigiel in Great Poland. The congregation at Kraków was declining under the pressure of Catholic persecutions at the capital, which fell on all Dissidents alike. That at Raków was becoming settled in normal life after the confusion of its early years, and on the way to being the metropolis of the whole movement. That at Lucławice, having absorbed a considerable part of the Arian wing which had at first gone after Farnowski, was growing in influence. But the centre of the church's strength was at Lublin, where the membership counted a considerable number of persons of high standing, and Czechowicz as minister and Niemojewski as Elder gave the church for twenty years an intellectual leadership that commanded respect. The social views fostered in the congregation were quite advanced, though community of goods was not practiced here as it had been at Raków.

Historians of the Reformation in Poland have often remarked that Protestantism in that country remained predominantly a religion of the upper classes, dominated by the gentry, showing little interest in the improvement of the humbler classes and peasantry and having little influence on them.[24] However true this may have been of the orthodox sects, it does not hold good of the Minor Church. Deeply impressed from early in its history with the doctrines and traditions of the Anabaptists, it was the most democratic of all the religious bodies in Poland.

Church, so long as they persist in their errors, can never come into union with the orthodox Protestants), Toruń, 1619. Answered by Valentin Smalcius, *Odpowiedź na książkę X. Jakuba Zaborowskiego, który dał tytuł, Ogień z wodą* (Reply to the Rev. J. Z's little book, which he entitled Fire with water), Raków, 1619. cf. Łukaszewicz, *Kościół Helwecki*, pp. 268–271; Bock, *Antitrinitar.*, i, 879–882; Zeltner, *Crypto-Socin.*, pp. 1194, 1208 f.

[24] cf. Wotschke, *Reformation*, p. 12 f.

While the magnates and higher nobility in large majority remained orthodox, many of the middle and lower nobility were found in the Minor Church, whose democratic atmosphere they found more congenial. The congregation at Lublin had convinced adherents in all classes of society, not only several score of the middle nobility, but many citizens of different levels in culture and wealth, professional men, merchants, artisans, and not a few of the lowest social status, including peasants and common laborers, of whom all took active part in the inner life of the church, and upon occasion would speak in its meetings.[25] Hence their opponents liked to refer to their congregations as sinks for the dregs of the human race. The extreme democracy at Raków has already been spoken of. In such a church the main emphasis was upon an ethical religious life in both personal and social relations, in conformity with the Sermon on the Mount. Doctrine was esteemed only in proportion to its simplicity and practical value, and the first full statement of it, supplementing the Catechism of 1574, was in Czechowicz's *Rozmowy*, which served until the appearance of the Racovian Catechism in 1605. Time wrought changes, of course, and the primitive simplicity of the Minor Church suffered modifications. Toward the end of the century the records of the synods reflect a growing worldliness in dress and food among the nobles, and an increasing indulgence in luxury and in worldly pleasures is frequently complained of, as many of the nobles became persuaded that after all they might retain their estates and live in the traditional manner of their class.[26] Nevertheless, to the end of their history the earlier ideals were earnestly proclaimed by the ministers, and however much a minority might disregard them, they were more or less adhered to in practice by the majority of the members.

[25] cf. Płokarz, *Jan Niemojewski*, p. 86; Powodowski, *Wędzidło*, p. 179, *v. infra*, p. 386.

[26] cf. the records of synods given by Dobrowolski, *Kronika*, pp. 169–171; and by Szczotka, *Synody*, p. 48 f; Helena Horwitzówna, 'Reformacja Polska a Zagadnienie Zbytku' (The Polish Reformation and the question of luxury), *Reformacja w Polsce*, iv (1926), 32 ff.

CHAPTER XXIX

THE MINOR CHURCH REACHES MATURITY. FAUSTUS SOCINUS UP TO HIS ARRIVAL IN POLAND

OUR HISTORY has now arrived at a point where the Minor Church may be said to have fairly found itself, not only in its essential inner character but also with relation to its general environment. We have seen it, under the broadly accepted principles of freedom, reason and tolerance, develop a body of doctrine on a purely scriptural basis which, while it negatively rejected the doctrine of the Trinity and of the eternal divinity of Christ, yet positively gave Jesus a very high rank as one whose human nature approximated the divine, and whose teachings Christians are bound to accept literally and to follow strictly. Its main emphasis, however, was not upon theological doctrines but upon the conduct of a life in which Christian teachings are put into actual practice in the private character and the social relations of individuals, and in one's public relations to the institutions and activities of the State. While no agreement in detail as to minor doctrines was reached or even thought necessary, the more important points had been comfortably agreed upon, and the rest were left to the issue of free discussion.

The membership of the church embraced all classes, and the spirit in its principal congregations was democratic, recognizing no class distinctions among members, since they were regarded as being all brethren in one Christian family. They were however firmly excluded from Christian fellowship with the other reformed confessions no less than with the Catholic Church. While they were at heart intensely loyal to their country and its government, their convictions as to rendering military service and holding public office laid them open to charges of disloyalty. Yet there was in all this no trace of a spirit of sedition or revolt, but simply the renouncement of public life.[1] Thus more or less isolated from the religious and political life of their time, they went their way alone with the deeper devotion to their cause. In the present

---

[1] cf. Stanislas Kot, *Le Mouvement Antitrinitaire au XVIe et au XVIIe Siècle* (Paris, 1937), p. 52.

chapter we shall see their divergent elements and conflicting views gradually and peaceably consolidated, and the Minor Church become an effective religious force under the persuasive leadership of Faustus Socinus.

The political background of the history of the Minor Church during this period was on the whole not oppressive. Henry of Valois had ruled only a few months in Poland when his brother, King Charles IX. of France, suddenly died, and Henry hastily and secretly left Kraków to claim the vacant throne in Paris. An interregnum of a year and a half followed, ending with the election of Stephen Batory (Báthory), Prince of Transylvania, as King of Poland (1576-'86). In his candidacy for the throne Stephen was very ably represented by his court physician, Dr. Giorgio Biandrata, whose acquaintance we have already made, and who had wide relations with the higher nobility and court circles in Poland. The orthodox Dissidents opposed him at first out of fear that he was an Antitrinitarian, though they afterwards accepted him in the belief that he favored the reformed cause. The Catholics on the other hand, including nearly all the Bishops, opposed his candidacy, thinking him of doubtful loyalty to the Church, and only one of the ten envoys sent to offer him the crown was a Catholic. All proved to be mistaken. Bishop Karnkowski before proposing Batory to the Catholics had informed himself exactly about Batory's religion. He had never ceased to be a practicing Catholic, and his family was one of the few in Transylvania that had remained consistently so.[2] In Poland he soon showed himself zealous for the Church, though no fanatic. He vigorously opposed the riots against Protestants which had of late been frequent and violent in the large towns, though he excepted Antitrinitarians from his protection in this respect.[3] But though he restored to the Catholics many of the churches that Protestants had taken from them, and much favored the Jesuits, he signed the *pacta conventa* guaranteeing protection to the Protestants, and scrupulously kept his promise when strongly urged to violate it, declaring that he was king of the people, not of their consciences.[4] For a time indeed there seemed

---

[2] cf. Artur Śliwiński, *Stefan Batory* (Warszawa, 1922), p. 218; Berga, *Skarga*, p. 190, n.; Karnkowski, *Epistolae*, pp. H. h. iii; I. i. iii; K. k. ii, and iii; D. d. ii and iii; C. c. ii; *Relacye Nunc.*, i, 277 (1575); Augustus Theiner, *Annales Ecclesiasticae* (Roma, 1856), i, 5; Antonio Possevino, *Transylvania* (Budapest, 1913), p. 94.

[3] cf. Berga, *Skarga*, p. 189 f; Friese, *Kirchengesch.*, II, ii, 66.

[4] Rex sum populorum, non conscientiarum . . . Nolo conscientiis dominari; siquidem Deus haec tria sibi reservarit: creare aliquid ex nihilo, nosse futura, et dominari consci-

great danger that the Racovians might suffer for their opposition to serving in war, and to holding public office; but nothing serious happened, and as time went on their views attracted less and less attention. But while the King himself showed tolerance, hostility now began to manifest itself from another quarter, that of the Catholic clergy. The controversy of Czechowicz with Canon Powodowski was briefly mentioned above.[5] Powodowski, being present at Lublin as a clerical member of the royal Tribunal or Supreme Court of the kingdom, which Stephen had recently established there, was stirred up by the boldness of Czechowicz's attacks upon the Roman Church and its doctrines, and challenged him to a debate. This was held in the Canon's house, and lasted eight hours, but it left each of the same opinion still. The matter was then continued in print.[6] This was practically the beginning of a long succession of public debates between the members of the Minor Church and the Catholics [7] (controversy with the Calvinists had by now largely ceased), who had hitherto been content to let the Dissidents waste their strength in controversy with one another, but henceforth accepted or seized every opportunity for debate, becoming ever more aggressive. Each side would make its points and claim the victory, and afterwards would usually print its own account. But though partisans were doubtless confirmed in the views they already held, few converts were made; appeals to popular feeling proved more effective than those to calm reason, and the main result was to widen the breach and deepen the enmity between the parties. In these controversies it was Czechowicz that was the able champion and the acknowledged authority of the Minor Church until he was superseded by Socinus.

---

entiis. cf. Wengerscius, *Slavonia*, p. 215. cf. also the King's tolerant utterance on releasing from prison Rodecki, punished for printing a heretical book (*v. supra*, p. 359, n. 12). quoted by Sandius, *Bibliotheca*, p. 82 f.   [5] *v. supra*, p. 379.

[6] cf. Jósefat Płokarz, *Niemojewski*, p. 90 ff. Hieronyn Powodowski, *Wędzidło na sprosne błędy a bluźnierstwa Nowych Arjanów . . . a mianowicie w Rozmowie Marcina Czechowicza opisanych* (A rebuke for the foul errors of the Neoarians . . . especially those set forth in the Dialogues of M. C.), Poznań, 1582; Czechowicz, *Epistomium na Wędzidło . . . Powodowskiego*, etc. (A demurrer to P's Rebuke), Wilno, 1583. cf. Brückner, *Różnowiercy*, pp. 259–266. Niemojewski also replied to Powodowski in *Obrona przeciw niesprawidlemu obwinieniu Powodowskiego . . . w swoim Wędzidło*, etc. (Defence against P's unjust accusation in the Rebuke), Raków, 1583.

[7] An interesting contemporary report of fourteen of these disputations from 1579 to 1620, probably made by Statorius, one of the participants, has survived. cf. Stanisław Kot, 'Disputacje Arjan Polskich' (Disputations of the Polish Arians), *Reformacja w Polsce*, viii (1936), 341–370.

It was at just this period, when the first leaders of the Minor Church were passing from the scene, leaving none to fill their places, and when for want of competent leadership the whole loosely organized movement was in grave danger of falling to pieces, that Faustus Socinus appeared on the scene, and through his ability, scholarship and persuasive speech won the confidence of the membership, and by his wise and tactful methods gave the church unity of spirit and aim, and fixed it in the characteristics that caused it eventually to be identified with his name as Socinianism, and launched it upon a new period in its history. It will therefore be convenient at this point to review the course of his life in preparation for his activity in Poland.

Faustus Socinus [8] (Fausto Sozzini) came of an ancestry long distinguished in Siena, where his family had lived since the middle of the fourteenth century, had been admitted to noble rank, and had held the highest offices.[9] His great-great-grandfather, Mariano Sozzini the elder (1397–1467), was Professor of Canon Law at Padua and Siena, a man of wide culture, and the most famous jurist of his time. If one may trust the almost incredibly flattering description of him written to a correspondent by Aeneas Sylvius (later Pope Pius II.) in 1444, he possessed in the superlative degree nearly every imaginable talent, skill, grace and accomplishment, physical, mental, moral and social.[10]

His grandson, Mariano the younger (1482–1556), was Faustus's grandfather, and was even more celebrated, being Professor of Law successively in the four universities of Siena, Pisa, Padua and Bologna, and was complimented with the title of *Princeps Jurisconsultorum*.[11]

---

[8] cf. Samuel Przypcovius, *Vita Fausti Socini*, prefixed to S's *Opera Omnia*, vol. i (*Bibliotheca Fratrum Polonorum*), Irenopoli, 1656; reprinted in P's *Cogitationes Sacrae* (Eleutheropoli, 1692), pp. 417–425; English trans. (London, 1653), and again, by Emily Sharpe (London, 1912); Bock, *Antitrinitar.*, ii, 654–850; Joshua Toulmin, *Memoirs . . . of Faustus Socinus* (London, 1777); Wallace, *Antitrin.*, ii, 306–339; Cantù, *Eretici*, ii, 486–498, 506–510; Alexander Gordon, 'The Sozzini and their School,' *Theological Review*, xvi (1879), 293–322, 531–571; Paul Lecler, *Fauste Socin* (Genève, 1885); David M. Cory, *Faustus Socinus* (Boston, 1932); Earl M. Wilbur, 'Faustus Socinus: an estimate of his life and influence,' *Bulletin du Comité international des Sciences Historiques*, no. 18, Février, 1933, pp. 48–60; *id.*, 'Faustus Socinus, Pioneer,' *Hibbert Journal*, xxxiii (1935), 536–548.

[9] cf. Antonio Mazzei, *Breve Storia della nobile e celebre famiglia senese dei Sozzini* (Siena, 1912).

[10] cf. Aeneas Sylvius Piccolomini, *Epistolae et varii tractatus* (Mediolani, 1496), ep. cxii. A recumbent bronze statue of him by Vecchietta is in the Bargello at Florence.

[11] cf. Guido Lanciroli, *De claribus legum interpretibus* (ed. 2, Venetiis, 1655), pp. 338–342. A monument to him is in the choir of San Domenico at Bologna. For Mariano the elder, cf. *id. op.*, pp. 456–459.

Of his eleven sons, the sixth was that Laelius whose career we have already followed; [12] while the eldest was Alessandro (1509–1541), father of Faustus. He bid fair to add further lustre to the family name, being appointed Professor of Civil Law at Padua at once after receiving his degree, and later at the new university at Macerata, where he died untimely at the early age of thirty-two. Of the three little children whom he left, Fausto, the second, was born December 5, 1539,[13] and was thus but two years old at his father's death. On his mother's side Fausto's ancestry was even more notable than on his father's. His mother was Agnese Petrucci, whose mother in turn was of the celebrated Piccolomini family, a grandniece of Pope Pius II., and an own cousin of Pope Pius III. Early bereft of his father, he spent his childhood and youth at the country place that his grandfather had lately bought, the villa of Scopeto, six miles east of Siena,[14] where he received careful training from his mother and grandmother. The young man's tastes ran rather to letters than to the law cultivated by his ancestors, which in fact he held in very low esteem,[15] and although he may have studied the rudiments of the subject, he seems to have made no serious attempt to master it. Thus, though he was considered a youth of high promise, he had an irregular and desultory education, and won no university degree. In a letter written but a few weeks before his death, he apologetically says of himself that he never studied philosophy nor applied himself to scholastic theology, and never dabbled even in Logic beyond the rudiments, and that very late in life.[16] It was however, this very

[12] v. supra, p. 239 ff.

[13] cf. his Opera, i, 490. His birthplace at Siena was in the Palazzo Sozzini, the town-house of his grandfather, at 21 Via Ricasoli (the street number was changed in 1932 to 9 Via di Pantaneto), later known as the Palazzo Malavolti with which it was incorporated, and later yet as the Palazzo Costa. Here Lelio was also born, and he and Fausto are commemorated by a tablet placed at the corner of the building in 1879, with a laudatory inscription, by liberal Sienese. Marble medallions of the two, sculptured by Prunai, are in the Loggia della Gloria on the Piazza dell' Indipendenza, placed, with inscription, in 1883. cf. Mazzei, op. cit., p. 29 f; W. M. Brady, 'Faustus Socinus,' Athenaeum, August 11, 1877, p. 180; E. A. Brigidi, Nuova guida di Siena (Siena, 1922), pp. 51, 117. v. supra, p. 239.

[14] The house still stands, much as it was, and contains the Sozzini arms, built into the wall. The Sozzini family at Siena became extinct early in the nineteenth century. Scopeto and the town-house above mentioned fell in 1845 to Count Malavolti. cf. Mazzei, op. cit., p. 28 n.

[15] cf. his letter of April 20, 1553, to Girolamo Bargagli, a fellow academician, printed in Cantù, Eretici, ii, 491 ff.; translation by Gordon in Theological Review above cited, p. 536.

[16] Quid . . . expectari a me potest, homine qui nec philosophiam unquam didicit, nec

deficiency in the conventional education of the time that contributed to his distinction as an original theologian, since when he came to work out a reformed system of doctrine he was not insensibly warped by traditional methods of thought, but approached the Bible text with an unbiased mind.

Though born the child of Catholic parents, Faustus in heart never gave allegiance to the Catholic Church.[17] The Protestant heresy was rife in the Sozzini family during his boyhood. Of his uncles, besides Lelio already mentioned, Camillo had to flee from the Inquisition, and was excommunicated; Cornelio was charged with heresy and for a time under arrest in Rome; and Celso was under suspicion. They evidently imbued him with their religious views, and when Lelio, whom he learned greatly to admire and revere, revisited Siena in 1552-'53,[18] he will have exerted a powerful influence on his young nephew.[19] His grandfather died in 1556, leaving Faustus a fourth of his estate; and whether for reasons of prudence or otherwise, as soon as he was of age, early in 1561, Faustus left Italy and took up residence at Lyon, perhaps for quiet study in a place where he need not be too much compromised by associations. Within a bare year, however, he received word from Zürich that his revered uncle had died, and he hastened thither to take possession of the books and papers that Lelio had left behind him. After a brief residence at Geneva, where he was enrolled as a member of the Italian church [20] but probably did not find himself spiritually at home, he returned to Lyon, where he composed his first work.[21] In this he proposed an interpretation of the prologue of the Fourth Gospel which did not take it as implying the doctrine of the Trinity.

By 1563 the persecution against members of his family having seem-

---

scholasticam (quam vocant) theologiam unquam attigit, et ipsius logicae artis, nihil nisi rudimenta quaedam, idque valde sero degustavit? *Opera*, i, 490.

[17] Vix dici potest me unquam Romanae Ecclesiae adhaesisse, cum simulatque per aetatem judicio in divinis rebus uti potui, fuerim in illis aliter atque Ecclesia Romana doceat, edoctus atque institutus. Letter to Vadovita, June 14, 1598, *Opera*, i, 476.

[18] *v. supra*, p. 243.

[19] cf. *Opera*, ii, 505, 118; i, 782.

[20] cf. Cantù, *Eretici*, iii, 104.

[21] *Explicatio primae partis primi capitis Evangelistae Johannis*; published anonymously at the request of friends with whom he had discussed the subject matter. In *Opera*, i, 75–85. Confessedly largely taken from conversations and writings of Laelius, to whom Zanchi and Beza (*Val. Gentilis*, praef., p. 15) attributed it, *op. cit.*, p. 497. Polish translation by Gregory Paulus, *Wykład na pierwszą kapitulę Jana Świętego Ewangeliej*, etc. n. p., n. d.). cf. Bock, *Antitrinitar.*, ii, 728 ff; Gordon, *op. cit.*, p. 544 f.

ingly abated, he returned to Italy, and accepted a post as secretary to Duke Paolo Giordano Orsini, husband of Isabella de' Medici and son-in-law of Cosimo I. In the brilliant but corrupt entourage of this Medicean court Faustus spent what he later regarded as twelve wasted years [22] (1563–'74), outwardly living the frivolous life of a courtier, dabbling in studies of the law and in efforts at poetry, living in outward conformity to the Church, yet in his serious moments evidently pondering the religious questions that his uncle's papers had stirred up in his mind. One result of these years at the Florentine court was his first important work, and the one that enjoyed the widest and longest popularity, his *De Sacrae Scripturae Auctoritate*, written in Italian about 1570 'at the request of a certain great man'.[23] This work, translated into four languages, published in half a score of editions, and in print for more than a century and a half, is a closely reasoned argument, addressed to any that question the authority of Scripture, and hence the truth of the Christian religion founded upon it.[24] Its design is to confirm the believer, reassure the doubter, and confute the unbeliever by showing that the authors of the Scriptures are worthy of credence, and that the Christian religion is not the outgrowth of superstition but has sound historical foundations. The question had hitherto not been searchingly investigated; but Socinus canvased it on rational and historical grounds so convincingly that he laid foundations of Apologetics that were to stand until the rise of modern biblical criticism rendered them obsolete. His little treatise was much esteemed by both Catholics and Protestants until its true authorship was discovered; and its argument was adopted in 1639 by Grotius in his famous work, *De Veritate*

---

[22] cf. *Opera*, i, 459, 474, 490; Bock, *op. cit.*, ii, 663 f.

[23] In gratiam magni cujusdam viri. Gordon (*op. cit.*, p. 542) seems to strain the meaning of *viri* too far when he conjectures that the reference is to the author's patroness, Isabella de' Medici. Can this be a veiled reference to his uncle Lelio?

[24] The earliest printed edition (copy in the Biblioteca Nacional, Madrid) is a translation hurriedly made by the author himself from the unpublished Italian original, but the preface was by some other hand, was done without the author's knowledge, and did not represent his views (*v. Opera*, i, 460). The work professes to be by Dominicus Lopez, S. J., and to have been published at Hispalis (Seville) in 1588. But there are good reasons for suspecting that these data are fictitious, and that the work was clandestinely published by liberals at Amsterdam who were unwilling to reveal its heretical origin. cf. Bock, *op. cit.*, ii, 744; also the preface to the text in Socinus, *Opera*, i, 265. Best edition, with preface by C. Vorst, Steinfurt, 1611; French and Dutch trans., 1592 and 1623; English trans. by the Rev. Edward Combe, Rector of St. Martin's, Worcester, at the instigation of Bishop Smalbroke, *An Argument for the Authority of Holy Scripture* (London, 1731).

Religionis Christianae, and by the Catholic Bishop Huet in his *Demonstratio evangelica*.

After the death of his powerful patron, the Grand-Duke Cosimo I., in 1574, the last bond that held Socinus in Florence was broken. In proportion as his interest in religious questions had deepened, his distaste for court life had also grown. Though there was no prospect that he would be dismissed from the court of Francesco, the new Duke, he voluntarily resigned from it, and left Italy never to return.[25] The Duke repeatedly urged him both by letter and through an important personal messenger to return to his position, which promised him enviable worldly advantages, but he modestly though firmly held to his purpose. Yet friendly personal relations continued, and as long as the Duke lived he forwarded to Socinus the revenues from the properties he had inherited at Siena, stipulating only that Socinus should not publish over his own name any work that might compromise his reputation. This condition Socinus faithfully observed during the twelve or thirteen years until the Duke's death in 1587. Leaving Florence, Socinus proceeded to Basel as a place where he might more conveniently and safely apply himself to the study of the Scriptures.[26] He remained at Basel for more than three years, and soon found himself the centre of a group of Italians of inquiring mind, who had known Laelius and been influenced by him, and who were especially interested in the question of salvation through Christ, which was often discussed among them. He held, as he had first learned from his uncle, that the common doctrine on this subject was a dangerous error. This was reported to a traveling French Protestant minister, Jacques Couet (Covetus), who was passing through Basel, and who challenged Socinus's view. The oral discussion that ensued was continued in writing for more than two years before Socinus was able to finish his contribution to it.[27] Even then it was not printed, though widely circulated in manuscript copies in Poland and elsewhere in Europe, until it fell into the hands of a Polish nobleman

[25] There is no ground for thinking that Socinus was moved by fear of prosecution for heresy. He repeatedly says that he left the country quite voluntarily—Italiae et patriae meae plane sponte valedicto. Me . . . mea ipsius sponte . . . patriae in perpetuum valedixisse. Patria . . . mea sponte relicta. cf. *Opera*, i, 379, 476; ii, 118. See also i, * * 2, Desperata ab invitissimis principibus missione sua, sponte patriam, amicos, spes et opes suas destituit.

[26] Ut commodius ac tutius Sacrarum Litterarum studiis possem incumbere. *Opera*, ii, 118.

[27] Socinus gives a full account of the origin and progress of the work in a preface to it, *Opera*, ii, 118 ff.

who insisted that it be published, undertook the matter himself, and gave it to the world in Poland in 1594, sixteen years after it was first written at Basel. Even then it was the first work published under his own name.

The work was entitled *De Jesu Christo Servatore*,[28] and it is the author's most original and most important contribution to systematic theology. The thesis of the work was, in brief, this: that Christ is called our Savior not because he suffered the penalty that was justly due to us, thus appeasing the wrath of an offended God; but because he made known to us the way of eternal salvation, which we may attain by imitating him. Such a view was not altogether new. It had long before been adumbrated by Abélard,[29] and Socinus himself owned that Ochino in his *Dialogues* pointed in the same direction.[30] But he now stated his view so boldly and clearly that it created a profound impression; for it was at once seen that it rendered several other orthodox doctrines superfluous, and was calculated to focus the Christian's effort not on an act of faith but on the conduct of life.[31] It was soon replied to by a Polish theologian, and (though Socinus was not aware of this) by Couet himself, and for a generation it was the object of attack by orthodox theologians; and when republished in Holland a generation later it stirred up the famous satisfaction controversy which lasted until the end of the century.

For Socinus himself the controversy soon brought consequences that he could not have foreseen, which determined the course of his whole future life. For echoes of it spread to Transylvania and reached the ears of Biandrata, who was now actively engaged in promoting a reformation in religion there as he had previously done in Poland. The movement had got out of hand, for its Bishop, Francis Dávid, had gone so far in doctrine as to oppose the worship of Christ as unscriptural,

---

[28] In using *servator* instead of *salvator*, the usual term for Savior, to denote the saving work of Christ, Socinus apart from perhaps wishing to avoid the theological associations of the latter term, may have wished to suggest a difference of meaning. The difference between the two might be said to be somewhat like that between prevention and cure.

[29] cf. his *Opera* (Paris, 1616), p. 553.

[30] cf. Socinus, *Opera*, i, 475.

[31] *v.* Socinus, *Opera*, i, 476. cf. Grzegorz Żarnowec, *Apokatastasis* (in Polish), Wilno, 1598; Latin trans. (Danzig, 1607); Jacobus Covetus, *Apologia de justificatione nostri coram Deo* (Tiguri, 1594); Michael Gittichius, *De gravissima quaestione*, etc. Basileae, 1612); Ludovicus Lucius, *De Satisfactione Christi* (*ibid.*, 1612); Otto Casmanus, *Anti-Socinus* (Ambergae, 1612). The work is summarized with the resulting controversies noted, in Bock, *op. cit.*, ii, 804–815.

and would not heed the warnings of Biandrata, who recognized in this a critical danger to his whole cause.[32] He discerned in Socinus a competent theologian who might be able to bring Dávid back to a more conservative view, and he sent him an urgent call for assistance. Thus in the autumn of 1578 Socinus came to Kolozsvár to spend several months in what proved a futile attempt to convert Dávid to his point of view. The full account of this episode properly falls in the next division of this history.

In his journey from Basel to Kolozsvár, Socinus had come by way of Kraków, taking occasion *en route* to seek out some of the friends that Laelius had made there twenty years before,[33] and to make acquaintance of the little congregation of the Minor Church of which Georg Schomann was then pastor. His mission in Transylvania ended, he therefore returned to Kraków in the spring of 1580, to spend in Poland the remaining twenty-five years of his life. It was natural that he should be attracted to this country. Switzerland was hardly a safe place for one whose mind was so rapidly moving from the old standards, while Poland was just then enjoying a brief fame as the most tolerant country in Europe. At Kraków itself he could enjoy many advantages in the intellectual and cultural capital of the country. Though as yet he knew no Polish, he could feel at home among his own countrymen, for there was a considerable company of cultivated and prosperous Italians settled there, of whom several sympathized with the liberal wing of the Reformed religion. His religious associations he sought with the poverty-stricken little group of Anabaptists.[34] They were an obscure and despised company in a Catholic capital, were not permitted to hold public worship, were divided in controversy over minor details, and their cause seemed to be declining; but they were earnest and united in their effort to maintain a doctrine purified of old errors and based solely on Scripture, and to lead lives in strictest accord with the teaching of Jesus. He did not indeed approve all their views, but of the several varieties of Protestants in Poland, these seemed to him to be the most nearly right.[35]

---

[32] This doctrine had been introduced into Transylvania by Palaeologus, who had perhaps derived it from Adam Neuser. An non ipse primus omnium in provincia ista, sententiam illam maxime impiam et detestendam de non adorando neque invocando Christo . . . docuit? Socinus to Squarcialupus, 1581; *Opera*, i, 365.

[33] cf. Szczęsny Morawski, *Arjanie Polscy* (the Polish Arians), Lwów, 1906, p. 93.

[34] Cum summa sit inter eos paupertas. Socinus to Radecki, 1586; *Opera*, i, 385.

[35] cf. Socinus to Radecki, 1584; *Opera*, i, 373.

Instead, however, of welcoming so distinguished an adherent with open arms, the little congregation received him with a caution bordering on suspicion. The brethren at Kraków had already, when he was on his way to Transylvania, asked him to give them his views on what they deemed the cardinal subject of baptism; and they were so much interested that when he returned they and the brethren at Lublin entreated him to put the matter in writing for them to read. He did so,[36] and from that time on expressed his opinion in public in various places as well as through letters, for he ardently desired that, if possible, they might all be of the same opinion with him.[37] But they could not be brought to see eye to eye with him. For in the reorganization of the little church effected by Ronemberg, baptism had been made one of its two corner-stones, and an essential condition of membership; while Socinus was convinced that baptism as then insisted on (i. e. the adult baptism of those already baptized in infancy) was proving a stumbling-block to large numbers that would otherwise be glad to join the Minor Church.[38] Moreover, he was firmly persuaded that neither Christ nor his Apostles had ever prescribed baptism as a lasting practice in the Church. It might be well enough to retain it for those that were coming to Christianity from another religion; but for those that had been born and brought up in the Christian Church it was not essential, but an indifferent matter, to insist on which as vital almost smacked of superstition.[39]

When, therefore, in 1580 at a synod at Raków Socinus publicly sought admission to membership in the church, making no secret of his dissent as to several minor doctrines as he deemed them, including baptism, and it was insisted that he must first receive adult baptism, he felt that as he had often expressed his views on this subject both in print and in speech he could not now stultify himself by submitting to the rite, unless he might first publicly protest that he did so not because he regarded it as in any way necessary or as a command of Christ, but only for the sake of having closer fellowship with the

---

[36] cf. De Baptismo aquae disputatio (1580); Opera, i, 709. To this, Alexander Witrelin, one of the ministers, made a reply (unpublished) in the worst possible spirit. cf. Opera, i, 384.

[37] Vehementer cupiam, ut si fieri possit, omnes ejusdem mecum sententiae sint. Socinus to Moskorzowski; Opera, i, 458.

[38] loc. cit.

[39] cf. Socinus to Radecki (1586), Opera, i, 383 f; to Moskorzowski, p. 458 f; to Ronemberg, p. 430.

brethren; and to this the brethren would by no means agree. His application was therefore rejected, and he was not admitted to their observance of the Lord's Supper.[40] Socinus felt his rejection keenly,[41] but however much he might regret being denied closer association with the brethren, he showed no resentment at the rebuff; nor did they on their part give him the cold shoulder. Ronemberg, Elder of the Kraków congregation and its most influential member, and the noble lady Siemichowska were still after three years beseeching him in the most urgent entreaties, in the name of God and Christ, for the sake of their poor and weak little church, to be baptized with the brethren; but he could not be moved, and he enumerated the many reasons that held him back.[42] However he might differ from them as to minor details, he was in sympathy with their general doctrinal position, and yet more with their earnest efforts to lead consistent Christian lives; so that he continued as long as he lived to worship with them and to share in the discussions at their synods and guide them by his counsels. Yet though he soon became their accepted leader, and their champion against opponents whether Calvinist or Catholic, and eventually set his stamp upon their theology, it is not of clear record that he was ever allowed membership in their church, or admitted to its sacrament. Was ever another such case in all Christian history? [43]

[40] cf. Sandius, *Bibliotheca*, p. 214; Szczotka, *Synody*, p. 31; Socinus to Siemichowska, *Opera*, i, 432; to Moskorzowski, i, 458 f.

[41] Deus novit quae et quanta diu propter hanc caussam sim passus, et adhuc patiar. Socinus to Siemichowska, *Opera*, i, 432.

[42] cf. Ronemberg to Socinus, Socinus to Ronemberg, and to Siemichowska, *Opera*, i, 428–433.

[43] The statement in an anonymous and undated Ms (Jagellonian Library, Kraków, No. 5433), that after being at Kraków four years Socinus was received into the church, can not be accepted without further confirmation. Still less is the question settled by his use of the expression, "our congregation" (in *nostro coetu*, cf. Socinus to Balcerowicz, 1593, 1594, *Opera*, i, 427 f.). It would seem, however, from a letter written but a few weeks before his death (Socinus to Smalcius, January 23, 1604; *Opera*, i, 468), that the general Synod had recently decided to admit to the Lord's Supper persons that had not been baptized; though the Lublin congregation had balked at this, and some were evidently withdrawing from the church on this account. Yet from this time on, baptism, though generally practiced to the end, was less and less insisted on. cf. Lubieniecius, *op. cit.*, p. 190; Zeltner, *Crypto-Socin.*, p. 1178, n. b.

CHAPTER XXX

THE MINOR CHURCH UNDER THE LEADERSHIP
OF SOCINUS, 1579–1604

THE COMING OF SOCINUS to the Polish churches at the time of their infant struggles must have seemed to them almost a dispensation of Providence. It had now been a score of years since their movement first began to germinate, and fourteen years since it had been cast off as a waif, at the mercy of both Catholics and Protestants whose hostility was bitter and undisguised. With organization and discipline still loose, their common church life was chaotic. They had no acknowledged leader; and though they disowned the authority of church traditions, councils and creeds, looking for guidance only to Scripture, yet they had adopted no common confession, and only the little congregation at Kraków had for its own apologetic purposes ventured to publish an elementary Catechism. They had no Melanchthon or Calvin to set their new faith in systematic order or to settle uncertain points of doctrine. They were indeed agreed upon rejecting the doctrine of the Trinity, but hardly upon any other doctrine, even as to the nature of Christ. They were well-nigh bewildered by the apparently inconsistent teachings that they found in the Bible, and their frequent synods were occupied with endless debates as they tried to settle this point or that. There were cautious conservatives on the one hand, and almost fanatical radicals on the other. Taking the country as a whole, there was a broad line of cleavage among them, between the churches of Little Poland in the south on the one hand, which in their Christology were conservative to the borders of orthodoxy, but in their social teachings were radical to a degree that finds an echo among many of the extreme social radicals of the twentieth century; and the churches of Lithuania far to the northeast on the other hand, which had been patronized by great magnates, and defended existing social institutions and customs, but in Christology were unitarian almost to the point of Judaism.

Within these broad limits they were much concerned, and much divided, over such questions as the proper form of baptism, the meaning of the Lord's Supper, the worship of Christ, the nature of the Holy Spirit, and the second coming of Christ. Their earlier leaders had now grown too old to exercise further leadership, and no new one had arisen who could speak with the authority of sound knowledge. Their movement therefore bid fair within a decade more to disintegrate hopelessly. It was at such a juncture that Socinus appeared, who, free from any bias of training in the old theology, had for four years been applying his fine native talents to the study of Scripture, had come to mature convictions on many points, and was prepared with magisterial authority to discuss many of the questions at issue. His competence was soon recognized, and although he never sought formal leadership, or tried to exert influence save by the method of rational argument, and was always modest as to his own attainments, yet ere long all instinctively looked to him as the one that could best guide them in their search for scripture truth, and could most ably defend them against the attacks of their adversaries.

Socinus exerted his influence not only in the doctrinal discussions at the church synods, but in a voluminous correspondence with both friends and opponents, by set debates to which he was challenged, and by printed works (anonymous until 1594) published at the solicitation of the church in answer to attacks upon it. Thus he debated the disputed question as to the invocation of Christ with Francken in 1584,[1] and in a letter to the synod at Węgrów the same year he exhorted the brethren to maintain this practice in their churches, since if it were given up they would lapse into Judaism or even into atheism.[2] Likewise he urged the synod at Chmielnik in 1589 to abandon as unscriptural, false, absurd, and ruinous, the wide-spread expectation of a millennial reign of Christ on earth, which Czechowicz was ardently proclaiming.[3] More privately he discussed various doctrines at length, now as disputant with an equal, now as teacher to learner; with Radecki who sought advice about gathering a congregation at Danzig; with Niemojewski who, as Elder of the church at Lublin, felt responsibility for the soundness of its doctrine; with the young Stoiński (Statorius) who in his first pastorate at Lucławice was rapidly outgrowing the theology of his father-in-law, Gregory Paulus; with Ostorod, Völkel and Smalcius who were ere long to carry on his work

[1] v. supra, p. 371.
[2] cf. his letter to the synod, Opera, i, 491.
[3] cf. epistle contra Chiliastas, Opera, i, 440 ff, and in another recension, ii, 457 ff.

of directing the thought of the Minor Church; and with Dudith, his peer in learning.

Socinus had not been long in Poland, however, when an urgent occasion arose for him publicly to champion the cause of his new brethren. In the preceding chapter an account has been given of the rise of the controversy as to the rightfulness of a Christian's bearing arms or holding a civil office which exercises the right of the sword.[4] Palaeologus had had the last word in the book that Budny published in 1580, which besides being extremely offensive in its tone, had so seriously misrepresented the real position of the Racovians, calling them disloyal, cowardly, downright wicked, and unworthy of the Christian name,[5] and was thus so much calculated to prejudice them in the eyes of the government, that they felt that it must not be allowed to go unanswered. Paulus, now grown aged and infirm, felt unequal to making a reply. The brethren therefore turned to Socinus, who in his brief residence in Poland had already won deep respect for his thorough knowledge of theology, his wide learning, his ability and skill in discussion, and his unvarying mildness and courtesy in debate; and notwithstanding that he had but lately been refused admission to their church he reluctantly accepted their commission, and in the summer of 1581 published his work.[6] Reasoning only from Scripture, he defended Paulus's position, and refuted Palaeologus's attack upon it. Although unsparing in criticism of what Palaeologus had written, and of the insulting manner of his attack upon Paulus, Socinus's book was temperate in its argument. While in general he defended the Racovian view, he avoided the extremes of some of the brethren; but he held that members of the church must obey the law of Christ. The command not to kill admits of no exceptions. Even defensive warfare can not be reconciled with the obligations of a Christian: the church must be pacifist. Also the *jus gladii* in the punishment of criminals is not a Christian office; hence believers may not exercise it nor co-operate with it. Yet one is bound to yield obedience to civil government so far as this does not conflict with the teaching of Christ, should pay taxes even though they be spent for war, may serve as magistrate if not inflicting

---

[4] *v. supra*, pp. 375–378.

[5] cf. *Defensio verae sententiae de magistratu politico* (Losci, 1580), pp. 1, 5, 32.

[6] *Ad Jac. Palaeologi librum . . . pro Racoviensibus responsio* (Cracoviae, 1581); also in *Opera*, ii, 1–114. Palaeologus, already in prison or on his way to the stake, could of course make no reply.

capital punishment, and may through the secular courts seek redress of injuries.[7]

This work of Socinus, published secretly and anonymously, produced no immediate effect. In Transylvania, indeed, where Palaeologus was admired for his shining abilities, and where the social views prevalent at Raków were not approved, it was sharply criticized.[8] But from the Jesuits there soon came a dangerous attack. This order, which had been introduced into the country by Cardinal Hosius in 1564, had now become well established, was just setting up a house at Kraków, and had already for some time conducted a college at Poznań, where the Jesuit fathers were now publishing a defence of the doctrine of the Trinity against its new deniers,[9] the first of a long series of Jesuit polemics against the Minor Church, soon to be followed by the violent attack on Czechowicz's *Dialogues* of 1575, which obviously pointed at Socinus, though unnamed, as discouraging loyalty to the magistrate.[10] When King Stephen, returning from his campaigns in the north, was thus told that a book had been published which was calculated to undermine the royal authority, his attention was aroused. Socinus, consciously innocent of any seditious thought, felt no fear;[11] but he was persuaded to act on the advice of experienced friends, and accepted the hospitality of the prominent noble, Christopher Morsztyn, in the little village of Pawlikowice some ten or twelve miles to the southeast, where on the estate of a nobleman even the King would have no right to molest him.[12] Waiting for any danger to pass, he stayed here for four years (1583–'87), though from time to time coming to Kraków

---

[7] The work is well summarized in Kot, *Ideologja*, pp. 57–74.

[8] cf. the letter to Socinus from his fellow-countryman, the antitrinitarian physician Marcello Squarcialupi, written from Gyula Fehérvár, the capital of Transylvania, and Socinus's reply in defence; *Opera*, i, 359–368.

[9] *Assertiones theologicae de trino et uno Deo*, 1581; answered by Socinus, at the request of the Synod, in 1583 in his notes appended to a reprint of the original—perhaps his ablest theological work. cf. *Opera*, ii, 423–436.

[10] cf. Powodowski, *Wędzidło; v. supra*, p. 386, n. 6.

[11] cf. his letter to Berzeviczy, 1583; *Opera*, i, 493.

[12] Not long after this, Martin Berzeviczy, the King's Chancellor in Transylvania (for Stephen still retained his throne as Prince of Transylvania, though he left the administration to his brother), offered Socinus an honorable station in that country. But he decided to remain where he was until the King should be persuaded of his innocence, rather than by fleeing the country to seem to plead guilty, as in fact it became rumored that he had done (cf. his letter to Dudith, March 6, 1583, *Opera*, i, 509). He did, however, express the hope that the Chancellor would try to persuade the King of his entire innocence of the charge against him. cf. his letter to Berzeviczy, March 12, 1583, *Opera*, i, 493.

for brief visits, until the death of the King made it quite safe for him to return thither.[13] In this safe retreat Socinus was able to lead an outwardly quiet life, but he wielded an ever busy pen in answer to the inquiries from all quarters as to points of doctrine or matters of policy.

At his new seat, Socinus was first occupied in an important controversial work on the nature and expiatory work of Christ, which in effect supplemented his early work on Christ the Savior, though the latter had not yet been published. One Andrew Wolan (Volanus), a theologian who held high position in Lithuania, and was regarded as the ablest champion of the Calvinist cause in Poland, had published a work accusing the liberals of reviving heresies of the first three Christian centuries, and attacking not only the whole church but also Socinus personally.[14] Socinus replied for the brethren in an authoritative exposition, amply fortified by Scripture, of their belief as to God, Christ, the Holy Spirit, and the forgiveness of sins.[15] At Pawlikowice he continued his investigation of theological questions, debated some of them with persons who sought to set him right, and gave counsel to inquirers orally or by letters. All seemed to turn to him with their questions. But the most important occurrence at this period was his marriage, probably in the summer of 1586, to Elizabeth Morsztyn, the daughter of his host. Not long afterwards, the King now having died, he returned to Kraków, where in the following spring a daughter was born to him.[16] But his happiness was soon cut short, for the young mother died a few months later. Socinus was overwhelmed with grief, his health, never robust, was shattered, and for the better part of a year he was unable to resume his normal occupations. Indeed, from now to the end of his life he suffered from attacks of various illnesses, and both hearing and eyesight were increasingly impaired. Nor did troubles come singly. Hitherto he had been comfortably supported by the

---

[13] The old Morsztyn manor-house where Socinus passed these four years still stands, now enlarged and transformed into a school for orphan boys. The site of Pawlikowice is about three miles south of the famous salt-mining town of Wieliczka.

[14] A. Volanus, *Paraenesis ad omnes in regno Poloniae Samosatenianae vel Ebioniticae doctrinae professores* (Spirae, 1582).

[15] The whole controversy, including two titles on each side, is comprised in his *De Jesu Christi Filii Dei natura*, *Opera*, ii, 371–422.

[16] Named Agnes, in honor of his mother. She married Stanislas Wiszowaty, and their son Andrew became one of the most able and active ministers before and after the banishment of the Arians. He edited the *Bibliotheca Fratrum Polonorum*, and died at Amsterdam in 1678. Agnes died at Rąbkowa, near Lucławice, in 1654.

revenues from his inherited estates in Italy; but when in 1587 death deprived him of the protection of his patron the Grand-Duke in Florence, he lost all his property in Italy by action of the Holy Office at Siena. Henceforth his life was one of poverty, in which however he never lacked the bounty and hospitality of generous friends.[17]

Socinus continued to live at Kraków, now busier than ever over correspondence with leaders of the church about their problems doctrinal or practical. Whenever well enough he attended synods in person, trying by calm discussion to bring about agreement on subjects in controversy, such as baptism, the Lord's Supper, the atonement, the second coming of Christ and above all the invocation of Christ, which he held to be the very touchstone of true Christianity; and when unable to attend he sent doctrinal tracts to be read as his contribution to the discussion. As early as 1588 at a provincial synod at Brześć (Brest) in Lithuania he reasoned so persuasively about the worship of Christ, and his nature, death and sacrifice, as to win over nearly all opponents,[18] and henceforth his authority in such matters was seldom questioned. Only two or three of the older generation like Czechowicz and Niemojewski still held out for a few years more while the younger ministers enthusiastically accepted his more liberal and reasonable interpretation of Scripture. As his authority in doctrinal matters came to be more and more acknowledged, so he was more and more called upon to champion the views of his church, especially against the Jesuits, who had now become the protagonists of the Catholic dogmas. Thus in 1590 Jacob Wujek, one of their most celebrated scholars, had published a book in Polish on the divinity of Christ and the Holy Spirit,[19] reproducing the arguments of the famous Jesuit theologian, Roberto Bellarmino, and when two years later the author was boasting that none of the 'Anabaptists' had yet made any adequate reply to it, the Synod entreated Socinus to publish a refutation; which indeed had from the first been his desire, though various causes had hindered him.[20] He now complied with their wish, and his work was at once translated

[17] For several years he was given a home with Dr. Filippo Buccella, who had succeeded Biandrata as the King's personal physician, and who provided him an annuity of 100 florins so long as he should live. cf. Jan Ptasnik, 'Z dziejów kultury włoskiego Krakowa' (History of Italian civilization at Kraków), *Rocznik Krakowski* (Kraków, 1906), p. 142.

[18] cf. *Opera*, i, p. **2b; Szczotka, *Synody*, p. 44.

[19] *O Bóstwie Syna Bożego* (On the divinity of the Son of God), Kraków, 1590.

[20] cf. preface to the work, *Opera*, ii, 529.

into Polish by Stoiński (Statorius).[21] It was a work of ample length, in which he proceeded step by step, in order, to a thorough and complete scriptural refutation. Although he had thus far written anonymously, Socinus's authorship was either known or suspected, and he was regarded as practically the acknowledged spokesman for the Minor Church. Hence he became the object of frequent attacks in print and from the pulpit; especially after the publication under his own name of his *De Jesu Christo Servatore* (1594), which was taken almost as a challenge of defiance to his opponents.[22]

It is easily seen that with the Catholic reaction already gathering force under the inspiration of the Jesuits such a publication was calculated to fan into a flame a fire that was already more than latent. In this very year Socinus became the victim of a brutal outrage in the streets of Kraków.[23] The city was full of soldiers in anticipation of an attack from the Tatars who were now ravaging Hungary, and discipline and good order were relaxed. Among those called to serve was a certain Kaspar Wiernek, a young Catholic noble from the Carpathian foothill district where 'Arian' churches were most numerous. He nourished a grievance against Socinus for having made a heretic of his father-in-law. Heated with wine, he was walking along the street with a troop of cavalrymen under his command, when he espied Socinus and ordered his men to drag him away. While Socinus shouted for help and a crowd came running up, Wiernek had Socinus's mouth stopped with filthy mud, and even his whole face smeared with filth, and then, having made him fall at his feet as a humble suppliant, he let him go. The outrage was not punished, but a common acquaintance secured from the assailant an apology for a deed done when he was drunk. Socinus forgave him, and even brought about a reconciliation of him with his father-in-law.

<hr />

[21] cf. Socinus to Balcerowicz, Dec., 1592, *Opera*, i, 427. Polish version, *Refutacya xiążek, które X. Wuiek Jezuita wydał w roku 1590*, etc. (Refutation of the books that the Jesuit priest Wujek published in 1590), n. p., 1593; Latin original, *Responsio ad libellum Jacobi Wuieki . . . de divinitate Filii Dei et Spiritus Sancti*, etc. (Racoviae, 1595). cf. Socinus to Morsztyn, Feb. 3, 1595; to Wojdowski, May 4, 1595, *Opera*, i, 456, 472; Bock, *Antitrinitar.*, ii, 834 ff. The publication was subsidized by brethren at Lublin and in Lithuania.

[22] The real reason for his now publishing his name as author was that he might else be thought afraid to avow openly the sentiments that his book expressed. cf. his preface, *Opera*, ii, 120.

[23] The date was October 6, 1594. cf. Socinus to Wojdowski, Oct. 7, 1594, and to

A much more serious occurrence took place in 1598.[24] Socinus, though living a very retired life, was by now regarded as one of the outstanding heretics in Kraków, and the great church festivals were occasions when outbreaks of violence against heretics were most apt to occur. University students often took the lead in the mobs that were frequent throughout all this period. As Ascension Day approached Socinus may have had a premonition of danger to himself, for to ensure safety from any attack, he secretly gathered together his most precious possessions and removed them to the dwelling of his landlord.[25] Some one had indeed hit upon him as a suitable victim for the holiday, and had informed the students where he was to be found. He was easily tracked to his hiding-place, which was near the University. The mob rushed to the dwelling, and forced their way in under threats of violence. Socinus was ill and in bed, but they dragged him out, struggling, bareheaded and barefoot, covered only with a cloak, to the great market-place in front of the Rathaus, and strewed in the mud or threw into the fire the books, papers and letters that they had taken from his room, threatening him with the same treatment unless he recanted. He replied with great firmness, 'I do not recant, but what I have been I am and will be, by the grace of the Lord Jesus Christ, as long as I live; and you may do whatever God permits you.' Though again threatened with a drawn sword he remained unmoved so that many marveled at his firmness. Somewhat abashed they decided to drown him instead, and started for the Vistula. As the throng was passing the University, the tumult was heard by one of the professors, who upon learning what they were at bade them bring the heretic to him, which they did, and he then locked his door against them. Having learned who his unfortunate visitor was, he showed him all possible kindness, and with the assistance of others took him

---

Morsztyn, Feb. 3, 1595; *Opera*, i, 473, 456, for Socinus's own account. Morawski, *Arjanie Polscy*, p. 117 f., gives a variant and less trustworthy account.

[24] For a circumstantial contemporary account of what follows, see Radecki's letter to Daems, Socinus's dear friend at Brussels, dated June 18, 1598 (the event took place on April 30, 1598), in Thomas Crenius, *Animadversiones philologicae et historicae* (Leiden, 1698 ff), iv, 233–242; reprinted in Bock, *Antitrinitar.*, ii, 492–497. cf. Adalbert Wengierski, *Chronik der Evangelischen Gemeinde zu Krakau* (Breslau, 1880), p. 16; Socinus, letter to Vadovita, *Opera*, i, 475–477.

[25] Socinus at this period occupied leased apartments on the first and second stories above the ground floor of the building (still standing, somewhat modernized) at the northwest corner of Bracka and Gołębia streets, one street distant from the Rynek and the University.

disguised to a safer place, whence having narrowly escaped another attack, which was broken up by a violent thunder and hail storm, he was removed at daybreak to the estate of an Italian friend at Igołomia, some fifteen miles to the east.[26]

Socinus had long since been urged to make his home at Igołomia, and would now have been glad to stay permanently in so agreeable a place but for two reasons: it lacked the books that he especially needed for his studies, and it was thought to be too near Kraków for his safety.[27] Hence as soon as he had recovered strength he removed to the village of Lucławice some forty-five miles southeast of Kraków, where he was to spend the rest of his life, under the patronage of the proprietor of the village and with the congenial companionship of his devoted disciple, Stoiński, who was minister of the congregation. He never ceased to lament the loss of his precious books and papers, but as long as his precarious health and his miserable eyesight permitted he continued to pursue his studies. His last important written work was in answer to the request of a friend in the Calvinist church that he explain why some of its most learned and worthy members should think their church inferior to that of the 'Arians.' The Calvinist church of Poland was in fact in a state of weakness under the attacks of the Catholics; its spiritual life seemed stagnant, its intellectual level was not above the average, and its political influence had declined, while the Minor Church, despite some of its singular views and practices, was increasing in strength and spiritual influence.[28] In this work, which he presently gave to the public,[29] he urged that all those that were

---

[26] The professor named was the young Dr. Martin Vadovita, Curate of St. Florian's, and the respected and beloved Professor of Theology at the University. Others mentioned as assisting in the rescue and deserving to be remembered are the Rector, Dr. Valentin Fontana, the Rev. Daniel Sigonius, instructor at the University, the Rev. Jan Godecki, Canon of St. Ann's, the brothers Myszkowski, and others. cf. Socinus, letter to Vadovita above cited; Włodzimierz Budka, 'Faust Socyn w Krakowie' (F. S. at Kraków), *Reformacja w Polsce*, v, no. 20 (1928), 120–122.

[27] cf. Socinus to Statorius, June 3, 1598; *Opera*, i, 436.

[28] cf. Kot, *Ideologja*, p. 90.

[29] cf. *Opera*, i, 691–707. *Quod Regni Poloniae et Magni Ducatus Lithuaniae homines, vulgo Evangelici dicti, qui solidae pietatis sunt studiosi, omnino deberent se illorum coetui adjungere, qui in iisdem locis falso atque immerito Arriani atque Ebionitae vocantur.* First published in Polish translation by Stoiński, *Okazanie*, etc. (Raków, 1600); Latin text as above (Raków, 1611). Also under the title, *De officio hominis Christiani*, etc. (Franeker, 1610); Dutch trans., *Het ampt van een Christen mensch* (n. p., 1630). The work was replied to by the Calvinist minister Jan Petrycy, *Krótka przestroga do Braciey Zboru Ewangelickiego*, etc. (Brief warning to the brethren of the Evangelical Church), 1600; which was answered in turn by Jerome Moskorzowski, *Odpowiedź na skrypt Przestroga nazwana* (Reply to a writing entitled Warning), Raków, 1602. Another reply

anxious for genuine religion really ought to join the Minor Church, miscalled Arian. He charged that the Calvinist church had not wholly purified itself of the errors of the Roman Church, and had retained some doctrines opposed to Christ's teachings, while ignoring some of his plain commands; and that it was a Christian's duty to belong to the church that is freest from error. He also complained that their moral standards were not strict, and that discipline and restraint of their members was slack, since many who did things that the church forbids were nevertheless admitted to the Lord's Supper. This lack of discipline had in recent years caused the church to lose many members and the Minor Church to gain many; while outsiders began to suspect that the doctrine of the latter was better than that of the orthodox, since its teachings were highly agreeable to Scripture and reason. This little work seems to have produced a deep impression, and it called forth several answers in defence for nearly a quarter of a century; but it is of particular interest for the evidence it shows of the deep concern of the Minor Church for purity of scripture doctrine, and for strictness of moral life in its members.

As the shadows grew longer, and Socinus was warned by his failing health that his remaining days must be few, he grew concerned for the future of the churches. Recognizing the leadership which was now by common consent given him, he called together a dozen of the leading ministers in the spring of 1601 at Raków to discuss important doctrinal questions.[30] Their gathering was unofficial, and was in fact a sort of theological seminar, conducted by Socinus, who presented his views on various questions and then threw them open for general discussion. No better method could have been chosen to harmonize differences and to promote final agreement. The sessions lasted three whole weeks, and covered such questions as the being of God, Christ, the Holy Spirit, man, sin, free will, the Scriptures, and sacraments. Emphasis was laid upon essential points, while subordinate details were left open as not being necessary to salvation. From these doctrinal questions Socinus went on to the social ones that had of late caused such sharp dissension: engaging in lawsuits, resistance to phys-

---

was by Prof. Baltazar Meissner of Wittenberg, *Brevis consideratio theologiae Photinianae*, etc. (Witebergae, 1623); answered in turn by Jonas Schlichting, *Quaestio num ad Regnum Dei possidendum*, etc. (Racoviae, 1635).

[30] cf. *Reformacja w Polsce*, vii (1935), 52–54; Smalcius, *Diary*, p. 1174. Smalcius, who participated, left an epitome of the discussions, which is still extant: Ms 3421 in the Krasiński Library, Warsaw.

ical evil, taking part in war, etc. All these Socinus treated in a spirit thoroughly Christian, but he avoided fanatical extremes by viewing them in the light of actually existing conditions. This meeting was found so profitable that a similar one was held at Raków late the following year, which lasted for twelve days and was attended by over a score of ministers and an equal number of Elders and other lay brethren.[31] Discussion of the doctrinal and social questions that had been left unfinished or untouched was now continued, and was enlivened by a spirited exchange of views between the progressive and rational Socinus and the literal and conservative Czechowicz. Here Socinus defended the holding of private property, and the taking of interest, but opposed luxury and a greed for wealth beyond one's needs. Thus step by step he toned down the exaggerated views of the Anabaptist extremists, while at the same time he still insisted on maintaining careful discipline among members of the church.[32]

After the turn of the century Socinus began also to collect and revise his various writings with a view to their being later published or reprinted.[33] They had in fact covered all the main and many of the minor topics in Christian theology as he had restated it. Indeed, he had begun as early as 1592 to reduce his teachings to an ordered system for use in the form of a catechism, though three years later he had been able to make little progress on it, and all but a fragment of the manuscript perished with the rest of his papers at the hands of the mob at Kraków in 1598.[34] But since the publication of Schomann's little Catechism in 1574, and of Czechowicz's *Rozmowy* in the following year, thought among the churches had made much progress, and under the constant discussions had steadily grown clearer and more definite, so that a new work was now urgently needed to assist in promoting harmony of teaching in the churches, and to set their doctrines in fair light before inquirers or opponents. No clear evidence is at hand that

---

[31] cf. *Reformacja w Polsce*, vii, 54 f; Sandius, *Bibliotheca*, p. 174 f.

[32] Even for some time after Socinus's death, and the publishing of a standard of faith in the *Racovian Catechism*, these informal seminars of ministers continued to be held for the threshing out of unsettled doctrinal questions. Thus during the three years from January, 1606 to January, 1609, at the house of Valentin Smalcius, minister at Raków, a series of such meetings was held at frequent intervals, sometimes almost weekly, though with one long interruption on account of war. cf. Sandius, *op. cit.*, p. 175; *Reformacja w Polsce*, vii, 57–59; Ms 527 in the Remonstrant Library at Rotterdam.

[33] cf. his letter to Radecki, 1603; *Opera*, i, 492, and to Smalcius, 1597; *ibid.*, p. 460.

[34] cf. his letter to Smalcius, Feb. 14, 1595; *Opera*, i, 459. For the surviving *Fragmentum Catechismi Prioris*, cf. *Opera*, i, 677–689.

the Synod itself authorized the composition of such a work. It was apparently rather the result of consultation among some of the younger ministers who, as followers of Socinus, wished to set forth a system of faith that might replace the now waning doctrine of Czechowicz. The work proposed was a 'reformation' of the existing Catechism; and direction of it was, after careful deliberation by the brethren concerned, left to Statorius (Stoiński), who lived near Socinus at Lucławice, and was his closest friend. Socinus was to devote to it all his spare time.[35] But he was already worn down by illness, and in a few weeks more he had to answer the last call. He died on March 3, 1604, at Lucławice.[36] Statorius performed the last offices for his master, and in a little more than a year followed him.

Busy as his pen had been during his life in Poland, Socinus had for want of funds been unable to publish much; and most of the ten or twelve works that had seen the light were printed through the interest of his friends. His other writings circulated only in manuscript, and as he could seldom afford an amanuensis, he had to spend much of his time in making the copies that were continually requested. After his death, however, the churches, realizing their loss, took measures to collect and preserve all his writings, and later to have the more important of them also published in German and Dutch translation.[37] Thus a pretty steady stream of his writings or of reprints of his earlier works kept issuing from the Raków press during the next quarter-century, whence they spread widely over western Europe, stimulating inquiry among scholars, arousing bitter controversy from orthodox theologians, and insensibly influencing Christian thought among both Protestants and Catholics. Socinianism became a factor that could no longer be passed by in silence, or dismissed with contempt, but had to be taken seriously into account, and for well-nigh two centuries those that undertook to refute it often laid themselves out at great length to do so. The complete collected works of Socinus were not published until 1668, in two stately folio volumes of the *Bibliotheca Fratrum Polonorum* at Amsterdam.

---

[35] cf. Socinus to Radecki, No. 23, 1603; *Opera*, i, 492.

[36] Socinus's grave was in the 'Arian' cemetery at Lucławice (modern spelling, Lusła-wice), and remained neglected and all but forgotten for generations until early in the twentieth century, when it was brought to the attention of western Unitarians. A handsome monument was at length erected in 1933. cf. Earl M. Wilbur, 'The grave and monument of Faustus Socinus,' *Proceedings of the Unitarian Historical Society* (Boston, 1936), iv, 25–42.   [37] cf. Bock, *Antitrinitar.*, ii, 850.

CHAPTER XXXI

THE RACOVIAN CATECHISM: THE SOCINIAN DOCTRINAL SYSTEM

THE RACOVIAN CATECHISM [1] got this name, by which it has been generally called, from that of the town of Raków (Lat., Racovia) where it was published, and to which the Socinians [2] looked from the beginning of the seventeenth century as practically their capital, where they annually held their general Synods, maintained their principal college, and published their books. As said at the end of the preceding chapter, the new Catechism was apparently the self-appointed work of some of the younger ministers who were disciples of Socinus. Statorius, living at Lucławice near Socinus, was to be the responsible editor, assisted by him as far as his time and strength permitted. It may be presumed that the *Christianae Religionis Institutio* (Socinus, *Opera*, i, 651–676), which was unfinished when death stayed his hand, was at least Socinus's first draft of the proposed work; [3] but if so, the draft was later entirely recast, so that the Catechism when finished, though representing his views, was in arrangement and expression the work of others. Within about three months Socinus died, and Statorius

---

[1] *Katechizm zbory tych ludzi, którzy w Królestwie Polskim, y w Wielkim Xięstwie Litewskim, y w innych Państwach do Korony należących, twierdzą, y wyznawaią, że nikt inszy, jedno Ojciec Pana naszego Jezusa Christusa, iest onym iedynym Bogiem Izraelskim, a on człowiek Jezus Nazarański który się z Panny narodził, a nie żaden inszy oprócz niego, abo przed nim, iest iednorodzonym Synem Bożym* (w Rakowie, 1605). (Catechism of the assembly of those people who in the Kingdom of Poland, and in the Grand Duchy of Lithuania, and in the other Dominions belonging to the Crown, affirm and confess, that no other than the Father of our Lord Jesus Christ is the only God of Israel; and the man Jesus of Nazareth, who was born of a virgin, and no other besides him, is the only-begotten Son of God.)

[2] For convenience we shall henceforth employ this name to denote those of the Minor Church, although they themselves objected to it as unjust. So Smalcius, *Odpowiedź na Książka Zaborowskiego* (*v. supra*, p. 381, n. 23), p. 14. Throughout the seventeenth century the name was in common use (along with Photinian, often preferred by German writers) by orthodox opponents, until it was gradually replaced by the name Unitarian. How the Socinians preferred to designate themselves may be seen from the title-page of the Catechism, as above.

[3] Zeltner, *Historia Crypto-Socin.*, p. 45 ff, is quite mistaken in ascribing the first draft to Soner.

was not long afterwards appointed minister of the congregation at Raków. Work on the Catechism was thus interrupted for more than a year, and had barely been resumed when Statorius himself died.[4]

The responsible authors of the Racovian Catechism were therefore Valentinus Smalcius (Schmalz), Hieronymus Moscorovius (Moskorzowski), and Johannes Völkel. Of these three Smalcius was probably the leading spirit. He was a German, born at Gotha in 1572, who had studied at several German universities, and having become intimate with a Socinian student at Strassburg visited Poland, joined the Minor Church, and after serving for five years as rector of a church school at Śmigiel, where he had an active correspondence with Socinus, was promoted to be one of the ministers of the important church at Lublin, succeeding Czechowicz. After seven years here he removed in 1605 to Raków, and there exercised a very active and influential ministry until his death in 1622.[5] A disciple of Socinus, he was in his time the leading minister among the Socinian churches, and their ablest and most zealous champion. He composed some fifty works, mostly polemical, and was unwearied in controversy with both Jesuits and Lutherans, in which he was often bitter and sarcastic as well as learned, able and persuasive.

Moscorovius was perhaps more distinguished than any other layman of his time for his noble birth, his large wealth, his wide learning, and his zeal for religion. He married the daughter of the celebrated Dudith, was an intimate friend of Socinus, and was repeatedly chosen a member of the national Diet. He was lavish in his support of church and college at Raków. With the Jesuits Skarga and Śmiglecki he carried on controversies, but on so high a plane of courtesy as to win their praise.[6]

Johannes Völkel was another German, coming from Grimma near Leipzig, who after studying at Wittenberg came to Poland and joined the Socinians. He was for a long time amanuensis to Socinus, and thus enjoyed his intimacy and became very familiar with his thought. He was a man of fine scholarship and independent mind. More competent persons for their task could hardly have been chosen to draw

---

[4] cf. Smalcius, *Diary*, in Zeltner, *op. cit.*, p. 1179: "1605, 25 Apr., Coepimus Catechesin componere, ego, Statorius, Moscorovius, et Volkielius. 9 Maji, Mortuus est Statorius."

[5] cf. Bock, *Antitrinitar.*, i, 836 ff.; Otto Fock, *Socinianismus* (Kiel, 1847), p. 188 f. His Diary, referred to above, is a rich mine of information.

[6] cf. Bock, *op. cit.*, i, 511–521; Ossoliński, *Wiadomości*, i, 245–279; Tadeusz Pasierbiński, *Hieronim z Moskorzowa Moskorzowski* (Kraków, 1931).

up the new Catechism; and for nearly two generations it was accepted by general consent as the standard exposition of the Socinian faith. The first Polish edition of the Catechism was published at Raków in 1605, and a second in 1619.[7] From the contents it is evident that in spite of its title and form this is not a catechism in the sense of being a book for the religious instruction of the young, so much as a manual of doctrines in question-and-answer form, intended largely for purposes of propaganda and defence. This purpose is the clearer from the fact that while but two editions were published in their own language for the use of Poles, eight editions or impressions were issued in Latin from 1609 to 1684 for the use of European scholars, besides three in Dutch, and two each in German and English.[8] A smaller catechism for the use of the young was also published at Raków in German by Smalcius in 1605, in Latin by Moskorzowski, and probably one in Polish, both in 1612.[9]

Smalcius lost no time in translating the Catechism into German for the enlightenment of those in his fatherland. This was published in 1608 and again in 1612,[10] in both cases with a preface addressed to the University at Wittenberg, where Smalcius had once been a student, and to which he sent a presentation copy by special messenger.[11] The gift was long ignored through a conspiracy of silence; since it was much feared that it would not be wise to bring these heretical doctrines to public notice through a printed refutation. At length, however, after

[7] No copy of the first edition is known to be extant; but in 1932 the writer discovered in the Czartoryski library at Kraków (No. 24685 I) four sheets (63 pp.) of it substituted in binding for corresponding missing sheets in a copy of the 1619 edition. Careful collation showed that save for insignificant typographical changes and a few added scripture references, the two editions are essentially identical in contents.

[8] Latin, 1609 (*bis*), 1651, 1665 ("1659"), 1680, 1681, 1684; Dutch, 1665, 1666, 1667; German, 1608, 1612; English, 1652, 1818, not to mention reprints in refutations by opponents.

[9] Little definite is known about these smaller catechisms, and that little is blurred by confusion with other and later catechisms for children. A copy of the *Catechesis Minor juventuti religione Christiana imbuendae conscripta* (Racoviae, 1612) is in the Jagellonian library at Kraków; and a perhaps unique copy of the German translation, reprinted in Transylvania by Bishop Valentin Radecki for the use of the Saxon Unitarian church at Kolozsvár, is preserved in the Brukenthal Museum at Hermannstadt (*Der kleine Katechismus zur Übung der Kinder in dem Christlichen Gottesdienst.* Clausenburg, 1620). Ms copy in the Unitarian library, Kolozsvár.

[10] *Catechismus der Gemeine derer Leute die da im Königreich Polen*, etc. (Rackaw, 1608).

[11] cf. Wolfgangius Franzius, *Augustanae Confessionis Articuli fidei . . . breviter explicati* (Witebergae, 1611), pref.

more than ten years, as the poison was seen to be spreading by means of private and public discussions and writings, and as Smalcius was boasting that no adequate reply had been made, Professor Friedrich Balduin in the name of the theological faculty at Wittenberg came out with a formal refutation, section by section, nearly twice as long as the original.[12] To reach a wider public Balduin followed this refutation of the German Catechism by a Latin refutation of the Latin one, which was not a mere translation of the German work, but added much new matter.[13]

The Latin version of the Catechism [14] was made by Moskorzowski. It was done in response to wide requests, and it aimed to be a faithful translation of the Polish original, from which it varied only in such minor omissions, additions or changes as criticism of the original had suggested.[15] The translator ventured to dedicate his work to King James I. of England, as a monarch celebrated for his devotion to the Protestant religion; but his Majesty, having glanced at it a little, was not well impressed, and expressed his detestation of the satanic work and its authors, the very offspring of Satan, whom he would severely punish if they fell into his power.[16] The work was consequently burnt by order of Parliament, April 1614.[17] Thus well launched into public notice both on the Continent and in England, the Racovian Catechism remained for a century and a half a thorn in the side of both Lutheran and Reformed theologians, and a standing object of attack by them in learned works, and by theological students in their dissertations and essays.[18] Though so often and so fully refuted, the questions it

---

[12] Ausführliche und gründliche Refutation des Deutschen Arianischen Catechismi, etc. (Wittenberg, 1619), cf. Vorrede.

[13] Solida refutatio Catechismi Ariani, etc. (Wittebergae, 1620).

[14] Catechesis Ecclesiarum quae in Regno Poloniae, etc. (Racoviae, 1609).

[15] Johannes Daniel Hoffman, 'Catechesis Racoviensis a Moscorovio translata,' Miscellanea Lipsiensia nova, ii (1743), 205–228, having collated the translation with the original, lists 22 pages of differences between the two.

[16] So reports Isaac Casaubon, Exercitationes ad Cardinalis Baronii prolegomena in Annales (London, 1614), pref., p. xxi.

[17] This burning is often confused (beginning with Sandius, Bibliotheca, p. 105) with that of the first English translation in 1652. cf. Johannes Hoornbeek, Summa controversiarum religionis (Trajecti ad Rhenum, 1658), p. 568.

[18] cf. inter alios multos, Franzius, cited above; J. H. Alting, Scriptores theologici (Amsterdam, 1646); J. H. Alsted, Theologia Polemica (Hanoviae, 1652); Nicolas Arnoldi, Religio Sociniana refutata (Franeker, 1654); Matthaeus Wren, Increpatio Bar Jesu (London, 1660); G. L. Oeder, Catechesis Racoviensis (Frankfurt, 1789). Catholic scholars outside of Poland did not much engage in published attacks upon it.

aroused kept continually recurring, with the inevitable result that the letter and the spirit of Protestant theology became insensibly yet surely modified, least in Germany, more in Holland, and most in England, as later chapters will show. The Catechism remained substantially unchanged in its various reprints for sixty years, until the Socinian exiles, having become subject to influences in Holland, considerably enlarged and modified its contents. The account of that period will be given later on. Meantime it remains to give a concise summary of the Catechism's characteristic teaching, as related to the prevailing orthodoxy of the seventeenth century.[19]

The Racovian Catechism was not built upon the customary lines and under the conventional categories of the existing Protestant confessions. While these, being framed by professional theologians, had hitherto started with a more or less traditional scheme of doctrine, and had then sought support for this from Scripture, Socinus, who had had no formal training in theology, and disowned the authority of the existing creeds, proceeded to form his doctrinal system independently of the past, and with a mind accustomed to legal methods of reasoning went to Scripture as to a *corpus juris*, explored its teachings inductively, and built up his system out of those. Hence its striking differences in both its method and its results from the Augsburg and the Helvetic Confessions. Instead of centering, as Luther's doctrine did, in faith in Christ, or as Calvin's did, in the sovereignty of God, the controlling interest in Socinus's teaching is the attainment of eternal life; and the Catechism sets out by defining the Christian religion as a divinely revealed way of attaining that life. This revelation is declared to have been made in the Scriptures, especially those of the New Testament, and reasons are shown why they may be accepted as a credible and true record. The truth of the Christian religion is established by the fact that its founder was proved, through the miracles that he wrought and his resurrection from the dead, to have been authenticated by God. These Scriptures contain all things necessary to salvation, and it is through them that man, who is by his nature mortal, must learn the way to attain immortality.

[19] In reading any account of the teaching of the Racovian Catechism, one should pay regard to which edition is referred to. Most accounts hitherto have been based on the later editions, published in Holland from 1665 on, and presenting a much expanded and modified form of the teaching. The present account is based on the earlier editions, and represents the original Socinian doctrine.

The way to salvation is plainly stated in the text (John xvii. 3), 'This is life eternal, that they might know thee, the only true God, and Jesus Christ whom thou hast sent.' It is thus *knowledge* of God and Christ, and acquaintance with God's will as revealed by Christ, that is the way to the supreme end, and it is therefore of crucial importance that this knowledge be correct, for if it is not correctly and truly held, then one's eternal salvation is jeopardized. After this introduction the Catechism goes on to elaborate what it regards as the correct views. Thus, knowledge of God comprises knowledge of both his nature and his will. In his nature he is only one, not three, and is eternal, and perfectly just, wise and powerful. Of these particulars the most important is that God is only one in person, namely the Father of our Lord Jesus Christ. After this positive statement the Catechism proceeds to refute the arguments offered in support of the doctrine of the Trinity, and to show that it has no sound foundation in Scripture.

Secondly, Jesus Christ is in his nature a real man, though not an ordinary man; for he was conceived by the Holy Spirit, and hence, though he has only a human nature, is God's Son. Here the Catechism in great detail (about a fifth of the whole book) proceeds to examine and refute the scripture proofs usually brought forward in support of the orthodox doctrine of Christ.

The office of Christ is treated under three aspects: as Prophet, as King, and as Priest. As *Prophet* we have Christ exercising the office of a teacher, declaring to men the will of God, which he had learned by ascending into heaven before his ministry (John iii. 13; vi. 38, 62; viii. 28b; cf. Socinus, *Opera*, i, 675), whence he was sent down again to earth, endowed with the Holy Spirit. This will of God consists in part of the commands of Moses in the Decalogue, to which Christ makes certain additions. Thus, the first command is that we should give God supreme worship, which consists in reverent adoration felt in the mind and heart and expressed in outward words and acts; and this Christ amplifies by prescribing a form of worship in the Lord's Prayer, whose meaning is explained in detail. A further addition is made in the requirement that we should pay divine honor to Christ as one that has divine authority over us, adoring him for his majesty and in all our necessities seeking his powerful aid, as many texts of Scripture illustrate. In doing this we still adore and worship God as the primary author of our salvation, but Christ as the secondary one; and although we may not thus invoke the Virgin or the Saints, yet

those that do not invoke Christ nor think him deserving of adoration
are in fact not Christians at all. The other commands of the Decalogue
are then taken up in like manner, with many applications to the situations of personal and social life, and with strong emphasis upon secular
and civil relations as subject to the will of God. Thus civil government
is not superfluous, and a Christian may hold office under it provided
he does not violate the laws and commands of Christ. One must obey
lawful magistrates as powers ordained of God. While common swear-
ing is forbidden, civil oaths are permitted in the greatest and most
solemn cases. The taking of usury is forbidden, though reasonable
interest is not. Christians, however, must not lay up wealth beyond
what the needs of life require, but should use any surplus to relieve the
poor, especially one's servants, rather than for luxury or bodily pleasure.
Going beyond the commands of Moses, Christ especially calls for self-
denial as to the bodily senses, wealth and pride; for bearing with patient
and uncomplaining endurance whatever cross may have to be borne
for his sake; and for imitating the example of Christ in his trust in
God, in love of God and of one's neighbor, even one's enemy, as oneself,
and in humility and constancy in prayer.

Only one sacrament is recognized, that of the Lord's Supper, which
is an act commemorating the death of Christ: other views of it are
vigorously controverted. Baptism is an outward act by which converts
to the Christian religion openly acknowlege Christ as their Master; but
it is not appropriate to infants, and it has no regenerative value. The
Holy Spirit is not a person in the Godhead, but a divine power in the
hearts of men.

Christ showed us the way to return to God, and how to be reconciled
to him. He was without sin, and lived a life of such holiness that no
one has ever approached him in sanctity, and he came next to God
himself in holiness. By the incomparable power to work miracles
which God would have given to no other, he proved his teaching true.
He suffered that he might give us an example how to bear our own
sufferings, though not to atone for our sins, for God forgives men
freely; and to reconcile us to God. Other views of the atonement are
fully refuted from Scripture. Faith is not merely believing that the
teaching of Christ is true, but such a belief as leads us to repent of our
sins and do the will of God to the utmost. Man's will is free, and
there is no such thing as original sin. The doctrine of predestination is
a great mistake, necessarily corrupting all religion, and attributing an

unworthy character to God. We are justified before God when he forgives our sins and gives us eternal life; but no one can be justified without faith in Christ; though saving faith is not mere belief, but such a trust as results in obedience.

Christ's office as King and as Priest receives much briefer treatment. In his *Kingly* office Christ exercises the supreme power given him after he rose from the dead and was seated at the right hand of God. In his natural body he rose from the dead, but his spiritual body is at God's right hand. In his *Priestly* office Christ in heaven makes intercession for us with God, and through the power that God gave him procures for us release from our sins and the punishment of them, by interceding for us and restraining us from all manner of sin, as well as by his own example.

Finally, the Church is the company, visible or invisible, of those that hold and profess saving doctrine. It is administered by regular officers, and it exercises upon offending members either private or public discipline. The unruly are corrected privately or if need be also publicly, and at the worst they are excluded from the Church.

Such, in briefest summary, are the outstanding lines of the Racovian Catechism in its original form. Every position taken is supported where necessary by ample citations of scripture texts in proof, which are accepted without question as final authority, and are in the main interpreted according to their plain sense as determined on lexical, grammatical and contextual grounds rather than by tradition. Obviously we have not here a manual of religious belief cast in the mold of twentieth century thought, for in various particulars its positions have long since been outgrown. In Scripture as its authority it sees not a collection of writings expressing the varied thought of various minds during centuries of time, but rather a single consistent work in which the word of God is revealed to man. Hence it often makes interpretations that later scholarship has rejected. It accepts the miraculous element in the record without hesitation, and founds doctrine upon it. Its apologetic purpose leads it at various points to leave positive doctrine for a time in order to engage in polemics against Catholic or Protestant teachings. It contains echoes of Schomann's Catechism of 1574, and especially emphasizes the points on which Socinus had strenuously insisted in the controversies within the Minor Church over the worship of Christ, baptism, relation to the civil power, and the social questions in general. It suffers from certain defects of arrangement, of relative emphasis, and of omission; but despite all its limitations the Racovian Catechism stands as a notable landmark on the way to more scriptural, simple and practical doctrine. For not only the central dogmas of the Trinity and the supreme deity of Christ, but such subordinate doctrines as original sin, total depravity, predestination, vicarious atonement, justification by faith, eternal punishment, and others that had been prominent in Christian teaching, and had long proved stumbling-blocks to many, were either passed by without notice, or were actively opposed as unscriptural, unreasonable or superfluous.

From what has been said above, the doctrinal characteristics of the Racovian Catechism will have been seen. It is noteworthy, however, that in its practical aspects its ultimate stress is laid upon the moral life of the Christian. This life is conceived as obedience to the revealed will of God, which is its immediate aim, as a necessary condition of attaining the supreme end in eternal life.

Various attempts have been made to account for Socinianism as an outgrowth of earlier systems or thinkers, or as dependent upon them; but none of them is convincing. There are, indeed, resemblances to the thought of Servetus; but Socinus emphatically denied that he had drawn his views from that source.[20] Of earlier heretics there is closest resemblance to Paul of Samosata and Photinus; but there is not a shred of evidence that he was acquainted with their doctrine unless through the brief references to it in Servetus. Finally, several distinguished scholars (Baur, Ritschl, Harnack) have been led to regard Socinianism as an outgrowth of the Scotism and Nominalism of the mediaeval philosophers. But Socinus testified that he had no acquaintance with philosophy or scholastic theology.[21] It is far more reasonable and simple to account for the characteristic views of the Socinian system as a lay scholar's plain and straightforward interpretation of the scripture text, merely on the background of Italian Humanism,[22] and unwarped by traditional philosophical or theological presuppositions.

Of course this first essay at giving formal expression to the Socinian doctrine could not be expected to prove adequate indefinitely, although it was a full sixty years before it received any substantial revision. Meanwhile it was admirably supplemented by other writings which gave the Socinian doctrine fuller treatment and better arrangement.

[20] cf. Socinus, *Opera*, ii, 535.
[21] cf. *Opera*, i, 490.
[22] cf. Dunin Borkowski, *Quellenstudien*, p. 135 f.

Of these the first was by Christoff Ostorodt, whose treatise on the chief points of the Christian religion [23] was in fact published a year earlier than the Catechism itself. He was son of a Lutheran pastor at Goslar in the Harz, and was educated at Königsberg. Having become converted to Socinian views, he went to Poland, joined the Minor Church in 1585, learned the Polish language, and after an apprenticeship as teacher became minister of the important church at Śmigiel in Great Poland,[24] where he engaged in an important debate with Canon Powodowski of near-by Poznań in 1592.[25] A few years later he went to Holland on a missionary journey which marked the first introduction of Socinianism into that country, of which an account will be given in a later chapter; and in 1605 he became minister at Busków near Danzig, where he died in 1611. He was a man of profound learning, conservative in his doctrinal and social views, and as minister held his people up to an extremely strict standard of Christian character. Deep interest in his fellow-countrymen led him to publish in German the treatise mentioned above. It is a popular presentation of the Socinian teaching, and adheres closely to the writings of Socinus. In order of topics and in substance of teaching it bears noticeable resemblance to the Racovian Catechism, though it is hard to say whether either was influenced by the other; but it goes into fuller detail as to doctrines, and it strongly emphasizes personal and social morals, thus showing influence from the Anabaptists, with whom the author had no little sympathy. The work remained in print for more than two generations, and was long highly esteemed as the best manual of Socinian doctrine. It must have had wide influence in Germany, as the writer desired, for theologians there attacked it repeatedly and savagely.[26]

For a decade and more after the publication of the Racovian Catechism, the presses of both Poland and Germany fairly swarmed with

[23] *Unterrichtung von den vornehmsten Hauptpunckten der christlichen Religion,* etc. (Rackau, 1604).

[24] If the questionable statement of Lubieniecius (*Historia*, p. 240 f.) be accepted as correct, that he was first minister of the church at Raków, his service there must have been brief.

[25] cf. C. Ostorodt, *Disputacia zboru Szmigielskiego,* etc. (Disputation in the Śmigiel church), n. p., 1592; Hieronim Powodowski, *Disputacia wtóra X. Hieronima Powodowskiego z Szmigielskiemi różnobożami* (Second disputation of the Rev. Hieronim Powodowski with the Śmigiel heretics), Poznań, 1592.

[26] So, e. g., Balduin, Feuerborn, Felwinger, Rost, Leuckenroth, Felgenhauer, Pelargus, and others.

attacks upon the Socinian teaching in general or some of its doctrines in detail. The ablest, most active and most effective champion for the defence was Smalcius. Of his half a hundred listed writings most were controversial, against Lutheran or Jesuit attacks. He had a clear and fluent style, and an unusual power of persuasive argument, but his manner of controversy was pugnacious and irritating, and intensified oposition where another might have softened it. Yet his bold and powerful advocacy won many supporters for his cause, and gave them assured confidence in it. His writings give the best representation of Socinianism in its aggressive mood.

The completest and best systematic treatment of Socinianism is the latest, that of Völkel.[27] It was largely composed by 1612, and in its first form was submitted to the Synod for approval, and then referred back to the author for revision. The work dragged, however, and was not yet finished when Völkel died in 1618, and it was a dozen years more before it was brought to completion. In fact, the first of its five books was found so inadequate that it was finally discarded, and replaced by one from the pen of Johannes Crellius, to whom the revision of the manuscript had been committed.[28] This work was held in the highest esteem by the Socinians as the standard exposition of their theology. Secretly reprinted at Amsterdam it was ordered burned by public authority, but afterwards saw the light at Rotterdam in Dutch translation; and it was judged worthy of being reprinted with an elaborate refutation in three volumes by a distinguished Dutch theologian.[29] The works here mentioned, together with others previously spoken of (Schomann's *Catechism* of 1574, Czechowicz's *Rozmowy*, the *Racovian Catechism*, Ostorodt's *Unterrichtung*, Smalcius's controversial works, and Völkel's *De vera religione*), furnish the inquirer with materials for an adequate survey of the development of Socinian doctrine from the beginning of the Minor Church to the time when the Socinians were banished from Poland. The considerable modifications that it received in its exile in Holland will be spoken of in a later chapter.

It was nearly two centuries before the Racovian Catechism began to receive due consideration and appreciation of its merits. The Protestant writers who dealt with it during the seventeenth and most of the

---

[27] Johannes Volkelius, *De vera religione libri quinque; quibus praefixus est Johannis Crellii liber De Deo et ejus Attributis* (Racoviae, 1630).

[28] cf. Bock, *Antitrinitar.*, i, 998 ff.

[29] Samuel Maresius, *Hydra Socinianismi expugnata*, etc. (Groningae, 1651–1662).

eighteenth century did so uniformly with a polemical purpose, seeking
to discover and confute its errors but largely ignoring its merits. All
such treatments were therefore prejudiced and one-sided. Catholic
writers, outside of Poland, on the other hand paid little attention to it
at all in their published writings, though it is evident from the correspondence of the celebrated Minorite scholar Marin Mersenne with the
Socinian scholar Martin Ruar,[30] that it was taken seriously in certain
Catholic circles. At the end of the eighteenth century, however, several
writings appeared that endeavored to do it justice.[31] The fear formerly
felt that Socinianism might prove a formidable enemy to Protestant
Christianity had largely died away, modern biblical criticism was paving the way for a revised theology, and the Socinian thought and spirit
began to be unconsciously absorbed in quarters where it had formerly
been only hated and opposed. A yet later survey of the Socinian system
of doctrine [32] endorses the judgment that 'Socinianism is by no means
mere Naturalism or Rationalism, but is a religion of revelation; that
the two Socini and their disciples were scholars and sincere theologians,
true children of the Reformation of the sixteenth century, of real piety
and laudable zeal, who wished to make true Christianity pure; that
they were passionate believers in free thought, the Bible was their only
guide, conscience their only light—true Christians and true Protestants.'

[30] cf. Ruar, *Epistolae*, pp. 191–222.

[31] cf. Johann Friedrich Flatt, 'Bemerkungen über Socins Philosophie und Theologie,
nach ihrem Verhältniss zur praktischen Vernunft betrachtet' in his *Beiträge zur christlichen Dogmatik und Moral*, chap. iii, pp. 117–152 (Tübingen, 1792); Wilhelm Carl
Ludwig Ziegler, 'Kurze Darstellung des eigenthümlichen Lehrbegriffs des Faustus Socinus,'
Henke's *Neues Magazin für Religionsphilosophie, Exegese und Kirchengeschichte*, iv
(1800), 201–276; Ernst Gottlieb Bengel, 'Ideen zur historischen-analytischen Erklärung
des Sozinischen Lehrbegriffs,' Süskinds *Magazin für christliche Dogmatik und Moral*,
xiv, 133–200; xv, 104–168; xvi, 90–157 (1808–'18).

[32] cf. Henri Amphoux, *Essai sur la doctrine Socinienne* (Strasbourg, 1850), pp. 79–81.

CHAPTER XXXII

SOCINIANISM FULL-BLOWN: PROPAGANDA, ORGANIZATION AND USAGES

THE DEATH OF FAUSTUS SOCINUS and the closely following publication of the Racovian Catechism mark an epoch in the history of Socinianism. During the next generation the little church on the one hand made rapid increase in its internal health and in vigorous outward activity, yet on the other hand began to feel a premonition of those increasing persecutions which were in another generation to put a period to its history in Poland. During a quarter-century the ripe scriptural knowledge and the persuasive reasoning of Socinus had brought about among practically all the members of the church a satisfactory agreement as to all the doctrines regarded as most important, and a broad tolerance as to the rest; and his practical good sense in the face of existing conditions had overcome the extreme views, doctrinal or social, that had once threatened to wreck the young church. With the divisions that had so seriously split its forces and sapped its strength thus comfortably brought together in unity upon essentials, the church was at length in a position to expand in adult strength. The high moral standards by which its adherents had from the first been distinguished were now observed more scrupulously than ever, appealed strongly to such as were seriously in earnest, commanded the respect of all, and were praised by even their adversaries. Their educated men also were putting forth works of literature of such excellence that though the smallest of the confessions in Poland, the 'Arians' outshone all others put together in the history of Polish letters.[1]

Inspired with fresh confidence in the truth of their doctrines and the future of their cause, of whose early triumph they felt sure, they burned with fervent missionary zeal to spread it as fast and far as possible. It

[1] The Catholic historian of Polish literature declares that the "Arians" were intellectually the most advanced, cultivated and talented of all Polish Dissidents, and that their life and doctrines left an enduring influence on the history of Polish culture and literature. cf. Alexander Brückner, *Geschichte der polnischen Literatur* (Leipzig, 1901), p. 119 f; *id.*, *Różnowiercy*, p. 137; Tadeusz Grabowski, *Literatura*.

was no mere vain boastfulness in Socinus when he appealed to all in the Reformed Church that were anxious to cultivate true piety, to abandon their lax and declining body and join the company of his brethren.[2] The vigorous life that the Minor Church had by now attained was expressed in various directions. A natural desire for sympathy and co-operation with other bodies seeking a purer and simpler form of Christianity early led the Socinians to seek some sort of union with them. Their attempt to come into fraternal relations with the Communists of Moravia, and their persistently attempted but always disappointed efforts to establish with the Reformed Church some alliance that, while allowing generous mutual tolerance on questions of doctrinal difference, should unite them for common religious ends, have already been mentioned.[3] There seemed better hopes of combining with the Mennonites at Danzig, since the two bodies not only agreed in general in the field of doctrine, but closely harmonized on the conspicuous subject of baptism. At the synod at Raków in 1613, therefore, negotiations were authorized, and representatives were appointed to discuss with the Mennonites a plan of union. The conference held, however, disappointed their hopes.[4]

Two years later a letter reached the Synod by which liberal churches in Holland urgently invited a visit from the brethren in Poland. The invitation was accepted, and Smalcius and Völkel were deputed, but before they could reach the Dutch border a war that had broken out compelled them to turn back.[5] When, however, shortly afterwards the Remonstrants in the Reformed Church of Holland were being bitterly persecuted by the strict Calvinists, and their ministers were deprived of their pulpits, and many of them had to leave the country for a time, the brethren at Raków, learning of this, sent Jonas Schlichting, a young man of great promise who had lately been a student under the Remonstrant professor Episcopius at Leiden, to offer them assistance and a welcome in Poland. This was the beginning of ever closer and warmer relations between Socinians and Remonstrants. Several of the latter[6] did in fact visit Poland and were cordially received there. From

---

[2] cf. his *Quod Regni Poloniae*, etc., *v. supra*, p. 404 f.

[3] *v. supra*, pp. 354 f, 380 f.

[4] cf. Smalcius, *Diary*, pp. 1193, 1200; Szczotka, *Synody*, p. 62.

[5] cf. Smalcius, *Diary*, p. 1203.

[6] Among them Samuel Naeranus and his son Jan, the latter of whom, when the Socinians in their turn were exiled from Poland a generation later, took the lead in raising large sums of money for their relief. *v. infra*, p. 496.

this time on the Socinian scholar and traveler Martin Ruar conducted an active correspondence with the Remonstrant ministers Naeranus (van der Neer), father and son, and so long as he lived endeavored to promote a closer approach between the two bodies.[7] At length in 1627, when the Remonstrants had been permitted to return to Holland and enjoy exercise of their religion, Ruar began to discuss with Naeranus the subject of a union of the two confessions. To promote this project, the Synod commissioned Ruar to go to Holland, which he did in 1632 in company with a number of other ministers.[8] But the time was not yet ripe, for the two confessions were not close enough in their teachings to make an attempt at union advisable. Each side wished first to convert the other to its own views; though one fruit of the sympathetic relations then cultivated was a little book designed to increase a spirit of mutual religious tolerance,[9] which was later of great influence in both Holland and England. Meanwhile the Socinians were forced to go their way alone, cut off from any close religious fellowship save with their brethren in Transylvania. A generation later, however, when they were banished from Poland, it was in Holland that the exiles had from both Remonstrants and Mennonites the kindest welcome, and from Remonstrant sources, through the efforts of Naeranus, that they received the most generous material aid.

In quite another direction the Socinians at the beginning of this period for a short time entertained an illusory hope of widely extending their field of influence—namely, in Russia. When the Czar Ivan the Terrible died in 1584 he left a young son Demetrius, and this son was supposed to have been murdered in childhood. But about 1600 a young man emerged from obscurity claiming that he himself was Demetrius, who had escaped death and until now had been kept in hiding. He had for some time been in one of the Socinian schools at Hoszcza in Volhynia, and had been confirmed in that faith; [10] and the Socinian leaders, believing in his genuineness and sincerity, therefore entertained great hopes of his influence in their favor, if he should come to the throne. Both in Russia and in Poland he won considerable support for his claim; and late in 1604 he invaded Russia with an army and

---

[7] cf. Ludwik Chmaj, *Marcin Ruar* (Kraków, 1921), pp. 48, 59, 62–65.

[8] cf. Szczotka, *Synody*, pp. 71, 74; Chmaj, *op. cit.*, p. 74 f; Bock, *Antitrinitar.*, i, 722.

[9] Samuel Przypkowski (Przipcovius), *Dissertatio de pace et concordia ecclesiastica* (Eleutheropolis=Amsterdam, 1628). English trans., by John Biddle (London, 1653).

[10] cf. Szczotka, *Synody*, p. 57.

defeated the forces of the Czar Boris. When a few months later the Czar suddenly died, Demetrius seized the crown that he claimed was rightfully his. Hence in 1605 the Synod sent to Moscow a delegation of five to enlist his active interest in their cause. Demetrius, however, had diplomatically sought wider support for his own cause by professing to be first a Roman and then a Greek Catholic; and the mission, after six months, returned disillusioned to Poland. Shortly afterwards Demetrius fell a victim to his enemies. He was only the first of three successive pretenders. It is now generally believed that he was an impostor, very possibly deluded by those that had brought him up and had made him a tool for their own political ends.[11]

With more conspicuous means of spreading their cause thus denied them, the Socinians had recourse to the slower but surer means of personal propaganda with individuals. This was carried on in two ways: through the extensive circulation of printed books, and through the missionary efforts of emissaries systematically sent to other lands. During this period the press at Raków was very active in the publication of works by Socinian authors. The unpublished writings of Socinus followed one another in rapid succession; the controversial works of Smalcius issued in a steady stream. Commentaries on books of the Bible, or essays on various doctrines, followed. Any attack from Calvinists or Jesuits at home, or from Lutherans abroad, was sure of a prompt and vigorous reply. All these, being the work of the ablest minds and of competent scholars, after having first received the scrutiny and revision of the Synod, were set forth in superior typography, and commanded attention wherever they went.[12] They were subsidized from general funds or from private gifts, and were sent in large numbers into the countries of the west. The comparative frequency with which, after well over three hundred years, books from the Raków press were still offered for sale by dealers in old books bears witness to their wide circulation; and the long series of ambitious works by

---

[11] cf. Aleksander Hirschberg, *Dymitr Samozwaniec* (the Pretender Demetrius), Lwów, 1898; Henryk Merczyng, 'Aryanie Polscy i Dymitr "Samozwaniec"' (The Polish Arians and the Pretender Demetrius), *Przegląd Historyczny*, iv (1907), 170–180; Hungarian trans., 'A Lengyel Unitáriusok és Pseudo-Demétrius' (The Polish Unitarians and the false Demetrius), *Keresztény Magvető*, xlii (1907), 189–200, Sonia D. Howe, *The False Dmitri* (London, 1916); Smalcius, *Diary*, pp. 1180, 1186; Bock, *Antitrinitar.*, i, 979 f; Dobrowolski, *Kronika*, p. 172. Demetrius is represented as one of the characters in Moussorgsky's opera, "Boris Godunoff."

[12] Over 500 titles or reprints came from the Raków press.

theologians, and the steady swarm of students' dissertations or essays at the Protestant universities, which during more than a century kept up an almost ceaseless attack against Socinian doctrines, are evidence of how seriously these Socinian books were regarded, and of how widely their influence was felt and feared. How effective they were in making proselytes, even in the face of the most bitter opposition, is to be seen in such names as those of Crellius, Smalcius, Ostorod, Völkel, Ruar, Schomann, Schlichting, Stegmann, Wolzogen and others, all of them German converts, who rose to leadership among the Socinians, and contributed immensely to the strength of their cause.

Yet more noteworthy was the influence of scholarly Socinian travelers that went abroad with missionary ends more or less in view. Open and avowed missionary propaganda or organization of Socinian churches in other lands would of course not have been allowed; but Polish noblemen were accustomed to send their sons to western Europe to complete their education by travel and by study at foreign universities. Two or three would often go at a time, with a tutor to supervise their studies and have an eye to their behavior. The tutor was likely to be a young theological graduate, or even an older minister, and he would take with him a stock of books for loan or distribution, overlooking no opportunity for religious discussion with such foreign scholars as he might meet. These secret missionaries easily won friends by their noble birth, good breeding and fine scholarship, their freedom from the usual theological rancor, their generous tolerance in discussion, and most of all their emphasis on the importance of freedom of conscience; and they would forward to Raków copies of any works published against Socinianism. Thus the Socinians had emissaries with their student retinue more or less frequently at most of the Protestant universities of Holland and Germany—Leiden and Franeker, Strassburg, Marburg, Heidelberg, Wittenberg, Jena, Helmstedt, Rostock—who cautiously broached their views and loaned their books. Hence in time a good many of the Protestant clergy in Holland and in France, and some even in Germany, became affected by Socinian views,[13] to the great alarm of the more orthodox; while even Catholic circles such as those of the Jansenists were not wholly untouched. Distinguished men like Grotius, then living in exile in France, the liberal Calvinist Sorbière

[13] cf. Andreas Carolus, *Memorabilia ecclesiastica* (Tubingae, 1697–1702), ii, 541 f.

and the Catholic Mersenne, carried on amicable exchange of views with the brethren of Raków.

Of all these interesting academic hot-beds of Socinianism, one became so notorious that it deserves more than casual mention. At Altdorf, a few miles distant from Nuremberg, there was early in the seventeenth century a flourishing academy (given the rank of a university in 1623, and eventually absorbed by Erlangen in 1809), which was patronized by Nuremberg as its own, and had an able faculty and attracted many foreign students, especially from Poland.[14] Among its earlier graduates was one Ernst Soner, who in the course of his post-graduate studies abroad spent some time at Leiden, at the very time when Ostorodt and his companion arrived there, as mentioned in the previous chapter.[15] He formed a close intimacy with them, and became a ready convert to their faith. In due time Soner became a professor at Altdorf, where he was one of the most popular teachers. He maintained a secret correspondence with his Socinian friends in Poland, and cultivated confidential relations with such students as came thence to Altdorf, often bringing books fresh from the Raków press, and cautiously spreading their views among susceptible fellow-students. While exercising the greatest caution as to what he did, Soner embraced the opportunity which his most private courses gave him, to rouse debatable questions in the minds of susceptible students, and to direct the course of their thought; and all this so inoffensively that when he met premature death by an incurable disease no one had entertained serious doubts of his orthodoxy. As the movement quietly spread, it developed into what was in effect a secret religious fraternity, whose members held meetings in one another's rooms, and there observed the Lord's Supper after the Socinian manner. About twenty students in all were concerned in the movement, and they were known for their devout piety and their exemplary lives.

After but seven years of fruitful teaching, Soner himself died in 1612, and his disciples, bereft of his guidance, mostly scattered to do missionary work in other centers. Of these one of the earliest was Johannes Krell (Crellius), who scenting danger fled in 1612 to Raków, where

[14] cf. A. G. Will, *Geschichte und Beschreibung der Nürnbergschen Universität Altdorf* (Altdorf, 1795). For an elaborate account of what is here to follow, cf. Zeltner, *Crypto-Socin.*; summarized by Earl M. Wilbur, 'Socinian Propaganda in Germany three hundred years ago,' U. H. S., Boston, iii (1933), 22–41.

[15] *v. supra*, p. 417.

he later became Rector of the College, and the most distinguished scholar among the Socinians. Another was Martin Ruar, who left Altdorf to spread the doctrine at Strassburg, and later became the most energetic propagator of Socinianism in foreign lands. Ere long, however, reports began to transpire of what had been going on behind the scenes, and the authorities of the Academy instituted a thorough investigation. Students under suspicion were examined, whereupon all but one denied any guilt. Two of the group, who had gone to spread their views at other universities, were brought back under guard, imprisoned, and labored with, until in view of what they might otherwise have to suffer, their resistance was finally broken down, and they made a solemn public recantation. Thus Socinianism was driven out of Altdorf, where it had been systematically cultivated and zealously promoted. In other universities, however, the same leaven continued silently to work wherever Socinian students were to be found, and through them it tended quietly to spread in the land.

Even at its most vigorous period the Minor Church was quite the smallest of the four Protestant confessions in Poland. No complete list of all the congregations during its century of existence is extant, and the synod records from which such a list might best be made up are, so far as has been discovered, no longer extant. Merczyng [16] compiled from the best sources available a list of 73 congregations in Poland and 4 in exile; of which 13 were in Lithuania and 7 in Great Poland, the greatest number being in the three Palatinates nearest Kraków, and in Volhynia; but the list is certainly quite incomplete. It is recorded that in a largely attended synod at Raków in 1611, 400 persons partook of the Lord's Supper; and that in 1618, at the largest gathering hitherto, 459 persons partook. [17] It would therefore probably not be going beyond bounds to estimate that first and last there were at least 125 Socinian congregations in Poland. [18] But many of these must have been short-lived, crushed by persecution or lost by a change of patron to one of another faith. Hardly one could trace its history throughout from 1565 to 1660. One of the most competent students of the movement estimates

---

[16] Henryk Merczyng, *Zbory i Senatorowie Protestanccy w Dawnej Rzeczypospolitej* (The Protestant congregations and Senators in the old Republic), Warszawa, 1905, pp. 105–120. cf. Dzieduszycki, *Skarga*, i, 405, n.

[17] cf. Szczotka, *Synody*, pp. 60, 67.

[18] Thus perhaps a third as many as the Reformed Church had. The author's previous estimate of 300 (*Our Unitarian Heritage*, p. 153) was undoubtedly much too high.

that at its most flourishing period it numbered not more than a thousand families, foreigners included.[19] Hardly a dozen of the congregations were in large towns. The rest were rural or village congregations on the estates of nobles, the minister being to all intents and purposes the patron's domestic chaplain, and the congregation being largely composed of his retainers. In the management of church affairs the influence of the gentry predominated, although in the congregations in the larger towns commoners and artisans took an active part. Yet although the Minor Church in its whole history could lay claim to but two great magnates in Lithuania and a half-dozen more in the distant Ukraine,[20] and only nine 'Arian' names are found in the list of lay Senators,[21] still for its size none had a more distinguished company of adherents. One of the most famous of these, writing in defence of their religious liberties soon after the Socinians had been banished from Poland, gives a list four or five pages long of early Antitrinitarians and later Socinians who had held public offices and dignities of highest distinction in the Kingdom,[22] and another declared in a suppliant letter to the Elector of Brandenburg about 1670, that in Poland and Lithuania not a family was found that was distinguished for its ancestry, services or wealth, including generals, princes and even the reigning King himself, which was not bound by ties of blood or marriage to some of the Socinians.[23]

During this vigorous period in its history the Minor Church was well organized and efficiently administered by faithful ministers and devoted lay leaders. In the essentials of polity it adhered closely to that of the Reformed Church from which it had sprung in 1565, though in time modifications were naturally made as experience suggested. The principles and practices of the church organization were, however, not formally codified until considerably later in the *Ecclesiastical Polity* of Peter Morzkowski (Morscovius—not to be confounded with the previously mentioned Moskorzowski, Moscorovius).[24] This work, which

---

[19] cf. Kot, *Mouvement*, p. 79.

[20] Jan Kiszka and Nicholas (the Black) Radziwiłł, who though he died just as the Minor Church was organizing, had shown unequivocal sympathy with the cause of its leaders.

[21] cf. Merczyng, *op. cit.*, p. 121 ff.

[22] cf. (Stanislaus Lubieniecius) *Vindiciae pro Unitariorum in Polonia religionis libertate*, in Sandius, *Bibliotheca*, pp. 282–286.

[23] cf. F. S. Bock, *Historia Socinianismi Prussici* (Regiomonti, 1754), p. 78.

[24] Peter Morscovius, *Politia Ecclesiastica*, etc. (Francofurti et Lipsiae, 1746). The Synod

represents the usages and ideals of the Socinian congregations at the middle of the seventeenth century, is in three books, covering 1) the general principles of church law, 2) the duties of the church officers, and 3) the church discipline. The matter is set forth in a series of 'aphorisms,' or concise statements of principles, which are then expanded as fully as necessary, and illustrated by reference to New Testament usage or to the writings of the Fathers as authority. Especial emphasis is laid on the office of the ministry, its sacred character and duties; and interesting detailed suggestions are offered as to the preparation and delivery of sermons. Baptism of infants is not sanctioned, but a rite of laying on of hands is substituted by way of recognizing the sacred obligation of parents in the rearing of their children. Adults are baptized by immersion, signifying that they recognize their obligation to live a Christian life; but rebaptism is not insisted on for any that were baptized in infancy. The Lord's Supper is not a sacrament but a commemorative rite, by which we are reminded of our baptismal vows. Much stress is laid on pastoral duties and a conscientious pastoral concern for the life of members of the church.

The administration of the affairs of the Minor Church was directed by its Synod, an annual assembly of all the pastors, elders and deacons of the whole body to provide in general for the welfare of the church.[25] There appears to have been in theory one general Synod inclusive of all congregations in both Poland and Lithuania; but in actual practice the Lithuanian churches, widely separated from those in Poland, not only in space but also in their doctrinal and social tendencies, seem in their provincial or local synods more or less to have gone their own way,

---

of Dążwa in 1646 appointed Morzkowski, the minister at Czarków, and formerly the pupil and amanuensis of Johannes Crellius, to prepare a digest of the rules and usages that the ministers and churches had from time to time adopted, or that seemed to be indicated as desirable. The manuscript of the work was duly presented to the Synod for approval, and was then submitted to others for additions and final revision before printing. The country was in confusion from various wars, and the work dragged, so that before it could be published the Socinians were banished from Poland. The manuscript was jealously preserved in the hope that it might yet prove useful for congregations dispersed abroad, and it thus came at length into the possession of the famous Socinian scholar, Samuel Crellius, from whom it passed in turn through two more hands into those of a Lutheran scholar, Georg Ludwig Oeder, whose ecclesiastical superior asked him to edit it for publication. He published the work in full, supplying it with copious notes, in which he seized every opportunity to carp at Socinianism as wanting the true basis of piety. cf. pp. 333–340 of the work itself; also Bock, *Antitrinitar.*, i, 501–506.

[25] cf. Morscovius, *op. cit.*, p. 312.

though when important issues were in question delegates from Poland would sometimes be sent to the synod meetings in Lithuania or *vice versa*. The earlier synods met at widely scattered points, though most often at Lublin and Chmielnik; but beginning with 1611 all synods with the exception of three at Lublin were held at Raków until its destruction in 1638, and after that generally in more remote places in the southeast.[26]

Besides the annual general Synod, there were also apparently local synods in various districts for settling questions of local interest. These seem to have been held only irregularly as occasion demanded. Matters not settled in these could be carried up to the general Synod for decision. In addition to the formal synods, groups of ministers from time to time met at Raków to discuss points of theology, and these were sometimes protracted for days or even weeks as aspects of doctrine were threshed out in what were in effect theological seminars. But as time went on, attention was centered less on doctrine than on the practical application of the principles of Christianity in the daily life of individuals or their duties to the State.

At meetings of the Synod, which lasted from one to two weeks,[27] there were two presiding officers, one a minister, the other a layman. There were prayers at the opening of the sessions, and at intervals thereafter. In the conduct of business, letters were read from persons unable to be present, or from other churches, and appropriate answers were authorized. Reports were made on the state of the churches, and the financial reports of their deacons were scrutinized. From the general treasury funds were voted for the support of feeble congregations or the foundation of new ones; assistance was given to needy promising students for the ministry, as also for those of special ability who were sent abroad for advanced study at foreign universities. Support was voted for retired ministers, and aid was granted for widows and children of those deceased, to such as were suffering persecution for their faith, and to prisoners or others suffering from war or public calamity. Any disorderly ministers were censured or removed from their office; young men suitably trained for the ministry were examined, and were ordained and appointed to their stations; and able men were sent abroad for purposes of propaganda.

[26] cf. Szczotka, *Synody*, for an account of all the synods in the history of the Minor Church.
[27] cf. Lubieniecius, *Historia*, p. 252.

Especial attention was given to schools under the direction of the Synod in connection with the larger congregations, and their Rectors and teachers were appointed by it; while private tutors for the sons of noble patrons at home or on their travels were chosen from the older and abler scholars. Stipends for ministers and teachers were paid by the Synod from common funds which were contributed by the various churches as apportioned to them by the Synod, and were supplemented by gifts from wealthy individuals. The Synod financed the publication of such religious works or school texts as were judged important, approved or revised their manuscripts, and subsidized the authors.

Questions of doctrine and of morals were earnestly discussed, often with much feeling, yet in a spirit so tolerant as often to win the admiration of those outside the church. Regulation of the private life of the brethren in accordance with Christian standards was a matter of serious concern, and discussion was often had of raising the standard of discipline in the congregations and in the moral life of the members. Even secular matters sometimes came into consideration, when members dissatisfied with the decisions of the civil courts, especially as to questions of property, appealed them to the Christian judgment of the Synod. Thus the Synod sought to deal effectively with all matters of general concern to members of the church; and when all its affairs were at length completed the session concluded with a solemn celebration of the Lord's Supper.[28]

In the earlier history of the Minor Church it had a titular head called Superintendent, chosen from one of the leading ministers, who convoked and presided over synods, visited the churches, and exercised general supervision over the Church as a whole, assisted by clerical or lay colleagues and district Elders. But after a short generation we hear no more of this office. In fact, the polity of the Minor Church seems to have grown much more simple, and its administration much freer, than that of the Reformed Church from which it was separated, and to have depended much more upon the weight of moral influence than upon administrative regulations.

The organization of the local congregations was simple.[29] At the head was the Patron, on whom, after the stipend granted the Pastor by the Synod, devolved the main responsibility for the material affairs of the church on his estate. Next after him was the Pastor, who instead

<hr>

[28] For further details as to all the above, cf. Bock, *Antitrinitar.*, i, 3–7; Szczotka, *op. cit.*, pp. 23–25. [29] cf. Morscovius, *op. cit.*, pp. 41–65.

of being chosen by the Patron or the congregation was appointed by the Synod, and after solemn ordination was installed by delegates in its name. He was assisted by Elders and Deacons, who attended respectively to the spiritual and the temporal details of the congregation. The Pastor's office was to conduct daily prayers, and to preach twice on Sunday, and also on Wednesday and Friday. The form of worship was plain and non-liturgical, consisting of a hymn and a prayer at the opening and the close of the service, together with a scripture lesson and a sermon on a chosen text or passage, the whole lasting about an hour, and followed by an examination of the young as to the main points of the sermon.[30]

Those wishing to become members of the church (normally at the age of fourteen) were before receiving their first communion prepared by the Pastor through careful instruction in its doctrine. Then, after expressing before the church their earnest purpose to lead a Christian life, they were baptized by immersion in some convenient body of water, and then received the sacrament.[31] By no means the least of the Pastor's duties was that of keeping careful watch over the members of his flock as to their faithful observance of religious duties, and their manner of life, and to reprove and warn them when necessary. This watchfulness over the lives of individual members was much more carefully observed by the Socinians than by other Protestant sects,[32] and it centered in the regular practice of 'church discipline,' which is to the modern mind one of the most striking features of the Minor Church. Discipline had been early practiced, and is well defined in Schomann's Catechism[33] as 'the frequent reminding of individuals of their duty, and the warning of such as sin against God or their neighbors, first privately, and then also publicly before the whole assembly, and finally the removal of the stubborn from the communion of the saints, that they may be ashamed and repent, or else be eternally lost.' Such discipline was commonly practiced four times a year just before the celebration of the Lord's Supper. In preparation for this solemn rite the congregation would meet on Saturday afternoon for worship and to confess their sins before God. Here, in a private session for members only, a searching examination was made of the conduct and conscience

---

[30] For a fuller account of the worship of the Socinians, cf. Bock, *Socinianismus*, pp. 89–92; *Acta Historico-ecclesiastica* (Weimar, 1753), xvii, 895 f.

[31] cf. Bock, *op. cit.*, p. 90 f.

[32] cf. Völker, *Kirchengeschichte*, p. 252.   [33] p. g 2.

of each member, and unsettled grievances were reported. This was followed by exhortation and correction from the Pastor or from fellow-members, and finally by expressions of repentance; [34] while the unrepentant were forbidden to come to the supper, and might even be ostracized by the other members. This periodical self-examination and discipline was no merely conventional form, but by all was taken very seriously. It had the tendency to maintain a high standard of conduct among the Socinians, which won them sincere respect, even from those that most disagreed with their doctrines. In fact, the Catholic historian whom we have more than once quoted declares that Polish 'Arianism' was the most influential page in Polish religious history, and that one reason why its adherents did not become more numerous was that its moral demands were too strict.[35]

The Socinians held the Lord's Supper in extreme reverence, and counted it a great disgrace to be forbidden it, and one of the greatest misfortunes to be prevented from being present at it. The rite was celebrated on Christmas, Easter, Whitsunday, and the Sunday after Michaelmas. No one that could possibly attend was willingly absent. On these occasions scattered members would gather from great distances, and to those dispersed abroad, far from any church, ministers were sent from time to time to administer the rite.

One more duty of the Pastor deserves mention. As an inheritance from a day before the Reformation when education was a care of the Church, the Protestant confessions accepted responsibility for the schooling of their children, not only in religious but also in secular learning. In perhaps a dozen of the larger congregations well staffed schools or academies were maintained by the Synod as a normal department of church work. Of these Raków was of course the chief; but in the smaller congregations it fell to the Pastor not only to catechise his young people in preparation for joining the church, but also to be responsible for rudimentary subjects. An assistant Pastor or a teacher would often be assigned to this work; while on the other hand a nobleman might be given a private tutor for his children.

[34] cf. Bock, *loc. cit.*; *Acta Hist.-eccl.*, xix, 248 ff.
[35] cf. Brückner, *Litteratur*, p. 48 f.
An interesting contemporary account of the life of a Socinian congregation as practiced toward the end of the sixteenth century is given in a letter that Ostorodt, minister at Śmigiel, wrote in 1591 to the Anabaptist congregation at Strassburg. cf. Theodor Wotschke, 'Ein dogmatisches Sendschreiben des Unitariers Ostorodt,' *Archiv für Reformationsgeschichte*, xii (1915), 137-154.

CHAPTER XXXIII

GROWING OPPOSITION TO THE SOCINIANS PROMOTED BY THE JESUITS

WHILE THE SOCINIANS were steadily gaining in strength and influence as their churches settled down to their work, ominous factors were also slowly and steadily taking form in the background, of which they themselves seemed to be sublimely unconscious, but which were eventually to bring about the ruin of their church. Serenely relying on the protection promised them in the King's coronation oath, they did not foresee that they were themselves on the way to be excluded from its provisions. Despite their undisguised pacifism, they had indeed enjoyed outward peace during the reign of King Stephen Batory. He had himself owed his election in no small measure to the efforts of his personal physician Biandrata, and kept at his court yet other 'Arians.' Even after his death the Socinians continued to prosper. Indeed in the period from 1580 to 1620, while Calvinism and Lutheranism were losing heavily, the Socinian churches enjoyed a marked development, and reached the apex of their strength.[1]

Sigismund III., who came to the throne in 1587 and reigned for forty-five years, was nephew of Sigismund Augustus, being son of his sister, the wife of John III. of Sweden. Jesuit fathers had brought him up strictly in the Catholic religion, and he was proud to be called the Jesuit King. 'Taciturn, tenacious and tardy,' he was much less interested in government than in religion and the arts; and he allowed his policy as King to be largely shaped by the Jesuits. His reign was therefore fateful for Protestantism in general, for he more and more refrained from appointing Protestants to senatorial offices, and many outrages against Protestants were allowed to go unpunished. Yet he did not persecute the 'Arians' as such, and they remained generally loyal to him, being content to live quietly aloof from public life. Indeed they were grateful to the government of a country that allowed them to live in peace at a time when their co-religionists in other lands were suffering

[1] cf. Völker, *Kirchengeschichte*, p. 252.

the most severe punishments; and when Smalcius published an important work on the divinity of Christ,[2] his patron Sieniński even ventured to dedicate it to the King, hoping thus to increase his favorable disposition toward them, by refuting the calumnious charge of blasphemy that their adversaries kept hurling at them.

Many of his subjects, however, grew discontented with Sigismund's rule. Not a few of even the Catholics were incensed at his subservience to Jesuit influence, and willingly joined hands with the Dissidents, who were exasperated by his overlooking them in the distribution of offices,[3] and by the frequent and unpunished aggressions of mobs against the Protestants. Though the King in his coronation oath had solemnly sworn to maintain peace between all religious parties, he made little pretence to fulfil his promise, for his religious advisers insisted that the *pacta conventa* had been illegal from the start, and encouraged him to disregard it. In fact, the Confederation [4] had become well-nigh a dead letter for want of any provision for enforcing it. From about the end of the century, therefore, both the Protestants and the Catholics that sympathized with them occupied many Diets with persistent demands for the establishment of what was called a 'confederation process,' (*proces konfederacyi*), that is, a method of legal procedure in prosecuting violations of the Confederation. The King at his coronation had explicitly promised this,[5] but had made no attempt to keep his word. In 1606, therefore, an armed rebellion broke out, known from the name of its leader as the Zebrzydowski rebellion, which smoldered for a year or two, but for want of unity and competent leadership collapsed without having accomplished anything. In fact, when it had been put down, large numbers of Protestants gave up as fruitless the struggle for equal rights and legal protection in their religion, and returned to the Church of Rome.[6] The Socinians for the most part held aloof from the uprising, both because it was against their religious principles to resist the established civil power, and because they had little to hope for even if it proved successful; since the orthodox Protestants had long been more

---

[2] *De divinitate Christi* (Racoviae, 1608).

[3] Especially the high offices that carried with them membership in the Senate. Thus at the beginning of Sigismund's reign in 1588 there were at least 45 Protestant Senators; while at his death in 1632 there remained only two. cf. Berga, *Skarga*, p. 219 n.

[4] *v. supra*, p. 363.

[5] cf. *Volumina Legum*, ii, 248, par. 214; *Encyklopedja Polska* (Kraków, 1923), V, ii, 165.

[6] cf. Załęski, *Jesuici*, ii, 42.

bitterly opposed to them than were even the Catholics.[7] While the rebellion was brewing, there had indeed even been some hope that if it succeeded, the throne might fall to Demetrius, who seems to have had an understanding with Zebrzydowski, and who might thus unite Poland and Russia under one crown, as well as improve the fortunes of the Minor Church.[8]

While the Socinians were thus vigorously growing in strength during the decade or two after the death of Socinus, with no serious interference from without, unrealized factors were gradually gathering force which were ere long to find expression in a rising tide of persecution. Apart from the political aspects to which reference has been made, the first and most effective of these factors was that of the public disputations and printed controversies between Socinians on the one hand and Catholics on the other. One of the earliest of these was at Śmigiel in Great Poland, where there was a strong and aggressive Socinian congregation, whose first minister, Jan Krotowski, debated the divinity of Christ and the doctrine of the Trinity with Canon Powodowski from the neighboring cathedral at Poznań, in the presence of a large company in the Śmigiel church at the end of 1581. A decade later occurred a sequel to this debate, when Powodowski debated the same question with Ostorodt, then minister at Śmigiel.[9] In the meantime Powodowski, whose polemic spirit was now fully aroused, made his heated attack on Czechowicz's *Rozmowy*, which has been referred to above.[10]

Protestants were now beginning to be apprehensive of a serious peril in the rapidly growing influence of the Jesuits in the kingdom. In the quarter-century since their arrival in Poland, they had for the most

[7] Jakob Sieniński, however, the Socinian proprietor of Raków, did join the rebellion, and Raków suffered in consequence, and was for a time deserted by its inhabitants, who feared the vengeance of the royal armies. cf. Lubieniecius, *Historia*, p. 241; Baliński i Lipiński, *Starożytna Polska* (Ancient Poland), Warszawa, 1843–46, ii, 294 f.

[8] cf. Wacław Sobieski, *Zabiegi Dymitra Samozwanca o koronę Polską* (The endeavors of the Pretender Demetrius for the Polish Crown), Kraków, 1909, p. 12 f; reprinted in his *Studya historyczne: Król a Car* (Historical studies: King and Czar), Lwów, 1912, pp. 59–166.

[9] Hieronym Powodowski, *Disputacia Księdza Hieronyma Powodowskiego z ministrem zboru nowoariańskiego Śmigelskiego Janem Krotowicyuszem*, etc. (Disputation between the Priest H. P. and the minister of the neo-Arian church at Śmigiel, J. K.), Poznań, 1582; id., *Disputacia wtóra . . . Powodowskiego z Śmigielskimi różnobożanich*, etc. (A second disputation of P. with the Śmigiel heretics), Poznań, 1592; Christoph Ostorod, *Disputacia Zbory Szmigielskiego która miał C. O. . . . z H. P.* (Disputation in the Śmigiel church which C. O. had with H. P.), n. p., n. d.

[10] *v. supra*, p. 386.

part devoted themselves to the work of their schools and colleges; but now their influence was becoming evident in other quarters. One of the first to realize what they were aiming at, and to see through their adroit methods, was the author of an anonymous pamphlet published in 1590.[11] This publication was a heated attack on the Jesuits, in which every possible charge against them was brought forward, whether well or ill founded. For example: they had already stirred up much mischief in Germany, England and Scotland; they were secret emissaries of the King of Spain, plotting a conquest for him; they were at the bottom of the recurring riots at Kraków and Wilno; they were introducing an artificial system of education, and under the guise of exceptional learning and piety were trying to undermine the wholesome discipline and ancient customs of the country. The work aroused much hard feeling, and called forth several replies in defence; [12] but it exposed the Jesuits to public criticism, forced them out into the open, and led them to more aggressive measures in pursuing their main purpose, which was to undermine and destroy the Protestant movement in Poland. Thus this little work was almost immediately followed by a series of controversies that lasted for a quarter of a century, in which Jesuits took a leading part.

Preliminary skirmishes of Socinus with Jesuit theologians have already been spoken of.[13] Public debates on doctrinal questions now became more frequent. They were ostensibly designed if possible to bring about harmony and mutual understanding, but the immediate purpose was evidently apologetic or polemic. They were generally conducted in strict academic form. The theses to be defended were pre-

---

[11] *Equitis Poloni in Jesuitas actio prima*; also German trans., *Schwarme des Heiligen Römischen Bienenkorbs*, etc. (n. p., 1592). Ostensibly by a Catholic gentleman, it was generally ascribed to Albert Calissius, Rector of the Arian school at Lewartów, perhaps in collaboration with others; though some attributed it to a disgruntled Catholic at the University of Kraków, who was jealous of the growing Jesuit influence in education. cf. Henryk Barycz, *Geneza i autorstwo "Equitis Poloni in Jesuitas actio prima"* (Source and authorship of the *Equitis Poloni*, etc.), Kraków, 1934; reviewed in *Reformacja w Polsce*, viii (1936), 407–409.

[12] cf. Stanislaus Rescius, *Spongia qua absterguntur convitia et maledicta equitis Poloni contra Jesuitas* (Cracoviae, 1590); Martinus Siscovius, *Pro religiosissimis S. J. Patribus, contra ficti Equitis Poloni actionem primam oratio* (Cracoviae, 1590); (Johannis Lans) *Poloni nobilis cujusdam pro Societatis Jesu Clericis oratio prima, in ficti Equitis Poloni in Jesuitas actionem primam* (Ingolstadi, 1599); answered by Albertus Calissius, *Speculum Jesuitarum*, etc. (n. p., 1590); Marcin Łaszcz, *Judicium albo Rozsądek* (A criticism . . . of the portrait of the Jesuits, etc.), Wilno, 1594.

[13] *v. supra*, pp. 399, 401 f.

viously submitted in print, and speakers, umpires and secretaries were appointed for each side. At first they were carried on with mutual courtesy and in good order, but as time went on and public feeling became inflamed, open disorders tended to break out, especially in such centres as Lublin, Kraków and Wilno. It is doubtful whether many converts were made on either side, but it is certain that enmities were often deepened as the hostility of the Catholic populace was kindled against those whom they were led to regard as desperately wicked heretics. Thus a foundation was laid for the persecutions that were later to become so wide-spread. The first of these disputations to attract wide attention at the time lasted for two days in January, 1592, at Lewartów (Lubartów), about twenty-five miles north of Lublin, where a flourishing 'Arian' school had been established, succeeding the earlier schools at Pińczów and Chmielnik. The disputants were a Jesuit, a Lutheran, a Calvinist, and an 'Anabaptist.' The Jesuit theses defended the deity of Christ against the 'Arians,' and transubstantiation against the orthodox Protestants. The debate, which attracted a great crowd of listeners, was conducted in the usual scholastic manner, with appeal to the authority of Scripture and the Fathers. The Jesuits maintained that the 'Arians' or 'Anabaptists' were in the same class with Jews, Tatars and Turks, a charge that was henceforth more and more frequently hurled at them. Both sides claimed the victory, and each published its own account of the debate.[14] The 'Arians,' dissatisfied with the conditions of this debate, returned to the contest in a further debate of the same theses at Lublin a few months later, with Statorius as their champion.[15]

No previous controversies, however, were to be compared in intensity and effect with the protracted one waged from 1604 to 1617 between Skarga and his successors on the one side and Smalcius and Moskorzowski on the other. The Jesuit father Peter Skarga,[16] born of middle-

---

[14] cf. Gregorz Piotrowski, *Pogrom Lewartowski* (The rout at Lewartów), Kraków, 1592, a Catholic account in verse, sometimes ascribed to Marcin Łaszcz, containing an interesting contemporary account of how Socinus looked. Answered by Jan Niemojewski, *Krótkie y prawdziwie opisanie Dysputacyey która była w Lewartowie*, etc. (A brief and authentic description of the disputation at Lewartów in 1592), Kraków, 1592.

[15] cf. Jan Przylepski, *Disputacia lubelska*, etc. (Disputation at Lublin between the Rev. Adrian Radzymiński and the Anabaptist minister Statorius, on the eternal divinity of Christ), Kraków, 1592; Kot, 'Dysputacye Arjan Polskich' (Disputations of the Polish Arians), *Reformacja w Polsce*, viii (1936), 351 f.

[16] cf. Dzieduszycki, *Skarga*; Berga, *Skarga*.

class parents in 1536 near Warsaw, in the ultra-Catholic province of Masovia, was the most eloquent pulpit orator that Poland ever had, and has been hailed as the Polish Bossuet. Entering the Jesuit order he had his earlier career at Wilno in Lithuania, where he was notably successful in winning Protestants back to the Catholic faith, and directed the religious instruction of the three younger sons of the great Prince Radziwiłł, when they abjured the Protestant religion. Upon the accession of Sigismund III. Skarga was called to Kraków as court preacher, and for twenty-three years he was a powerful influence in public affairs. Passionately believing that the only true way to national prosperity was through faithfulness to the Catholic religion, he considered the Reformation a disaster to Poland and a crime against God, and the attempt of the Warsaw Confederation to give Protestantism legal recognition he regarded with indignation and horror. Though not approving the use of force or violent persecution against heretics, he insisted that they be excluded from public office, and that every effort be made by reason to bring them back as fatally misguided brethren.

Soon after the destruction of the Reformed and the 'Arian' places of worship at Kraków, and the burning of the Reformed church at Wilno, in 1591, when all Protestants were roused to a high pitch of excitement over unpunished excesses of the Catholics, Skarga published an anonymous *Admonition to Protestants*,[17] calling on them not to feel too much aggrieved over troubles that they had brought upon themselves by their own oppression of Catholics, and their seizure and plundering of 2,000 Catholic churches.[18] A violent outburst of passions followed; while Skarga in several successive publications [19] energetically opposed all efforts of the Dissidents to secure from the Diet a legal enforcement of their rights as promised. All these writings, as well as Skarga's famous sermons before the Diet, were full of intense intolerance against the religion of the Protestants as damnable heresy, and the Dissidents themselves as dangerous enemies of the State.

[17] *Upominanie do Ewanjelików* (Kraków, 1592). Well summarized by Berga, *op. cit.*, pp. 231–234.

[18] He later raised the figure to 3,000. In either case it is allowed to have been grossly exaggerated. cf. Berga, *op. cit.*, p. 232, n.

[19] *Proces Konfoederaciey* (The Confederation process) (Kraków, 1593); revised and enlarged as *Proces na Konfoederacia* (Process against the Confederation) (1596); *Diskurs na Konfoederacya* (Discourse against the Confederation), Kraków, 1607. Summarized in Berga, *op. cit.*, pp. 237–240.

This polemic had been directed against Dissidents in general; but when Skarga a decade later felt impelled to return to the fray, he directed his attack not against the orthodox Dissidents, whose number had by now sensibly fallen off,[20] but only against the 'Arians,' whose numbers, under the stimulus given at Raków and the wise leadership of Socinus, had of late been increasing with alarming rapidity. This new controversy began in 1604 when Skarga, encouraged by the Bishop of Kraków, began a campaign against the 'Arians' with two Trinity Sunday sermons in which he defended the orthodox doctrine at length on scriptural grounds. Smalcius, now minister at Raków, hearing of this, preached a vigorous sermon in refutation. Skarga rejoined at the end of the year by publishing a notable work entitled *The Shame of the Arians* [21] in which he maintained that they are not Christians but Pagans; that they have no right to appeal to the Christian Scriptures; that they stand condemned by Christ, his Apostles, the Councils of the Fathers, the teachings of the Church, the martyrs, and the laws of all ages. Identifying them with the Arians of old,[22] he recites their history, and calls on them to repent; and citing in proof (pp. 69–73) a series of articles of faith that have been reported to him as being taught in the school at Raków, he declared that they leave none of the foundations of Christianity standing.

Smalcius was quick to reply to Skarga in his usual hard-hitting fashion; but, not to mention several subordinate skirmishes on each side, the strongest antagonist on the 'Arian' side was Moskorzowski, a competent scholar and polished gentleman, with whom Skarga debated on a plane of mutual respect. He took up Skarga's points in order,

---

[20] cf. Józef Łukaszewicz, *O kościołach Braci Czeskich* (The churches of the Bohemian Brethren in Great Poland), Poznań, 1835, p. 173; German trans. (Grätz, 1877), p. 146.

[21] *Zawstydzenie Arianów* (Kraków, 1604), including the two sermons above mentioned. The chief titles in the ensuing controversy are (Smalcius), *Zawstydzenie Xiędza Skargi* (The shame of the Priest Skarga), Raków, 1608; Hieronim Moskorzowski, *Zniesienie zawstydzenia*, etc. (Erasure of the shame that Skarga strove to fix upon the church of the Lord Jesus of Nazareth), Raków, 1607; Skarga, *Wtóre zawstydzenie Arianów* (Second shame of the Arians, in answer to Moskorzowski), Kraków, 1608; Moskorzowski, *Zniesienie wtórego zawstydzenia*, etc. (An erasure of the Second Shame), Raków, 1610; Skarga (posthumously edited), *Messiasz Nowych Arianów* (The Messiah of the Neo-Arians), Kraków, 1612; Smalcius, *Wtóre Zawstydzenie X. Skargi* (The second shame of the priest Skarga), Raków, 1615.

[22] On the ground that, though it be admitted that they do not in all points agree with Arius, yet they do in the chief and essential point of denying that Christ is true God and consubstantial with the Father, which was the principal doctrine of Arius. cf. Martinus Smiglecius, *Nova monstra Novi Arianismi* (Nissae, 1612), p. 172.

analyzed his arguments in logical form without heat or invective, exposed his flaws in reasoning, and in a dedicatory preface to the King set forth the authentic Socinian faith in fourteen articles.[23] There was rejoinder and counter-rejoinder, for the most part in fairly good spirit, with the effort on each side to convict the other of errors and flaws in reasoning, until the controversy ran to a whole dozen of works. Increasing emphasis was laid by the Catholics on the charge that the 'Arians' were not Christians, but came near to being Mohammedans, and that their views had long since been universally condemned as heretical.

The controversy proper ended with the death of Skarga in 1612; but the matter was still protracted for six years more between the Jesuit father Martin Śmiglecki (Smiglecius) on the one side and Moskorzowski and Smalcius on the other. Śmiglecki was a theologian of high repute, who had been Rector of three colleges, and had years before made a contribution to the controversy on the divinity of Christ between Socinus and Wujek.[24] He now took up the question again, addressing himself to the errors of the various 'Arian' writers hitherto, also introducing the subject of baptism. Both Smalcius and Moskorzowski were quick to reply, and the battle of the books continued until Śmiglecki's death in 1618. The scope and spirit of this controversy can best be gathered from the titles of the works comprised in it.[25] While this controversy was in progress, Śmiglecki also stirred up another, as to the validity of the Protestant ministry, maintaining that Protestant ministers are not properly called or ordained, are not real priests, and hence have no valid authority to remit sins or administer the sacraments. Such a charge greatly provoked the Protestants, and was vigorously answered on the part of the 'Arians' by both Smalcius and Völkel; but both Śmiglecius and Völkel died in 1618.[26] The outcome

[23] Reprinted in Pasierbiński's *Moskorzowski*, pp. 155–157.

[24] cf. his *O bóstwie przedwiecznym Syna Bożego*, etc. (On the eternal divinity of the Son of God), Wilno, 1595.

[25] Smiglecius, *Nova monstra Novi Arianismi* (Nissae, 1612); Moscorovius, *Refutatio appendicis . . . Nova Monstra Novi Arianismi* (Racoviae, 1613); Smalcius, *Responsio ad . . . Nova Monstra Novi Arianismi* (Racoviae, 1613); Smiglecius, *De baptismo* (Cracoviae, 1615); Smiglecius, *De erroribus Novorum Arianorum* (Cracoviae, 1615); Smalcius, *Examinatio centum errorum quos Martinus Smiglecius*, etc. (Racoviae, 1615); Smiglecius, *De Christo vero et naturali Dei Filio* (Cracoviae, 1615); Smalcius, *Examinatio centum quinquaginta septem errorum* (Racoviae, 1615); Smalcius, *Refutatio duorum M. Smiglecii librorum* (Racoviae, 1616); Smalcius, *De Christo vero et naturali Dei Filio* (Racoviae, 1616); Moscorovius, *Refutatio libri de baptismo Martini Smiglecii Jesuitae* (Racoviae, 1617).

[26] cf. Smiglecius, *Nodus Gordius, seu de vocatione ministrorum disputatio* (Cracoviae,

of these warm and long controversies was in the main this: that the convinced adherents of either side were more and more confirmed in their views; that those that were wavering were more likely now to make their choice, which would be much determined by the weight they allowed to tradition and old associations on the one hand, or to the letter of Scripture on the other; that between the two parties differences were sharpened and antagonisms deepened; and that thus the background was prepared for the religious persecutions that were soon to become increasingly common and severe.

1609); Volkelius, *Nodi Gordii a Martino Smiglecio dissolutio* (Racoviae, 1613; Smiglecius, *Refutatio vanae dissolutionis nodii Gordii*, etc. (Cracoviae, 1614); Smalcius, *Notae in libellum M. Smiglecii quem Refutationem vanae dissolutionis Nodi sui Gordii appellat* (Racoviae, 1614); Volkelius, *Responsio ad vanam refutationem dissolutionis Nodi Gordii a Smiglecio nexi* (Racoviae, 1615).

CHAPTER XXXIV

GROWING PERSECUTION AND OPPRESSION: THE DESTRUCTION OF RAKÓW

In the preceding chapter it has been seen how during something like a generation around the beginning of the seventeenth century the natural antagonism between the Socinians on the one hand and the Catholics on the other was steadily deepened and sharpened by published doctrinal controversies and public debates on disputed points of doctrine. Still enjoying uninterrupted religious liberty, the Socinians were tempted to abuse it in acrimonious writings and oral attacks upon the dominant Catholic religion. While these discussions were going on, however, they seem never once to have suspected that they were fanning a fire that might one day consume them. Blindly relying on the protection that the Warsaw Confederation was supposed to ensure them, serenely confident that their views of Christian truth, as the only ones justified by Scripture, were therefore certain to prevail, and elated by the steady accession to the number of their adherents and the corresponding decline in the vigor of their rivals in the Reformed Church, they eagerly seized every opportunity to proclaim their own views and to hold up to scorn the errors of their opponents. Little did they realize that their safety lay in avoiding the notice of the ruling powers; and that to become more aggressive meant not so much to win more converts as to stir up greater confessional hatred, inviting persecution from those in power, and passion and violence from the populace. While the printed controversies, often in Latin, appealed to the educated classes and employed every available weapon of scholarship, logic or rhetoric, oral appeals to the people tended to degenerate into sarcasm, ridicule, bitter invective or even personal abuse; and those whom repeated admonitions from the pulpit had already predisposed to look upon heresy not only as fatally poisonous to individual souls, but as treason subverting the State, were all too ready to respond in scenes of disorder and acts of mob violence. For the background was already laid in the view, fostered by the Catholic clergy, that Dissidents as such had no legitimate claim to protection; and the temptation was therefore great for them to take the punishment of heretics into their own hands if the authorities seemed loath to proceed against them. In all this the Socinians had a double burden to carry, for the tradition was being steadily fostered, in which the orthodox Dissidents willingly joined the Catholics, that they not only were heretics, but as blasphemers of the accepted doctrines of God and Christ, were quite outside the Christian pale. The charge was even made and reiterated in high quarters that they worshiped the Devil as a God; and their places of worship therefore came popularly to be called Hell (*piekło*), a designation that survives at Nowy Sącz to this day.[1]

With such a background of bigoted conviction on the one hand and passionate hatred on the other, instances of religious persecution might easily break out on the slightest provocation. Already before the end of the sixteenth century sporadic attempts had been made and sundry outrages perpetrated upon Dissidents at Kraków, in which Socinians suffered, while the young King paid little heed to their complaints and made little attempt to punish the guilty. Such were the two assaults upon Socinus referred to in a previous chapter;[2] a similar attack by University students at Kraków on the venerable and noble Socinian minister Lubieniecki as late as 1627;[3] the destruction of both the Reformed and the 'Arian' places of worship at Kraków in 1591, and the repeated outrageous attacks upon Protestant funerals and plundering of Protestant graves at Kraków.[4] Local disturbances of this sort occurred in various places during most of the long reign of Sigismund III., and little serious effort was made either to prevent or to punish them. It was not until toward the end of his reign that a law was passed in 1631 which expressly and unreservedly forbade religious

---

[1] Now applied to the suburban quarter to which the Arian church was required to remove. cf. Załęski, *Jesuici*, ii, 423, n.; Morawski, *Arjanie*, p. 88.

[2] *v. supra*, pp. 402–404.

[3] cf. Jan Wielewicki, *Dziennik Spraw . . . Jezuitów . . . w Krakowie* (Diary of the doings of the Jesuits at Kraków (Kraków, 1881–'99), xvii, 265; Załęski, *Jesuici*, ii, 297. It was apparently Christopher Lubieniecki, minister at Lublin. The Lubienieckis were among the most distinguished families of the Polish nobility. The three brothers Andrew, Christopher and Stanislas were living at the court of King Stephen, when to the astonishment of all Andrew resigned the prospect of high honors that he might have had, left the court at Kraków and went to Wieliczka near by and received adult baptism while in court dress. He entered the ministry of the Minor Church, serving at his own charges. His two younger brothers followed his example. cf. Lubieniecius, *Historia*, p. 191 f; Morawski, *op. cit.*, p. 88.

[4] cf. Węgierski, *Chronik, passim.*

tumults.[5] An outstanding exception was in 1620 at Szczebreszyn, where an 'Arian' funeral was attacked by a mob, and the bereaved were insulted, while the authorities looked on indifferently. Complaint was lodged with the court, and a heavy fine was imposed upon both the delinquent authorities and the citizens at large; though at the same time the 'Arians' were strictly admonished, under penalty, not to give the Catholics offence on occasion of public ceremonies or gatherings.[6] It is evident therefore that the disturbances that occurred were sometimes invited or provoked, where they might have been avoided by more conciliatory measures.

As contrasted with these earlier and irregular outbreaks of popular violence, acts of persecution began early in the seventeenth century to be more systematic and deliberate, and to be conducted more or less under the forms of law. The earliest and most conspicuous case of this sort was that of the martyrdom of Iwan Tyszkiewicz (Jan Tyskiewicz or Tyszkowicz) in 1611, which created a profound and enduring impression upon the whole Socinian world.[7] Tyszkiewicz was an honored and influential citizen of Bielsk in Podlasie, who had abandoned the Russian Church and become an ardent Socinian, active in defence of his faith, hence much disliked by both Roman and Greek Catholics, who would gladly have been rid of him. They envied him the more when he and his brother inherited a large property from their grandfather, and they incited the Mayor, who was a more distant relative, to invent some way to keep him from his inheritance. To this end, though he had always preferred a quiet life, and shunned public office, they all but forced him to accept the responsible office of public steward, not requiring him to take the usual oath of office, to which on religious grounds he would at once have objected. At the end of his term he rendered his accounts, whereupon the Mayor, seeking to make trouble, insisted on his taking oath that he had performed faithful service. This he at first declined to do, as being contrary to the teaching of Christ, but at length he yielded, consenting to swear by the name of God and

---

[5] cf. *Volumina Legum*, iii, 226, sec. 32.

[6] cf. Morawski, *op. cit.*, p. 132.

[7] For contemporary accounts cf. Lubieniecki, *Poloneutychia*, p. 216 ff (Ossoliński Ms 112, p. 177 ff; Smalcius, *Diary*, p. 1191 f; *Brevis relatio de Johannis Tyscovicii martyrio*, in Sandius, *Bibliotheca*, p. 205 f); Ms account in Unitarian Library, Kolozsvár, cf. *Sprawozdanie z poszukiwan na Węgrzech* (Report of researches in Hungary), Kraków, 1919, p. 228; Wallace, *Antitrin.*, ii, 528–530. Catholic accounts are few and scanty; but cf. Guichard, *Socinianisme*, i, chap. xxiv.

his Son the Lord Christ, though not upon the crucifix offered him, nor by the Trinity. Record of his refusal was made, and the case was postponed. A few days later he was summoned before the local court and questioned as to his religious beliefs by a priest, who hoped to ensnare him. His answers angered the priest, who struck him a blow and had him and his brother lodged in jail, though innocent and not convicted of any crime. Influential friends intervened, however, and they were given easy confinement in the town hall, where their friends visited and encouraged them.

When the case was resumed, in the presence of a great crowd, and Iwan's friends protested against proceedings in violation of the Warsaw Confederation, their protest was unheeded, the trial was conducted in a high-handed way, and the accused were denied their rights. Notice was therefore given of an appeal of the case to the Tribunal. The magistrate did not admit this, and remanded the case to the King's court for review, and then released the accused under heavy bail. But Iwan's friends, guided by advice previously taken, had already commenced suit before the Tribunal, charging the Bielsk magistrate with having taken action contrary to the law, and when the King was absent from the country in Muscovy. When the Tribunal gave judgment, the two brothers were discharged, and a heavy fine was imposed on their prosecutors for their illegal proceedings. But when now the case came up for review before the King's court at Warsaw, it was found that the accusation was quite changed. The charge now was that Iwan had thrown down a crucifix and cast it on the ground, that he had blasphemed the Almighty in court, and that he had inveighed against the court and inflicted insults and great injury upon it by haling the magistrate before the Tribunal. The supporting evidence was denied by the accused as false, and the case was remanded to Bielsk, where it was decreed that Iwan should sell all and leave town within six weeks, and pay a considerable fine; and that his brother also should remove, under pain of death. The King's court had in fact advised leniency; but some of their friends still urged an appeal to the King's court, promising complete satisfaction at the next Diet. Arrived at Warsaw at the appointed time, their friends were asked in private conference with the judges not to trouble the Diet with the case, and were promised that when the time came they should have a satisfactory decree. But the prosecution was represented by an attorney, who pressed stronger charges than ever, while the defendants, relying on the promise given, had only a lay representative who was however allowed to speak in their defence, and made a general denial of the charges. The judges then submitted their report to the King, expecting an early decree, which only Iwan remained to hear.

What had gone on, or now went on, behind the scenes, the earliest extant account could not learn, though a later account [8] states that the accusers quietly carried the matter up to Queen Constance, a fervent Catholic, in whose personal domain Bielsk lay, and that she, as the supreme authority there, confirmed the magistrate's sentence, and ordered it put into execution. In view of what followed, this seems likely enough, and also that she used her influence with the King; for his decision, in which the judges concurred, was that Tyszkiewicz should be put to death. At all events, he was soon thrown into a dungeon among condemned prisoners, where for several weeks priests and monks repeatedly labored with him, seeking by various means to move him to change his religion, threatening him with a frightful death on the one hand, and promising him life and peace on the other. Through it all he remained unshaken, betraying no fear even when the death sentence was read to him. The sentence was this: Since he has blasphemed almighty God and the Virgin Mary, his tongue is to be cut off as a blasphemer; since he has resisted the magistrate of his town, opposing him and haling him before the Tribunal, and has not been content with the decree of his magistrate, he is to be beheaded as a rebel; since he has thrown a crucifix from the table down upon the ground, his hand and foot are to be cut off; and finally, since he is a heretic, he is to be burned. After the sentence was read, Iwan continued to assert his innocence, and to protest that he had been condemned on the testimony of false witnesses, until the sheriff ordered the executioner to proceed; when he met his death with a firmness and constancy like that of the early Christian martyrs. This took place in the forenoon of December 16, 1611, in the great market-place at Warsaw.[9] It will have been noted that in this case what began as a plot simply to deprive a Dissident of an inheritance ended, when the plot miscarried, by being transformed through clerical influence into a prosecution for heresy.

[8] cf. *Brevis relatio*, in Sandius, *Bibliotheca*, p. 203.

[9] In more recent times it has been known as the old market-place (Stary Rynek). In the center of it stood the City Hall, and in front of this was the place of execution. Buildings that antedated the death of Tyszkiewicz were still standing, little changed, on the west side of the square at least as late as 1939.

Not forgetting the death of Servetus and of Gentile, which occurred before the movement had become distinct whose history we are following, it is fair to reckon Iwan Tyszkiewicz as the first martyr in historical Unitarianism.

The martyrdom of Tyszkiewicz was in a way a sort of echo of one that had been suffered by a Calvinist at Wilno earlier in the same year. Francus di Franco [10] was a young Italian who had embraced the Protestant faith after coming to Poland, and was eager in promoting it at Wilno, where he adhered to the Reformed Church. Carried away by his zeal he interrupted the Catholic ceremonies on Corpus Christi day (a festival observed by Poles with the greatest solemnity) by a public attack upon such idolatry, as he regarded it. He was severely beaten by the crowd whose feelings he had outraged, but was taken away to safety. When later questioned by the authorities he eloquently and even defiantly defended his action, not weakening even when put to torture, and apparently courting martyrdom. Protestant nobles interceded for him in vain, and as he could not be brought to escape by denying his faith he was privately executed in prison in much the same way as Tyszkiewicz, after which the quartered parts of his body were publicly exposed. Following this a mob burned the Reformed church at Wilno, and religious tumults continued for three weeks.[11]

From this time on, the prevailing state of popular feeling and the constitution of the courts were such that upon slight occasion a violent case of persecution might at any time be stirred up, with little hope of relief or redress from the Tribunal in case of appeal. The seat of the Little Poland Tribunal was at Lublin,[12] and when this was in session many important persons came thither, as did young men destined for the law, as a part of their legal education. Lublin had thus almost the dignity of a capital. It was also the seat of a flourishing Jesuit college, whose students were easily excited to mischief against Protestant here-

---

[10] cf. Wengerscius, *Slavonia*, pp. 252–255.

[11] cf. Wielewicki, *Dziennik*, xiv, 64 ff.

[12] King Stephen in 1578 had organized Tribunals, or high courts of appeal (at Lublin, Piotrków, and later in Lithuania), to hear civil cases that hitherto had been tried before the King himself. cf. *Encyklopedja Polska*, V, ii, 147. These were mixed courts, whose deputies were both lay and clerical; the former chosen by their dietines, the latter by the clergy in their cathedral chapters. It is easy to see that before a court so constituted, cases involving the religious rights of Protestants would from the start be seriously prejudiced. The long series of trials of 'Arians' before Tribunals mark significant steps in the progressive suppression of the Socinian churches in Poland.

tics; and at the same time of perhaps the most flourishing 'Arian' church in Poland, led by able ministers, and patronized by a large number of distinguished nobles.[13] The leaders of the church here were especially aggressive and eager to engage in debates in a place where they might hope to win influential converts. When therefore the distinguished Jesuit scholar Nicholas Łęczycki came from Lwów and challenged both Calvinists and 'Arians' to debate in 1615, though the Calvinists avoided the challenge, the young 'Arian' minister Jan Stoiński readily accepted it, and the debate was held before a crowded church and in the presence of most of the members of the Tribunal. In the interest of good order, the populace were excluded, and the debate, on the sufficiency of Scripture and the eternal divinity of Christ, lasted three hours, being conducted on both sides quietly and with entire courtesy.[14] Another public debate, in which Stoiński accepted a challenge given by a Dominican monk named Waleryan Grocholski, was held in the Lublin Dominican church in the following year. The subjects debated were the Trinity, the incarnation, and the charge that the respondents were Arians. The discussion was in Latin, for the Dominicans would not consent to a debate before the people in their native tongue.[15] The debate broke off abruptly for want of time, but ended without disturbance, and the 'Arians' were conducted in safety to their own meeting-place. Later in the evening, however, a riot broke out against the Calvinists, whose meeting-place was destroyed, and it then spread against the 'Arians', as being equally heretics with them. The age of toleration was evidently passing, and confessional hatred was increasing throughout the land; for in the same year at Nowogródek in Lithuania a crowd drove the Antitrinitarians away, so that they dared not hold their intended synod.[16]

The chief centre of disorder, however, continued to be at Lublin, for it was here that the two elements in maximum strength oftenest came into conflict; and as time went on, and the Socinians continued aggres-

---

[13] cf. Lubieniecius, *Historia*, Book iii, chap. 13.

[14] For an account by Stoiński himself, with a summary of the arguments, cf. Kot, *Dysputacje Arjan polskich*, pp. 354–364; Wielewicki, *Dziennik*, xiv, 159. There is disagreement as to the exact date.

[15] For a report cf. Kot, *op. cit.*, pp. 364–370; Johannes Stoieński, *De Jesu divinitate*, etc. (Racoviae, 1618); *Disputatio habita a Reverendis Patribus Discalceatis . . . contra Arianos* (Zamoscii, 1617). For a third disputation held in 1620, cf. Krzystof Pawławski, *Disputatio inter Carmelitas . . . et Johannem Statorium* (Cracoviae, 1621).

[16] cf. Szczotka, *op. cit.*, p. 67.

sive, their public worship became increasingly offensive to the Catholics. Relations grew steadily worse until 1627, when an unfortunate incident occurred which caused the impending storm to break in full force.[17] It happened that some Jesuit students fell into an altercation with some Protestant German mercenaries drinking in a public house, in which it came to blows and ended in bloodshed. The students at once raised a call to arms, and a wild mob of Sunday idlers soon gathered, bent on taking vengeance upon all Protestants without distinction, and on sharing in the plunder. Both the Calvinist and the Socinian church were demolished in the following night, and the homes of their leading members were attacked, while judges of the Tribunal gave tacit approval, and no just punishment was inflicted upon the rioters. On the contrary, the Protestant Palatine, though himself a member of the Tribunal, and the Castellan, together with other patrons of the destroyed churches, were called into court, as being ultimately responsible for the disturbance. A heavy fine was imposed, and both churches were sentenced to perpetual proscription; though the Diet annulled the decree in the same year as illegal.[18] In the years immediately following, however, there were repeated instances in which leading noblemen of the Socinian congregation were brought to trial before the Tribunal, and on flimsy charges and in defiance of law and right were sentenced to heavy fines or long and severe imprisonment,[19] until in 1635 the church was by decree of the Tribunal closed forever.[20] The site of the Socinian meeting-place then fell into the hands of the Jesuits. Driven thus from Lublin, the remnants of the church there found refuge for a dozen years or so on the estate of a wealthy noble at Piaski a few miles distant, and then for a decade more at Siedliska near by, until the war with Sweden brought it to an end.

Though Lublin had long rivaled Raków as the most influential centre of the Socinian movement, Raków now became the uncontested capital for three short years, when it too was destined to receive the fatal blow. For after their success in the instances thus far related, it was becoming evident that a deliberate policy of extermination was now being adopted by the Catholics, to be applied wherever and when-

---

[17] A detailed account of the whole occurrence and its sequel is given in Lubieniecius, *op. cit.*, p. 260 ff.

[18] cf. *Volumina Legum*, iii, 263, sec. 13; 346, sec. 7.

[19] cf. Lubieniecius, *op. cit.*, pp. 256–269.

[20] cf. Merczyng, *Zbory*, p. 112. Yet domestic worship still continued at Lublin, where Christopher Lubieniecki was minister until his death in 1648.

ever any excuse could be found. Such an excuse unfortunately soon offered itself at Raków. At the end of the first quarter of the seventeenth century Raków had attained a high degree of prosperity. It had now grown to be an active little city of perhaps from 20,000 to 30,000, with flourishing manufactures of paper, cloth, pottery and cutlery. It had a college ranking as the best in Poland, whose fame drew to its faculty able scholars from western universities, and to its student body youth not only from all parts of Poland, but in considerable numbers also from Germany and other countries abroad; and from orthodox Protestant confessions, and even from Catholic families, as well as from Socinian sources. Its press was sending forth a steady stream of books which were widely circulated in Poland and Transylvania, and were also secretly exported by way of Danzig to Holland, France and England, where they were eagerly read by those into whose hands they fell, and had not a little influence in mellowing the religious views of both Protestants and Catholics. Under the assured protection of the Socinian proprietor of Raków, the Racovians, even if no longer quite confident of the guarantees promised under the Warsaw Confederation, felt secure against the persecutions to which they might elsewhere have been exposed; and in the course of its history it had so often escaped threatening calamity that its inhabitants were ready to believe that it was under the special guardianship of Providence.[21] No wonder, then, if they were sometimes tempted to be unwisely bold and aggressive toward the adherents of other confessions.

Meantime clouds were slowly gathering for the storm that was to come. The oral debates and the printed controversies of the Socinians with Jesuits and others were having their effect in various quarters; and the often repeated warnings and denunciations of parish priests nourished feelings of antagonism in the people at large. The Socinians, indeed, were not wholly blind to the rising Catholic reaction and its dangers for them, for as early as 1624 their synod commissioned one of their ablest scholars to prepare a special treatise *De concordia et unione inter coetus Evangelicos et Unitarios*, which they had much at heart; and six years later the rising tide of intolerance led to a renewal of the commission.[22] The Evangelicals, however, seem not to have been interested, but to have regarded Socinians as more dangerous to their cause than Catholics.

[21] cf. Lubieniecius, *op. cit.*, book iii, chap. 12.
[22] cf. Szczotka, *op. cit.*, pp. 70, 72 f; Bock, *op. cit.*, p. 645.

Ladislas (Władysław) IV., who succeeded to the throne in 1632, was tolerant in spirit, disliked the Jesuits and would not admit them to his court, at once assured Protestants of complete freedom of worship in their private homes, and gave them some share in public offices, so that in the first five years of his reign the Socinians in the main enjoyed peace. Nevertheless, Catholic strength and influence in government steadily increased. Hence while it had hitherto been generally assumed without question that 'Arians' were included among the Dissidents referred to in the Confederation, this now began to be denied. Already in 1636 at a Prussian dietine at Grudziądz the Bishop of Chełmno had asserted that 'Arians' were not included in the guarantees of religious freedom to Dissidents, and held that their deputies should be excluded from the Prussian Diet.[23] The stage was therefore set for a fierce act of persecution whenever a plausible excuse might offer. In 1638 an excuse was unexpectedly offered at Raków itself.[24] Contemporary accounts of the occurrence are not satisfactory, being warped by prejudice, and partly based on popular rumor, but in essence they relate events about as follows: Jakob Sieniński, the eminent and noble proprietor of Raków, had a quarrel about their boundary line with a poor neighboring noble named Rokicki,[25] who to spite the former, though ostensibly out of piety,[26] erected a crucifix by the roadside bordering Raków, where it might annoy the Racovians. One day early in March, 1638, as some younger scholars of the Raków school were taking a walk with two of their teachers, they came to this crucifix, whereupon two of them, named Falibowski and Babinecki, threw stones at it as at a mark, and thus broke it down.[27] Unfortunately the act was seen by laborers at a

---

[23] cf. Gottfried Lengnich, *Geschichte der Preussischen Lande Königlich-Pohlnischen Antheils* (Danzig, 1722–55), vi, 102.

[24] For the best general account of what follows, cf. Józef Stanko, *Upadek Rakowa* (The fall of Raków), Brzeziny, 1926, in *Sprawozdanie Dyrekcji Gimnasjum Koła Polskiej Macierzy Szkolnej w Brzezinach Łódzkich*, 1916–'26. Reviewed in *Reformacja w Polsce*, iv (1926), 239 f. For contemporary accounts, cf. Ruar's letter to Naeranus, May 4, 1638, appended to Zeltner, *Historia*, p. 319; Albrycht Stanisław Radziwiłł, *Pamiętniki* (Memoirs), Poznań, 1839, i, 370 ff; *Anonymi epistola*, in Sandius, *Bibliotheca*, pp. 233 f, 278, n. cf. also Lauterbach, *Socinismus*, pp. 462–465; Łukaszewicz, *Szkół*, i, 349 ff; Morawski, *Arjanie*, p. 150 f; Samuel Przypkowski, Account of the case of Sieniński before the Diet of 1638, from a Warsaw Ms, in Ludwik Chmaj, *Samuel Przypkowski* (Kraków, 1927), pp. 203–226.

[25] cf. Czartoryski Ms No. 135.

[26] The Catholic historian Łukaszewicz unhesitatingly pronounces this judgment; *op. cit.*, i, 360, n.

[27] One rumor was that Sieniński's wife had been heard to say, 'What a shame that no

distance, and was reported to the parish priest, who in return reported it to his Bishop, Jakób Zadzik of Kraków. The Bishop, perhaps seeing at once that here was a hoped-for opening for striking a telling blow at the Socinians, was quick to act. He first arranged several public meetings in the vicinity, where complaint was made of the insult offered to the Divine Majesty, so that public feeling was greatly aroused. At the same time a rumor was set afloat that the Raków press was in process of publishing a book entitled *Tormentum throno Trinitatem deturbans*, by an Arian named Letus, which insulted the principles of the Catholic faith.[28] Casimir Sieniński himself, third son of the Socinian proprietor of Raków, having become an ardent Catholic while studying in Vienna, now turned against his father and fervently espoused the Catholic cause in this case. Meantime the matter had reached the ears of Sieniński himself, who through messages to the Bishop and letters to his friends sought to make all possible amends. It was in fact but the rash act of irresponsible schoolboys, deserving to be punished in the usual way; and indeed, as soon as their parents heard of it, they punished the boys and removed them from the school.[29] This however was not enough to satisfy the Bishop, who, as the event showed, chose to interpret the occurrence as a deliberate insult to the Catholic religion, for which the whole Raków community, and especially its proprietor, should be held ultimately responsible. He therefore carried the matter up to the Diet then in session at Warsaw, of which the majority were zealous Catholics, and appealed to their feelings by exhibiting fragments of the broken crucifix.[30] A great outcry was raised, and a demand for punishment of the guilty. The affair was reported to the King, who was much impressed and agreed to an im-

---

one throws this crucifix down', and that this furnished the instigation to the act. Another ran that they shot at it with arrows, or even with a gun, and having broken it in pieces buried them.

[28] But the Socinian Jonas Schlichting, who was in a position to know, declares in his *Apologia pro veritate accusata* (1654), p. 42, that no such book ever existed, and that the author of this fable was a Moravian refugee, Johannes Laetus, who later gave it wider currency in his *Compendium Historiae Universalis* (Lugduni Batavorum, 1643), p. 766. Uzoni (*Historia* i, 474) reports Leydecker as saying in his notes to G. Hornius, *Historia ecclesiastica* (Frankfurt, 1704) that this was the title of Christian Francken's work suppressed by the authorities at Kraków in 1584 (*v. supra*, p. 371, n. 18). Legend may thus have confused this with the Raków episode.

[29] Upon later espousing the Catholic faith they escaped any civil punishment. cf. Jagellonian Ms 2274.

[30] cf. *Scriptores Polon.*, xvi, 61.

mediate investigation, though a good many of the deputies still felt that the case ought to be dealt with by local authorities in the ordinary way, and were jealous of infringement of their rights by the Diet. After much maneuvering, however, it was finally agreed to send to Raków an investigating committee of four, two representing the Diet, and one each the Senate and the King, reserving to the Diet, however, the right of judging the case.

On the Sunday preceding the investigation the local parish priest gave notice of it, inviting the attendance of any that could give evidence in the case, and reporting that two teachers, named Paludius and Andreas, were said to have taken part in the wicked deed. Considering arrest as sure and torture likely, the two therefore took hasty flight, and when sought by the investigators could nowhere be found. When the latter reached Raków and delivered their orders to Sieniński, a panic seized the inhabitants, who now first realized the danger that threatened them, and took to prayer and fasting. Sieniński left nothing undone that might avert the impending ruin, offered a site for a Catholic church, which had long been sought in vain though the population at Raków was more than half Catholic, and promised a generous gift for building, but all to no purpose. The official inquiry brought out nothing that was not already known, and the report was sent to Warsaw under seal and delivered to the King. Though it had been stipulated that the report be given to the Chamber of Deputies for decision,[31] clerical pressure prevailed and it was instead handed over to the Senate, which, being overwhelmingly Catholic, might more surely be relied upon for an unfavorable verdict. A fanatical majority here insisted that the case be not left to the slow process of debate in the Chamber of Deputies, but be dealt with in the Senate by swift summary process. Strong and influential opposition from members of all parties was made to such a procedure, lest it set a precedent that in future might be used to the prejudice of the rights of the nobility; but even the services of the venerable Sieniński, who in time of grave public danger had sacrificed his fortune for the Republic, and had thus often been hailed in the Diet as the Father of his Country,[32] were not enough now to secure him from unjust persecution. The opposition at length yielded, under the plea that it was for this time only, and that a law should be passed that

[31] For the Diary of the Diet, cf. Jagellonian Ms 2274, pp. 1–28; Czartoryski Ms 390, p. 405.

[32] cf. *Anonymi epistola*, p. 233.

in any such case in future summary process should be excluded.[33] The Senate therefore took charge of the case, and cited Sieniński, as the one ultimately responsible, to appear and answer the charges against him;[34] and when at length he protested that a decree could not legally be passed against him as a free nobleman, anger against him was so great that he barely escaped with his life. He was required to take an oath of innocence, confirmed by six other nobles of the same rank, that he had in no way been directly or indirectly guilty of the crime charged, nor privy to it; and he was thereupon adjudged innocent. Within a few days a decree was drawn up,[35] ordering that the two accused teachers should within six weeks present themselves before the court, under pain of perpetual infamy; that the school which had given chief cause to the crime should within four weeks be destroyed and never be restored; that the Raków press which had for so many years been issuing works against the Catholic faith should be abolished, and its prints be destroyed wherever found; that the teachers, ministers, and Arian inhabitants should leave Raków within four weeks, under pain of perpetual infamy and death; and that neither school nor press should ever be rebuilt, nor Arian ministers imported, under pain of loss of civil rights and a fine of 10,000 gold florins.

Before adjournment a protest against the decree was laid before the Diet and formally entered in the records of the trial, remonstrating against the gross violation of the rights of the nobility, and freedom of conscience. It bore the signatures of some of the most distinguished men in the country, not only Socinians but also Calvinists, and even some of the more liberal Catholics and members of the Orthodox Greek Church,[36] but it produced no result. The provisions of the decree were rigorously carried out. Church, school and press were abolished,[37] and the remnants of the congregation set up a place of worship in the

---

[33] No such law appears to have been passed.

[34] Text of the citation in Jagellonian Ms 2274, p. 48 f; reprinted in Chmaj, *Przypkowski*, pp. 213–215 n.

[35] April 29. For the text of the decree, cf. Jagellonian Ms 2274, p. 50 f; Czartoryski Ms 135, pp. 225–227; Ms 2476, pp. 4–8. Printed in (Szymon Starowolski) *Braterskie Napomnienie* (A brotherly admonition), 1644, p. 18; Ossoliński, *Wiadomości*, i, 294–296.

[36] cf. (Stanislaus Lubieniecius) *Vindiciae pro Unitariorum . . . libertate*, in Sandius, *Bibliotheca*, p. 278, n. For the text of the protest, cf. Samuel Przypkowski, *Braterska Deklaracja na niebraterskie Napomnienie*, etc. (A brotherly statement in answer to the unbrotherly Admonition), 1646, pp. 83–85. See also Jagellonian Ms 2274, p. 59 f.

[37] A large part of the printing establishment was shipped down the Vistula to Danzig, where there were bright hopes of establishing a new centre. cf. Bock, *Socinianismus*, p. 26.

neighboring village of Radostów, where it survived for fourteen years more. Sieniński, seventy years old, heart-broken with grief and cares, died within the year, leaving his estate to a widowed sister, who turned Catholic. Ministers, teachers and pupils scattered in various directions and went into hiding, as will presently be seen. The inhabitants were given three years in which to dispose of their property, much of which was bought up by Jews, it is said, at ridiculous prices. Thus, as a Socinian writer of the next generation pathetically laments, 'the very eye of Poland was plucked out, the sanctuary and refuge of exiles, the shrine of religion and the muses.' [38] From that day to this Raków has declined, often overrun in war and several times ravaged by fire, until, when the writer visited it in 1924, it was a wretched, unkempt town of a thousand or so inhabitants, mostly poor Jews, with nothing but vague memories of its former importance.[39] On the spot where the Socinian church had stood, Bishop Zadzik in 1640 laid the foundations of a new Catholic church. He died before construction was completed, but had liberally provided for it at his own expense, doubtless feeling that the destruction of heresy at Raków was the crowning act of his life.[40]

[38] *Anonymi epistola, loc. cit.*

[39] Only names survive to recall the past. A little meadow lying south of the Franciscan church still bears the name *drukarnia*, witnessing that this was the site of the Raków press. A mill on the bank of the Czarna is still called *papiernia*, evidently carrying on the memory of the old paper mill. A space by the pond west of the church is known as *bursa*, indicating the site of the students' quarters; and a sandy hill beyond this was the old 'Arian' cemetery, where bones and other relics have been turned up. cf. Wiśniewski, *Dekanat Opatowski*, p. 376.

[40] The new church was finished in 1654, and still stands. Over the west portal is the inscription: Dei Unius et Trini gloriae, Sanctorum Apostolorum Petri et Pauli, Majoris et Minoris Jacobi honori, sacram hanc aedem, in aeternum proscripta hinc Ariana impietate, restitutoque Romani Catholici ritus cultu, Illustrissimus et Reverendus Jacobus Zadzik, Episcopus Cracoviensis, Dux Severiae, studio ac opera posthuma executorum amicorum, erexit anno Salutis MDCXLV. Precare bene Praesuli tuo, tibique gaude Rakovia, quod ubi Filium et Spiritum Sanctum Patre minorem impie credebas, ibi jam aequalitatem Trinitatis adores. cf. Simon Starovolscius, *Monumenta Sarmatorum* (Cracoviae, 1655), p. 679. Another crucifix was erected in place of the one destroyed; but it too was wrecked in 1805, this time by a storm. cf. Orgelbrand, *Encyklopedja powszechna* (Warszawa, 1859–'68), xxxi, 928.

CHAPTER XXXV

CONTINUED PERSECUTION IN THE UKRAINE
AND ELSEWHERE

THOUGH STAGGERING from the brutal blow they had received at Raków, the Socinians spent no time in wringing their hands, but at once rallied to secure their future. Late in that very month they convened a general Synod at Kisielin, the seat of their strongest church in Volhynia.[1] In this quarter of Poland, in the Palatinates of Volhynia and Kijów, the region now known as the Ukraine, Socinianism had long found quiet shelter, and in the first quarter of the seventeenth century a whole series of churches and schools had sprung up here, which in the end numbered probably thirty or more. They won numerous and powerful adherents among the great landed proprietors, and were patronized by magnates whose domains were wide and whose wealth was princely, especially the Czaplices of Kisielin, the Sienutas of Lachowce, the Niemiryczes of Uszomir, and the Hojskis of Hoszcza.[2] Socinians were indeed so numerous among the nobility that in the local dietines they had the majority, though the dominant religion in these parts was not Roman Catholic but that of the Greek Church. Prince Konstanty Ostrogski, however, though orthodox by profession, was suspected of being a Socinian at heart, was sympathetic with the Socinians, and gave them his protection; for his daughter was wife of Jan Kiszka, the great Socinian magnate in Lithuania. It was therefore natural for the shattered church to try to re-establish itself in this region, distant from Catholic centres, and presumably safe from Catholic persecution. One of the first acts of the Synod was to send a letter soliciting the help and counsel of Prince Christopher Radziwiłł, who though a Calvinist was not an enemy of the Socinians. The letter was sent by the hand of one of his councilors, Samuel Przypkowski,

---

[1] cf. Szczotka, *Synody*, pp. 79–81; Chmaj, *Przypkowski*, p. 34.

[2] The Czaplices put their Christianity into practice by freeing their peasants from taxes and socage. cf. Lewicki, *Socynjanie*, pp. 204–234; Sandius, *Bibliotheca*, p. 283, n.; Lubieniecius, *Historia*, book iii, chap. 16; Aleksander Brückner, *Dzieje kultury Staropolskiej* (History of old Polish Culture), Kraków, 1930, ii, 496.

who was an eminent Socinian and could give a full account of what had taken place. The letter bore an impressive list of signatures of both Socinians and Greek Catholics.[3] Radziwiłł in turn addressed a letter to the Palatine Stanislas Lubomirski of Kraków, asking for aid and consideration for the Socinians; but the answer to it was a downright refusal to do anything for such wicked heretics.[4]

The Synod also sent representatives to the Reformed Synod at Krasnobród in September to see whether a political union might be formed with the Calvinists with a view to joint action at the next Diet in defence of religious toleration; but the proposal was rejected.[5] At the same time Martin Ruar,[6] who had for several years been in active correspondence with Hugo Grotius, then self-exiled from Holland and living in Paris as Swedish ambassador, wrote him a full account of the tragedy at Raków, as did also Jan Stoiński, asking his intervention.[7] Grotius wrote in turn to the Swedish Chancellor Oxenstiern, lamenting the event, and foreseeing that this present attack by intolerant Catholics upon the weakest of the Protestant sects foreboded a danger threatening also the stronger ones in time to come.[8]

Besides these emergency measures, the Synod dealt with measures for carrying on church life in an unbroken sequence. Still obsessed with the notion that by reasoned arguments they could convince the Catholics of one's natural right to religious freedom, and restrain them from intolerant acts, they requested Przypkowski to finish his work on freedom of conscience and that on the Confederation, and charged Ruar to prepare for press an unfinished work of the late Joachim Stegmann on religious controversies. To fill the place of the college at Raków, it

---

[3] cf. Czartoryski Ms 2573, no. 47. Also Wjaczesław Łypyńckyj, 'Arjanskij sejmyk w Kysełeni na Wołyny w Maju 1638 r.' (An Arian synod at Kisielin in Volhynia in May, 1638) Zapiskyj Towarzystwa Szewczenka (Lwów), iv (1910), 96.

[4] cf. Czartoryski Ms 1657, p. 317 f.

[5] cf. Szczotka, Synody, p. 80, citing Warsaw National Library Ms Różnoj Q iv, 22, pp. 85–104; Chmaj, op. cit., p. 34.

[6] Ruar was one of the most learned men among the celebrated Socinians. Born in Holstein, he had become Socinian at Altdorf, studied at Strassburg, and traveled extensively in western Europe, everywhere forming relations with distinguished scholars. He declined a professorship offered him at Cambridge, but in 1621 became Rector of the college at Raków. His later years were spent as minister at and near Danzig, where he died in 1657. cf. Ludwik Chmaj, Ruar.

[7] cf. Ruari Epistolae, p. 164; Ludwik Chmaj, 'Hugo Grotius wobec Socynjanismu' (H. G. in relation to Socinianism), Reformacja w Polsce, iv (1926), 89; id., Przypkowski, p. 34.

[8] cf. Hugo Grotius, Epistolae (Amsterdam, 1687), epp. 1006, 1001.

was voted to bring the school at Kisielin up to the Racovian standard, to bring the Raków professors thither, and to appoint from influential noble families seven directors for the Socinian community, in order to provide against fresh dangers.[9] The new college and its theological department, together with a branch at Beresko, soon won a reputation that drew students from all confessions, and for some five years it enjoyed high prosperity. Kisielin became the new capital of Socinianism, and a center of vigorous propaganda; but the rapid growth that now took place also aroused enmity among the other confessions. As early as 1640 therefore the clergy cited three brothers Czaplic before the court, charged with giving shelter to ministers and teachers expelled from Raków, arbitrarily opening an 'Arian' academy and other schools to corrupt Christian youth, holding sectarian synods, and in general propagating the 'Arian' sect forbidden by decrees of Diets and Tribunals and declared by common law and universal opinion to be diabolical. All 'Arian' ministers and teachers at Kisielin and Beresko were also included in the summons. The case dragged on for four years, but ended with a decree of the Tribunal ordering the churches and schools closed, their buildings burned, and the heretics banished, besides a fine of 1,000 florins and a threat of infamy for George Czaplic if he did not produce the ministers and teachers before the court. As the latter had fled, Czaplic was branded with infamy, and further fined 10,000 florins. Nor did punishment of the living suffice. Matthew Twardochleb and Joachim Rupniowski, sometime ministers at Kisielin and Beresko, but already in their graves, were also declared infamous, and a fine was demanded for them as well, so that Czaplic had in all to pay over 20,000 florins.[10] Thus after less than six years the school at Kisielin came to an end.[11] Czaplic testified at his trial that the ministers and teachers at Kisielin had in fact never held office at Raków, but his testimony was disregarded; and when the case was tried before the supreme Tribunal, to which it had been appealed, the 'Arian' members of the court were excluded from its deliberations.[12]

At about the same time a similar case was brought against the noble Sienuta, proprietor of Lachowce, charged with secretly sheltering Jan Stoiński, banished from Raków. The case issued in a decree of the Lublin Tribunal in 1644, condemning all 'Arians' there to banishment,

---

9 cf. Szczotka, *op. cit.*, pp. 79–81.

10 cf. *Anonymi epistola*, p. 237.

11 cf. Lewicki, *Socynjanie*, p. 220 f.   12 cf. *Anonymi epistola*, p. 237.

touching Stoiński with infamy and depriving him of his noble rank, and heavily fining Sienuta.[13] To mention but one instance more, George Niemirycz was the chief patron of the Socinians in the Ukraine, and had valiantly supported them in the Diet when the Raków case was on trial, and enjoyed the favor of the King to such an extent that despite the fanatical opposition of both the Bishop and the Palatine, he was appointed Chamberlain of Kijów. After several unsuccessful attempts to reach him, his enemies finally had him prosecuted in 1643 for sheltering fugitive ministers and teachers from Raków, organizing new churches on his domains, and spreading heresy in general. At Kijów the case seems to have been decided in his favor, but on appeal to the Lublin Tribunal he was convicted and sentenced in 1646 to pay a fine of 10,000 florins, and was ordered to close the churches on his estates.[14] Under a government and courts overwhelmingly Catholic, the guarantees of the Confederation of Warsaw had by this time become a dead letter, especially for Socinians, who could no longer look to the other Protestants for support, and whom the Catholics were now professing to regard not as Dissidents, nor even as mere heretics, but as blasphemers and atheists wholly outside the Christian pale. Through their representatives in the Diet they might still appeal to their constitutional rights, but their appeals fell on deaf ears. In various other parts of the Ukraine at this period similar suits were brought against 'Arians,' all leading to heavy fines, infamy, banishment and the like, and all aiming at the same end, the extinction of 'Arianism.' These cases were tried before a Tribunal composed half of Catholic clergy, and with 'Arian' members excluded. To the nobility of the region, of all confessions, such prejudiced trials gave general offence, but their protests before the national Diet, and their demands that the decrees of the Tribunal be annulled, were inevitably defeated by the fanaticism of the Catholic party. Such was the desperate situation of Socinianism in the southeastern provinces of Poland when the Cossack war overwhelmed the country, and hastened the churches there to a ruin from which they never rallied.

Kisielin was not the only place to which members of the college at Raków withdrew after their expulsion from there. Many of the students and several of the ablest teachers removed to Lucławice,[15] a convenient location in a territory where the Socinian population was very

[13] cf. Lewicki, *op. cit.*, pp. 221–223.
[14] *Op. cit.*, pp. 225–229.   [15] cf. Morawski, *Arjanie*, p. 168.

numerous, and where there was one of the oldest and strongest of their churches. Here, where Socinus had spent his last years, they might find safe protection on the estates of sympathetic nobles; and here there had long been a Socinian school, which was now raised to the rank of a college in which advanced studies were pursued, including theology. It took on a marked growth after the closing of Kisielin, especially under the seven years' rectorship of Valentin Baumgart, a graduate of Königsberg who had been converted by Ruar and had already been Rector at Kisielin.[16] As the school lay near the Hungarian border, it had active relations with the Unitarians of Transylvania, of whom many sent their sons here to learn Polish and finish their education. The college was finally broken up when the country was overrun during the war with Sweden; but both church and school at Lucławice had already fallen victims to local mob violence in 1651, and 'Arian' homes had been sacked. In the end the buildings of both were given to the neighboring Franciscan monastery by the proprietor, Achacy Taszycki, who had now become Catholic, and were then torn down.[17]

While these events were disturbing the outward face of Socinian affairs, the inner life of their churches seems to have proceeded soberly. Annual synods were held as usual, and the needs of churches and ministers were attended to. Ministers were ordained and appointed to their stations; appropriations were voted to promising students to continue their studies abroad. With a view to an indefinite future, a manual of their ecclesiastical polity was ordered to be prepared, provision was made for writing a careful history of their movement thus far, and a collection of hymns in German was authorized for use in the growing number of German congregations.[18] Especially noteworthy were the evidences of literary activity, for at nearly every synod one or more books were approved for publication, though the printing must be done in greatest secrecy in Poland, or else by sympathetic presses in Holland. The ablest pen at this period was wielded by Jonas Schlichting. Born of a noble family, he had been highly educated and was widely traveled, and was relied upon to undertake various important affairs. As a matter of course he became the champion of the Socinian

---

[16] cf. Lubieniecius, *Historia*, book iii, chap. 15; Bock, *Socinianismus*, pp. 35, 42–47.

[17] cf. Morawski, *Arjanie*, p. 187.

[18] Respectively: Morscovius, *Politia ecclesiastica*, finished and submitted to the Synod in 1652 (cf. Szczotka, p. 92), but not published until 1746, *v. supra*, p. 427, n. 24; Lubieniecius, *Historia Reformationis Polonicae*, posthumously published, 1685; Johann Preuss, *Herzliches Seytenspiel* (Frankfurt, 1657), cf. Szczotka, p. 93.

cause in a protracted debate with the Catholics. It was the longest and most intense of any in Socinian history, lasted from 1641 to 1662, and comprised no fewer than twenty-five separate items.[19]

The controversy began in 1641 when a Jesuit professor, Nicholas Cichowski of Poznań, one of the most active and persistent foes of the Socinians, published a book, expanding a discussion had with Jan Stoiński two years before into a hundred arguments for the supreme divinity of Christ, addressed to 'Arians,' and urging that the Diet pass a law of banishment against them. One of these arguments was that the 'Arians' regard the Devil as a God,[20] and worship him accordingly, a statement that he was to repeat in later works with great popular effect. As the Socinians had now lost their press, they were unable to reply; but to the surprise of all, a little book of twenty-six pages appeared the following year, with no indication of author or place,[21] designed to support the Socinian faith by showing that it was in entire agreement with the Apostles' Creed. It took the Creed article by article, explained the simple meaning of each, and quoted supporting texts of Scripture, concluding that as the Socinians sincerely believed this Creed they should be recognized as Christians. It altogether ignored, however, many teachings current among the Socinians which are not supported by the Creed, but were regarded by Catholics as heretical.

The Catholics were scandalized that such a book should have been published so boldly, not because there was heresy in it, for when the Bishops requested an opinion from the University professors they were told that the book contained nothing but what is said in Scripture,[22]

---

[19] cf. Stanisław Estreicher, *Bibliografia Polska*, Część III, xxvii, 21. The more important items in the controversy are these: Nicolaus Cichovius (Cichowski), *Centuria argumentorum*, 1641; Jonas Schlichting, *Confessio fidei Christianae*, 1642; C., *Credo Arrianorum*, 1649; S., *Confessionis Christianae ad rogum damnatae . . . vindices*, 1652; S., *Centuria argumentorum caesa*, 1652; C., *Epistola paraenetica ad . . . Schlichting*, 1655; C., *Pogrom Diabła Arriańskiego* (Defeat of the Arian Devil), 1659; C., *Triumphus sanctissimae et aeternum adorandae Trinitatis*, 1662. For a running sketch of the whole controversy, cf. Grabowski, *Literatura*, pp. 479–487.

[20] *v. supra*, p. 443, n. 1.

[21] *Confessio fidei Christianae illarum ecclesiarum, quae in Polonia unum Deum, et Filium eius unigenitum, Iesum Christum et Spiritum Sanctum corde sancte profitentur, per divinae veritatis confessorem.* Also Polish, German, Dutch and French translations. Perhaps unique copy in the Bibliothèque Nationale, Paris. Cichowski guessed it must have been printed at Amsterdam, where Schlichting was known. It had in fact been printed on a little press set up in great secrecy in the house of Stanislas Wiszowaty in the secluded village of Wrocmirowa, a few miles south of Lucławice. cf. Morawski, *Arjanie*, p. 155.

[22] cf. Samuel Grondzki, *Historia Belli Cossaco-Polonici* (Pesth, 1789), p. 344.

but because it so openly defied the prohibitions of the Raków decree. The matter was brought before the Diet, and again trial was had by summary process. As Schlichting, whose authorship had now become known, did not answer the summons to appear, a decree was passed in 1647 condemning him to death, confiscating his property, touching him with infamy, proscribing him from the Kingdom, ordering his books publicly burned by the executioner, suppressing all 'Arian' schools and printing-presses, and threatening with banishment and confiscation of goods any one offering him shelter or circulating or even keeping his books.[23] Schlichting had to flee the country, and for several years lived in remote exile beyond the Dnieper, or was in hiding around Lucławice. It was 1651 before feeling had subsided enough for him to venture to show himself in Poland. The new decree much depressed the other Socinians, who began to see clouds foreboding worse storms to come. The printed controversy with Cichovius went on, however, without interruption. Schlichting was an eager controversialist, too hasty to be careful, while Cichovius, cool, keen and adroit, was quick to take advantage of every opening, attacked his opponent first on one side and then on another, employing invective, logical argument, or appeals to feeling as the case might be. He was right in his contention that the Apostles' Creed was not a true summary of characteristic Socinian teaching, which in its most offensive doctrines was as far beyond the belief of the early Church as it was contrary to the Catholic tradition. But in truth argument between the two was wasted, for the situation had drifted beyond the field of logical reasoning, and the case was already prejudged, and only awaited formal decision and a final verdict.

One brief ray of hope relieved the general discouragement of these times. King Ladislas was much concerned to promote the internal strength of his country by securing peace among the contending religious parties, and when one of his secretaries, who had been a Lutheran and a Calvinist minister, but had lately accepted the Catholic faith, urged upon him that it might be easy to unite all the Christian confessions if only a friendly discussion could be brought about, he gladly

---

[23] For the text of the decree, cf. Ossoliński Mss 1453, p. 239 f; 224, p. 978; Jagellonian Ms 2274, pp. 55–57. Printed in Chmaj, *Przypkowski*, p. 46, n. 2. The penalty of infamy, already several times referred to, was more feared than any other short of death. It deprived one of rank, honors, citizenship, and all legal rights, withdrew legal protection from him, and made him virtually an outlaw and shunned of all men.

fell in with the idea. Hence came the celebrated *Colloquium charita-tivum* or friendly conference of Thorn (Toruń),[24] to which the King and the Catholic Synod issued invitations for the Protestants. The proposal aroused high hopes among all the non-Catholics, not least among the Socinians. Their synod at Siedliska appointed as delegates Schlichting, Ruar and Christopher Lubieniecki,[25] who were the first to arrive and present their credentials on the day appointed, October 10, 1644. The other Protestant confessions refused to make any joint appearance with them at the proposed discussion; and when they presented themselves alone and the presiding Bishop asked which confession they represented, they said, the Christian. He politely replied that discussion had been authorized with only the Lutherans and the Calvinists, and asked to be excused for the present from having any further conference with them.[26] They were of course disappointed, yet in fact little was lost. The conference was deferred until the following August to accommodate the Protestants; but when met, the parties quarreled from the beginning, the Lutherans being most intractable of all. Neither side was willing for the sake of harmony to yield any ground; and although 50,000 guests had crowded the city, and enormous expense had been incurred, the assembly came to an end after 36 fruitless sessions without any result except increased acrimony between the Protestants. Indeed, a prominent historian has expressed the opinion that this was probably the real purpose in arranging the discussion at all.[27]

Although after the fall of Raków 'Arianism' was theoretically tolerated (except in those on whom the Raków decree had fallen), the decrees of the Tribunal against such 'Arians' as came before it grew steadily more frequent and severe. The printed controversy between Schlichting and Cichowski kept the flame of hatred against them constantly fanned, and not a few of the younger generation yielded to pressure and returned to the Roman Church. One Abraham Hulewicz, who had been convicted before the Tribunal of blasphemy against the Trinity, escaped the decreed punishment by making public recantation of his 'Arianism' in 1647.[28] After the Protestant fiasco at Thorn, the

---

[24] cf. Krasinski, *Reformation*, ii, chapter 11; Stanislaus Lubieniecius, *Fidelis relatio transactorum Thorunii . . . MDCXLIV*, in Bock, *Socinianismus*, pp. 115–121.

[25] cf. Szczotka, *op. cit.*, p. 85.

[26] cf. Lubieniecius, *op. cit.*, p. 118 f.

[27] cf. Lengnich, *Geschichte*, vi, 226.

[28] cf. Czartoryski Ms 1657, p. 403 f; Sandius, *Bibliotheca*, p. 237.

Catholic reaction gathered fresh strength and vigor. Simon Starowolski, Canon of Kraków, published in 1644 a *Fraternal Admonition to the Dissidents*,[29] citing various unrepealed laws against heretics, and attacking the guarantees of the Warsaw Confederation as illegal and invalid; and thus showing on what dangerous ground they stood, he urged them in their own interest to remain quiet and stir up no disturbance in the Diets or elsewhere.

Though the writing was not addressed especially to the Socinians, they felt that it called for a prompt and decisive reply, which the synod asked Przypkowski to make.[30] He made a general and detailed denial of his opponent's assertions, and a strong appeal for religious toleration as a foundation of civil liberty. In Prussia during all this period, though the prevailing religion was strongly Lutheran, there were many secret Socinians who had their own congregations for religious worship. They made some notable converts, insomuch that the authorities were aroused to take aggressive action to prevent the heresy from spreading further. Thus in 1647 the King issued an edict prohibiting 'Arians', especially in Prussia, from making converts, under pain of death, loss of property, and expulsion of all the sect from the Kingdom.

The interregnum after the death of King Ladislas in 1648, and the election of a new King, furnished an opportunity for a fresh outbreak of religious hatred. The new King, Jan Casimir (Kazimierz), took the usual oath at his coronation, to maintain peace and tranquility among Dissidents as to the Christian religion, and to allow no oppression on account of religion;[31] but this oath no longer had any practical meaning for the Socinians, for the term Dissidents, which had at first signified all religions without distinction, and had later come to be used of the Protestant sects alone, had now by deliberate interpretation been restricted to the three orthodox sects subscribing the *Consensus Sendomiriensis*, from which 'Arians' had been expressly excluded.[32] The

---

[29] *Braterskie napomnienie ad Dissidentes in religione, aby się skromnie i w pokoju zachowali* (1644). (A fraternal admonition . . . to behave modestly and quietly.)

[30] cf. Szczotka, *op. cit.*, p. 86. (Samuel Przypkowski) *Braterska deklaracia na niebraterskie Napomnienie . . . ad Dissidentes in Religione* (A fraternal statement in reply to the unfraternal Admonition, etc.), 1646. Sometimes wrongly ascribed to Niemirycz.

[31] cf. *Volumina Legum*, iv, 98.

[32] For a time there was a quibble between the expressions dissidentes *de* religione (the original language of the *pax dissidentium*) and dissidentes *in* religione which was used more or less interchangeably with it, or even *a* religione; and it was urged that 'Arians' were not *in* religion at all, but wholly outside it. But if they were now to be regarded as not being included in the compact, it did not matter which preposition was used. cf. (Stanislaus

way was therefore more than ever open to persecution of the Socinians on any pretext or on none at all.

As early as 1636 at a Prussian dietine at Grudziąz the Bishop of Chełmno had argued that the 'Arians' were not included in the provisions of the Confederation, and moved that the Arian deputies to the Diet be excluded;[33] and in 1648 the Bishops issued a manifesto to the same effect.[34] At the Diet in 1648 at which Jan Casimir was elected King, protest was made against the vote of George Niemirycz as an 'Arian,' and Paul Iwanicki, another 'Arian', was refused a vote; but though he was permitted to remain, he was advised not to present himself as a deputy again. It was voted that 'Arian' nobles might indeed stay in the country, but might not build more churches or buy more land.[35] In the same year, when at a dietine at Proszowice a resolution had been voted concerning religious rights and immunities, several formal protests were entered against the acts being subscribed by 'Arians' or Anabaptists; [36] and repeatedly at Diets and local dietines in the first decade of King Jan's reign, things were said and measures adopted showing that the Socinians could no longer expect to enjoy the political rights and privileges that were open to the other nobles,[37] but must submit to being classed with Tatars, Cossacks and heathen. Thus year by year and month by month the bands that were slowly strangling them were drawn closer and closer, until the prime source of all their ills, as one of their writers later called it,[38] but in reality only the final and fatal blow, fell upon them in the outbreak of the Cossack war in 1648, which laid all Poland prostrate, and brought the Socinian churches within immediate sight of total extinction.

NOTE: It must not be concluded that Socinians, though they were the chief, were the only victims of Catholic persecution at this period. Encouraged by their success at Raków, the Jesuits in the following year tried the same procedure against the Calvinists at Wilno. Two young noblemen, merry with wine, when shooting with bow and arrow at jackdaws, accidentally hit an image of the Archangel Michael on the church of the Clare Nuns. A

Lubieniecius) *Vindiciae pro Unitariorum in Polonia religionis libertate*, in Sandius, *Bibliotheca*, p. 280 f.

33 cf. Adryan Krzyżanowski, *Dawna Polska* (Ancient Poland), Warszawa, 1857, ii, 320; Lengnich, *Geschichte*, vi, 102; *v. supra*, p. 451.

34 cf. Johannes Matthias Schröckh, *Christliche Kirchengeschichte* (Leipzig, 1810), ix, 428.

35 cf. Lengnich, *op. cit.*, pp. 13, 19 f.

36 cf. Czartoryski Ms 1657, p. 443 f.

37 cf. Lengnich, *op. cit.*, pp. 6–200 *passim*.

38 Prima nobis malorum origo, Lubieniecius, *Historia*, p. 279.

tumult followed, incited by the priests. The youths were let go, but the Calvinist church, school and hostel were seized, and all their worship, public or private, was henceforth forbidden in the city. The Rector of the school barely escaped with his life, and many homes of Protestant merchants were pillaged. Similar outrages took place in Podlasie and White Russia (cf. Wengerscius, *Slavonia*, pp. 256–264). Likewise in 1658 the church and school of the Bohemian Brethren at Leszno (Lissa) were destroyed (cf. Krzyżanowski, *op. cit.*, I, lxlviii [*sic!*]). The misfortunes of the Socinians were thus but a prophecy of what, under the same policy of repression or persecution, were in another generation or two to fall upon all the Dissidents.

CHAPTER XXXVI

SOCINIANISM OVERWHELMED AND BANISHED FROM POLAND

TOWARD THE END of the reign of Ladislas IV. a long smoldering unrest among the peasant population of the Ukraine, under the oppression of the magnates and other land-owners who lorded it over them, came to a head in open revolution. The leader of the movement was Bogdan Chmielnicki, son of a Polish noble who had removed from Masovia and taken a Cossack wife. Chmielnicki had been outrageously wronged by one of the magnates, and he stirred up a general uprising in the Ukraine, in which the Cossacks formed against Poland a league with the ferocious Tatars of the Crimea, who had formerly been their greatest enemies. In its deeper causes, however, this was a social and religious uprising, on the one hand of the peasantry against oppression by their masters the nobility, and on the other of Greek Catholics against the Jesuits and the Jews. Even the King was suspected of sympathizing with the revolt, as tending to curb the rapacity of the nobles.[1] The rebellion burst on the country like lightning out of a clear sky, and in the first great battle the flower of the Polish nobility were slain or taken captive. The death of the King five weeks later was the beginning of long years of defeat and misfortune for Poland. The Cossacks and Tatars, moved by savage hatred, ravaged the land as far west as the Vistula, torturing, killing, plundering, destroying all with fire and sword.[2] Whole cities were wiped out amid frightful atrocities, and those that were taken alive were carried away into slavery. Over a thousand of the Socinians, who were especially numerous in the Ukraine, left everything behind them and fled headlong and all but naked, and sought refuge with their scattered brethren in western Poland.[3] Though the Cossacks were not, as has sometimes

---

[1] cf. Anatol Lewicki, *Zarys historyi Polskiej* (Outline of Polish history), Warszawa, 1907, p. 291 f.

[2] For a vivid fictional picture of this war, cf. Sienkiewicz's historical novel, *With Fire and Sword*.

[3] cf. Lubieniecius, *Historia*, p. 287 f; Sandius, *Bibliotheca*, p. 241.

been asserted,[4] more fierce against the Socinians than against the other religions, they vented their wrath without distinction against all their noble oppressors, those of their own Greek Church not excepted. They were at length defeated, though not before all the Socinian churches in the Ukraine had been irretrievably ruined, and any of their patrons that had not escaped from the country had been either slain or transported into slavery among the Tatars. Thus their already greatly weakened community lost in a single year perhaps half of their remaining congregations.

It was in the midst of this Cossack rebellion that Jan Casimir, younger brother of King Ladislas, came to the throne of Poland. Though he had been a Jesuit priest and a Cardinal, he was dispensed from his vows by the Pope, that he might the better serve the interests of the Church as King. Brave and energetic, but impulsive, capricious and unstable, he had a reign marked by incessant and disastrous wars with nearly all his neighbors at once; so that after twenty harassed years he gladly sought escape from his troubles by resigning his crown and seeking the refuge of a cloistered life in France.[5] Though the Cossacks were decisively defeated in 1651, they were not pacified, and intermittent warfare went on until 1655, when they sought an alliance with Poland's inveterate foe Russia, which was easily persuaded to take advantage of her weakened condition by carrying on a war of unspeakable barbarity in the northeast, which wiped out whatever Socinian churches had still survived in Lithuania. While Russia was thus invading Poland from the east, Charles X. of Sweden, ambitious to extend his realms, and having an eye on the crown of Poland,[6] invaded it from the north and west, on the flimsy pretext of protecting it from the Russians and Cossacks. Only feeble resistance was offered, for during the recent struggle for power between the King and the nobles in Poland, large numbers of the nobles, especially the Dissidents

---

[4] cf. Sandius, *loc. cit.*; Lewicki, *Socynjanie*, p. 230.

[5] He had taken as his Queen the energetic widow of his brother Ladislas; but in 1668, the year after her death, he abdicated his throne and retired to the abbey of Saint Germain in Paris, of which he became Abbot. He died at Nevers in 1672. His remains were later removed to Poland and entombed on the Wawel at Kraków; but his heart was placed in a chapel in the church of Saint Germain-des-Prés, where the inscription on his monument records as his most memorable achievement that he expelled the Socinians from Poland.

[6] By intermarriage between the Polish house of Jagiełło and the Swedish house of Vasa, Jan Casimir and Charles were second-cousins. There had already been some designs of uniting both countries under one crown, and in some circumstances Charles might have had a presumptive claim to the Polish crown.

(who at all events had more to hope for from the rule of the Lutheran Charles than from the ex-Jesuit Jan), had become estranged from their King, and without drawing a sword strove to outdo one another in putting themselves under the protection of the Swedish King. In the end even generals and their troops entered his service. Charles quickly took the capital at Warsaw, and pursued the fleeing King and his army to Kraków, which soon surrendered; while the Elector Friedrich Wilhelm undertook the 'protection' of East Prussia.[7]

As practically the whole of Poland was in the hands of his enemies, the King, after wandering about the land for a time, fled from the country and took refuge in Silesia, in the domain of the Emperor of Austria. And now a marvelous thing happened. In the hour when King Jan's cause seemed, humanly speaking, to be utterly lost, when nothing seemed to be left of Poland but a few score exiles in Silesia, a few towns that had happened not to surrender, and a wandering remnant of the Polish army, an unexpected turn for the better took place. The Swedes, who had been so widely welcomed as emancipators from the oppressions of the King, were now found to be wolves in sheep's clothing, ravaging and pillaging wherever they went, treating the inhabitants with contempt, sacking homes and desecrating the Catholic churches. A spontaneous insurrection took place in all sections of the nation. The magnates who had welcomed Charles withdrew their support from him; even the peasants sprang to arms. The heroic defence of Częstochowa against an overwhelming force inspired enthusiasm, and Lwów (Lemberg) refused to surrender even when its fall seemed certain. The generals of the national army returned to their allegiance, and formed a confederation at Tyszowce at the end of 1655 in defence of faith and fatherland. At the same time both King and Queen, who had in the meantime been indefatigable in foreign diplomacy, had set causes in train that were to result in the formation of a general league of other nations against Sweden, whose rapid conquests had aroused fears in the rest of Europe.[8]

Hearing how the tide was turning at home, the King, after some three months in exile, secretly made his way through Carpathian forests back to Poland, where Lwów, which had remained stedfastly loyal to

---

[7] For a picture of Poland during these invasions, cf. Sienkiewicz's historical novel, *The Deluge*.

[8] For a clear account of events of this period, cf. Lewicki, *Zarys*, p. 298 ff; Józef Szujski, *Dzieje Polski* (History of Poland), Lwów, 1864, iii, 360–391.

him, received him with enthusiasm. It was at this solemnly critical juncture in his life that on April 1, 1656 the King, following a custom then not unknown in a time of crisis, made a celebrated vow in a little chapel adjoining the Lwów cathedral. In the presence of a crowd of clergy and gentry, he knelt with his Senators on the altar steps before a picture of the Holy Virgin, and took her as his patroness and the Queen of his dominions, and committing all to her especial protection and imploring her aid, promised that he would henceforth with all diligence spread her worship everywhere in his territories; and that if he gained the victory over his enemies, especially the Swedes, he would when peace was established take every means to relieve the peasants of their unjust oppressions.[9] A sweeping victory soon ensued; though the King never fulfilled the second part of his vow, which would indeed have been impossible save with the unlikely co-operation of the landholding nobles in the Diet. From now on for a time affairs went more favorably for the King. Victories over the Swedes followed, and at the end of June the united Polish forces stood before Warsaw. It was again a critical moment for the King, and again he would make a vow, encouraged by Jesuit priests who as usual were with him. On the day before the final assault on the capital, wishing to invoke divine aid, he made the vow which they suggested to him, having in view the final step toward which they had been pressing for half a century. Yielding to their persuasions that God had been punishing King and country for their treachery in tolerating in Poland such blasphemers of the deity of Christ, he solemnly vowed that he would banish the Arians from the land.[10] It is not to the purpose here to follow the course of Poland's struggle with her enemies further than to say in brief that in what was at once a political and a religious struggle, of Poland against invasion, and of Catholics against Protestants, the Swedes after wavering fortunes were gradually driven back; peace was concluded with Russia and with the Elector of Brandenburg, in which Poland lost East Prussia and Livonia; an invasion from Transylvania in 1657 under Prince George Rákóczy, inspired by the Swedes, was repulsed with frightful loss to the invaders; and shortly after the death of

---

[9] Original Polish text in Ludwik Kubala, *Wojna Szwecka w roku 1655 i 1656* (The Swedish war in 1655 and 1656), Lwów, 1913, pp. 307–309; and in Orgelbrand, *Encyklopedya Powszechna*, xii, 945; Latin translation in Vespasianus Kochowski, *Annalium Poloniae, Climacter secundus* (Cracoviae, 1688), p. 106 f; and in Andrzej Załuski, *Epistolae historico-familiares* (Brunsbergae, 1709), i, 5.

[10] cf. Załęski, *Jesuici*, iii, 113. Writers have generally confused this vow with that previously made at Lwów, but it is entirely distinct from it in place, date and substance.

Charles X. in 1660, peace with Sweden was concluded by the treaty of Oliva in the same year.[11]

The period embracing the Cossack, Russian and Swedish wars was not only one of unprecedented calamities for Poland as a whole, but also one that brought complete ruin to the few surviving Socinian churches. The one remaining part of the country where there still was, as there had long been, a considerable group of these was the foot-hill country southeast of Kraków, known as Podgórze, and lying between the Vistula and the Carpathians, a district roughly forty or fifty miles square. When the invading Swedish forces overran this territory, the gentry of the district, seeing that the King had fled from the country and that there was no Polish army to defend them, left their homes and for a time sought whatever refuge they could find. When the invaders had swept by, leaving only a garrison at the chief town, Sącz, they returned to their homes; though within three months trouble again broke out in this district. In the peasant uprising at the end of 1655, referred to above, the peasants were encouraged to expel the garrison the Swedes had left behind them, and as a reward were promised the estates and homes of the 'Arians,' whom they were told in the market-places and publicly from the pulpit that they might attack and kill, and then plunder their possessions. Thus a peasant mob of over 3,000 attacked Sącz, murdered the garrison, and then under the guidance of their priests, and armed with rustic weapons, proceeded without warning to attack the estates of the 'Arians' and ravage all with fire and sword. Any that would not renounce their faith were brutally slain, men, women, and children alike,[12] or were left wounded and half-dead. Leaving their most precious possessions behind, those that could escape made their way by night, in the intense cold of a Polish winter, across the Vistula to a Socinian community in the village of Czarków, whence after a few weeks they were forced again to flee before the plundering invaders. Taking hasty counsel they realized that in the open country they had no protection against the raging peasantry, and that any attempt to cross the border would expose them there to danger of attack from robbers and assassins. Their only safety seemed to lie in their going to Kraków, which was well fortified and had been held by the Swedes for half a year, and in

[11] For the course of events in this period, cf. Lewicki, *Zarys*, pp. 298–302; Szujski, *Dzieje*, ii, 388–403.

[12] For a contemporary relation, *v. Anonymi epistola*, p. 244 f; cf. Sygański, *Nowy Sącz*, i, 156–160; Lubieniecius, *Historia*, p. 280.

seeking shelter, as many others from the vicinity had already done, both Catholics and Protestants. Some thirty families took this step, and were kindly received by the Swedish governor. Several of their ablest ministers were of the number—Schlichting, Lubieniecki, Stegmann, and Socinus's grandson Andrew Wiszowaty—and with leave of the governor they regularly held religious worship and observed church discipline and the sacrament, to the great comfort of the fugitives;[13] while their ministers continued their study of the Scriptures, and Schlichting prepared a commentary on a great part of the New Testament.[14] Thus they continued for a year and a half, in which the city was four times under siege, suffering much from hunger and cold.

Meantime the tide of war began to turn strongly against the Swedes, and to stem this Charles devised a plan for dividing Poland among the envious neighboring powers. Under this plan he dangled before the eyes of Prince George Rákóczy of Transylvania the prospect of wearing the Polish crown, and invited him in pursuit of it to invade Poland from the south and join forces with the Swedes. Rákóczy was quick to respond, and at the beginning of 1657 he invaded Poland on the Galician frontier with a motley army of 40,000, composed of Hungarians, Wallachians, Gypsies and Cossacks, chiefly bent upon plunder. When the Poles refused to accept his 'protectorship', he ravaged the country mercilessly, including the district where the remaining Socinian communities had been, and then, after reenforcing the Swedish forces at Kraków, proceeded to a union with King Charles farther north. But just at this juncture the Danes attacked Charles in the west, and he at once hastened to meet them, thus leaving Rákóczy alone to face the Poles. As these had already invaded Transylvania in his rear, and Austrian allies of Poland now stood at the gates of Kraków, Rákóczy hastily beat a retreat, which soon turned into a disorderly rout. His Cossacks deserted him, the Polish forces pursued him and harassed his rear, the remnant of his army fell into the hands of the Tatars, who cut them to pieces, and Rákóczy himself barely escaped, and reached his capital only to be deposed by his Diet.[15]

The Swedish forces evacuated Kraków at the end of August, and the

---

[13] After Rákóczy had occupied the city in 1657, with his Hungarian troops, among whom were many Unitarians from Transylvania, they held services in Latin for them, which were gladly attended and much appreciated.

[14] Included in the *Bibliotheca Fratrum Polonorum* (Irenopoli, 1666).

[15] cf. Szujski, *Dzieje*, p. 404 f.

Socinian refugees, since their district was now cleared of enemies, turned back to the homes from which they had fled, only to find their houses pillaged and in ruins, and everything of value carried away. With devotion unshaken by all they had endured they at once set about gathering their congregations together and re-establishing their churches; but before they had been able to do more than take breath a prostrating blow fell upon them. This blow had been long preparing. Even at the time of the accession of King Jan Casimir in 1648 the banishment of the 'Arians' had been under consideration in a dietine at Marienburg in Prussia, where the feeling against them was especially strong, though the measure was not deemed practicable as yet for the whole country; and they were publicly compared to Tatars, Cossacks and heathen, and were forbidden to build churches or buy land.[16] Also at the national Diet of 1648 after the election of the new King, the great Socinian magnate, George Niemirycz of Kijów, was not permitted to sign the Constitution, since he was an 'Arian.'[17] These and other similar occurrences were clear portents of what was destined soon to overwhelm what was left of the Minor Church.

[16] cf. Lengnich, *Geschichte*, vii, 13, 20, 65, 88.

[17] *loc. cit.* The later history of Niemirycz deserves to be recorded here. After his valiant championship of the Raków Socinians at the Diet in 1638, and his persistent advocacy of their cause at later Diets, he still continued for some years loyal to the Polish State. But when the government had so completely collapsed under the Swedish invasion that no Diet met for three years, and the King had fled from his kingdom, a notable number of the Ukrainian nobles, he among them, espoused the cause of Sweden as offering the best prospect of escape from Catholic religious oppression. When Sweden withdrew from the scene he joined the Cossacks, and enjoyed great influence among them. He now ardently espoused a scheme for a free South-Russian republic, to be federated with Poland; and as this seemed to him to offer hope of religious freedom which had been taken from them in Poland, he urged his Socinian brethren to unite with the Greek Church as he himself had done. (cf. Lewicki, *Socynjanie*, pp. 231–234.) To this end he published an appeal (no longer extant), to all Dissidents, but especially to Socinians, to follow his example and thus become full citizens of the new State. He emphasized the advantage of membership in one true and universal church rather than in a small sect without authority. Such an appeal, coming from one that had but lately been their chief champion, and at a time when many in the face of growing intolerance were beginning to waver or to return to the Catholic faith, seriously threatened the endurance of the Socinian cause. Samuel Przypkowski, therefore, promptly issued in both Polish and Latin a reply (*Responsio ad scriptum . . . Niemiricii*; printed in his *Opera* (Eleutheropolis, 1692), pp. 533–590, in which he discussed the grounds of the authority of the true Church, the necessity of using one's private judgment in religion, the errors in his author's reasoning, and the objectionable doctrines of the Greek Church. (cf. Chmaj, *Przypkowski*, pp. 58–62.) Events moved too fast for Niemiricz. Among those whose cause he had espoused and was trying to direct, suspicion arose that he meant to bring them again under the power of Poland, and while commanding a division of their army he was murdered by a mob of them in 1659.

Despite the confusion and ruin of the years of war, the Jesuits had never been diverted from the pursuit of their main purpose, the utter destruction of 'Arianism' in the Kingdom. The controversy that Cichowski had begun in 1641 [18] was not allowed to lapse or be forgotten. Schlichting, to be sure, no longer having access to a press, was unable to carry on his part in it, and after 1554 made but one more contribution; but Cichowski, safe from war's alarms in the seclusion of his college at Poznań, still poured forth a steady stream of attacks— nine in eight years—despite the difficulty of publishing in a time of chaos. By reiterating that 'Arians' had no legitimate claim to toleration, asserting the age-honored authority of the Roman Church, attacking the wickedness of the 'Arian' doctrines, urging that the national misfortunes of the time were divine punishments for the nation's toleration of wicked heresies, he caused these ideas in time to become, by sheer force of repetition, an accepted part of the national consciousness. With the ground thus long and carefully prepared, nothing was wanting but a favorable opportunity for consummating the long-delayed action. As soon, therefore, as the Swedes had cleared the country, as they had by the beginning of 1658, a council of the Senate was held at Warsaw, which decided that while amnesty should be granted to all others that had been guilty of treasonable action in the late war, the 'Arians,' who had been especially guilty, and were most abominable heretics besides, should upon pain of death either recant or else be banished from the country within a year. [19]

After an interval of over three years, the Diet met again in June, 1658, and at the instigation of the King's confessor and court preacher, the Jesuit father Karwat, it took up religious matters at the very beginning. In his sermon before the Diet Karwat urged the King now to fulfil the vow that he had made at Warsaw two years before, and the Diet to show its gratitude to God by deeds in exterminating the heretics. The King and the Diet were in a mood to comply readily, and a decree was therefore enacted against the 'Arians,' reaffirming an antiquated decree against heretics published by King Ladislas Jagiełło in 1424, and aimed especially at the Hussites. [20] The new decree called

---

[18] v. supra, p. 461.

[19] cf. Załęski, Jesuici, iii, 109; Biegeleisen, Aryanie, p. 490.

[20] cf. Morawski, Arjanie, p. 495. For the decree of 1424, cf. Volumina Legum, i, 38. It covered heresy in general, though that of the Hussites was particularly aimed at and specified. Though under Sigismund Augustus measures had been taken that practically

for capital punishment of any duly convicted of 'Arianism,' who would not renounce their faith; but as an act of clemency any such were granted three years within which to sell their estates and collect their debts, with possession of their homes and estates in the meantime. In the interval they were to hold no public worship nor perform any official duties.[21]

The decree was not passed without opposition, for there were still 'Arians' in the Diet. But immediately after the opening it had been proposed and agreed to that an 'Arian' is not a Dissident but a heretic, and as such may not sit in the Diet as a Deputy; and they were for excluding forthwith Iwanowicz, Cupbearer from Czerniechów. When he afterwards approached with others to do homage to the King by kissing the royal hand, he was denied unless he would turn Catholic. These things took place in the Senate; but later when the Deputies had withdrawn to their chamber, they voted that no 'Arian' might sit among them.[22] When it came to a vote on the decree, an 'Arian' Deputy, Tobias Iwański (or Iwanicki),[23] sought to block proceedings by expressing his disapproval, but this was disregarded as coming from one whose right to a voice was denied.[24]

---

nullified it, it had never been actually repealed; and it was susceptible of application to all Protestants as well as to 'Arians.'

[21] Original Polish text in *Volumina Legum*, iv, 238; also in Krzyżanowski, *Dawna Polska*, ii, 325 f; and in Morawski, *Arjanie*, p. 496 f. Latin version in Sandius, *Bibliotheca*, p. 248 f; Lubieniecius, *Historia*, p. 293 f; Krasinski, *Reformation*, ii, 397 f; Lauterbach, *Socinismus*, p. 471 f; Fock, *Socinianismus*, p. 229; Fischer, *Reformation*, ii, 376; Wallace, *Antitrin.*, iii, 582.

[22] cf. Krzyżanowski, *op. cit.*, ii, 325; Morawski, *op. cit.*, p. 497; Lengnich, *Geschichte*, v, 587.

[23] This lone brave champion of religious liberty and tolerance deserves to be remembered by his right name, as here given. By a palpable misreading of indistinct chirography, the name has usually been taken to be Szwański (so by Krasinski—corrected in the Polish translation—Fock, Szujski, Załęski, Wallace and others, or Żwański (Morawski). Query: whether Iwanowicz (Iwanowitz, Iwanowski) mentioned above is not another variant for the same person. His name appears in a document addressed in 1663 to Prince Michael Apafi of Transylvania by the Polish Unitarian refugees at Kolozsvár. cf. Ms no. 1663, III. f. in the Unitarian library there.

[24] Under an ancient custom in most European countries, unanimous consent was necessary to the passage of legislation, so that the objection of even a single member might defeat a proposed measure or dissolve the assembly. This was known as the *liberum veto*. It had first been invoked in Poland as recently as 1652, and in subsequent history was grossly abused, to the great damage of the country. The present instance has sometimes been spoken of as the only case in Polish history when it was disregarded; but, as said above, this was because Iwański, being an 'Arian,' was deemed to have no right to participate in proceedings at all.

The Socinians were struck well-nigh dumb by the passage of the decree, finding it hard to believe that its terms were meant quite seriously. Their members in the Diet sought support among the other Deputies, and appealed to the King, who was believed to be merciful, to revoke the sentence of banishment; but he replied that he was commanding, not arguing, and that they should come over to Catholicism as the only true faith. There were, however, not a few, even of the Catholics, who opposed the execution of the decree, and for a considerable time the authorities were reluctant to enforce it. To break down such opposition, and place the 'Arians' in the worst possible light, one of the Catholic nobility now put into circulation an anonymous tract of a score of pages which, instead of attacking them on the ground of their blasphemous heresies, as the decree had done, now changed the accusation and sought to pillory them as traitors who had been conspicuous in the recent wars by joining with the Swedes, Cossacks and Hungarians against their own country.[25] This tract had immense influence upon Polish minds, and greatly intensified their hatred of the 'Arians;' and it furnished the favorite materials for whatever *apologia* Poles later felt called upon to make for the crowning intolerance that blemished their history. It was largely based on the writer's experiences at Kraków during the Swedish occupation, and it charged that at Kraków the 'Arians' stood higher in Swedish favor than did the other Dissidents there, and were more faithful to the Swedish cause; that they took an oath of loyalty to the Swedish King; that the Governor employed eminent 'Arians' as his confidential secretaries, who composed his Polish proclamation to the people; that they encouraged and assisted in the Swedish invasion, and also induced Rákóczy to invade the country and enjoyed his favor; that 'Arians' fought with Swedes against the Poles and betrayed their plans, and rejoiced at Swedish

---

[25] *Przysługa Aryańska, która się Koronie Polskiey pod czas woyny Szwedzkiej przysłużyli. Wydana przez Szlachcica Polskiego pod ten czas z miasta Krakowskiego Obywatela* (The service of the Arians, which they rendered to the Polish Crown in time of the war with Sweden. Published by a Polish gentleman, at the time a citizen of the town of Kraków). Undated, but the date has generally been supposed to have been 1657. This however must be a mistake, for the text refers to the decree as already passed. Its intent was thus not to assist in the passage of the act but to support the enforcement of it. Two other titles are reported, of which little or nothing is known: *Zdrady Aryańskie* (Arian treason), and *Proditiones Arianorum*, of which the former may well be an inaccurate reproduction of the title given above, while the latter is doubtless a Latin version of one or the other. A reply was written by Schlichting in 1659, *Memoriale in causa Fratrum Unitariorum*, but it is not known to have been printed.

successes; that they reviled the King and blasphemed the Catholic religion, and were atheists and hypocrites who had been excluded from the Dissidents. Some of these charges were based on gossipy rumor, some were exaggerations, some were suspicions or misinterpretations, and all were naturally colored by prejudice and bitter hatred, and hence deserved critical examination. But as the Socinians had no press with which to reply, the charges being undenied were generally taken at face value.

When at length a vindication of their course could be published, it was too late to avert their fate.[26] In the defence at length prepared on their behalf, however, it was replied that in putting themselves under Swedish protection in Kraków, the 'Arians' did only what many other citizens of that province were also doing, Catholics and Protestants alike, when their own King and armies had left them with no protection, and there was no other way of escaping the fury of the Cossacks and Russians who were then mercilessly ravaging the land. Though all refugees were indeed required to swear fidelity to the King of Sweden,[27] they did not join in his plans nor take up arms against their country. They had kept faith with King Jan up to the moment of his flight, furnishing him supplies, fighting in his forces, losing many sons in battle, and being ever ready to die for him; nor had they given the Swedish Governor any help, except that one, of German birth, had sometimes been employed by him to write Latin letters for him. But many of the Socinians in other parts of the country, on the other hand, had never sworn allegiance to King Charles, but had borne arms against him with the rest; and many others had made their escape into Hungary or Silesia, as all would have done had it been possible. Even if some individuals acted otherwise, the whole Socinian community was not bound to answer for what they had done, and it was not fair to rouse suspicions and persecutions in the popular mind against them all.[28] Yet in spite of all that was said in defence, one still gets the impression that the Socinians were, in all the existing circumstances, somewhat deficient in complete loyalty. Of their unqualified love of their

[26] cf. *Vindiciae pro Unitariorum in Polonia Religionis Libertate, ab Equite Polono conscriptae* (by Stanislas Lubieniecki), in Sandius, *Bibliotheca*, pp. 265–296, especially pp. 291–296. Perhaps prepared in support of efforts to have the 'Arians' included in the amnesty under the treaty of Oliva.

[27] For the text of the oath required of the refugees at Kraków, cf. Czartoryski Ms 1657, p. 318.

[28] cf. *Vindiciae*, pp. 281–295.

country there can be no doubt; but when the existing government for twenty or thirty years, and their King for ten, had shown a steadily growing hostility to them and their faith, it is easy to understand why they may have been ready to believe that a change of ruler from Catholic to Protestant might improve their condition. Nevertheless, the exceptional fact in the whole matter is that while all the others that had for a time given their allegiance to Sweden were granted amnesty, the Socinians were denied it; or rather, that having already been banished from the Kingdom by the decree of 1658, they were unable to claim the amnesty secured under the treaty of Oliva in 1660.

This bitter little tract was perhaps published early in the summer of 1658, soon after the proclamation of the decree of banishment, and must have had immediate and strong effect, for early in September the King found it necessary to issue a mandate forbidding any violence or oppression of 'Arians,' and guaranteeing them in the appointed interval of three years peaceable possession of all their goods and enjoyment of all rights and privileges even as other citizens, except that of public worship.[29] For his zeal in purifying his realm of heresy King Jan was highly praised by Pope Alexander VII., who conferred upon him the title of *Rex orthodoxus*.[30] Undeterred by all that was happening, the Socinians, after three years' intermission during the wars, again held their synods in 1658 and 1659. The attendants must have been only a handful, and the meetings held in secrecy; but they continued to make plans, and even ordered the publication of two works by Crellius, and voted that Morzkowski's long delayed work on Ecclesiastical Polity be revised and prepared for the press.[31] At the Diet in March, 1659 the Jesuit Karwat again set the key in his opening Diet sermon, in which he urged that for the sake of peace and prosperity in the country they must resist all efforts to interfere with the state of religion, and not yield a hair from the decree already passed; and he also persuaded them to reduce the interval before banishment from three years to two.[32] The provision was annexed that the decree should not affect any

---

[29] cf. Czartoryski Ms 1657, p. 445; Morawski, *Aryanie*, p. 498.

[30] For the papal decree conferring this honor, cf. Mikołaj Zalaszowski, *Jus Regni Poloniae* (Poznań, 1697–1702), i, 59 f; Andrzej C. Załuski, *Epistolae Historico-familiares* (Brunsberga, 1709–'11), i, 69.

[31] cf. Szczotka, *Synody*, p. 96.

[32] cf. Krzyżanowski, *Dawna Polska*, ii, 326 f; Morawski, *Arjanie*, p. 499 f. Text of the law, *Volumina Legum*, iv, 272; Latin translation, Lubieniecius, *Historia*, p. 294; Lauterbach, *Socinismus*, p. 473; Fischer, *Reformation*, p. 377; Wallace, *Antitrin.*, iii, 582.

that had been converted to the Catholic Church, thus preventing any more from going over to the Reformed Church, as some of the more wealthy had already done. The fatal date was thus fixed at July 10, 1660, precisely two years from the passage of the decree. Lest there be any reluctance or failure to enforce it, however, Cichowski continued his campaign of attack upon the 'Arian' cause, issuing yet seven or eight works after the passage of the decree, in one of which he undertook the defence of those 'Arians' that had returned to the Catholic Church, and in another opposed Catholics in the Diet who favored patient indulgence to the 'Arians', and urged proceeding without hesitation to execute the decree.[33]

It was evident that there had been wide-spread lack of sympathy with the plan to banish the 'Arians,' and that (as has often happened in history, when laws were passed that did not command general approval) there might in some quarters be considerable opposition to seriously enforcing the decree. But when the Diet of 1659 had now confirmed the decree and stiffened its terms, the hopes of its victims grew steadily dimmer. They still kept trying, indeed, in influential quarters to win sympathy for their situation, but they now found themselves seriously driven to plan what should be done if all their efforts failed. Their predicament was more tragic than can readily be conceived. They must make the choice between forever leaving their native land, homes, possessions, life-time friends and kindred, to go out they knew not whither (for there was scarcely a country in all Europe where they could be sure of a welcome and of freedom from persecution), or on the other hand, for the sake of worldly advantage, abjuring their religious faith, violating their conscience, surrendering their honor and self-respect, and all hope of the spiritual freedom that they had enjoyed for a century. As for the humbler classes among them, there was little choice left: it was practically impossible for them to emigrate to another land. For themselves and their children they must perforce accept

---

[33] The works referred to were respectively: *Obrona zacnych y pobożnych ludzi którzy . . . do kościoła się s. katolickiego udali* (Defence of the worthy and pious folk that . . . have come over to the Holy Catholic Church), Kraków, 1660; and *Namowa do ich Mościów Panów koronnych, aby przy konstytucji przeciw Arjanów . . . statecznie stali i do egzekucji przystępowali* (A suggestion to the honorable gentlemen of the Diet to stand firmly by the law passed against the Arians, and proceed to execute it), 1661. The latter tract was answered from his place of exile by Przypkowski in his *Judicium sinceri et antiqui majorum moris retinentis*, etc., printed in his *Opera* (Eleutheropoli, 1692), pp. 435–450. Chmaj, *Przypkowski*, pp. 61–67.

baptism in the Catholic Church. Whatever faith they still secretly cherished in their own hearts, their posterity would live in a faith that they themselves had abhorred. Even the gentry had to choose between home comforts and associations, all worldly prospects and public honors, and going forth in their declining years to face privation, hardship and misery, not only for themselves but also for their wives and children. The ampler their possessions the more they must sacrifice in leaving them, and the greater temptation to compromise with conscience instead. Small wonder, then, that the greater part of the wealthier ones chose the easier alternative, while comparatively few chose a life in exile.[34] It stands recorded, however, that in not a few instances the wives and daughters remained stedfast even after their husbands or fathers had yielded.

Nearly a year before the decree of banishment was passed, the Swedes had evacuated Kraków, and the Socinians that had taken refuge there departed at the same time. Now that the country was again pacified, those that had come from the Palatinate of Kraków returned to their desolated estates, accompanied by their devoted pastor, Andrew Wiszowaty. Three prominent Socinians, however, who had enjoyed the Swedish governor's favor, followed in the Swedish train: Jonas Schlichting, whose life as one long since proscribed would not now be safe in Poland;[35] Christian Stegmann, and Stanislas Lubieniecki.[36] These hoped that the Swedish King, who had given them protection at Kraków, might be induced to have the Socinians included in the amnesty provided for in the treaty of peace. Hence Lubieniecki continued to live for a year and a half in close association with influential Swedes until, through the mediation of France, the treaty of peace between

---

[34] *Plures ditiorum . . . paucioribus.* cf. Lubieniecius, *Historia*, p. 297.

[35] The remaining four years of his life, incessantly busy with his pen, he spent in exile in Brandenburg. He died at Züllichau (Selchów) near the Polish border in 1661. His son Vespasian had been lately captured by Polish soldiers while carrying despatches, and though he was given the opportunity to save his life by renouncing his faith, he refused, and was hanged by General Czarniecki at Pińczów. cf. Sygański, *Nowy Sącz*, i, 158; Jonas Schlichting, *Opera* (Irenopoli, 1666), p. * * b; Krzyżanowski, *Dawna Polska*, ii, 319; Morawski, *Arjanie*, p. 641.

[36] As Lubieniecki could no longer return to Poland, he spent the rest of his life abroad, largely at Hamburg, chiefly engaged in literary occupations, though making many efforts in behalf of his exiled brethren. He died of mysterious poisoning in 1675 at Hamburg. Of his various published works the most valuable is his posthumous *Historia Reformationis Polonicae* (Freistadii, 1685), often referred to in the present work, which stands, though left unfinished, as the only history of Socinianism in Poland by a contemporary hand, and is hence of inestimable importance. A brief life of the author is prefixed to it.

Poland and Sweden was signed in May, 1660 at Oliva, a Cistercian abbey near Danzig. The treaty in its second article declared a general amnesty to all, of whatever state, condition or religion; and the Swedish commissioners later added a declaration that they understood that no one was to be excepted for having taken the part of the King of Sweden.[37] It very soon became evident, however, that the Polish government did not mean to extend amnesty to 'Arians'; doubtless holding that they were already outlawed and excluded from the body politic by the decree of 1658, the execution of which had merely been suspended until a later date.

The final months before the date fixed for their banishment were doubtless spent by the Socinians in anxious preparations for their departure; but there were still many that almost to the last were reluctant to abandon their comfortable life and personal connections, and were therefore wavering in religion. Evidently in the forlorn hope that perhaps the Catholics might somehow be persuaded that the doctrines of their opponents were less offensive than had been supposed, and might after all agree to toleration, these now urgently requested as a last resort that a friendly conference on religion might be arranged between the Catholics and the 'Arians.' The Bishop of Kraków gave his consent, and the distinguished Jan Wielopolski, one of the leading Senators of the Kingdom, in whose neighboring castle at Roznów Wiszowaty had twice sought refuge during the peasant uprising four years earlier,[38] offered his castle for the purpose.

Some of those that were invited to attend and participate were suspicious of a plot and therefore held aloof, some were dissuaded by their friends, some arrived too late; but Wiszowaty, disregarding any danger, appeared on the day appointed, and was received by the Castellan with enviable cordiality. The conference lasted through five days (March 11–16), and was attended by a score or more, in approximately equal numbers on each side.[39] Save for occasional brief interjections, Wiszowaty was the sole debater on the 'Arian' side; while the Catholics were represented first by the Provincial of the Bernardine monks, and later by Cichowski and another Jesuit from Kraków. Wielopolski pre-

[37] Text of the treaty in *Volumina Legum*, iv, 344–354. cf. Lubieniecius, *Historia*, pp. *3b–*4b, *7a–b; J. G. Boehmius, *Acta Pacis Oliviensis inedita* (Vratislaviae, 1763–'66).

[38] cf. *Anonymi epistola*, p. 244 f.

[39] cf. the narrative in Sandius, *Bibliotheca*, pp. 251–253; and an abbreviated summary of the discussions in Wengerscius, *Slavonia*, pp. 538–586, taken down by Andrew Lachowski, Socinian, under the pseudonym of Andrew Jovedecius.

sided, and as the priests refused to use Polish, the discussion was conducted in Latin, with dignity and in good spirit, and in strict academic form and close adherence to the canons of logic. The topics canvassed were, the Church as interpreter of Scripture, Ecclesiastical traditions, the infallibility of the Church, the eternal divinity of Christ, the Eucharist, infant baptism. Arguments were very acute; but the priests were no match for Wiszowaty, who single-handed often cornered them. One of them, on being asked by the Castellan what he thought of the debate, replied, 'If all the devils were to come out of hell, they could not defend their religion more strongly than this one man'.[40] The result that had been fondly hoped for was not attained, but it was admitted that the disposition of the Catholics was rendered milder toward their opponents; while on the other hand not a few that had been wavering in their religion were confirmed in their adherence to it. A few days later Wiszowaty was invited again to be Wielopolski's guest, when several days were spent in friendly conversation on religion; and he was urged to change his religion, and promised life-use of a fine estate, and a generous annuity from other magnates, but he remained stedfast rather than forfeit a clear conscience.[41]

[40] This conference has often been represented as a last despairing attempt to secure toleration by proving that the doctrines of the Socinians were after all not different in essentials from those of the Catholics; and as a pitifully weak willingness to compromise in the face of danger. There is nothing in the extant record of the debate to support this view. Wiszowaty was throughout direct, straightforward and unequivocal in his opposition to the views of his opponents.

[41] cf. Sandius, *op. cit.*, p. 253.

CHAPTER XXXVII

SOCINIAN EXILES SEEK TRANSYLVANIA. HEROIC LEADERSHIP OF ANDREW WISZOWATY

THE FINAL MONTHS before the date of the exile of the Socinians were full of confusion and anxiety for those that had still to dispose of their property before leaving the country. Poland had suffered frightful losses and ruin during the recent years of war, and money was scarce and high in value. Buyers took advantage of the necessities of the exiles and drove shrewd bargains. Very few were able to sell what they owned at any price, since the remaining inhabitants realized that property left behind must inevitably fall into their hands. Cases were reported where property valued at 1,000 thalers brought only 300 florins, and where values of 10,000 thalers realized only 8,000 florins. Many had to be content with a tenth, a fifteenth, or even a twentieth of a fair price. Some, trusting to the good faith of purchasers, accepted a mere promise to pay, only to be disappointed of this when a new decree forbade any one to have the least communication with the exiles, under penalty of confiscation of goods without recourse.[1] Hence even the friends that most pitied them dared give them no aid or comfort for fear of the law.

As the day for their departure drew near, the exiles from various places scattered in different directions, crossing the border at whatever point promised to be most convenient. How many were of the number can only be guessed. Probably there were only a few hundred families altogether. It was estimated that a thousand families, unable to emi-

---

[1] cf. Sandius, *Bibliotheca*, p. 254 f; Lubieniecius, *Historia*, p. 281 f, 296 f. Martin Adelt, *Historia de Arianismo olim Smiglam infestante* (Danzig, 1741), p. 30 f, relates a gruesome revenge taken upon one that sought to evade a promise of this sort. Two brothers Arciszewski of a family that had been patrons of the 'Arian' church at Śmigiel, disposed of their inheritance there to the Catholic proprietor, who bound himself by a secret contract to send them their money abroad at a stated time. When he paid no attention to repeated demands, they came to Warsaw disguised as Poles, with a troop of a hundred men. Having tracked the culprit down, they followed him out of town to near Śmigiel, where they attacked him, wreaked bloody vengeance, and made their escape over the border. As one of them was an officer in the Dutch army they escaped punishment. cf. Lauterbach, *Socinismus*, p. 407 f.

grate, were left behind in want; while others were shifting for themselves or were still wavering and in hiding with their friends.[2] Much
the largest company was composed of those that lived south of the
Vistula, where Socinians had been the most numerous. A train of more
than 380 of these, with 200 wagons,[3] made their way across the southern border toward Transylvania, where they had chosen Kolozsvár
(Clausenburg) for their future home.[4] Here they would be surrounded
by those of their own faith, in the Unitarian capital of the country, and
under the protection of laws that specifically gave toleration to the
Unitarians as one of the four religions formally recognized by the
government. The churches here had for nearly a century had friendly
intercourse with those in Poland, had drawn teachers, ministers, and
even a Bishop from there, and had often sent their sons thither to supplement their education. Hardly had the caravan crossed the Carpathians into Hungary, where they planned to take breath under the
protection of a famous Protestant noble, Count Francis Rhédei [5] at
Huszt in Máramoros County, when a roving band of Imperial soldiers
(secretly incited, it was rumored, by enemies in Poland) fell upon them
unexpectedly, pitilessly robbed them of their money, plundered the few
goods they had been able to rescue from their homes, seized their provisions for the journey, and stripped them of the very clothes they
wore.[6] This calamity, and the threat of new wars just beginning there,
led the greater part of them to retrace their steps and seek shelter in
East Prussia, which since the treaty of Oliva was no longer subject to
Poland, but under the rule of the Elector of Brandenburg. The rest,
with minds resolute in face of danger, persevered in their journey,
joined perhaps by others that had first been given refuge at Késmárk
in Szepes (Zips) County by the Governor, Count Stephen Thököly.[7]

[2] cf. Lubieniecius, *Historia*, p. 283 f.

[3] cf. Lubieniecius, *op. cit.*, p. 297, quoting from a letter of the exiles at Kreuzburg, June,
1661. The author himself elsewhere says (p. 272), "a wretched band of over 500." So also
Anonymi epistola, p. 255.

[4] The principal sources for the story of this company are Lubieniecius, *Historia*, pp.
271 ff, 282, 297 f; *Anonymi epistola*, pp. 255–257, supplemented by Hungarian authorities cited below.

[5] When a certain fanatical English minister declared that this hospitable act deserved
an anathema as heretical, the Count promptly replied that the opinion of the Englishman
himself seemed to deserve it more for its cruelty. cf. Bock, *Socinianismus*, p. 67.

[6] cf. *Anonymi epistola*, p. 255; Lubieniecius, *op. cit.*, pp. 271 f, 282, 298; Josephus
Benkö, *Transsilvania* (Vindobonae, 1778), ii, 582, speaks of only 50 being thus plundered.

[7] The *Anonymi epistola* latinizes this name as Tekeli, which has sometimes been mistaken for the well-known Hungarian Teleki.

Thus in 1661 a company of about 200 at length reached their destination at Kolozsvár,[8] whither Prince János Kemény had granted them safe-conduct in January. The brethren at Kolozsvár, though they had themselves recently been ravaged and plundered in repeated incursions of Turks and Tatars, who had exacted almost all their money, and plundered even the funds of their churches, when they heard of the approach of the exiles and of their wretched condition, went out many miles on the road to meet them with wagons and supplies of provisions and clothing, gave them shelter in their own homes, and did everything for them that brotherly love could suggest. But the pilgrims' troubles were not yet at an end. The severe weather there was especially hard on them, and a plague that was just then prevalent attacked them, worn as they were with their hardships, with the most fatal results, and out of their whole number left barely thirty surviving. At long last their situation began to improve. Two years later, in 1563, the new Prince, Michael Apafi, granted them the right to stay in the country,[9] and they made arrangements for permanent settlement, in which others doubtless joined them latter on. They were granted the right of citizenship, and a separate church in Inner Monostor street was provided for them to worship in their own tongue. As they dispersed in the country, three other congregations were organized. That at Bethlen lasted until 1745, though those at Ádámos and Bánffy Hunyad were short-lived.[10] They were long poverty-stricken, and as late as 1710 they were forced to appeal to sympathetic friends whom they had left behind in Poland for aid in relieving their various necessities.[11] During this period of pressing want some of them thought to better their condition by returning to Poland, and collected funds to that end; but when the attempt was made in 1711, the sight of their

[8] This date is given by Ferencz Kanyaró, *Unitáriusok Magyarországon*, etc. (Unitarians in Hungary) Kolozsvár, 1891, p. 223.

[9] cf. the petition in their behalf presented to the Prince, Ms 1663. III. f, in library of the Unitarian College, Kolozsvár.

[10] cf. Sándor Székely, *Unitária Vallás Történeti Erdélyben* (History of the Unitarian faith in Transylvania), Kolozsvár, 1839, p. 208 f; Benkö, *op. cit.*, p. 583; Kanyaró, *op. cit.*, p. 222.

[11] In response to this appeal Achacy Taszycki, probably a grandson of one of the same name who was proprietor of Lucławice in the time of Socinus, sent from Königswalde in Brandenburg, where he was living in exile, donations amounting to 24,000 thalers, intended as a permanent fund for the church; and Dutch sympathizers sent a gift of over 5,000 florins. cf. *Sprawozdanie*, pp. 173–175; Domokos Simén, 'Origo piarum fundationum apud Polonos Claudiopoli,' etc. *Keresztény Magvető*, xi (1876), 335.

ruined homes, and the religious hatred that the inhabitants still cherished, discouraged them from carrying out the plan.[12]

The church of the Socinian exiles at Kolozsvár, after loyally sustaining their cause for nearly four generations, at length succumbed to the inevitable fate of any small foreign colony in a strange land. The original exiles died, their children intermarried with Transylvanians and gradually scattered, and they eventually forgot their mother tongue and became absorbed into the surrounding population. They kept up occasional correspondence with the brethren in other lands, and sometimes sent delegates to the synods in Silesia or Prussia that attempted to hold them all together. They maintained worship in the Polish language, and had Polish ministers. But it became increasingly difficult to secure ministers, and their congregations slowly dwindled. Before their last Polish minister died in 1792 his congregation had already coalesced with that of the local Unitarian church. Their descendants, however, gratefully remembered the Christian kindness of their hosts. Some of them rose to high position in public life; and one of them, Pál Augustinowicz, who had been Judge in the Royal Hungarian Supreme Court, as well as Chief Curator of the Unitarian Church, when he died in 1837 left the Church a bequest of 100,000 florins, which long amounted to more than all the rest of the church funds put together.[13]

During all this period of tragic affliction, one able, devoted and heroic figure stands out before all his brethren. Their faithful teacher, wise counselor, unfailing comforter, devoted friend, bold champion, intrepid leader from the beginning to the end was Andrew Wiszowaty;[14] and his active career so strikingly embodies and expresses the character and spirit of the surviving Socinian group that he deserves more than this passing mention. He was born in 1608 near the Prussian border in Lithuania, where his father was for a time Vice-Starost under Christopher Morsztyn, whose daughter had married Faustus Socinus. He was of noble family, and his mother was Socinus's only daughter, Agnes. After his early schooling with Morsztyn's sons he was sent to

---

[12] cf. Kanyaró, *Unitáriusok*, p. 224.

[13] cf. Áron Buzogány, 'Augustinowicz Pál életrajza,' etc. (Biography of P. A.), *Keresztény Magvető*, iv (1864, 11–36.

[14] cf. *Anonymi epistola exhibens vitae ac mortis Andreae Wissowatii . . . historiam* (1680), appended to Sandius, *Bibliotheca*, pp. 221–263; Ludwik Chmaj, 'Andrzej Wiszowaty jako działacz a myśliciel religijny' (A. W. as religious doer and thinker), *Reformacja w Polsce*, i (1921), 189–207, 284–308.

Raków, where he enjoyed the privilege of living in the family of Jan Crellius, minister of the Raków church, and of being under the stimulating influence of Smalcius, Stoiński and Moskorzowski, who were members of the community, and of Ruar, who was Rector of the College. He thus advanced rapidly. A public career had been planned for him; but his teachers so strongly urged that the first male descendant of Socinus should devote himself to the ministry, that his parents consented. After finishing at Raków, he served for a year as tutor to the son of a Catholic magnate and then, with a subsidy from the Church, was sent abroad to continue his studies. He had Ruar, Niemirycz and other prominent Socinians for his companions to Holland, where he studied first at Leiden, and later at the new Remonstrant seminary at Amsterdam, where he heard famous teachers and formed intimate acquaintance with the liberal theologians, Episcopius and Courcelles. Here he met an old friend, Arciszewski, a Socinian from Śmigiel, who was leading a military expedition to Brazil, where Holland was then trying to found a colony, and who invited him to join him, with the hope of promoting his faith in a fresh field. The temptation was great, but he resisted it, and continued his travels, first visiting England, where he met some distinguished men, and then traveled widely in France, heard lectures at the Sorbonne in Paris, and formed acquaintance with such men as Grotius, Gassendi and Mersenne. On all occasions, privately with individuals or publicly in universities, he was ready to defend or promote his faith.

At length, after six profitable years abroad, he returned home in 1637 and became tutor to a young nobleman. The fall of Raków occurred at this period, but unterrified by this he appeared before the Diet at Warsaw the next year and fearlessly defended his faith in the Chamber of Deputies, discussing its articles with both Catholics and Protestants, as he never shrank from doing whenever opportunity offered. The next year he again went abroad, visiting Germany, Holland and France as traveling tutor, and renewing his acquaintance with distinguished men whom he had previously met. After this preliminary period, protracted for more than a dozen years, Wiszowaty finally returned to Poland prepared to enter upon his work as a minister. Never, perhaps, had a young man among the Socinians entered upon his career so richly furnished for it, nor had one ever faced a longer and heavier succession of calamities than were to fall to his lot, or confronted them with more devoted consecration or a spirit more unafraid.

His first charge was brief, but must have been phenomenally successful; for the Calvinist proprietor on whose land his church at Piaski stood soon ordered it closed, out of fear, she said, lest all the people of the place should be converted to his religion. He was next appointed assistant minister of a church in the Ukraine, where before the year was out he had news that his father had been murdered by night robbers on his estate in the Podgórze; [15] but he at once buried his grief in work, and warmly commended himself to his people and his patron. In 1644 he was given charge over four important congregations in Volhynia. It was at the time when the Catholic reaction, encouraged by the destruction of Raków, was rapidly gathering force, and was attacking the Socinians in their new centre in the Ukraine. As was related in a previous chapter, the Socinian patrons in this region were haled into court and heavily fined for fostering 'Arianism' on their domains, their churches were ordered destroyed, and their worship was forever abolished. [16] Nevertheless Wiszowaty kept on with his work there in face of continued opposition from his adversaries. Priests often haled him into the local courts, though these evidently favored him, and once he was even brought before the supreme Tribunal at Lublin, where he barely escaped banishment from the country for conducting religious worship; so that he had already resolved to remove to Holland, had not the brethren dissuaded him, so highly did they value his counsel and help.

Having fortunately escaped these threatening dangers, he now married the daughter of one of the leading ministers in 1648. It was a year of great disturbance in Church and State. Feeling was still high over Schlichting, who had been proscribed; a new King had just come to the throne; and the Cossack war was about to break out. At this juncture the Synod transferred Wiszowaty to the important congregation that had had to remove from Lublin to Siedliska, and had just lost its minister. He was barely settled there when the congregation scattered in fright before the invading Cossacks, and he with his family and many of his people sought safety in East Prussia, where he spent the winter, not in idleness but in busily ministering to three congregations near Danzig, preaching three times a week, and administering the sacrament in Polish to those that used that language. When the storm of war had passed in the spring, he returned to Lublin, gathered

---

[15] cf. *Anonymi epistola*, p. 235; Morawski, *Arjanie*, pp. 155–159.
[16] *v. supra*, p. 458 f.

his scattered flock, and went on as before. But not for long, for within the year the Synod again transferred him to Radostów to minister for three years to what was left of the church at Raków near by. Diligent in his calling as ever, besides his regular duties he thrice a week held meetings for brethren coming from Raków, which on fast-days lasted all day. It was not long before the growth of his congregation roused the hostility of a neighboring priest, who tried with threats of danger to frighten him away. When this plan failed, trumped-up charges against him and his people were laid before the Diet at Warsaw, and he and his leading members were cited to defend themselves there. Before they could answer the summons, the matron of the church died, her estate fell into Catholic hands, and the Socinians were deprived of their place of worship. Wiszowaty then removed to the Podgórze and became minister at Rąbkowa, close by the place where his father had met his death and his mother still lived. Here he was to pass the last eight active years of his broken and troubled ministry. Besides the care of his own flock, he was appointed to supervise that at Lucławice, and he also ministered to shut-ins in another village in the vicinity where he went to hold services, despite the constant opposition of Catholic neighbors. Such leisure as these occupations left he occupied with his pen, annotating the whole New Testament,[17] making a Polish translation of the Psalms in verse for church use, together with numerous hymns. The Synod also appointed him to write an answer to Cichowski's 'Thirty Reasons why self-respecting men should abominate the Arian Church'; [18] but in the disorders that soon followed, the manuscript perished with the rest of his books.

The two years of anarchy and desolation in Poland, lasting from the capture of Warsaw by the Swedish forces to their evacuation of Kraków, and their devastating effect upon the churches in Little Poland, have been spoken of in the preceding chapter,[19] and need not be reviewed here further than to say that the one that gathered the people together when the peasants had risen and in their drunken fury were sweeping on ready to pillage or burn everything and to murder

[17] His commentary on the Acts, James and Jude were published in the second volume of Wolzogen's works in the *Bibliotheca Fratrum Polonorum*. The others remained unpublished.

[18] *Trzydzieści przyczyń*, etc. He also wrote several other works in reply to Cichowski, but they remained unpublished. cf. Bock, *Antitrinitar.*, i, 1026 f.

[19] cf. *supra*, p. 471 f.

every one in their way; that guided them through the bitter cold of a winter night across the Vistula to a refuge at Czarków; that so long as they could stay there gathered the fugitives together again from all directions and kept their spirits strong by daily religious services, as their custom was, both before morning light and during the day; that when danger pressed close again led the company to Kraków as the safest place for them, and obtained from the commanding general permission for them to enjoy his protection; that once again, when safe, made it his first care to establish the customary offices of religion as their greatest solace in adversity, observing as usual their daily prayers, as well as their regular fasting and church discipline and the Lord's Supper; that when Transylvanian forces entered Kraków arranged religious services for the many Unitarians among them in a language that they could understand; and that at last, when the country was again at peace, at once returned to his station in the foot-hills with its wasted fields and ruined homes, and set about his work again as though nothing had happened, visiting those whom he could find, and writing letters to those that were scattered, and starting to rebuild his ruined work from the foundations—that one was the heroic Socinian minister, Andrew Wiszowaty. Was ever a Christian minister braver in danger, wiser in disaster, more resolute under discouragement, more devoted to his calling?

In the few months that elapsed between his return to his station and the publishing of the decree of banishment, Wiszowaty could accomplish little toward reviving his work, though he did that little with his accustomed diligence. At a time when many, shrinking from the miseries of exile, looked first to their own safety, abandoning their own cause and deserting to the Catholic camp or to that of Calvin, he remained unshaken, and performed his duties as before, heedless of the dangers and plots to which he was daily exposed. And when new orders were issued by the King, strictly forbidding the 'Arians', on pain of imprisonment, to meet for religious worship, even then he did not shrink from the duties of his office; for when the proprietor of the estate on which his church stood dared not allow further use of it, he did not hesitate to invite his people to meet for worship in his own home in a neighboring village, to which some came openly, others under cover of darkness, while he went in person to confirm in their faith yet others that could not or dared not come at all. Thus he held almost daily worship in his home, sustaining courage in face of threatening danger. His final service to his cause, in the debate with the Catholics in the castle at Roznów, was mentioned above.[20]

Before the final day for exile arrived, Wiszowaty, forewarned of plots being made against him, anticipated the time and withdrew with his family across the border into Silesia. Here he stayed for half a year, occupied as ever in serving the religious needs of those that had fled thither. Then as winter drew on, and the country had grown somewhat more quiet, he stole back into Poland, where some of the brethren, and especially widows and orphans who had lacked the means to remove, had remained. Not a few of these, when they heard of his coming, flocked to him; and as long as he stayed he gave them such counsel, encouragement and help as he could. All this exposed him to constant danger, which might have cost him his life had he been discovered; so that advised by his friends he again left the country and crossed into northern Hungary, where he spent the summer at Késmárk with an old friend, a Scottish physician named John Patterson, who had been a resident of Poland, but had left it for the same reason as himself.[21] As many Socinians were believed still to be lying concealed in the country, the Diet in the spring of 1661 passed a third decree, requiring all officers and magistrates to enforce the decree against them.[22] This however did not deter Wiszowaty from making another visit to the brethren the following winter, though again at the risk of his life, that he might remind them of their duty and confirm them in their religion, especially women whose husbands had now apostasized. In the spring he returned to Késmárk, where he stayed the year through, since there no longer seemed any hope of his being able to accomplish anything in Poland. For at the Diet that summer (1662) a yet more stringent law was passed.[23]

Seeing that there were many in the country that were ignoring the severity of the law, it was declared that it applied to all women as well,

---

[20] cf. *supra*, p. 481 f.

[21] cf. *Anonymi epistola*, p. 256.

[22] As a final effort the Socinians sought the intervention of friendly members of the Diet in their behalf, and even appealed to the King to take pity on the sufferings of so many noted families. cf. Załęski, *Jesuici*, iii, 110; Kochowski, *Annales*, ii, 505. Text of the decree in *Volumina Legum*, iv, 323; Krzyżanowski, *Dawna Polska*, ii, 327 f; Morawski, *Arjanie*, p. 501 f; Latin trans. in Lubieniecius, *Historia*, p. 294 f; Krasinski, *Reformation*, ii, 404; Lauterbach, *Socinismus*, p. 475 f; Fischer, *Reformation*, ii, 378 f; Wallace, *Antitrin.*, iii, 583.

[23] cf. *Volumina Legum*, iv, 389 f; Krzyżanowski, *Dawna Polska*, ii, 331 f.

even to wives of men that had accepted the Catholic faith but continued to live with 'Arian' wives, and to any that kept 'Arian' servants, or corresponded with 'Arian' ministers, or allowed their children to be taught 'Arian' errors, or aided 'Arians' in any way, etc. All such were subject to confiscation of property, the half to go to the informer. To give this law the more certain effect, all of any standing whose names were known were now proscribed, without any hearing, and their names were publicly read and posted at Warsaw, including even women, widows and young girls, without exception, or the indulgence of brief delay granted in case of any that were aged, infirm or ill.[24] As a triumphant finale to his twenty years' polemic against the 'Arians,' Cichowski now celebrated the centenary of the Society of Jesus in Poland by publishing a jubilant commemorative volume.[25]

The indefatigable Wiszowaty did not even now sit down in idleness in a quiet retreat at Késmárk. He ministered to those within reach and kept up correspondence with the scattered exiles, considering the while where he should now go. Both Transylvania and lower Hungary attracted him as promising fields of service to the churches there, and he even went to Kolozsvár for a short time to learn the difficult Hungarian language.[26] But at just this time a messenger came to him from a company of exiles at Kreuzburg in Silesia, summoning him to attend an important synod there, at which plans for the future were to be considered. He at once responded, and hastening through Poland, bristling with dangers for him, presented himself, with results for his future and his cause that will soon be related.

While the little company of surviving fugitives were getting settled in Transylvania, the brethren remaining in Poland were concerned in making plans for the future of their cause. They had no idea where it might find another home, but they had no mind to let it perish for want of care. They therefore met in a synod held in greatest secrecy in 1662 at some place not recorded, but doubtless near the Silesian border. It was the last Socinian synod in Poland.[27] They were concerned for the early publication of a work in defence of religious

---

[24] cf. Lubieniecius, *Historia*, p. 295.

[25] *Triumphus sanctissimae et aeternum adorandae Trinitatis, de Socinistis, vulgo Arrianis.* (Cracoviae, 1662.)

[26] His name appears among those signed to the petition to Prince Apafi and dated March 7, 1663, to which reference has been made above.

[27] cf. Szczotka, *Synody*, p. 97 f; Bock, *Socinianismus*, p. 61 f.

liberty.[28] Besides, now that their history threatened to be approaching its term, they were more than ever anxious to have that also committed to writing, and this duty as well was laid upon Przypkowski at the same time, while all the brethren were requested to assist him in collecting materials. More pressing obligations would seem constantly to have interfered with this one, of which he was finally reminded again by the synod at Kreuzburg in 1663.[29] They also authorized Schlichting to publish his commentaries on the New Testament (Amsterdam, 1666). Seweryn Morsztyn and his son were appointed to stay on in Poland and have a care for the brethren, which was faithfully done until 1668 or later; [30] and a minister was appointed to serve the exiles in Silesia, and another to look after the exile congregations in Prussia, and a third to go to Holland to try to bring about a union with the Remonstrants, and on the way to visit brethren scattered about in Silesia and Brandenburg, and two more to go to minister to brethren at Mannheim on the Rhine. Finally, still with a view to an indefinite future, they charged two of the ministers to preserve and continue the records of the synods.[31]

[28] The writing of such a work had first been delegated to Przypkowski as early as 1627, but as he had repeatedly postponed it, it was finally done by Lubieniecius: the eloquent and able *Vindiciae pro Unitariorum in Polonia religionis libertāte, ab Equite Polono conscriptae*, appended to Sandius, *Bibliotheca*, pp. 267–296.

[29] At the synods of 1643 and 1644 the matter was taken out of his hands and entrusted to Pastorius, though with no better result. cf. Szczotka, *Synody*, p. 84 f. Whether Przypkowski, being already over seventy, ever actually performed this task seems doubtful, though it was later reported that his manuscript was destroyed by fire when he fled from Poland. cf. Bock, *Antitrinitar.*, i, 682. At all events, the history was at last undertaken by Lubieniecius in exile at Hamburg about 1668, though it was only half done when he met his tragic death in 1675. This was at length published in 1685 as the *Historia Reformationis Polonicae*, so often cited in the present work.

[30] cf. Bock, *op. cit.*, i, 510 f.

[31] cf. Szczotka, *Synody*, p. 97 f; Bock, *op. cit.*, i, 429, 582, 649, 1009, 252; *id.*, *Socinianismus*, p. 62. These synod records in two large manuscript volumes were in Bock's hands before the middle of the eighteenth century, and extensively used by him in his writings here cited; but they have disappeared and eluded all search hitherto. He unfortunately did not live to publish the history of Polish Socinianism as he had intended. cf. his *Historia Antitrinitariorum*, i, preface and pp. 1–4; and his *Historia Socinianismi Prussici*, preface.

CHAPTER XXXVIII

SOCINIAN EXILES AT KREUZBURG, MANNHEIM AND
FRIEDRICHSTADT AND IN BRANDENBURG. DEVELOP-
MENT OF SOCINIANISM IN EAST PRUSSIA AND DANZIG

WHILE THE COMPANY of exiles that set out for Transylvania was
doubtless the largest of those that left Poland, their number
was soon so greatly reduced by misfortune and disease that
but few survived to carry on. Quite the most important group, therefore, and the most influential on the history of their movement, was
that which for more than ten years sojourned at Kreuzburg in Silesia.[1]
This was a convenient place for the exiles to stop, take breath, and form
their plans, being but a dozen miles from the border; so that they could
easily return from here to settle their affairs, and the ministers could
secretly go back to visit their members, or be visited by them. Antitrinitarians had been known here a full ninety years before,[2] and for
the better part of a century the Polish Brethren had received recruits
from Silesia, of whom several reached high standing among their
ministers;[3] while in the recent years Socinians had fled from the dangers of the Swedish war in Poland and sought the protection of Duke
George of Liegnitz, whose territory, though he was a Protestant, lay
in the domain of the Austrian Emperor.[4] When the first band of refugees reached Kreuzburg in 1660, they were ordered to leave the city
within three days, and a few did so; but most stayed and addressed to
the Duke a petition for leave to stay longer, not with a view to permanent settlement, but to see whether the sentence against them in
Poland might not yet be modified, and to save what they could of their
property, and quietly look about for a place to settle.[5] Their petition

---

[1] cf. Theodor Wotschke, 'Die Polnischen Unitarier in Kreuzburg,' *Correspondenzblatt des Vereins für Geschichte der evangelischen Kirche Schlesiens*, xii (1911), 1–28.

[2] cf. Wotschke, 'Die Reformation in Kosten,' *Correspondenzblatt*, etc., ix (1905), 179, 183.

[3] cf. Ludwik Chmaj, *Ślązący wśród Braci Polskich* (Silesians among the Polish Breth-ren), Katowice, 1936.

[4] At this time the clergy of the Bohemian Brethren at Leszno (Lissa) did their utmost to have Socinian fugitives refused admission to the country. cf. Wotschke, *Kreuzburg*, p. 12.

[5] Text of the petition in Wotschke, *Kreuzburg*, pp. 23–26.

was warmly supported by Prince Bogusław Radziwiłł, formerly their fellow-countryman, but now in the service of the Elector of Brandenburg as Governor of Prussia. The desired indulgence was granted for three months, on condition that they furnish a list of their families, and abstain from any propaganda and from holding public worship. The inhabitants, who the year before had suffered from a great conflagration, were sympathetic and helpful; the Lutheran ministers, whose public worship they attended, were kind; [6] their domestic worship was not interfered with; and they were granted a special place to bury their dead. Their minister during the first few months was Andrew Wiszowaty, who was succeeded by Christopher Crellius.

When their leave had expired, and there was no complaint against them, they continued to stay on. They were evidently in sore need, for in June, 1661, twenty-six of them, nearly all bearing the names of noblemen, addressed an elaborate letter to the Remonstrant churches in Holland, setting forth at length the long history and the wide reach of their misfortunes, and their present desperate need, and humbly beseeching for generous relief. They related that their stay at Kreuzburg was precarious and liable at any time to be cut short. Though the most of their company were of noble birth, many had not enough to live from. Some had been officials in the State, others had lived from the rentals of their own estates, and some had managed the estates of others; but all these sources had now been cut off. The ministers were in great destitution, and some of them were aged and enfeebled by their long misfortunes. Their craftsmen, being foreigners, were not permitted to follow their trades. Their very speech was a hindrance. All in all their situation was most pitiable. Even if they were deemed to be in error as to their beliefs, it was for conscience' sake rather than subscribe to the opinions of the Pope; and this should commend them even to those that disagreed with their views, especially as to mysteries beyond human understanding. Forty years ago they had offered a refuge in Poland to the Remonstrants when they in their turn had been exiles for conscience, and they now appealed for like treatment for themselves.[7] This letter, dated June 17, 1661, was at once entrusted to the Rev. Christopher Crellius, son of the celebrated Raków professor,

[6] cf. Lubieniecius, *Historia*, p. 299.

[7] Ms of the original, with Dutch translation, in the Remonstrant Library, Rotterdam, 529 g. no. 2; printed as chap. xviii. of Lubieniecius, *Historia*.

who bore a confidential letter of the same date,[8] and in due time delivered it to the Rev. Jan Naeranus (van der Neer), Remonstrant minister at Oudewetering (Oudewater), whose father Samuel had visited Ruar at Danzig thirty years before,[9] and had had a long and intimate correspondence with him. He in turn had the letter translated into Dutch and forwarded to all the Remonstrant ministers.[10] From Holland Crellius went on to England, where the Socinians had long had sympathetic friends and correspondents. There he seems to have had only moderate success in collecting funds,[11] but from the brethren in Holland the response was generous. After a year, as the number of exiles at Kreuzburg was diminishing, and those in East Prussia were increasing, remittances were made to the latter, and by them were carefully distributed to the scattered brethren in need. A careful record was kept, and a due report was rendered to the generous givers. The brethren at Kreuzburg expressed their heartfelt appreciation upon receipt of the first gift in 1662 (not without a note of disappointment that it was only 2,200 thalers, and that no more could be confidently expected); but the gifts kept coming on for three years as the condition of the exiles was more fully realized, and in the end they amounted to ten or twelve thousand thalers. When in 1665 the aid was at an end, the Synod in Prussia voted a formal letter of thanks for the generous gifts, adding that 'it is the more grateful and acceptable to us for the reason that, though you differ from us in certain opinions about religion, this did not detract from nor lessen your benevolence to us.' [12]

In the meantime, while these hard days were passing, the members of the Kreuzburg company were gradually slipping away. Some of them found new homes in the neighboring Principalities of Oppeln and Ratibor, whose owner, the Queen of Poland, allowed them to settle on her hereditary territories. Some dispersed through other parts of Silesia, or in Brandenburg. Yet more removed to East Prussia, where

---

[8] cf. Ms 529, Remonstrant Library, Rotterdam.

[9] cf. Ruar, *Epistolae*, p. 129.

[10] *ibid*.

[11] cf. his long and interesting letter to Naeranus from London, July 28, 1662; Ms 1784 in the Remonstrant Library, Rotterdam. Some funds were collected in London by the Unitarian philanthropist, Thomas Firmin, of whom more will be said in a later division. cf. Stanisław Kot, 'Oddziaływanie Braci Polskich w Anglii' (Reaction of the Polish Brethren in England), *Reformacja w Polsce*, vii (1936), 235–242.

[12] For the interesting correspondence connected with this whole matter, cf. Remonstrant Library, Rotterdam, Mss 527 and 1455, and Amsterdam University Library, Remonstrant collection, Mss N 78 a-k, N 102 a-b.

the confident hope was entertained that the Elector would allow them to live in security. Some had already removed to Mannheim on the Rhine, where there seemed to be good promise; so that when a synod was held at Kreuzburg in 1663, with delegates present from all quarters, Wiszowaty, who had been summoned to come from Kolozsvár, was appointed to remove thither to look after them. The leadership of the whole Church was given to Przypkowski, and he removed ere long to East Prussia, where he oversaw the distribution of the aid that the friends abroad were now asked to send thither; and Iwański was appointed one of the ministers to the church at Kolozsvár.[13] Still hovering between life and death, the churches now began to make more determined efforts than ever to ensure their continued existence. Correspondence was maintained with all the scattered groups; the education of a new generation of ministers was planned; the publication of needed books was ordered. Only one more synod was held at Kreuzburg. But three noble families remained there in 1669, and the Austrian government at Vienna now announced that even these might no longer be tolerated.[14] They asked the new King of Poland, Michael Wiśniowiecki, to intercede for them, and further indulgence was granted. But a traveling Jesuit discovered them and demanded their expulsion, and the Duke found himself reluctantly forced to send them away.[15] They left Kreuzburg in March, 1671, and apparently went to East Prussia, where their old pastor, Christopher Crellius, after returning from England and holding a short pastorate of the exiles at Friedrichstadt (see below), was now minister of a little congregation at Kąsinowo (Andreaswalde). Yet some still remained secretly in Silesia, to whom Crellius went from time to time to visit and administer the Lord's Supper. It was while on such a pastoral visit in the winter of 1680 that death overtook him.[16]

Next, geographically, to the company of exiles at Kreuzburg were a few scattered groups here and there in the Neumark of Brandenburg. The population here was more or less mixed, and many Poles had long lived here. A few Socinian communities had long existed here, and though not legally tolerated were connived at under the tolerant government of the Great Elector Friedrich Wilhelm, who needed colonists

---

[13] cf. Wotschke, *Kreuzburg*, p. 14.   [14] *id. op.*, p. 19.

[15] Since the Emperor Leopold I. had two months before proscribed them throughout the whole Empire.

[16] cf. Bock, *Antitrinitar.*, i, 158 f; and for all the above, Wotschke, *op. cit.*

and granted them admission and protection. Perhaps the earliest of these was at Meseritz, east of Frankfurt on the Polish border, where an Anabaptist movement had developed into a Socinian one. This movement existed long before it had a regular minister or its own place of worship, and held its meetings now at Meseritz, now at Bobelwitz on the Polish side of the border, drawing its members from both communities. It was patronized by several important noble families.[17] Other centres of Socinianism of which we find mention were Selchów (Züllichau), where Schlichting died in 1661 worn out by his constant labors and the persecutions of many years; also Möstchen, Griesel, Neuendorf, Landsberg, and Königswalde, all within some fifty miles eastward from Frankfurt on the Oder. In most of these the brethren, following a characteristic Socinian custom, gathered for simple domestic worship in the manor-house of one of the patrons. Of these centres records are scanty; but the one that survived longest was that of Königswalde. A considerable group of Socinians lived here after the exile from Poland, and had for their minister Johannes Preuss. Toward the end of the century he was succeeded by his son-in-law, Samuel Crellius, son of the Christopher Crellius above mentioned, who had been born in the very year of the exile.[18] After studying in England and Holland and being ordained in 1687 he established his home at Königswalde, where he ministered to the congregation for some forty years.

After the death of the Great Elector, the clergy began to urge the extermination of the Arian heresy. Crellius met the demand with a little book arguing that both Lutherans and Calvinists ought to tolerate them and admit them to the Lord's Supper.[19] For some time this re-

---

[17] cf. Theodor Wotschke, 'Die Unitarische Gemeinde in Meseritz-Bobelwitz,' *Zeitschrift der Historischen Gesellschaft für die Provinz Posen*, xxvi (1911), 161–223.

[18] When Crellius later sought admission to the new University of Halle, he was refused on account of his religion (cf. *Hessische Hebopfern*, i, 130, quoted by G. W. Götten, *Das jetztlebende gelehrte Europa*, Braunschweig, 1735–'40, iii, 281); and he was also denied access to the shelves of the Bodleian Library at Oxford, lest like Sandius before him he should there find material to adorn his cause (cf. Bock, *Antitrinitar.*, i, 164 f).

His two sons, Stephen and Joseph, were admitted to the celebrated Joachimsthal gymnasium in Berlin; but after two years they were told that if they were to stay longer they would have to conform to the Reformed Church, which they were unwilling to do. cf. Johannes Sembrzycki, 'Die polnischen Reformirten und Unitarier in Preussen,' *Altpreussische Monatsschrift*, xxx (1893), 53.

[19] *Kurze und einfältige Untersuchung, ob, und warum die Reformirte Evangelische Kirche die also genannte Socinianer mit gutem Gewissen dulden, oder auch in ihre Gemeinschaft aufnehmen könne und solle.* n. p., 1700.

sulted in more tolerant treatment; but in 1716, when he saw that the younger generation were now forgetting Polish and speaking German, Crellius published for them a brief catechism [20] which was so well received that two years later he published a much larger edition for general circulation,[21] which as much as possible softened doctrines that might give offence. The Lutheran Superintendent took notice and complained to the King, who issued a warning against further Unitarian meetings. Crellius responded with a petition, setting forth that their numbers had so fallen off that in the whole Neumark there were now but 72 persons all told professing the Unitarian faith, and in Königswalde not more than 20; that their meetings were held within closed doors, and that no proselyting or controversy was carried on. They therefore begged his Majesty either to allow them to continue their private services, or else to order Lutherans and Reformed to admit them to their celebration of the Lord's Supper, as they had before requested.[22] They remained quiet and were not further disturbed. But the little group rapidly declined, and ere long yielded to the inevitable; and in 1725 Crellius, who had served them with unshaken loyalty for forty years, took his leave of them and joined his countrymen in Holland. He had given himself much to studies and the writing of learned works, and had from time to time visited Frankfurt or Berlin, Holland or England, where he had eminent literary friends, and enjoyed the reputation of being one of the most learned men of his time. There will be occasion to speak of him again further on.

Even with their pastor gone the scattered individuals in Brandenburg were not forgotten or wholly neglected. The brethren in East Prussia felt responsible for them, and every year a minister would go from there to visit them and administer the Lord's Supper, which they so deeply

[20] It was a revised translation into German of a brief Polish catechism published thirty years before. cf. Bock, *Antitrinitar.*, i, 42, 1029.

[21] *Kurzer Unterricht in der christlichen Religion* (1717), 56 pp. cf. Wotschke, *Meseritz*, p. 199.

[22] cf. Wotschke, *op. cit.*, pp. 200 f, 217–219; Paul Schwartz, 'Unitarier in der Neumark,' *Schriften des Vereins für Geschichte der Neumark*, x (1900), 61–72. The matter of the Sacrament seriously concerned them. When in 1717 two absent members of his flock, the brothers Stephen and Thomas Widawski, officers in the Prussian army, wrote from Cleve to inquire whether it was right for them, being so far from a church of their own faith, to commune with the Reformed, he advised them to do so. But the Berlin theologians opposed such a concession to the Unitarians in the Mark, and the King allowed them to continue their private worship. cf. Bock, *Antitrinitar.*, i, 202 f.

valued.[23] But from this time on they disappear from the record. In 1750 but one of the brethren was reported, still loyal to the faith of his fathers, and even he had a Lutheran wife, and his children were brought up in their mother's faith.[24]

As has been already related above, some of the exiles had early gone from Poland to Mannheim in the Rhine Palatinate. The Elector Karl Ludwig was now making every effort to build up this city after the damage it had suffered in the Thirty Years' War, and to that end he had welcomed as settlers those that had suffered religious oppression elsewhere, including Protestant refugees from Holland and Anabaptists from Moravia, with enjoyment of religious freedom.[25] At the last Socinian synod held on Polish soil in 1662, two ministers were appointed to go thither to minister to their brethren.[26] Their reports were evidently favorable, for Stanislas Lubieniecki, who was then more or less at the Danish court, and in correspondence with many of the ruling princes in Europe, had evidently made the Elector well-disposed to the exiled Poles,[27] so that at the Kreuzburg synod the following year, to which Wiszowaty was summoned from Kolozsvár, he and Joachim Stegmann were appointed to repair to Mannheim, where the Elector, already sympathizing with them in their misfortunes, had granted them a place of residence under his patronage. They at once set out on the long journey with their families, and dwelt at Mannheim for three years, happy under the Prince's protection.[28] They held their worship and observed the various rites of their religion in their own dwellings, but they also made every effort to commend their faith to others.[29] The

---

[23] cf. Bock, *Socinianismus*, p. 86.

[24] cf. Wotschke, *Kreuzburg*, p. 22. Yet later than this we hear of scattered Unitarians living here and there in the Mark or elsewhere. cf. Wotschke, 'Zur Geschichte der Unitarier in der Mark,' *Jahrbuch des Vereins für Kirchengeschichte der Provinz Brandenburg*, vii, viii, 227–241 (Berlin, 1911–'12). See also two interesting letters from G. F. Redoch, dated from Hamburg, 1652, and Lichtenberg, 1654, in Boysen's *Allgemeines historisches Magazin*, i, 385–392; ii, 319–324 (Halle, 1767, 1763). He gives an account of a group of prominent Socinians meeting in deep secrecy at Hamburg; and writes to unnamed brethren in the Mark to counsel them to observe great caution and prudence as to their religion.

[25] cf. Wotschke, *Kreuzburg*, p. 13. His great-great-grandfather, Friedrich II., "the pious," had been less tolerant a hundred years before, when he prosecuted Neuser and Sylvan. *v. supra*, Chap. xviii.

[26] cf. Bock, *Antitrinitar.*, i, 1009, 252.

[27] cf. Lubieniecius, *Historia*, p. *4b.

[28] For the whole Mannheim episode, cf. *Anonymi epistola*, p. 257 f.

[29] A company of exiles farther down the Rhine at Neuwied had also been assigned to their pastoral care. This town had recently been founded by Count Friedrich von Wied,

Elector showed Wiszowaty his favor, sometimes inviting him to the castle, sometimes coming down with the members of his court to visit Wiszowaty, when they would talk intimately, especially about religion. But when it was discovered that through conversation or the circulation of books and writings the faith of some of the citizens was being shaken, the clergy had the Socinians called before the authorities at Heidelberg, where they were enjoined from discussing religion or giving religious books to any subject of the Elector. This restriction of their religious liberty deprived them of their greatest happiness; and as war with Lorraine had broken out and the plague had smitten the city, they decided to remove. They were urged to join the exiles in Prussia, Brandenburg, Silesia or elsewhere; but Wiszowaty had long felt attracted to Holland, and in 1666 he therefore took his family down the Rhine to Amsterdam, where many of the brethren already were, where he was to spend the rest of his life, and where we shall meet him again. Stegmann, however, went to Kolozsvár in Transylvania, where he became minister of the German-speaking Transylvanians. Both died in 1678.

One more attempt to establish in a foreign land a colony of Socinians was made. It will be recalled that when the Swedes evacuated Kraków in 1657 Stanislas Lubieniecki was one of those that followed with them, hoping through Swedish influence to get the Socinians included in the general amnesty when the treaty of peace should be drawn. Disappointed in this hope, since he could not return to Poland he went on with his family to Copenhagen, with the plan of obtaining from the Danish King some place in his dominion where the exiles might settle. He was received with much favor at court, and did get from the King assurance that he would connive at their dwelling at Altona. He himself therefore took up his residence at Hamburg near by. While here, he received from the brethren a request to procure permission for them to settle at Friedrichstadt, a tidy Dutch-looking little city on the western coast of Schleswig-Holstein near the mouth of the Eider. It had been built some forty years before by the enlightened and liberal young Duke Frederik III. of Holstein-Gottorp as a city of refuge for the Dutch Remonstrants, who had in 1619 been excluded from the Reformed Church and forbidden to hold religious assemblies in Holland.

---

who invited settlers without distinction of religion; and the much mixed religious population have lived together there in great harmony ever since. cf. Baedeker's *Rhine*, s. v.; Bock, *Antitrinitar.*, i, 1016.

The Duke offered to build them a town with complete religious freedom, saying, 'I do not understand how any one can be forced in respect to his conscientious convictions.' Thus in an intolerant age Friedrichstadt soon became conspicuous as a haven for the persecuted. Soon after the Remonstrants came the Mennonites, then Lutherans, Catholics, and finally Quakers and Jews, who have now lived side by side in tolerance and peace for more than three centuries.[30] Lubieniecki went at once to Friedrichstadt, and early in 1662, having explained to the Magistrate that his people would join in with the Remonstrants, he was assured that they would be gladly received. The Synod upon learning this requested Lubieniecki to do all possible in their behalf, and especially to conclude a union with the Remonstrants. He made great efforts, and spared no expense of his own property to remove the brethren thither and aid them after their arrival.[31] The brethren sent several of their ministers, Preuss, Crellius, and young Martin Ruar, besides several members from the Danzig congregation, to prepare the way; and early in the autumn seventeen Polish Brethren were enrolled among the Remonstrants, and many others were on their way, assisted by funds sent from Holland.[32] Unfortunately all their hopes were soon dashed to the ground. The Lutheran Superintendent Johannes Reinboth thwarted their plans. He prevailed upon the new Duke, Christian Albert, a more conservative man than his father, to expel the Socinians from the city, with the excuse that the Magistrate had not consulted him before admitting them.[33] The Remonstrant brethren intervened, but in vain. The Polish Brethren tried to move the Superintendent to show a milder spirit, again in vain. In October, 1663, after barely a year's happy residence, a new order of expulsion was issued, and they too went on to Holland. Thus the last attempt to form a compact colony of the exiles under conditions of religious liberty fell to the ground.[34]

[30] cf. Harry Schmidt, *Bilder aus der Geschichte der Stadt Friedrichstadt a. d. Eider* (Friedrichstadt, 1931). cf. Joannes Tiedeman, *Frederikstad ann de Eider en hare Hollandsche Gemeente* (Rotterdam, 1852).

[31] cf. Lubieniecki's Life, prefixed to his *Historia*, p. *5b.

[32] cf. J. J. van Vollenhoven, *Beiträge zur Geschichte der remonstrantisch-reformirten Gemeinde in Friedrichstadt* (Friedrichstadt, 1849).

[33] cf. Lubieniecius, *Historia*, p. *5b; Theodor Wotschke, 'Schleswig-Holstein und die Polnischen Brüder,' *Schriften des Vereins für Schleswig-Holsteinische Kirchengeschichte* (1926), pp. 14–18; Schmidt, *op. cit.*, p. 26.

[34] Crellius now went to join the exiles in Prussia, where he was active in his ministry at Andreaswalde until 1680. Preuss returned to his itinerant ministry in Brandenburg, for

It has now been seen that, aside from the exile church at Kolozsvár, which dragged out a feeble existence for 130 years, none of the other groups of exiles that have been mentioned took root or held together for more than a few years. Their tenure of residence was too precarious, and the pressure of the orthodox confessions was too strong and steady, for them firmly to establish new centers of church life. In East Prussia, however, conditions were somewhat more favorable to their continuing their existence and perhaps even extending their work. From 1525 Ducal Prussia, as it was called, though governed by its own hereditary Prince, had been bound to Poland by ties of feudal allegiance, and was practically, if somewhat loosely, a part of the Polish State. Its population was predominantly German, and its religion after the rise of the Reformation was strongly Lutheran; though there was also a large infiltration of Poles, especially along the eastern border. But in the settlement of affairs by treaty after the war with Sweden, Poland was obliged to renounce all claims to sovereignty over Prussia, and it became henceforth a part of Germany, ruled by the Elector of Brandenburg, and locally by a Governor appointed by him. At the time of the exile of the Socinians the Governor was Prince Bogusław Radziwiłł, who was related to the Great Elector. In the recent war he had, as a magnate in Lithuania who was discontented with the rule of King Jan, given powerful help to the Swedes and Germans, and in 1657 he was rewarded with this office.[35] Though he was of the Reformed Church, he was not unfriendly to the Socinians, with whom he had many con-

---

which he suffered imprisonment, and later became minister at Königswalde, where he died in 1696. Early in 1664 Lubieniecki appeared at Lübeck with a number of the exiles, and sought from the Council permission to settle there with free exercise of their religion. The Council voted to grant them leave, with freedom of domestic worship, and eventual citizenship, but first referred the matter to the Lutheran Superintendent. He disapproved on account of their religion, and the Council therefore rescinded its vote, unless they would accept the Nicene Creed; whereupon they soon departed. cf. W. Brehmer, 'Polnische Socinianer in Lübeck,' *Mitteilungen des Vereins für Lübeck'sche Geschichte*, vi (1894), 156 f. Lubieniecki continued to reside at Hamburg, drawing an annual salary from the King as a confidential correspondent who should report to the King such news as he gathered through his wide correspondence in Europe. At Hamburg he roused the enmity of the clergy by his efforts to spread his faith, and was required to leave the city. After living several years at Altona he returned, but was again ordered to leave, on the ground that he had corrupted the faith of a Lutheran divinity student who was tutor to his children. But before he could comply with the order, he fell fatally ill from eating poisoned food, which caused not only his death in 1675 at the untimely age of 52 years, but also that of his two daughters. cf. Bock, *Antitrinitar.*, i, 442 f; Lubieniecius, *Historia*, pp. *5b–7a.

[35] cf. Sembrzycki, *Reformirten*, pp. 21–23.

nections, and whose cause at Kreuzburg he supported with the local
government there in 1660; [36] and his cousin Janusz had championed
their cause in the Diet when the fate of Raków was at stake in 1638.
Hence on all accounts Prussia seemed to offer the exiles a promising
refuge, even though it had long had provincial laws against 'Arians.'
Long before 1660, however, pioneers of Socinianism had appeared in
Prussia; and although they arose more or less independently of the
movement we have been following in Poland, yet they had such
affinities and eventual connection with it that their record deserves to
be given here.

Not counting Lismanino and Alciati, who in 1563 and the following
year had taken refuge in Prussia but had excited no disturbance by
their views, the earliest recorded instance of Antitrinitarianism here is
found in 1574. In this year one Ralph Rutter [37] of London, who had
for some years been active in eastern Europe as a trader in the service
of the Muscovy Company, but was now trading on his own account,
formed an acquaintance with Simon Budny, Antitrinitarian minister
at Łosk, who through him opened correspondence with John Foxe, the
English martyrologist.[38] But it appears also that through their conversations on religious matters Rutter became a convert to Budny's
views, and undertook to make them more widely known. For in the
following year (1575) a book by the Lutheran Bishop Johannes
Wigand [39] of Pomesania appeared at Königsberg, from which it is
evident that Rutter had been spreading among university students at
Königsberg dangerous views as to the deity of Christ.[40] There is no

[36] *v. supra*, p. 494.

[37] Budny's Ms (see below) calls him Raph Rutter, but another early source says Ralfe.
Wigand says, D. Raphael Ritter, apparently taking Raph as an abbreviation of Raphael, and
the unfamiliar English Rutter as a mistake for the familiar German Ritter. The initial D.
may stand for Dominus as well as for Doctor. There is thus poor foundation for the assumption that R. was a German physician born or resident in London.

[38] cf. Kot, *Oddziaływanie*, 219 ff, 316 ff; *id.*, 'Anglo-Polonica,' *Nauka Polska*, xx
(1935), 105 ff.

[39] Wigand won his spurs this very year by an able critique of Servetus and his doctrine
(*De Servetianismo, seu de Antitrinitariis*, Regiomonti, 1575), and by several other works
earlier or later showed himself one of the strongest opponents of the developing Antitrinitarianism. He was chosen one of the disputants sent by the University to assist the orthodox
in their debate with the 'Arians' at Lewartów in 1580; *v. supra*, p. 381; Bock, *Socinianismus*, p. 94 f.

[40] *Nebulae Arianae per D. Raphaelem Ritterum Londinensem sparsae, luce veritatis
divinae discussae per D. Johannem Wigandum, Episcopum Pomesaniensem* (Regiomonti,
1575).

evidence that Rutter himself had published these views, or was the author of them. It seems rather that they formed a brief appendix to a recent book of Budny's on the two natures of Christ,[41] and were now circulated as a separate reprint, or else in manuscript, with the title, *Brevis demonstratio, quod Christus non sit ipse Deus qui Pater*, etc. It was a brief and lively polemic against the current view of Christ as God, equal with the Father, and the related doctrine of the Trinity; and it contended that Christ was a man of wholly human origin. Wigand reprinted the tract entire in his book, and then undertook to refute it sentence by sentence.[42] What the immediate result was we do not know, for Rutter was a bird of passage and did not pause to reply.

It was not many years, however, before signs of heresy were again discovered. For about 1580 a congregation of 'Anabaptists' was gathered at Danzig, which had relations with the brethren of the Minor Church in Poland. Its meetings were doubtless held in great secrecy; but in 1592 they received a notable accession. Matthew Radecki, a native of Danzig and a graduate of Königsberg, who had for twenty-six years been Secretary of the city, but had led a restless and wandering religious life, received immersion and joined this congregation. When this fact became known to the city Council he was removed from office, and left town with his wife and eight children.[43] He then became a Socinian minister and served his churches for the twenty remaining years of his life. One of these churches was at Busków, a near suburb of Danzig, whither many from Danzig went to worship when their meetings were forbidden in town; and another near by was at Straszyn.

A generation later, about 1626, trouble broke out at St. Peter's Reformed church in Danzig itself. Joachim Stegmann, who had already been under suspicion when minister of a church in Brandenburg, and had at that time been in communication with the Racovians, was now for a short time minister at St. Peter's, where he was discovered to be holding Socinian opinions. He was therefore dismissed, and went at once to Raków as Rector of the college there. Two years later he was

<hr/>

[41] cf. Sandius, *Bibliotheca*, p. 55.

[42] cf. Kot, *Oddziaływanie*, pp. 221–223; Sandius, *Bibliotheca*, p. 55.

[43] cf. Matthaeus Radecke, *Ursachen warumb sich Matthaeus Radeke welcher der Stad Dantzigk 26 jahr lang für ein Secretarium gedienet, von dar gemachet, undt sich mit den seinen ann andere ort begeben hat* (Racków, 1593). See also Socinus's letters to him in 1584–'86, *Opera*, i, 373–395.

called to be minister of the Saxon Unitarian church at Kolozsvár in
Transylvania, where he died in 1633. A printed controversy ensued at
Danzig, which tended much to spread Stegmann's views. It was begun
and ended by Johannes Botsak, minister of Trinity church and Rector
of the gymnasium there.[44]

At the time of Stegmann's dismissal from his church, the Raków
Synod began to be interested in pushing forward the work at Danzig,
where the number of adherents was rapidly growing, and made an
appropriation toward the cause; and in 1631 Martin Ruar, who had
several years before spent some time at Danzig, took up his permanent
residence there. He was ostensibly and actively the factor for various
Polish gentlemen in their commercial affairs; but he was at heart above
all devoted to spreading his religious faith in that influential centre.
Ruar,[45] born in 1589, was a native of Krempe in Holstein, son of a
Lutheran school Rector. Early distinguished as a student, he went to
the Academy at Altdorf, where he was converted to Socinian views by
Professor Soner, and became an ardent and life-long propagandist of
his new faith. He traveled extensively in France and England, Italy,
Holland and Germany, became a man of the broadest culture, highly
accomplished in nearly half a score of languages, and was offered a
professorship in history at the University of Cambridge on very flattering terms, but declined the tempting offer rather than compromise his
religious freedom, as he would have had to do.[46] Later for one short
year he was Rector of the College at Raków; but the restrictions of
academic life did not suit him, and he had ten years more of unsettled
life, ranging like a bee, as he said of himself,[47] among flowers of the
classics, studying to perfect his style and enrich his mind as a preparation for practical life. Thus by the time he settled at Danzig Ruar had
come to be widely known as one of the most learned men in Europe.
In religion, though agreeing in general with the Socinians, he was no
narrow sectarian, but was tolerant and irenic in spirit, and for many
years tried to bring about union with the Remonstrants and the Men-

---

[44] cf. Johannes Botsaccus, *Einfältige Warnung für der new photinianischen oder Arianischen Lehre*, etc. (Danzig, 1633); Joachim Stegmann, *Prob der einfältigen Warnung*, etc.
(Rackaw, 1633); Botsaccus, *Anti-Stegmannus*, etc. (Gedani, 1635).

[45] cf. Chmaj, *Ruar*; Bock, *Antitrinitar.*, i, 713–735.

[46] cf. Ruar, *Epistolae*, pp. 56, 60. It was the then recently founded Fulke-Greville professorship.

[47] cf. Ruar, *Epistolae*, p. 88.

nonites. His activity, however, was that of a layman, for he was not ordained to the ministry until late in life.

Soon after his arrival in Danzig, the brethren in Poland commissioned Ruar to purchase a piece of land in a convenient location for a church, and also a house for the regular minister; and he used to preach to the Socinian congregations in German, since the regular minister knew only Polish. These meetings were of course private assemblies; though once or twice, being invited to do so, he took part in a public discussion, and defended his cause against misrepresentation.[48] But his more effective work was done by recommending and distributing books from the Raków press, and by cautious and skilful private conversations and discussions with individuals or small groups, mostly with common people.[49] The results of this activity could not well escape the notice of the Council of the city, who since Stegmann's case had already put some pressure upon the congregation of the Socinians; and now that these were increasingly active, and Ruar himself, having married into one of the prominent families of the city, had converted to his faith not only his wife but her relations, the Council were aroused to drastic action. Encouraged by what the Diet had done that very year in the case of Raków, they notified Ruar in 1638 to leave the city and thus free the church from further danger,[50] on the ground that he not only professed the 'Arian' religion but was leader in spreading it in the city.

He answered [51] that it was next to impossible for him to leave at once, since that would cause great loss to several Polish magnates whose interests there he had in charge, and he asked meantime to be heard in his own defence and legally tried before punishment. He had borne, he said, a good reputation throughout learned Europe, and had chosen Poland out of all places for its boasted golden freedom of conscience and its tolerant laws; and he had liked Danzig the more as a place of residence because here adherents of various religions were freely allowed to dwell and to practice their religion publicly or (by connivance) secretly. He had lived here for seven years without complaint

---

[48] cf. his *Epistolae*, p. 635.

[49] Ruar gives a detailed and most interesting account of his method of winning converts, in a letter to an intimate friend. cf. his *Epistolae*, pp. 123–126; also Bock, *Socinianismus*, p. 25 f.

[50] cf. Hartknoch, *Kirchen-Historia*, p. 284 f; Bock, *op. cit.*, pp. 26–29.

[51] cf. his *supplex libellus* in his *Epistolae*, p. 622 ff.

from any, and had married into an honorable family. In religion he had nothing in common with Arius, and chose Scripture alone as the standard of his faith and life. He had never been ordained or acted as a minister, but only as a private Christian; had never discussed religion with any student, nor forced his views on any one in private, nor persuaded any one in the city to change his religion; had loaned religious books only when asked; and had done nothing against the laws or customs of the city. Finally, he hoped that at a time when religious persecution of the innocent was rife elsewhere it would not be permitted in this free state to begin with him.

Ruar also asked the intercession in his behalf of some of the leading nobles in Poland whose factor he had been, of whom more than a dozen, persons of the highest standing, addressed a letter to the Danzig Council.[52] The Council yielded to these influences, and suspended the decree, on condition that Ruar should not slyly spread his religious views. Five years later, finding these conditions irksome, and seeking wider liberty, Ruar through the influence of two friends at court obtained from King Ladislas an appointment as member of his court,[53] which was supposed among other things to secure him immunity from arrest. This distinction, however, proved of little advantage to Ruar, for under the royal privilege granted to the city a certain precedence had been assured to the Lutheran Church.[54] When therefore in 1643 it became known that he had again been actively making converts, including several of note, he was again ordered to leave the city. Ruar hastened to Warsaw where he again found influential friends to intercede for him, urging that though the city might be within its rights under its charter, it would be safer policy to exercise there the same toleration that prevailed in the Republic at large; since if the principle of general toleration were abandoned, all Protestants might soon suffer persecution from the Catholics. The Council so far yielded as to grant Ruar leave to enter the city to transact his business, but he must reside outside it and give up his propaganda, a condition that he had thus far failed to fulfil.[55] He therefore removed to Straszyn, a (German)

---

[52] cf. the extensive correspondence ensuing, Ruar, *Epistolae*, pp. 626–643.

[53] cf. the diploma in *Epistolae*, p. 684. This honor was renewed by King Jan in 1649; cf. *id. op.*, p. 686 f.

[54] For the privilege granted by King Ladislas IV. in 1633, cf. Hartknoch, *Kirchen-Historia*, p. 820. An earlier privilege in 1558 also included the Reformed Church, but extended no further; *op. cit.*, p. 678 f.

[55] cf. *Epistolae*, pp. 644 f, 648 f, 655 f.

CHAPTER XXXIX

THE SOCINIAN EXILES IN EAST PRUSSIA

AFTER THUS TURNING ASIDE from the main course of our narrative to trace that of the somewhat detached kindred movements in East Prussia, we return to follow those exiles from Poland who in 1660 and later sought to reestablish themselves and their church life in what had until recently been Polish Prussia. When the decree of banishment against the 'Arians' was passed in 1658, one of the first to leave the country seems to have been Samuel Przypkowski.[1] He had long been close to public life as secretary to one of the Radziwiłłs, and had been an active and aggressive champion of toleration in the face of the rapidly growing intolerance of the Catholic reaction. At the accession of Ladislas IV. in 1632 he had addressed an eloquent panegyric to the new King, extolling the value of religious peace and freedom of conscience, deprecating the rising danger of intolerance, and especially pleading for religious freedom for the Polish Brethren.[2] Unfortunately the writing did not have the desired effect, for intolerance remained unchecked. He had also published a bold apology defending Prince Janusz Radziwiłł against the charge of treason in the war with Sweden;[3] and had made an eloquent reply to Cichowski's final attack upon the 'Arians' in 1661.[4] Being known as a man of brilliant talents and wide experience in public life, when he left Poland he found a ready welcome at the court of Bogusław Radziwiłł at Königsberg, and became a member of his Council.[5] Here he was able to render useful service not only to the Governor but also to the exiles. Numerous others are said also to have removed to Königsberg, and to have held their religious worship privately in one of their dwellings in the Rossgarten,[6]

---

[1] cf. Chmaj, *Przypkowski.*

[2] cf. Przypcovius, *Opera*, pp. 405–416 (*Bibliotheca Fratrum Polonorum*).

[3] cf. *Opera*, pp. 403*–410*.

[4] *v. supra*, p. 479, n.; cf. *Opera*, pp. 435–450.

[5] I am bound to believe that Sandius's statement (*Bibliotheca*, p. 123), repeated on the title-page of Przypcovius's *Opera*, that he was Councilor to the *Elector*, is an error, to be corrected as above.

[6] cf. Hartknoch, *Kirchen-Historia*, p. 647; Bock, *Socinianismus*, p. 70.

having for some time a regularly appointed minister. Under existing laws, Arians might not buy nor inherit property, although the law was evaded by taking life-leases which might pass on to survivors. Thus the Elector in 1663 granted life-use of a large property at Rudawki to Zbigniew Morsztyn, perhaps the most distinguished of all the exiles, and afterwards made him one of his Council, with a residence in the castle at Königsberg, and employed him in diplomatic service of great importance.[7] The Governor was well-disposed to the exiles, and did all in his power to protect them, having many of them in his employ. Przypkowski was thus doubtless able to pave the way for more of the brethren to remove to Prussia, where they settled mostly near the border in the southeast corner of the Duchy, leasing large estates on which the poorer brethren could live around them in villages, in the traditional Polish custom, with meetings for worship in the hall of the manor-house. No sooner, however, had the exiles begun to arrive and settle than the Lutheran clergy grew apprehensive lest their territory become widely infected with 'Arianism,' and began to work for their banishment. The Diet requested the Elector to have the laws against 'Arians,' etc. enforced, and some repressive legislation was at length passed in 1663, though extant records do not show what it was.

Meantime the brethren in exile held a synod in 1663,[8] and appointed two ministers to serve the congregations in Prussia. They also voted that, as they entertained a strong hope that they were to find a permanent and sure settlement in Prussia under the Elector's protection, all the brethren should henceforth send to Prussia all their records, and the money collected elsewhere, especially in Holland, Holstein and England; and that as Przypkowski had great experience in public affairs he should be directed to write a petition to the governing powers, and do all possible to get a safe place appointed for them to settle,[9] also that he should compose in Latin an accurate account of all their sufferings in the Russian and Swedish wars and forward it to Holland, to stir up compassion for them.[10] The confidence thus reposed in Przyp-

---

[7] cf. Sembrzycki, *Reformirten*, p. 30.

[8] Bock says (p. 61) at Claudiopolis (Kolozsvár) in Transylvania. This is perhaps a mistake for Kreuzburg, where a synod was held that year; but it is hardly likely that another one was also held the same year with the little handful at Kolozsvár so far away.

[9] cf. Bock, *op. cit.*, p. 61.

[10] This is the letter given in Lubieniecius, *Historia*, pp. 278–285; English trans. in (Gaspard de Tende) *Account of Poland*, etc. (London, 1698), p. 238 ff. Also in preface to Przypcovius's *Opera*.

kowski is the more noteworthy since he was an eclectic in religion, and had alienated some of the brethren by his dissentient views about Christ and other subjects, and had suffered harsh abuse for it.[11] Pressure upon the exiles now relaxed a little. Stragglers from Poland kept arriving for several years, and in 1665 they ventured to hold a synod at the village of Kessel near Johannisburg, with delegates even from Transylvania, as well as from scattered places in Prussia.[12] Here, taking thought for their future, they voted that their synod records should be preserved and continued; that aid be sent as far as possible to the brethren at Kolozs-vár, though they could not now provide a minister for them; that money sent from Holland should be distributed to the brethren still remaining in the Kraków district; and that a sum of money be sent to the destitute widow of one of their distinguished leaders in Silesia. It was not long, however, before the authorities ordered that no more assemblies be held until further notice. The brethren, therefore, fearing that a storm was about to break upon them, presented to the Elector the petition that Przypkowski had been asked to draw up.[13]

The *Apologia* that Przypkowski presented to the Elector in behalf of the Unitarians, as they now preferred to be called, was designed to defend them against the charges that were evidently being made by the Lutherans; namely, that they blaspheme the Trinity, offend the majesty and dignity of Christ, and dishonor the Holy Spirit. These charges are stoutly denied. In other articles of religion they hold to nothing blasphemous or heretical, or at variance with the Apostles' Creed. They uphold the office of the Magistrate. Though differing as to various matters, they believe that Jesus is the Christ, and prove their faith by uprightness of life, holding that service of him lies not in one's opinions but in obedience to his commands; and they do not own the name of Anabaptists or Arians, but detest their errors. They are faithful subjects, have no strange laws, and have introduced no evil customs. After over five years here their worst enemies can not point out one that they have even tried to lead astray. Liberty of conscience is a gift of God, and error is to be put down by spiritual weapons, not by force. Their

---

[11] cf. Bock, *Antitrinitar.*, i, 668 f.

[12] cf. Bock, *Socinianismus*, p. 62.

[13] *Apologia afflictae innocentiae*, etc. Printed in Bock, *Socinianismus*, pp. 63–69; also in Przypcovius, *Opera*, pp. 451–453. Several versions are extant, more or less differing from one another. For one, cf. *Fortgesetzte Sammlung von Altem und Neuem* (Leipzig, 1722), pp. 43–60. The *Apologia* was followed by *Hyperaspistes, seu Defensio Apologiae, Opera*, pp. 450–474 (paging duplicated).

brethren have been granted citizenship by William of Orange in Holland, and have been received by Protestant princes in Silesia, by the Queen of Poland in her Duchies, by the Princes of Transylvania and Hungary, and by the Elector at Mannheim. Can Prussia be less kind? The appeal closes with an eloquent plea for liberty of conscience as the foundation of civil liberty, and a moving reference to the pitiable case of the exiles if they should now be denied room even on the sandy and waste fields that they have but just begun to restore.

This petition was presently followed by a supplementary writing, an extended defence of the *Apologia* entitled *Hyperaspistes*. In six chapters it sets forth the doctrine of Jesus Christ as the Son of God, with especial regard to the radical views that had been espoused by Budny, Palaeologus and Dávid, and had drawn down criticism upon the Socinians. Both these documents were quite irenic in spirit, and went as far as possible to state the faith of the exiles in terms that might not seem too heretical to their opponents. With the same design a Confession of Faith of the Exiles was soon afterwards dedicated to the Elector.[14] It followed in the footsteps of Jonas Schlichting's Confession of 1642, stating the main articles in brief and simple form, with proof-texts cited for every item, and the obvious purpose of showing that this faith in every particular is agreeable to Scripture and the Apostles' Creed.

No immediate result followed these efforts, but they apparently made a favorable impression, for with the silent connivance of the Elector, doubtless encouraged by the Governor, leave was allowed the exiles to stay in Prussia at least for a time; and it is noteworthy that at just this time Przypkowski and another of the brethren were allowed, with the Elector's approval, to acquire, subject to mortgage, the village of Kąsinowo (Andreaswalde),[15] which was henceforth to become the centre of Socinianism in Prussia.

The Governor, Bogusław Radziwiłł, who had from the beginning shown himself a sympathetic friend of the exiles, died on the last day of 1669.[16] Hereupon the Diet at once seized the opportunity to obtain from the Elector early in 1670 an edict, which was publicly posted,

---

[14] cf. Bock, *Socinianismus*, pp. 71–76. It is said to have been by Benedict Wiszowaty, minister at Andreaswalde. cf. *Zeitschrift für Kirchengeschichte*, xviii (1897), 141.

[15] In 1666. cf. Bock, *op. cit.*, p. 88; Sembrzycki, *op. cit.*, p. 36.

[16] Przypkowski, who had lived at his court for some ten years, now withdrew to the estate that he had acquired at Andreaswalde as just mentioned.

denying the exiles any right to remain in Prussia after three years from date.[17] They therefore presented to him another petition,[18] appealing to his pity, mercy, and sense of justice: they were not criminals, had a clear conscience, could remove to no place where they would be safe from violence; they could claim kinship with all the noblest families in Poland and Lithuania, even with Princes and the present King, and they prayed most earnestly to be spared this last calamity. The King consulted his intimate Councilors: though he had acquiesced in their desire, yet could they not find some other way in view of this piteous appeal? For himself, he felt that at least public posting of the decree should be avoided, and that other means might be found. Their opponents, however, were not satisfied, and kept urging the proscription of the Socinians. These therefore turned again to King Michael of Poland, who two years before had interceded for the exiles at Kreuzburg.[19] He then addressed letters to the Elector, the Governor of Prussia, and the Prussian Diet, making the personal request that the exiles, being of noble birth and closely related to leading men in Poland and Lithuania, might, out of Christian tolerance and as a favor to him, be permitted to remain in Prussia. Such a request could not well be disregarded, so that, from 1673 on, means were sought by which on the one hand the Socinians might be protected, and on the other the danger of their infecting the country with their heresy might be overcome; the Elector favoring only very moderate procedure, while the Diet continually pressed for exile, especially in 1679. In this year the Elector, after being reminded that orders four times given in the past ten years had been allowed to be treated as dead letters, issued a new decree of banishment within six weeks; [20] nevertheless, on one pretext or another, execution of the decree was from time to time deferred.

Meanwhile the exiles, though conscious of a sword continually hanging over their heads, slowly grew reassured, and prepared for an indefinite stay. Thus in 1678 representatives from congregations in Brandenburg and in Prussia met in synod at Rudawki, appointed a regular minister for the congregation there, voted for shorter sermons and more prayers, and to observe church discipline more strictly. At another synod in 1684, the inner life of the church and domestic wor-

---

[17] cf. Przypcovius, *Opera*, pref., p. **3a.
[18] cf. Bock, *op. cit.*, p. 78 f.
[19] *v. supra*, p. 497.
[20] *id. op.*, p. 83 f.

ship were considered, with emphasis on personal virtues. Though meetings for worship were apparently held at or near Andreaswalde by about 1662, with occasional visits from ministers delegated by the synods at Kreuzburg, the exiles there had a regular minister beginning with 1670, the first being Christopher Crellius, now returned from his visit to Holland and England; and he also paid annual visits to dispersed groups in Silesia. Later they also had a school, and their church life was uninterrupted until the death of the last minister about 1803. There were in all eight ministers in succession.[21] Somewhat later a church with a regular minister was established on the Morsztyn estate at Rudawki (Rudowken, Rutów),[22] which had a succession of seven ministers; but the worship ceased in 1752 when the estate passed into the hands of strangers. No other Socinian congregation with regular church life is known to have existed in East Prussia,[23] though private domestic worship was doubtless held on various Socinian estates, in accordance with traditional Socinian custom.

The best account we have of the mode of worship among the Socinians comes from the hand of a contemporary who enjoyed their confidence in Prussia at the middle of the eighteenth century.[24] Their worship, extremely simple, and without ceremonial, was held in a private home, similar as they believed to those in which the first Christians met, whose rites and customs they strove to imitate. Their place of worship at Andreaswalde [25] was in a common house suited for domestic purposes, in whose plain *hypocaustum* they met for worship

[21] cf. Henryk Merczyng, 'Ostateczny koniec Aryan polskich' (The last end of the Polish Arians), *Przegląd Historyczny*, xii (1908), 86; Bock, *op. cit.*, pp. 85–88.

[22] About thirty miles northwest of Lyck.

[23] Merczyng, *Zbory*, p. 120, lists one at Orzys (Arys), as having lasted to the beginning of the eighteenth century, but no authority is given.

[24] cf. Bock, *op. cit.*, pp. 89–92.

[25] In November, 1924 the author visited Andreaswalde, a little farming village about ten miles southwest of Lyck, and a mile from Baitkowen station. So far as known no other Unitarian had ever done so. The place of Paul Crellius's residence (grandson of Professor John Crellius of Raków), where he was living at an advanced age at the middle of the eighteenth century, was easily identified, as was the pond at the foot of the knoll on which it stood, where the Socinians immersed their members by night in order to avoid a sensation. Across the road was a large old farm-house with thatched roof, 'the Arian church,' in whose ample living-room the brethren used to worship. My visit was none too soon. Half the old building had been torn down and reconstructed in the preceding summer, and the remaining part was to follow in the next season. On the estate is a hill known as the Arianer Berg (locally, "Oriander"), which was no doubt their burial place. cf. the author's illustrated article, 'The last Socinian Church Visited,' *Christian Register*, civ, 627 ff (June 25, 1925).

on Sundays and holy days. The service began with the singing of a hymn from Preuss's German hymn-book, *Herzliches Saytenspiel*, followed by a brief introduction to the sermon. The minister then knelt to invoke the divine blessing on the word, with other prayers not in prescribed form but according to the dictates of the heart. The scripture passage to be dwelt on was then read, with comments and an application. The sermon did not exceed an hour, after which the younger people present were examined upon it by question and answer. The service ended with prayers and a hymn. The afternoon service had a briefer sermon, but more catechizing. The Lord's Supper and baptism and church discipline were observed with the utmost seriousness, as related in a previous chapter.[26] The minister was assisted in administering the church funds by a Deacon, an elderly man of upright life, who relieved widows, orphans and the poor, as well as paid the minister's salary, which was meager indeed, amounting to no more than 100 florins a year. Morsztyn had left the church a legacy of 6,000 thalers, whose income supplemented the church funds.

From the point our narrative has now reached, the church life of the Socinians in Prussia proceeded normally, and not too seriously disturbed, for over a hundred years. They had of course to take care not to arouse Lutheran opposition by doing anything to spread their faith, as by holding public services, engaging in discussions, or circulating their books; but they held their synods, long remained in communication with the brethren in Transylvania and with Remonstrants and Mennonites in Holland, whither they sent their young ministers to be educated, and maintained their traditional standards of devout piety and strict Christian morals. Though for the most part they went their way quietly and gave little offence, the over-zealous had now and then to be admonished not to engage in propaganda. By 1721 the cause at Andreaswalde seemed to be taking on fresh vigor. The members were showing themselves aggressive, and had now built a special house of worship and employed a schoolmaster; and they were said not to be paying due regard to the local Lutheran church administration. The Lutheran clergy became concerned and complained to the King, Frederick William I., who ordained restrictions for the Socinians, with accompanying threats of punishment. This was done in 1721 and again ten years later; but nothing happened. The danger of banishment had

---

[26] *v. supra*, p. 431 f.

passed. Despite repeated complaints and occasional decrees, the Socinians had maintained their existence and held their worship here for seventy years.

Henceforth there was no real question of exile, but only of a measure of religious freedom. Nevertheless from this time on their cause showed a gradual decline. Some twenty families or more are known to have sought refuge in Prussia; [27] but in 1754 only ninety Polish Arians were reported in Prussia, of whom seventy were at Andreaswalde; while worship had now ceased at Rudawki. They were mostly agriculturists, and some of them were poor. They could no longer employ a teacher for their young. They had lost connection with their distant brethren in Transylvania. Worship was still conducted in Polish, but a German catechism was gradually replacing the Polish one, which the children could no longer understand. Their members steadily grew fewer. Some died, some removed to join the brethren in Holland or elsewhere, some went over to the Lutheran or the Reformed Church, some married Lutheran or Reformed wives who brought up their children in their own faith. Although a few of them were placed in important administrative offices, as a rule they were debarred from public office and from the professions. They might not buy estates or invest their money profitably.[28] In short, they were steadily succumbing to the fate of a weak minority in a hostile environment; and when in 1776 King Frederick the Great at length granted them permission to build a new church, with guarantee of unrestricted religious freedom, they were grown so few and so poor that after a dozen years more they had gone no further than gather some materials for it, and there is no indication that it was ever built.[29] In fact, there was now no longer any good reason why they should continue to live in Prussia in face of such odds; for in 1767 religious freedom had been proclaimed in Poland, and 'Arians' were no longer liable to prosecution there. Undoubtedly some of them then returned to the homeland, though no record of them remains. We can trace but one individual. One of the owners of Andreaswalde late in the eighteenth century was the family Sierakowski; and of this family came General Karol Sierakowski, who won fame under Kościuszko in the war against Russia. He re-

---

[27] cf. Merczyng, *op. cit.*, pp. 87–89.

[28] cf. Sembrzycki, *op. cit.*, p. 40.

[29] cf. Sembrzycki, *op. cit.*, p. 39; Ludwig Ernst von Borowski, *Neue Preussische Kirchenregistratur* (Königsberg, 1788), pp. 251–266; Merczyng, *op. cit.*, p. 89 f.

mained true to the faith of his fathers to the end of his life at Warsaw in 1824, and is said to have been the last Socinian in Poland.[30]

Those that remained in Prussia held together a little while longer. With the death of their last minister, a Schlichting, in 1803 their public worship will have ceased, and henceforth they worshiped in the Protestant parish in which they lived, in the persuasion, as one of them bore witness, 'that true worship is not a matter of name or forms, but of an upright life, which was the chief basis of the old "Arian" religion.' The dissolution of the group was now only a question of time. The members still held in common the lands at Andreaswalde; but in 1811 the seven surviving members decided to sell the village to the present tenant and divide the proceeds among themselves.[31] An inquiry made in 1838 showed two of the members as still living, both very old men, a Morsztyn and a Schlichting. Of these two, Karol Henryk Morsztyn died in 1852, and is recorded as the last Polish Arian in Prussia.[32] All the rest had now, with their families, become assimilated to the surrounding German churches, though the old Polish names still survive in Masuria in families that in religion and language have long been completely German. Thus ends the history, at once heroic and pathetic, of the Socinians in Poland, the simple Polish Brethren, who united with the widest doctrinal freedom the most eager missionary zeal and the most fervent piety, as they conscientiously tried to live strictly after the literal teachings of Jesus. But though its body had ceased to exist its spirit lived on, widely diffused, as we shall see, in Western Europe, and its teachings insensibly but surely modified the rigors of western orthodoxy. As an orthodox German historian has said of the Socinians, 'the distinguishing mark of their life, the showing of love toward every one, their demand for freedom of the religious life from all civil compulsion, praised even by Luther but forgotten again in early Protestantism, has entered on its victorious march in the social and liberal thoughts of the whole civilized world.' [33]

It is worth while for a moment in concluding this story to glance back at Poland and see what happened after the Socinians had been disposed of. Their banishment, as we have seen, was hastened and

---

[30] cf. Józef Zajączek, *Pamiętnik* . . . *albo historya revolucii* . . . *r. 1794* (Memoirs, or history of the revolution of 1794), Poznań, 1862, chaps. 8 and 9; Merczyng, *op. cit.*, p. 88.

[31] cf. Merczyng, *op cit.*, p. 90 f.

[32] cf. Merczyng, *op. cit.*, p. 88; Krasinski, *Reformation*, ii, 403.

[33] cf. Wotschke, *Meseritz*, p. 203.

facilitated through the willing cooperation of the orthodox Protestants with the Catholics. Unfortunately the former did not realize until too late that they were used as tools to dig their own graves. With the Socinians out of the way, Catholic pressure upon the others soon began. The Bohemian Brethren, the next weakest sect, were banished a year after the Socinians; and by 1668 the power of Protestantism in Poland was practically crushed. In 1716 freedom of worship was forbidden to Protestants except in their older churches, and in 1733 and 1736 their political rights were taken from them.[34] When after a long struggle the old rights of Dissidents were again restored in 1767, it was not only forever too late for the Socinians, but also too late to do much good to the Protestant cause in Poland, which has never regained more than a mere fraction of its former vigor.

[34] cf. Krasinski, *Reformation*, pp. 290, 423, 488.

CHAPTER XL

SOCINIAN LEAVEN AT WORK IN GERMANY AND FRANCE

W E HAVE NOW reached the end of the history of Socinianism as an organized movement in Poland and in the little handful of congregations that for a time survived in exile. Yet though the body of this movement perished as we have seen, its spirit still survived, and in the end became perhaps even more widely diffused than if its corporate existence had not been brought to an end, but had lived on unopposed in the land of its origin. Before we proceed, however, to follow what may be called the supplementary history of the movement, among the gradually disappearing remnants of the Socinians in Holland, something deserves to be recorded of the extent to which Socinian principles and beliefs permeated and influenced lands where no organized movement would have been tolerated.

Except in Poland, Socinian thought never came to any extent into active conflict with Catholicism. In other lands Catholic writers largely ignored it; and even in Poland it won comparatively few converts except by way of the Reformed Church, many of whose ablest converts from Catholicism soon passed on into the Minor Church. It was from this source, indeed, that the membership of the latter was chiefly recruited; which is no doubt a main reason for the bitter hatred and persistent opposition with which the Calvinists pursued the Socinians. Nor did Socinianism make much impression upon the Lutherans in Poland; while in Germany the Lutheran clergy were so vigilant that any converts made there either had to remain such in secret, or else found it necessary to leave the country and join the Socinians in Poland. These latter at length made a company notable for their ability, and for leadership in thought and scholarship, witness the names of Crellius, Ostorodt, Preuss, Ruar, Schomann, Smalcius, Stegmann, Völkel and others. The Socinian movement in Poland, however, was fairly well developed before theologians in other lands became much concerned about it. Two or three theologians in Western Europe did, it is true, incidentally attack early writings of Gonesius and Budny,[1] though their writings can have fallen into but few hands, and will soon have been forgotten.

Apart from individual personal efforts of Socinian students at the universities, or of traveling scholars, no means of widely spreading their faith abroad were open to the Socinians much before the first decade of the seventeenth century, when their recently established press at Raków began to be active in publishing writings by Socinus and his followers. These were subsidized by the Synod or by individuals of means, and as they were intended largely for propaganda and defence, every opportunity was embraced for circulating them far and wide. Socinians traveling abroad would take copies of these works with them and, though they might not be placed on sale publicly, would discreetly place them in hands where they would do most good to their cause. Thus Socinian views came to be secretly and quietly diffused in whatever universities the Polish students frequented. Though it was only at Altdorf that their influence spread so far as to become a public scandal, yet in at least a score of the German universities the seed was thus sown and converts were quietly made, or sympathy awakened, or prejudices softened. Such influences, and corresponding efforts to counteract them, were especially active in the period immediately following the publication of the Racovian Catechism, and again for thirty years about the middle of the century. Smalcius's dedication of the German edition of the Catechism to the University of Wittenberg was equivalent to an outright challenge to reply, but as we have seen in a previous chapter, a policy of silence was at first adopted, and for more than a decade no reply was attempted by the University. Professor Franz, however, had already attacked the smaller Raków catechism and a work of Socinus; while at about the same time Professor Grawer of Jena had also come out with a work attacking writings of Socinus and Ostorodt, to both of which Smalcius promptly published refutations.[2]

---

[1] Simler, Wigand, and Zanchi; v. supra, p. 292, n. 33; 369, n. 9.

[2] cf. Wolfgang Franzius, Augustanae Confessionis Articuli fidei . . . adversus . . . Antitrinitarios . . . breviter explicati et ex Verbo Divino confirmati (Witebergae, 1611); Smalcius, Refutatio thesium . . . Frantzii, etc. (Racoviae, 1614); Albert Grawius, De novo ac horrendo errore circa doctrina de satisfactione Christi, etc. (Jenae, 1619); id., Theses de aeterna deitate et incarnatione Filii Dei (ibid., 1612); id., Vindicatio incarnationis aeterni Filii Dei (ibid., 1613); Smalcius, Refutatio thesium . . . Graweri . . . de incarnatione aeterni Dei Filii (Racoviae, 1615); id., Refutatio disputationis de persona Christi (ibid., 1615).

From this time on, controversial writings came thick and fast, and lasted with little intermission until after the middle of the eighteenth century. The Wittenberg theologians in 1613 considered the refutation of Socinianism a common task for the Saxon universities, whose professors were to meet and consult about a common work in confutation; and in 1616 it was even planned to call a large assembly of German theologians to this end.[3] The work of counteracting the rapidly increasing infection of Socinian doctrines was, however, not confined to the Saxon universities. Wittenberg, indeed, took the lead, closely followed by Jena, Leipzig, Helmstedt and Rostock; but first or last in at least a score of the German universities anti-Socinian or anti-Photinian dissertations were presented or disputations held by students under the supervision of the faculties.[4] Such exercises appear to have been the favorite means employed by young theologues to establish their reputation for orthodoxy and by their teachers to confirm them in it, and they treated the subject in every possible aspect and in the most minute detail. Apart from these polemical efforts at the universities directed against Socinianism in general or in detail, a large number of solid works were published by individual theologians, either to controvert works that issued with increasing frequency from the Raków press, hardly one of which, it would seem, was suffered to go unanswered, or to attack the Socinian system or one of its doctrines in particular. In fact, out of the eighty years following the publication of the Racovian Catechism in German, there were but fifteen in which an attack of some sort was not published in Germany. Of all these opponents, the most notable was Abraham Calovius, Lutheran dogmatic theologian, professor successively at Rostock and Wittenberg, whose *Socinismus profligatus* (Wittenberg, 1652) devoted over 1,100 pages to his theme,

---

[3] cf. Wotschke, *Schleswig-Holstein*, p. 21 f; *id.*, 'Wittenberg und die Unitarier Polens,' *Archiv für Reformationsgeschichte*, xv (1918), no. 57, 58, pp. 73, 66.

[4] The writer has found in print over 700 such products of the universities, and the list must be far from complete. The dates range between 1595 and 1797. The responsible professors would sometimes make a collection of their students' dissertations and publish them as a more or less comprehensive refutation of Socinianism. Thus Scherzer of Leipzig published a collection of 154 dissertations as *Collegii Anti-Sociniani* (1672), filling over 1,300 pages; Josua Stegmann of Rinteln collected 56 under the title of *Photinianismus* (1623), running to over 900 pages; Becmann of Zerbst in *Exercitationes Theologicae* (1639) collected 17 long dissertations, which occupied over 1,000 columns; and Crocius of Bremen combined 28 disputations into *Antisocinismus contractus* (1639). The separate items usually extended to about 20 pages, but sometimes reached the proportions of a moderate-sized book.

and whose other *Scripta Anti-Sociniana* (Ulm, 1677–'84) filled three portly folio volumes,[5] of nearly 2,000 pages in all.

The significance of this struggle of German Lutheranism against the influence of Socinianism, which was thus protracted with serious intensity for a full century and a half, and even continued for nearly a hundred years after the Socinian movement in Poland had ceased to exist, does not lie in what was advanced on either side. This never varied far from the customary arguments based upon Scripture, tradition and reason, however skilfully and forcibly presented; and the considerations urged have long since lost much of the force or interest that they once had, or have ceased to be relevant. Its importance in this history is in the witness it bears to the acute, wide-spread and long-continued fear lest the Protestant religion be fatally corrupted and undermined by this heresy. For Socinianism, so far from being regarded as the negligible vagary of an obscure foreign sect of a few scattered congregations on the fringe of western Europe, was taken very seriously, and feared as an insidious and dangerous enemy of true Christianity, against whose slightest manifestations it behooved the guardians of the faith to be constantly alert. Of the outcome of the struggle between forces so unevenly matched there could of course be no real doubt. The only means the Socinians had of spreading their faith was through the clandestine circulation of their books, which can have reached but comparatively few hands, or through the personal contacts of an occasional venturesome missionary; and any rare convert might avow himself as such only at the serious risk of his personal safety. Hence any little flame of heresy was bound to be smothered almost as soon as lighted. Nevertheless, even those that strove to confute Socinian views, or read or heard the confutations, could not escape being to some degree influenced and modified in their religious thinking, if only because long acquaintance with an enemy tends at length to make him seem less dangerous; so that if by the middle of the eighteenth century the theological atmosphere of Germany had come to be by no means so rigid as it had been at the beginning of the seventeenth, the leaven of Socinian views had no doubt made a substantial contribution to the change. The rise of Rationalism in the age of the Enlightenment, and the growth of modern biblical criticism, but illustrated tend-

[5] Johann Georg Walch, *Einleitung in die Religions-Streitigkeiten ausser der Lutherischen-Evangelischen Kirche*, etc. (Jena, 1736), iv, 322–330, mentions several of the Lutheran clergy who were accused of Socinianism at the beginning of the eighteenth century.

encies in religious thought to which the Socinians, with their persistent advocacy of reason and tolerance had led the way.[6]

In France the influence of Socinianism was not nearly so wide or deep as it was in Germany. It was more remote from Poland, the Raków prints penetrated there but rarely and were difficult to obtain, there were no Socinian exiles in the country, and only an occasional traveler or scholar came thither. As compared with the great number of Anti-Socinian writings published in Germany, barely a dozen appeared in France or in French in the seventeenth century, though there was eventually a good deal of unconfessed Socinianism of a sort in both Calvinistic and Catholic quarters. As early as the summer of 1618 Jonas Schlichting was in Paris as traveling tutor to a young Socinian nobleman, together with quite a number of others, several of whom were Socinians.[7] Also immediately after the Synod of Dort in 1619 some Polish students under the charge of Ruar, fearing an outbreak of intolerance in Holland, removed from Leiden to Paris to complete their studies, doubtless also lured by the desire to form relations with liberal-minded theologians there and to continue their relations with Remonstrant fugitives there. After staying at Blois for some time Ruar was in Paris for nearly a year, and after leaving France in 1620 he continued his interest in the religious affairs of the country, and afterwards sent desired Socinian books to Grotius in exile there.

When Grotius returned to Paris in 1632 he became the centre of a circle of Polish youth, who seem to have been largely Socinians. Andrew Wiszowaty in the course of his wide travels had intimate relations not only with him but also with Gassendi, Mersenne and other distinguished men. One of the most interesting of these was Samuel Sorbière, member of a prominent Calvinist family, who had been designed for the Protestant ministry but had left it for medicine, and finally ended a Catholic. Wiszowaty made his acquaintance, interested him in Socinian thought, and for several years corresponded with him. Ruar thought him very near the Socinian camp, and by the Calvinists he was even charged with being a Socinian. These liberal-minded Frenchmen appreciated the lack of passion with which the Socinians

---

[6] In the field of church history this change of atmosphere is strikingly illustrated in Gottfried Arnold's *Unpartheyische Kirchen- und Ketzer-Historie* (Franckfurt a/M, 1729), with its prevailingly tolerant sympathy toward the heretics; J. L. von Mosheim's *Vollständige Kirchengeschichte* (Heilbronn, 1786–'96); and Schröckh's *Kirchengeschichte*.

[7] cf. Ludwik Chmaj, 'Propaganda Braci Polskich w Paryżu w xvii wieku' (Propaganda of the Polish Brethren in Paris in the 17th century), *Reformacja w Polsce*, v (1928), 105.

discussed disputed points in theology, and their decent way of treating their opponents; attracted by their tolerant principles, they did not hesitate to have cordial relations with them. But though the Socinians would have been glad to establish a center for their propaganda in Paris, on the basis of mutual toleration, they lacked an acknowledged leader, their activity was only occasional and accidental, and they faced the renascent Catholicism of the counter-reformation. Sympathy with them was therefore not sufficiently wide-spread for them to strike deep root as they were able to do in Holland, where all their propaganda was henceforth to be carried on.

Not long after this time an interesting correspondence arose between Martin Ruar, of whose career at Danzig an account was given in a previous chapter, and the celebrated Minorite scholar in Paris, Marin Mersenne, friend of Pascal and Descartes. Though primarily a mathematician and physicist, he had a deep interest in religious matters, and felt seriously concerned at the rapid spread of scepticism, deism and atheism in the country. He had already read some works of Socinus and Crellius, and these had so much interested him that he was eager to learn whether other Socinian writings might not help him in his struggle with the growing French infidelity. Having heard of Ruar's reputation as a highly educated and influential Socinian, he opened correspondence with him, asking him to send him some Socinian books.[8] The correspondence soon passed on to a wider range of questions in theology, the Reformation doctrines, the main doctrines of the Catholic Church, the fundamental differences between the churches, and the evils of sectarian divisions. They amicably discussed the doctrines of the divinity of Christ and the Trinity, which Mersenne was pained that Ruar could not endure; but he praised the mildness of the Socinians in controversy, and wished that they would join in the combat with libertinism, in which cause he was glad to employ their arguments against atheism.[9]

The earliest evidence in print of the influence of Socinian thought in France appears in 1647, when an anonymous writing of Jonas Schlich-

[8] The correspondence is preserved in a series of letters (dated 1640–'44) among Ruar's *Epistolae*, pp. 191–222. cf. Chmaj, *Ruar*, chap. ix; Grabowski, *Literatura*, p. 324 f.

[9] It was shortly after this that Michel de Marolles, Abbé de Villeloin, writing to the eminent Socinian, Stanislas Lubieniecki, June 23, 1650, expressed the feeling that they were not far apart in doctrine, and said, "What you have in a positive way advanced in your Catechism will doubtless be approved by all." cf. *Clarorum virorum epistolae . . . ex musaeo Johannis Brant* (Amsterdam, 1702), pp. 192–196.

ting attacking the doctrine of the Trinity [10] was answered paragraph by paragraph by a French Catholic priest, the Rev. Joseph de Voisin.[11] To another Catholic writer in East Prussia this answer seemed so weak and inadequate that he came out with a swaggering improvement on it,[12] which was anonymously answered in turn by a Dutch scholar, whose work long remained in manuscript, and was not published until a half-century later.[13] This work indicates that Socinianism was beginning to be regarded as a danger to the Catholic faith in France.

In another quarter an insidious danger to religious faith was discerned and opposed. It was in the new intellectual movement that was asserting itself in France. The works of Descartes, father of modern philosophy, were winning wide acceptance in France among both Catholics and Calvinists, to many of whom they offered a welcome relief from out-moded Scholasticism and the dogmatism of the Jesuits. Progressive spirits were reassured to discover that they might rest their religion on solid grounds of reason instead of on the questionable foundation of mere faith. The influence of the new philosophy was manifest both in liberal Catholic quarters, as among the Jansenists of Port Royal, and among Calvinists, especially at their theological college at Saumur on the Loire. It is interesting, however, to note that one of the first to scent danger in this movement was a leading Socinian, Johann Ludwig von Wolzogen.[14] When men prominent in the Church, like the Jansenists and even Bossuet, seemed blind to it, he foresaw that if reason were to replace Scripture as the source of reli-

---

[10] *Disceptatio de Verbo* (Irenopoli = Amsterdam, 1643). Reprinted in Vorst's work cited below.

[11] *Disceptatio theologica orthodoxa de Sanctissima Trinitate*, etc. (Parisiis, 1647).

[12] Johannes Stephanus Rittangel, *Libra veritatis*, etc. (Elbingae, 1650). The author had been successively Catholic, Jewish proselyte, and Catholic again. He dedicated his writing to King Jan Casimir.

[13] (Willem Hendrik Borst) *Bilibra Veritatis*, etc. (Freistadii = Amsterdam, 1700) replied to both the preceding books.

[14] Wolzogen was by birth an Austrian, born at the end of the sixteenth century. A man of large inherited wealth, and celebrated for his learning, he resisted strong worldly temptations to conform to the Catholic faith, and adhered to that of Calvin. Presumably for the sake of greater religious liberty, he removed to Poland, where he joined the Socinians and also engaged in public life and fulfilled various important political missions. He had long been much given to mathematical and physical studies, but the study of the Scriptures more and more absorbed him; and his excellent commentaries on the New Testament make up two volumes of the *Bibliotheca Fratrum Polonorum*. He was an intimate friend of Ruar. He died in Silesia in 1661. cf. Bock, *Antitrinitar.*, i, 1030–1039; Fock, *Socinianismus*, p. 202; Ludwik Chmaj, '*Wolzogen przeciw Descartes'owi*' (W. against D.), in *Archiwum Komisyi do Badania Historyi Filozofii w Polsce*, Tom i, Część i (Kraków, 1915), pp. 90–132.

gious truth, the way would be wide open to infidelity, and religion would have but an arbitrary and shifting basis. He therefore wrote and published some trenchant criticisms on the Cartesian philosophy in its religious implications.[15] Descartes had already died, and there was no one to reply for him; but his thought had spread too far for much attention to be paid to the criticisms of a Socinian theologian unknown in the West. Wolzogen had spoken too late; and the increasing emphasis, in the later history of Socinianism, upon the claims of reason as compared with Scripture, tended to justify his apprehensions.

A clearer trace of infection with Socinian thought is seen in 1670 in a book on the reunion of Christendom, by a professor of theology in the Calvinist college at Saumur.[16] The author had for several years been interested in the cause of the Remonstrants in Holland, and had eagerly read Socinian books. Applying Cartesian principles to religion, he proposed in his work a union of all Christians on the fewest possible articles of faith, and those only such as are the most plainly set forth in Scripture. The guardians of the faith were quick to see that this would be to neglect as non-essential many of the distinctly orthodox doctrines, and thus to open the door wide to Arminians and Socinians. The Synod at Saumur therefore condemned the author and his book, and when he still persisted deposed him from his chair and from the ministry, and excommunicated him from the church the same year.[17] The movement thus started, with its inclusive spirit of toleration, spread, however, especially after the revocation of the Edict of Nantes in 1685 exposed the Huguenots to renewed persecution, and made religious toleration more than ever a matter of vital interest; while its most active and able opponent was the Calvinist pastor and professor, Pierre Jurieu, a man of great learning and uncommon vigor in polemics, which made him the strongest controversialist of his time.

Determined at all hazards to keep the Reformed churches free of all looseness in doctrine, and at the same time smarting under increasing persecutions from the Catholics, Jurieu sought to convince the Catholic

---

[15] *Annotationes in Meditationes metaphysicas Renati Des Cartes* (Amsterdam, 1657); also printed at the end of vol. ii of his works above mentioned. cf. Fock, *Socinianismus*, p. 203, n.

[16] (Isaac d'Huisseau) *La réunion de Christianisme, ou la manière de rejoindre tous les Chrétiens sous une seule confession de foi* (Saumur, 1670).

[17] cf. Guichard, *Socinianisme*, p. 177 f; Francesco Ruffini, *Religious Liberty* (London, 1912), pp. 116–118.

Church itself of fostering heresy in its own bosom. On the authority of a work by Bishop Huet of Avranches,[18] he charged that Catholic France was full of deists and free-thinkers, and that infidelity was spreading, especially at court and among the intellectuals. In a little book on the French clergy,[19] he declared (as though it were the admission of a Catholic) that the most dangerous enemies of the Catholic religion were the large numbers of those who, while professing the strongest attachment to it, do not accept its doctrines or respect its worship. Some of them call in question the main truths of Christianity, and are in fact Socinians, and this is the religion not only of young priests, but of some serious associations (meaning the Jansenists), who make a great show of their austere morals and their loyalty, yet doubt even the Trinity and the incarnation. Among these are to be numbered those Protestant pastors who to avoid threatening persecution lately joined the Catholic Church out of policy, subscribing to its doctrines as mere symbols of the Christian religion, while in fact disbelieving them. Jurieu's charges, though it was admitted that there was a limited basis for them, naturally aroused much resentment among the Catholics. They were, however, overdrawn, and were duly answered and rebutted. Feeling against Jurieu was so strong that he found it best to withdraw to Rotterdam, where he became pastor of the French Protestant refugees (Huguenots) who had fled from France after the revocation of the Edict of Nantes.[20] Here he was now attacked from another quarter. It was being said that many of the French Protestant pastors sympathized with the views of the Remonstrants in Holland who had revolted from the high Calvinism of the Reformed Church, and consequently approved their tolerant attitude toward Socinianism. A French pastor who had been successively Catholic in France and Reformed in Holland, and had recently been dismissed by the latter as Socinian, now published at Amsterdam an anonymous work aimed at Jurieu, to prove that members of the Reformed Church were bound

[18] *Demonstratio Evangelica* (Parisiis, 1679), preface.

[19] *La Politique du clergé de France* (La Haye, 1681), p. 90 f.

[20] A fuller account of this controversy is to be found in Guichard's *Histoire du Socinianisme*, chaps. xxxvi–xxxviii. This work was written by a contemporary, but not published until about a quarter of a century later. It is Catholic and partisan in tone, but is the fullest treatment of the general subject published before the twentieth century. It has sometimes been attributed to Bernhard l'Ami (Lamy). An English translation of the first and more important part is appended to the English translation of the second volume of Maimbourg's *History of Arianism* (London, 1726).

in all reason and Christian charity to extend to all other Christians, including Socinians and Quakers, the same toleration that they claimed for themselves; [21] and in a supplementary work he sought to show that there was only a verbal difference between the currently accepted interpretation of the doctrine of the Trinity and Socinianism, and hence no valid objection to the toleration of the latter.[22]

The discussion thus now shifted ground from the secret heresies in the Catholic Church in France to the subject of toleration in general in the Protestant churches in Holland, where the Remonstrants were urging complete freedom to preach, print, teach, and interpret Scripture and the Catechism, as also among the churches of the French Protestant refugees, in which a large number, while professing opposition to Socinian doctrines, yet openly favored toleration of Socinianism. Jurieu, knowing full well that the source of all this was Socinianism itself, now came out with a new book,[23] written in hot indignation at those who under the pretence of charity wished utterly to overthrow the Christian faith. He condemned toleration as a 'Socinian doctrine, the most dangerous of all those of that sect, since it was on the way to ruin Christianity and place all religions on the same plane'.[24] He sharply criticized the Socinian doctrines as stated by Socinus, Crellius and Völkel, likened Socinians to Moslems and pagans, attacked the Remonstrant theologian Episcopius, calling Arminianism the precursor of Socinianism, which was not Christian at all, but a species of atheism. Those that tolerated it out of charity were great enemies of the faith. Not satisfied with printed attacks, he got the Synod of Amsterdam in the same year to pass decrees condemning a policy that 'under the misleading names of charity and tolerance tends to insinuate into unsophisticated minds the poison of Socinianism.' [25] As over 4,000 Protestant refugees and more than fifty pastors had taken refuge at Amsterdam after the revocation of the Edict of Nantes, and as they were here exposed to currents of the Socinian influence then rife among their Remonstrant neighbors, the question of how much toleration should be allowed became an urgent one, and discussion of it was active. Isaac

---

[21] (Noël Aubert de Versé) *Le Protestant pacifique* (Amsterdam, 1684).

[22] *Le Tombeau du Socinianisme*, etc. (Francfort, 1687).

[23] *Le Tableau du Socinianisme* (La Haye, 1690).

[24] *Des Droits des deux Souverains en matière de religion* (Rotterdam, 1687), p. 14.

[25] Cited by Ruffini, *op. cit.*, p. 134. At this same synod a letter from the refugee pastors in London complained that many of their company there were infected with Socinianism and trying to spread it among their people. cf. Cordemoy, *Traité* (*v. infra*), pp. 11–13.

Jaquelot in an anonymous book [26] undertook to refute Jurieu, whose position he thought extreme, and urged tolerance of Socinianism, though he was not a Socinian himself. Pastor Gédéon Huet also wrote in defence of true toleration,[27] but his work was condemned by the Synod. Jacques Philipot, another refugee pastor at Amsterdam, continued the strife,[28] answering Jaquelot, and cautioning against the consequences of too wide a toleration. Thus one writing led to another until at length the debate lost its edge, and died out with the death of the fiercest disputants.

The centre of the discussion now returned from that of Protestant tolerance of Socinianism, and ended where it had begun, among the Catholics. De Versé at length brought his wanderings full-circle by returning to Rome and doing what he could to counteract the evil of his earlier writings by publishing a refutation of them, in which he answered Socinian objections to the Catholic doctrines.[29] A few years later the Abbé Louis de Cordemoy published, at Bossuet's request, a volume of solid controversy against the Socinians, based on the doctrine of the first Christian centuries, and holding that of all sects none was more dangerous than that of the Socinians. He followed it by another defending belief in eternal punishment, also directed against the Socinians.[30] Both these books are evidence that the leaven of Socinianism was still working in Catholic circles in France.

Only two other works deserve attention in this connection: one by the Huguenot pastor Philippe Mesnard, called forth by Le Clerc's recent French translation of the New Testament, moderately written, and showing that tolerance had gained ground; [31] and the other the ablest and most thorough doctrinal polemic that the French Protestants produced against Socinianism, written by a refugee pastor from La Rochelle.[32] After this comparatively brief and narrowly limited struggle against the quiet spread of Socinian doctrines and principles on French soil or among exiled French congregations, the disturbance quieted

---

[26] *Avis sur le Tableau du Socinianisme* (1690).

[27] *Apologie pour les vrais tolérans*, etc. (Dordrecht, 1690).

[28] *Les justes bornes de la tolérance*, etc. (Amsterdam, 1691).

[29] *L'Anti-Socinien, ou nouvelle apologie de la foi Catholique, contre les Sociniens et les Calvinistes*, etc. (Paris, 1692.)

[30] *Traité contre les Sociniens . . . en parlant de la Trinité, & de l'Incarnation* (Paris, 1697), p. 13; *l'Éternité des peines de l'enfer, contre les Sociniens* (Paris, 1707).

[31] *Essai sur le Socinianisme* (La Haye, 1709).

[32] Theodore le Blanc, *Principes contre les Sociniens* (Hambourg, 1718).

down. If some of the priests in the Catholic Church still privately held Socinian opinions but were not aggressive about it, they were not disturbed so long as they conformed to the usual outward observances; and if among the Huguenot congregations there were those that were drawn more to Socinus than to Calvin, the tolerant spirit had now grown so strong in Holland that there was no danger of civil persecution, and little of church discipline. The further course of our story will therefore be concerned with the gradual and quiet absorption of the Socinian thought and spirit among the native Dutch churches.

CHAPTER XLI

PRECURSORS OF SOCINIANISM IN HOLLAND. A KINDRED MOVEMENT IN THE REMONSTRANTS' STRUGGLE FOR TOLERATION

IT WILL BE RECALLED from the preceding chapters that apart from the two colonies that permanently established themselves in Transylvania and East Prussia, all the other scattered exiles tended sooner or later to find their way to Holland.[1] It was on various accounts quite the most natural place for them to seek refuge. The most frequent line of communication between Poland and western Europe was by sea from Danzig to Amsterdam, and students and other travelers had been taking this journey since before the beginning of the century; various Socinian scholars had formed friendly relations with liberal theologians there; a number of Socinians had for various reasons already taken up their residence there; for more than a generation efforts had from time to time been made to arrange some sort of union between the Socinians of Poland and the Mennonites or the Remonstrants of Holland; and the tradition of religious toleration which had long been more or less observed there made Holland the only remaining land in Europe where the exiles might hope to enjoy at least a fair measure of religious freedom. For ever since William (the Silent) of Orange had thrown off the yoke of Spain in 1578, it had been understood that freedom of worship was permitted to all; and although for well-nigh a century and a half there were occasional and sometimes serious lapses, and although public worship was still legal only for the Reformed Church, yet the ideal of religious toleration remained a national ideal, and was more or less adhered to in practice.

Antitrinitarian thought had appeared in Holland long before Socinianism began to exert its influence there. Adam Pastor, the Unitarian Anabaptist, whose activity was just at the middle of the sixteenth cen-

---

[1] The best general accounts of Socinianism in Holland are by W. J. Kühler, *Socinianisme in Nederland* (Leiden, 1912); and J. C. van Slee, *Geschiedenis van het Socinianisme in de Nederlanden* (Haarlem, 1914). The two complement each other admirably, Kühler being chiefly interested in the theological aspects of the history, van Slee in its external manifestations. cf. Chmaj's review of both in *Reformacja w Polsce*, iv (1926), 237–239.

tury, has already been spoken of in an earlier connection;[2] but there were precursors even before him. The first heretic to suffer death in Friesland was Wybrant Jansz van Hartwerd, who in 1530 was 'burned to powder because he did not believe that Jesus Christ is really God and man'.[3] Adam Pastor at his death in 1552 left numerous disciples who shared his views. One of these may have been the Herman van Vlekwijk who in 1569 was burned at the stake in Bruges for denying the Trinity and the deity of Christ, after a lengthy dispute with a Franciscan monk who sought to convert him.[4] Another early Antitrinitarian was Erasmus Johannis, a German by birth, and an accomplished Hebrew scholar, who after studying in Switzerland, where he seems to have become acquainted with heretical views, was made Rector of the Latin school at Antwerp. Here he secretly and anonymously published a book [5] whose contents were found so heretical (apparently Arian) that he was removed from his office and required to leave the city. He fled to Poland, and there had a debate with Socinus, sustaining the Arian view of Christ,[6] and thence went on to Transylvania, where he was appointed preacher at Kolozsvár, on condition that he should not teach Arianism from the pulpit.[7] The final one of the precursors of Socinianism in Holland to be mentioned here is Cornelis Daems, a lawyer who had been active at Mechlin, Brussels and Antwerp. Probably in the course of his legal studies in Italy he had come to know Socinus, with whom he maintained an affectionate and life-long friendship.[8] While living at Gouda he paid a visit to

---

[2] v. supra, p. 41 f.

[3] cf. Johannes Reitsma, *Hondert Jaren uit de Geschiedenis der Hervorming . . . in Friesland* (Leeuwarden, 1876), p. 33 f.

[4] Original account in *Historie der Doopsgezinde Martelaaren* (Haarlem, 1615), ii, 135 (but omitted from the later editions); reprinted in Tieleman J. van Braght, *Het bloedig Tooneel* (ed. 2, Amsterdam, 1685), ii, 437–452; Gerard Brandt, *Historie der Reformatie . . . in de Nederlanden* (ed. 2, Amsterdam, 1677–1704), i, 501–507; *id. op.*, French trans. (La Haye, 1726), i, 176–189; abridged English trans. by de la Roche (London, 1725), i, 123–131; Wallace, *Antitrin.*, ii, 272–280. The credibility of the debate as given is called in question as fictitious; cf. S. Cramer in *Doopsgezinde Bijdragen*, xxxix (1899), 94 f, 144–152.

[5] *Antitheses doctrinae Christi et Antichristi de uno Deo* (1585). Reprinted with a refutation, by Girolamo Zanchi, *Opera* (Heidelberg, 1619), viii, 849–938.

[6] cf. Socinus, *Opera*, ii, 489–528, *De Unigeniti Filii Dei existentia . . . Disputatio*. See also letters, *id. op.*, 437 f.

[7] cf. Brandt, *Historie*, i, 74–76; Bock, *Antitrinitar.*, i, 419 ff; van Slee, *Socinianisme*, pp. 35–39.

[8] He had won the degree of D. C. L. in Italy, and in 1585 was intending to remove to Poland; at which time Socinus wrote of him to Radecki at Danzig, calling him "Amicus

Utrecht in 1587, apparently meaning to spread liberal religious views there through some books and papers that he took with him. His purpose was suspected, and the sheriff seized books and papers for examination, though he himself escaped arrest by flight; but before anything happened the government changed, and he recovered his books and papers. It was to him that Radecki wrote ten years later giving an account of the outrage upon Socinus at Kraków in 1598.[9]

These few names (and more might have been added) are not to be regarded as in any true sense marking the beginnings of the Socinian movement in Holland. Though preceding it in time, they had actually little if any connection with it; but they are interesting as isolated and sporadic instances of what was at this period stirring in the minds of many in the Netherlands, who lacked however the organization and competent leadership that a cause requires. This was to come from abroad with the arrival in Holland, in gradually increasing numbers, of missionaries, travelers, students, and finally exiles from the Socinians in Poland.

The first of these missionaries arrived in 1598, in the persons of Christopher Ostorodt and Andrew Wojdowski. We have met Ostorodt before as minister of the Socinian congregation at Śmigiel.[10] Still fervent with the zeal of a proselyte, he gladly embraced the opportunity to accompany Wojdowski to Holland with a missionary purpose in view. Wojdowski was a young nobleman who enjoyed a warm friendship with Socinus, as the letters of the latter show.[11] Some years previously when a student at Strassburg he had made a notable convert in the person of Valentin Smalcius. Again in 1597 he had brought two young Polish nobles and their tutor from Strassburg to Leiden, and at the same time had used his opportunity to try to make some converts to his views. It was through him that Ernst Soner was won, who later was centre of the Socinian propaganda at Altdorf.[12] He may also have known Arminius, who was then preaching at Amsterdam; but there is little reason to suppose, as was later loosely charged by an irresponsible and hostile Calvinistic writer, that there was an intimate acquaintance

---

meus summus, & mihi in religione potissimum, omnium quos habeo conjunctissimus." cf. Socinus, *Opera*, i, 378.

9 *v. supra*, p. 403. cf. van Slee, *op. cit.*, pp. 32–35.

10 *v. supra*, p. 417.

11 cf. Socinus, *Opera*, i, 469–473.

12 *v. supra*, p. 425 f; cf. Zeltner, *Crypto-Socin.*, pp. 29–33.

between them, and that this was the source of Arminius's heresies.[13] A year later, since their tutor had now died, Wojdowski was persuaded to return to Holland and have temporary oversight of the two students. Ostorodt would seem to have accompanied him purely with a missionary purpose in mind.

The two emissaries landed at Amsterdam about the beginning of August, 1598, after a voyage of nearly five weeks.[14] While staying for a few days at their hotel to rest up after their long voyage, they were ordered to deliver to the city Council the books and papers they had brought with them, and to appear at the town hall the next day to give account of themselves. This was mysterious enough, though it presently transpired that one of the clergy, whom Wojdowski had known the year before and had supposed to be his sympathetic friend, had reported their arrival to the authorities, who were keenly on the watch to prevent any outbreak of heresy in Holland. They appeared before the Council as ordered, showed proper passports, and were questioned as to their purpose, which they declared was to visit some noble Polish students at Leiden. Meantime members of the Council had examined their books and papers, and reported that they contained blasphemous doctrines; and presuming that these were intended for missionary use, they refused to return them to the visitors, who were bidden, under threat of punishment, not to debate with any one about their religion. The books would be returned to them when they were ready to sail; but when they replied that they meant to return to Poland by another route, it was decided to forward the books to the Leiden Council, who in turn submitted them to the theological faculty for examination, and then forwarded them to the States General at the Hague, with the faculty's opinion about them.[15] The faculty stated that they had glanced through the writings in question (of which one was Socinus's *De Jesu Christo Servatore*), and found that they were not far from the

[13] cf. Jacobus Triglandus, *Kerkelycke Geschiedenissen* (Leiden, 1650), p. 285; van Slee, *Socinianisme*, p. 59 f.

[14] The early authorities for what follows are: Ostorodus et Voidovius, *Apologia ad Decretum . . . Ordinum Provinciarum Foederatum Belgii*, etc. (n. p., 1600); also in Dutch; Pieter Bor, *Nederlantsche Oorloghen* (Amsterdam, 1621), V, boek xxxv, p. 586; Johannes Uytenbogaert, *Kerckelicke Historie* (Rotterdam, 1646), pp. 307–309; Triglandus, *op. cit.*, p. 28; Brandt, *Historie*, i, 839 f; Wallace, *Antitrin.*, ii, 394–398; but above all, the critical retelling in van Slee, *op. cit.*, pp. 44–65.

[15] The faculty's rescript is given in Johannes Cloppenburg, *Theologica opera omnia* (Amstelodami, 1684), ii, 332 f.; Zeltner, *Crypto-Socin.*, p. 31 f, n.; Wallace, *Antitrin.*, iii, 557 f; and van Slee, *op. cit.*, 299 f.

religion of the Turks; they denied the deity of Christ and the Holy Spirit, the saving work of Christ, the office of baptism, and the worship of Christ as true and eternal God, and that Christ by his death had satisfied the justice of God, and many like things too blasphemous to be borne by Christians. They therefore hoped that the men who were circulating these things might not be allowed to stay long in the land, and that their writings might not fall into innocent hands.

Meanwhile Wojdowski and Ostorodt, having attended to the affairs of their charges at Leiden, went on to the Hague to recover their books. They were sent from one person to another, and repeated delays followed, while they were given various excuses until at length they began to suspect that something evil for them was on foot, decided to cease asking for their books, and disappeared from town. At length, more than five weeks after their landing, the committee of Deputies to whom the case had been referred brought it before the session of the States General, together with the written opinion of the Leiden theologians. It was then decreed that on the following day the books in question should be publicly burned in the presence of their owners, and that they themselves should be charged and strictly ordered to leave the country within ten days, under penalty; and that the several Provinces should be warned of the action taken.[16] But the two visitors were by now no longer at the Hague, and their whereabouts were unknown. The books could thus not be burned in their presence, and the notice given could not be delivered to them. Nor were the books burned, for when the fire was lighted they were not forthcoming; for they had been locked up in a secret place, whence some of the Deputies took them home and read them out of curiosity.[17] Ostorodt did not stay long in Holland. Finding that his plans for spreading his faith were so effectually blocked, he departed toward the end of October, and at the end of January was again back in Poland.[18] Where Wojdowski spent the next six months is uncertain. The two may have gone together as far as Friesland, where they are said to have stayed a while before separating,[19] perhaps at Franeker, where a promising university had lately been established; and on the way they apparently visited Hans de Ries,

[16] For the text of the decree cf. the references in the preceding note.
[17] cf. van Slee, *op. cit.*, p. 54, and authorities there cited.
[18] cf. *Apologia*, p. 13; Smalcius, *Diary*, p. 1171.
[19] cf. Uytenbogaert, *Historie*, p. 309.

an influential Mennonite preacher at Alkmaar.[20] There were doubtless opportunities enough as they went to find sympathetic points of contact with Mennonites, whose views as to baptism and non-resistance would bring them together. However, by the middle of March the authorities at the Hague learned that Wojdowski was back again at Leiden. The Magistrate there, under orders from the Hague, summoned him to the town hall, gave him a copy of the decree, and warned him to depart within ten days; and though the Polish students under his charge made a strong plea for an extension of time, the plea was denied.[21] Wojdowski obeyed the decree, and before the end of May left the country. In August the two returned missionaries met in Poland and composed an Apology for their cause, addressed to the States General, and sent it to Franeker, where it was published in a Dutch version. A Latin version soon followed in Poland. A sealed package of the Apologies was privately delivered to the Clerk of the Deputies at the Hague, and thus the case ended. The Apology gave a straightforward account of the writers' experiences in Holland, and then went on to answer the charge that they held and had wished to spread blasphemous doctrines undermining the main truths of Christianity. They complained of having been condemned without a hearing, and by prejudiced judges. They pleaded that free exercise of religion might be granted, and only sectarian strife be forbidden, since the progress of truth cannot be stopped by force. Thus ended the first direct attempt to introduce Socinianism into Holland, which was checked so decisively that it was nearly a generation before another attempt was made. In the meantime the ground was being mellowed for the reception of Socinian seed by the steady growth of the spirit of freedom and tolerance in the liberal party of the Dutch Reformed Church.

At the beginning of the seventeenth century a strong ferment of doctrinal unrest was rising in the Reformed Church in Holland. Though this was the state church, and the only one for which public worship was lawful, yet two wings were developing in it. The conservatives with stubborn obstinacy held to the doctrines of Calvin in all their strictness; while the moderate Calvinists rebelled at some of these, and favored a modification or at least a loose interpretation of them, with a generous allowance of tolerance for differing shades of

---

[20] cf. van Slee, *op. cit.*, pp. 61–63; Hans de Ries, *Ontdeckinghe der dwalingen*, etc. (Hoorn, 1627), p. 127.

[21] For copies of the documents, cf. van Slee, *op. cit.*, pp. 302–307.

opinion. Both wings were represented on the theological faculty at Leiden; the former by Professor Gomarus, whose party were known as the Gomarists, the latter by Jacobus Arminius, who in 1603 came from the pulpit of a church at Amsterdam to represent the liberal interest in the University teaching, whose followers were called Arminians, and whose theological system later gave rise to that of the Methodists in England. He was bitterly opposed by Gomarus, and when he died in 1609 the question of his successor was a critical one. A candidate was sought who was reputed not only for his learning, but also for his tolerant spirit. The choice at length fell upon Dr. Konrad Vorst, Professor in the academy at Steinfurt (now Burgsteinfurt) in Westphalia, where he had won a reputation and was very highly esteemed; and after long hesitation he was persuaded to accept the call, and removed to Leiden in 1611.[22] But even before he could take his chair the most violent opposition to him was stirred up on all sides by the orthodox party, until the Governors of the University found themselves obliged, for the sake of peace in the church, to ask him not to enter upon his duties at once, but to retire on salary to Gouda, until peace should be restored. In fact, he never did enter upon the active discharge of his office. His opponents combed his whole past in search of evidence that he was not sound in the faith. The desired evidence was indeed not too hard to find. In his student days at Heidelberg some ten years before, he had called in question the doctrine of predestination and had shown that he had evidently been influenced by Socinus's book on Christ the Savior. He had admitted at the time that he had read Socinian writings, but had declared that he rejected their errors. He thus satisfied the Heidelberg faculty, and for some years he was generally accepted as an orthodox and moderate theologian.

But at the very time when his appointment was still pending he published a work that roused a fierce storm of indignation,[23] and was attacked on all hands as full of Arian and Socinian errors. Various fugitive rumors of what Vorst had sometime said or written or done were now pressed into service: he had corresponded with Socinians and had obtained and loaned Socinian books; he had used Socinian inter-

---

[22] On his call and the ensuing controversy cf. Brandt, *Historie*, ii, 145–170; iii, 581–597; Hendrik C. Rogge, 'Het beroep van Vorstius tot hooghleeraar te Leiden,' *de Gids*, xxxvii (1873), 31–70, 495–558; van Slee, *op. cit.*, pp. 66–90.

[23] *Tractatus theologicus de Deo*, etc. (Steinfurti, 1610); cf. Alex. Schweizer, 'Conradus Vorstius,' *Theologische Jahrbücher*, xv, xvi (1856–'57), 435–486, 153–184.

pretations of Scripture; he had been offered the principalship of a
Socinian school in Poland; [24] in short, anything was grasped at that
might tend to brand him as an utter Socinian. The Heidelberg theologians were induced to condemn his book, and he replied in defence
of it. His case had, however, been much prejudiced in the meantime
by the reprinting in Friesland of Socinus's *De officio hominis Christiani*,[25] with its vigorous criticism of the doctrines of the Trinity and
the atonement, which though published entirely without his knowledge was nevertheless laid to his charge, since the students responsible
for it had formerly been under him at Steinfurt. Unconscious or re-
gardless of the rising storm, Vorst at about the same time had also
reprinted Socinus's early anonymous work *On the Authority of Holy
Scripture*, with a preface by himself.[26] His opponents now interested
King James I. of England in the matter, who had been reared as a strict
Scotch Calvinist, and took very seriously his title of Defender of the
Faith. He caused the book to be burned at St. Paul's Cross and at the
two Universities in 1611 (the year of the King James's version of the
Bible), wrote a confutation of it, and informed the States General that
he should be much displeased if such a monstrous heretic were tolerated; and when they demurred at his interference, he threatened to
break off relations.[27] Although Vorst made a very favorable impression
on the Deputies when he pleaded his cause before them in 1612, and
ably defended himself in several printed writings, they felt it prudent
to yield to the pressure, and he was dismissed from the University.

Despairing of any early settlement in his favor, Vorst now withdrew
from the scene at Leiden and removed to Gouda, where he lived without reproach for seven years. It was not until 1619 that the National
Synod at Dort, after having deposed the Remonstrant ministers from

[24] cf. *Praestantium Eruditorum Virorum Epistolae*, etc. (ed. 3, Amstelaedami, 1704),
epp. 164, 166, 167, 623. The Synod at Lublin in 1600 invited him to be Rector of the
school at Lucławice (cf. Sandius, *Bibliotheca*, p. 98; Szczotka, *Synody*, p. 50); and Moskorzowski sent him the invitation by special messenger, but he declined it at once because
he did not agree with their doctrine.

[25] *v. supra*, p. 404, n. 29.

[26] Steinfurt, 1611. *v. supra*, p. 390. The work was so far from being heretical that
it had already been reprinted at Basel without opposition. Vorst declared that he did not
know at the time that the true author was Socinus (cf. his *Prodromus* (Leiden, 1612),
p. 61; and his *Oratio apologetica*, quoted by Schweizer, *op. cit.*, xv, 471), though even if
this were literally true, he did know that it had been ascribed to him. cf. *Praestantium
Epistolae*, ep. 259.

[27] cf. James I., *Opera* (London, 1619), pp. 347–380.

their pulpits, took up Vorst's case, voted him unworthy to teach in the Reformed Church, and begged the States General to remove him from the country. No one ventured to take his part, and the vote was unanimous. The States General banished him, and for two years he lived in concealment and constant fear. He declined an invitation to return to Steinfurt, but in 1622 sought refuge under the government of the Duke of Holstein, who had just given the exiled Remonstrants permission to build themselves a new town at Friedrichstadt.[28] But he had been well-nigh hounded to death by his implacable theological enemies; and within three months from his arrival at a place where he hoped at last to enjoy peace, he passed to his rest. His body was entombed at the new Friedrichstadt on the site where the Remonstrant church was later built.[29] It would be as unfair to claim Vorst for an outright Socinian as it was unjust to brand him such in his lifetime. Like the Remonstrants in general, he disapproved some of the articles in the Calvinistic system, especially that about predestination, and having naturally an open, inquiring mind, he did not shrink from inquiry in any direction that promised new light. Hence, while he rejected the Socinian system in the main, some of its teachings won his approval, whereupon his opponents charged him with accepting them all. Though he be presumed to have been sincere in his professed opposition to Socinianism, he may yet have gone further in that direction than he realized at the time. The bitter enmity of his opponents, their unfairness in judging him, and the sting of the persecutions he suffered, may well have alienated him in the end from the church he had wished to serve. At all events, in his dying statement calmly made he said, 'I have expressly declared, and hereby declare, that I make a difference between the Lord Jesus the Son of God, our only and eternal Savior, and the only true and almighty God, herein following the words and meaning expressed in the New Testament.'[30] His beliefs seem then to have been eclectic, lying somewhere between strict Calvinism and Socinianism, with a strong inclination to tolerance of divergent views. He comes into our history because his case gives concrete illustration of a stage in the development of Socinian influence in Holland, when Socinian books, formerly very rare and difficult to obtain, were more and more being

[28] *v. supra*, p. 501 f.

[29] For an account of the last three years of his troubled life, cf. Brandt, *Historie*, iv, 827–849.

[30] cf. Brandt, *op. cit.*, iv, 842.

brought or sent into the country, and increasing numbers were tending to become more liberal and reasonable in their beliefs, and more tolerant in spirit.

In contrast and opposition to the unyielding dogmatism of the leaders of the Reformed Church in Holland, who sometimes seemed to be trying to outdo Calvin himself, a movement favoring a spirit of religious tolerance in individuals, and a policy of toleration in government, had for some time been gathering force and winning adherents among both those that stood more or less aloof from the church and those that were active in it. The pioneer of this movement was Coornhert,[31] who had been deeply imbued with the spirit of Castellio, two of whose tracts he translated into Dutch (1581, 1582), and whose views he eagerly propagated. By the beginning of the next century, indeed, the idea of tolerance was gaining so much favor that the orthodox sought to counteract it and to confirm minds of the faithful by reprinting at Franeker in 1601 a Dutch version of Beza's *De Haereticis*. The effect of this work was countered in turn by the publication (supposedly at Amsterdam) of Castellio's anonymous *Contra Libellum Calvini* in 1612, which had hitherto circulated only in manuscript, and by a Dutch version of his works the following year. His thought had marked influence on the Arminians, as may be judged from the fact that the five articles (see below) that they opposed to five points of Calvinism were almost literally the conclusions of some of Castellio's writings.[32] Another bold champion of religious and civil liberty was also inspired to use his pen in support of greater religious freedom. Reinier Telle (Regnerus Vitellius), teacher and man of letters at Amsterdam, in 1514 translated Servetus's first book on the Trinity,[33] intending by its publication to soften existing prejudice against Servetus; but he first showed it to Episcopius. The latter was aghast at a plan that would only pour oil on the fire by confirming the charge that the Arminians were secretly fostering a blasphemous heresy, and he begged Telle to abandon his plan.[34] Telle complied, and the translation was not published until 1620, when Telle had already died, and the Remonstrants had been turned out of their pulpits.

Within the church at this period increasing friction was developing.

[31] *v. supra*, p. 207 f.
[32] *v. supra*, pp. 198–200, 202.
[33] *v. supra*, p. 60.
[34] cf. Episcopius to Vitellius, June 17, 1614, *Praestantium Epistolae*, ep. 228, p. 383.

The Arminians, acknowledging only the Bible as the standard of their belief and life, opposed the imposition of man-made creeds, and as to points on which they did not think alike they advocated freedom of conscience and mutual tolerance. On the other hand, the conservatives, greatly in the majority, insisted on strict adherence to the current doctrines of Calvinism, and put all possible pressure on the Arminians. The latter were therefore driven to unite for self-defence, so that early in 1610 nearly fifty of their ministers and others met at Gouda and drew up a document asking that a promised revision of doctrinal standards be now made. They declared their principles and convictions, and asserted the rights and freedom that they claimed from the supreme authority in the State. They set forth five points in the doctrine of the Reformed Church which they deemed in conflict with Scripture and could not therefore with good conscience accept, and expressed their own view in five other points. This famous Remonstrance (which gave rise to their name, Remonstrants) was presented to the States General. On these points of difference they desired mutual toleration, and a resolution was therefore passed that the signers of the Remonstrance, and others like them in future, should not be disturbed for holding these convictions. Again, in 1614, the States General issued an edict tolerating the opinions of both parties, and forbidding further dispute. Peace however did not ensue. The Remonstrant party steadily grew and was favored by the political liberals in the government, and the country became more and more divided religiously and politically. The Remonstrants continued to be persistently accused of being Socinians in disguise, and of aiming to introduce Socinianism into the country. To set the whole controversy at rest, therefore, the issue was brought before a national Synod at Dort in 1619. Here the Remonstrants were from the outset treated as wicked conspirators against the truth, and were shown scant consideration. Their ministers were removed from their pulpits and from any office they might hold under the State. The States General confirmed the sentence of the Synod. About 200 ministers were concerned, and 80 of them were put into wagons and sent into exile across the border. Public proclamations forbade those that remained in the country to hold any meetings, even in secret. The quarrel had infected the government of the country. The ruling Prince of Orange sided with the Contra-Remonstrants, and caused Oldenbarnevelt, the most prominent liberal stateman in the government, and a Remonstrant, to be put to death for alleged treason; and the great Hugo Grotius, who was also prominent in the same cause, was sentenced to life imprisonment, from which he afterwards escaped, to spend the rest of his life in exile. In a few years, however, the wave of fanatical intolerance subsided, for it was discovered that the Remonstrant party was after all not dangerous to the State. The exiles gradually returned, and in 1630 were given freedom of residence and liberty to erect churches and schools; and in 1633 they established at Amsterdam a seminary for the training of their own ministers.

CHAPTER XLII

GROWING INFLUENCE OF SOCINIANISM AMONG THE REMONSTRANTS. INCREASED REPRESSION BY THE ORTHODOX

THE PERSECUTION of the Remonstrants and the banishment of their ministers naturally awakened deep sympathy among the Socinians in Poland. A token of this was given when Jonas Schlichting, who had been one of the Socinian students at Altdorf and later at Leiden, was a pupil of Arminius's successor, Episcopius (who had been the leading champion of the Remonstrants at Dort), sought out the latter in his exile at Antwerp.[1] At the instance of the brethren at Raków[2] he had made the long journey from Poland on purpose to offer the exiles any help in their power to give. If they were disposed to remove to Poland, he assured them of a hearty welcome and of all needed assistance. So generous an offer could not be declined outright, and was carefully considered; but Episcopius replied the following evening, with thanks for the offer, that their present necessities were provided for, and that they felt they could serve their people better by remaining near them than by removing to a distant land. Another and conclusive reason might also have been given: that any such connection with the Socinians at this time would have seemed to their enemies a tacit confession of Socinianism, which they had hitherto indignantly denied. The offer, however, was not forgotten, but was recalled forty years later when the Socinians themselves had to go into exile. It was in all probability prompted by the thought that it might lead to closer relations between the Socinians and the Remonstrants.

Even before this time Martin Ruar, whose life-long passion was the hope of church union, had been trying to foster a *rapprochement* between the two. He had been at Leiden in 1617 when hostility to the Remonstrants was at its height, had then attended the lectures of Episcopius, and had made the acquaintance of several of the professors,

---

[1] cf. Kühler, *Socinianisme*, p. 87 f; Johannes Tideman, *De Stichting der Remonstrantsche Broederschap* (Amsterdam, 1871–'72), ii, 443.

[2] cf. Ruar, *Epistolae*, p. 502. *v. supra*, p. 421.

with whom he later corresponded.[3] In 1619 he was again in Holland visiting persecuted Remonstrants. He also formed a friendship with Samuel Naeranus, pastor at Ammersfort, who went into exile with the rest, and was a wanderer for the most of his life thereafter. When Ruar had returned to Poland he wrote an affectionate letter in 1623 to Naeranus, who had then wandered with his family as far as Rostock, and urged him to undertake a ministry at Danzig, where he might enjoy religious liberty and find a numerous following; but Naeranus preferred, when the storm should have subsided, to return to Holland.[4] An active correspondence between them continued, however, on the subject of union of the two churches, as also with Naeranus's son Jan, and bore rich fruit later when the Socinians themselves were driven into exile, and Jan Naeranus raised bountiful aid for them among the Dutch Remonstrants.[5] Throughout this period Ruar played an important rôle in keeping connections open between the two communions; and he even tried to get Jan Geisteran, who had been deprived of his pulpit at Alkmaar, to become Rector of the Raków school, though the offer was declined on account of divergent views about social questions.[6]

Not the least interesting and important of Ruar's Remonstrant correspondents was Hugo Grotius.[7] Ruar had long admired him, and when on the way from Danzig to Amsterdam in 1631 [8] was so fortunate as to meet him in Hamburg, where he was at the time in exile. A correspondence between them followed, which continued for over eight years; [9] and as we have already seen, Grotius in Paris soon afterwards had association with the numerous Socinian youth who gathered there for study.[10] Though by profession a jurist, and by occupation a distinguished publicist, he was also deeply interested in religious questions, and in the Protestant world was as famed for his theological writings as in the secular world for his classical work, *De Jure Belli et*

---

[3] cf. Ruar, *Epistolae*, p. 45 and n., 58–63.

[4] cf. Ruar, *Epistolae*, pp. 304–324. Naeranus did, however, go to Ruar at Danzig in 1631, apparently for only a short time; *op. cit.*, p. 129.

[5] *v. supra*, p. 496.

[6] cf. Ruar, *Epistolae*, p. 503 f.

[7] cf. Ludwik Chmaj, 'Hugo Grotius wobec Socynjanizmu' (H. G. in relation to Socinianism), *Reformacja w Polsce*, iv (1926), 74–99.

[8] cf. Ruar, *Epistolae*, p. 503 f.

[9] cf. Ruar, *op. cit.*, pp. 126–162, *passim*; Chmaj, *Ruar*, pp. 83–95.

[10] *v. supra*, p. 527.

Pacis (1625), which won him lasting renown as the founder of international law. Indeed for some time he seemed to take more interest in religious questions than in legal ones. He had long been saturated with the thought of Socinus in some of its phases, through the latter's controversy with Palaeologus,[11] although unaware of the authorship of that anonymous work; and he had more lately come into contact with Socinus's theology in his work *De Jesu Christo Servatore*, and had undertaken to controvert it in a work of his own,[12] which though it was widely circulated was allowed even by the orthodox to be a rather ineffective performance.[13] He had long before declared the Polish Brethren to be unworthy even of the name of heretics, being not very different from Mohammedans,[14] and was the most distinguished opponent of Socinianism in Holland; and in this and a later work he had spoken of the doctrine of Socinus as the worst of heresies. Grotius's work was at length answered (though not until six years later, when he was now in exile) by Crellius[15] in a work so marked by both thorough scholarship and moderation of tone as to win the respect of Grotius, who did not venture to reply to it, though other writers carried on an active controversy over it—the so-called Satisfaction controversy.[16]

Grotius became in time familiar with various Socinian writings which Ruar had recommended to him, calling his attention to some views of the Polish Brethren which corresponded with those held by the Remonstrants;[17] and both Ruar and the students in Paris supplied him with many of the Raków prints as they appeared. Hence his opinions and judgments were gradually modified; and as his interest in unity among the different confessions increased, his emphasis upon the doctrinal differences between them declined. He thus tended to give greater weight to the rational grounds of religion as supported by natural law, and to relegate the authority of Scripture to a second place. Thus in his work *De Veritate Religionis Christianae* (1627) he defended Christianity on grounds of reason, and avoided any positions that reason might call in question, not even mentioning the doctrine of

---

[11] *v. supra*, p. 398.

[12] *Defensio fidei catholicae de Satisfactione Christi adversus Faustum Socinum* (Lugduni Batavorum, 1617).

[13] cf. Bock, *Antitrinitar.*, ii, 814 f; van Slee, *Socinianisme*, p. 98 f.

[14] cf. Chmaj, *op. cit.*, p. 85 n.

[15] *Ad librum Hugonis Grotii . . . responsio* (Racoviae, 1623).

[16] cf. Bock, *Antitrinitar.*, i, 140–145.

[17] cf. Ruar, *Epistolae*, p. 132 f.

the Trinity. In the end he made the test of true Christianity consist not in the correctness of one's belief but in the moral quality of one's life. While this was laying the emphasis precisely where the Socinians laid it, yet it did not prove that he accepted the whole Socinian system. Though he agreed to some of its characteristic doctrines, he was quite opposed to some of the others. But, doctrines apart, he did sympathize strongly with its broad, irenic spirit and its persistent plea for tolerance. It was but natural, then, that the Socinians both then and later should be fain to regard him as on their side; while on the other hand both Catholics like Bossuet and extreme Calvinists like Jurieu and Lutherans like Calovius were equally ready to call him a Socinian or even an atheist.[18] Such verdicts were extreme and unjust. Despite his catholic attitude toward other confessions and his appreciation of their good points, he remained a moderate Calvinist, holding nevertheless that the heart of religion lies not in the creed that one professes, but in the life that one lives.

In the year after the appearance of Grotius's work on the truth of the Christian religion, a little Socinian book appeared holding a very similar position. Samuel Przypkowski,[19] member of a prominent Socinian family, after studying at Altdorf up to the time when Socinianism was suppressed there, spent several years at Leiden when affairs there were approaching a crisis. All over Europe the question of religious harmony lay upon the hearts of many, and various solutions were proposed. Przypkowski's experiences in Holland had forced it upon his attention, and now that the Remonstrants were beginning to return from their exile he published his contribution to the subject (anonymously) in a little book that he had printed at Amsterdam.[20] He argued that the way to religious peace was for the churches to require not agreement on elaborate statements of doctrines often hard to understand, but union about the fundamental things absolutely necessary to salvation, which are very few and very simple. All that is required is sincere love to God and Christ; and errors of the understanding concerning divine mysteries, which are not essential to salvation, will not condemn a man. He took occasion also to add that Socinians, even if mistaken in their belief as to these non-essentials, deserve sympathy as

---

[18] cf. Guichard, *Socinianisme*, 2. partie, chap. xlii.

[19] cf. Chmaj, *Przypkowski*. His activity in behalf of the exiles in East Prussia a generation later has already been noted. *v. supra*, pp. 513–516.

[20] *De Pace et Concordia Ecclesiae*, 1628, 1630. *v. supra*, p. 422.

conscientious and God-fearing, and that heretics in general instead of being excommunicated ought rather to be tolerated and if possible set right. The book at first attracted little attention, but when a new edition appeared, a supposed similarity of style and thought caused it to be ascribed to Episcopius, and its plea for the Socinians therefore brought new reproach upon the Remonstrant cause. Denials were prompt and decisive, but the episode made the Remonstrants more cautious than ever about showing sympathy with Socinianism. The little book, however, had no little influence both now in Holland and later in England, in promoting simplicity in beliefs and generous tolerance of differences.

Undeterred by their failures hitherto to bring about closer relations between the two communions, the brethren at Raków early in 1632 took advantage of the fact that Ruar was about to go with a number of others to Holland, and by him sent to the Remonstrant brethren there a letter signed by eleven of the leading ministers, congratulating them upon the return of happier days, and offering to furnish any needed aid in their power. Ruar was also instructed to approach them tactfully with regard to forming closer relations of friendship between the two churches.[21] Unfortunately the leaders of the Remonstrants did not think it advisable to make any reply to the communication, though Episcopius afterwards wrote Ruar an evasive apology for their shabby silence.[22] The truth doubtless was that in view of all that had been charged against them they still feared becoming involved with the Socinians. The progress of Socinianism now went on quietly for several years, and though accusations continued to be made that the Remonstrants were Socinians in belief, no evidence of Socinian activity was discovered. There can be no doubt, however, that Socinian books were now coming in an increasing stream from the busy Raków press, and that letters continued to pass between the Polish Brethren and kindred spirits in Holland, so that the field was insensibly prepared for a harvest to come.[23]

The calm was suddenly broken in 1638. The Socinians had lately

---

[21] For the correspondence, cf. van Slee, *Socinianisme*, pp. 311–316; Tideman, *Stichting*, p. 441 f.

[22] cf. van Slee, *op. cit.*, p. 203 f.

[23] In the nine years, 1630–'38 inclusive, at least ten Dutch translations of Socinian writings (Socinus, Smalcius, Völkel) were published, ostensibly at Raków, though it is probable that this was only a blind for Amsterdam.

been forced to leave Raków by decree of the Diet,[24] and Jan Stoiński (Statorius, and, by error, Sartorius), who had lately been minister of the Raków church, but was now apparently in Holland recovering from serious illness,[25] and had been outlawed by the decree, was homesick for the brethren. He therefore addressed a letter to Adam Franck, minister of the 'Saxon' (i. e., German-speaking) Unitarian church at Kolozsvár, saying, *inter alia*, that 'there is a great harvest here, but also many opponents, and not a few that are Unitarians; but the most of them are either Arians or near-Arians, who admit that knowledge of the doctrine (of the Trinity, etc.) is not necessary, and that they ought to treat us as brethren.'[26] This letter never reached its destination, for it was intercepted by the Calvinist Prince George Rákóczy I. of Transylvania, and by him was, 'out of love to the Christian religion, and to put the Dutch on their guard,'[27] sent to Professor Bisterfeld of Gyulafehervár, who was then at Utrecht preparing an answer to a work of Crellius. The theologian to whom it was reported interpreted it, rightly or wrongly, as evidence of a Socinian scheme to introduce into Holland a colony of refugees from Raków whom the Prince, as he himself had written, had denied residence in Transylvania as being outlaws from another country, and blasphemers and disturbers of the public peace.[28] The letter was at once translated into Dutch, with appropriate notes, and posted at the city gates, on the doors of the churches and the University, and even of the meeting-place of the Remonstrants. The purely incidental mention in it of the name of Uytenbogaert, Remonstrant minister at the Hague, brought fresh and undeserved reproach on both him and his cause; and the letter itself stirred up the Synod to fresh efforts to defend the faith.

Already ten years before, in 1628, the church had tried to get the government to take action against the infection of Socinianism, when

[24] *v. supra*, p. 454.

[25] cf. Bock, *Antitrinitar.*, i, 938 f.

[26] cf. translation of the letter in the Royal Library at the Hague. cf. Heinrich Ludolff Benthem, *Holländischer Kirch- und Schulenstaat* (Frankfurt & Leipzig, 1698), i, 383 f.

[27] cf. van Slee, *op. cit.*, p. 110.

[28] cf. F. K. van Ommen Kloeke, 'Socinianen en de Zuid-Hollandsche Synode in 1639,' *Nederlandsch Archief voor Kerkegeschiedenis*, N. S., xi (1914), 244–256. The statement here ascribed to the Prince was categorically denied by Jonas Schlichting in his *Apologia* (1664), p. 39, *v. infra*, pp. 555–556. The translator may have hastily misinterpreted an action taken not against refugees from Raków, but against the semi-Judaizing group of the Unitarians in Transylvania, who were subjected to severe discipline, as will be related in another division of this history.

the North and South Holland Synod petitioned the States General not to tolerate the Socinians, lest the Republic give offence to all Christendom, but the petition was not granted.[29] Now again in 1639 the Synod addressed to the States General a lengthy remonstrance, setting forth the chief heresies of the Socinians and the methods employed in spreading them, and asking that appropriate action be taken, as had been done forty years before in the case of Ostorodt. The States, who had also been warned by the English ambassador Boswell that exiles from Raków had already come as far as Danzig on their way to Holland, acknowledged receipt of the remonstrance and made a rather evasive answer, but urged the brethren to keep their eyes open, undertaking to take appropriate action if any were found attempting to enter the country.[30] The States however adopted a resolution under which Socinian books were seized and burned at Leiden, Amsterdam and Rotterdam.[31] Again in 1641 the Friesland Synod moved the provincial Estates to take similar action, and books were burned also at Leeuwarden, where, as Courcelles wrote Ruar, it seemed to them easier to throw them into the fire than to refute their arguments.[32] In the following year at Amsterdam the sheriff, acting without proper legal warrant, seized 550 copies of Völkel's *De Vera Religione* at the booksellers' and burned them in public, also sentencing the holders to a fine of 2,000 gulden, which the chief magistrates later annulled. The book was however published at Rotterdam in Dutch translation in 1649.[33]

The fact is that the States General as a whole did not share the zeal of the Synods for repressing the Socinians, for an influential number of them favored the policy of complete religious liberty, which had now for more than a generation been more or less in eclipse. Decrees might indeed be passed in response to group pressure from the Synods; but whether they were enforced was likely to depend upon the local authorities, whose sympathies, especially in the larger towns, and above all in Amsterdam, inclined them to wink at infractions. Thus affairs went on for a decade or two. The fears of an invasion of Socinian refugees from Raków seem not to have been realized. Schlichting wrote in 1654 that so far as he knew there had been none save some

---

[29] cf. Guichard, *Socinianisme*, p. 146.
[30] cf. Kloeke, *op. cit.*, pp. 245–256.
[31] cf. van Slee, *op. cit.*, p. 254.
[32] cf. Ruar, *Epistolae*, p. 326.
[33] cf. Ruar, *Epistolae*, p. 327 f; Bock, *Antitrinitar.*, i, 1000 f.

young men who had been drawn to Holland to pursue their studies.[34] But books were imported in increasing numbers, or were published in Dutch translation, and were circulated in ever wider circles; and for these it would seem that Dutch correspondents of Polish scholars were chiefly responsible. If any meetings for public worship were attempted, they were soon suppressed by the authorities.[35] It is evident, however, that private groups of Socinians were wont to gather in one another's houses after the custom of primitive Christianity which they liked to observe, to pray, sing their hymns, read the Scriptures, and exhort one another to lead strictly Christian lives. To such meetings sympathetic outsiders would also be cautiously admitted. We have from a mild Calvinist source a contemporary account of these gatherings.[36]

They hold private meetings in which they offer fervent prayers to God, with groans and tears. All present are permitted to speak. One of them begins with reading a chapter of Scripture, and when he has read a few verses, or a complete passage, he and the hearers speak their minds on the meaning of the words read. Though the most of them are shop-keepers, artisans, uneducated and often illiterate, yet they seem to have a special talent for understanding and expounding Holy Writ. Their lives are holy and blameless so far as can be judged by what one sees, and they govern themselves entirely by the teachings of Jesus Christ, caring little for this world's goods, but apparently only for works of piety and charity, and for the salvation of their souls. They give themselves chiefly to reading the word of God, in which they are so well versed that one would say that the most of them know it by heart.

The records of the church Synods during this period bear witness that the Reformed Church was keenly alive to the 'in-creeping Socinianism.' At almost every meeting the members were admonished to keep a watchful eye against Socinians and the circulation of their books,

---

[34] *Apologia*, p. 35.

[35] cf. Benthem, *Kirch- en Schulenstaat*, i, 884–890.

[36] (Lt. Col. Jean Baptiste Stouppe) *La religion des Hollandois*, etc. (Cologne, 1673), pp. 54–56; cf. Guichard, *op. cit.*, p. 152 f. Stouppe, a native of the Grisons, had studied theology and been minister of the Walloon church in London, but later entered military service with the Swiss. In 1672 he was appointed commandant at Amsterdam, whence in the following year he wrote to a friend at Bern his impressions of religion in Holland, as published in this book. His account was resented by the orthodox in Holland, and was answered by the Groningen professor Johannes Braun. cf. Jean Brun, *La véritable religion des Hollandois* (1675); K. C. Meinsma, *Spinoza en zijn kring* ('s Gravenhage, 1696), p. 364 ff.

and plans for repressive action were discussed.[37] It all came to little. Despite all the measures adopted during twenty years, Socinianism was reported as rapidly spreading (of course among the Dutch themselves) in almost all the provinces, especially those of Holland, Friesland and Groningen.[38] Resolutions might be passed and proclamations posted, but a strict enforcement of them was an entirely different thing. The reiteration of proclamations was in itself evidence that the measures of the government had produced little or no result. At length, however, in 1651 the National Synod presented to the States General a remonstrance so strong that it could not well be disregarded. The latter sought advice of the theological faculty at Leiden, who at once supported the remonstrance in all respects: the doctrine of the Socinians was in short the uprooting of the Christian faith, a fusion of many errors, hardly different from paganism. Thus spurred on from both sides the States General in 1653 issued against the Socinians an edict which in its severity left little to be desired.[39] All men were forbidden to import or circulate Socinian books or hold (Socinian) meetings, on pain of banishment for the first offence, and of arbitrary punishment for the second. Printers and booksellers were forbidden to print, import or sell Socinian books in any language, under penalty of a fine of 1,000 gulden for the first offence and of banishment for the second. All such books were at once to be delivered to the Magistrate, with oath that none was withheld, under suitable penalty.

The decree produced a temporary effect, and at least the Socinians did not attempt again to hold public worship. But it is significant that more than a year was allowed to elapse before the decree was given to the officers to enforce; [40] and it was not long before the Socinians began again to be active in publishing, translating and selling their books, and in spreading their doctrines through other channels, as will be seen below. In the meantime a powerful voice was raised in defence of the Socinians. A 'Polish Knight' (Jonas Schlichting) published in 1664 a dignified defence of his brethren against the unjust accusations that had been made against them in the Synod's remonstrance which

---

[37] cf. W. P. C. Knuttel, *Acta der Particuliere Synoden van Zuid-Holland*, 1621–1700 ('s Gravenhage, 1908–'16), *passim*.

[38] cf. Kühler, *Socinianisme*, p. 142.

[39] For the text, see Benthem, *Kirch- en Schulenstaat*, i, 885–889; also in Meinsma, *Spinoza*, Bijlage iv, p. 3; and in Cocceius, *v. infra*.

[40] cf. van Slee, *op. cit.*, p. 260.

had led to the decree of the previous year.[41] It was written with a self-restraint and moderation that contrasted favorably with the passionate recriminations of the remonstrance. It answered one by one the charges that the Socinians taught wicked heresies, corrected various errors in statements that had been hastily made on insufficient grounds, and ended with a noble plea for tolerance and patience rather than force in the treatment of errors. The Synod could not afford to let this Apology go unanswered, and entrusted the task to the Leiden faculty, who appointed Professor Johannes Cocceius to undertake it, since it was he that had prepared the original remonstrance. He accepted the commission with alacrity, and in due time published a reply to Schlichting's defence.[42] It was not a very convincing reply, for instead of squarely meeting the main points at issue it consisted mainly of bickering objections to a large number of trivial ones; but the Synod expressed entire satisfaction with the refutation. As we have seen, the decree had only a tardy and half-hearted execution. The Synods continued to complain, and the Estates from time to time posted new proclamations forbidding printing and sale, but all to little purpose. While in the smaller towns and remote provinces the law was more or less enforced, in the larger ones the magistrates, jealous of their own authority, resented the interference of the church, and the law was largely a dead letter.[43]

Thus matters drifted on for nearly ninety years after the passing of the decree. The Socinian infection continued steadily to spread, and Socinian books were imported, translated and printed in increasing numbers. On the other hand the provincial Synods continued to pass their resolutions and to discipline any ministers charged with heresy, and to prod the States General to go through the form of issuing proclamations, which local authorities were increasingly reluctant to enforce; [44] until the fires of controversy gradually burned out with the

[41] *Apologia pro veritate accusata, ad Illustrissimos & Potentissimos Hollandiae & West-Frisiae Ordines. Conscripta ab Equite Polono.* Also a Dutch version, *Verantwoordinghe,* etc.

[42] *Equitis Poloni apologia adversus edictum . . . examinata* (Lugduni Batavorum, 1656). Prefixed were the original remonstrance of the Synod presented to the States General, their reference of it to the Leiden faculty, the advice of the latter, and the resulting decree, all given in both Dutch and Latin. Cocceius gives the *Apologia* in full, with his examination and rejoinder in the form of extensive foot-notes. The whole is reprinted in his *Opera omnia theologica* (Amstelodami, 1701), vol. viii.

[43] cf. van Slee, *op. cit.*, p. 263 f.

[44] cf. *passim*, Cau en van Leeuwen (comps.), *Groot Plakkaatboek* (11 vols., 's Graven-

realization that the results of the heresy were not so fatal as had been feared, that Socinianism was actually doing little serious harm, and that their efforts to suppress it were doing little good, and that when let alone those holding Socinian views nevertheless fitted comfortably into the religious and social life of the Republic. The fires of persecution lasted longest in Friesland, and finally flickered out in 1742.

The events that we have related were in the open field of action by church assemblies, with the half-hearted co-operation of the civil authorities. But in the field of thought the theologians also put forth their strongest efforts. The number of polemic works issued in Holland against the Socinians was considerable, and the anti-Socinian disputations and dissertations in the universities ran into the hundreds. Five theologians, however, are outstanding, and deserve record here. Johannes Hoornbeek, Professor at Utrecht, published at the height of the struggle with Socinianism a confutation of it in three ample volumes, which was so highly esteemed that an abridgement of it was called for more than a generation later. He also directed his students in presenting anti-Socinian disputations as a part of their training, of which he collected more than a hundred and published them in two large volumes.[45] He early discovered the affinity between Socinians and Mennonites, which he declared in an often-quoted epigram: *Anabaptista indoctus Socinianus; Socinianus autem doctus Anabaptista.*[46] Professor Johannes Cloppenburg of Franeker published there in 1652 a *Compendiolum Socinianismi confutati*, which was prefaced by a careful *Praefatio historica de origine et progressu Socinianismi*; also a work *Anti-Smalcium de Divinitate Christi* (*ibid.*, 1652). Both are contained in his *Theologica opera omnia* (Amstelodami, 1684), ii, 318–449. The most pretentious work of all, though hardly the ablest, was by Samuel Maresius (des Marets), a French Calvinist who was Professor at Groningen. His *Hydra Socinianismi expugnata* (3 vols., Groningae, 1651–'62) was a refutation of Völkel's *De vera religione* with the work of Crellius prefixed to it. It reprints Völkel in full, divided into short

<hr>

hage, 1658); Nikolaas Wiltens (comp.), *Kerkelijk Plakkaat-boek* (5 vols., 's Gravenhage, 1722).

[45] cf. his *Socinianismus confutatus* (3 vols., Amstelodami, 1650–'64) including *Apparatus ad controversias et disputationes Socinianas* of 103 pp. in vol. i; answered by Daniel Zwicker, *Irenico-Mastygis pars specialis* (Amstelodami, 1667). Also his *Disputationes theologicae Anti-Socinianae* (2 vols., Lugduni Batavorum, 1654–'62); *Socinianismi confutati compendium* (*ibid.*, 1690).

[46] cf. his *Socinianismus confutatus*, i, 371.

sections, each of which was assigned to a student to defend as a thesis, with critical notes and comments. It was said that Maresius, in venturing thus to reprint a work which was under the ban, followed the advice of the bookseller, who hoped by this means to promote the sale among those that would be curious to read a forbidden book.[47] The three writers just mentioned wrote in scholarly Latin, and thus only for the educated. Petrus de Witte, Reformed minister at Leiden, wrote in common Dutch for the uneducated his *Weerlegginge der Sociniaansche Dwalingen* (Amsterdam, 1622), in which he dipped his pen in gall and leveled a wealth of passionate and abusive epithets against both the Socinians and their confederates the Remonstrants and Mennonites, as being no better than Turks, though he offered not a single argument that had not often been used already. But the ablest and most dignified of the Reformed polemics against Socinianism was by the venerable Abraham Heydanus, Professor at Leiden, who in his *De origine erroris*, and his *Diatribe de Socinianismo* appended to it (Amsterdam, 1678), clearly discerned that the root of the matter lay in giving human reason precedence over Scripture in any disputed question of religious belief.[48]

Besides these comprehensive treatises by leading theologians against the Socinian system as a whole, several minor works deserve mention, which tried to prove the practical identity of the Remonstrant position with Socinianism by calling attention to the close resemblances between the two; although their strategy allowed them to pass by without notice the many and important divergences between the two systems. The Remonstrants in reply brought forward the latter in defence of their position, but the denials could never quite keep up with the accusations. Thus Nicolaas Bodecher, who had formerly been a Remonstrant, but at the Synod of Dort deserted his brethren and went over to the camp of the contra-Remonstrants, justified his change by publishing, with the approval of the Leiden faculty, a book designed to prove that the Remonstrants agree with the Socinians either in fact, or in words, or even in method, in many parts of their confession.[49] Episcopius felt himself so much implicated in this attack that he replied in a book contemptuously entitled, *Bodecherus ineptiens*. Nicolaas Vedelius, Pro-

---

[47] cf. Bock, *Antitrinitar.*, i, 1002 f.

[48] cf. van Slee, *op. cit.*, p. 249; Krüger, *Socinianisme*, p. 224.

[49] *Sociniano-Remonstrantismus, hoc est evidens demonstratio, qua Remonstrantes cum Socinianis sive re ipsa, sive verbis, sive etiam methodo, in pluribus confessionis suae partibus consentire ostenditur* (1624).

fessor at Deventer, followed up with a book entitled *De arcanis Arminianismi* (1631), which has been characterized as a lampoon full of diabolical hatred, but was yet so much esteemed by Professor Voet of Utrecht that he had it translated into Dutch. Episcopius was reluctantly pressed again to reply, in his *Vedelius Rhapsodus, seu vindicatio doctrinarum Remonstrantium a criminationibus et calumniis Vedelii* (1633). Not to mention other controversial works along the same line, perhaps the most effective indictment of the Remonstrants was that of Johannes Pelt, Reformed minister at Schiedam, whose *Harmonia Remonstrantium et Socinianorum* (1633) printed in deadly parallel columns the views of Remonstrants and Socinians on various characteristic doctrines, that the reader might judge for himself. When so much agreement was shown to exist, it availed little to show that in many other important points there was disagreement.

It must not be supposed that these long and persistent efforts to prevent or suppress Socinianism in Holland were only the expression of a principle of political intolerance and religious bigotry.[50] For the Dutch were by native temperament as heartily devoted to liberty as those who had long suffered under despotism might be expected to be; and the original broadly tolerant policy of William the Silent embodied a basic ideal of the people. But in the period of the Catholic reaction for a century or more after the Council of Trent, the fear of the Dutch was sincere and acute that by insidious steps they might again be brought under the oppression of Rome, which had been more cruel and merciless in the Netherlands than in any other country. Hence any relaxing of the strictest standards of Protestantism was at once under suspicion as perhaps the first step back toward Rome. Hence the opposition to the Remonstrants with their tolerant spirit in matters of doctrine. Hence yet more the opposition to Socinianism, which was regarded as retaining in the principle of Nominalism the fundamental error of the Roman Church.[51] It was on this ground that the most competent Dutch theologians rested their argument against the Socinian doctrine.

[50] cf. van Slee, *op. cit.*, pp. 247–253.

[51] The author doubts whether the theology of Socinus was historically based, as some have contended, upon the nominalist philosophy. Whatever affinities may be discovered between the two systems may rather be regarded as largely accidental. Socinus disclaimed knowledge of philosophy, and based his teaching on Scripture reasonably interpreted, independently of either church tradition or philosophical theory.

CHAPTER XLIII

SOCINIANISM AMONG THE MENNONITES
AND COLLEGIANTS

THE EVENTS thus far related have for the most part concerned the growing influence of Socinianism among the Remonstrants and the unwearied efforts of the Reformed theologians to combat it in that quarter. Concurrently with this, however, Socinianism was quietly and even more deeply affecting the Mennonite body. Early in this history we noted a strong undercurrent of antitrinitarian doctrine among the Anabaptists in the Netherlands in the sixteenth century; and when Socinian emissaries and Socinian books penetrated Holland in the first quarter of the seventeenth century they found a ready response in many Mennonite hearts. Between the two bodies there were from the start strong points of contact in the effort of both to cultivate Christian faith and life in its primitive simplicity, in their reliance upon the letter of Scripture rather than upon ecclesiastical tradition, in their emphasis upon Christian conduct and character rather than upon creedal orthodoxy, in their view of baptism, their opposition to warfare, to holding of civil office, to oaths, and to worldly pleasures and luxuries.

Ostorodt and Wojdowski are said while in Holland in 1598 to have visited Hans de Ries of Alkmaar, one of the most respected and influential Mennonite leaders; and from 1606 to 1612 negotiations were attempted by the Synods in Poland, through a congregation of Dutch Mennonites at Danzig, to establish closer relations between the two bodies.[1] The Danzig congregation sought the counsel of de Ries, and the matter was seriously considered in Holland; but there proved to be too strong disagreement about it among the Mennonites, not only as to doctrinal matters, but especially because it was felt that, as they already stood in considerable disfavor with the government, it was not advisable to make their case yet worse by an alliance with the Socinians. The matter therefore fell through. Nevertheless Socinian influence

[1] cf. van Slee, *Socinianisme*, pp. 140–143; W. J. van Douwen, *Socinianen en Doopsgezinden* (Leiden, 1898), pp. 133–144.

more and more penetrated the Mennonite communities, and doctrinal differences naturally developed between the conservative members and the progressives. Thus in the congregation at Haarlem a heated controversy over doctrine took place, which was nominally settled in 1626 by an agreement upon a series of articles which were signed by both sides. But these were so vaguely drawn as to leave loop-holes, and Socinianism remained unchecked.[2] It made greatest progress, however, in the congregation at Amsterdam,[3] where a circle of liberally minded spirits in the Mennonite congregation began about 1646 to hold meetings for discussion of religious doctrines, in which the greatest freedom of expression was exercised. The leading spirits were Daniel de Breen (Brenius),[4] Adam Boreel, and Galenus Abrahamsz de Haan. Of these the last was easily the most influential. He was by profession a physician, but was deeply interested in promoting progressive religion; and he showed himself so broad of mind and so eloquent in speech that he was early chosen as preacher to the Mennonite congregation. In his preaching he ardently espoused religious freedom and mutual toleration. A cleavage in the congregation developed ere long between the conservatives, who laid primary emphasis on confession of orthodox doctrine as necessary to salvation, and the progressives, who set comparatively little store by doctrines, but insisted first of all on a religious conduct of life. Between these two factions a stubborn controversy was waged for many years. Galenus boldly and publicly held, as to such doctrines as the Trinity, the deity of Christ, the incarnation, and satisfaction, views that at least had a strong Socinian tinge, and were opposed accordingly. Eventually the consistory of the Reformed Church intervened in a matter that they had long followed with interest, and filed with the city Council a remonstrance charging that in place of a Mennonite congregation one clearly Socinian had been opened in defiance of law. Galenus was charged before them with being a Socinian, but was discharged by the court and declared a good Mennonite. They issued a proclamation, however, and sought to secure peace in the congregation by forbidding pulpit discussion of the points in controversy. It was to no purpose. The inevitable division of the

---

[2] cf. van Slee, *op. cit.*, pp. 143–151; Kühler, *Socinianisme*, pp. 106–113.

[3] cf. van Slee, *op. cit.*, pp. 152–160; Kühler, *op. cit.*, pp. 149–173.

[4] He was a pupil of Episcopius, but later withdrew from the Remonstrants. His large volume of *Opera Theologica* (Amsterdam, 1664) is sometimes taken as supplementary to the *Bibliotheca Fratrum Polonorum*.

congregation took place. About 700 conservative members withdrew, and became known as Zonists from the building ("de Zon") where they set up their meetings, while the Galenists continued to meet in their old place, "het Lam," and were called Lamists.

A similar development took place in the Mennonite congregations in many other towns [5]—Rotterdam, Leiden, Utrecht, in fact in all the more important centers in Holland. Socinian influences penetrated, were complained of, and were opposed in various ways; preachers were here and there removed from their pulpits, religious meetings were forbidden, members were excommunicated, fined, imprisoned or banished, and Socinian books were banned or burned. Yet nowhere were repressive measures effective save in limited regions and for brief periods. The last instance was in Friesland, where Johannes Stinstra, a Mennonite preacher of outstanding gifts and the highest character at Harlingen, was accused of Socinianism and in 1642 suspended from his pulpit, which he was not allowed to enter again for fifteen years.[6] By that time the old repressive laws had become dead letters. Even twenty years before this, in 1722, when the States of Friesland had been prevailed upon by the Reformed leaders to require the Mennonite preachers to subscribe Trinitarian articles, the whole company of them, 150 in number, refused almost to a man to bind themselves to any human confession, though it meant that for a time their places of worship were closed throughout the whole province.[7]

Although Socinian thought considerably influenced many of the leaders of the Remonstrant brotherhood, it was among the Mennonites that it penetrated most deeply and widely. The latter had no authoritative standards of faith to limit their freedom of thought and its expression, and they had a welcome therefore, without regard to differences in doctrine, for any that aimed to practice the Christian religion in all the relations of daily life. Socinianism was almost from its beginning a fusion of two different elements, the rational and the practical; the former deriving from Italian Humanism, and the latter from Anabaptist sources. It was the predominant emphasis of both upon the latter element, together with their relative indifference to the

---

[5] cf. van Slee, *op. cit.*, pp. 160–198; Kühler, pp. 173–179.

[6] cf. A. J. van der Aa, *Biographisch Woordenboek* (Haarlem, 1868), xvii, 1008; Steven Blaupot ten Cate, *Geschiedenis der Doopsgezinden in Friesland* (Leeuwarden, 1839), pp. 211–243, 327.

[7] cf. Kühler, p. 264 f.

former, that made Mennonites and Socinians so congenial to each other. It was, however, the existence of a third group that was the effective means of bringing them together, and we must therefore give some account of the very interesting company of independent Dutch Christians known as Collegiants, or less frequently, from the village where they held their general gatherings, as Rijnsburgers.[8]

In 1619, when the leading Remonstrant ministers had been driven from the country, and others were permitted to remain only on condition of giving up their ministry, many of their members seriously felt the lack of religious meetings. Among these was one Gijsbert van der Kodde, lately an Elder of the church at the village of Warmond near Leiden, whose religious views had been shaped by reading Acontius, Castellio and Coornhert. He deemed it important to hold the members of the church together, even though they were deprived of the leadership of a minister. He therefore proposed to some kindred spirits that they should nevertheless meet now and then to read the Scriptures, offer prayers, and contribute whatever else might seem good as the Spirit might move. The plan was approved and soon put into execution. The movement throve, and the members discovered that they could do without professional preachers so well that when the next year the church leaders in exile at Antwerp appointed a minister to come back secretly to serve the brethren at Warmond, he was given to understand that he was not welcome, since his presence if discovered would imperil them all; and he was advised to go and learn some trade. In fact the movement early began to take on the character of one definitely averse to church organization, to a professional ministry, and to any officially adopted beliefs; and to glory in its emancipation from most of the traditional marks of churches. The members were better satisfied to do the speaking and the praying themselves than to be merely passive listeners to ministers who tended too much to magnify their office. When the Remonstrant congregations at length began to resume activity with settled ministers, van der Kodde and his followers persistently held aloof from their meetings, and resisted all attempts of the ministers to win them over. Their movement, in fact, a little ante-

---

[8] For full contemporary accounts of them, cf. the *Opregt berigt van den tegenwoordigen staet der Collegianten of Rynsburgers*, appended to Simeon Frederik Rues, *Tegenwoordige staet der Doopsgezinden of Mennoniten*, etc. (Amsterdam, 1745); and the anonymous (Elias van Nimwegen) *Historie der Rijnsburgers* (Rotterdam, 1775); also the exhaustive study by Jacob Cornelis van Slee, *De Rijnsburger Collegianten* (Haarlem, 1895).

dated the separate organization of the Remonstrant brotherhood, and as a perfectly free and democratic fellowship of laymen it had already discovered some valued features which they were unwilling to give up. They therefore rented a separate house for their gatherings, which were generally called *collegia* (hence their name, Collegiants), and were at first held but monthly. The procedure in these meetings was simple. Some passages of Scripture were read, a prayer was offered, and one or more made an edifying address.[9] An invitation was then given for any one that felt so moved to speak. Such addresses sometimes lasted an hour, and in case of several in succession the meeting would run far into the night. In this way they aimed to revive the practice of the first Christian churches.

In order to escape continued friction with the Remonstrants, van der Kodde and his brothers presently removed their meetings from Warmond to the neighboring village of Rijnsburg, where they met secretly after each new moon, and observed the Lord's Supper and baptized their members after their own way. This final separation from the Remonstrants was much regretted, though in fact it did little or nothing to weaken the Remonstrant cause. But whereas hitherto all the Collegiants had come from Remonstrant sources, henceforth their main strength was to come from the Mennonites and their chief influence was to be felt among them. From such humble beginnings in an obscure village, the Collegiant movement gradually spread in the seventeenth century until 'colleges' were formed in about a dozen of the larger towns and yet more of the smaller places, to the number of some thirty in all. They did not mean to be organized churches, competing with existing ones, but only free gatherings of persons from all churches or from none, who wished to meet to promote one another's religious life and thought by free and tolerant discussion of matters of common interest. Despite its small compass, this movement, says its latest historian,[10] 'deserves to be reckoned, for the singular freshness and the great breadth of spirit that characterized it, as one of the most remarkable phenomena in the field of the religious life of the seventeenth and eighteenth centuries.'

Of the local meetings of Collegiants, the most important were at Amsterdam, referred to above,[11] and at Rotterdam and Groningen, but

[9] Later on singing of hymns was introduced.
[10] cf. van Slee, *Collegianten*, p. 56.
[11] *v. supra*, p. 561.

the character of all of them was in general the same. The membership of the Collegiants was composed of some from the Remonstrants, a few from the Reformed and many that were not committed to any confession; but by far the largest number came from the Mennonites. It was never thought necessary for one to leave another church to join them, and even some of the ministers of churches attended their gatherings. Their meetings were usually held on Sunday, but there were often week-day meetings as well. Baptism (by immersion) was practiced as a valued sign of adherence to Christianity, but was not insisted on; and the Lord's Supper was observed as a token of Christian fellowship, to which any were admitted who acknowledged in any sense that Jesus was the Christ, the Son of the living God. The Scriptures were their only rule of faith: no creed or confession was set up as a test of membership in their company or of participation in their meetings. The controlling principles of the *collegia* were that the utmost freedom of speech was allowed to all participants (though women, on scriptural grounds, were not permitted to take part), and that in the free fraternal discussion that followed the largest mutual tolerance of divergent views was practiced. Followers of Socinus and their opponents, Remonstrants, Mennonites, rationalists, scripturalists, Jews, all enjoyed equal 'liberty of prophesying,' and respected one another's rights. Amid all the natural diversities of opinion there was no repression of free speech, and only once in a century and a half was there any schism, between the followers of Jan Bredenburg, influential merchant of Rotterdam, who held that reason gives man a natural knowledge of God, and Frans Kuyper, ex-Remonstrant preacher, who insisted on the supernatural origin of Christianity in the Scriptures and the miracles that they report. This, however, ceased with the death of the two leaders.[12]

What has been said above relates to the local 'colleges' in various towns; but with 1640 general meetings of the whole Collegiant connection began to be held at Rijnsburg. Local monthly or weekly meetings were still held here until 1660, when the leading members had died or removed, but the general meetings became great occasions. Twice a year, at Easter (later at Whitsuntide) and at the end of August, Collegiants gathered at Rijnsburg from all parts of the country, to celebrate the Lord's Supper in token of mutual fellowship, to have baptisms, and

[12] cf. Kühler, *Socinianisme*, pp. 241-248.

to hold religious meetings for three days. The centre for these gatherings was at 'the Great House' (*het Groote Huis*), an extensive building at the east end of the village, containing a large number of rooms for the accommodation of guests, together with provision for their entertainment, and a large baptismal pool in the garden. This was established by one of the members and became the property of their orphanage at Amsterdam.[13] The religious meetings were held in a separate meeting-house. These general gatherings continued until late in the eighteenth century, though after the middle of the century they began steadily to grow smaller until 1787, when they ceased in the troubled times of French oppression. In the same period the local 'colleges' were one by one disbanding until 1810, when only one remained.[14] Apart from any damage they may have suffered from the repeated charge that they were nests of Socinianism, they apparently came to an end because there was no longer serious need of them, since the existing churches had by now grown so free and tolerant as to give them all the liberty that they desired to use. Most of their members were absorbed by the Mennonites, from whom many of them had come and with whom they had so much in common.

Of all the persons connected with the Collegiant movement in the course of its history, perhaps the most celebrated was the philosopher Benedict Spinoza, the young Spanish Jew who, after having been put out of the synagogue of his people for being unable to accept the teachings of the rabbis, found among the Collegiants the friendly sympathy and religious fellowship that he was denied elsewhere.[15] He came into connection with the 'college' at Amsterdam about 1654, when he was but twenty-two years old and they were much occupied with the interpretation of Scripture, and thenceforth he had much to do with them, attending their meetings and sharing in their discussions. As long as he lived, some of his best friends were Mennonite Collegiants;

[13] cf. illustrations in Bernard Picart, *Naauwkierige Beschryving der uitwendige Godsdienstplichten* (Amsterdam, 1738); also appended to van Slee, *Collegianten.*

[14] No visible remains of the Collegiants are now extant, at Rijnsburg or elsewhere, except at Amsterdam, in their orphanage, "de Oranjeappel," in the Heerengracht, and the old people's almshouse, "de Rozenhofje."

[15] cf. Meinsma, *Spinoza*; W. Meijer, 'Wie sich Spinoza zu den Collegianten verhielt,' *Archiv für Geschichte der Philosophie*, x (1902), 1932; *id.*, 'Spinoza's demokratische Gesinnung und sein Verhältnis zum Christentum,' *ibid.*, xvi (1903), 455–485; Adolf Menzel, 'Spinoza und die Collegianten,' *ibid.*, xv (1902), 277–298; Ludwik Chmaj, 'De Spinoza a Bracia Polscy' (Spinoza and the Polish Brethren), *Reformacja w Polsce*, iii (1924), 48–88.

and when for the sake of greater quiet and study he removed in 1661 to Rijnsburg he continued his relations with them. He was drawn to them by their deep concern for a sincere religious life, their interest in its rational basis and its application in practical morals, and their broad-minded tolerance; and though he could not fully agree to the particular Christian teachings and practices that they held, in other respects they undoubtedly influenced him deeply. It was among the Collegiants that Spinoza formed contact with the Polish Brethren. Some of them were presumably in the Collegiant circle earlier than Spinoza, and a notable accession will have arrived soon after their banishment from Poland in 1660. Their culture, their tolerant spirit, and their method of interpreting Scripture appealed to him, and his view of the Bible: that Scripture never teaches what is in conflict with our reason; that it can easily be understood by every one; and that it leaves reason free—might almost have been taken directly from Socinus.[16] It should not be claimed, however, that Spinoza accepted the Socinian doctrine in general, for his conception of God was radically different, and his theology had sounder philosophical grounds, and was carried through much more consistently, that that of the Socinians. He was no doubt familiar with many works of the leading Socinian thinkers, which were published during his life-time, and the catalogue of his library at Rijnsburg shows that he owned several important works by Socinian authors, and an engraved portrait of Socinus.

It has been said above that an effective agency through which Socinianism permeated the Mennonite body was the Collegiant movement, in whose free and tolerant meetings Socinians had all the opportunity they could have wished to express their views and win adherents to them. Naturally converts were made; and when persecutions grew heavy in Poland, the little stream of stragglers seeking a new home with freedom of faith would readily attach themselves to the Collegiant movement, and eventually to the Mennonite congregations. When the decree of banishment from Poland was finally enforced, yet larger numbers of Socinians kept arriving in Holland for several years. How large the whole number was it is quite impossible to guess, for only a few names have been recorded. There may at most have been a hundred or two, or at least perhaps only a score or two. They could not under the law have set up avowed Socinian places of worship and con-

---

[16] cf. *Tractatus theologico-politicus*, trans. L. Meyer, p. 46.

tinued their old organization even had they desired to do so; but they were admitted without question to the worship and the sacraments of the Remonstrants, and equally so to those of the Mennonites, without question as to their doctrinal beliefs. As they were generally of noble birth and of superior education and culture, they would feel intellectually and socially most at home in Remonstrant circles; but their views as to baptism, their creedless scriptural Christianity, their attitude toward the civil government, especially as to war, offices, capital punishment, oaths, courts, etc., gave them strong affinities with the Mennonites, despite any differences in belief. It was quite unfair to accuse the whole body of either Collegiants or Mennonites of being Socinian, by the familiar device of holding guilty of a whole system of heresy those who had accepted only a minor part of its teachings though rejecting the rest. Yet the Collegiant Dirk Rafaelsz Camphuysen, famed as a hymn-writer, was in 1625 or earlier invited to be a professor at Raków, and refused largely on account of his wife's reluctance;[17] and he later translated several works of Socinus into Dutch; and Jan Geesteran, after being deprived of his pulpit at Alkmaar, was called in 1622 to a teaching office in Poland, which he also declined. It is not too much to say that about 1660 a Socinian tendency was evident among the Mennonites in all parts of the country.[18] The difference between the two most remarked was, curiously enough, not as to doctrines, but that the Socinians lived a more disciplined life than others, were austere in their morals, abjured frivolous worldly pleasures, and gave themselves much to prayer, fasting and almsgiving.[19]

Apart from direct personal contacts, Socinianism was widely spread in Holland through printed books. These first came to inquiring scholars, as they issued in Latin from the Raków press, and naturally circulated only among the educated. Then, to reach the unlettered, a long series of Dutch translations came from the press, mostly as inexpensive little books, usually published by the enterprise or at the expense of Collegiants or Mennonites of means—over twenty-five of Socinus's works, twenty or more of Crellius, and the most important writings of Smalcius, Schlichting, Ostorodt, Völkel, and several others;

[17] cf. Leon A. Rademaker, *Didericus Camphuysen* (Gouda, 1898), pp. 100, 113.

[18] cf. Kühler, *Socinianisme*, p. 174.

[19] cf. Steven Blaupot ten Cate, *Geschiedenis der Doopsgezinden in Holland*, etc. (Amsterdam, 1847), ii, 173; Kühler, *op. cit.*, p. 195. Their strict ethical views are set forth at length in Johannes Crellius, *Ethica Christiana*, reprinted at Amsterdam, 1681; and in Dutch translation at Rotterdam already in 1651.

and after Wiszowaty, Zwicker, Sandius and Samuel Crellius became residents they contributed their part by numerous works in which they made their contribution to the religious thought of their time. These numerous publications provided the Mennonites, who were poor in competent theological scholars, with a body of divinity well developed and ready to hand; and taken together had a powerful influence upon the development of liberal religion among the Dutch. But by far the most important, as well as the most extensive of these publications, was the celebrated *Bibliotheca Fratrum Polonorum*.[20] Now that the Raków press had long been silenced, its publications had become exceedingly rare and commanded high prices, and the arrival of the distinguished exiles from Poland stimulated lively interest in their cause, a plan for publishing a *corpus* of outstanding Socinian works, which is said to have been first broached in 1628,[21] was revived. The works were published with a fictitious publisher's name, Irenæus Philalethius, which roused much speculation. Suspicion at first and for a long time centered upon Frans Kuyper, who had originally been for a brief time Remonstrant preacher at Vlaardingen, but left the pulpit and became a publisher at Amsterdam. He was a zealous Collegiant, and author of several controversial books. The actual printing is attributed to the famous press of the Blaeuw brothers, who were of the Remonstrant camp, and favored Courcelles and the Socinians. They had already got into trouble by printing Völkel's work in 1642. Of late other guesses have been made; but the question remains unanswered.[22]

---

[20] *Bibliotheca Fratrum Polonorum, quos Unitarios vocant, instructa operibus omnibus, Fausti Socini Senensis, Nobilissimi Itali, Ioannis Crellii Franci, Ionae Schlichtingii a Bucowietz, Equitis Poloni, exegeticis et Ioannis Ludovici Wolzogenii Baronis Austriaci, quae omnia simul iuncta totius Novi Testamenti explicationem complectuntur* (Irenopili, post annum Domini 1656), 8 vols., large folio (also a handsome large-paper edition), with authors' portraits; Socinus, 2 vols.; Crellius, 4 vols.; Schlichting, 1 vol. in 2 parts; Wolzogen, 1 vol. in 2 parts. Irenopolis is a printer's blind for Amsterdam; the vague date is really for 1668 (cf. Sandius, *Bibliotheca*, p. 79), though the first two volumes of Crellius and the exegetical works of Schlichting were published 1665 (*ibid.*, pp. 118, 131). Samuel Przypcovius, *Cogitationes Sacrae*, etc. (Eleutheropoli, 1692), though published much later, is sometimes reckoned as a supplementary volume of the set. cf. Bock, *Antitrinitar.*, i, 46–54; Johannes Fabricius, *Historia Bibliothecae Fabricianae* (Wolfenbüttel, 1718), ii, 57–80; Xawery Godębski, '*Bibliotheca Fratrum Polonorum*' *poszukowanie bibliograficzne* (a bibliographical investigation), Lwów, 1868.

[21] cf. Kühler, *Socinianisme*, p. 140. It has been conjectured that Étienne Courcelles, professor in the Remonstrant seminary at Amsterdam, and correspondent of Ruar, first proposed and planned the work, and that Wiszowaty took over and completed the task that Courcelles had begun. cf. Bock, *Antitrinitar.*, i, 52; Ruar, *Epistolae*, p. 608, n. Publication had already begun the year before Wiszowaty reached Amsterdam.

[22] cf. Kühler, *op. cit.*, p. 140; van Slee, *Socinianisme*, pp. 243–245.

The work belied its title, for it contained (apart from some brief items by Stegmann and Wiszowaty in the Wolzogen volume) the writings of only four authors; and of Schlichting's works not all, but only those composed during and after the Swedish war. On the other hand there are lacking the writings of such important authors as Smalcius, Völkel, Ostorodt, Moskorzowski and others of the classical literary period of Socinianism, not to mention the Racovian Catechism. Except for the commentaries of Crellius and Schlichting, the editorial work of arranging, correcting, annotating, etc. was diligently performed by Andrew Wiszowaty, who also furnished a brief preface to the whole series. The work was at first sold very quietly to trusted persons, but as usually happens with forbidden books it was ere long sold openly and bought by many.[23] In less than a year it came to the notice of the Consistory of the Reformed Church, then as ever on the watch for heresy.[24] Investigation followed, and the matter was reported to the civil government, and finally, after long delay and official reluctance, the *Bibliotheca Fratrum Polonorum* was proscribed by the States General in 1674 as a blasphemous and soul-destroying work, and its sale was forbidden in pursuance of the decree of 1553.[25] Sale continued nevertheless, and it was reported that the work might be openly bought in Amsterdam for 100 gulden.[26] It became a token of respectability to own it, and it was said that it might be found in the libraries of many that had not the learning to read its Latin, but were glad to possess it as a monument.[27] To the guardians of orthodoxy it was of course anathema. Thus a Tübingen professor declared, 'Opus est orco non prelo dignum; quod utinam suppressum fuisset, non impressum;' and for such a sentiment was duly rebuked.[28] On the other hand Lavater admitted that one finds in the doctrines and explanations of Socinus many incomparable solutions of unpalatable difficulties in the orthodox system.[29]

[23] cf. Annaeus Ypey, *Geschiedenis van de Kristlijke Kerk in de achttiende Eeuw* (Utrecht, 1797–1811), ix, 49.

[24] For sundry decisions of the Court of Holland, and votes of the various synods concerning the Bibliotheca, 1671–'76, cf. J. Freudenthal, *Lebensgeschichte Spinoza's* (Leipzig, 1899), pp. 125–153.

[25] cf. Meinsma, *Spinoza*, pp. 325 f, 386 f.

[26] cf. Guichard, *Socinianisme*, p. 151.

[27] cf. Bock, *Antitrinitar.*, i, 53, quoting Crenius, *Animadversiones philologicae et historicae* (Rotterdam, 1695), i, 43.

[28] cf. Andreas Carolus, *Memorabilia ecclesiastica* (Tübingen, 1697–1702), ii, 150; Gottfried Arnold, *Ketzer-historie*, ii, 558.   [29] cf. Ypey, *op. cit.*, ix, 63.

CHAPTER XLIV

THE LAST SOCINIANS IN HOLLAND. CHANGES IN DOCTRINAL AND SOCIAL VIEWS

BESIDES the *Bibliotheca Fratrum Polonorum*, the only other publication issued with general Socinian sanction in the post-exile period was the Racovian Catechism in several successive editions, to be spoken of below. Any other works published were purely individual matters. In such an environment as has been indicated, Socinianism as a distinct movement now began gradually to fade away. No further recruits could be expected from Poland, and only an occasional one still came from East Prussia, Silesia or Brandenburg. No distinct organization or propaganda might be maintained for the winning of converts and the continuance of the movement, and the surviving exiles either died off or were assimilated to the existing churches. The broken narrative has therefore to be followed in the story of the separate individuals in whose hands its torch finally flickered out.

Easily first of these was Andrew Wiszowaty, the account of whose earlier life has already been given.[1] He removed to Amsterdam from his brief ministry at Mannheim in 1666, at the age of 58, to spend the remaining twelve years of his life in the peace and quiet that he had long craved and so little enjoyed. Those, however, were not years of idle ease. From all quarters the scattered exiles turned to him for the advice, comfort and encouragement that his letters gave them; while near at hand his mind was full of concern for brethren who were tempted to desert the faith of their fathers or were likely to be misled by the new philosophies of the time, and his pen was active in meeting the continued attacks of enemies, or the vagaries of friends. The struggle of the new philosophy of Descartes with the old scholastic philosophy was under way, and skepticism of every hue was rife. Views long abandoned were reappearing under the guise of Platonism, a ferment of philosophical and religious thought was universal, the scriptural foundations of theology were being modified or outgrown. He was driven to recognize that besides Scripture there are other ways to

[1] *v. supra*, pp. 486–492, 500.

the truth, and he inquired into these. The mature fruit of his thought was given in a work which he highly valued on Rational Religion, which was not published until some years after his death.[2] In this little book he strove to vindicate the claims of reason as a source of religious truth and the arbiter in religious questions. This was a radical and epoch-making departure from views hitherto held among the Socinians. Socinus had definitely denied that man has by nature any knowledge of God apart from revelation from above. Hence his total reliance upon Scripture as the source of religious truth. Ostorodt wholly agreed, and so did the earlier Racovian Catechism, despite some obvious difficulties and inconsistencies involved. Crellius, however, acknowledged natural sources of religious knowledge; while his pupil Wiszowaty, now living in an atmosphere where the new philosophical views of Descartes, and especially of Spinoza, were the subject of lively discussion, and were causing the serious schism among the Collegiants mentioned above,[3] was forced to think the question through, and he came to the conclusion that sound reason is the touch-stone of truth, the inner eye given us by God to see and explore it and distinguish it from the false. Though revelation has come to us, all religious controversies arising about it must be decided in the court of reason; and anything in Scripture conflicting with plain reason should be rejected. True philosophy does not contradict the teaching of Christ but agrees with it. Thus a way was opened into new fields of thought and new methods of religious thinking. In the field of ethics one other work of Wiszowaty was published;[4] and he left half a hundred manuscripts that were never put into print. He died at Amsterdam in 1678 at the age of 70 years, and his devoted wife a year later. His two sons were both ministers, Benedict at Andreaswalde, and Andrew over the Polish exiles at Kolozsvár.[5]

Contemporary with Wiszowaty at Amsterdam was Christopher Sand (Sandius), Jr., already spoken of.[6] Though a definite Antitrinitarian,

---

[2] *Religio rationalis seu de rationis judicio, in controversiis etiam theologicis, ac religiosis, adhibendo, tractatus* (n. p., 1685). Also a German translation (Amsterdam, 1703). This work was immediately criticized in an inaugural dissertation at Kiel by Professor Bartholomaeus Kempen, 1685. For an illuminating discussion of the work, cf. Kühler, *Socinianisme*, pp. 227–241.

[3] *v. supra*, p. 565.

[4] *Stimuli virtutum, frena peccatorum* (Amstelaedami, 1682); Dutch translation, 1703.

[5] cf. again the works referred to above (p. 486, n. 14), and Bock, *Antitrin.*, i, 1010–1025.   [6] *v. supra*, p. 511 f.

he never identified himself with the Socinian tradition, but all his life adhered to the Arianism which he had accepted from his father, thus contenting himself with a phase of doctrinal development which the Socinians had outgrown early in their history. After coming to Amsterdam to oversee the publication of a work by his father, he obtained a place as corrector for the press, and spent the rest of his life in writing theological works, in which he showed himself so much given to Platonism that Wiszowaty felt bound to oppose him in a book against Arianism, to which Sand replied, followed by a rejoinder and another reply.[7] Sand also wrote works explaining difficult passages in the Gospels in an Arian sense, on the origin of the soul, and on the Holy Spirit, which Wiszowaty, as a defender of the Socinian position, felt called upon to answer. These controversies were an indication that the old Socinian views were being called in question even by their friends, and were precursors of impending modifications called for by a new environment and new tendencies of thought. Sand's Arian writings received considerable attention in England during the Trinitarian controversy of the seventeenth century.

Another witness of changing thought among the Socinians in Holland was Jeremias Felbinger, born in Silesia as a Lutheran, who after teaching for years in Germany adopted the Socinian faith, became an ardent opponent of Trinitarian views, and suffered much for his boldness in attacking them. He at length came to Amsterdam, where he published several religious works, and translated into German a Socinianizing version of the New Testament by Courcelles, professor at the Remonstrant seminary. But he had become an eclectic in theology, inclined to Arianism, and therefore was denied a pension by the Socinians, and dragged out a miserable life by teaching and correcting proof.[8]

A very interesting figure more or less connected with the history of Socinianism in Holland is that of Dr. Daniel Zwicker, whose earlier career has been spoken of.[9] He was associated for some years with the congregation of the Polish Brethren at Danzig, was a zealous promoter of their cause, and was therefore forced to leave the city along with Ruar, Crusius and the rest. He was a restless spirit, by temperament

[7] C. S., *Dissertatio de Verbo*; A. W., *Objectiones contra opinionem*, etc.; C. S., *Contra objectiones*; A. W., *Defensio objectionum*; C. S., *Notae in objectiones*, 1673–'78. cf. Bock, *Antitrinitar.*, *s. vv.* Sandius and Wissowatius.

[8] cf. van Slee, *Socinianisme*, pp. 216–219; Bock, *op. cit.*, i, 340–355.

[9] *v. supra*, p. 510.

much inclined to controversy, and a zealot almost to the point of fanaticism for whatever cause he espoused; and seeing little hope of progress
in Ruar's little congregation now excluded from Danzig, he sought a
field of activity elsewhere. In 1644 he visited the colony of Moravian
Brethren at Sobotišt, Hungary, whither they had gone into exile from
Moravia over twenty years before. He became persuaded that their
way of life was the true way of imitating Christ, and became an enthusiastic devotee of their system. He had an extensive correspondence
with Ruar about the excellence of the Moravian system and enthusiastically urged a union of the Socinians with the communistic Anabaptists among whom he was then living.[10] Ruar did not share his
enthusiasm, but Zwicker decided to join their community. They were
so much flattered by receiving such an able convert that they waived
certain conditions to which he objected, and ordained him as Minister
of the Word, and commissioned him to do missionary work in Prussia
and Poland.[11] This was in 1654; but the results were evidently disappointing, for in 1657 he removed to Holland, where he was to spend
the rest of his life agitating for religious and social reform. He had
previously formed the acquaintance of Jan Amos Comenius (Komen-
ski), one of the outstanding minds of his time. Comenius was Bishop
of the Bohemian Brethren, and in a celebrated school at Leszno (Lissa)
in Great Poland he had won enduring fame as an educational reformer;
for he believed that the regeneration of the world was to be attained
through a new system of education.[12] As a step toward that universal
and enduring peace for which so many in that turbulent period longed,
he called first of all for a union of all Protestant churches. He had
recently been forced to leave Poland and seek refuge in Holland, and
Zwicker now renewed acquaintance with his fellow-exile and discussed
with him the great theme of church union. Though he did not reveal
his heretical views to Comenius, he found that there was otherwise
such deep sympathy between them that he felt encouraged to publish
a book on the subject.[13] He cherished the illusion that all men with
normal faculties could by rational proofs be persuaded to become Christians, and by the same token members of the same universal Church.
The truths of religion as laid down in the Bible are simple, open, and

---

[10] cf. Ruar, *Epistolae*, cent. i, epp. 70–75.
[11] cf. Beck, *Wiedertäufer*, pp. 486–490; Kot, *Ideologja*, pp. 107–111.
[12] cf. Jan Jakubec, *Johannes Amos Comenius* (Prague, 1928).
[13] *Irenicum Irenicorum*, etc. (116 words in the title!) (Amsterdam, 1658).

demonstrable to the ordinary mind. Professing to be committed to none of the many existing sects, in each of which there was some good, but to be devoted only to Truth,[14] he proposed for the investigation of truth these three standards: sound reason, Holy Scripture, and the tradition of early Christian writers.

Not content, however, with laying down these general principles, Zwicker proceeded to apply them forthwith, by demonstrating that by each of these three standards it is clear that not Christ, but only the Father, is God over all.[15] This was too much for Comenius. After reading the first part he said he had never read so clever a book, and Courcelles deemed it irrefutable;[16] but he felt outraged that some expressions in the book seemed to commit him to the author's doctrine, which he now felt bound to attack decisively, since he considered the book only a mask for Socinian tendencies. Hence ensued a long and bitter controversy, which more and more degenerated into mutual abuse and personal invective.[17] During the course of this controversy or soon after it, Zwicker published a number of other works, mostly controversial, on toleration,[18] office-holding, pacifism, criminal law and prisons, and on various doctrinal questions in which he sometimes defended Socinian writers, sometimes opposed them. In them all he reflected the tendency of the time, in which writers of Socinian antecedents were showing independence and bearing witness that the Socinian system was gradually dissolving in the atmosphere of a new age and a changed environment.

The only other person that needs to be considered as a significant factor in the declining history of Socinianism in Holland is Samuel

---

[14] cf. *Irenicum Irenicorum*, p. 79.

[15] Zwicker was threatened with confiscation of his book and banishment for himself, and he was closely watched for a whole year. For a full sketch of his thought, cf. Cornelis B. Hylkema, *Reformateurs* (Haarlem, 1900), ii, 295–312; i, 220.

[16] cf. Bock, *Antitrinitar.*, i, 1055.

[17] Following *Irenicum Irenicorum* came successively, Comenius, *Irenicum Irenicorum, hoc est . . . ad omnes Christianos facta admonitio* (Amstelredami, 1660); Zwicker, *Irenico-Mastyx perpetuo convictus et constrictus* (Amst., 1661); Comenius, *De iterato Sociniano Irenico iterata ad Christianos admonitio* (Amst., 1661); Zwicker, *Irenico-Mastyx iterato victus et constrictus, imo obmutescens* (Amst., 1662); Comenius, *Admonitio tertia adversus Zwickerum* (Amst., 1662); Zwicker, *Irenico-Mastygis pars specialis, seu confutatio finalis Comenii*, etc. (Amst., 1662). Besides the chief items were also lateral contributions from Maukisch, Przypcovius, Bishop Bull of England, Felwinger, Hoornbeek, and Maresius.

[18] Especially noteworthy in his *Vereenings-Schrift der Christenen*, etc. (1661), and the Latin version, *Henoticum Christianorum* (1662), being a condensed translation of Mino Celso's *In haereticis coercendis; v. supra*, p. 206.

Crellius, whose earlier course in Germany we have already traced.[19] After having to leave his little congregation at Königswalde, he went first to England, where he renewed earlier friendships and formed new ones with distinguished scholars, enjoyed the patronage of Lord Shaftesbury, received a singular token of sympathy from Sir Isaac Newton,[20] then far advanced in age, and had intimate conversation with several distinguished Anglican divines. His chief occupation in England, however, was to attend to the publication of his best known work, which the generosity of an unorthodox English sympathizer enabled him to bring out.[21] The purpose of this work,[22] in two handsomely printed volumes, was to demonstrate on the ground of a corrected Greek text of John i. 1, and of the witness of early Fathers, that the chief scriptural foundation of the dogma of the deity of Christ was a corrupt text. The thesis was argued with great cleverness and an encyclopaedic knowledge of early Christian writings, and the work created a great sensation by its impressive weight of learning. Its edition of 1000 copies soon went out of print. It naturally called forth numerous replies;[23] but for our present purpose the point of most interest is in the preface, in which he says (p. xv): 'You have seen that I am not an Arian nor an Athanasian; you now see that I am not a Socinian either. What distinguishes Socinianism from all other denominations and views in Christendom is not the doctrine concerning one God the Father, and the person of Christ; . . . but the erroneous view about our justification, the sacrifice and priesthood of Christ, is what properly constitutes Socinianism. . . . Socinus, in opposing the crude view of Christ's satisfaction, fell into the opposite extreme.' As to the doctrine of satisfaction, then, he forsook Socinus and followed

---

[19] v. supra, p. 498 f.

[20] As they parted, Newton placed two guineas in his hand for his personal use. cf. Charles Étienne Jordan, Recueil de littérature (Amsterdam, 1730), p. 44; Crellius to la Croze, July 17, 1727, Thesaurus epistolicus Lacrozianus (Lipsiae, 1742), i, 105.

[21] Matthew Tindal; cf. Götten, Gelehrte Europa, iii, 284–293; cited by Bock, Antitrinitar., i, 182.

[22] Initium Evangelii S. Joannis Apostoli ex antiquitate ecclesiastica restitutum, etc. Per L. M. Artemonium (London, 1726). The initials L. M. in the pseudonymous author's name stand for Lucas Mellierus, a name formed from Samuel Crellius by a transposition of letters. Artemonius was an early heretic whose views Crellius felt were nearest his own. The disguise was adopted to avoid the odium that the publication of a famous Socinian name would be sure to invite.

[23] cf. Johannes Philippus Baraterius, Anti-Artemonius, etc. (Norimbergae, 1735), and the long list given by Götten, op. cit., iii, 295–303.

the Remonstrants, and late in life he declared that he was sure that few if any remained who could properly be called Socinians. But as to the doctrine about God, he remained to his last breath a Unitarian.[24]

The last twenty years of his life Crellius spent quietly in Amsterdam, occupied with studies and literary work. He associated with both Collegiants and Remonstrants. The Collegiants long gave him a yearly contribution from their funds, to make up for the salary he had forfeited when he left Königswalde; and as he lived very modestly he spent much of this on the new books that he was always eager to read until his vision became impaired.[25] He regretted the rise of an anti-Socinian spirit among the Remonstrants, fostered by their Professor Adriaan van Cattenburgh in order to soften the hostility of the Reformed Church, but he declared that after the Collegiants he knew no better people than the Remonstrants.[26] He died at Amsterdam in 1747, honored by the learned world for his extensive and accurate scholarship, and beloved by all that knew him for the virtues and graces of his character. His intimate friend and correspondent for many years, Professor Mathurin Veyssière la Croze at the French college in Berlin, who grieved only that Crellius was not properly sound in saving faith, wrote Mosheim of him that, heresy apart, he was the best and most lovable man in the world.[27] He may be said to have been the last surviving Socinian of importance. He was survived by two sons, Stephen and Joseph, who emigrated to the colony of Georgia in America, which was settled 1733–'38 by Protestant refugees under English auspices. Their joining the colony may be presumed to have been facilitated by English friends of their father. Stephen held there the office of Justice of the Peace, and Joseph followed agriculture. Both were married, but left no male offspring.[28] They are the only Polish Socinians known to have

---

[24] cf. *Thesaurus epistolicus*, i, 110; Bock, *Antitrinitar.*, i, 168.

[25] cf. Rues, *Collegianten*, p. 323 f.

[26] cf. van Slee, *Collegianten*, p. 395. Van Cattenburgh succeeded the very liberal Philip van Limborch in the Remonstrant Seminary at Amsterdam, and opposed several of the characteristic Socinian views as unfounded. cf. his *Specimen controversiarum inter Remonstrantes et Socinum*, etc. (Amsterdam, 1728). The Remonstrants had grown timid in the face of orthodox criticism, and for some time deferred calling to a chair in their Seminary the renowned New Testament scholar, Johann Jakob Wettstein, who had been dismissed from his pulpit at Basel for alleged Socinianism. cf. van Slee, *Socinianisme*, p. 121 f; Kühler, *Socinianisme*, pp. 252–256; Willem Johan Lente, *Leven en Werken van Johan Jakob Wettstein* (Leiden, 1902).

[27] Quoted in Bock, *op. cit.*, i, 167, and in Fock, *Socinianismus*, p. 240.

[28] cf. Bock, *Antitrinitar.*, i, 168 f.

gone to the New World, but persistent efforts to trace them or their descendants there have met with no success.

The preceding pages have taken note of a growing tendency among the surviving leaders of thought in the Socinian tradition, to criticize and depart from some of the doctrines taught by Socinus and in the Racovian Catechism. This tendency began to appear, indeed, soon after the death of Socinus, and grew stronger as time went on and conditions changed. These modifications are in part reflected in the later editions of the Racovian Catechism, as will be noted below; and they gradually went on until the surviving Socinians had become fairly assimilated to the liberal churches in Holland, and there was no longer any important difference between them. What is thus said relates to the theological teachings of the Socinians, but in their social teachings, as to the duties of Christians as citizens of the State, thought was still very active at this period, and deserves attention as we pass. It will be remembered that early in the history of the movement we have been following in Poland its members, in the effort to follow New Testament teachings punctiliously, felt bound to depart from the existing usages in relation to the State. The matter of bearing arms, engaging in warfare, paying military taxes, taking judicial oaths, holding the office of Magistrate, indulging in luxury in dress and food, and joining in demoralizing social amusements, was deemed to be something with which religion had directly to do, and the Socinians surpassed all others in their high ideals in these respects and their strict adherence to them. It is true that their earliest leaders, Paulus, Czechowicz, and Niemojewski went to almost fanatical extremes; but the saner teachings of Socinus introduced a more reasonable standard, and while the commoners and artisans in the churches remained for the most part socially radical, the nobles for the most part tended to be less rigorous in practice. Socinus gradually relaxed his social teaching, and Völkel and Crellius in the next generation taught a more practicable system of Christian ethics.

In the Collegiant circles in Holland, where the writings of all these writers were now known, nearly all the questions they treated would naturally come up for discussion, and among them that of the relation of Christians to the State. As a result of the interest thus existing, Daniel van Breen (Brenius), a leading Collegiant of Amsterdam, in 1641 published a work [29] in opposition to the social conservatism of his

---

[29] *Tractatus de qualitate regni Christi, contra Sim. Episcopii librum, cui titulus: An*

master, Episcopius, giving the most consistent expression of the radical view of the Christian's political duties. Christ's kingdom (the Church) is entirely different from the State in structure and purpose. Its members rule themselves strictly by his commands and thus are subject to no other. They do not disturb the foundations of society, but though they may not take part in civil government, wage war or resist evil, they are bound to obey the authorities. This pronouncement of Brenius made a strong impression upon the Polish Brethren, for it revived teachings that had been widely accepted at the beginning of their movement. It was followed by two contrary reactions, the one from the element that as far as possible held aloof from public activity, and for its spokesman had Wolzogen, and the other from the gentry or nobles who, despite all the oppressions they had lately suffered from an intolerant government, were heroically trying to maintain the fragment of the rights they had enjoyed under Sigismund Augustus. The idealistic standpoint of Brenius was championed by Wolzogen in a work [30] that was both longer and more extreme than that of Brenius. In Christ's kingdom secular rulers have no place, and Christians may take no part in secular government. Wolzogen maintains his cause unflinchingly, and answers all objections confidently.

Such a doctrine could not be allowed to pass unchallenged as the teaching of the Polish Brethren, and the most prominent member of the church, Jonas Schlichting, pupil of Crellius and the main champion of Socinianism against its Protestant opponents, came forward to uphold the more realistic view of the conservatives. Following the teaching of St. Paul,[31] he saw no reason why others might hold public office, but not Christians: if all were Christians, must they still be ruled by unbelievers? Reasoning thus, he wrote against Wolzogen a work no longer extant, whose argument is seen from the latter's reply, to which Schlichting made a rejoinder, to be met by a closing response by Wolzogen.[32] Apart from this controversy, in which Schlichting abandoned

---

homini Christiano conveniat officium magistratus gerere (Amsterdam, 1641, 1657); also in his Opera (Amstelaedami, 1666); Dutch trans., Van de hoedanigheyd des Rijcks Christi (Amsterdam, 1641, 1657). Summarized in Kot, Ideologja, p. 112 f.

[30] De natura et qualitate Regni Christi ac religionis Christianae, part ii, pp. 241–296 of his Opera in Bibliotheca Fratrum Polonorum. Really a translation of Brenius, with many additions. Summarized by Kot, op. cit., pp. 114–116.

[31] Commentary on Rom. xiii, Schlichting, Opera (Bibliotheca Fratrum Polonorum), i, 302.

[32] Respectively, J. S., Quaestiones de magistratu, bello, defensione privata; J. L. W.,

the old standpoint as to arms, war, offices, etc., and tried to consult practical requirements of the citizen, Wolzogen also supported Brenius further in another work.[33] A yet more powerful voice was now raised in favor of sober conservatism on social questions by Samuel Przypkowski, whose active life had been largely connected with public affairs at court and in the field, and who held a statesmanlike view quite out of sympathy with fanatical extremes. In opposition to Brenius, who held that there was an essential moral opposition between Church and State, and that one must choose which to serve, he maintained in a work that he wrote in 1650 [34] that one must accept a positive relation to the State; for he had long been convinced that the general dislike, hatred and secret machinations to which the Polish Brethren had been subject were largely due to the social-political views that they had held since the beginning of their movement. He therefore felt the crying need for a revision of these views. In this work the most talented of the Socinian writers followed the arguments of Brenius step by step in brilliant style. It was one of the ablest works produced in the Socinian circle, as the author proceeded by strict logical reasoning and with perfect courtesy to expose the absurdity of his opponent's positions. In this work he was settling matters with the extremists, and for certain reasons did not think best to publish it at the time, but Grotius's great work *De jure belli et pacis* had removed any doubt Przypkowski may have cherished as to the soundness of his position, and he therefore prepared for publication another work, addressed to the moderate group.[35] In this he spoke out more boldly than before, and declared that Socinus, great and incomparable as he had been in many points, had been mistaken in this respect: complete non-resistance was not only opposed to declarations of Scripture and of reason, but also to all order, justice, and peace. This was the reason why their adherents had never grown in number

Annotationes ad Quaestiones Jonae Schlichtingii; J. S., *Annotationes oppositae memoratis J. L. Wolzogenii Annotationibus*; J. L. W., *Responsio ad Jonae Schlichtingii Annotationes in Annotationes*. cf. Wolzogen's *Opera*, iii, 63–78, 91–132, in *Bib. Frat. Polon.* The exact dates of the various items are not known, but they must have fallen within a few years just preceding 1650. cf. Kot, *op. cit.*, pp. 117–123, for a summary of the arguments.

33 The first part of his *Praeparatio ad utilem sacrarum litterarum lectionem* (*Opera*, ii, 241–296); Dutch translation, with additions, by the Collegiant Dr. Pieter Langedult, *De weerloose Christen, verbeeldende de natuur en hoedaenigheyd van het rijcke Christi*, 1676.

34 *Animadversiones in libellum cui titulus De Qualitate Regni Christi*, etc., in his *Opera* (*Cogitationes Sacrae*), Amsterdam, 1692, pp. 621–681. cf. Kot, *op. cit.*, pp. 124–130.

35 *De jure Christiani magistratus et privatorum in belli pacisque negotiis* (1650); in *Opera*, pp. 685–736. cf. Kot, *op. cit.*, pp. 130–133; Chmaj, *Przypkowski*, pp. 163–168.

and respect. Surely men might seek justice and defend themselves. Even war was no sin, still less the holding of office.

For a Socinian this was revolutionary doctrine indeed, and it provoked two replies. The first was by Joachim Stegmann, one of the younger ministers, who having seen a copy of what Przypkowski had written, attacked his work in a writing which is not extant, though its contents can be made out from Przypkowski's rejoinder.[36] He was not an extreme fanatic, but he was under the influence of Wolzogen, and totally opposed to war. Though he held Przypkowski in high esteem, he reproached him for raising the question at this unfortunate time, when it would be better to let it remain in abeyance; he was undermining the established good order in the church, and many were beginning to take up arms; nor should he have shown such disrespect for Socinus. Finally he repeated all the known arguments against military service, and predicted that the church would not follow Przypkowski, but that all worthy members would condemn his untimely stand. Przypkowski could not let such reproaches go unanswered, and now produced a large and powerful work,[37] in which he undertook to undermine his opponent's position and shatter his authority. In this work, nearly as long as Socinus's reply to Palaeologus, he brought into action not only all his powers of argument, but the weapons of sarcasm, derision and mockery, and in the greatest detail he annihilated the traditional arguments of Stegmann and reduced them to absurdity.

The other reply which Przypkowski's work on the Magistrate evoked was made by Dr. Daniel Zwicker in the form of objections. Zwicker's writing is not extant, but the reply to it concludes the volume of Przypkowski's collected works.[38] In this work the author again observes the limits of calm and reasonable argument. With this the main controversy had spent its force and the disputants relapsed into silence as the wars that overwhelmed Poland removed the subject from the field of controversy. It should be kept in mind that this, however, was not a printed controversy spread before the whole public, but a written one addressed to the leaders of Socinian thought through manuscripts that had a limited circulation. The significance of this discussion there-

36 See the following note.
37 *Apologia prolixior tractatus de jure Christiani magistratus*; in *Opera*, pp. 739–851. cf. Chmaj, *op. cit.*, pp. 168–171.
38 *Vindiciae tractatus de magistratu contra objectiones Danielis Zwickeri*; in *Opera*, pp. 855–880. cf. Kot, *op. cit.*, p. 136 f.

fore lies not in the breadth and depth of its immediate influence, but
in the unmistakable evidence it gives that in what had for half a century been the fairly uniform thought among the Socinians, there were
now developing sharp differences in social ideals no less than in doctrinal views—in the one case under the pressure of disturbed conditions
of national and international life, in the other, in response to new currents of thought in philosophy. The ferment we have just been tracing
began in Holland, with the work of Brenius in 1641; it overflowed
among the Socinians in Poland when their cause there was declining;
and in Holland again it flickered out. Dying echoes of the controversy
continued even after the exile of the Socinians from Poland. The contentious Zwicker continued to discuss it with Stegmann, and published
his latest views in 1666,[39] still condemning war, capital punishment,
prisons and the use of force. The final publication of which we need
take note is that of Jan Hartigveld, an influential and wealthy merchant among the Collegiants at Rotterdam, who espoused the cause of
Brenius against Przypkowski, reasserting the extremest positions to
the last.[40]

The changes that Socinianism had undergone in the eighty years
since Socinus's death may be clearly seen in the later editions of the
Racovian Catechism. No new edition or revision of it had taken place
since Moskorzowski's Latin version in 1609 and the second Polish edition in 1619; and meanwhile thought had moved on as the current of
history, the criticisms of opponents, and a new foreign environment
raised new questions. Even Moskorzowski had introduced a considerable number of minor changes into his translation, which then remained the standard text for half a century. The modifications, corrections or additions that experience suggested were made by several
scholars in Poland authorized by vote of the Synod, evidently with a
view to the preparing of a revised edition, and it was further revised
several years later by Johannes Crellius, who died in 1633, and finally,
after long delays doubtless due to the increasing persecutions and exile
of the Socinians, it was prepared for the press by Jonas Schlichting,

[39] *Ecclesia antiqua inermis.* Dutch trans., *De weerloose oude Kercke,* 1668.

[40] *De recht weerloose Christen* (Rotterdam, 1678). cf. van Slee, *Collegianten,* pp. 98–
100. Though published under the name of Hartigveld, this was not a new and independent
work, but Brenius's book of 1641, annotated by Wolzogen, enlarged by Langedult (*De
Weerloose Christen*), finally revised and given a new title by Hartigveld, and after his death
reedited and published by Brenius's nephew, Frans Kuyper. cf. preface by the latter.
Hartigveld was a generous contributor to the Socinian exiles after 1660.

with an appendix of notes by Martin Ruar and some answers by Schlichting. It was at length brought out at Amsterdam in 1665 at the expense of an anonymous patron;[41] with a long preface by Joachim Stegmann, Jr., and Andrew Wiszowaty, pleading for a reasonable freedom in teaching and liberty of conscience, with generous mutual tolerance. 'While we compose a Catechism,' says the preface, 'we prescribe nothing to any man; while we express our own views, we oppress no one. Let each man be free to express his own mind in religion, provided we too be permitted to bring forward our own thoughts about religious matters, without wronging or attacking any one.' A particular occasion for publishing this edition at this time was the fact that in 1659 Jan Knol (Cornelis), an influential Collegiant at Amsterdam, took the liberty of bringing out a translation of the (1612) Catechism into Dutch, but on his own authority made arbitrary additions, omissions (especially of the chapters on baptism and the Lord's Supper), and alterations to such an extent that the responsible surviving Socinians felt that they could not acknowledge it as their own.[42] Hence the revised Latin edition here referred to, and an authorized Dutch translation of it in 1667.[43] This newly revised edition was in contents more than half as large again as the first edition, thus bearing witness to the plastic state of Socinian thought, in contrast to the fixed and unyielding form of the Augsburg Confession and the Heidelberg Catechism, which made no provision for change or growth. In this feature the editors took pride, saying in their preface, 'We do not think the we need blush if our Church advances in some things. We ought not in every case to cry out, We believe, I stand fast in the ranks, here

---

[41] The date on the title-page, "Irenopili: post annum Domini 1659," is intentionally misleading, to avoid persecution. The correct date is given by Sand, *Bibliotheca*, pp. 114, 117, 130.

[42] cf. last paragraph of the preface to the "1659" edition.

[43] Two later Latin editions were published in Holland: (1) (Stauropoli = Amsterdam, 1681) in 4°, appended to Crellius's *Ethica* (1880), esteemed the best and most correct edition. The text is essentially the same as that of the "1659" edition, except that the minor verbal corrections by Ruar and Schlichting noted in the appendix to the latter are here made in the text, which was otherwise left unchanged by the editor, Andrew Wiszowaty. The notes by the editor, his scholarly nephew Benedict Wiszowaty, Ruar, and Schlichting were intercalated in the appropriate places. This edition was prepared at the urgent request of distant brethren. cf. the address to the reader, following the preface; also Johann C. Koecher, *Catechetische Geschichte*, etc. (Jena, 1768), pp. 94–111. (2) The last edition, published in 1684, was apparently made up of unsold sheets of the "1659" edition with which it exactly agrees, save for a new title-page and an appendix containing the additional notes.

I plant my foot, I will not allow myself to be moved from here ever so little.' [44] This edition made a few brief omissions of matters that had grown obsolete in thought or practice, and in many places made expansions of the text or extensive additions to it. Quite noteworthy are the large number of passages which have been revised in contents, modified in expression or rewritten in substance: especially the greatly strengthened chapter on the Person of Christ, that on Christian morals and religious practices, those on the Sacraments, on Eternal Life, the Holy Spirit, Free Will, and above all on the Death of Christ. This last was greatly revised and expanded, and shows the influence of the Remonstrant theologians by treating the death of Christ as an expiatory sacrifice. Comparison of the changes made in this edition with the various orthodox refutations of the earlier editions shows that many significant changes were made to answer or disprove the criticisms that had been made.[45] One significant feature in the newer editions of the Catechism is their frequent appeal to reason in support of positions taken, and their objection to current doctrines as repugnant to reason.

It is by no means easy to estimate fairly the extent to which Socinianism and the other religious bodies in Holland influenced each other. As for the Socinians, they held unwaveringly to their belief in the strict unity of God as contrasted with any interpretation of the doctrine of the Trinity; nor did they waver as to the person of Christ as a being subordinate to the Father, though in their latest period an Arian construction made to a significant number a stronger appeal than bare humanitarianism. On the other hand, as their predominant emphasis upon practical Christian virtues and graces led them to attach the less importance to speculative dogmas, they tended to find the Remonstrant doctrine of the religious meaning of the death of Christ more satisfying to their religious experience than the rather superficial doctrine that Socinus had handed down to them; and, still enjoying entire freedom of individual belief and speech, they gradually coalesced with the prevailing religious life of their tolerant neighbors.

The Remonstrants, on the other hand, though persistently called Socinians by their orthodox contemporaries in the Reformed Church, never fairly deserved the reproach. In one or two prominent doctrines they may have accepted the Socinian view, but the whole body of

---

[44] This edition was translated into English, with an important historical introduction: Thomas Rees, *The Racovian Catechism, with notes and illustrations* (London, 1818).

[45] For a citation of the most important refutations, *v. supra*, p. 411, n. 18.

Socinianism did not attract them. Nevertheless in the series of professors in the Remonstrant Seminary at Amsterdam,—Episcopius, Courcelles, van Limborch, van Cattenburgh, Le Clerc, Wetstein—we see, with the exception of the reactionary van Cattenburgh, an ever increasing sympathy with the teaching and the spirit of Socinianism. Though they still counted themselves Trinitarians, yet they were not orthodox as to the relation of Christ to God; and they accepted wholeheartedly the Socinian principles of scientific method, grammatical and historical exegesis of the Scriptures without dogmatic presuppositions, moral freedom, full tolerance, and admission of the claims of reason in religion.[46]

The Mennonites, especially the Collegiant element among them, went further in their approach to the Socinians, and some of their influential leaders went the whole way; but as a whole they never embraced Socinianism, but repeatedly denied such a charge, even while giving Socinians the most unstinted welcome, as being equally with themselves devoted to governing themselves by the principles of the Gospel in every relation of life. The affinities of the Socinians in Holland were on the intellectual and social side more with the Remonstrants; on the practical side more with the Mennonites.[47]

Here, at the point where Socinianism as a distinct movement has run its course, where its surviving adherents have been happily assimilated to the freer religious bodies about them, and when its intellectual tendencies are being absorbed in the broader current of the Rationalism of the eighteenth century, we take leave of the Socinians, not without warm admiration for their depth of religious devotion, the sincerity of their efforts, at the cost of whatever sacrifice, to follow the way of life that Jesus had taught and the early Christians had illustrated, and for the heroism with which they remained stedfast at the cost of nearly every earthly advantage. But though their body perished their spirit and thought survived and lived on transformed in other lands. In the first half of the eighteenth century, at the time when Socinianism was

---

[46] It will not be forgotten in this connection what proof the Remonstrants gave of sympathetic fellowship with the Socinians in the tragedies of their exile during several years after 1660, in the generous sums sent through Naeranus (v. supra, p. 496), nor that when the Unitarians of Kolozsvár in Transylvania were overwhelmed by a great conflagration in 1691 an appeal from their churches for assistance was promptly answered by a generous gift. cf. van Slee, Socinianisme, p. 240 f; Ms 529 in the Remonstrant library at Rotterdam.

[47] cf. van Slee, Socinianisme, pp. 123–135, 197 f.

drawing to its close in Holland, currents of religious reform were stirring in England, and the relations between progressive minds in England and the liberal theologians in Holland were active. Scholars and theologians passed back and forth, books were circulated in both directions, and much community of thought and feeling existed. Thus Socinianism, somewhat changed in form, was destined to experience a new life in England. There we shall in a later division of this history be able to follow its further course. Before doing that, however, we must return to Eastern Europe, and follow in Transylvania the almost exactly contemporaneous and yet largely distinct history of an allied movement, which is again marked by devotion, sincerity and heroism.

At this close of our survey of the history of Socinianism it is fitting to estimate, apart from its doctrinal or social aspects, what measure of progress the movement has made toward the three major ends of freedom, reason and tolerance in religion. It totally escaped from bondage to creeds and ecclesiastical tradition; and though it still acknowledged the authority of Scripture, it accepted it in the end only in so far as it corresponded with the inner authority of reason and conscience. In the successive editions of the Racovian Catechism, it set forth not an authoritative creed to define and limit belief, but a convenient summary of generally accepted beliefs, always subject to criticism and revision in the light of new thought. For religious faith was conceived not as static and unchangeable, but as vital, plastic and progressive.

It required a little struggle at first to assert clearly and without flinching the paramount claim of reason in religion, though Socinus himself realized that if ever a clear conflict arose between reason and Scripture, reason must be accepted as final. It remained for Wiszowaty, however, to state the view boldly and without evasion or equivocation. Henceforth the religious faith of the Socinian must be not only perfectly free but perfectly reasonable.

Finally, tolerance of differing views or practices was almost from the beginning the Socinian's very breath of life; and even in the early history of the movement it was infringed only in aggravated cases. But the whole history of the movement gives repeated proofs of how the most varied views of religious truth could peaceably coexist with unity of spirit in the bond of peace, and of how conflicting views could either be resolved in the alchemy of free and reasonable discussion, or else could be left behind as minor details not much worth contending for.

This point was reached even while Socinus lived, and largely as a result of his own practice; and if any, like the followers of Stancaro or Farnowski, could not peaceably endure divergence from their own views, they naturally gravitated to a body which preferred the bondage of dogma to the freedom of tolerance. The further history of our movement in other lands, with other origins, and in other circumstances, will show how perfectly these three principles were achieved, and how faithfully they were maintained.

PRONOUNCING TABLE

THERE are many names in the text that the reader unaided might find it difficult to pronounce. Names from the more common languages of western Europe are presumed to offer no particular difficulty; but Polish and Hungarian follow other rules. The table here given is designed to help the reader by indicating approximately correct pronunciations. A few additional names or words are included as likely otherwise to be mispronounced.

In Polish the accent is invariably on the penult; in Hungarian, on the first syllable. The marks over vowels in Hungarian denote not accent but a long vowel sound.

In the table below,

 1. *gh* is like *g* in *go*
 2. ʜ denotes a strongly aspirated *h*
 3. ɴ denotes the nasal *n* as in French words
 4. *ñ* is to be pronounced as in *cañon*
 5. *zh* is like *z* in *azure*, or the French *j*

Ádámos (ah'-dah-mosh)
Albin (ahl'-bin)
Alexandrowice (ahl-ex-an-dro-veet'-seh)
Apafi (aw'-paw-fee)
Arciszewski (ar-chi-shef'-skee)
Augustinowicz (ow-goos-tee-no'-vich)

Babinecki (Bah-bee-net'-skee)
Balcerowicz (bahl-tser-o'-vich)
Bánffy (bahn'-fy)
Batori (bah-to'-ree)
Bełżyce (bel-zhyt'-seh)
Beresko (berr-es'-ko)
Berzewiczy (berr-zheh-vich'-y)
Bethlen (bet'-len)
Biała (be-ah'-wah)
Bielsk (byelsk)
Bogusław (bo-goos'-wahf)
Bonar (bon'-ahr)
Bracka (braht'-skah)
Brześć (bzheshch)
Brzeżiny (bzhezh-ee'-ny)
Budny (bood'-ny)

Budżiński (bood-zhiñ-skee)
Bychawa (by-ʜah'-vah)

Ciechanowiec (tseʜ-ah-no'-vyets)
Chełmno (ʜelm'-no)
Chełmski (ʜelm'-skee)
Chmielnicki (ʜmee-el-ñit'-skee)
Chmielnik (ʜmee-el'-ñik)
Chrzczęcice (ʜzhchaɴ-cheet'-seh)
Cichowski (chi-ʜof'-skee)
Csánad (chah'-nawd)
Czaplic (chahp'-lits)
Czarków (chahr'-koof)
Czarna (char'-na)
Czarniecki (char-ñet'-skee)
Czartoryski (char-to-rys'-kee)
Czechowicz (cheʜ-o'-vich)
Czerniechów (cher-ñe'-ʜoof)
Częstochowa (chaɴ-sto-ʜo'-va)

Daems (dahms)
Dávid (dah'-vid)
Dązwa (doɴz'-va)

Dłuska (dwoo'-ska)
Domanowski (do-ma-nov'-skee)
Dubiecko (doob-yets'-ko)
Dudith (doo'-dit)

Falibowski (fah-lee-bof'-skee)
Farnowski (fahr-nof'-skee)
Filipowski (fil-ip-of'-skee)
Firley (feer'-lay)

Gamrat (gahm'-raht)
Gentile (jen-tee'-lay)
Giezek (ghyez'-ek)
Gilowski (ghee-lof'-skee)
Gniezno (gñez'-no)
Godecki (go-det'-skee)
Gołębia (go-waNb'-ya)
Goniądz (go'-ñoNdz)
Grudziąz (grood'-zhoNz)
Gyula-Fehérvár (joo'-law-fe'-herr-vahr)

Hojski (hoy'-ski)
Hoszcza (hosh'-cha)
Hulewicz (hoo-lev'-ich)
Hunyad (hoon'-yahd)
Hus (hoos)
Huszt (hoost)

Igołomia (eeg-o-wom'-ya)
Inowracław (ee-no-vrahts'-wahf)
Iwanicki (ee-vah-ñits'-kee)
Iwanowice (ee-vahn-o-veet'-say)
Iwanowicz (ee-vahn-o'-vich)
Iwański (ee-vahñ'-ski)

Jagiełło (yah-ghee-ew'-wo)
Joris (yo'-ris)

Kalisz (kah'-lish)
Karniński (kar-ñiñ'-skee)
Karnkowski (karn-kof'-skee)
Karwat (kar'-vaht)
Kąsinowo (koN-shi-no'-vo)
Kazimierz (kahzh'-myezh)
Kemény (keh'mayñ)
Késmark (kaysh'-mahrk)

Kijów (kee'-yoof)
Kisielin (kish-yel'-in)
Kiszka (kish'-ka)
Kolozsvár (ko'-lozh-vahr)
Korczyn (kor'-chin)
Koryto (ko-ryt'-o)
Kościelec (kosh-chel'-ets)
Kościeński (kosh-cheñ'-skee)
Koźminek (kozh-mee'-nek)
Krajewski (krah-yef'-skee)
Kraków (krah'-koof)
Krasnobród (krahs-no'-brood)
Krawiec (krahv'-yets)
Krotowski (kro-tof'-skee)
Krzyżak (kzhyzh'-ahk)
Kujawy (koo-yah'-vy)

Lachowce (lah-HOV'-tse)
Lachowski (lah-HOV'-skee)
Łańcut (wahñ'-tsoot)
Lasicki (lah-shits'-kee)
Łaski (wah'-skee)
Lasocki (lah-sot'-skee)
Łęczyca (waN-chit'-sa)
Łęczycki (waN-chits'-kee)
Leśniowolski (lesh-nee-o-wol'-ski)
Leszno (lesh'-no)
Lewartów (lev-ahr'-toof)
Lipowiec (lip-ov'-yets)
Lubartów (lu-bahr'-toof)
Lubecz (loo'-betch)
Lubieniecki (loo-byeñ-yet'-skee)
Lublin (loob'-lin)
Lubomirski (loo-bo-meer'-skee)
Lucławice (loots-wah-veet'-seh)
Lutomirski (loo-to-meer'-ski)
Lutomirsko (loo-to-meer'-sko)
Lwów (lvoof)

Maciejowski (mah-tcheh-yof'-skee)
Mączyński (moN-chiñ'-skee)
Mały rynek (mah'-wy ryn'-ek)
Máramaros (mahr'-aw-maw-rosh)
Mężyk (maN'-zhyk)
Mieczysław (myech-ys'-wahf)
Mieszko (myesh'-ko)

Mikołai (mik-o'-wye)
Modrzewski (mod-zhef'-skee)
Monostor (mon'-osh-tor)
Mordy (mor'-dy)
Morsztyn (mor'-shtin)
Morzkowski (mozh-kof'-skee)
Moskorzowski (mos-ko-zhof'-skee)
Myszkowski (mish-kof'-skee)

Naeranus (nay-rah'-noos)
Niedżwież (ñedzh'-vyezh)
Niemojewski (ñem-o-yef'-skee)
Niemojówka (ñem-o-yoof'-ka)
Niemyricz (ñem-eer'-ich)
Nieśwież (ñesh'-vyezh)
Nowogródek (no-vo-groo'-dek)
Nowy Sącz (no'-vy soɴch)

Oleśnicki (o-lesh-ñit'-skee)
Orzechowski (o-zhe-ʜof'-skee)
Orzys (ozh'-ys)
Ostrowski (os-trof'-skee)
Ostroróg (os-tror'-oog)

Paklepka (pah-klep'-ka)
Parczów (par'-choof)
Pawlikowice (pahv-lik-o-vee'-tseh)
Pécs (paych)
Pełsznica (pewsh-ñeet'-sa)
Petrycy (pet-ryt'-sy)
Piaski (pee-ah'-skee)
Piekarski (pyek-ar'-skee)
piekło (pyek'-wo)
Pińczów (piñ'-choof)
Piotrków (pee-otr'-koof)
Podgórze (pod-goo'-zhe)
Podlasie (pod-lah'-sheh)
Podole (po-do'-leh)
Powodowski (po-wo-dof'-skee)
Poznań (poz'-nahñ)
Proszowice (prosh-o-veet'-seh)
Przasnysza (pzhahs-ny'-sha)
Przypkowski (pzhip-kof'-skee)
Pulchranin (pull-ʜrah'-ñin)

Rąbkowa (roɴp-ko'-va)

Radecki (rah-det'-skee)
Radostów (ra-dos'-toof)
Radziwiłł (rahd-zhee'-view)
Rákóczy (rah'-ko-tsy)
Raków (rah'-koof)
Rhédei (ray'-deh-ee)
Rodecki (ro-det'-skee)
Rogów (rog'-oof)
Rokicki (ro-kit'-skee)
Rozmowy (roz-mo'-vy)
Roznów (roz'-noof)
Rudawki (roo-dahf'-kee)
Rupniowski (roop-ñoff'-skee)
Rutów (root'-oof)
rynek (ryn'-ek)

Sącz (soɴch)
Sandomierz (sahn-do'-myezh)
Sarnicki (sar-ñits'-kee)
Secemin (set-sem'-in)
Sejm (same)
sejmiki (say-mee'-kee)
Selchów (sel'-ʜoof)
Siedliska (shed-lis'-ka)
Siekerzyński (shek-ezh-yñ'-skee)
Siemichowska (shem-ee-ʜof'-ska)
Sienkiewicz (shen-kyev'-ich)
Sienuta (shen-oo'-tah)
Simons (see'-mons)
Skrzynno (skzhyn'-no)
Słomniki (swom-ñee'-kee)
Śmigiel (shmig'-yel)
Śmiglecki (shmig-let'-skee)
Sokolowski (so-ko-lof'-skee)
Stadnicki (stahd-ñit'-skee)
Starowolski (stahr-o-vol'-skee)
Stary rynek (stah'-ry ryn'-ek)
Sternacki (sterr-naht'-skee)
Stoieński (sto-yeñ'-skee)
Stoiński (sto-iñ'-skee)
Straszyn (strah'-shin)
Szepes (sep'-esh)
szlachta (shlaʜ'-ta)

Taszycki (tah-shits'-kee)
Thököly (tö'-köll) (ll as in million)

Toruń (tor'-ooñ)

Trecy (tret'-sy)

Trzycieski (tzhy-ches'-kee)

Twardochleb (tvahr'-do-нlep)

Tyskiewicz (tys-kye'-vich)

Tyszowce (tysh-of'-tseh)

Uszomir (oo-sho'-meer)

Voet (voot)

Waiglowa (vy-glo'-va)

Wawel (vah'-vel)

Wędrogowski (van-dro-gof'-skee)

Węgrow (van'-groof)

Widawski (vee-dahf'-skee)

Wieliczka (vyel-ich'-kah)

Wielopolski (vyel-o-pol'-skee)

Wiernek (vyer'-nek)

Wierzbowski (vyezh-bof'-skee)

Wilkowski (vil-kof'-skee)

Wilno (vil'-no)

Wiśniowiecki (vish-ñov-yet'-skee)

Wiszowaty (vish-o-vah'-ty)

Witebsk (vit'-epsk)

Witrelin (vit-rel'-in)

Włodysław (vwo-dys'-waf)

Wojdowski (voy-dof'-skee)

Wojewoda (vo-ye-vo'-da)

wojewódstwo (vo-ye-voodst'-vo)

Wola Justowska (vo'-la joost-of'-ska)

Wolan (vo'-lahn)

Wujek (voo'-yek)

Xiąż (książ) (kshyoнzh)

Zadzik (zahd'-zhik)

Zagrobelny (zah-gro-bel'-ny)

Żak (zhahk)

Zalaszowska (zah-lah-shof'-ska)

Żarnów (zhahr'-noof)

Zbąszyn (zbon'-shin)

Zbigniew (zbig'-ñef)

Zborowski (zbo-rof'-skee)

Zebrzydowski (zeb-zhyd-of'-skee)

Żmudż (zhmoodzh)

INDEX OF ABBREVIATIONS

FULL bibliographical citation of works referred to is given but once. Subsequent references are abbreviated as given below. The full citation can be found on pages here noted.

INDEX OF ABBREVIATIONS

FULL bibliographical citation of works referred to is given but once. Subsequent references are abbreviated as given below. The full citation can be found on pages here noted.

GENERAL INDEX

Abelard, 12, 392

Acontius (Aconzio), Italian scholar at Basel, 188, 205, 206

Admonition to Protestants (Skarga), 438

Adrian VI., Pope, 129

Against the whole world since the Apostles (Campanus), 35–36

Ailly, Pierre d', 62

Aix-la-Chapelle, Charles V. crowned at, 89

Albin, Matthias, Polish Anabaptist, 332n., 342

Alciati de la Motta, Gianpaolo, 81, 321, 504; Italian liberal in Switzerland, 108, 224, 225, 227–229; flees to Poland, 266, 312, 314, 315; last days, 321

Aleandro, Girolamo, quoted on Servetus, 58n.; papal representative at court of Charles V., 72

Alesius, Alexander, 192

Alexander VII., Pope, 478

Alfabeto Cristiano (Valdés), 90, 91

Aliod, Claude d' (Claudius Aliodus), 73–74

Altdorf, Socinianism at, 425–426, 524

Althamer, Andreas, Humanist leader, 24

Anabaptism, beginnings of, 22–23; in Poland, 331–336

Anabaptists, seek reform of Christian doctrines, 17, 19, 20–23, 76–77; persecution of, 21, 22, 23, 27, 30, 31, 33, 41, 44; not pioneers of Unitarian doctrine, 47–48; in Italy, 77–78, 79–87; views on baptism, 331; Calvinists and Lutherans attack, at Lublin, 339–340; Catholics oppose, in Poland, 343; in Moravia, 354–355. *See also* Antitrinitarians, Arians, Minor Reformed Church, Socinians, Unitarians

Andreaswalde, Socinians at, 516, 518–519, 520, 521

Angleria, Pedro Martir de, 89

Antidota (Gentile), 233–234, 314

Antidotum (Paulus), 318

Anti-Smalcium de Divinitate Christi (Cloppenburg), 557

Antitrinitarianism, beginnings of, 23; outbreak of, at Heidelberg, 258–264; in Poland, 283, 326–327; in Lithuania, 329–330

Antitrinitarians, 3n.; in Grisons, 98–99, 108–112; persecution of, in Poland, 318, 321, 322, 325, 339–342; reject Athanasian doctrine of Trinity, 344; at Raków, 352; uphold pacifism, 375–377. *See also* Anabaptists, Arians, Minor Reformed Church, Socinians, Unitarians

Apafi, Prince Michael, 485

Apologhi (Ochino), 250

Apologia (Przypkowski), 515

Apology (Servetus), 123–125

Apostles' Creed, 8, 461

Apostolic Brethren, 28

Aquinas, St. Thomas, 127

Aretius, 237–238

Arianism, 3n.; outlawed in Roman Empire, 11; Sarnicki defines, 321–322

Arians, 8, 345; in Poland, 290, 327, 328; Calvinists attack, 339–340; attempted disbarment from Warsaw Confederation, 365–366. *See also* Anabaptists, Antitrinitarians, Ditheists, Minor Reformed Church, Socinians, Unitarians

Arius, 8, 10, 291–292

Arminianism, 207

Arminians, 541, 544, 545

Arminius, Jacobus, 537–538, 541

Arneys, Antoine, 151, 152

Arnoullet, Balthazar, publishes *Chris-*

manist, 200, 214–216, 230, 234, 266; his orthodoxy questioned, 217–220, 222; arrest and trial of, 220–222; doctrines of, 222–223, 262–263

Griesel, Socinians at, 498

Grisons, described, 97; Antitrinitarians in, 98–99, 108–112

Grocholski, Waleryan, 448

Grotius, Hugo, publicist and religionist, 390, 424, 457, 527, 546, 548–550

Grynaeus, Simon, 65

Guéroult, Guillaume, prints *Christianismi Restitutio*, 138, 140

Guinter, Jean, 119

Haan, Galenus Abrahamsz de, 561–562

Haetzer, Ludwig, Anabaptist leader, 29–32, 59

Haller, Berthold, 65, 69; supports Calvin against Servetus, 175, 176, 177, 187

Harmonia Remonstrantium et Socinianorum (Pelt), 559

Hartigveld, Jan, 582

Hartwerd, Wybrant Jansz van, 536

Harvey, William, 147

Heidelberg, outbreak of Antitrinitarianism at, 258–264

Heidelberg Catechism, 583

Helvetic Confession, 111, 237, 353

Henry of Valois, King of Poland, 267, 364–365, 377n., 385

Heraklides, establishes reformed religion in Moldavia, 317

Heresy, persecution of, 191–192, 197–198, 199, 210n. *See also* Tolerance

Herzliches Saytenspiel (Preuss), 519

Hesshusen, Tileman, quoted on Servetus, 161n.

Hetzer, Ludwig, *see* Haetzer, Ludwig

Heydanus, Abraham, 558

Hilarius, 33

Histoire de Genève (Spon), 210

Historia de morte Serveti, 204

History of the Polish Reformation (Lubieniecki), 81

Hofmann, Melchior, radical Anabaptist, 33, 40–41, 59

Hojskis, patrons of Socinians in Ukraine, 456

Holkot, Robert, scholastic theologian, 62

Holland, Unitarianism in, 4; Anabaptists in, 19, 22, 40–48; Socinianism in, 417, 502, 535–540, 547–559, 568–578; Remonstrants in, 532

Hoornbeek, Johannes, 557

Hosius, Cardinal, 255, 324; campaigns against Protestantism in Poland, 318, 319; introduces Jesuits into Poland, 399

Hoss, Christopher, 65

Hotoman, on Castellio and Calvin, 205

Hubmaier (Hübmeier, Hubmör), Balthasar, Anabaptist Leader, 32

Huet, Bishop, 391

Huet, Gédéon, 533

Hugo, Cardinal, 283, 296

Huguenots, 531, 534

Hulewicz, Abraham, 463

Humanism, 13

Humanists, seek reform of Christian doctrines, 20; Italian, further ideals in Poland, 282

Hus, Jan, 266, 270

Hussites, 272, 474

Hydra Socinianismi expugnata (Maresius), 557–558

Hyperaspistes (Przypkowski), 516

Ibn An-Nafîs, 149

Ilanz, Diet of, opens toleration to Protestants, 97–98

Imitation of Christ, 6, 21, 25

In Haereticis coercendis (Celso), 110

In Leonardum Fuchsium Apologia (Servetus), 117–118

Inquisition, 197; investigates Servetus, 72; in Republic of Venice, 78–79; established in Italy, 95, 97; in Poland, 270